"Movies Were Always Magical"

"Movies Were Always Magical"

Interviews with 19 Actors, Directors, and Producers from the Hollywood of the 1930s through the 1950s

LEO VERSWIJVER

FOREWORD BY RONNIE PEDE

McFarland & Company, Inc., Publishers
Jefferson, North Carolina, and London

Library of Congress Cataloguing-in-Publication Data

Verswijver, Leo.
"Movies were always magical" : interviews with 19 actors, directors, and producers from the Hollywood of the 1930s through the 1950s / Leo Verswijver ; foreword by Ronnie Pede.
p.   cm.
Includes index.

ISBN 0-7864-1129-5 (softcover : 50# alkaline paper)

1. Motion picture industry—California—Los Angeles. 2. Motion picture actors and actresses—United States—Interviews.
3. Motion picture producers and directors—United States—Interviews.   I. Title.
PN1993.5.U65 V47   2003   384'.8'0979494—dc21   2002153189

British Library cataloguing data are available

©2003 Leo Verswijver. All rights reserved

No part of this book may be reproduced or transmitted in any form or by any means, electronic or mechanical, including photocopying or recording, or by any information storage and retrieval system, without permission in writing from the publisher.

Cover photograph: Joan Leslie and Humphrey Bogart in the 1941 film *High Sierra*

Manufactured in the United States of America

McFarland & Company, Inc., Publishers
Box 611, Jefferson, North Carolina 28640
www.mcfarlandpub.com

To my children, Koen and Sabrina,
my mother, Hortensia,
and in loving memory of my father, Renaat (1922–1963)

ACKNOWLEDGMENTS

I would never have been able to accomplish this on my own, so I am deeply grateful to a number of people who were extremely supportive along the way and who helped me considerably to get in touch with all of those talented and fascinating actors and actresses and the august, legendary filmmakers: Janet Saint Pierre (Pat Boone's administrative assistant); Gene H. Walsh & Associates (representing Beverly Garland); Rorri Feinstein (executive assistant to Samuel Goldwyn, Jr.); Phill Norman (Sheree North's personal manager), as well as Sheree North herself who introduced me to Curtis Roberts, the award winning theatrical, television and motion picture producer—he arranged the interviews with Kathryn Grayson and Janis Paige; former screen actress, Golden Globe winner (1954) and current producer Karen Sharpe Kramer (wife of Stanley Kramer for over 35 years); Kristi Kittendorf (assistant to Janet Leigh); DeeDee Sadler (personal assistant to Robert Wise); Linda Ayton (Fred Zinnemann's secretary) and Jerry Anker and his wife, former child actress Marguerite Campbell, who introduced me to Paula Raymond. I was able to get in touch with all the other interviewees on my own—they all were equally warmhearted, elegant and gracious. It is difficult for me to describe how grateful I am to all of them.

I'm also very appreciative of everything film director and producer Kevin Brodie has done on my behalf: his enthusiasm, dedication and love for the "old Hollywood" and for the art of filmmaking deeply impressed me.

In Flanders, the Flemish-speaking part of Belgium where I live, I appreciate all the support I got from Alain Keytsman and Paul Breuls (two of our leading film producers), from film director Erik Van Looy, Christiaan De Schutter (festival media and industry executive of the Ghent Film Festival), and film critics Willy Magiels and Lukas De Vos. Last but not least, I wish to thank Ronnie Pede, chief editor of the prestigious Belgian film magazine *Film en Televisie* (published since 1956, it is one of the longest-running film magazines in the entire world) for his assistance, his never-ending support and for allowing me to use his outstanding DOCIP Film Archive for numerous photographs included in this book, as well as for extensive research. My own file system which was compiled over the last three decades also provided various facts and figures, and I also credit the impressive Internet Movie Data Base (www.imdb.com).

Also, I would never have been able to start this book (or finish it for that matter) without my brothers Gilbert, Marc and Gustaaf Verswijver, along with Rik Frans, Ludo De Lee, Eric Verhoeven, Tom Tilleman, Véronique Sturm, Saskia Vander Mast, Veerle Van Wallendael, Paul Peeters, Liliane Van den Cruyce and Josiane Van den Bril—they were all terribly helpful to me in one way or another.

Finally, Rudy Caverneels, Annik Loncke, Werner Schuybroeck, Alex Elemans, Céline Verschave, Nadia Holemans, Karina Van der Steen, Joery Belderbos, Gregory Van Loock and Patrik Wouters all indirectly helped me to get where I had to be and I'm grateful they didn't forget about me.

Leo Verswijver
February 2003
Kapellen, Belgium

TABLE OF CONTENTS

Acknowledgments vii
Foreword by Ronnie Pede 1
Preface 3

Pat Boone   5
Jeff Corey   14
Beverly Garland   29
Samuel Goldwyn, Jr.   43
Kathryn Grayson   53
Jane Greer   64
Stanley Kramer   75
Janet Leigh   93
Joan Leslie   107
Sheree North   121
Janis Paige   132
Luise Rainer   142
Paula Raymond   148
John Saxon   156
Vincent Sherman   173
Robert Wise   188
Jane Withers   202
Jane Wyatt   217
Fred Zinnemann   228

Index   243

FOREWORD

It may be unusual these days that a European and more specifically a Belgian film lover, so fond of the old Hollywood, wants to preserve that particular film past by interviewing the still living Hollywood legends. Unusual because most European countries try to counter the actual (commercial) domination of American films by smothering the name of Hollywood as if it were a four letter word. But these "Hollywood Alltimers," as we call them, who really created "more stars than there are in heaven" (MGM being only a *pars pro toto*), do have European roots and their cinema was multicultural *avant-la-lettre*.

So when reading the interviews with for example the late Stanley Kramer, the still very vivacious Joan Leslie or Vincent Sherman, one understands very well that the cultural European heritage these people treasured was well reflected in their art of filmmaking, whether it was producing, directing or acting.

Leo Verswijver catches these reflections with wit and with the correct historical insight, acknowledging that these men and women created America's true cultural heritage, a heritage that not only needs preservation through film archives all over the world, but also needs perpetual comment as presented in this series of wonderful interviews.

> Ronnie Pede,
> Chief Editor,
> *Film en Televisie* (Belgian film magazine)

PREFACE

This book would never have been published if it weren't for the kindness and the generosity of the 19 dear and wonderful people I was able to meet and interview, and who are included in this book. Initially I had the pleasure of growing up with their films, so I was familiar with their achievements as first-rate, all-round artists. Their huge contribution to the films that came out of Hollywood over the years influenced me more than they could possibly have imagined. Through their work, I became so fascinated years ago with the American film industry that I always hoped to become a part of it in some way. So in the late 1970s, when I was fortunate to begin writing film reviews and essays, I also started interviewing actors and directors. It was like a dream come true—a dream in which I was able to share my own enthusiasm and passion for Hollywood and everything it stood for with anyone out there who was interested in reading it.

The interview with the most energetic 93-year-old Vincent Sherman, whom I first met in April 1999, was the first of the interviews that would be included in this book—apart from an earlier interview I had with director Fred Zinnemann in 1993, which I wouldn't dream of excluding. During the next three years, right up until February 2002, I was able to meet several other equally fascinating screen personalities in London and in the Los Angeles area. All had witnessed the studio system that made Hollywood so powerful; all were involved in the film classics made at those very same studios; all were there when history was made, history that would never have been as colorful, as rich and as enriching without their precious and invaluable contribution. Through learning about their careers, I hoped it would be possible to reflect on the studio system that flourished when Hollywood was at its peak, when the "Golden Era" of Hollywood produced numerous film classics which, because of their innocence, sincerity and honesty, will never lose their appeal.

Needless to say I'd like to express my deepest appreciation to all of those 19 most talented artists for their confidence and faith in me. Despite their hectic schedules, they all took the time and trouble to allow me into the privacy of their own homes. It was a pleasure, an honor, a privilege for me to meet them in person and to have them share, so passionately and so beautifully, their wealth of thoughts and countless experiences in the film industry.

Each interview in this book is followed by a filmography for the interviewee, with general information about each film: the U.S. distributor (during the studio era it was usually the same as the production company), the year the film was released, the director (DIR), producer (PROD), screenwriter (SCR). Also indicated is whether the film was based on a (short) story, play or novel and who the author was. Other credits include director of photography (CAM), editor (ED), composer (MUS), the running time and the major cast.

Notes are included to provide a little more biographical background information on key figures in America's engrossing film history.

The photographs are from my own collection, except as noted.

PAT BOONE

When I entered a shopping mall recently, all of a sudden I heard the voice of Pat Boone. They were playing "Speedy Gonzales," one of his many immortal hit songs, and because they played it so unexpectedly, his refreshing voice and the uplifting way he was singing this delightful tune, made me forget all about the terrible storm weather we were having that day.

Pat Boone was one of America's leading and most successful recording artists for many years; after all, who can ever forget "Ain't That a Shame" (1955), "I Almost Lost My Mind" (1956), "Bernadine" (1957), "Love Letters in the Sand" (1957), "April Love" (1957), "Sugar Moon" (1958), "Moody River" (1961) or "Speedy Gonzales" (1962, female backing voice by Robin Ward)? He was an entertainer with all-American looks, a smooth voice, a clean-cut image and white buck shoes that became his trademark. In the 1950s, only Elvis Presley was more successful than he was, and according to renowned record industry statistician Joel Whitburn, as indicated in his *Pop Annual 1955-1999* (published by Record Research, Inc.), to this day Mr. Boone still is the tenth most successful singles artist of *all* time.

One of the distinctions he still holds is that of being on the U.S. charts for 200 consecutive weeks. No other artist has ever approached that—during the following decades, Elton John came closest. Mr. Boone: "I never knew this until *long* after the fact. But there was a period for about four years when I was always on the charts with at least one record, sometimes two, even three records."

His music is what he always will be best remembered for, but on the other hand, he also had a long and very interesting career in films which started in 1957 with *Bernadine*. "My idol, my role model was Bing Crosby. He had appeared in all these musicals, and that's what I wanted to do as well," Mr. Boone says. And he became a leading actor, a good one and a successful one, and on top of that, he is also known to be a very devoted Christian who has written several books on the subject and regularly focuses on how living according to the Christian guidelines can solve all kinds of teenage problems.

On the strength of his first few years as a singer, Buddy Adler,[1] head of 20th Century Fox, offered him a seven year contract, making him one of the last to be offered such a contract by a major studio. Adler immediately gave him the leading role in *Bernadine* (the first teenage musical ever), opposite veteran actress Janet Gaynor in her final role—she was the first actress to win an Academy Award for best actress (1927). It turned out to be a solid and assured performance by Mr. Boone and he was also allowed to demonstrate his vocal talent and exercise his tonsils for the first time on the screen. Besides the title song, the soundtrack included songs such as "Technique" and "Love Letters in the Sand" as well.

His next film, *April Love* (1957), a musical remake of Henry Hathaway's *Home in Indiana* (1944) with Walter Brennan, co-starred Shirley Jones as his girl-next-door; the film had strong production values and made Boone a bankable star: "I really liked *April Love* from which my theme song came and which is the kind of movie I wish I could have made 20 more of: a musical, appealing characters, some drama, a good storyline, a happy ending, it's the kind of film which makes you feel good. I never wanted to make a depressing or an immoral film. Another film I consider a highlight in my career so far, is *The Cross and the Switchblade* [1970], a straight drama, which is the true story of David Wilkerson. I took a huge gamble with that film. Financially it didn't pay off, because I did it for next to nothing—I virtually did it as a charity, but I don't regret it at all. Within its budget limitations, it was a very well made film about David Wilkerson, a very wonderful human being. The drug fighting organization called T Challenge is to this day by far the most successful drug rehabilitation and rescue program *ever*. It's got a 75 percent cure rate, meaning that three out of four people who commit to their recovery program never go back."

Studio portrait of Pat Boone in the late 1950s. (Courtesy of DOCIP Film Archive, Brussels, Belgium.)

While he appeared in several films in the late 1950s and early 1960s, he had one hit song after the other and in the meantime he hosted his own TV variety show from 1957 till 1959, making him one of the busiest performers in the entertainment industry. Surprisingly, in those days he also appeared in the title role of a science fiction film, *Journey to the Center of the Earth* (1959), based on the novel by Jules Verne. *20,000 Leagues Under the Sea* (1954) and *Around the World in Eighty Days* (1956), also based on his writings, turned out to be money makers, but the casting of Pat Boone in *Journey to the Center of the Earth* seemed very odd. Mr. Boone: "It was a very good movie and even to this day it is shown in theaters around the world and on video, but I didn't want to do a Jules Verne picture or a science fiction film. When they offered me to do this film, it wasn't even an *in* thing and they wanted me, a singer, in a science fiction film. So I was pretty resistant. Twentieth Century Fox then said they'd put songs in it, but it would still be a science fiction film. It seemed odd to me, so they had to keep twisting my arm and finally they offered me 15 percent of the film—that was unheard of! My agent and my manager told me I couldn't possibly turn this down. Reluctantly I said, 'Okay, all right, I'll do it.' Later on, I was very glad I did it, because it was fun to do, it had some good music and it became a very successful film. In fact, executives at 20th Century Fox told me years later that this film saved the studio, because it came out at a time when they were trying desperately to get through filming of *Cleopatra* with Liz Taylor and Richard Burton. That film was over budget and over schedule, it was a scandal and a sensation, but the bankers were not impressed and they were about to close 20th Century Fox down. Then out came *Journey to the Center of the Earth*, which immediately racked up big grosses and it convinced the bankers to play along with 20th a little while longer. So they were able to finish *Cleopatra*, edit it and put it out and finally, the science fiction film that I didn't want to do, saved the studio. Every year I still get checks of the exhibition of the film and the videos—who dreamed at that time there would ever be income of a then uninvented process called videotape."

Up until now, he gets scripts offered but hasn't played any screen roles since *The Cross and the Switchblade*. Mr. Boone: "I turned down a lot more films than I made. They can't twist my arm hard enough to make me do a film where the character I play is either immoral or unredeemed, or when the basic storyline is immoral. For instance, I risked suspension while everything was going great at 20th Century Fox. What happened was, I had turned down a film and this really upset Buddy Adler, but I had refused it on religious grounds: they wanted me to play a Catholic priest who falls in love with a young girl and who has to decide whether he would continue to be faithful to his vows as a priest, or has to succumb to the love of this girl. It was a Bing Crosby type of role, but at that time I was so serious about my church involvement that I really didn't want to play a Catholic priest, certainly not play one who was considering renouncing his vows, and who'd do the reverse of what he had committed to God. It made me feel very uncomfortable; Buddy Adler really threatened me with suspension. He said, 'If you don't do this film, we'll suspend you and you won't be able to make any records, do television, you'll be finished.' So I said to him—and this was a long distance conversation on the phone, I was in Rome at the time—'Mr. Adler, I know you have to do what you have to do and I don't expect you to understand or agree with my religious or moral convictions: they're mine. But I hope you can understand I must do what I feel is right too. So if you'll have to suspend me, then I'll understand.' It was then that they offered me *Journey to the Center of the Earth*, so that's another reason why I accepted that film. I couldn't turn down two films in a row, particularly when my only objection to the second one was that it was a science film while in the meantime I had already turned down the other one.

"Later on, when Spyros [P.] Skouras[2] was the head of the studio, I turned down a film with Marilyn Monroe. We were both under contract at Fox and they wanted us to do a William Inge play, I think it was called *Celebration*, about a fading, but still lovely and appealing singer [Marilyn Monroe]—in a way, it was the same kind of character she played in *Bus Stop*, also written by Inge. It was tailor-made for her: she comes back to her little town and has to decide what she's going to do with the rest of her life. They intended me to play this young college-aged kid who falls completely heads over heels in love with her. It was really like a forerunner of *The Summer of '42*, about an impossible romance with a young guy who falls in love with this woman, while she's attracted to him because of his young and dynamic energy. She then realizes this is certainly not going to be her future and leaves to go back on the road and work. The message is, no real harm done, it was just a poignant experience for the young kid and she goes on with her life and he goes on with his. Now that's the very kind of film I don't want to see and I don't ever want to make. I don't want to be a part of it, because it says to the young people, *hey, a little immoral escapade, no harm done!* I don't believe that and so I turned it down. It hurt, you know, I didn't want to turn down a movie with Marilyn Monroe, but I just couldn't do it. Eventually it was made with Joanne Woodward and Richard Beymer [as Franklin J. Schaffner's *The Stripper*, 1963]—they really didn't know where they were going and it might have been different if it had been with Marilyn Monroe and with me, it might have been on a different level of interest. But I don't regret it at all."

There were several occasions when his own firm religious beliefs and convictions restricted him to playing a certain role or do certain scenes. Mr. Boone: "I once worked with producer Ray Stark, he saw in me a dramatic actor and he wanted me to play dramatic roles. I thought, 'Well, that's probably the only way to keep on working, because in the 1960s there weren't too many musicals made by anybody, and that's why I did *The Main Attraction* [1962]. It's the story of an amoral young drifter who winds up in an Italian circus and lives in the trailer of an older woman, played by Mai Zetterling, and it was understood that we were having some kind of an affair—in a way I was portraying the kind of guy I didn't want to portray with Marilyn Monroe. Then this virginal, young Nancy Kwan falls for me—I played sort of the bad guy, not a *bad* guy, but someone who's not exactly a saintly person [laughs]. My character is accused of murder and runs away from the circus. She follows him, they wind up together and at one point they stay in an abandoned chalet in the Alps. A romance develops—he doesn't want it, he knows she's a sweet, innocent young girl attracted to him and he knows that he's running from what he believes is a fatal situation. For the first time in his life, he resists and rejects an offer to go just with her and have an immoral relationship because he respects her.

"And yet, when we get to the scenes in the chalet, Stark and the screenwriter John Patrick said they really needed those characters to *sleep* together. They said, 'Well, they are in the chalet alone, it is his opportunity to get her madly in love with him, she can feel real love for him, why wouldn't they?' I took him aside and I said, 'Ray, the reason I agreed to do this script is because the subtext here is that this guy finally comes to care for somebody beside himself and he's even willing to deny what he wants for her own good. To me this is the story!' No, nobody would believe that, they should have one, tense night together in bed and then he'd leave her. I said, 'That would leave her wounded and hurt; why would he do that if he really cares for her? He *knows* he's going to leave, why would he do this?' Well, he told me I had to think in terms of what the public wants [laughs], but I didn't want to do it. I wanted to go home and just drop out of the film. My lawyer said, 'They got script approval, so they can sue you for the cost of the whole film.' I had to go and do it, but I refused to get in bed with Nancy Kwan, so what they did in this scene, when the night is falling and they're alone in the chalet, was that he bends down and kisses her and she reaches up while he's still over her, she's lying on the bed and she turns out the light. In the morning, my character is shaving in front of the mirror and it *looks* that my character has gotten out of bed, it is *indicated* that we were in bed together, but I would not shoot any scenes that we were actually in bed. Again, I risked legal action because they wanted to see the two of us in bed and I didn't want to do it.

"The film literally got banned in Boston. The film reviewers there said that young people who go to see a Pat Boone film with a scene which indicates they spend the night together, that's out of the question! The exhibitors wouldn't show the film unless that scene was cut out—in the light of what goes on today in films and television, this is unbelievable. Ray Stark refused to do so, he thought 'Banned in Boston,' let's use that in the promo! And he did use it in a slogan: '*The Main Attraction* ... Pat Boone in trouble!' What he wanted to tell the public, was 'Hey, buy your ticket, come and see this!' My fans were not interested to see me play that kind of a part and it wasn't even *that* kind of a part, it was really a warm romantic adventure. So many times, I have been offered parts, completely the opposite of what I try to be. Look, I'll play Judas in the life of Christ if necessary, but then at least I'll know that the story has an uplifting message. I just don't want to be a part of films that I don't want my own children or grandchildren to see. I'm just astonished that top actors and actresses will do virtually *anything* on the screen. A raunchy, graphic sex scene seems to be required in any film today, and those films are often nominated for Academy Awards. To me it is so beneath dignity, beneath moral, beneath self-respect for actors and actresses to do these things. What will they tell their children? What will their children say? 'I've seen my Mom do this on the screen in front of millions.... Why shouldn't I do it in the back of a car?'

"If you are going to invest in a movie, you got a far better chance of recouping your investment and making money with a G-rated film that the whole family can see. Anybody who is going to invest in any business would like to have the best chance of return, and yet the movie business is one business where they throw those normal considerations to the winds. They would purposely go for a salacious, scandalous taboo or make an R-rated film with violence and sex, and hope they'll get a home-run while most of the time they *don't*. Mostly they lose their shirts, but occasionally a film with all those harmful elements will succeed so that everybody flocks to make more movies like that. Meanwhile the statistics show year after year, without exception, that if you want to make money on a film, you got a far better chance of getting your money back and on top of that making a *lot* of money if you got a film that the whole family can see. Yet, that does not motivate them.

"Families always looked forward to going to movies together. If they went once a week or once a month, it was always a happy event, something the whole family enjoyed: it was a shared experience. I think that's when the movie business was the healthiest and stood a great chance of being profitable. Now they borrow 80 million dollars and make a film with tremendous production values and with a PG rating, or better an R rating—then there'll surely be some stuff that'll be raunchy. I often said to Jack Valenti, 'If they had offered me your job and if I had accepted it, I probably would have kept it for six months.' I would have tried to block the film industry from this headlong rush over into degradation and depravity. Now PG is the equivalent of what X used to be, or R at least, because they just keep lowering the standards. I think it is *bad* for the film industry—not that I am for censorship—although I think that is not a bad word in a healthy society, but I think it is irresponsible, it is shortsighted. I don't go to movies much anymore, I certainly don't think about taking my family to the movies, and I have always been in the movie business.

"They always say that art is depicting life. Well, there is a lot of life that doesn't belong up there on a movie screen. A lot of things that people are capable of, we don't need to show graphically on the screen. We all go to the bathroom several times a day and that's also winding up in films—to me, that's one of the last things you should show on the screen. Filmmakers try to figure out if there's anything now that they haven't shown yet. In *Hannibal* there's a scene where they're eating a human brain; things like that will not kill the industry, but they will certainly poison it.

"I was very lucky, I came in at the tail end when they were still making films for the family, when the film industry felt—and I think it still should—that movies were for families, that they were trying to make things that the whole family could experience and enjoy together. Most of the scripts that I've been offered for the last 15 years, I just can't do them. There are things that are more important to me in my life than just my career. For that reason I never wanted to encourage young people to go into the entertainment business; I'd always tell them to try and find something else they're good at. Movies and music are so unpredictable and so capricious—just because you're good, that doesn't guarantee anything. There are terrific actors and actresses that never get a break."

There are also several similarities between him and Elvis Presley: they are both from Tennessee, both from the same generation, started singing at the same time and both went to Hollywood to make movies. Elvis was Boone's opening act in Cleveland in the fall of 1955, when "Ain't That a Shame" was heading for number one, just prior to the release of "Heartbreak Hotel" (1956), Elvis' first national hit song.

The only major difference is that Presley died over 25 years ago while Pat Boone is still around, looking better than ever and still going strong. "Elvis Presley and I used to visit each

Pat Boone in *The Yellow Canary* (1963), based on a script by Rod Serling. (Courtesy of DOCIP Film Archive, Brussels, Belgium.)

other when we were both making films at 20th Century Fox," he says. "We both leased houses in a section called Bel Air, a really swanking rich area, and I had a house with my wife and four children [Mr. Boone has been married for 48 years now to Shirley Foley; they have four daughters, including singer Debbie, and 15 grandchildren]. He had another house nearby and we visited back and forth. He'd come over in the afternoon; my four little girls would jump out of the swimming pool, jump on him and get him all wet. 'Girls, stop it,' I'd say. And Elvis would say [imitates Elvis], 'Leave them alone, man, I like it.' And he *did*. That's why he came over, he was *wanting* a wife and kids for himself. I didn't know it at the time, I guess. Priscilla was still a girl living in Graceland, back in Memphis, and eventually they did get married and he thought, 'Ah, now I got a wife and a kid!' One of his great life goals had been realized, but he kept his buddies with him all the time. His entourage was like a group of high school kids and they adopted this girl in his group who happened to be his wife. After a while that wore very thin. Unfortunately [in 1973] their marriage ended in divorce [after six years, they had one daughter, Lisa Marie Presley, b. 1968]. So this cherished dream and ambition of Elvis escaped him: he had fame, he had all his movies, all his money, he was the recognized king of rock 'n' roll, but his marriage fell apart. He became increasingly unhealthy and died *much* too young [1977 at age 42]. Very sad."

During the past decades, Mr. Boone has recorded over a dozen Christian albums, several with his wife and children as the Boone Family Singers. He continued to make live appearances into the '90s, was frequently involved in charity work and hosted religious-themed radio and television shows: "I'm not trying to shove anything down anybody's throats and I am not an evangelist, but I live my life based on precepts that I first read in the Bible and tried in my life. And they *work!* They kept my marriage together, which I'm very grateful for, they have given me a wonderful family and a stable life, they gave me the opportunity to indulge and experiment in a lot of businesses, athletic and a lot of other things I never dreamed I would have the opportunity to do. Because it has worked for my family and myself, I'm sure it is God's wish for all of us. The reason He gave us the Commandments, was not to restrict us, but really to give us guidelines by which to live successful, happy, fulfilled lives, the same way we put lines on the streets or stoplights at the intersections. It's all to create order and to give everybody a fair chance to get them where they're trying to go without killing each other. That's the way it all seems to me and I'm happy to share that with others, but I sure don't want to send out some other kind of message in the entertainment that I do. I've had many entertainers come up to me, privately, who say, 'We've made jokes about you over the years, about how square you seem to be, but we now know you're not, that you have a great sense of humor and the way you live your life has *produced* inner peace and happiness.'

"I think peace comes in individual packages. Jesus, who is called the Prince of Peace, didn't speak to governments, he talked to individuals. If I am going to know peace in my life, it won't be because there's peace in the world—it would be great if there is, but I don't have a solution for that—it will only be because there is peace inside *me*. If enough people have internal peace, that could tend to promote a universal kind of peace. Films can help that, they don't have to be preachy films, they should tend to show the best people are capable of, the good should always prevail, the good people should be rewarded for being good and not ridiculed.

"So there should be a higher goal than just the money. On the subject of censorship, if you use that word in this town, it sends shivers up everybody's spine, yet I think it is not only good, but essential, in a healthy society, as long as three provisos are met: voluntary, self-imposed and majority-approved. That means they're always subject to change and it is the majority who sets the standard, they can say, 'We don't want those four-letter words in the presence of our children.' We've gone way beyond that when you see the gutter language in films. I guess they must think it is cute or funny or something, but it is shocking when you see a boy or a girl and out of that child's mouth comes really filthy language. You *know* it is in the script, the screenwriter *wrote* it, the director *rehearsed* it, and now it is a part of that child's career and resume. It is corrupting the morality of minors, but they do it for money and it's on the screen, so they get away with it. We take people, their tax money, and we fund something that is completely sacrilegious and immoral; it's a miscarriage of justice. I think a majority of people should say, 'We will not support, we will not fund, nor do we even want to allow in our society and in the presence of our women and children obscene language and graphic violence. We will not tolerate it.' If you want to call that censorship, so be it. So just like the traffic light on the corners, and we have laws and rules in traffic, movies also do need a form of censorship: it ought to apply to the arts as well."

In 1997 Mr. Boone recorded a heavy metal CD, *No More Mr. Nice Guy*, and 42 years after his first hit songs, he entered the pop charts again after many years of absence. That's another distinction he holds. And for those who have any doubts about it, the future will always be bright for Pat Boone.

Interview: Hollywood, February 13, 2002

Notes

1. Buddy Adler (1909–1960) entered films in 1935 at MGM writing short stories. In 1947 he became a producer at Columbia and in 1956 he replaced Darryl F. Zanuck as production chief at 20th Century Fox. According to his contract at Fox, no artistic decisions could be made without his final approval. His films (as producer) include *From Here to Eternity* (1953, Academy Award for best picture), *Love Is a Many Splendored Thing* (1955), *The Left Hand of God* (1955), *Bus Stop* (1956), *Anastasia* (1956), *Heaven Knows, Mr. Allison* (1957), *South Pacific* (1958) and *The Inn of the Sixth Happiness* (1958). He was married to actress Anita Louise (1915–1970) who had started her career as a child star in silent films.

2. Spyros P. Skouras (1893–1971), son of a Greek shepherd who arrived in the U.S. in 1910, was instrumental in the merger of Fox and 20th Century in 1935. He became president of 20th Century Fox in 1942, a position he held for 20 years. He then became chairman of the board. In the 1950s, when competing with television, he introduced the publicity campaign "Movies Are Better Than Ever" and he was one of the driving forces behind CinemaScope.

Filmography

Bernadine (20th Century Fox, 1957). DIR Henry Levin. PROD Samuel G. Engel. SCR Theodore Reeves (play by Mary Chase). CAM Paul Vogel. ED David Bretherton. MUS Lionel Newman. RUNNING TIME 94 min. CAST: **Pat Boone** (Arthur "Beau" Beaumont); Terry Moore (Jean Cantrick); Janet Gaynor (Mrs. Ruth Wilson); Dean Jagger (J. Fullerton Weldy); Dick Sargent (Sanford Wilson); James Drury (Lt. Langley Beaumont).

April Love (20th Century Fox, 1957). DIR Henry Levin. PROD David Weisbart. SCR Winston Miller (novel by George Agnew Chamberlain). CAM Wilfrid M. Cline. ED William B. Murphy. MUS Alfred Newman, Cyril J. Mockridge. RUNNING TIME 98 min. CAST: **Pat Boone** (Nick); Shirley Jones (Liz Templeton); Dolores Michaels (Fran Templeton); Arthur O'Connell (Jed Bruce); Matt Crowley (Dan Templeton).

Mardi Gras (20th Century Fox, 1958). DIR Edmund Goulding. PROD Jerry Wald. SCR Winston Miller, Hal Kanter (story by Curtis Harrington). CAM Wilfrid M. Cline. ED Robert Simpson. MUS Lionel Newman. RUNNING TIME 107 min. CAST: **Pat Boone** (Pat Newell); Christine Carere (Michelle Marton); Tommy Sands (Barry Denton); Sheree North (Eadie); Gary Crosby (Tony Runkle); Fred Clark (Curtis).

Journey to the Center of the Earth (20th Century Fox, 1959). DIR Henry Levin. PROD Charles Brackett. SCR Charles Brackett, Walter Reisch (novel by Jules Verne). CAM Leo Tover. ED Stuart Gilmore, Jack W. Holmes. MUS Bernard Herrmann. RUNNING TIME 130 min. CAST: **Pat Boone** (Alec McEwan); James Mason (Professor Oliver Lindenbrook); Arlene Dahl (Carla); Diane Baker (Jenny); Thayer David (Count Saknussem).

All Hands on Deck (20th Century Fox, 1961). DIR Norman Taurog. PROD Oscar Brodney. SCR Jay Sommers (novel *Warm Bodies* by Donald R. Morris). CAM Leo Tover. ED Fredrick Y. Smith. MUS Cyril Mockridge. RUNNING TIME 98 min. CAST: **Pat Boone** (Lt. Victor Donald); Buddy Hackett (Shrieking Eagle Garfield); Dennis O'Keefe (Lt. Com. Brian O'Gara); Barbara Eden (Sally Hobson); Warren Berlinger (Ensign Rush).

State Fair (20th Century Fox, 1962). DIR José Ferrer. PROD Charles Brackett. SCR Richard Breen (novel by Philip Stong, adaptation by Oscar Hammerstein II, Sonya Levien, Paul Green). CAM William C. Mellor. ED David Bretherton. MUS Richard Rogers. RUNNING TIME 118 min. CAST: **Pat Boone** (Wayne Frake); Bobby Darin (Jerry Dundee); Pamela Tiffin (Margie Frake); Ann-Margret (Emily Porter); Tom Ewell (Abel Frake); Alice Faye (Melissa Frake).

The Main Attraction (MGM, 1962). DIR Daniel Petrie. PROD-SCR John Patrick. CAM Geoffrey Unsworth. ED Geoffrey Foot. MUS Andrew Adorian (title song: **Pat Boone**, Jeff Corey). RUNNING TIME 87 min. CAST: **Pat Boone** (Eddie); Nancy Kwan (Tessa); Mai Zetterling (Gina); Yvonne Mitchell (Elenora); Lionel Blair (Clown); Golda Casimir (Peasant Woman).

The Yellow Canary (20th Century Fox, 1963). DIR Buzz Kulik. PROD Maury Dexter. SCR Rod Serling. CAM Floyd Crosby. ED Jodie Copelan. MUS Kenyon Hopkins. RUNNING TIME 93 min. CAST: **Pat Boone** (Andy Paxton); Barbara Eden (Lissa); Steve Forrest (Hub Wiley); Jack Klugman (Lt. Bonner); Jessie White (Ed Thornburg); Jeff Corey (Joe).

The Horror of It All (20th Century Fox, 1963). DIR Terence Fisher. SCR Ray Russell. CAM Arthur Lavis. ED Robert Winter. MUS Douglas Gamley. RUNNING TIME 75 min. CAST: **Pat Boone** (Jack Robinson); Erica Rogers (Cynthia Marley); Dennis Price (Cornwallis Marley); Andree Melly (Natalie Marley); Valentine Dyall (Reginald Marley).

Never Put It in Writing (Allied Artists, 1964). DIR-SCR Andrew L. Stone. PROD Andrew L. Stone, Virginia Stone. CAM Martin Curtis. ED Virginia Stone, Noreen Ackland. MUS Frank Cordell (title song: **Pat Boone**). RUNNING TIME 93 min. CAST: **Pat Boone** (Stephen Cole); Milo O'Shea (Danny O'Toole); Fidelma Murphy (Katie O'Connell); Reginald Beckwith (Lombardi); Harry Brogan (Mr. Breeden).

Goodbye Charlie (20th Century Fox, 1964). DIR Vincente Minnelli. PROD David Weisbart. SCR Harry Kurnitz (play by George Axelrod). CAM Milton Krasner. ED John W. Holmes. MUS André Previn. RUNNING TIME 116 min. CAST: Tony Curtis (George Tracy); Debbie Reynolds (Charlie/The Woman); **Pat Boone** (Bruce); Joanna Barnes (Janie); Ellen Burstyn (Franny); Walter Matthau (Sir Leopold Sartori).

The Greatest Story Ever Told (United Artists, 1965). DIR-PROD George Stevens. SCR George Stevens, James Lee Barrett (novel by Fulton Oursler). CAM William C. Mellor, Loyal Griggs. ED Frank O'Neill, Argyle Nelson, Jr. MUS Alfred Newman. RUNNING TIME 221 min. CAST: Max von Sydow (Jesus); Dorothy McGuire (Mary); Robert Loggia (Joseph); Charlton Heston (John the Baptist); Roddy McDowall (Matthew); Sidney Poitier (Simon of Cyrene); Carroll Baker (Veronica); **Pat Boone** (Young Man at the Tomb); Angela Lansbury (Claudia); José Ferrer (Herod Antipas); Claude Rains (Herod the Great).

The Perils of Pauline (Universal, 1967). DIR Herbert B. Leonard, Joshua Shelley. PROD Herbert B. Leonard. SCR Albert Beich (play by Charles W. Goddard). CAM Jack A. Marta. ED Sam E. Waxman. MUS Vic Mizzy. RUNNING TIME 107 min. CAST: **Pat Boone** (George); Terry-Thomas (Sten Martin); Pamela Austin (Pauline); Edward Everett Horton (Caspar Coleman); Hamilton Camp (Thorpe); Kurt Kasznar (Consul General).

The Cross and the Switchblade (Dick Ross, 1970). DIR Don Murray. PROD Dick Ross. SCR Don Murray, James Bonnet (novel by David Wilkerson, John Sherrill, Elizabeth Sherrill). CAM Julian C. Townsend. ED Angelo Ross. MUS Ralph Carmichael. RUNNING TIME 106 min. CAST: **Pat Boone** (David); Erik Estrada (Nicky); Jackie Giroux (Rosa); Jo-Ann Robinson (Little Bo); Dino DeFilippi (Israel).

JEFF COREY

Jeff Corey was one of Hollywood's busiest and most reliable character actors from 1940 through the end of the twentieth century. He made his screen debut in *Bitter Sweet* (1940) opposite Jeanette MacDonald and Nelson Eddy, and then appeared in over a hundred feature films and numerous TV shows. He became friends with some of the industry's most respected stars such as Leslie Howard and Gary Cooper, and, more importantly, as a teacher of his own acting classes, he taught some of the most prominent directors and actors and encouraged them to enter films or to improve their skills. These include directors such as Steven Spielberg, Taylor Hackford, Roger Corman, Irvin Kershner and actors such as Jack Nicholson, James Dean, Sheree North, Sally Kellerman, Rita Moreno, Dean Stockwell, Richard Chamberlain, Donna Reed, Kirk Douglas, Anthony Quinn, Anthony Perkins, Dick Van Dyke, Barbra Streisand, Ann-Margret, Ursula Andress, Matthew Modine, Tuesday Weld, Jane Fonda, Peter Fonda, Candice Bergen, Steve Allen, Ellen Burstyn, Carol Burnett, Pat Boone, Melissa Gilbert, Robin Williams, Kim Darby, Diane Varsi, Tab Hunter and Dorothy Dandridge. Need I say more?

It was a joy meeting this "man of a thousand faces" (a name he acquired in consideration of the wide range of characters he portrayed over the years) at his Malibu home. I had sent him a letter with a request for an interview; he then confirmed it by fax, telling me I could come over. A couple of minutes after his fax arrived at my office, his wife called me to ask if it came through all right. It surely did.

Sadly, Jeff Corey passed away on Friday, August 16, 2002, after suffering complications from a fall. As the end of this interview shows, Mr. Corey was cheerful and gracious in his last years, clearly grateful for a life well lived.

Mr. Corey: "My wife and I have been married since 1938. One of my daughters asked me recently, 'What keeps your marriage going?' I told her simply, 'I love looking at her!' Which is an interesting thing, because you see older people and they walk with their eyes unfocused." Jeff Corey on the other hand, born in New York in 1914, still was very vivid and bright, probably because he never stopped working and because he was known to be a devoted actor who always took his craft very seriously.

His acting career began when he was in his early twenties. "I consider myself a very lucky man," he said. "When I was 22 years old, I was in the production of Hamlet with Leslie Howard, playing Rosencrantz, and we traveled all over the country. I had been in the theatre for quite some time and had also worked in New York. But I always wanted to settle down, have children and buy a house in the suburbs someday—by then we were living in a marvelous little apartment in Greenwich Village, close to the Washington Square Park. I actually went to the Brooklyn Engineering Institute to study blueprint reading and wanted to work in the construction business.

"My wife had several hundreds of dollars in the bank, left by her mother and we bought a Ford model A for 70 dollars. She said to me, 'You talked about how much you loved California when you toured with Leslie Howard'—we had played in places like Fresno, San Jose, Los Angeles, San Diego—'well, before you give up acting, let's just go there, see what happens, and then we'll come back.' We were 18 days on the road and we spent 80 dollars and 30 cents. We came up Highway 66, we turned left on Sunset Boulevard and there was a sign, *Room for rent, $3.00 a week*. So we went into that place and I wanted to show my wife Hollywood. As we went down Sunset Boulevard, towards Vine Street, I happened to spot Lee J. Cobb—in New York we had worked together in a Clifford Odets play, *Till the day I die*."

"He told me how glad he was we ran into each other again, and he gave me the addresses of all the New York people I knew, including [director] Jules Dassin, who was an apprentice to Garson Kanin for *They Knew What They Wanted* [1940] with Carole Lombard and Charles Laughton. So I called him up, and he said, 'I'm so glad you called. My wife is expecting our second child, will you come over and stay with us.' He had this new, very nice house, way up on Vine Street, up in the Hollywood hills. And they were so glad to have us baby-sit for their boy as we took care of him! We had our own segment of the house and while we were there, I thought, why don't I get myself an agent. In New York it's different from here in Hollywood. There you go from agency to agency and try to get work. Here things are quite different, I didn't know that. So the first agent I went to, said, 'No.' The second one said, 'I'll think about it.' The third one, 'Okay, I like you'—and the next day I was working in *Bitter Sweet* [1940]."

From then on, he got job after job: "One day, [director] William Dieterle saw my name in the *Players' Guide*—he was a man with a social conscience, he believed in numerology and astrology, and both he and his wife looked at my name and my picture and, as I was told by my agent, Dieterle had suggested that I go to RKO right away and get into an outfit for a certain role in his upcoming film, which I did. That's how I got a part in *The Devil and Daniel Webster* [1941], one of the all-time great movies."

During the 1940s Mr. Corey appeared in numerous films, playing character parts in films such as *My Friend Flicka* (1943) with Roddy McDowall, the crime drama *The Killers* (1946) opposite Burt Lancaster and Ava Gardner, Joseph L. Mankiewicz' *Somewhere in the Night* (1946), *California* (1947) with Ray Milland and Barbara Stanwyck, Cecil B. De Mille's *Unconquered* (1947), *Brute Force* (1947) directed by his friend Jules Dassin, *Joan of Arc* (1948) starring Ingrid Bergman, *Home of the Brave* (1949), one of the first films produced by Stanley Kramer, and Michael Curtiz' *Bright Leaf* (1950) with Cary Cooper, Lauren Bacall and Patricia Neal.

For Jeff Corey and most of his contemporaries, it was never really a problem to find a proper supporting role in those days, basically because people were respectful of actors. "Today it is quite the opposite, a terrible thing is happening: they audition actors for a part, that didn't happen in the 1930s and 1940s. The producer would call you in and tell you if you were interesting enough for the part. You didn't have to read for it, they saw your film and that was it. Today it is just terrible, they film actor after actor who does the scene, they don't have any respect for the actors, but unfortunately it is the only way to get a job. I remember doing a screen test for *Bright Leaf* with Gary Cooper for Michael Curtiz; we were treated totally different. They were respectful of actors and we got to know each other very well—I became very close to Gary Cooper and Patricia Neal.

"If you are a good actor, it shows. Back then, when they were casting for a part, they preferred to get an actor they could rely on. Stanley Kramer wanted me for *Home of the Brave*; he had just seen my work in [general], so he wanted to meet me. In his autobiography he wrote he immediately understood I was the guy for the part, he even didn't want me to read for him, he sensed I was the right guy."

By then, Mr. Corey had begun his second career as a teacher of his acting classes in Hollywood and, as he claims, "Gary Cooper sat in on my first classes, he was very interested in acting." He started teaching in 1949 (for many years, his acting class was called the "Actors Craft," an idea he got from Stanley Kramer's 1965 classic *Ship of Fools*) and practically to the day he died, he still had 25 students in a daytime class. They rehearsed, discussed and talked about acting in a spacious area above his garage. Mr. Corey: "At one time I taught ten classes a week, now it is one class a week—it's good for my brain to keep on working, you keep remembering things. A psychiatrist friend of mine always says, 'Whenever you forget something, if it's important, it'll come back.' Very frequently I forget a name or something, but then it almost always comes back in a minute. I don't use the Method jargon in my class, like what's your reaction, what were you indicating, stuff like that. I have a way of working with people by having them do the scene and then change the circumstances, try this, try that.

Jeff Corey played opposite Joan Bennett (1910–1990) in *Girl Trouble* (1942). She was the sister of actresses Barbara and Constance Bennett. Here Miss Bennett is seen with the April 1949 copy of the Belgian film magazine *Film en Toneel*.

"The interesting thing is that I have never been listed in the phone book and I never advertised, so actors who wanted to attend my classes, really had to *find* my phone number. But not all of them I worked with in classes. Some of those people I worked with privately, like I did with Kirk Douglas and Dick Van Dyke; this was one on one.

"I have an exercise that a lot of screenwriters have adopted: I give the students the opportunity to improvise a scene or whatever, without making a single reference to the plot, in other words, the dialogue I want to hear, is a subtext, what's *underneath* the dialogue is important. I saw Jack Nicholson recently, we talked about it, about improvising a person's plot without mentioning the plot at all. He was just crazy about that. Screenwriter Bob Towne said publicly in a paper that my ideas about doing that, provided him with a way of writing a screenplay [his credits include *Chinatown* and *The Firm*]. Carole Eastman based her screenplay of *Five Easy Pieces* [1970, credited as Adrien Joyce] on that very same procedure." Both were former students of his.

"I was once at the University of Texas where the teachers watched me teach, they took notes which pleased me, and then I had dinner with three teachers who were the head of that

Jeff Corey (left) and Pat Boone in *The Yellow Canary* (1963). (Courtesy of DOCIP Film Archive, Brussels, Belgium.)

particular department at the university. The students had a chance to talk about the experience, they could comment on it and they described what they thought about my teaching. In one voice they all said, 'You're a hands-on teacher!' That made me feel very proud."

Mr. Corey was extremely influential to numerous actors, directors and screenwriters who attended his classes over the past five decades. One of them was Steven Spielberg. Mr. Corey: "He was 17 when he first came to my class. He directed me later on in one of his early pictures [*Something Evil*, 1972]. He liked the way I taught, I liked the way he directed. He really worked his way up, he used to climb over the fences at Universal to find an empty office and started using it, so people thought he belonged there."

Shortly after becoming a renowned acting teacher (Washington's *National Observer* once described his workshop rightfully as a major influence on the motion picture industry), his career took a whole different turn as he was accused of affiliations with the Communist party during the so-called McCarthy era, probably the most terrible chapter in the history of Hollywood. Consequently he couldn't find an acting job in Hollywood from 1951 to 1963. Mr. Corey: "The blacklisting was a major set-back, not only for the motion picture industry, but for the entire country. It was a terrible thing that happened back then. It was all based on fear and it was illegal to do these things to people. Arthur Miller was very brave: he didn't take the Fifth Amendment, so he could be jailed, but a judge said his sentence had been suspended, so he didn't have to go to jail. I had three citations for my work as a motion picture combat photographer during World War II on the USS *Yorktown*, I was in Yokohama harbor

Director Steven Spielberg at work on the set of his masterpiece E.T. (1982). He was one of Jeff Corey's pupils.

when the peace was signed. In late 1945 I even received a citation from the Secretary of the Navy, James Forrestal, and from Captain Edward Steichen which mentioned: 'His sequence of a Kamikaze attempt on the Carrier Yorktown, done in the face of grave danger, is one of the great picture sequences of the war in the Pacific, and reflects the highest credit upon Jeff Corey and the U.S. Navy Photographic Service.' The other citations I got from the members of the photo lab. I always thought I was a good and responsible American citizen, I certainly demonstrated it during the war, but they simply wouldn't let me mention it, they didn't even want to *hear* about it. But in the end, it didn't make any difference at all, because I didn't want to be cleared by the House Un-American Activities Committee, I just turned my back on them and made a life for myself. When they asked me to come and testify before the committee, I took the Fifth Amendment, and when I began to read my war record, they said that Darren McDonald was in the armed service and he betrayed the country, so then they assumed that I also betrayed the country, which is nonsense. But that's how narrow-minded they were, it was just terrible. Finally, the head of the House committee wound up in the same jail as Ring Lardner, Jr.,[1] who was serving time for contempt of Congress.

"I used to know Elia Kazan pretty well, I knew all of the Group Theatre people. John Houseman wanted me to play the part of a doctor with Bobby De Niro in *The Last Tycoon* [1976], so he asked me to come over and talk to him. Kazan was there too—they used to play tennis, he'd get mad if he didn't win. Kazan put his arms around me and said, 'Oh Jeff, we've been a couple of survivors.' And I said, 'Well, not on the same raft' [laughs]. I think he's been very uncomfortable, I don't think he's had a good life: he got stuck with it. But I didn't suffer through the blacklisting, I didn't fall apart, I would just not *let* myself fall apart.

"There was a young woman in my class, she was very successful in Paris and was known as the 'American Songbird.' She played at nightclubs in Paris. When she came to America, she lived with a producer at 20th Century Fox. In the class she kind of found herself, she found her *own* self, I guess she was quite independent, despite being this guy's mistress. My agent once went to see him and suggested me for a part and he said, 'I'll *never* hire that Fifth Amendment Commie!' There were also so many right-wing people in my class, like [actress] Marie Windsor [1919–2000]; she loved my class and she invited me to her house for dinner or to play tennis. We all got along just fine.

"When I was mentioned, I still was able to do radio. I did one more film, *Superman and the Mole Men* [1951], and a couple of insignificant shorts, but then it all stopped. I was the first one to work again, in the early 1960s. So throughout the 1950s, when I was unable to act, I concentrated on my teaching. Still, my best years were still ahead. I always considered 1969 as my best year. In that calendar year, I played in *True Grit*—the director, Henry Hathaway, told me that when he read Marguerite Roberts' screenplay, he was fascinated as the first paragraph referred to Tom Chaney, the villain, and he said, 'As soon as I read that, I had an image of you in the part, so I called [producer] Hal [B.] Wallis and said I want Jeff Corey for that part.' I did several movies for Arthur Penn, like *Mickey One* [1965] in Chicago, and when I was working at Fox on *Beneath the Planet of the Apes*, he wanted me to play Wild Bill Hickok in *Little Big Man*. I was very pleased to play that part, and the third part I played that year was in *Butch Cassidy and the Sundance Kid*." Up until the decade before his death, Mr. Corey still appeared

Dustin Hoffman (left) with Jeff Corey as Wild Bill Hickok in *Little Big Man* (1970). (Courtesy of DOCIP Film Archive, Brussels, Belgium.)

in films; his last efforts include *Bird on a Wire* (1990), *Deception* (1992), *Beethoven's 2nd* (1993) and *Color of Night* (1994) opposite Bruce Willis.

In between he also worked as a director of several TV shows. "I did a lot of shows of 'Night Gallery.' I liked directing. I once asked Robert Blake, who was a student of mine, 'Why didn't I do a *Baretta*?' He said, 'You had an enemy in the tower.' I don't know who it was, somebody just didn't like me. I began directing in my fifties, when I was approaching 60, and I was beginning to feel my age at that time."

Despite his devotion to film and television, the theatre was always very dear to him. "Six years ago Matthew Modine put together an invitation only one-week performance in Beverly Hills of *Twelve Angry Men* with actors like Leo Penn, F. Murray Abraham, Seymour Cassel, myself. The audience *loved* it, they were crazy about it. But my ability to memorize dialog now has become a test at my age. When I was a kid, I did summer stock. One week we'd do a frivolous play, next we'd do *Hedda Gabler*. I'd get a script on Monday night and the opening night would be on Saturday. We'd have four and a half days to work on it. My memory was very good back then. Looking back on my life, I feel good about it. It is like the French say, *j'ai quatre-vingt-six ans—I have 86 years*."

Interview: Malibu, February 28, 2001

Note

1. Screenwriter Ring Lardner, Jr. (1915–2000), was one of the ten directors, screenwriters and directors who refused to co-operate with the investigators of the House Un-American Activities Committee. Subsequently they all went to jail for a period of between six months and one year. Known as the Hollywood Ten, they were Lardner, director Edward Dmytryk (1908–1999), producer-writer Adrian Scott (1912–1973; he produced four Dmytryk films), producer-director-screenwriter Herbert J. Biberman (1900–1971; his wife actress Gale Sondergaard also refused to testify), screenwriters Alvah Bessie (1904–1985), Lester Cole (1904–1985), John Howard Lawson (1894–1977), Albert Maltz (1908–1985), Samuel Ornitz (1891–1957) and Dalton Trumbo (1905–1976; like most of the other victims he kept on writing screenplays under various pseudonyms and even won an Academy Award in 1956 for his [motion picture] story of *The Brave One*, using the pseudonym of Robert Rich).

Filmography

Bitter Sweet (MGM, 1940). DIR W.S. Van Dyke II. PROD Victor Saville. SCR Lesser Samuels (operetta *Bitter Sweet* by Noel Coward). CAM Allen Davey. ED Harold F. Kress. MUS Herbert Stothart. RUNNING TIME 92 min. CAST: Jeanette MacDonald (Sarah Millick); Nelson Eddy (Carl Linden); George Sanders (Baron von Tranisch); Ian Hunter (Lord Shayne); Felix Bressart (Max); **Jeff Corey** (Man on stairs).

You'll Find Out (RKO, 1940). DIR-PROD David Butler. SCR James V. Kern (story by David Butler, James V. Kern). CAM Frank Redman. ED Irene Morra. MUS Roy Webb. RUNNING TIME 95 min. CAST: Kay Kyser (Kay); Peter Lorre (Fenniger); Boris Karloff (Judge Wainwaring); Bela Lugosi (Prince Saliano); Helen Parrish (Janis); **Jeff Corey** (Mr. Brown).

The Reluctant Dragon (RKO, 1941). DIR Alfred R. Werker (Ford Beebe, Jasper Blystone, Jim Handley, Hamilton Luske, Erwin L. Verity dir. of the cartoon sequences). SCR Ted Sears, Al Perkins, Larry Clemmons, Bill Cottrell (story by Kenneth Grahame). CAM Bert Glennon, Winton Hoch. ED Paul Weatherwax. RUNNING TIME 73 min. CAST: Robert Benchley (Himself); Frances Gifford (Doris); Buddy Pepper (Humphrey); Nana Bryant (Mrs. Benchley); Alan Ladd (Story Artist); **Jeff Corey** (Uncredited).

The Lady from Cheyenne (Universal, 1941). DIR-PROD Frank Lloyd. SCR Warren Duff, Kathryn Scola. CAM Milton Krasner. ED Edward Curtiss. MUS Frank Skinner. RUNNING TIME 84 min. CAST: Loretta Young (Annie); Robert Preston (Steve); Edward Arnold (Cork); Frank Craven (Hank Foreman); Gladys George (Elsie); **Jeff Corey** (Uncredited).

You Belong to Me (Columbia, 1941). DIR-PROD Wesley Ruggles. SCR Claude Binyon (story by Dalton Trumbo). CAM Joseph Walker. ED Viola Lawrence. MUS Frederick Hollander. RUNNING TIME 93 min. CAST: Barbara Stanwyck (Helen Hunt); Henry Fonda (Peter Kirk); Edgar Buchanan (Billings); Roger Clark (Vandemer); Ruth Donnelly (Emma); Melville Cooper (Moody); **Jeff Corey** (Greener).

Small Town Deb (20th Century Fox, 1941). DIR Harold Schuster. SCR Ethel Hill (story by Jerrie Walters [*nom de plume* of Jane Withers]). CAM Virgil Miller. ED Alexander Troffey. MUS Emil Newman. RUNNING TIME 72 min. CAST: Jane Withers (Patricia Randall); Jane Darwell (Katie); Bruce Edwards (Jack Richards); Cobina Wright, Jr. (Helen Randall); Cecil Kellaway (Mr. Randall); **Jeff Corey** (Hector).

The Devil and Daniel Webster, a.k.a. *All That Money Can Buy* (RKO, 1941). DIR-PROD William Dieterle. SCR Dan Tetheroh, Stephen Vincent Benét. CAM Joseph August. ED Robert Wise. MUS Bernard Herrmann. RUNNING TIME 100 min. CAST: Edward Arnold (Daniel Webster); Walter Huston (Mr. Scratch); Jane Darwell (Ma Stone); Simone Simon (Belle); Gene Lockhart (Squire Slossum); **Jeff Corey** (Tom Sharp).

Petticoat Politics (Republic, 1941). DIR Erle Kenton. SCR Ewart Adamson, Taylor Caven. CAM Jack Marta. ED Edward Mann. MUS Cy Feuer. RUNNING TIME 67 min. CAST: Roscoe Karns (Joe Higgins); Ruth Donnelly (Lil Higgins); Spencer Charters (Grandpa); George Ernest (Sidney Higgins); Alan Ladd (Don Wilcox); **Jeff Corey** (Henry Trotter).

Paris Calling (Universal, 1941). DIR Edwin L. Marin. PROD Benjamin Glazer. SCR Benjamin Glazer, Charles S. Kaufman (story by John S. Toldy). CAM Milton Krasner. ED Edward Curtiss. MUS Richard Hageman. RUNNING TIME 93 min. CAST: Elizabeth Bergner (Marianne); Randolph Scott (Nick); Basil Rathbone (Benoit); Gale Sondergaard (Colette); Lee J. Cobb (Schwabe); **Jeff Corey** (Benoit's Secretary).

Mutiny in the Arctic (Universal, 1941). DIR John Rawlins. SCR Maurice Tombragel, Victor McLeod (story by Paul Huston). CAM John W. Boyle. ED Edward Curtiss. MUS H. J. Salter. RUNNING TIME 60 min. CAST: Richard Arlen (Dick); Andy Devine (Andy); Anne Nagel (Gloria); Addison Richards (Ferguson); Don Terry (Cole); **Jeff Corey** (Cook).

Roxie Hart (20th Century Fox, 1942). DIR William A. Wellman. PROD-SCR Nunnally Johnson (play *Chicago* by Maurine Watkins). CAM Leon Shamroy. ED James B. Clark. MUS Alfred Newman. RUNNING TIME 72 min. CAST: Ginger Rogers (Roxie Hart); Adolphe Menjou (Billy Flynn); George Montgomery (Homer Howard); Lynne Overman (Jake Callahan); Nigel Bruce (E. Clay Benham); **Jeff Corey** (Orderly).

North to the Klondike (Universal, 1942). DIR Erle C. Kenton. SCR Clarence Upson Young, Lou Sarecky, George Bricker (story by William Castle). CAM Charles Van Enger. ED Ted Kent. MUS H. J. Salter. RUNNING TIME 58 min. CAST: Broderick Crawford (John Thorn); Evelyn Ankers (Mary Sloan); Andy Devine (Klondike); Lon Chaney, Jr. (Nate Carson); Lloyd Corrigan (Doctor Curtis); **Jeff Corey** (Lafe Jordon).

The Man Who Wouldn't Die (20th Century Fox, 1942). DIR Herbert I. Leeds. SCR Arnaud D'Usseau (novel *No Coffin for the Corpse* by Clayton Rawson). CAM Joseph P. MacDonald. ED Fred Allen. MUS Emil Newman. RUNNING TIME 73 min. CAST: Lloyd Nolan (Michael Shayne); Marjorie Weaver (Catherine); Helene Reynolds (Anna); Henry Wilcoxon (Dr. Haggard); **Jeff Corey** (Coroner Larson).

The Postman Didn't Ring (20th Century Fox, 1942). DIR Harold Schuster. PROD Ralph Dietrich. SCR Mortimer Braus (story by Mortimer Braus, Leon Ware). CAM Joseph MacDonald. ED Nick DeMaggio. MUS Emil Newman. RUNNING TIME 68 min. CAST: Richard Travis (Daniel Carter); Brenda Joyce (Julie Martin); Spencer Charters (Judge Colt); Stanley Andrews (Insp. Brennon); William Bakewell (Robert Harwood, Jr.); **Jeff Corey** (Harwood Green).

Who Is Hope Schuyler? (20th Century Fox, 1942). DIR Thos. Z. Loring. SCR Arnaud D'Usseau (novel *Hearses Don't Hurry* by Stephen Ransome). CAM Virgil Miller. ED Louis Loeffler. MUS Emil Newman. RUNNING TIME 57 min. CAST: Joseph Allen, Jr. (Tom Mason); Mary Howard (Diane Rossiter/Hope Schuyler); Sheila Ryan (Lee Dale); Ricardo Cortez (Anthony Pearce); Janis Carter (Vesta Hadden); **Jeff Corey** (Coroner).

Girl Trouble (20th Century Fox, 1942). DIR Harold Schuster. PROD Robert Bassler. SCR Ladislas Fodor, Robert Riley Crutcher (story by Ladislas Fodor, Vicki Baum, Guy Trosper). CAM Edward Cronjager. ED Robert Fritch. MUS Alfred Newman. RUNNING TIME 82 min. CAST: Don Ameche (Pedro Sullivan); Joan Bennett (June Delaney); Billie Burke (Mrs. Rowland); Frank Craven (Ambrose); Alan Dinehart (Barrett); **Jeff Corey** (Mr. Mooney).

The Moon Is Down (20th Century Fox, 1943). DIR Irving Pichel. PROD-SCR Nunnally Johnson (novel by John Steinbeck). CAM Arthur Miller. ED Louis Loeffler. MUS Alfred Newman. RUNNING TIME 90 min. CAST: Sir Cedric Hardwicke (Lanser); Henry Travers (Orden); Lee J. Cobb (Albert Winter); Dorris Bowdon (Molly); Margaret Wycherly (Sarah); **Jeff Corey** (Albert).

Frankenstein Meets the Wolf Man (RKO, 1943). DIR Roy William Neill. PROD George Waggner. SCR Curt Siodmak. CAM George Robinson. ED Edward Curtiss. MUS H. J. Salter. RUNNING TIME 73 min. CAST: Ilona Massey (Baroness Elsa Frankenstein); Patric Knowles (Dr. Mannering); Lionel Atwill (Mayor); Bela Lugosi (Monster); Maria Ouspenskaya (Maleva); **Jeff Corey** (Grave Digger).

My Friend Flicka (20th Century Fox, 1943). DIR Harold Schuster. PROD Ralph Dietrich. SCR Lillie Hayward (novel by Mary O'Hara). CAM Dewey Wrigley. ED Robert Fritch. MUS Alfred Newman. RUNNING TIME 89 min. CAST: Roddy McDowall (Ken); Preston Foster (Rob); Rita Johnson (Nell); James Bell (Gus); Diane Hale (Hildy); **Jeff Corey** (Tim).

The Killers (Universal, 1946). DIR Robert Siodmak. PROD Mark Hellinger. SCR Anthony Veiller (short story by Ernest Hemingway). CAM Woody Bredell. ED Arthur Hilton. MUS Miklos Rozsa. RUNNING TIME 105 min.

CAST: Burt Lancaster (Anderson, a.k.a. Pete Lund); Ava Gardner (Kitty Collins); Edmond O'Brien (James Riordan); Albert Dekker (Charleston); Virginia Christine (Lilly); **Jeff Corey** (Blinky Franklin).

Somewhere in the Night (20th Century Fox, 1946). DIR Joseph L. Mankiewicz. PROD Anderson Lawler. SCR Joseph L. Mankiewicz, Howard Dimsdale (story by Marvin Borowsky). CAM Norbert Brodine. ED James B. Clark. MUS Emil Newman. RUNNING TIME 110 min. CAST: John Hodiak (George Taylor); Nancy Guild (Christy Smith); Lloyd Nolan (Donald Kendall); Richard Conte (Mel Phillips); Josephine Hutchinson (Elizabeth Conroy); **Jeff Corey** (Bank Teller).

It Shouldn't Happen to a Dog (20th Century Fox, 1946). DIR Herbert I. Leeds. PROD William Girard. SCR Eugene Ling, Frank Gabrielson (short story by Edwin Lanham). CAM Glen MacWilliams. ED Robert Fritch. MUS Emil Newman. RUNNING TIME 70 min. CAST: Carole Landis (Julia Andrews); Allyn Joslyn (Henry Barton); Margo Woode (Olive Stone); Henry Morgan (Gus Rivers); Reed Hadley (Valentine); **Jeff Corey** (Sam Black).

California (Paramount, 1947). DIR John Farrow. PROD Seton I. Miller. SCR Frank Butler, Theodore Strauss (story by Boris Ingster). CAM Ray Rennahan. ED Eda Warren. MUS Victor Young. RUNNING TIME 97 min. CAST: Ray Milland (Jonathan Trumbo); Barbara Stanwyck (Lily Bishop); Barry Fitzgerald (Michael Fabian); George Coulouris (Pharaoh Coffin); Albert Dekker (Mr. Pike); **Jeff Corey** (Uncredited).

Hoppy's Holiday (United Artists, 1947). DIR George Archainbaud. SCR J. Benton Cheney, Bennett Cohen, Ande Lamb (characters created previously by Clarence E. Mulford). CAM Mack Stengler. ED Fred W. Berger. MUS David Chudnow. RUNNING TIME 60 min. CAST: William Boyd (Hopalong Cassidy); Andy Clyde (California Carlson); Rand Brooks (Lucky Jenkins); Andrew Tombes (Mayor Patton); Leonard Penn (Dunning); **Jeff Corey** (Jed).

The Gangster (Allied Artists, 1947). DIR Gordon Wiles. PROD Maurice King, Frank King. SCR Daniel Fuchs (based on his novel *Low Company*). CAM Paul Ivano. ED Walter Thompson. MUS Louis Gruenberg. RUNNING TIME 82 min. CAST: Barry Sullivan (Shubunka); Belita (Nancy); Joan Lorring (Dorothy); Akim Tamiroff (Nick Jammey); Henry Morgan (Shorty); **Jeff Corey** (Brother-in-Law).

The Flame (Republic, 1947). DIR John H. Auer. SCR Lawrence Kimble (story by Robert T. Shannon). CAM Reggie Lanning. ED Richard L. Van Enger. MUS Heinz Roemheld. RUNNING TIME 96 min. CAST: John Carroll (George MacAllister); Vera Ralston (Carlotta Novak); Robert Paige (Barry MacAllister); Broderick Crawford (Ernie Hicks); Henry Travers (Dr. Mitchell); **Jeff Corey** (Stranger).

Miracle on 34th Street (20th Century Fox, 1947). DIR George Seaton. PROD William Perlberg. SCR George Seaton (story by Valentine Davies). CAM Charles Drake, Lloyd Ahern. ED Robert Simpson. MUS Alfred Newman. RUNNING TIME 95 min. CAST: Maureen O'Hara (Doris Walker); John Payne (Fred Gailey); Edmund Gwenn (Kris Kringle); Gene Lockhart (Judge Harper); Natalie Wood (Susan Walker); **Jeff Corey** (Reporter).

Unconquered (Paramount, 1947). DIR-PROD Cecil B. DeMille. SCR Charles Bennett, Fredric M. Frank, Jesse L. Lasky, Jr. (novel *Unconquered: A Novel of the Pontiac Conspiracy* by Neil H. Swanson). CAM Ray Rennahan. ED Anne Bauchens. MUS Victor Young. RUNNING TIME 146 min. CAST: Gary Cooper (Capt. Holden); Paulette Goddard (Martha "Abby" Hale); Howard da Silva (Martin Garth); Boris Karloff (Guyasota); Cecil Kellaway (Jeremy Love); Ward Bond (John Fraser); Katharine DeMille (Hannah); **Jeff Corey** (Trapper).

Ramrod (United Artists, 1947). DIR André de Toth. SCR Jack Moffitt, Graham Baker, Cecile Kramer (novel by Luke Short). CAM Russell Harlan. ED Sherman A. Rose. MUS Adolph Deutsch. RUNNING TIME 94 min. CAST: Joel McCrea (Dave Nash); Veronica Lake (Connie Dickason); Don DeFore (Bill Schell); Donald Crisp (Jim Crew); Preston Foster (Frank Ivey); **Jeff Corey** (Bice).

Brute Force (Universal, 1947). DIR Jules Dassin. PROD Mark Hellinger. SCR Richard Brooks (story by Robert Patterson). CAM William Daniels. ED Edward Curtiss. MUS Miklos Rozsa. RUNNING TIME 94 min. CAST: Burt Lancaster (Joe Collins); Hume Cronyn (Capt. Munsey); Charles Bickford (Gallagher); Ann Blyth (Ruth); Ella Raines (Cora); **Jeff Corey** (Freshman).

The Wreck of the Hesperus (Columbia, 1948). DIR John Hoffman. PROD Wallace MacDonald. SCR Aubrey Wisberg (story by Edward Huebsch, based on the poem "The Wreck of the Hesperus" by Henry Wadsworth Longfellow). CAM Allen Siegler. ED James Sweeney. MUS Mischa Bakaleinikoff. RUNNING TIME 67 min. CAST: Willard Parker (John McReady); Edgar Buchanan (George Lockhart); Patricia White (Deborah Allen); Holmes Herbert (Pastor West); Wilton Graff (Caleb Cross); **Jeff Corey** (Joshua Hill).

Homecoming (MGM, 1948). DIR Mervyn LeRoy. PROD Sidney Franklin. SCR Paul Osborn (story by Sidney Kingsley). CAM Harold Rosson. ED John Dunning. MUS Bronislau Kaper. RUNNING TIME 112 min. CAST: Clark Gable (Delby Johnson); Lana Turner (Lt. Jane McCall); Anne Baxter (Penny Johnson); John Hodiak (Dr. Robert Sunday); Gladys Cooper (Mrs. Kirby); **Jeff Corey** (Cigarette Smoker).

Wake of the Red Witch (Republic, 1948). DIR Edward Ludwig. SCR Harry Brown, Kenneth Gamet (novel by Garland Roark). CAM Reggie Lanning. ED Richard L. Van Enger. MUS Nathan Scott. RUNNING TIME 106 min. CAST: John Wayne (Capt. Ralls); Gail Russell (Angelique Desaix); Gig Young (Sam Rosen); Adele Mara (Teleia Van Schreeven); Luther Adler (Mayrant Ruysdaal Sidneye); **Jeff Corey** (Loring).

Joan of Arc (RKO, 1948). DIR Victor Fleming. PROD Walter Wanger. SCR Maxwell Anderson, Andrew Solt (play *Joan of Lorraine* by Maxwell Anderson). CAM Joseph Valentine. ED Frank Sullivan. MUS Hugo Friedhofer. RUNNING TIME 100 min. CAST: Ingrid Bergman (Joan of Arc); José Ferrer (Charles VII); Richard Derr (Jean de Metz); Ray Teal (Bertrand de Poulengy); **Jeff Corey** (Prison Guard).

Kidnapped (Monogram, 1948). DIR William Beaudine. PROD Lindsley Parsons. SCR W. Scott Darling (novel by Robert Louis Stevenson). CAM William Sickner. ED Leonard W. Herman. MUS Edward J. Kay. RUNNING TIME 81 min. CAST: Roddy McDowall (David Balfour); Sue England (Fairlie); Dan O'Herlihy (Alan Breck); Roland Winters (Capt. Hoseason); **Jeff Corey** (Shuan).

Let's Live Again (20th Century Fox, 1948). DIR Herbert I. Leeds. PROD Frank N. Seltzer. SCR Rodney Carlisle, Robert Smalley (story by Herman Wohl, John Vlahos). CAM Mack Stengler. ED Bert Jordan. MUS Ralph Stanley. RUNNING TIME 67 min. CAST: John Emery (Larry Blake); Hillary Brooke (Sandra Marlowe); Taylor Holmes (Uncle Jim); Diana Douglas (Terry); James Millican (George Blake); **Jeff Corey** (Bartender).

A Southern Yankee (MGM, 1948). DIR Edward Sedgwick. PROD Paul Jones. SCR Harry Tugend (story by Melvin Frank, Norman Panama). CAM Ray June. ED Ben Lewis. MUS David Snell. RUNNING TIME 91 min. CAST: Red Skelton (Aubrey Filmore); Brian Donlevy (Kurt Devlynn); Arlene Dahl (Sallyann Weatharby); George Couloris (Drumman/The Grey Spider); Lloyd Gough (Capt. Lorford); **Jeff Corey** (Union Cavalry Sgt.).

I, Jane Doe (Republic, 1948). DIR John H. Auer. SCR Lawrence Kimble (short story by Faith Baldwin). CAM Reggie Lanning. ED Richard L. Van Enger. MUS Heinz Roemheld. RUNNING TIME 85 min. CAST: Ruth Hussey (Eve Meredith Curtis); John Carroll (Stephen Curtis); Vera Ralston (Jane Doe/Annette Dubois/Annette Fontaine); Gene Lockhart (Arnold Matson); **Jeff Corey** (Immigration Officer).

Canon City (Eagle-Lion Films, 1948). DIR-SCR Crane Wilbur. PROD Robert T. Kane. CAM John Alton. ED Louis H. Sackin. MUS Irving Friedman. RUNNING TIME 82 min. CAST: Scott Brady (Sherbondy); **Jeff Corey** (Carl Schwartzmiller); Whit Bissell (Heilman); Stanley Clements (New); Charles Russell (Tolley); DeForest Kelley (Smalley).

Roughshod (RKO, 1949). DIR Mark Robson. PROD Richard H. Berger. SCR Geoffrey Homes, Hugo Butler (story by Peter Viertel). CAM Joseph Biroc. ED Marston Fay. MUS C. Bakaleinikoff. RUNNING TIME 88 min. CAST: Robert Sterling (Clay); Gloria Grahame (Mary); Claude Jarman, Jr. (Steve); John Ireland (Lednov); Jeff Donnell (Elaine); **Jeff Corey** (Jed Graham).

Bagdad (Universal, 1949). DIR Charles Lamont. PROD Robert Arthur. SCR Robert Hardy Andrews (story by Tamara Hovey). CAM Russell Metty. ED Russell Schoengarth. MUS Milton Schwarzwald. RUNNING TIME 82 min. CAST: Maureen O'Hara (Princess Marjan); Paul Christian (Hassan); Vincent Price (Pasha Ali Nadim); John Sutton (Raizul); **Jeff Corey** (Mohammed Jad); Frank Puglia (Saleel).

Home of the Brave (United Artists, 1949). DIR Mark Robson. PROD Stanley Kramer. SCR Carl Foreman (play by Arthur Laurents). CAM Robert de Grasse. ED Harry Gerstad. MUS Dimitri Tiomkin. RUNNING TIME 86 min. CAST: Douglas Dick (Major Robinson); Steve Brodie (T. J.); **Jeff Corey** (Doctor); Lloyd Bridges (Finch); Frank Lovejoy (Mingo); James Edwards (Moss).

Hideout (Republic, 1949). DIR Philip Ford. SCR John K. Butler (story by William Porter). CAM John MacBurnie. ED Richard L. Van Enger. MUS Stanley Wilson. RUNNING TIME 61 min. CAST: Adrian Booth (Hannah Kelly); Lloyd Bridges (George Browning); Ray Collins (Arthur Burdette/Philip J. Fogarty); Sheila Ryan (Edie Hansen); **Jeff Corey** (Beecham).

Follow Me Quietly (RKO, 1949). DIR Richard O. Fleischer. PROD Herman Schlom. SCR Lillie Hayward (story by Francis Rosenwald, Anthony Mann). CAM Robert de Grasse. ED Elmo Williams. MUS C. Bakaleinikoff. RUNNING TIME 60 min. CAST: William Lundigan (Lt. Harry Grant); Dorothy Patrick (Ann Gorman); **Jeff Corey** (Sgt. Art Collins); Nestor Paiva (Benny); Charles D. Brown (Mulvaney).

City Across the River (Universal, 1949). DIR-PROD Maxwell Shane. SCR Maxwell Shane, Dennis Cooper (novel *The Amboy Dukes* by Irving Shulman). CAM Maury Gertsman. ED Ted Kent. MUS Walter Scharf. RUNNING TIME 90 min. CAST: Stephen McNally (Stan Albert); Thelma Ritter (Katie Cusack); Luis Van Rooten (Joe Cusack); **Jeff Corey** (Lt. Louie Macon); Sharon McManus (Alice Cusack).

Bright Leaf (Warner Bros., 1950). DIR Michael Curtiz. PROD Henry Blanke. SCR Ranald McDougall (novel by Foster Fitz-Simons). CAM Karl Freund. ED Owen Marks. MUS Victor Young. RUNNING TIME 109 min. CAST: Gary Cooper (Brant Royle); Lauren Bacall (Sonia Kovac); Patricia Neal (Margaret Singleton); Jack Carson (Christopher Malley); Donald Crisp (James Singleton); **Jeff Corey** (John Barton).

Singing Guns (Republic, 1950). DIR R. G. Springsteen. SCR Dorrell McGowan, Stuart McGowan (novel by Max Brand). CAM Reggie Lanning. ED Richard L. Van Enger. MUS Nathan Scott. RUNNING TIME 91 min. CAST: Vaughn Monroe (Rhiannon/"John Gwyn"); Ella Raines (Nan Morgan); Walter Brennan (Jonathan Mark); Ward Bond (Sheriff Caradac); **Jeff Corey** (Richards).

The Outriders (MGM, 1950). DIR Roy Rowland. PROD Richard Goldstone. SCR Irving Ravetch (also story). CAM Charles Schoenbaum. ED Robert J. Kern. MUS André Previn. RUNNING TIME 94 min. CAST: Joel McCrea (Will Owen); Arlene Dahl (Jen Gort); Barry Sullivan (Jesse Wallace); Claude Jarman, Jr. (Roy Gort); James Whitmore (Clint Priest); Ramon Navarro (Don Antonio Chaves); **Jeff Corey** (Keeley).

The Next Voice You Hear... (MGM, 1950). DIR William A. Wellman. PROD Dore Schary. SCR Charles Schnee (short story by George Sumner Albee). CAM William Mellor. ED John Dunning. MUS David Raskin. RUNNING TIME 82 min. CAST: James Whitmore (Joe Smith); Nancy Davis (Mrs. Smith); Gary Gray (Johnny Smith); Lillian Bronson (Aunt Ethel); Art Smith (Mr. Brannan); **Jeff Corey** (Freddie).

Rock Island Trail (Republic, 1950). DIR Joseph Kane. SCR James Edward Grant (novel *A Yankee Dared: A Romance of Our Railroads* by Frank J. Nevins). CAM Jack Marta. ED Arthur Roberts. MUS R. Dale Butts. RUNNING TIME 90 min. CAST: Forrest Tucker (Reed Loomis); Adele Mara (Constance Strong); Adrian Booth (Aleeta); Bruce Cabot (Kirby Morrow); Chill Wills (Hogger); **Jeff Corey** (Abe Lincoln).

The Nevadan (Columbia, 1950). DIR Gordon Douglas. PROD Harry Joe Brown. SCR George W. George, George F. Slavin (story by George W. George, George F. Slavin). CAM Charles Lawton, Jr. ED Richard Fantl. MUS Arthur Morton. RUNNING TIME 80 min. CAST: Randolph Scott (Andy Barkley); Dorothy Malone (Karen Galt); Forrest Tucker (Tom Tanner); Frank Faylen (Jeff); George MacReady (Edward Galt); **Jeff Corey** (Bart).

Only the Valiant (Warner Bros., 1951). DIR Gordon Douglas. PROD William Cagney. SCR Edmund H. North, Harry Brown (novel by Charles Marquis Warren). CAM Lionel Linden. ED Walt Hannemann. MUS Franz Waxman. RUNNING TIME 104 min. CAST: Gregory Peck (Capt. Lance); Barbara Payton (Cathy Eversham); Ward Bond (Cpl. Gilchrist); Lon Chaney, Jr. (Trooper Kebussyan); Neville Brand (Sgt. Murdock); **Jeff Corey** (Joe Harmony); Steve Brodie (Trooper Onstot).

Red Mountain (Paramount, 1951). DIR William Dieterle. PROD Hal Wallis. SCR John Meredyth, George W. George, George F. Slavin (story by George W. George, George F. Slavin). CAM Charles B. Lang, Jr. ED Warren Low. MUS Franz Waxman. RUNNING TIME 84 min. CAST: Alan Ladd (Brett); Lizabeth Scott (Chris); Arthur Kennedy (Lane Waldron); John Ireland (Quantrell); **Jeff Corey** (Skee); James Bell (Dr. Terry).

Fourteen Hours (20th Century Fox, 1951). DIR Henry Hathaway. PROD Sol C. Siegel. SCR John Paxton (story by Joel Sayre). CAM Joe MacDonald. ED Dorothy Spencer. MUS Alfred Newman. RUNNING TIME 91 min. CAST: Paul Douglas (Dunnigan); Richard Basehart (Robert Cosick); Barbara Bel Geddes (Virginia); Debra Paget (Ruth); Agnes Moorehead (Mrs. Cosick); Grace Kelly (Mrs. Fuller); **Jeff Corey** (Sgt. Farley).

New Mexico (United Artists, 1951). DIR Irving Reis. PROD Irving Allen. SCR Max Trell. CAM Jack Greenhalgh, William Snyder. ED Louis Sackin. MUS Lucien Moraweck, Rene Garriguene. RUNNING TIME 84 min. CAST: Lew Ayres (Capt. Hunt); Marilyn Maxwell (Cherry); Robert Hutton (Lt. Vermont); Andy Devine (Sgt. Garrity); Raymond Burr (Pvt. Anderson); **Jeff Corey** (Coyote).

The Prince Who Was a Thief (Universal, 1951). DIR Rudolph Maté. PROD Leonard Goldstein. SCR Gerald Drayson Adams, Aeneas MacKenzie (story by Theodore Reiser). CAM Irving Glassberg. ED Edward Curtiss. MUS Hans J. Salter. RUNNING TIME 87 min. CAST: Tony Curtis (Julna); Piper Laurie (Tina); Everett Sloane (Yussef); **Jeff Corey** (Mokar); Betty Garde (Mirza); Marvin Miller (Hakar).

Rawhide (20th Century Fox, 1951). DIR Henry Hathaway. PROD Samuel G. Engel. SCR Dudley Nichols. CAM Milton Krasner. ED Robert Simpson. MUS Sol Kaplan. RUNNING TIME 87 min. CAST: Tyrone Power (Tom Owens); Susan Hayward (Vinnie Holt); Hugh Marlowe (Zimmerman); Dean Jagger (Yancy); Edgar Buchanan (Sam Todd); Jack Elam (Tevis); **Jeff Corey** (Luke Davis).

Never Trust a Gambler (Columbia, 1951). DIR Ralph Murphy. PROD Monty Shaff, Louis B. Appleton, Jr. SCR Jerome Odlum, Jesse L. Lasky, Jr. (story by Jerome Odlum). CAM Allen Siegler. ED Al Clark. MUS Arthur Morton. RUNNING TIME 78 min. CAST: Dane Clark (Steve Garry); Cathy O'Donnell (Virginia Merrill); Tom Drake (Ed Donovan); **Jeff Corey** (Lou Brecker); Myrna Dell (Dolores Alden); Rhys Williams (Quinten McClory).

Superman and the Mole Men (Lippert, 1951). DIR Lee Sholem. PROD Barney A. Sarecky. SCR Richard Fielding. CAM Clark Ramsey. ED Al Joseph. RUNNING TIME 67 min. CAST: George Reeves (Superman/Clark Kent); Phyllis Coates (Lois Lane); **Jeff Corey** (Luke Benson); Walter Reed (Bill Corrigan); J. Farrell MacDonald (Pop Shannon).

The Main Attraction (MGM, 1962). DIR Daniel Petrie. PROD-SCR John Patrick. CAM Geoffrey Unsworth. ED Geoffrey Foot. MUS Andrew Adorian (title song: Pat Boone, **Jeff Corey**). RUNNING TIME 87 min. CAST: Pat Boone (Eddie); Nancy Kwan (Tessa); Mai Zetterling (Gina); Yvonne Mitchell (Elenora); Kieron Moore (Ricco); John Le Mesurier (Bozo).

The Yellow Canary (20th Century Fox, 1963). DIR Buzz Kulik. PROD Maury Dexter. SCR Rod Serling. CAM Floyd Crosby. ED Jodie Copelan. MUS Kenyon Hopkins. RUNNING TIME 93 min. CAST: Pat Boone (Andy Paxton); Barbara Eden (Lissa); Steve Forrest (Hub Wiley); Jack Klugman (Lt. Bonner); Jessie White (Ed Thornburg); **Jeff Corey** (Joe).

The Balcony (Continental, 1963). DIR Joseph Strick. PROD Ben Maddow, Joseph Strick. SCR Ben Maddow (based on the play *Le Balcon* by Jean Genet). CAM George Folsey. ED Chester W. Schaeffer. MUS Robert Craft. RUNNING TIME 84 min. CAST: Shelley Winters (Madam Irma); Peter Falk (Police Chief); Lee Grant (Carmen); Ruby Dee (Thief); Peter Brocco (Judge); Kent Smith (General); **Jeff Corey** (Bishop).

Lady In a Cage (Paramount, 1964). DIR Walter Grauman. PROD-SCR Luther Davis. CAM Lee Garmes. ED Leon Barsha. MUS Paul Glass. RUNNING TIME 93 min. CAST: Olivia de Havilland (Mrs. Hilyard); Ann

Sothern (Sade); **Jeff Corey** (the Wino); James Caan (Randall); Jennifer Billingsley (Elaine); Rafael Campos (Essie).

Der Schatz der Azteken, a.k.a. *Treasure of the Aztecs* (1965). DIR Robert Siodmak. PROD Arthur Brauner. SCR Ladislas Fodor, Georg Marischka (novel by Karl May). CAM Siegfried Hold. ED Walter Wischniewsky. MUS Erwin Halletz. RUNNING TIME 101 min. CAST: Lex Barker (Karl Sternau); Gérard Barray (Count Alfonso di Rodriganda y Sevilla); Rick Battaglia (Capt. Lozoro Verdoja); Ralf Wolter (Andreas Hassenpferrer); **Jeff Corey** (Abraham Lincoln).

Die Pyramide des Sonnengottes, a.k.a. *The Pyramid of the Sun-God* (1965). DIR Robert Siodmak. PROD Arthur Brauner. SCR Ladislas Fodor, Georg Marischka (novel by Karl May). CAM Siegfried Hold. ED Walter Wischniewsky. MUS Erwin Halletz. RUNNING TIME 98 min. CAST: Lex Barker (Karl Sternau); Gérard Barray (Count Alfonso di Rodriganda y Sevilla); Rick Battaglia (Capt. Lozoro Verdoja); Ralf Wolter (Andreas Hassenpferrer); **Jeff Corey**.

Once a Thief (MGM, 1965). DIR Ralph Nelson. PROD Jacques Bar. SCR Zekial Marko (also novel). CAM Robert Burks. ED Fredric Steinkamp. MUS Lalo Schifrin. RUNNING TIME 106 min. CAST: Alain Delon (Eddie Pedak); Ann-Margret (Kristine Pedak); Van Heflin (Mike Vido); Jack Palance (Walter Pedak); John Davis Chandler (James Sargatanas); **Jeff Corey** (Lt. Kebner).

The Cincinnati Kid (MGM, 1965). DIR Norman Jewison. PROD Martin Ransohoff. SCR Terry Southern, Ring Lardner, Jr. (novel by Richard Jessup) CAM Philip H. Lathrop. ED Hal Ashby. MUS Lalo Schifrin. RUNNING TIME 113 min. CAST: Steve McQueen (the Cincinnati Kid); Edward G. Robinson (Lancey Howard); Ann-Margret (Melba); Karl Malden (Shooter); Tuesday Weld (Christian); Joan Blondell (Lady Fingers); **Jeff Corey** (Hoban).

Mickey One (Columbia, 1965). DIR-PROD Arthur Penn. SCR Alan M. Surgal. CAM Ghislain Cloquet. ED Aram Avakian. MUS Jack Schaindlin. RUNNING TIME 93 min. CAST: Warren Beatty (Mickey One); Alexandra Stewart (Jenny); Hurd Hatfield (Castle); Franchot Tone (Ruby Lopp); Teddy Hart (Berson); **Jeff Corey** (Fryer).

Seconds (Paramount, 1966). DIR John Frankenheimer. PROD Edward Lewis. SCR Lewis John Carlino (novel by David Ely). CAM James Wong Howe. ED Ferris Webster, David Webster. MUS Jerry Goldsmith. RUNNING TIME 106 min. CAST: Rock Hudson (Antiochus Wilson); Salome Jens (Nora Marcus); John Randolph (Arthur Hamilton); Will Geer (The Old Man); **Jeff Corey** (Mr. Ruby); Richard Anderson (Dr. Innes); Murray Hamilton (Charlie Evans).

In Cold Blood (Columbia, 1967). DIR-PROD Richard Brooks. SCR Richard Brooks (novel by Truman Capote). CAM Conrad Hall. ED Peter Zinner. MUS Quincy Jones. RUNNING TIME 134 min. CAST: Robert Blake (Perry Smith); Scott Wilson (Dick Hickock); John Forsythe (Alvin Dewey); Paul Stewart (Reporter); Gerald S. O'Loughlin (Harold Nye); **Jeff Corey** (Dick's Father).

The Boston Strangler (20th Century Fox, 1968). DIR Richard Fleischer. PROD Robert Fryer. SCR Edward Anhalt (novel by Gerold Frank). CAM Richard H. Kline. ED Marion Rothman. MUS Lionel Newman. RUNNING TIME 116 min. CAST: Tony Curtis (Albert DeSalvo); Henry Fonda (John S. Bottomly); George Kennedy (Phil DeNatale); Mike Kellin (Julian Soshnick); Hurd Hatfield (Terence Huntley); Murray Hamilton (Frank McAfee); **Jeff Corey** (John Asgeirsson).

Impasse (United Artists, 1969). DIR Richard Benedict. PROD Hal Klein. SCR John C. Higgins. CAM Mars Rasca. ED John F. Schreyer. MUS Philip Springer. RUNNING TIME 100 min. CAST: Burt Reynolds (Pat Morrison); Anne Francis (Bobby Jones); Lyle Bettger (Hansen); Rodolfo Acosta (Draco); **Jeff Corey** (Wombat); Clarke Gordon (Trev Jones).

True Grit (Paramount, 1969). DIR Henry Hathaway. PROD Hal Wallis. SCR Marguerite Roberts (novel by Charles Portis). CAM Lucien Ballard. ED Warren Low. MUS Elmer Bernstein. RUNNING TIME 128 min. CAST: John Wayne (Rooster Cogburn); Glen Campbell (La Boeuf); Kim Darby (Mattie Ross); Jeremy Slate (Emmett Quincy); Robert Duvall (Ned Pepper); Dennis Hopper (Moon); **Jeff Corey** (Tom Chaney).

Butch Cassidy and the Sundance Kid (20th Century Fox, 1969). DIR George Roy Hill. PROD John Foreman. SCR William Goldman. CAM Conrad Hall. ED John C. Howard, Richard C. Meyer. MUS Burt Bacharach. RUNNING TIME 110 min. CAST: Paul Newman (Butch Cassidy); Robert Redford (Sundance Kid); Katharine Ross (Etta Place); Strother Martin (Percy Garris); Henry Jones (Bike Salesman); **Jeff Corey** (Sheriff Bledshoe).

Beneath the Planet of the Apes (20th Century Fox, 1970). DIR Ted Post. PROD Arthur P. Jacobs. SCR Paul Dehn (story by Paul Dehn, Mort Abrahams; characters created by Pierre Boulle). CAM Milton Krasner. ED Marion Rothman. MUS Leonard Rosenman. RUNNING TIME 95 min. CAST: Charlton Heston (Taylor); James Franciscus (Brent); Kim Hunter (Zira); Maurice Evans (Dr. Zaius); Linda Harrison (Nova); **Jeff Corey** (Caspay).

Getting Straight (Columbia, 1970). DIR-PROD Richard Rush. SCR Robert Kaufman (novel by Ken Kolb). CAM Laszlo Kovacs. ED Maury Winetrobe. MUS Ronald Stein. RUNNING TIME 124 min. CAST: Elliott Gould (Harry Bailey); Candice Bergen (Jan); **Jeff Corey** (Dr. Willhunt); Max Julian (Ellis); Robert F. Lyons (Nick); Cecil Kellaway (Dr. Kasper).

They Call Me MISTER Tibbs! (United Artists, 1970). DIR Gordon Douglas. PROD Walter Mirisch. SCR Alan R. Trustman, James R. Webb (story by Alan R. Trustman, characters created by John Ball). CAM Gerald Finnerman. ED Bud Molin. MUS Quincy Jones. RUNNING TIME 108 min. CAST: Sidney Poitier (Virgil Tibbs); Martin Landau (Rev. Logan Sharpe); Barbara McNair (Valerie Tibbs); Anthony Zerbe (Rice Weedon), **Jeff Corey** (Capt. Marden).

Little Big Man (National General, 1970). DIR Arthur Penn. PROD Stuart Miller. SCR Calder Willingham (novel by Thomas Berger). CAM Harry Stradling, Jr. ED Dede Allen. MUS John Hammond. RUNNING TIME 150 min. CAST: Dustin Hoffman (Jack Crabb); Faye Dunaway (Mrs. Pendrake); Martin Balsam (Allardyce T. Merriweather); Richard Mulligan (Gen. Custer); Chief Dan George (Old Lodge Skins); **Jeff Corey** (Wild Bill Hickock).

Cover Me Babe (20th Century Fox, 1970). DIR Noel Black. PROD Lester Linsk. SCR George Wells. CAM Michel Hugo. ED Harry Gerstad. MUS Fred Karling. RUNNING TIME 89 min. CAST: Robert Forster (Tony); Sondra Locke (Melisse); Susanne Benton (Sybil); Robert S. Fields (Will); Ken Kercheval (Jerry); Sam Waterston (Cameraman); **Jeff Corey** (Paul).

Shoot Out (Universal, 1971). DIR Henry Hathaway. PROD Hal B. Wallis. SCR Marguerite Roberts (novel *The Lone Cowboy* by Will James). CAM Earl Rath. ED Archie Marshek. MUS David Grusin. RUNNING TIME 94 min. CAST: Gregory Peck (Clay Lomax); Pat Quinn (Juliana); Robert F. Lyons (Bobby Jay); Susan Tyrrell (Alma); **Jeff Corey** (Trooper); James Gregory (Sam Foley).

Catlow (MGM, 1971). DIR Sam Wanamaker. PROD Euan Lloyd. SCR Scott Finch, J. J. Griffith (novel by Louis L'Amour). CAM Ted Sciafe. ED John Glen, Alan Killick. MUS Roy Budd. RUNNING TIME 101 min. CAST: Yul Brynner (Catlow); Richard Crenna (Cowen); Leonard Nimoy (Miller); Daliah Lavi (Rosita); Jo Ann Pflug (Christina); **Jeff Corey** (Merridew).

Clay Pigeon (MGM, 1971). DIR Tom Stern, Lane Slate. PROD Tom Stern. SCR Ronald Buck, Buddy Ruskin, Jack Gross, Jr. (story by Buddy Ruskin, Jack Gross, Jr.). CAM Alan Stensvold. ED Danford Greene. MUS Gavin Murrell. RUNNING TIME 93 min. CAST: Telly Savalas (Frank); Robert Vaughn (Henry); John Marley (Police Captain); Burgess Meredith (Freedom); Ian Dixon (Simon); Tom Stern (Joe); **Jeff Corey** (Doctor).

Paper Tiger (Joseph E. Levine, 1975). DIR Ken Annakin. PROD Euan Lloyd. SCR Jack Davies. CAM John Cabrera. ED Alan Patillo. MUS Roy Budd. RUNNING TIME 101 min. CAST: David Niven (Walter); Toshiro Mifune (Ambassador); Hardy Kruger (Muller); Ando (Koichi); Ivan Desny (Foreign Minister); **Jeff Corey** (King).

The Last Tycoon (Paramount, 1976). DIR Elia Kazan. PROD Sam Spiegel. SCR Harold Pinter (novel by F. Scott Fitzgerald). CAM Victor Kemper. ED Richard Marks. MUS Maurice Jarre. RUNNING TIME 122 min. CAST: Robert De Niro (Monroe Stahr); Tony Curtis (Rodriguez); Robert Mitchum (Pat Brady); Jeanne Moreau (Didi); Jack Nicholson (Brimmer); Donald Pleasence (Boxley); **Jeff Corey** (Doctor).

The Premonition (Avco Embassy, 1976). DIR-PROD Robert Allen Schnitzer. SCR Robert Allen Schnitzer, Anthony Mahon, Louis Pastore. CAM Victor C. Milt. ED Sidney Katz. MUS Henry Mollicone, Pril Smiley. RUNNING TIME 90 min. CAST: Sharon Farrell (Sheri); Richard Lynch (Jude); **Jeff Corey** (Det. Denver); Ellen Barber (Andrea); Edward Bell (Miles).

Oh, God! (Warner Bros., 1977). DIR Carl Reiner. PROD Jerry Weintraub. SCR Larry Gelbart (novel by Avery Corman). CAM Victor Kemper. ED Bud Molin. MUS Jack Elliott. RUNNING TIME 97 min. CAST: George Burns (God); John Denver (Jerry Landers); Teri Garr (Bobbie Landers); Donald Pleasence (Dr. Harmon); Ralph Bellamy (Sam Raven); **Jeff Corey** (Rabbi).

Moonshine County Express (New World, 1977). DIR Gus Trikonis. PROD Ed Carlin. SCR Hubert Smith, Daniel Ansley. CAM Gary Graver. ED Gene Ruggiero. MUS Fred Werner. RUNNING TIME 95 min. CAST: John Saxon (J. B. Johnson); Susan Howard (Dot); William Conrad (Starkey); Morgan Woodward (Sweetwater); Claudia Jennings (Betty); **Jeff Corey** (Preacher Hagen).

Jennifer (American International, 1978). DIR Brice Mack. PROD Steve Krantz. SCR Kay Cousins Johnson (story by Steve Krantz). CAM Irv Goodnoff. ED Duane Hartzell. MUS Porter Jordan. RUNNING TIME 90 min. CAST: Lisa Pelikan (Jennifer); Bert Convy (Jeff); Nina Foch (Mrs. Calley); Amy Johnston (Sandra); John Gavin (Senator Tremayne); **Jeff Corey** (Luke).

The Wild Geese (Allied Artists, 1978). DIR Andrew V. McLaglen. PROD Euan Lloyd. SCR Reginald Rose (novel by Daniel Carney). CAM Jack Hildyard. ED John Glen. MUS Roy Budd. RUNNING TIME 132 min. CAST: Richard Burton (Col. Faulkner); Roger Moore (Lt. Flynn); Richard Harris (Capt. Janders); Hardy Kruger (Lt. Coetzee); Stewart Granger (Sir Edward Malherson); **Jeff Corey** (Martin).

Butch and Sundance: The Early Years (20th Century Fox, 1979). DIR Richard Lester. PROD Gabriel Katzka, Steven Bach. SCR Allan Burns (characters created by William Goldman). CAM Laszlo Kovacs. ED Antony Gibbs, George Trirogoff. MUS Patrick Williams. RUNNING TIME 110 min. CAST: William Katt (Butch Cassidy); Tom Berenger (Sundance Kid); Jill Eikenberry (Mary); Paul Plunkett (Bobby); Wesley Burgess (Sam); **Jeff Corey** (Ray Bledshoe).

Up River (1979). DIR Carl Kitt. CAST: Morgan Stevens (Jacob Taylor); **Jeff Corey** (Bagshaw); Dale Wilson (Keeler); John Bear Curtis (Mungal); David Crowley (Jules); Mikal Dughi (Judith).

Battle Beyond the Stars (New World, 1980). DIR Jimmy T. Murakami. PROD Ed Carlin. SCR John Sayles (story by John Sayles, Anne Dyer). CAM Daniel Lacambre. ED Allan Holtzman, Bob Kizer. MUS James Horner. RUNNING TIME 104 min. CAST: Richard Thomas (Shad); Robert Vaughn (Gelt); John Saxon (Sador); Darlanne Fluegel (Nanelia); George Peppard (Cowboy); Sam Jaffe (Dr. Hephaestus); **Jeff Corey** (Zed).

The Sword and the Sorcerer (Group I, 1982). DIR Albert Pyun. PROD Brandon Chase, Mariane Chase. SCR Albert Pyun, Thomas Karnowski, John Stuckmeyer. CAM Joseph Mangine. ED Marshall Harvey. MUS David Whittaker. RUNNING TIME 100 min. CAST: Lee Horsley (Talon); Kathleen Beller (Alana); Simon MacCorkindale (Mikah); George Maharis (Machelli); Richard Lynch (Cromwell); **Jeff Corey** (Craccus).

Rooster: Spurs of Death (1983). DIR Brice Mack. SCR John F. Eastman. RUNNING TIME 92 min. CAST: Gene Bicknell (Stoke); **Jeff Corey** (Kink); William Dial (Willard); Kristine De Bell (Melody).

Conan the Destroyer (Universal, 1984). DIR Richard Fleischer. PROD Raffaella De Laurentiis. SCR Stanley Mann (story by Roy Thomas, Gerry Conway, characters created by Robert E. Howard). CAM Jack Cardiff. ED Frank J. Urioste. MUS Basil Poledouris. RUNNING TIME 103 min. CAST: Arnold Schwarzenegger (Conan); Grace Jones (Zula); Wilt Chamberlain (Bombaara); Mako (Akjiro The "Wizard"); Tracey Walter (Malak); **Jeff Corey** (Grand Vizier).

Creator (Universal, 1985). DIR Ivan Passer. PROD Stephen Friedman. SCR Jeremy Laven (also novel). CAM Robbie Greenberg. ED Richard Chew. MUS Sylvester Levay. RUNNING TIME 114 min. CAST: Peter O'Toole (Harry); Mariel Hemingway (Meli); Vincent Spano (Boris); Virginia Madsen (Barbara); David Ogden Stiers (Sid); **Jeff Corey** (Dean Harrington).

Messenger of Death (Cannon, 1988). DIR J. Lee Thompson. PROD Pancho Kohner. SCR Paul Jarrico. CAM Gideon Porath. ED Peter Lee Thompson. MUS Robert O. Ragland. RUNNING TIME 92 min. CAST: Charles Bronson (Garrett Smith); Trish Van Devere (Jastra Watson); Laurence Luckinbill (Homer Foxx); Daniel Benzali (Chief Doyle); **Jeff Corey** (Willis Beacham).

Tajna Manastirske Rakjie, a.k.a. *Secret Ingredient* (1989). DIR Slobodan Sijan. SCR Ric Hardman, Christopher Longshadow (story by Ric Hardman). CAST: Rick Rossovich (Bogoljub/Prior Nakamia); Catherine Hicks (Ella Frazier); Gary Kroeger (Charles Lawrence); **Jeff Corey** (Col. Frazier); Brad Dexter (Veljeko Pantovich); Sam Wanamaker (Ambassador Morley).

Bird on a Wire (Universal, 1990). DIR John Badham. PROD Rob Cohen. SCR David Seltzer, Louis Venosta, Eric Lerner (story by Louis Venosta, Eric Lerner). CAM Robert Primes. ED Frank Morriss, Dallas Puett. MUS Hans Zimmer. RUNNING TIME 113 min. CAST: Mel Gibson (Rick Jarmin); Goldie Hawn (Marianne Graves); David Carradine (Eugene Sorenson); Bill Duke (Albert Diggs); **Jeff Corey** (Lou Baird).

Ruby Cairo, retitled *Deception* (Miramax, 1993). DIR Graeme Clifford. PROD Lloyd Philips. SCR Robert Dillon, Michael Thomas (story by Robert Dillon). CAM Laszlo Kovacs. ED Caroline Biggerstaff. RUNNING TIME 90 min. CAST: Andie MacDowell (Bessie Faro); Liam Neeson (Fergus Lamb); Viggo Mortensen (Johnny Faro); Jack Thompson (Ed); Paul Spencer (Johnny Faro as a Boy); Chad Power (Niles); **Jeff Corey** (Joe Dick).

Beethoven 2nd (Universal, 1993). DIR Rod Daniel. PROD Michael C. Gross, Joe Medjuck. SCR Len Blum. CAM Bill Butler. ED Sheldon Kahn, William D. Gordean. MUS Randy Edelman. RUNNING TIME 88 min. CAST: Charles Grodin (George Newton); Bonnie Hunt (Alice Newton); Nicholle Tom (Rye Newton); Christopher Castile (Ted Newton); Sarah Rose Karr (Emily Newton); **Jeff Corey** (Janitor).

The Judas Project (RS Entertainment, 1993). DIR-SCR-MUS James H. Barden. CAM Bryan England. ED Noreen Zepp Linden. RUNNING TIME 97 min. CAST: John O'Banion (Jesse); Ramy Zada (Jude); Richard Herd (Arthur Cunningham); Gerald Gordon (Jackson); **Jeff Corey** (Poneras).

Color of Night (Hollywood Pictures, 1994). DIR Richard Rush. PROD Buzz Feitshans, David Matalon. SCR Matthew Chapman, Billy Ray (story by Billy Ray). CAM Dietrich Lohmann. ED Jack Hofstra. MUS Dominic Frontiere. RUNNING TIME 121 min. CAST: Bruce Willis (Dr. Bill Capa); Jane March (Rose); Ruben Blades (Martinez); Lesley Ann Warren (Sondra); Scott Bakula (Dr. Moore); **Jeff Corey** (Ashland).

Surving the Game (New Line Cinema, 1994). DIR Ernest Dickerson. PROD David Permut. SCR Eric Bernt. CAM Bojan Bazelli. ED Sam Pollard. MUS Stewart Copeland. RUNNING TIME 96 min. CAST: Ice-T (Mason); Rutger Hauer (Burns); Charles S. Dutton (Cole); Gary Busey (Hawkins); F. Murray Abraham (Wolfe, Sr.); **Jeff Corey** (Hank).

Ted (1998). DIR Gary Ellenberg. SCR Gary Ellenberg, Daniel Passer, A. J. Peralta. CAM Stops Langensteiner. ED John Wolfenden. MUS Evan Eder. RUNNING TIME 85 min. CAST: Daniel Passer (Ted); Edie McClurg (Mother); Richard Fancy (Father); **Jeff Corey** (Professor); Paul Provenza (Brother); Andy Dick (Sheriff).

Television Movies

The Movie Murderer (1970). DIR Boris Sagal. CAST: Arthur Kennedy; Warren Oates; Tom Selleck; **Jeff Corey** (Collier Landis); Robert Webber; Elisha Cook, Jr.

A Clear and Present Danger (1970). DIR James Goldstone. CAST: Hal Holbrook; E. G. Marshall; Joseph Campanella; Jack Albertson; **Jeff Corey** (Beiseker).

Something Evil (1972). DIR Steven Spielberg. CAST: Sandy Dennis; Darren McGavin; Ralph Bellamy; **Jeff Corey** (Gehrmann); Johnny Whitaker.

Set This Town on Fire (1973). DIR David Lowell Rich. CAST: Chuck Connors; Carl Betz; Linda Day George; Charles Robinson; **Jeff Corey** (Walter Stafford).

The Gun and the Pulpit (1974). DIR Daniel Petrie. CAST: Walter Barnes; Jason Clark; **Jeff Corey** (Head of Posse); Melanie Fullerton.

Banjo Hackett: Roamin' Free, a.k.a. *Banjo Hackett* (1976). DIR Andrew V. McLaglen. CAST: Chuck Connors; L. Q. Jones; **Jeff Corey** (Judge Janeway); Anne Francis; Slim Pickens.

Captains Courageous (1977). DIR Harvey Hart. CAST: Karl Malden; Jonathan Kahn; Fred Gwynne; **Jeff Corey** (Salters); Fritz Weaver; Ricardo Montalban.

Testimony of Two Men (1977). DIR Leo Penn, Larry Yust. CAST: David Birney; Barbara Parkins; Ralph Bellamy; Ray Milland; **Jeff Corey** (William Simpson).

Curse of the Black Widow (1977). DIR Dan Curtis. CAST: Anthony Franciosa; Donna Mills; Patty Duke; June Allyson; **Jeff Corey** (Aspa Soldado).

The Pirate (1978). DIR Ken Annakin. CAST: Franco Nero; Anne Archer; Olivia Hussey; Christopher Lee; Eli Wallach; **Jeff Corey** (Prince Feiyad).

The Greatest Heroes of the Bible (1978). DIR James L. Conway. CAST: Julie Adams; John Carradine; John Saxon; Robert Vaughn; **Jeff Corey** (Saul).

Homeward Bound (1980). DIR Richard Michaels. CAST: David Soul; Moosie Drier; Barnard Hughes; **Jeff Corey** (George).

Cry for the Strangers (1982). DIR Peter Medak. CAST: Patrick Duffy; Cindy Pickett; Lawrence Pressman; Brian Keith; **Jeff Corey** (Riley).

Father of Hell Town (1985). DIR Don Medford. CAST: Robert Blake; James Gammon; Fran Ryan; **Jeff Corey** (Sam).

Final Jeopardy (1985). DIR Michael Pressman. CAST: Richard Thomas; Mary Crosby; **Jeff Corey** (Derelict); Jonathan Goldsmith.

Second Serve, a.k.a. *I Changed My Life* (1986). DIR Anthony Page. CAST: Vanessa Redgrave; Martin Balsam; Louise Fletcher; **Jeff Corey** (Harry Benjamin).

A Deadly Silence (1989). DIR John Patterson. CAST: Heather Fairfield; Charles Haid; **Jeff Corey** (Judge); Sally Struthers.

The Rose and the Jackal (1990). DIR Jack Gold. CAST: Christopher Reeve; Kevin McCarthy; **Jeff Corey**; Madolyn Smith-Osborne.

To My Daughter (1990). DIR Larry Shaw. CAST: Rue McClanahan; Samantha Mathis; Ty Miller; **Jeff Corey** (Travis).

Payoff (1991). DIR Stuart Cooper. CAST: Keith Carradine; Kim Greist; Harry Dean Stanton; John Saxon; **Jeff Corey** (Don Anzia).

Sinatra (1992). DIR James Steven Sadwith. CAST: Philip Casnoff; Olympia Dukakis; Joe Santos; Gina Gershon; **Jeff Corey** (Quinlin).

The Lottery (1996). DIR Daniel Sackheim. CAST: Dan Cortese; Keri Russell; Veronica Cartwright; **Jeff Corey** (Albert Smith).

BEVERLY GARLAND

Beverly Garland made her screen debut in Rudolph Maté's prestigious film noir *D.O.A.* (1950; as Beverly Campbell); she then became one of Roger Corman's leading actresses in several of his films in the 1950s, until she made a very successful transition to television. In 1957 she became the first actress in American television to star in the title role of a dramatic series when she appeared as television's first policewoman, undercover cop Casey Jones, in *Decoy*. Later she played the wife of screen veterans like Bing Crosby and Fred MacMurray in other popular TV series.

The Santa Cruz, California, native, born as Beverly Lucy Fessenden on October 17, 1926, is now in what she calls "my second 50 years in show business." She received her star on the Hollywood Walk of Fame in 1983 and on January 19, 2001, the City of Los Angeles, in recognition of her 50 years in films and television, declared that day "Beverly Garland Day" in the city.

Miss Garland, who in 2002 continued as a recurring regular on two TV series and made guest starring appearances in others, spends most of her time off-camera at her office in the impressive Southern California mission-style, luxurious 255 room Beverly Garland's Holiday Inn (www.beverlygarland.com) in North Hollywood, California, where I got to meet her. The hotel was built in 1971 by her late husband, developer Fillmore Crank, and is only a few blocks from the main entrance to Universal Studios Hollywood. It teamed with the Holiday Inn about ten years ago, but Miss Garland still manages, operates and owns it.

Always acting and writing poetry as a young girl, she was destined to become an artist. Miss Garland: "I had done a few plays in Glendale before I joined [former Broadway actress] Anita Arliss—she was the sister of George Arliss,[1] a very remarkable character actor. She taught acting, but those weren't really acting lessons compared to what you could learn later on: mainly she trained your voice. In those days voice teachers were very big at the studios: the studios *listened* to them, also because she was very well-known, but unfortunately a little later she died of a heart attack [in 1945]. Subsequently, I did a lot of radio work and had my own show for the Salvation Army. After I graduated in 1945, I took drama lessons at Glendale College.

"I then decided to quit college and got into summer stock to get my Equity card, and I did a lot of plays. My parents had a friend who knew an agent by the name of Ray Cooper; he came down to see me at Laguna Beach and he suggested to represent me. He got me an interview for *D.O.A.* [1950], I tested with Eddie [Edmond O'Brien] and I got the part."

Miss Garland played the role of William Ching's secretary, a very promising start it seemed, but due to an unfortunate misunderstanding, she became the victim of studio blacklisting. "After the film was finished, my publicity man took me to dinner to meet a number of people. Somebody at the table asked me if I thought that D.O.A. could win the Academy Award. I said, 'No, I don't think so'—there was another picture I thought would win, but I can't remember which one it was. The next day, my publicity man went back to the producers and said, 'You know, this girl doesn't appreciate anything you've done for her. You took her on when she was unknown, and last night she said she didn't think the picture could win the Academy Award. I think she is very ungrateful.'"

"Meanwhile my agent got me up for several other pictures and he told the producers, 'All you have to do is talk to the producers of D.O.A. and they'll tell you how good she is.' Well of course, when they called the producers of D.O.A., they said, 'Well, we don't recommend that young girl, she doesn't appreciate what we've done for her.' This went on for a couple of months and one day, my agent met the producers and he said, 'You know, I sent Beverly out and I had a number of producers call you, and nothing ever happened!' They said, 'Oh really?' They told the whole story, and I decided to walk up to their office myself. They were both sitting at their desk and I said, 'I feel very badly about this, I certainly *do* appreciate everything you did for me and I should not have said that I didn't think D.O.A. couldn't win the Academy Award.' They looked me straight in the eye and said, 'We don't know what you are talking about.' I sat down and thought, I'm not getting anywhere here. So I left and I was blackballed for a few years.

"I was a young girl, I had to work, I had to *support* myself and worked in between as a waitress, an elevator operator, worked for a doctor, did a few plays and some television work—television was just starting out then. I joined the Players Ring, a small theater in Hollywood, appeared in a show which got great reviews, and a lot of people saw me working again."

She resurfaced and appeared in films again, playing small parts in pictures like *The Glass Web* (1953) opposite Edward G. Robinson and William Wyler's *The Desperate Hours* (1955), while in between she did a lot of television. When Roger Corman[2] cast her in *Swamp Women* (1955), it was a turning point in her career: Miss Garland became a leading lady in several cheaply made Westerns, science fiction and horror films (all popular with the drive-in audiences) and over the years several of those became cult-classic B-films. Miss Garland: "Roger Corman was very instrumental in my career and he wanted to put me under contract, but I didn't want that—I was hoping I could do something else beside monster movies for the rest of my life. But he was very efficient: he was a brilliant man, he could do nearly anything and he had good, young and dynamic writers who all worked very well together.

"I remember we once were on location for *Gunslinger* [1956], we were in this little barn. Allison Hayes[3] came riding in on her horse right before lunch, and they were wondering if they were going to have lunch or not. All of a sudden she fell from her horse and broke her arm—I think she wanted to get out of the movie—then Roger Corman ran over and said, 'Oh Allison, you'll be okay!' They called a doctor and took her to the hospital, they put her arm in a sling and she finished the movie, with a broken arm [laughs]."

That was also the movie in which Miss Garland played the sheriff and in one of the scenes she had to run up to the bar where all the girls were, fight with them and then kick them out of town. Miss Garland: "That was the last scene of the movie that we shot, and Roger decided to rent a studio for that one scene where we'd be more contained. The day before, we were shooting the scenes where you see me going in the bar and where you see me coming out—that's *after* the fight which was going to be filmed the following day, and as I come down, Roger says to me, 'I want you to come right down the stairs, jump on your horse and ride out of town.' I am not a stunt girl, so I said, 'Jump on my horse and ride out of town?' 'Yeah!' Okay then, so I came down the stairs, and I said to myself, 'Think high, Beverly, think high!'

Beverly Garland in a posed publicity still for Roger Corman's *It Conquered the World* (1956). (Courtesy of Beverly Garland.)

John Ireland and Beverly Garland in *Gunslinger* (1956), another film made by Roger Corman. (Courtesy of Beverly Garland.)

I *ran* down the stairs, *jumped* on my horse, I went right over the horse and fell down. The cameraman said, 'She came up, but she never hit the saddle!'

"So I had to do it again: I ran down the stairs, but then I twisted my ankle and I couldn't walk. In the evening I went home, put my foot in hot water and the next morning my ankle was *this* big. I knew then I couldn't do the fight scene. On the set, I told Roger, 'You know I twisted my ankle yesterday. I can't walk, I can't do this fight scene.' He looked at me and said, 'Okay.' After a while this doctor came in, he gave me five shots in my ankle, he taped everything up and I worked all day. I did all the fights, I felt great! But after that, I didn't work for a month, because I couldn't walk. Those are the kind of things that happened with Roger Corman, never say *no* [laughs]. He'll do it, no matter what."

That same year, she appeared in *Curucu, Beast of the Amazon* (1956), shot on location in Brazil. "There we did everything ourselves," she remembers, as there was no dressing room, no trailer, not even a bathroom on the set. On top of that, it was very difficult to communicate with director Curt Siodmak[4] as he mainly spoke German and Portuguese. There is a famous scene in the film when she has to struggle with a snake—not just an ordinary snake, it turned out to be a boa constrictor. Miss Garland: "I was terrified. It was a *looong* snake; when they brought it on the set, three natives were holding the snake at one end and three at the other end. Then they wrapped it around me, and when they started shooting, I was lying on the ground, fighting with the snake and screaming. All of a sudden Curt Siodmak says, 'Cut! Cut!' I asked, 'What's the matter?' And he said, 'Are you all right?' I said, 'Sure,

Studio portrait of Beverly Garland. (Courtesy of Beverly Garland.)

I'm okay! Aren't I supposed to be *screaming* with this thing around me?' 'Yes, but I just wanted to make sure you were all right.' I said, 'I'm all right, let's do the damn scene and get out of here!'"

Other films she made in those days include *It Conquered the World* (1956), with Miss Garland playing the wife of scientist Lee Van Cleef who initially collaborates with an alien force (remade in 1968 as *Zontar, The Thing from Venus* with John Agar); *Not of This Earth* (1957), with its leading character Paul Birch who, as the title indicates, comes from outer space (the film was remade three times); and *The Alligator People* (1959), directed by veteran Roy Del Ruth, with Miss Garland trying to locate her husband (Richard Crane)—when she finally tracks him down in Louisiana, he's partly transformed into an alligator. Her Westerns include *Badlands of Montana* (1957), playing the part of outlaw Emile Meyer's daughter, and *The Saga of Hemp Brown* (1958) with Rory Calhoun as a former U.S. cavalry officer who intends to capture the killers of an ambush which cost the lives of several soldiers as well as his colonel's wife. Most of those low-budget films had a hard time competing with the blockbuster films released by the major studios, but in the end they often proved to be very original, interesting, stimulating, honest, skillful and rewarding. Furthermore they could rely on a strong and fast-paced dialogue. Miss Garland: "Back then, they were only shown in drive-in theatres, but now there's a whole cult to see these films, because they're so real, while today you don't know if it's done digitally or not. In those days you *knew* that that's the way it was and that people got a kick out of them. Roger Corman used to shoot an entire picture in nearly one week or ten days at the most; we all worked our heads off, we were all very young and we did the very best we could. We didn't look at those pictures as *quickies*, we considered them good movies and that's why I think some of his films have held up very well. We took it very seriously."

While appearing in B-films, she was approached to play opposite Frank Sinatra in *The Joker Is Wild* (1957) as Eddie Albert's wife. Miss Garland: "That was a wonderful opportunity for me, but right after I finished that movie, a producer came up to me and asked if I would be interested in doing a television show, called *Decoy*, which was the story of a New York police woman who goes undercover and plays different parts, from housewives and secretaries to prostitutes and prisoners. I thought it was the most wonderful thing that ever happened, so I accepted. I went to New York where I did 39 shows." As a result of this rewarding and successful experience and because of her body of work in television, appearing in several guest

Rory Calhoun and Beverly Garland in *The Saga of Hemp Brown* (1958). (Courtesy of Beverly Garland.)

starring roles before *Decoy* (and earning an Emmy nomination in 1954 in the category "Best Actress in a Single Performance" for her role in "White Is the Color"), the *Los Angeles Times* crowned her "Television's First Lady" in 1957.

After she finished *Decoy*, Miss Garland returned to Hollywood: "Unfortunately if you had done television, you had a black spot on your forehead, meaning it would be very difficult to work in pictures again. So when I went back to television, I became a television *child*, appear-

Publicity still of Beverly Garland in *The Alligator People* (1959), directed by veteran Roy Del Ruth. (Courtesy of Beverly Garland.)

ing in numerous TV shows. Still, I think I lived in the best time, the only bad part is that there was transition of movies and television, that made it very difficult: if you did television, you couldn't do movies and if you did movies, you didn't want to do television because you wouldn't be able to do a movie.

"I remember I did the pilot of *Dr. Kildaire* with Richard Chamberlain and I went to MGM for wardrobe; I had worked there before and I knew where the wardrobe department was, so I walked in and said, 'Hi, I'm Beverly Garland and I'm doing the pilot for the television show with Dick Chamberlain.' This lady said, 'Just sit over there and I'll call you.' I sat there for maybe 45 minutes and then I said, 'Hello, I'm here to do wardrobe for *Dr. Kildaire*.'' She said, 'Oh my dear child, we do motion pictures here and when there is enough time for you, we'll let you know. Just be seated, I'll call you.' If you look at television now, it is *everything*, they even advertise pictures on television, they *use* television, but in those days they believed that television was something that wouldn't last and they didn't want their actors, for whom people spent money to go to the motion picture show, to see those same people on free television in your living room. Some major stars like Dick Powell also worked for television—he had his own company with Ida Lupino, David Niven and Charles Boyer [the four of them founded the Four Star Playhouse TV Show which became Four Star Television]—but they were all such big stars that they were able to appear both on television and in pictures at the same time."

Unfortunately most people don't remember who Dick Powell, Charles Boyer or Ida Lupino were or what they achieved. Miss Garland: "That's too bad, isn't it? They were such wonderful people—I worked with Charles Boyer, he was a wonderful actor, but they could only film one side of his face. He thought the other side of his face didn't look right. I remember I had to walk around a whole couch to get to the other side of his face, we almost had to choreograph this so that only the 'right' side of his face was shown. Just as most people have forgotten about him, 40 years from now, people will not remember the stars of today either, except only a few who will be remembered always, like Marilyn Monroe, Mae West or Charlton Heston."

Her TV series include *The Bing Crosby Show* which was canceled in 1965 after one season because Bing Crosby wasn't too happy with the ratings, she joined Fred MacMurray and the rest of the cast of *My Three Sons* (1969–72), and played Kate Jackson's mother in *The Scarecrow and Mrs. King* (1983–86). Miss Garland: "When the producers approached me to do *The Bing Crosby Show*, they told me, 'In this series, you are very much in love with Bing Crosby[5] and that has to come over in the television show. He will not give you anything, he will not be affectionate, he's very undemonstrative, so it is entirely up to you to let us see you are in love with him.' Still, he was a fascinating man, because he had a photographic memory. While I was studying my lines like crazy, he would go over the script, page by page, just look at his lines, and he knew them! He also knew every song he had ever sung. We had a piano player on the set because he *loved* to sing, he had to have music around him. He was not particularly cold, but he was kind of *away* from everybody. He didn't socialize with anybody on the set, he didn't participate. When Christmas came, big stars used to give presents to their co-stars, so we were all fascinated with what he would give to us [laughs]. He gave everybody a 8 × 10 picture of himself. We didn't think that was so sharp [laughs]. He was tight, let's put it that way."

What about Fred MacMurray? Miss Garland: "Fred MacMurray[6] was a sweetheart of a man, very conservative, and he probably ended up having the first dime he ever made. There's a wonderful story about him, more specifically about a man who goes up to God and says, 'Oh, I'm here, God, but I can't just sit around here on cloud nine and do nothing. I have got to be busy, can You give me something to last me 70,000 years?' God says, 'Okay, here's a teaspoon, you take all the sand of the Mojave Desert and put it in the Sahara Desert.' All of those 70,000 years go by, and he did it! So he goes back to God and says, 'Could You please

Charles Boyer (1897–1979), French actor who became a major screen star in the United States, was one of the founders of Four Star Television.

Fred MacMurray with Beverly Garland, the children (left to right: Don Grady, Dawn Lyn, Barry Livingston, Stanley Livingston) and Tramp the dog in the television series *My Three Sons*. (Courtesy of Beverly Garland.)

give me something to last while I'm here, 100,000 years?!' 'Okay, here's a teaspoon, you take all the water of the Atlantic Ocean and put it in the Pacific Ocean.' He does it again, so he goes back to God and says, 'I really need something to last an eternity!' And God says, 'Okay, why don't you go to the Los Angeles Country Club, sit at the bar and wait for Fred MacMurray to buy you a drink!' [laughs]. There was a time when Bob Hope, Bing Crosby and Fred Mac-Murray were the richest men in Hollywood, they had a lot of property and all that."

In between her frequent TV roles, she occasionally played supporting or character roles in various films, such as Dana Andrews' wife in *Airport 75* (1974) and Michael Douglas' mother in *It's My Turn* (1980). In 1968, she appeared opposite Anthony Perkins and Tuesday Weld in *Pretty Poison*. "Tony Perkins was the most gracious man you could imagine. In a crucial scene, Tuesday Weld's character shoots me and I have to fall down a stairs. Although it looked very steep, I thought I could do it. But Tony said, 'Wait a minute, wait a minute. I don't know if you should do that.' I said, 'What do you mean, Tony?' 'Well, this stairs is very steep, let me try and if I can do it, you can do it.' And he did it, *okay I'm shot*, he fell down, and then he said, 'Okay Beverly, this is what you do,' and he explained the fall. He was a very nice man: if he didn't break his neck, he was sure I wouldn't break mine."

Beverly Garland today. (Courtesy of Beverly Garland.)

After a career in films and television which spans more than 50 years, can Miss Garland best be described as a working actress? "That's right, I was. As a working actress, you did your *gig* and you never dreamed that anybody would ever care. I never thought that anybody would ever see any of these movies. I never stopped working, I worked all the time and as long as I couldn't work in major motion pictures, I did all those Roger Corman movies and anything else that came along. Whenever I had a job, I did my job. I went home, paid my bills and my rent and waited for the phone to ring for the next movie. It *never* entered my mind that anybody would ever—in a million years—talk to me 20, 30 or 40 years later about what I did. I remember once somebody said to me, 'Gee, I saw *The Alligator People* and I loved it!' I mean, back then I didn't pay any attention at all, and now they are cult films."

She was indeed more than just an attractive, dignified and competent actress. "I always had a tremendous amount of energy. In all the years that I worked, I also took care of my children and they came first. I always cooked dinner for them and for my husband [her first husband from 1949 to 1953 was actor Richard Garland; her second husband from 1959 was businessman Fillmore Crank]. Early in the morning, before I rushed to the studio, he used to say to me, 'I know that you're going to work today, because I can smell the onions cooking right now, for whatever dish you're making!'"

Interview: Los Angeles, February 14, 2002

Notes

1. George Arliss (1868–1946), legendary British stage and screen actor who arrived in America at the turn of the century and who often appeared on the stage and on the screen with his wife Florence. He made his first films in the early 1920s. With the 1929 remake of *Disraeli* (1921)—his first talking picture—he earned an

Academy Award for best actor which made him an even bigger star than he already was. His films include *The Devil* (1921), *Disraeli* (1921), *The Man Who Played God* (1922), *$ 20 a Week* (1924), *Disraeli* (1929), *Alexander Hamilton* (1931, also story), *The Man Who Played God* (1932), *House of Rothschild* (1934) and *Dr. Syn* (1937), his final film. He then retired from the screen to take care of Florence (1871–1950) who had gone blind. Their son is director-writer Leslie Arliss (1901–1987). He published his autobiography in 1927 (*Up the Years from Bloomsbury*), followed by a second volume in 1940 (*My Ten Years in the Studios*).

2. Roger Corman (b. 1926), one of the most efficient and all-round filmmakers of all time, has made countless low-budget pictures since he entered films in the early 1950s. He is best remembered for launching the careers of countless directors, screenwriters, actors and actresses who all learned their craft when they started working for him. The long list includes Diane Ladd, Charles Bronson, Bruce Dern, Robert De Niro, Sandra Bullock, Sally Kirkland, Sylvester Stallone, Talia Shire, Peter Fonda, Francis Ford Coppola, Peter Bogdanovich, Martin Scorsese, Jonathan Demme, John Sayles, Ron Howard, Paul Bartel, Joe Dante and Robert Towne. His autobiography *How I Made a Hundred Movies in Hollywood and Never Lost a Dime* was published in 1990.

3. Allison Hayes (1930–1977), began her career at Universal and made her screen debut in *Francis Joins the Wacs* (1954). However B-movie fans will remember her in the title role of *Attack of the 50 Foot Woman* (1958). Later on she was also able to demonstrate her talent as a comedienne opposite Dean Martin in *Who's Been Sleeping in My Bed?* (1963). Her final film was *Tickle Me* (1965) with Elvis Presley.

4. Curt Siodmak (1902–2000) was born in Germany where he worked as an extra on Fritz Lang's *Metropolis* (1926). He co-directed *Menschen am Sonntag* (1930) with his brother Robert (1900–1973) and Fred Zinnemann before arriving in Hollywood in the late 1930s where he became a very productive screenwriter of mostly low-budget films until the early 1970s. In the 1950s he directed a handful of films, including *Bride of the Gorilla* (1951), *The Magnetic Monster* (1953), *Love Slaves of the Amazon* (1957) and *Tales of Frankenstein* (1958).

5. Bing Crosby (1903–1977) was one of America's greatest and most popular entertainers, both as a singer and as an actor, who made his first films in 1930, appearing as himself. Initially, he was the star of several musicals until he gradually became a leading actor who won an Academy Award for best actor for playing a priest in *Going My Way* (1944). His films include *Going Hollywood* (1933), *Mississippi* (1935), *Pennies from Heaven* (1936), *Holiday Inn* (1942), *White Christmas* (1954), *The Country Girl* (1954, playing an alcoholic opposite Grace Kelly), *High Society* (1956), *Let's Make Love* (1960, uncredited) and *Stagecoach* (1966). He will always be associated with Bob Hope (more information: interview with Janis Paige, note 2) and Dorothy Lamour (1914–1996) for their frequent and rewarding collaboration on seven *Road to...* pictures: *Road to Singapore* (1940), *Road to Zanzibar* (1941), *Road to Morocco* (1942), *Road to Utopia* (1945), *Road to Rio* (1947), *Road to Bali* (1953) and *The Road to Hong Kong* (1962). As a singer, which he was in the first place, "White Christmas" and "True Love" (duet with Grace Kelly in *High Society*) are just a few of the numerous songs he immortalized.

6. Fred MacMurray (1908–1991), a star in the true sense of the word, entered films in the mid-1930s and instantly became a leading actor on the Paramount lot, appearing opposite Claudette Colbert in *The Gilded Lady* (1935) and Katharine Hepburn in *Alice Adams* (1935) and co-starring with Carole Lombard in *Hands Across the Table* (1935), *The Princess Comes Across* (1936), *Swing High, Swing Low* and *True Confession* (both 1937). He played a crook in Billy Wilder's tense and exciting crime drama *Double Indemnity* (1944), which is considered to be his most memorable portrayal. Other highlights in his long career include *Where Do We Go from Here?* (1945), *The Egg and I* (1947), *The Caine Mutiny* (1954), *Day of the Bad Man* (1958), *The Shaggy Dog* (1959), *The Apartment* (1960) and *The Absent Minded Professor* (1961). From 1954 he was married to actress June Haver (b. 1926).

Filmography

D.O.A. (United Artists, 1950). DIR Rudolph Maté. PROD Leo C. Popkin. SCR Russell Rouse, Clarence Greene. CAM Ernest Laszlo. ED Arthur H. Nadel. MUS Dimitri Tiomkin. RUNNING TIME 83 min. CAST: Edmond O'Brien (Frank Bigelow); Pamela Britton (Paula Gibson); Luther Adler (Majak); **Beverly Campbell** (Miss Foster); Lynn Baggett (Mrs. Philips).

A Life of Her Own (MGM, 1950). DIR George Cukor. PROD Voldemar Vetguluin. SCR Isobel Lennart. CAM George Folsey. ED George White. MUS Bronislau Kaper. RUNNING TIME 108 min. CAST: Lana Turner (Lily Brannel James); Ray Milland (Steve Harleigh); Tom Ewell (Tom Caraway); Louis Calhern (Jim Leversoe); Ann Dvorak (Mary Ashlon); **Beverly Garland** (Girl at Party—uncredited).

Strictly Dishonorable (MGM, 1951). DIR-PROD Melvin Frank, Norman Panama. SCR Melvin Frank, Norman Panama (play by Preston Sturges). CAM Ray June. ED Cotton Warburton. MUS Lennie Hayton. RUNNING TIME 94 min. CAST: Ezio Pinza (Augustino Caraffa); Janet Leigh (Isabelle Perry); Millard Mitchell (Bill Dempsey); Gale Robbins (Marie Donnelly); Maria Palmer (Countess Szadvany); Esther Minciotti (Mme. Maria Caraffa); **Beverly Garland** (uncredited).

Fearless Fagan (MGM, 1952). DIR Stanley Donen. PROD Edwin H. Knopf. SCR Charles Lederer (story by Eldon W. Griffiths, Sidney Franklin, Jr.). CAM Harold Lipstein. ED George White. RUNNING TIME 79 min. CAST: Janet Leigh (Abby Ames); Carleton Carpenter (Floyd Hilston); Keenan Wynn (Sgt. Kellwin); Richard Anderson (Capt. Daniels); Ellen Corby (Mrs. Ardley); Barbara Ruick (Nurse); **Beverly Garland** (Smudge-faced WAC).

Problem Girls (Columbia, 1953). DIR Ewald André Dupont. PROD-SCR Jack Pollexfen, Aubrey Wisberg. CAM Jack Rabin, John L. Russell. ED Fred R. Feitshans, Jr. MUS Albert Glasser. RUNNING TIME 71 min. CAST: Helen Walker (Miss Dixon); Ross Elliott (John Page); Susan Morrow (Jean Thorpe); Anthony Jochim (Professor Richards); James Seay (Max Thorpe); **Beverly Garland** (Nancy Eaton).

The Neanderthal Man (United Artists, 1953). DIR Ewald André Dupont. PROD-SCR Jack Pollexfen, Aubrey Wisberg. CAM Stanley Cortez. ED Fred R. Feitshans, Jr. MUS Albert Glasser. RUNNING TIME 78 min. CAST: Robert Shayne (Professor Clifford Groves); Joyce Terry (Jan Groves); Richard Crane (Ross Harkness); Doris Merrick (Ruth Marshall); **Beverly Garland** (Nola Mason).

The Glass Web (Universal, 1953). DIR Jack Arnold. PROD Albert J. Cohen. SCR Robert Blees, Leonard Lee (novel by Max S. Ehrlich). CAM Maury Gertsman. ED Ted J. Kent. MUS Joseph Gershenson. RUNNING TIME 81 min. CAST: Edward G. Robinson (Henry Hayes); John Forsythe (Don Newell); Marcia Henderson (Louise Newell); Kathleen Hughes (Paula Ranier); Richard Denning (Dave Markson); **Beverly Garland** (Sally).

Bitter Creek (Allied Artists, 1954). DIR Thomas Carr. PROD Vincent M. Fennelly. SCR George Waggner. CAM Ernest Miler. ED Sam Fields. MUS Raoul Kraushaar. RUNNING TIME 74 min. CAST: William "Wild Bill" Elliott (Clay Tindal); **Beverly Garland** (Gail Bonner); Carleton Young (Quentin Allen); Claude Akins (Vance Morgan); Jim Hayward (Dr. Prentiss).

The Desperado (Allied Artists, 1954). DIR Thomas Carr. PROD Vincent M. Fennelly. SCR Geoffrey Homes [Daniel Wainwaring] (novel by Clifton Adams). CAM Joseph M. Novac. ED Sam Fields. MUS Raoul Kraushaar. RUNNING TIME 80 min. CAST: Wayne Morris (Sam Garrett); Jimmy Lydon (Tom Cameron); **Beverly Garland** (Lauren Bannerman); Rayford Barnes (Ray Novak); Dabbs Greer (Sheriff Jim Langley); Lee Van Cleef (Paul/Buck Crayton).

The Killer Leopard (Allied Artists, 1954). DIR-SCR Ford Beebe. RUNNING TIME 70 min. CAST: Johnny Sheffield (Bomba); Russ Conway (Maitland); Bill Walker (Jonas); Milton Wood (Conji); Barry Bernard (Charlie Pulham); **Beverly Garland** (Linda Winters).

Two Guns and a Badge (Allied Artists, 1954). DIR Lewis D. Collins. PROD Vincent M. Fennelly. SCR Daniel B. Ullman. CAM Joe Novak. ED Sam Fields. MUS Raoul Kraushaar. RUNNING TIME 69 min. CAST: Wayne Morris (Deputy Jim Blake); Morris Ankrum (Sheriff Jackson); **Beverly Garland** (Gail Sterling); Roy Barcroft (Bill Sterling); William Phipps (Dick Grant).

Rocket Man (20th Century Fox, 1954). DIR Oscar Rudolph. PROD Leonard Goldstein. SCR Lenny Bruce, Jack Henley (story by George W. George, George F. Slavin). CAM John F. Seitz. ED Paul Weatherwax. MUS Lionel Newman. RUNNING TIME 79 min. CAST: Charles Coburn (Mayor Ed Johnson); Spring Byington (Justice Amelia Brown); John Agar (Tom Baxter); Anne Francis (June Brown); **Beverly Garland** (Ludine).

Miami Story (Columbia, 1954). DIR Fred F. Sears. PROD Sam Katzman. SCR Robert E. Kent (also story). CAM Henry Freulich. ED Viola Lawrence. MUS Mischa Bakaleinikoff. RUNNING TIME 75 min. CAST: Barry Sullivan (Mick Flagg); Luther Adler (Tony Brill); John Bear (Ted Delacorte); Adele Jergens (Gwen Abbott); **Beverly Garland** (Holly Abbott).

The Desperate Hours (Paramount, 1955). DIR-PROD William Wyler. SCR Joseph Hayes (also novel and play). CAM Lee Garmes. ED Robert Swink. MUS Gail Kubik. RUNNING TIME 112 min. CAST: Humphrey Bogart (Glenn Griffin); Fredric March (Dan C. Hilliard); Arthur Kennedy (Dep. Sheriff Jessy Bart); Martha Scott (Eleanor Hilliard); Gig Young (Chuck Wright); Mary Murphy (Cindy Hilliard); **Beverly Garland** (Miss Swift—uncredited).

Sudden Danger (Allied Artists, 1955). DIR Hubert Cornfield. PROD Ben Schwalb. SCR Daniel B. Ullman, Elwood Ullman (story by Daniel B. Ullman). CAM Ellsworth Fredericks. ED William Austin. MUS Marlin Skiles. RUNNING TIME 85 min. CAST: William "Wild Bill" Elliott (Det. Lt. Anthony Doyle); Tom Drake (Wallace Curtis); **Beverly Garland** (Phyllis Baxter); Dayton Lummis (Raymond Wilkins); Helene Stanton (Vera).

Swamp Women (Favorite Films, 1955). DIR Roger Corman. PROD Bernard Woolner. SCR David Stern (also story). CAM Fred West. ED Ronald Sinclair. MUS Willis Holman. RUNNING TIME 70 min. CAST: **Beverly Garland** (Vera); Carole Matthews (Lee Hampton); Mike Connors (Bob Matthews); Marie Windsor (Josy); Jil Jarmyn (Billie); Susan Cummings (Marie).

New Orleans Uncensored (Columbia, 1955). DIR William Castle. PROD Sam Katzman. SCR Orville H. Hampton, Lewis Meltzer (story by Orville H. Hampton). CAM Harry Freulich. ED Al Clark, Gene Havlick. MUS Mischa Bakaleinikoff. RUNNING TIME 76 min. CAST: Arthur Franz (Dan Corbett); **Beverly Garland** (Marie Reilly); Helene Stanton (Alma Mae); Michael Ansara (Floyd "Zero" Saxon); Stacy Harris (Scrappy Durant); William Henry (Joe Reilly).

The Steel Jungle (Warner Bros., 1956). DIR-SCR Walter Doniger. PROD David Weisbart. CAM J. Peverell Marley. ED Folmar Blangsted. MUS David Buttolph. RUNNING TIME 86 min. CAST: Perry Lopez (Ed Novak); **Beverly Garland** (Frances Novak); Walter Abel (Warden Keller); Ted de Corsia (Steve Marlin); Kenneth Tobey (Dr. Lewy).

Gunslinger (American Releasing Corp., 1956). DIR-PROD Roger Corman. SCR Charles Griffith, Mark Hanna. CAM Fred West. ED Charles Gross. MUS Ronald Stein. RUNNING TIME 71 min. CAST: **Beverly Garland** (Marshal Rose Hood); John Ireland (Cane Miro); Allison Hayes (Erica Page); Jonathan Haze (Jake); Martin Kingsley (Major Polk).

It Conquered the World (American International Pictures, 1956). DIR Roger Corman. PROD Roger Corman, Samuel Z. Arkoff. SCR Lou Rusoff. CAM Fred E. West. ED Charles Gross. MUS Ronald Stein. RUNNING TIME 71 min. CAST: Peter Graves (Paul Nelson); **Beverly Garland** (Claire Anderson); Lee Van Cleef (Tom Anderson); Sally Fraser (Joan Nelson); Russ Bender (General Pattick).

The Go-Getter (1956). DIR Leslie Goodwins, Leigh Jason. RUNNING TIME 78 min. CAST: Hank McCune (Henry R. "Hank" McCune); Hanley Stafford (Lester Mayberry); Thurston Hall (Mr. Higgins); Ray Collins (J. P. Miller); **Beverly Garland** (Peggy); Andrew Tombes (Mr. Symington).

Curucu, Beast of the Amazon (Universal, 1956). DIR-SCR Curt Siodmak. PROD Richard Kay, Harry Rybnick. CAM Rudolph Lesey. ED Terry Morse. MUS Raoul Kraushaar. RUNNING TIME 75 min. CAST: John Broomfield (Rock Dean); **Beverly Garland** (Andrea Romar); Tom Payne (Tupanico); Harvey Chalk (Father Flaviano); Larri Thomas (Vivian); Wilson Viana (Tico).

Not of This Earth (Allied Artists, 1957). DIR-PROD Roger Corman. SCR Charles Griffith, Mark Hanna. CAM John Mescall. ED Charles Gross. MUS Ronald Stein. RUNNING TIME 67 min. CAST: Paul Birch (Paul Johnson); **Beverly Garland** (Nurse); Morgan Jones (Harry Sherbourne); William Roerick (Frederick W. Rochelle); Jonathan Haze (Jeremy Perrin).

Chicago Confidential (United Artists, 1957). DIR Sidney Salkow. PROD Robert E. Kent. SCR Raymond T. Marcus. CAM Kenneth Peach, Sr. ED Grant Whytock. MUS Emil Newman. RUNNING TIME 75 min. CAST: Brian Keith (Jim Fremont); **Beverly Garland** (Laura Barton); Dick Foran (Artie Blaine); Beverly Tyler (Sylvia Clarkson); Elisha Cook, Jr. (Duggan).

Naked Paradise (American International Pictures, 1957). DIR-PROD Roger Corman. SCR Charles B. Griffith, Mark Hanna. CAM Floyd Crosby. ED Charles Gross, Jr. MUS Ronald Stein. RUNNING TIME 68 min. CAST: Richard Denning (Duke Bradley); **Beverly Garland** (Max MacKenzie); Lisa Montell (Lanai); Dick Miller (Mitch); Leslie Bradley (Zach Cotton).

The Joker Is Wild (Paramount, 1957). DIR Charles Vidor. PROD Samuel J. Briskin. SCR Oscar Saul (book *The Life of Joe E. Lewis* by Art Cohn). CAM Daniel L. Fapp. ED Everett Douglas. MUS Walter Scharf. RUNNING TIME 126 min. CAST: Frank Sinatra (Joe E. Lewis); Mitzi Gaynor (Martha Stewart); Jeanne Crain (Letty Page); Eddie Albert (Austin Mack); **Beverly Garland** (Cassie Mack); Jackie Coogan (Swifty Morgan).

Badlands of Montana (20th Century Fox, 1957). DIR-PROD-SCR Daniel B. Ullman. CAM Frederick Gately. ED Neil Brunnenkant. MUS Irving Gertz. RUNNING TIME 75 min. CAST: Rex Reason (Steven Brewster); **Beverly Garland** (Susan Hammer); Emile Meyer (Henry); Keith Larsen (Rick Valentine); Margia Dean (Emily Branton).

The Saga of Hemp Brown (Universal, 1958). DIR Richard Carlson. PROD Gordon Kay. SCR Robert Creighton Williams (story by Bernard Girard). CAM Philip H. Lathrop. ED Tony Martinelli. MUS Joseph Gershenson. RUNNING TIME 80 min. CAST: Rory Calhoun (Hemp Brown); **Beverly Garland** (Mona Langley); John Larch (Jed Givens); Russell Johnson (Hook); Fortunio Bonanova (Serge Bolanos).

Gundown at Sandoval (1959). DIR Harry Keller. SCR Frank D. Gilroy, Maurice Tombragel. RUNNING TIME 72 min. CAST: Lyle Bettger; Harry Carey, Jr.; Dan Duryea; **Beverly Garland**; Norma Moore; Judson Pratt.

The Alligator People (20th Century Fox, 1959). DIR Roy Del Ruth. PROD Jack Leewood. SCR Orville H. Hampton (story by Orville H. Hampton, Charles O'Neal). CAM Karl Struss. ED Harry W. Gerstad. MUS Irving Gertz. RUNNING TIME 74 min. CAST: **Beverly Garland** (Joyce Webster/Jane Marvin); Bruce Bennett (Eric Lorimer); Lon Chaney, Jr. (Manon); George Macready (Mark Sinclair); Frieda Inescort (Mrs. Hawthorne).

Stark Fear (Ellis Films, 1963). DIR Ned Hockman. PROD Ned Hockman, Joe E. Burke, Dwight V. Swain. SCR Dwight V. Swain. CAM Robert E. Bethard. MUS Lawrence V. Fisher. RUNNING TIME 86 min. CAST: **Beverly Garland** (Ellen Winslow); Skip Homeier (Gerald Winslow); Kenneth Tobey (Cliff Kane); Hannah Stone; Paul Scovil.

Twice Told Tales (United Artists, 1963). DIR Sidney Salkow. PROD-SCR Robert E. Kent. CAM Ellis W. Carter. ED Grant Whytock. MUS Richard La Salle. RUNNING TIME 119 min. CAST: Vincent Price (Alex Medbourne/Dr. Rappaccini/Gerald Pyncheon); Sebastian Cabot (Carl Heidegger); **Beverly Garland** (Alice Pyncheon); Richard Denning (Jonathan Maule).

Pretty Poison (20th Century Fox, 1968). DIR Noel Black. PROD Noel Black, Marshal Backlar. SCR Lorenzo Semple, Jr. CAM David Quaid. ED William Ziegler. MUS Johnny Mandel. RUNNING TIME 89 min. CAST: Anthony Perkins (Dennis Pitt); Tuesday Weld (Sue Ann Stepanek); **Beverly Garland** (Mrs. Stepanek); John Randolph (Azenauer); Dick O'Neill (Bud Munsch); Clarice Blackburn (Mrs. Bronson).

The Mad Room (Columbia, 1969). DIR Bernard Girard. PROD Norman Maurer. SCR Bernard Girard, A. Z. Martin (play *Ladies in Retirement* by Reginald Denham, Edward Percy). CAM Harry Stradling, Jr. ED Pat Somerset. MUS Dave Grusin. RUNNING TIME 92 min. CAST: Stella Stevens (Ellen Hardy); Shelley Winters (Mrs. Armstrong); Skip Ward (Sam Aller); Carol Cole (Chris); Severn Darden (Nate); **Beverly Garland** (Mrs. Racine).

Where the Red Fern Grows (Doty-Dayton, 1974). DIR Norman Tokar. PROD Lyman Dayton. SCR Eleanor Lamb, Douglas C. Stewart (novel by Wilson Rawls). CAM Dean Cundey. ED Bob Bring, G. Daniel Greer. MUS Lex De Azevedo. RUNNING TIME 97 min. CAST: James Whitmore (Grandpa); **Beverly Garland** (Mother); Jack Ging (Father); Lonny Chapman (Sheriff); Stuart Peterson (Billy).

Airport 75 (Universal, 1974). DIR Jack Smight. PROD William Frye. SCR Don Ingalls (inspired by *Airport* [1970], based on the novel by Arthur Hailey). CAM Philip Lathrop. ED Terry Williams. MUS John Cacavas. RUNNING TIME 107 min. CAST: Charlton Heston (Alan Murdock); Karen Black (Nancy Pryor); George Kennedy (Joe Patroni); Dana Andrews (Scott Freeman); Myrna Loy (Mrs. Devaney); Martha Scott (Sister Beatrice); **Beverly Garland** (Mrs. Scott Freeman); Gloria Swanson (Herself).

Sixth and Main (1977). DIR-SCR Christopher Cain. CAST: Leslie Nielsen (John Doe); **Beverly Garland** (Monica); Roddy McDowall (Skateboard); Leo Penn (Doc); Joe Maross (Peanuts).

Roller Boogie (United Artists, 1979). DIR Mark L. Lester. PROD Irwin Yablans, Bruce Cohn Curtis. SCR Barry Schneider (story by Irwin Yablans). CAM Dean Cundey. ED Byron "Buzz" Brandt, Edilberto Cruz, Howard Kunin, Edward Salier. MUS Bob Esty. RUNNING TIME 103 min. CAST: Linda Blair (Terry Barkley); Jim Bray (Bobby James); **Beverly Garland** (Lillian Barkley); Roger Perry (Roger Barkley); James Van Patten (Hoppy); Kimberly Beck (Lana).

It's My Turn (Columbia, 1980). DIR Claudia Weill. PROD Martin Elfand. SCR Eleanor Bergstein. CAM Bill Butler. ED Byron Brandt, Marjorie Fowler, James Coblentz. MUS Patrick Williams. RUNNING TIME 91 min. CAST: Jill Clayburgh (Kate Gunzinger); Michael Douglas (Ben Lewin); Charles Grodin (Homer); **Beverly Garland** (Emma); Steven Hill (Jacob).

Gamble on Love (1982). DIR Jim Balden. CAST: **Beverly Garland**; Louis Jourdan.

Television Movies

The Nine Lives of Elfego Baca (1958). DIR William Beaudine, Norman Foster. CAST: Robert Loggia; Robert F. Simon; Skip Homeier; Arthur Hunnicutt; James Coburn; Annette Funicello; **Beverly Garland** (Suzanna O'Brien).

Cutter's Trial (1969). DIR Vincent McEveety. CAST: John Gavin; Manual Padilla, Jr.; Marisa Pavan; **Beverly Garland** (Maggie); Joseph Cotton.

Say Goodbye, Maggie Cole (1972). DIR Jud Taylor. CAST: Susan Hayward; Darren McGavin; Michael Constantine; **Beverly Garland** (Myrna Anderson); Richard Anderson.

The Weekend Nun (1972). DIR Jeannot Szwarc. CAST: Joanna Pettet; Vic Morrow; Ann Sothern; James Gregory; **Beverly Garland** (Bobby Sue Prewitt); Kay Lenz.

The Voyage of the Yes (1972). DIR Lee H. Katzin. CAST: Desi Arnaz, Jr.; Mike Evans; **Beverly Garland** (Agatha Markwell); Skip Homeier; Dick Powell, Jr.

Unwed Father (1974). DIR Jeremy Paul Kagan. CAST: Joseph Bottoms; Kay Lenz; **Beverly Garland** (Estelle); Kim Hunter; Joseph Campanella.

The Healers (1974). DIR Tom Gries. CAST: John Forsythe; Pat Harrington, Jr.; Katherine Woodville; Season Hubley; **Beverly Garland** (Laura Kier).

The Day the Earth Moved (1974). DIR Robert Michael Lewis. CAST: Jackie Cooper; Stella Stevens; Cleavon Little; William Windom; **Beverly Garland** (Helen Backsler).

This Girl for Hire (1983). DIR Jerry Jameson. CAST: Bess Armstrong; Celeste Holm; Cliff De Young; José Ferrer; **Beverly Garland** (Evan Picard); Roddy McDowall; Elisha Cook, Jr.

Scarecrow and Mrs. King (1983). DIR Burt Brinckerhoff. CAST: Kate Jackson; Bruce Boxleitner; **Beverly Garland** (Dottie West); Mel Stewart; Martha Smith.

Beanpole (1990). DIR Linda Day. CAST: Hayley Brown; Molly Cheek; Heather Lind; **Beverly Garland** (Margaret); Pat Hingle.

The World's Oldest Living Bridesmaid (1990). DIR Joseph L. Scanlan. CAST: Donna Mills; Brian Wimmer; Winston Rekert; Art Hindle; **Beverly Garland** (Mother).

Finding the Way Home (1991). DIR Rob Holcomb. CAST: George C. Scott; Hector Elizondo; **Beverly Garland** (Arlene); Eddie Flores.

Hellfire (1995). DIR David Tausik. CAST: Ben Cross; Jennifer Burns; **Beverly Garland** (Carlotta); Doug Wert; Lev Prygunov.

SAMUEL GOLDWYN, JR.

In his autobiography *A Tree Is a Tree* (1953, published by Samuel French Trade, Hollywood, CA), legendary film director King Vidor wrote about veteran producer Sam Goldwyn: "He was the first producer to inveigle the best literary minds to write his scripts. This was quite an innovation in the early days of the silents, when the emphasis was on action rather than words. He was the first to try to lure to Hollywood such writers as H.G. Wells, Sinclair Lewis, Somerset Maugham, and George Bernard Shaw (who said, 'The trouble, Mr. Goldwyn, is that you are interested in art and I am interested in money')."

Perhaps that sums up the essence of Samuel Goldwyn (1879–1974), one of the very first film pioneers who in 1913, along with Jesse L. Lasky and Cecil B. De Mille, founded the Jesse L. Lasky Feature Play Company (their first picture that same year was *The Squaw Man*). After collaborating with others, he formed Samuel Goldwyn Productions in 1923. He was a totally independent filmmaker for nearly four decades (until his final film *Porgy and Bess*, 1959); his only real *associate* was his second wife, former Broadway star Frances Howard (1903–1976).

Over the years he made films such as *Ben-Hur* (1925), *Dodsworth* (1936), *Stella Dallas* (1937), *The Westerner* (1940), *The Pride of the Yankees* (1942), *The Best Years of Our Lives* (1946, earning him an Academy Award for best picture) and *Guys and Dolls* (1955). The opening words *Samuel Goldwyn Presents* introduced films that excelled in combining talent and quality; they were an absolute guarantee that the audience would be entertained with the very best that one of the most creative film producers could possibly offer. His tremendous film output went far beyond the mere financing and administration of numerous first-rate productions over the years.

To this day, almost 80 years after the company bearing his name was initially founded, the Los Angeles based film company named Samuel Goldwyn Productions[1] still exists, being headed now for several decades by his son and also independent filmmaker, Samuel Goldwyn, Jr., who was born in Los Angeles on September 7, 1926. Besides being a film producer, he also distributes foreign and American films in the U.S. (both mainstream and artistic features).

I met Mr. Goldwyn at his office and it was a pleasure talking to this man who has a huge knowledge of film, and not only of its history—he also has a true vision of what filmmaking is really all about and, just like his illustrious father, knows how to put it up there on the screen. A humorous man all the way through, he was able to talk about his career, as well about his father, in a most enjoyable way. While he did the talking, I couldn't stop listening.

Mr. Goldwyn: "I always loved the movies, I think the first movie I saw as a kid was *Skippy* [1931] with Jackie Cooper. Movies were always magical to me and they were all we ever talked

Legendary film pioneer Samuel Goldwyn. (Courtesy DOCIP Film Archive, Brussels, Belgium.)

about at home. My father had a tremendous love for movies. There's a joke about him that says, 'This is a movie I want to do and I don't care what people think, as long as everybody goes to see it' [laughs]. I grew up with his enthusiasm, watching his enthusiasm, and his belief in this enthusiasm. I always enjoyed going to the movies; when I had a free day or on a Saturday afternoon, I would go out and see one of them. I thought for a while I would become a journalist; I was very taken with making documentaries which I did at one point, but there is no better way to tell a story than making a movie. It's a wonderful medium and its power gets greater and greater because there are more ways you can tell a story today than you could years ago.

"My father made the films he wanted to make, he never turned people loose by saying, 'Go make a movie.' He didn't work that way. He was enormously involved in every single aspect of the movies. His feeling about movies was you are telling a story, and once you went in with a story, you'd better come out with a story. He was a very tough guy to work for, very demanding and he had a great respect for talent, but he was difficult for people, even if they were very talented. He had the longest running producer-director relationship with Billy Wilder; sometimes they fought like cats and dogs, always about how to make a picture better." (Wilder once reportedly said, "Just because Sam Goldwyn is a shit, doesn't mean that being a shit makes you Sam Goldwyn.'")

"The screen now has become much more sophisticated than it was, but what we miss today, are the stars. They had great stars back then. Despite all its problems, the star system was wonderful, it *worked*. You went to see movies to see the stars. They invested in creating stars and they created a generation of stars who have lived for so long. Joan Crawford is still Joan Crawford; Davis is still Davis. The system was focused on delivering star pictures and they were made with those people in mind. That very same system was able to exist and survive for so long because the studios owned theaters; people went to the movies and as each studio made 50 or 60 pictures a year, they had to cast their stars to please the audience."

One of the great stars today is Julia Roberts, who was cast by Mr. Goldwyn in Mystic Pizza (1988) which launched her career. "She is a star in the true meaning of the word. It is a funny thing what happened with her back then, when we made Mystic Pizza. We wanted to make a movie about working class girls. A few years before I saw Diner [1982], a brilliant film made

Julia Roberts, Lili Taylor and Annabeth Gish in *Mystic Pizza* (1988). (Courtesy of DOCIP Film Archive, Brussels, Belgium.)

by Barry Levinson, about young men and about their expectations of life. I wanted to do the same thing about girls. So I started looking for a story and I found a script on which a lot of rewriting was done. Basically it was about three girls whose prospects in life were limited by their background. It was a small movie and there was an actress we wanted to get, but she couldn't decide whether the part was right and big enough for her. So one day the director, Donald Petrie, said to me, 'I think I saw a girl for that part,' and he shot a little video on her. Unfortunately, when I saw it, she was awful. He said, 'Sam, she's going to be good.' I said, 'Well, this is wrong, that is wrong, that has to be changed, etc.' A little while later, he came back with another video of her. I said, 'Is this the *same* girl?' All the habits she got, like biting on her lip and all that, it was all there. And, most importantly, there was a kind of a fire and a lost quality at the same time, which people love, it was all there! After two days of rushes, it was very clear: she would become a star. And she is, she's a wonderful actress.

"Michael Curtiz had a phrase about acting schools. He used to say, 'In acting schools they can teach you how to act, but only God can make a star!' [laughs]. A friend of mine, Tom Ewell, once did a movie with Marilyn Monroe called *The Seven Year Itch* [1955]. When I asked him, 'What's it like to work with her,' he said, 'Well, I'll tell you what it's like to work with her: she's always late, she doesn't know her lines, she's got the wrong costume on, her hair is still a mess, she stumbles around, she can't hit the marks, but then there's that moment when that little red light goes on...! Now I understand why it took me forty plays to get to Hollywood!' [laughs]. *That's* a star! I watched Billy Wilder when he was shooting *Some Like It Hot* [1959]. He was going nuts, he was complaining, screaming, yelling, it was awful. He never knew when she was going to show up, she always had all these people around her and all that, but then again, whatever she brought to that picture, was more than what was on the paper. That's the *extra* thing you get from a star. It is still something people want. One of the things about the old system was that it nurtured them over a period. Of the hundreds of people who got contracts, it often didn't amount to anything, but each year, there was somebody going up the ladder. Now we do very little to develop people—we develop stories, we develop directors, but very little to develop personalities. Only television does something about it, but the movies don't do anything about it anymore. I think that's a shame.

"Today when you start working on a movie, you got X in mind; when you find out you don't get X, you start to change until you can work with Y or Z. When you think of the number of stars they had then, compared to the number of stars the system produces today and also look at the shorter lives that they're having now ... back then they all had 25 year careers whereas today you see them coming and going so fast.

"Whenever I make a film, I also start with names in the back of my mind. One of the films I distributed and am very proud of, is *The Madness of King George* [1994]. I went to the theater, saw that play and told author Alan Bennett I wanted to do the film with Nigel Hawthorne, the guy who was playing it. I was determined that the writer, the star and also the director of the play, Nicholas Hytner, would do the film. So you always start out to do a movie with so-and-so." Ultimately, *The Madness of King George* proved to be a hugely successful film, winning an Academy Award for John Fenner (art direction) and a nomination for a first-rate Nigel Hawthorne in the leading role of George III in the best actor category.

"I was very lucky to have a father who said, 'You're only as good as what you do.' He believed that it's not what you did yesterday, but what you're going to do tomorrow that was important. That's a very interesting philosophy, so I thought about that when I was growing up.

"Today a star is only as good as his last picture and you deal with different subject matters you couldn't deal with back then. Married people slept in separate beds, there was no divorce, you never got away with a murder, etc. The morality of the world has changed a great deal. We've headed to a very bad time in American pictures because I think too few pictures are working. This megabuck movies era, when everything just seems a big action picture, I don't know if that's going to last. They try to reach audiences worldwide; [because] only 35 percent of the income of movies comes from the United States, ... they have got to work all over the world and their common language now is action. But despite that, there are still a lot of good movies that come out of here.

"What I am more depressed about, is the tendency of European pictures to copy American pictures; that's a big mistake. One of our sources is European pictures. European filmmakers have a different point of view on life, so when they start making American type of pictures, I don't think that is going to work. Also, their films often don't work in their own countries and if that happens, usually they don't work abroad. They tend to lose their individuality. In the United States the movie industry has become a part of a vast communications company, while it used to stand on its own. If you look at the pictures these old guys made, every movie *had* to stand on its own feet.

"Take my father's pictures, he borrowed money from the bank and if the picture didn't pay the bank back, he was in trouble. That's how he worked his *whole* life. People often ask me what it was like to be brought up in Hollywood, and I would say, 'What do you mean?' 'Well, you know, the movie stars and everything!' And then I would say, 'You really want to know what I remember being brought up? That is the day my father was able to pay back the cost of a movie, that was a celebration in our family. At least, then he didn't owe the bank any money.' This was combined with the personality of a man who was a compulsive gambler.

Samuel Goldwyn, Jr.: "Joan Crawford is still Joan Crawford; [Bette] Davis is still Davis."

He *had* to do it: when he was making a movie, he was throwing the dice. The more I study his fascinating life, the more I realize that.

"After his death in 1974, I reflected on the death of a parent and sometimes your perception of a parent changes. I was involved for some time with A. Scott Berg, a man who did a wonderful biography of him [called *Goldwyn*, first published in 1989] and who spent eight years on that book. What I learned from his research, was pretty consistent with the man I knew. I remember so many times when my father would see a movie, which was not his movie, and he'd turn to me and say, 'You see what you can do, you see what you can do with this! You see how wonderful it is! God, I wish I could have made it!' He took great pleasure in somebody else's movies; he never felt threatened by other people's success.

"His attitude towards films had a wonderful quality and he also made mistakes that way. But it made him less afraid to make any mistakes and that is very important, because you shouldn't be making pictures if you're afraid to make any mistakes."

Could Mr. Goldwyn, Sr., be compared with another of Hollywood's august filmmakers, independent producer David O. Selznick (1902–1965) who made films as *King Kong* (1933), *Anna Karenina* (1935), *A Star Is Born* (1937), *Gone with the Wind* (1939), *Rebecca* (1940), *Since You Went Away* (1944) and *Spellbound* (1945)? "David O. Selznick was more complex than my father. I knew him very well, I adored him. But he had this enormous success when he was in his thirties with *Gone with the Wind*. We once talked about death and he said to me, 'You know what's so terrible? I know what the headline of my obituary will be: *David O. Selznick, producer of Gone with the Wind, dies.* And that film was made such a long time ago, that's the frightening thing.' My father adored him, he respected him too and he tried to get him to work at one point, but David had a self-destructive mechanism. My father on the other hand was a survivor, that was one of his qualities. This is a business for survivors. It isn't one hit, two failures, one hit. You have to survive all the time and stay in the game. My father was bought out of the company which later on became Paramount [1916], he was thrown out of the company which would become MGM [1922], but he survived them all. That I think is about character and personality, that's more than just picture making. That's what I learned from him and it made me a rich man, you know. I was able to get it sitting at the table and that was very valuable. Fortunately, it was there when I needed it often. He was a difficult guy, terrible rages of temper which he couldn't control, but he was a very, very interesting man. He didn't speak English very well, but he was always trying to say something meaningful. He taught me a lot more than just about movies. After all, he was a man who walked across Poland at age 13, he got beaten so many times in the game and he always said, 'They're not going to kill me, I will come right back.' That's what happens so much in this business, you see people with great talent, great flair, great success and then they're gone."

In regard to his misuse of the English language, Mr. Goldwyn, Sr., was known for his *Goldwynisms* such as "include me out," "I can answer you in two words: im possible" and "anyone seeing a psychiatrist, should have his head examined."

It is very interesting to see that most of the Hollywood film pioneers had more or less the same background and had their roots in European countries like Russia, Poland, Germany and Hungary: Mr. Goldwyn was born in Warsaw; Louis B. Mayer came from Minsk (Belorussia); Carl Laemmle, president of Universal, was born in Laupheim (Germany); Adolph Zukor, president of Paramount, came from Risce (Hungary); William Fox had German parents and was born in Tulchva (Hungary); Lewis J. Selznick, film executive in the silent era and father of Myron and David O. Selznick, was born in Kiev (Ukraine); Harry Cohn, president of Columbia, and Irving G. Thalberg, MGM's production executive, were both born in New York to European parents, and the Warner brothers' parents were immigrants from Poland. All of those pioneers (or in some cases their parents) were born in a 500 miles radius from one another and they wound up in Los Angeles within 15 miles where they would eventually create the American dream on the screen for the entire world to see. Just a coincidence?

Samuel Goldwyn, Jr.: "Well, there was really no place for them to go to in Europe. They weren't wanted there. Most of them were poor Jews, there was little employment for them, they weren't educated, they could never become lawyers, bankers or doctors, they could never move to that side of society. So they came to America and the best most of them could do, was work in the rag trade, like my father who was a glove cutter. And then something happened: even though most of them hardly spoke any English and came from the lower class of their own society, they were all smart enough to see and take a look at the future—they were guys like uneducated versions of what Bill Gates is now. They all saw this new idea and they took their chance. They brought their culture with them; some of the morality of their movies is probably very much affected by this. Also, it was important that they integrated into the society, that they could become part of it and be accepted by it.

"I knew a few of them, I didn't know Mayer, but I knew his daughter Irene Mayer Selznick[2] very well; she was married to David. She was the godmother of one of my children and always was a very dear friend. My father didn't like Mayer, they always disliked each other. I also knew Harry Cohn, Jack Warner, all of those people. The same thing also is true for the talented people who came over here in the 1930s, like Michael Curtiz, Fred Zinnemann and Billy Wilder. They were all the same, except that they were educated; they knew they *had* to make it in this culture because they also knew there was no way to go back."

Samuel Goldwyn, Jr. (Courtesy of Samuel Goldwyn, Jr.)

Was it more difficult in those early days to make films as an independent producer, or is it much tougher nowadays? Mr. Goldwyn, Jr.: "I often used to say to my father, 'Well, it was easy in your time, there was no television so people had nothing to do but go to the theater.' And then he would say, 'Well, have you ever thought what it was like when they didn't want to go to the theater!' [laughs]. We're becoming a lot like Broadway—everything has got to be a hit, that makes it very difficult. After I got back from the military, I worked for CBS, but I was not happy with corporations and with their regimes. I probably missed something, maybe I was spoiled. If I were more disciplined, I would better be able to deal with that. But I was never good at dealing with politics and these politics of survival are very difficult at studios, although as a producer I have also done pictures at studios.

"Darryl F. Zanuck would wake up in the morning, read the newspaper and say, 'I see a story here about a chain gang. We're going to make a chain gang movie!' So he came in the office, threw the newspaper on the table, a bunch of people looked at it and they said, 'Great idea, Darryl!' He was going to do it anyway, whether they liked it or not. Then he'd say, 'Any ideas for a title?' *I Am a Fugitive from a Chain Gang!* They'd announce they would make it, they had directors, writers and directors under contract. 'We'll put that aggressive fellow in it, what about Paul Muni, maybe that would be good too!' And the next thing ... they had a movie! You can't do that today, there's too much at stake with every movie, everybody involved with it has a reason to be 'frightened.' When they make a film for let's say 60 or 70 million dollars, they spend 35 to 40 million marketing; most of that is spent within about four weeks. That's a lot of money.

"As an independent producer it is very difficult to compete with that. I have to come up with pictures that in some form are completely unique. That's very enjoyable, but also very difficult. You have to look for something that is fresh, something that is different. A picture like *The Full Monty* has that quality and every year, you see a couple of pictures like that. But you're fishing for needles in a haystack really and the guys who make those 100 million dollar films, say those are hard to find too. Basically we're all gambling, but that's the fun of it— you take that away and what have you got left? I couldn't imagine not waking up at three o'clock in the morning and not worry about something [laughs]. My father told me once, 'The night you will not solve the problem, write it down and you'll deal with it tomorrow because it will not be as bad as it seems,' and I still work with that all the time. Am I going to finish this movie on time? I got to do retakes and when am I going to get all the people to do it because some actors will be doing other things? etc., things like that.

"I am not sure that those old boys would have survived because they did not see television coming. That was a big, *big* mistake. Just like nobody at this moment really knows what the impact of the Internet will be. This Internet business is really big. Just think about this—and I don't know the answer—just as you can download music, you can download movies. I can download a movie and pass it on to you; technically it is possible. Just think about the implications, what it is going to do, how it is going to change the business. The movie business didn't see television coming, they didn't see video coming, neither of which they own—while they *could* have owned television and video. Each time one of these changes takes place, it takes you further and further from what those guys were about. My father used to talk about television; he didn't like it—it wasn't movies! But he also saw the implications of it. Also the whole method by which we project movies is changing, it is all becoming digital now. If anyone builds a movie theater today without digital capability, that would be a huge mistake. All these things affect how you make movies, how you go about doing it all—it's all part of the same package, you know, it's a revolving thing.

"So history is repeating itself. Sound changed the business; it took the industry nearly a year and a half to adapt to sound. When Al Jolson sang in *The Jazz Singer* [1927], those companies were loaded with two years of product they first had to get rid of. So they had to stick sound and music on it one way or the other, so that they could advertise with sound. It killed a whole generation of actors—one of the stars my father had at that time was Vilma Banky.[3] She was a star, had appeared in *The Son of the Sheik* [1926] with Rudolph Valentino in his final film, but she was Hungarian and she couldn't speak two words of English. After sound came, she simply retired from acting."

Several of the film pioneers who began their careers in the silent era had sons named after them: Jesse L. Lasky, Jr., Jack L. Warner, Jr., Carl Laemmle, Jr.,[4] Charles Chaplin, Jr., and Irving Thalberg, Jr. They all carried the family name and, with the exception of Irving Thalberg, Jr., they all entered show business. What effect did it have on Samuel Goldwyn, Jr.: "For me it was not difficult to carry the family name: I always had a good life, went to a good school, didn't always take advantage of every opportunity that I was offered, but I learned. I grew up with the Chaplin boys, Charles and Sydney, I went to school with them, but theirs is a whole different story. They had a pretty rough childhood because their parents didn't get along, they barely took time. Actually Charles was very talented and Sydney had a pretty good career in the theater, he was in *Funny Girl* with Barbra Streisand and all that."

Some of them, including Jesse L. Lasky, Jr. and Charles Chaplin, Jr., wrote autobiographies as did screenwriter and novelist Budd Schulberg,[5] the son of B.P. Schulberg (head of Paramount in the late 1920s and discoverer of Clara Bow, a.k.a. the "It Girl"). Mr. Goldwyn, Jr.: "Budd's story is sadder than mine. His father, B.P. Schulberg, was the head of Paramount and every year he got presents from Clara Bow and from all the directors and the writers. Then, one day, his father was fired from Paramount just before Christmas and there were no presents. So his mother and father went out, bought them themselves and wrote the names of the people on them. He wrote a short story about this, "The Christmas Presents." It had a very profound impact on Budd and his brother. The marriage of their parents broke up, his mother became a very successful agent but it was the end of his father. Again, that's where my father was so unique: whenever they thought he was defeated, he always kept coming back.

"My father was quite a character. I remember when I was a child, we went up to Lake Tahoe on a fishing trip. When we arrived there, we checked in the hotel and he told [them] his name. So this guy said, 'Oh, Goldwyn, like Metro-Goldwyn-Mayer?' 'No,' my father said, 'like the Metro-Goldwyn Company.' I said, 'Why don't you straighten it out with Mayer?' He said, 'Would that get us a better room?' [laughs]. Sometimes he'd laugh about such things, sometimes he could get all worked up over something. If I brought a bad report card home from school, he'd say, 'I got to have a talk with you.' I knew then what was coming, I knew exactly the dialogue that was coming: 'As I look at you, I look at somebody facing two forks on the road: one, a chance to be a great man, the other is prison' [laughs]. I'd say, 'Is there any chance in the middle?' And he'd say, 'That's no way no look at it!' [laughs]. Then there'd be a long lecture about the opportunity that I had and that he hadn't had, and then he'd say, 'Now, I know which direction you're going to take and we're not even going to think about the other,' so at least I knew I wouldn't be going to prison! [laughs]. That was the kind of personality he was—larger than life!"

The third generation of the Goldwyn family has been in show business for quite some time now. His son Tony (born in 1960) is an actor who has appeared in films such as *Gaby–A True Story* (1987), *Ghost* (1990), *Kuffs* (1992), *The Pelican Brief* (1993), *Nixon* (1995), *Reckless* (1995), *The Substance of Fire* (1996) and *Kiss the Girls* (1997). Mr. Goldwyn, Jr.: "Another son of mine works at Paramount and another one wants to make documentaries, one daughter also tries to put a documentary together and another daughter writes music for the Internet. So they're all in show business. I once asked them, 'Don't you want to make an honest living in your life?' They said, 'Well, what about you?'" [laughs].

Interview: Los Angeles, August 14, 2000

Notes

1. Samuel Goldwyn Company is the parent company of Samuel Goldwyn Productions and Samuel Goldwyn Films. The Samuel Goldwyn Foundation is a charitable organization, mostly dealing with helping children.
2. Irene Mayer Selznick (1907–1990) became a successful and well respected Broadway producer after her divorce from David O. Selznick in 1948, with plays as *A Streetcar Named Desire*, *Bell, Book and Candle* and *The Chalk Garden* to her credit. When producing *A Streetcar Named Desire* on Broadway, she once had a dispute with director Elia Kazan and told him: "I have survived Louis B. Mayer and David O. Selznick, so you'd better lay off!" She published her memoirs, *A Private View*, in 1983.
3. Vilma Banky (1898–1991), born near Budapest, had made several films in Hungary, Germany and Austria before she was discovered in Europe by Samuel Goldwyn who brought her to Hollywood in 1925. She immediately rose to fame when she co-starred with Rudolph Valentino in *The Eagle* (1925) and *The Son of the Sheik* (1926); she also teamed with Ronald Colman in *The Dark Angel* (1925), *The Winning of Barbara Worth* (1926), *The Night of Love* (1927), *The Magic Flame* (1927) and *Two Lovers* (1927). Meanwhile, she was billed as the "Hungarian Rhapsody." In 1927 Samuel Goldwyn personally supervised her wedding in Beverly Hills to silent screen matinee idol (and another Goldwyn discovery) Rod La Rocque. They remained a couple till La Rocque's death in 1969 at age 73. Miss Banky died in Los Angeles in 1991.
4. Carl Laemmle, Jr. (1908–1979), son of film pioneer Carl Laemmle (1867–1939), was the only one of the "second generation" to run a studio, after his father put him in charge of Universal as a birthday present when he turned 21 in 1929. In 1936 he became an independent producer.
5. Budd Schulberg (b. 1914) wrote his autobiography, *Moving Pictures: Memories of a Hollywood Prince*, in 1981 and described his childhood growing up on the Paramount lot. He was a screenwriter whose credits include *On the Waterfront* (1954, based on his own story—earning him an Academy Award), *A Face in the Crowd* (1957) and *Wind Across the Everglades* (1958). During World War II he worked with John Ford's documentary unit.

Filmography (as producer only)

Good Time Girl (1950). DIR David MacDonald. PROD Sydney Box. ASS PROD **Samuel Goldwyn, Jr.** SCR Muriel Box, Sydney Box, Ted Willis. CAM Stephen Dade. ED Vladimir Sadovsky. MUS Lambert Williamson. RUNNING TIME 93 min. CAST: Jean Kent (Gwen Rawlings); Dennis Price (Red Farrell); Griffith Jones (Danny Mortin); Flora Robson (Court Chairman); Herbert Lom (Max); Bonar Colleano (1st Deserter).

Man with the Gun (United Artists, 1955). DIR Richard Wilson. PROD **Samuel Goldwyn, Jr.** SCR Richard Wilson, N. B. Stone, Jr. CAM Lee Garmes. ED Gene Milford. MUS Alex North. RUNNING TIME 83 min. CAST: Robert Mitchum (Clint Tollinger); Jan Sterling (Nelly Bain); Karen Sharpe (Stella Atkins); Henry Hull (Marshal Sims); Emile Meyer (Saul Atkins); John Lupton (Jeff Castle).

The Sharkfighters (United Artists, 1956). DIR Jerry Hopper. PROD **Samuel Goldwyn, Jr.** SCR Lawrence

Roman, John Robinson (story by Jo Napoleon, Art Napoleon). CAM Lee Garmes. ED Daniel Mandell. MUS Jerome Moross. RUNNING TIME 74 min. CAST: Victor Mature (Ben Staves); Karen Steele (Martha Staves); James Olson (Harold Duncan); Philip Coolidge (Leonard Evans); Claude Akins ("Gordy" Gordon); Rafael Campos (Carlos).

The Proud Rebel (Buena Vista, 1958). DIR Michael Curtiz. PROD **Samuel Goldwyn, Jr.** SCR Joe Petracca, Lillie Hayward (story by James Edward Grant). CAM Ted McCord. ED Aaron Stell. MUS Jerome Moross. RUNNING TIME 100 min. CAST: Alan Ladd (John Chandler); Olivia de Havilland (Linnett Moore); Dean Jagger (Harry Burleigh); David Ladd (David Chandler); Cecil Kellaway (Dr. Enos Davis); Dean Stanton (Jeb Burleigh).

The Adventures of Huckleberry Finn (MGM, 1960). DIR Michael Curtiz. PROD **Samuel Goldwyn, Jr.** SCR James Lee (novel by Mark Twain). CAM Ted McCord. ED Frederic Steinkamp. MUS Jerome Moross. RUNNING TIME 90 min. CAST: Tony Randall (The King); Eddie Hodges (Huckleberry Finn); Archie Moore (Jim); Patty McCormack (Joanna); Neville Brand (Pap); Mickey Shaughnessy (The Duke).

The Young Lovers (MGM, 1964). DIR-PROD **Samuel Goldwyn, Jr.** SCR George Garrett (novel by Julian Halevy). CAM Joe Biroc. ED William A. Lyon. MUS Sol Kaplan. RUNNING TIME 109 min. CAST: Henry Fonda (Eddie Slocum); Sharon Hugueny (Pam Burns); Nick Adams (Tarragoo); Deborah Walley (Debbie); Beatrice Straight (Mrs. Burns); Malachi Throne (Prof. Schwartz).

Cotton Comes to Harlem (United Artists, 1970). DIR Ossie Davis. PROD **Samuel Goldwyn, Jr.** SCR Arnold Perl, Ossie Davis (novel by Chester Himes). CAM Gerald Hirschfeld. ED Robert Q. Lovett, John Carter. MUS Galt McDermot. RUNNING TIME 97 min. CAST: Godfrey Cambridge (Grave Digger Jones); Raymond St. Jacques (Coffin Ed Johnson); Calvin Lockhart (Rev. Deke O'Malley); Judy Pace (Iris); Redd Foxx (Uncle Budd); John Anderson (Bryce).

Come Back, Charleston Blue (Warner Bros., 1972). DIR Mark Warren. PROD **Samuel Goldwyn, Jr.** SCR Bontche Schweig, Peggy Elliott (novel *The Heat's On* by Chester Himes). CAM Dick Kratina. ED Gerald Greenberg, George Bowers. MUS Quincy Jones, Donny Hathaway. RUNNING TIME 100 min. CAST: Godfrey Cambridge (Grave Digger Jones); Raymond St. Jacques (Coffin Ed Johnson); Peter DeAnda (Joe); Percy Rodriguez (Capt. Bryce); Jonelle Allen (Carol); Maxwell Glanville (Uncle Caspar).

The Golden Seal (Samuel Goldwyn, 1983). DIR Frank Zugina. PROD **Samuel Goldwyn, Jr.** SCR John Groves (novel by James Vance Marshall). CAM Eric Saarinen. ED Robert Q. Lovett. MUS John Barry. RUNNING TIME 94 min. CAST: Steve Railsback (Jim Lee); Penelope Milford (Tania Lee); Michael Beck (Crawford); Torquil Campbell (Eric); Sandra Seacat (Gladys); Seth Sakai (Semeyon).

Once Bitten (Samuel Goldwyn, 1985). DIR Howard Storm. PROD Dimitri Villard, Robby Wald. EXEC PROD **Samuel Goldwyn, Jr.** SCR David Hines, Jeffrey Hause, Jonathan Roberts (story by Dimitri Villard). CAM Adam Greenberg. ED Marc Grossman. MUS John Du Prez. RUNNING TIME 97 min. CAST: Lauren Hutton (Countess); Jim Carrey (Mark Kendall); Karen Kopins (Robin Pierce); Cleavon Little (Sebastian); Thomas Ballatore (Jamie); Skip Lacey (Russ).

Mystic Pizza (Samuel Goldwyn, 1988). DIR Donald Petrie. PROD Mark Levinson, Scott Rosenfelt. EXEC PROD **Samuel Goldwyn, Jr.** SCR Amy Jones, Perry Howze, Randy Howze, Alfred Uhry (story by Amy Jones). CAM Tim Suhrstedt. ED Marion Rothman, Don Brochu. MUS David McHugh. RUNNING TIME 104 min. CAST: Julia Roberts (Daisy Araujo); Annabeth Gish (Kat Araujo); Lili Taylor (Jojo Barboza); Vincent Phillip D'Onofrio (Bill Montijo); William R. Moses (Tim Travers); Adam Storke (Charles G. Winsor).

Stella (Touchstone, 1990). DIR John Erman. PROD **Samuel Goldwyn, Jr.** SCR Robert Getchell (novel by Olive Higgins Prouty). CAM Billy Williams. ED Jerrold L. Ludwig. MUS John Morris. RUNNING TIME 106 min. CAST: Bette Midler (Stella Claire); John Goodman (Ed Munn); Trini Alvarado (Jenny Claire); Stephen Collins (Stephen Dallas); Marsha Mason (Janice Morrison); Eileen Brennan (Mrs. Wilkerson).

The Program (Touchstone, 1993). DIR David S. Ward. PROD **Samuel Goldwyn, Jr.** SCR David S. Ward, Aaron Latham. CAM Victor Hammer. ED Paul Seydor, Kimberly Ray. MUS Michel Colombier. RUNNING TIME 114 min. CAST: James Caan (Coach Sam Winters); Halle Berry (Autumn Haley); Omar Epps (Darnell Jefferson); Craig Sheffer (Joe Kane); Kristy Swanson (Camille Schaeffer); Abraham Benrubi (Bud-Lite Kamanski).

The Preacher's Wife (Touchstone, 1996). DIR Penny Marshall. PROD **Samuel Goldwyn, Jr.** SCR Nat Mauldin, Allan Scott (based on the screenplay of *The Bishop's Wife* [1947] by Robert E. Sherwood and Leonardo Bercovici, from the novel by Robert Nathan). CAM Miroslav Ondricek. ED Stephen A. Rotter, George Bowers. MUS Hans Zimmer. RUNNING TIME 124 min. CAST: Denzel Washington (Dudley); Whitney Houston (Julia Biggs); Courtney B. Vance (Rev. Biggs); Gregory Hines (Joe Hamilton); Jennifer Lewis (Marguerite Coleman); Loretta Devine (Beverly).

Tortilla Soup (Samuel Goldwyn Films, 2001). DIR María Ripoll. PROD John Bard Manulis, Lulu Zezza. EXEC PROD **Samuel Goldwyn, Jr.** SCR Ramón Menéndez, Tom Musca, Vera Blasi (based on the screenplay of *Yin Shi Nan Nu*, a.k.a. *Eat Drink Man Woman* [1994] by Ang Lee, Hui-Ling Wang, James Schamus). CAM Xavier Perez Grobet. Ed Andy Blumenthal. MUS Bill Conti. RUNNING TIME 122 min. CAST: Hector Elizondo (Martin); Jacqueline Obradors (Carmen); Tamaro Mello (Maribel); Constance Marie (Yolanda); Raquel Welch (Hortensia).

KATHRYN GRAYSON

Legendary movie star Kathryn Grayson was extremely instrumental and, frankly, equally timeless and priceless as well, in MGM's long history of engrossing and lavish musicals, made during the reign of its founder Louis B. Mayer.[1] Her delightful and thoroughly engaging portrayals of colorful characters such as the love interest of Gene Kelly and Frank Sinatra[2] as two sailors on leave in Hollywood (*Anchors Aweigh*, 1945), the part of Magnolia Hawks in the third and most prestigious screen version of *Show Boat* (1951, immortalizing the song "Make Believe"), or her dynamic performance in *Kiss Me, Kate* (1953), based on Shakespeare's *The Taming of the Shrew*, are just a few examples to indicate how versatile Miss Grayson's talent really was.

She was graced with an enormously powerful coloratura soprano singing voice which made her an established star at the studio in the 1940s and early 1950s. Along with her close friend and predecessor Jeanette MacDonald,[3] she was one of the very few to combine popular and classical music, and introduce the latter genre to a broad audience.

Born Zelma Kathryn Hedrick on February 9, 1922, in Winston-Salem, North Carolina, she was discovered and signed to an MGM contract in 1939. She finished school at MGM's Little Red School House and made her screen debut in *Andy Hardy's Private Secretary* (1941), playing Mickey Rooney's secretary. As it turned out, it would only be the beginning of a career in motion pictures as one of MGM's top leading ladies; in those days, the early 1940s, when Greta Garbo[4] and Norma Shearer[5] stars such as eventually retired from the screen, Miss Grayson was able to follow into their footsteps ever so convincingly.

About her early days at MGM, she recalls: "One day I was sitting down to have lunch. I had just done my screen test, but I hadn't even seen it. We had recorded some popular songs, some comedy and dramatic singing, it was quite a long and expensive test. Katharine Hepburn came running over and said, 'Oh Kathryn, I just saw your test, you are the greatest young actress I have ever seen,' and she kissed my hand. So I thought, if she likes it that much, I should go and see it. So I went over to the executive building and saw it—I *hated* myself, I thought I was terrible. I went to Mr. Mayer and said, 'Mr. Mayer, you have been very kind and I want to thank you very much, but I can see I am not the right person to be in pictures.' He then said, 'Are you *crazy*? We spent so much money on that test, everybody loves it, people from other studios even asked for it and we had sent it to them.' On Sunday nights they'd have dinner and they would run a picture or somebody's test or something, I guess mine was a very popular test—I wish I could find it."

So it only took her a short while to convince her boss she would be able to make a valuable contribution to the successful string of musicals they were making at MGM. After her screen debut opposite Mickey Rooney, Miss Grayson appeared in *Rio Rita* (1942) with Bud Abbott and Lou Costello (both on loan-out from Universal) and she became the leading lady in veteran director Frank Borzage's *Seven Sweethearts* (1942), incidentally the first film producer Joe Pasternak[6] made at MGM. He previously had handled Deanna Durbin's career at Universal and was assigned to guide Miss Grayson's career at Metro. With Miss Grayson, he made many successful musicals such as *Thousands Cheer* (1944, MGM's wartime musical extravaganza, focusing on a star-studded camp show organized by Miss Grayson), *Anchors Aweigh* (1945, with Miss Grayson singing "All of a Sudden My Heart Sings" and "Jalousie"), *Two Sisters from Boston* (1946, with her song "Take a Chance on Romance" as a standout), *The Kissing Bandit* (1948, songs include duets "What's Wrong with Me?" and "Senorita" with her co-star Frank Sinatra), and finally the first two films Mario Lanza[7] appeared in, *That Midnight Kiss* (1949) and *The Toast of New Orleans* (1950, with their duet "Be My Love" as one of the highlights).

After seeing her screen test, Katharine Hepburn told Kathryn Grayson: "You are the greatest young actress I have ever seen."

She did work with the very best, as she also frequently collaborated with two other top producers at MGM. For Arthur Freed,[8] she appeared in the 13th and final sequence of the all-star musical *Ziegfeld Follies* (1945, singing "Beauty"), the Jerome Kern biography *Till the Clouds Roll By* (1946, as Magnolia Hawks in the *Show Boat* sequence) and *Show Boat* (1951, singing "After the Ball" and duets with co-star Howard Keel including "Why Do I Love You" and "Make Believe"). Jack Cummings[9] on the other hand was the producer of *It Happened in Brooklyn* (1947, with Miss Grayson as a music teacher who sings a delightful duet with her leading man Frank Sinatra, "La Ci Darem la Mano" from *Don Giovanni*), *Lovely to Look At* (1952, a remake of *Roberta* [1935], with duets with Howard Keel such as "You're Devastating" and "Lovely to Look At") and *Kiss Me, Kate* (1953, with other highly enjoyable duets with Howard Keel including "So in Love" and "Wunderbar"). She was not only one of Hollywood's major box-office attractions, she was also a most appealing and highly respected star because of her solid, skilful and imaginative performances. This made her one of the most popular stars on the lot.

Miss Grayson: "Over the years, they were always so kind to me at MGM. I always loved walking in the rain and I will never forget the limousine drivers, even before I made my first picture—I was there a year before I made my first picture. If the drivers of Garbo or Crawford or Greer Garson saw me, they'd say, 'Kathryn, you get in here, you shouldn't be walking in the rain.' They treated me beautifully. The studio for example bought a lot of wonderful things for me, such as *Peg o' My Heart* [filmed in 1933 with Marion Davies], they made a dancing picture out of one they bought for me with Gene Kelly, Van Johnson and Cyd Charisse [*Brigadoon*,

Gene Kelly, Frank Sinatra and Kathryn Grayson in George Sidney's *Anchors Aweigh* (1945).

1954], but I never got a chance to do them. Back then, people often asked me, 'Why can't you do great stories with great music?' And Mr. Mayer always said, 'The public likes you the way you are with the things you're doing, you make them happy!' I'd argue with him—I remember director Victor Fleming once was walking through the commissary, he took me aside and said, 'Oh Kathryn, it's just too bad that you weren't old enough to play Scarlett, we'd have to tame you down while we always had to build Vivien up!' And I said, 'What do you mean?' He said, 'She just didn't have the *fire* you have.' The studio always had me playing the *goodie-goodie* girl, except in *Kiss Me, Kate* I got to do a little of me [laughs].

"If Louis B. Mayer didn't have people stabbing him in the back, he would have been able to accomplish a lot more than he already had achieved. He was so far ahead of his time. He once said that television could do only such an amount of films on a lower scale, we should do great films to get and to keep our audience. Mr. Schary[10] went back to making cheaper films, they weren't the pictures that Mr. Mayer would have made. I think Mr. Mayer was the *real* 'Wizard of Oz.' He once said he didn't believe in television, but he wined and dined with NBC and CBS. He told me, 'Look, I'd rather have that motion pictures run television than television running motion pictures.' How right he was. But the stockholders were horrified that Mr. Mayer wanted to blend in with television—well, it happened that way anyway, but if Mr. Mayer had been ahead of it, we would have had great quality in television. He *believed* in quality, we would have had beautiful, wholesome television.

"When MGM was selling its props and back lots in the late 1960s, early 1970s, it broke my heart. They could have had a much better tour than Universal could ever have: we had the second and the third lot; there was the lot of the Tarzan pictures; Esther Williams' swimming pool was over there too; then there was the lot up the hill with the Show Boat; I think

Kathryn Grayson. (Courtesy of Kathryn Grayson and Curtis Roberts.)

Kathryn Grayson. (Courtesy of Kathryn Grayson and Curtis Roberts.)

it was there that we also did *Seven Sweethearts*. Mr. Mayer always brought in the best craftsmen, they were wonderful artists. He would leave an empty set one day, and come back to a beautiful set the next morning. To me, making all those films at MGM was like going from one home to another home."

What about the directors she worked with at MGM—anyone in particular who can be considered her favorite? Miss Grayson: "George Sidney made my first test. We sort of grew up together at MGM; his wife was the drama coach at the studio. I adored her, she was a great friend. I loved Georgie, but I think the greatest director that I ever worked with, was Frank Borzage.[11] He was the first director to receive an Academy Award. He gave you things to do with your character that no other director did. I was also looking forward to work on *The Vagabond King* which we made at Paramount, with Mike Curtiz, who was such a wonderful director for actresses like Bette Davis, but he was having a nervous breakdown at the time; that was very unfortunate for everyone. He would have hundreds of extras on the set without having planned the day's work. That made it very difficult. And my mother died just before we started the picture. He said, 'Darling, I'm so sorry about your mother, I'm going to give you two weeks off to get yourself together.' Then I got a call from Paramount, they said, 'Look, you can't have two weeks off.'"

"As for my co-stars, Fred Astaire was wonderful with his feet, he had a brilliant choreography. But the one thing that always bothered me about Fred was his hands, he didn't know what to do with them. My favorite dancer was Gene Kelly, his mannerisms were pretty much the same in each picture. If you look at his films, one after another, his expressions were very much the same. I didn't realize that at the time. Frank Sinatra was terribly kind and so sweet, he had a lot of people working for him and they had already made him a big star before he ever arrived at the studio. Despite all the fame, all the girls screaming and all that, he was the kindest man you could imagine. He was very lovable, I liked him very much. But he was so skinny. In our first two pictures I wouldn't kiss him, so they wrote it so that I got someone else in the end—the love story always started with us, but I ended up with someone else. So finally, producer Joe Pasternak even padded his legs in the last picture we did together, *The Kissing Bandit*, and he said, 'You *have* to kiss him now, Kathryn!' Well, I thought he had something terminal, he was just so skinny [laughs].

"All the singers that I worked with put their feet on the piano bench, and so I decided to make a needle point cover for the piano bench. When I finished a concert tour in Australia, we landed in Singapore and I decided to get off the plane, walk around and stretch my legs a little bit. When I got back on the plane, my needle point cover was gone, I had just about maybe twenty rows to go to the bottom, it was almost finished, somebody just took it [laughs]."

Screen actress Greer Garson (1904–1996).

What was the best lesson Miss Grayson was taught? "We were taught that your *eyes* told the story and they showed us how Spencer Tracy, who is probably considered to be the greatest film actor in the business, was able to show that. He wouldn't have to say a word, it was just his expression while he was listening to people. When you saw his eyes, you could see what he was thinking. He would steal a scene without saying a word, you were looking at him for his reactions, it was fascinating. He didn't have to move his arms or make faces—as an actor you only have to *think* and that's exactly what he did."

After *Lovely to Look At* Miss Grayson left the MGM lot, made two films at Warner Bros., *The Desert Song* and *So This Is Love* (both 1953), returned to MGM once more for *Kiss Me, Kate* (also 1953) and made her final film, *The Vagabond King* (1956), at Paramount. She then retired from the screen and dedicated her time and energy strictly to stage musicals (*The Merry Widow*, *Naughty Marietta*, *Kiss Me, Kate*, *Show Boat*, *Camelot*), nightclub appearances, concerts and straight plays (*Night Watch*)—a second career, equally successful as the one she had in motion pictures, and which to this very day still is going strong.

Miss Grayson: "I still work professionally. I do concerts. I have my own one-woman show [*An Evening with Kathryn Grayson*] and appeared with Van Johnson in *Love Letters* in the past years. I also do straight dramatic things, it's fun. People, especially in Europe, are not aware that I have been working all the time. I never looked for any kind of publicity, perhaps that's why they don't realize it. You know, there's a picture of all of us in Greer Garson's book, when we all went on the third war bond tour during the second World War, and I am looking down—I don't like big bunches of people, so I sort of hid from the camera. On one of the anniversaries of MGM, I believe it was in 1945, I didn't want to show up. Mr. Mayer was furious, he had sent two policemen and a limousine for me. I was so angry, I put my raincoat on and came there with a *glare* on my face, because I didn't want to be there [laughs]. The policeman was so sweet, everyone was so good to me at the studio—Eleanor Powell said, 'The most spoiled brat of our studio, is Kathryn Grayson' [laughs]. Even the telephone operators, if they didn't want me to speak to someone they thought wasn't nice enough for me to speak to, they'd say, 'No, she's been doing such and such, you can't talk to her!' I would go into the commissary and order a big luncheon and I'd only get a chicken soup and a small salad [laughs], that's what Mr. Mayer thought I should have!"

Music has always been a driving force for Miss Grayson in anything she has done professionally: "I learned my first opera when I was 11 years old. When I had just moved here [to Los Angeles], I started singing at church and at school. Because we were of different ages, my brothers and sisters went to different schools, but we were always chosen to be the soloists at church and at school. We thought it was natural, because we had been singing all our lives; we always sang along with all of the records we had, we'd even hum the orchestral parts in between. We were fortunate to be raised with the great music. We all sang, we all had over four octave ranges. When we were chosen to sing solos, we took it very naturally. We didn't think were any better than anybody else, we just *sang*."

"Later on, Edward Johnson, who was the head of the Metropolitan, wanted me to make my debut there with *Lucia*, the first opera I had learned, but Mr. Mayer said, 'No, people will think you are an opera singer and your career won't last very long, while as a motion picture star, you will be a star for the rest of your life.' But I have sung opera since my contract at MGM ended [debuting in 1960, performing in operas such as *Madame Butterfly*, *La Traviata* and *La Bohème*] and the opera world is a very small world. The funny thing is that when I go in, a lot of the young people come in and say, 'Oh, I became a singer because I saw you in films.' The three great tenors of today also became tenors because of Mario Lanza.

"When we'd go to New York or tour the country back then, people would tear your clothes off, we'd need police escorts. Once a fan took her scissors out of her purse and almost cut my hair to the scalp. So I would have to brush my hair over that place and pushed it over where she cut. When I came home, the hair stylist at the studio cut all my hair and made little short curls, which became very fashionable later on.

"Anyway, I do thank God for everything I was allowed to do, because it was really a joy in those days. It never was a problem to get up early in the morning and be at the studio at seven for make-up. Everybody loved everybody, it was like a family, we were all very close. Mr. Mayer wanted to create a family and that's exactly what he did. Even today, a lot of us are still great friends. I don't like all the things some of those people do, but I love them. We all miss that era, it was very joyful. And if you look around, there's not much joy in the world today, and that's particularly sad for the young people who should have a very happy, carefree life.

"You know, they took music out of our schools. I'd like to go to Washington and see that they have music appreciation back in our schools, because there weren't gangs, there was no shooting back then. Somehow, good music makes everybody happy: it can be very uplifting, it elevates the spirits. Back then we were taught about Mozart, Brahms, etc. Once we were driving to Palm Springs, I had the classic music station on in the car and Annie Miller said, 'Oh, can't we get something else, that sounds so funereal!' [laughs]. She's so funny, she's still a good friend of mine.

"I teach music now and I give scholarships for the Sunbelt Communications—I work for them. We also build music centers. I really enjoy working with these young people. Of all the schools I've

Kathryn Grayson. (Courtesy of Kathryn Grayson and Curtis Roberts.)

been in, there's one school in southern Utah, with one fine teacher and a lot of students with beautiful voices consequently. There are a few good voices here and there, but they don't have teachers. Today they're pushing everybody's voice down in the chest, that's why a few stars got into trouble with their voice. I noticed that a lot of people are even putting the children's voices down, that's a criminal thing to do. They have high piping beautiful little voices and they should not tamper with that."

Those were the final thoughts Miss Grayson shared with me; as she was on a pretty tight schedule and had a lot of work to do, she gracefully waved me out and before leaving her home, she handed me two compilation CDs of songs she had recorded over the years.[12] When I got back home, I heard no complaint at all from my neighbors as they too were able to enjoy the wonderful voice of Kathryn Grayson.

Interview: Los Angeles, March 1, 2001

Notes

1. Louis B. Mayer (1885–1957) will always be one of the most important and leading figures in the history of motion pictures. A former junk dealer, he formed his own company, Louis B. Mayer Pictures, in 1916, which merged with Metro and the Goldwyn Company into Metro-Goldwyn-Mayer (1924). He reigned at the studio and was MGM's vice-president in charge of production until his forced departure in 1951 when he was replaced by Dore Schary. He was assisted by perhaps the best production chief ever, Irving G. Thalberg, from 1924 to 1936 (when Thalberg died at age 37). Mayer had a huge influence on the whole process of filmmaking. After all, MGM was Hollywood's most prestigious studio, with "more stars than there are in heaven." Mayer was one of the founding members of the Academy of Motion Picture Arts and Science (1927) and received an honorary Oscar in 1951 for his "distinguished services to the motion picture industry."

2. Frank Sinatra (1915–1998), another screen legend and icon in the world of show business, got his first acting role in the RKO musical *Higher and Higher* (1943) opposite French actress Michèle Morgan, but it wasn't until *Anchors Aweigh* (1945) that he became fully recognized as an all-round actor, singer and dancer. Over the years, he appeared in numerous musicals and played character roles as well; one of them, the part of Angelo Maggio in Fred Zinnemann's *From Here to Eternity* (1953), earned him an Academy Award for best supporting actor. Sinatra's other films include *Take Me Out to the Ball Game* (1949), *On the Town* (1949), *The Man with the Golden Arm* (1955, Academy Award nomination for best actor), *High Society* (1956), *The Pride and the Passion* (1957), *Pal Joey* (1957), *Some Came Running* (1959), *Can-Can* (1960), *The Manchurian Candidate* (1962), *None but the Brave* (1965, also dir. and prod.), and *Von Ryan's Express* (1965). In 1970 he was awarded the Jean Hersholt Humanitarian Award by the Academy. He is regarded by many as the greatest and most popular singer of the 20th century. Even in the 1990s, he topped the charts with his *Duets* CDs. From 1951 to 1957 he was married to actress Ava Gardner (1922–1990).

3. Jeanette MacDonald (1901–1965) appeared in stage musicals and operas before arriving in Hollywood. Director Ernst Lubitsch cast her in *The Love Parade* (1929) and opposite Maurice Chevalier in *One Hour with You* (1931) and *The Merry Widow* (1934), but it wasn't until she joined MGM in 1933 and teamed up with Nelson Eddy in *Naughty Marietta* (1935) that she enjoyed phenomenal popularity. They also appeared in *Rose Marie* (1936), *Maytime* (1937), *Girl of the Golden West* (1938), *Sweethearts* (1938), *New Moon* (1940) and *Bitter Sweet* (1940). Because of their many films together, they were known as the screen's "Singing Sweethearts." However when World War II broke out, the innocent days were over. Their collaboration came to an end and for both of them it also meant the end of their careers in films. In between, she also played dramatic roles in films such as *San Francisco* (1936, with Clark Gable and Spencer Tracy); her operettas include *Romeo and Juliet* and *Faust*.

4. Greta Garbo (1905–1990), the legendary and mysterious "Divine Garbo" and Swedish-born pre–World War II star of MGM. She arrived in Hollywood in 1925, and immediately became one of Hollywood's top stars in 1926 when *The Torrent*, her first U.S. film, was released (the other leading ladies at that time included Clara Bow, Dolores Del Rio and Louise Brooks). She made films until 1941 (*Two-Faced Woman* was her final feature) when she decided to retire from films at age 36, while she still was at the peak of her career. After that time she lived as a total recluse, dividing her time between homes in Switzerland, Sweden and New York's Upper East Side where she once in a while was spotted window shopping (photographers frequently tried to follow and photograph her, although mostly in vain). A comeback never materialized. On the screen, she often played tragic and tormented heroines. Her films include *The Torrent* (1926), *Flesh and the Devil* (1927), *Love* (1927), *A Woman of Affairs* (1928), *The Kiss* (1929), *Anna Christie* (1930, her first talkie, announced with

the tag line "Garbo Talks!"—Academy Award nomination for best actress), *Romance* (1930, Academy Award nomination for best actress), *Mata Hari* (1931), *Susan Lenox: Her Fall and Rise* (1931), *Grand Hotel* (1932), *As You Desire Me* (1932), *Queen Christina* (1933), *Anna Karenina* (1935, remake of her 1927 silent *Love*), *Camille* (1937, Academy Award nomination for best actress—also filmed in 1915 with Clara Kimball Young, in 1917 with Theda Bara and in 1921 with Nazimova), *Conquest* (1937) and *Ninotchka* (1939, released with the slogan "Garbo Laughs!"—Academy Award nomination for best actress).

5. Norma Shearer: more information, interview with Janet Leigh, note 1.

6. Joe Pasternak (1901–1991), Hungarian-born producer who worked in films from 1923 to 1968, arrived in the U.S. in 1921. He became a dishwasher at Paramount's Astoria Studios in New York but he worked his way up until he became an assistant director at Universal in the late 1920s. He then returned to Europe for a few years, made films in Germany and Hungary and came back to the U.S. in 1936 with his favorite director, Hermann Kosterlitz (Henry Koster). At Universal he made ten films with Deanna Durbin (and consequently saved Universal from bankruptcy), he revived the career of Marlene Dietrich in the late 1930s, and from 1941 until his retirement in 1968, he worked at MGM as one of the studio's top producers. In all, he made over 80 films, including *Destry Rides Again* (1939), *The Unfinished Dance* (1947), *A Date with Judy* (1948), *The Great Caruso* (1951), *Easy to Love* (1953), *The Student Prince* (1954), *Party Girl* (1958) and his final film, *The Sweet Ride* (1968).

7. Mario Lanza (1921–1959), Philadelphia-born tenor, was discovered at the 1942 Tanglewood Music Festival (Mass.). He was signed for a nationwide concert tour which was interrupted by his World War 2 service. In 1948 Louis B. Mayer heard him singing at the Hollywood Bowl and offered him a contract, resulting in a successful but short career in films such as *That Midnight Kiss* (1949), *The Toast of New Orleans* (1950), *The Great Caruso* (1951) and *Because You're Mine* (1952). He spent his final years in Italy and died at age 38 in a Rome hospital of a heart attack. Lanza was known for his temper which, along with personal problems such as a bout with alcohol, shortened his career.

8. Arthur Freed (1894–1973), legendary lyricist and one of history's most prestigious film producers, was first hired by Irving Thalberg in 1929 when producing a play in Hollywood, and remained with MGM till 1969. One of the first songs he wrote for the screen, was "Singin' in the Rain" for MGM's legendary all-star revue *The Hollywood Revue of 1929* (1929)—later on, he wrote about 150 other songs used in various films (including "Broadway Rhythm," "Pagan Love Song," "You Were Meant for Me"). His endless list of credits as producer includes films such as *Babes in Arms* (1939), *Strike Up the Band* (1940), *For Me and My Gal* (1942), *Meet Me in St. Louis* (1944), *The Clock* (1945), *The Harvey Girls* (1946), *The Pirate* (1948), *Easter Parade* (1948), *Annie Get Your Gun* (1950), *Show Boat* (1951), *An American in Paris* (1951, Academy Award for best picture), *Singin' in the Rain* (1952), *Brigadoon* (1954), *Silk Stockings* (1957) and *Gigi* (1958, Academy Award for best picture). He produced over 45 films at MGM which grossed over $280,000,000, making him probably the most successful producer during the studio era.

9. Jack Cummings (1905–1989), the nephew of Louis B. Mayer, worked his way up and started working at age 17 as an office boy, then script clerk, assistant director and short subjects producer/director until 1935 when he produced his first feature, *The Winning Ticket*. His films include *Born to Dance* (1936), *The Broadway Melody of 1938* (1937), *Bathing Beauty* (1944), *The Stratton Story* (1949), *Texas Carnival* (1951), *Seven Brides for Seven Brothers* (1954), *The Last Time I Saw Paris* (1954), *Can-Can* (1960) and *Viva Las Vegas* (1964).

10. Dore Schary: more information, interview with Janet Leigh, note 3.

11. Frank Borzage (1893–1962), two-time Academy Award winner as best director for *Seventh Heaven* (1927, starring Janet Gaynor) and *Bad Girl* (1931, starring Sally Eilers and James Dunn), started out as an actor in 1912 in Thomas Ince films and directed his first film in 1917. His credits include *Humoresque* (1920), *Lazybones* (1925), *The River* (1929), *A Farewell to Arms* (1932), *Desire* (1936), *Mannequin* (1938), *The Mortal Storm* (1940) and *Stage Door Canteen* (1943). He made his final film in 1959, *The Big Fisherman*.

12. Miss Grayson released a total of three compilation CDs: *Remember*, *Softly* and *Make Believe*—none of them are available in record stores, however. For orders ($15.00 each, plus $2.00 for shipping in the U.S.), write to Miss Grayson's secretary Sally Sherman, AZEL Music, Box 281, 513 Wilshire Blvd., Santa Monica, CA 90401, U.S.A.

Filmography

Andy Hardy's Private Secretary (MGM, 1941). DIR George B. Seitz. SCR Jane Murfin, Harry Ruskin (characters created by Aurania Rouverol). CAM Lester White. ED Elmo Veron. MUS Herbert Stothart. RUNNING TIME 98 min. CAST: Lewis Stone (Judge Hardy); Mickey Rooney (Andy Hardy); Fay Holden (Mrs. Hardy); Ann Rutherford (Polly Benedict); Sara Haden (Aunt Milly); **Kathryn Grayson** (Kathryn Land).

The Vanishing Virginian (MGM, 1941). DIR Frank Borzage. PROD Edwin Knopf. SCR Jan Fortune (novel by Rebecca Yancey Williams). CAM Charles Lawton. ED James E. Newcom. MUS David Snell. RUNNING TIME 96 min. CAST: Frank Morgan (Robert); **Kathryn Grayson** (Rebecca Yancey); Spring Byington (Rosa Yancey); Natalie Thompson (Margaret Yancey); Douglas Newland (Jim Shirley); Mark Daniels (Jack Holden).

Rio Rita (MGM, 1942). DIR S. Sylvan Simon. PROD Pandro S. Berman. SCR Richard Connell, Gladys Lehman. CAM George Folsey. ED Ben Lewis. MUS Herbert Stothart. RUNNING TIME 90 min. CAST: Bud Abbott (Doc); Lou Costello (Wishy); **Kathryn Grayson** (Rita Winslow); John Carroll (Ricardo Montera); Patricia Dane (Lucette); Tom Conway (Maurice Craindall).

Seven Sweethearts (MGM, 1942). DIR Frank Borzage. PROD Joe Pasternak. SCR Walter Reisch, Leo Townsend. CAM George Folsey. ED Blanche Sewell. MUS Franz Waxman. RUNNING TIME 99 min. CAST: **Kathryn Grayson** (Billie Van Maaster); Van Heflin (Taggart); Marsha Hunt (Regina); Diane Lewis (Mrs. Nugent); S. Z. Sakall (Mr. Van Maaster); Frances Raeburn* (Cornelius Van Maaster).

Thousands Cheer (MGM, 1944). DIR George Sidney. PROD Joe Pasternak. SCR Paul Jarrico, Richard Collins. CAM George Folsey. ED George Boemler. MUS Herbert Stothart. RUNNING TIME 125 min. CAST: **Kathryn Grayson** (Kathryn Jones); Gene Kelly (Pvt. Eddie Marsh); Mary Astor (Hillary Jones); John Boles (Col. Bill Jones); Ben Blue (Chuck Polansky); Frances Rafferty (Marie Corbino).

Anchors Aweigh (MGM, 1945). DIR George Sidney. PROD Joe Pasternak. SCR Isobel Lennart (story by Natalie Marcin). CAM Robert Planck, Charles Boyle. ED Adrienne Fazan. MUS Georgie Stoll. RUNNING TIME 138 min. CAST: Frank Sinatra (Clarence Doolittle); **Kathryn Grayson** (Susan Abbott); Gene Kelly (Joseph Brady); José Iturbi (Himself); Dean Stockwell (Donald Martin); Pamela Britton (Girl from Brooklyn).

Ziegfeld Follies (MGM, 1945). DIR Vincente Minnelli. PROD Arthur Freed. SCR Peter Barry, David Freedman, Harry Tugend, George White, Robert Alton, Al Lewis, Irving Brecher. CAM George Folsey, Charles Rosher. ED Albert Akst. MUS Lennie Hayton. RUNNING TIME 110 min. CAST: Fred Astaire (Himself/Imposter/Tai Long); Fanny Brice (Norma Edelman); Judy Garland (Great Lady); **Kathryn Grayson** (Singer); Lena Horne (Singer); Gene Kelly (Himself); Esther Williams (Dancer).

Two Sisters from Boston (MGM, 1946). DIR Henry Koster. PROD Joe Pasternak. SCR Myles Connolly. CAM Robert Surtees. ED Douglass Biggs. MUS Charles Previn. RUNNING TIME 112 min. CAST: **Kathryn Grayson** (Abigail Chandler); June Allyson (Martha Canford Chandler); Lauritz Melchior (Olstrom); Jimmy Durante ("Spike"); Peter Lawford (Lawrence Patterson, Jr.); Ben Blue (Wrigley).

Till the Clouds Roll By (MGM, 1946). DIR Richard Whorf. PROD Arthur Freed. SCR Myles Connolly, Jean Holloway (story by Guy Bolton). CAM Harry Stradling, George J. Folsey. ED Albert Akst. MUS Lennie Hayton. RUNNING TIME 120 min. CAST: June Allyson (Guest Star); Lucille Bremer (Sally Hessler); Judy Garland (Marilyn Miller); **Kathryn Grayson** (Magnolia in "Show Boat" number); Van Heflin (James I. Hessler); Lena Horne (Julie); Van Johnson (Band Leader).

It Happened in Brooklyn (MGM, 1947). DIR Richard Whorf. PROD Jack Cummings. SCR Isobel Lennart. CAM Robert Planck. ED Blanche Sewell. MUS Johnny Green. RUNNING TIME 103 min. CAST: Frank Sinatra (Danny Webson Miller); **Kathryn Grayson** (Anne Fielding); Peter Lawford (Jamie Shellgrove); Jimmy Durante (Nick Lombardi); Gloria Grahame (Nurse); Marcy McGuire (Rae Jakobi).

The Kissing Bandit (MGM, 1948). DIR Laszlo Benedek. PROD Joe Pasternak. SCR Isobel Lennart, John Briard Harding. CAM Robert Surtees. ED Adrienne Fazan. MUS Georgie Stoll. RUNNING TIME 99 min. CAST: Frank Sinatra (Ricardo); **Kathryn Grayson** (Teresa); J. Carrol Naish (Chico); Mildred Natwick (Isabella); Mikhail Rasumny (Don Jose); Billy Gilbert (General Torro); Sono Osato (Bianca).

That Midnight Kiss (MGM, 1949). DIR Norman Taurog. PROD Joe Pasternak. SCR Bruce Manning, Tamara Hovey. CAM Robert Surtees. ED Gene Ruggiero. MUS Charles Previn. RUNNING TIME 99 min. CAST: **Kathryn Grayson** (Prudence Budell); José Iturbi (Himself); Ethel Barrymore (Abigail Trent Budell); Mario Lanza (Johnny Donnetti); Keenan Wynn (Artie Geoffrey Glenson); J. Carrol Naish (Papa Donnetti).

The Toast of New Orleans (MGM, 1950). DIR Norman Taurog. PROD Joe Pasternak. SCR Sy Gomberg, George Wells. CAM William Snyder. ED Gene Ruggiero. MUS Georgie Stoll. RUNNING TIME 98 min. CAST: **Kathryn Grayson** (Suzette Micheline); Mario Lanza (Pepe Abellard Duvalle); David Niven (Jacques Riboudeaux); J. Carrol Naish (Nicky Duvalle); James Mitchell (Pierre).

Show Boat (MGM, 1951). DIR George Sidney. PROD Arthur Freed. SCR John Lee Mahin (musical play by Jerome Kern, Oscar Hammerstein II; novel by Edna Ferber). CAM Charles Rosher. ED John Dunning. MUS Adolph Deutsch. RUNNING TIME 107 min. CAST: **Kathryn Grayson** (Magnolia Hawks); Ava Gardner (Julie LaVerne); Howard Keel (Gaylord Ravenal); Joe E. Brown (Capt. Andy Hawks); Marge Champion (Ellie May Shipley); Gower Champion (Frank Schultz).

Grounds for Marriage (MGM, 1951). DIR Robert Z. Leonard. PROD Samuel Marx. SCR Allen Rivkin, Laura Kerr (story by Samuel Marx). CAM John Alton. ED Frederick Y. Smith. MUS Bronislau Kaper. RUNNING TIME 89 min. CAST: Van Johnson (Dr. Bartlett); **Kathryn Grayson** (Ina Massine); Paula Raymond (Agnes Young); Barry Sullivan (Chris Bartlett); Lewis Stone (Dr. Young); Reginald Owen (Delacorte).

---

*Frances Raeburn (1924–1976), born Frances Hedrick, was Miss Grayson's younger sister who also appeared in Joe Smith, American *(1942),* The Canterville Ghost *(1944) and* Swing Out, Sister *(1945) opposite Billie Burke.*

Lovely to Look At (MGM, 1952). DIR Mervyn LeRoy. PROD Jack Cummings. SCR George Wells, Harry Ruby (musical comedy *Roberta* by Otto A. Harbach; book by Alice Duer Miller). CAM George J. Folsey. ED John McSweeney, Jr. MUS Jerome Kern. RUNNING TIME 101 min. CAST: **Kathryn Grayson** (Stephanie); Red Skelton (Al Marsh); Howard Keel (Tony Naylor); Marge Champion (Clarisse); Gower Champion (Jerry Ralby); Ann Miller (Bubbles Cassidy); Zsa Zsa Gabor (Zsa Zsa).

The Desert Song (Warner Bros., 1953). DIR Bruce Humberstone. PROD Rudi Fehr. SCR Roland Kibbee (play by Lawrence Schwab, Otto Harbach, Oscar Hammerstein II, Sigmund Romberg, Frank Mandel). CAM Robert Burks. ED William Ziegler. MUS Max Steiner. RUNNING TIME 110 min. CAST: **Kathryn Grayson** (Margot); Gordon MacRae (Paul Bonnard/El Khobar); Steve Cochran (Capt. Fontaine); Raymond Massey (Yousseff); Dick Wesson (Benjy Kidd); Allyn McLerie (Azuri).

So This Is Love (Warner Bros., 1953). DIR Gordon Douglas. PROD Henry Blanke. SCR John Monks, Jr. (autobiography by Grace Moore). CAM Robert Burks. ED Folmar Blangsted. MUS Ray Heindorf. RUNNING TIME 100 min. CAST: **Kathryn Grayson** (Grace Moore); Merv Griffin (Buddy Nash); Joan Weldon (Ruth Obre); Walter Abel (Colonel Moore); Rosemary De Camp (Aunt Laura Stockley); Jeff Donnell (Henrietta Van Dyke).

Kiss Me, Kate (MGM, 1953). DIR George Sidney. PROD Jack Cummings. SCR Dorothy Kingsley (musical comedy by Samuel Spewack, Bella Spewack; music and lyrics by Cole Porter). CAM Charles Rosher. ED Ralph E. Winters. MUS André Previn, Saul Chaplin. RUNNING TIME 109 min. CAST: **Kathryn Grayson** (Lilli Vanessi/Katherine); Howard Keel (Fred Graham/Petruchio); Ann Miller (Lois Lane/Bianca); Keenan Wynn (Lippy); Bobby Van (Gremio); Tommy Rall (Bill Calhoun/Lucentio).

The Vagabond King (Paramount, 1956). DIR Michael Curtiz. PROD Pat Duggan. SCR Ken Englund, Noel Langley (operetta by Rudolf Friml, William H. Post, Brian Hooker; play by Justin Huntly McCarthy). CAM Robert Burks. MUS Victor Young. RUNNING TIME 88 min. CAST: **Kathryn Grayson** (Catherine De Vaucelles); Oreste Kirkop (François Villon); Rita Moreno (Huguette); Cedric Hardwicke (Tristan); Walter Hampden (King Louis XI); Leslie Nielsen (Thibault).

JANE GREER

Like Clark Gable will always be associated with Rhett Butler, the character he played in *Gone with the Wind* (1939), or like Anthony Perkins will go down in history as Norman Bates in Hitchcock's *Psycho* (1960) and in its sequels, so will screen actress Jane Greer always be remembered fondly for her huge contribution to the *film noir* of the 1940s, most notably for her impressive portrayal of Kathie Moffat in Jacques Tourneur's classic *Out of the Past* (1947).

Even though she had only been occasionally in films for the past few decades, this versatile actress still had the charisma and the elegance of many of the charming roles she played over the years, when I met her for the first time in April 1999. She resided in her beautiful house on top of one of the hills of Bel Air, was extremely at ease, in great shape and bright as ever, and she followed closely what was going on in the film industry.

Born on September 9, 1924, she took part in several beauty and talent contests as a youngster and started modeling professionally when she was 12. Miss Greer: "In the 1930s my mother and I used to go to the movies all the time. We lived in Washington, D.C., in Georgetown. There was a theater down the street, it was ten cents I believe in those days. My mother loved pictures and she always wanted me to be in pictures. Those were the days of Shirley Temple and if I could ever become a movie star, I wanted to be like her of course. I never thought of studying acting, so when I finally got a chance in Hollywood, I really didn't know a thing. But RKO, the studio where I started, was a very good training ground for all of us."

She was brought out to Hollywood by Howard Hughes in 1943 who had her under contract for a year before she went to RKO in 1944. "It was that kind of wonderful, young, small, *great* studio, I hated leaving it years later. They had been so good to me. I know a lot of people from my era didn't like the studio system. They didn't want to be *owned* by a studio or be told what to do and given films that they may or may not like. I liked it because I had done nothing yet and I didn't know if I could do anything. We had a dramatic coach, a casting man who sat in on a lot of sessions, a song coach, we had anything you want. The people there were so terrific. First they offered me little parts, then a little bit bigger. My first part was four lines. I was Eve Arden's secretary in *Pan-Americana*. I said 'Yes, DJ,' initials of some sort, and then 'No, DJ,' that was my part."

Although RKO (short for Radio-Keith-Orpheum, a production, distribution and exhibition company that emerged in 1928) didn't really have the impact of Hollywood's major studios, it was nevertheless a prestigious studio that made lots of outstanding films in the 1930s and 1940s, including nearly all of the Astaire-Rogers musicals, comedies starring Cary Grant and Katharine Hepburn and numerous other prestigious productions such as Orson Welles' *Citizen Kane* (1941) and Hitchcock's *Suspicion* (1941).

First billed as Bettejane Greer (her real name), it was changed to Jane Greer early on in her career, and among her first films were *Dick Tracy* (1945), *The Falcon's Alibi* (1946, in which she sings two songs) and *Sinbad the Sailor* (1947), a highly profitable adventure film with a flamboyant Douglas Fairbanks, Jr. in the title role. Can her next film, *They Won't Believe Me* (1947), be considered a turning point in her career? Miss Greer: "Joan Harrison[1] was the producer of this picture and she put me in it. She had written screenplays for a number of Hitchcock films and they were very close. She liked my work—she had seen me in some rushes or whatever. She said, 'I want to test you.' It was opposite Robert Young. She told me that I should lighten my hair. I had dark hair and I also dyed it dark—I was playing heavies and they wanted dark hair. I said, 'Fine.' She said, 'I'm not going to make you blonde, but I'm going to make you look like a young woman. Now you look like Gale Sondergaard.' So she did that and it looked better, I felt better, I loved it! She tailored a suit to fit me and tested me with Robert Young. Generally you were tested with another actor on the lot. Before that, I did several tests with Steve Brodie for other roles.

"So she put me into this picture, it was a sort of a *film noir*. But with this film Robert Young didn't have a chance with the audience; he played a heavy and they hated it. People didn't want to see it, and so it didn't do well at all," Miss Greer said. *They Won't Believe Me* (1947), an interesting James M. Cain–type character study and melodrama with Robert Young in an unsympathetic role as a philanderer, focuses on the three women in his life: Jane Greer, Susan Hayward as his partner's secretary and Rita Johnson as his wife.

"It did lead to *Out of the Past* however; I think it was Robert Sparks[2] who put me in that picture. I'm sure they had a lot of people who wanted to be in it, but it turned out to be me. It was a wonderful part, with a wonderful introduction for the character; this was a girl of which one man says, 'She shot me, I want her back, go find her.' People wanted to see what she looked like! And when I finally did show up twenty minutes later, people had heard so much about me that they thought, 'She must be something!' And they said, 'My God, she's stunning! Look at that hat!' and all that. It was all contrived, you know.

"People sometimes write things that we supposedly did—I had people say, 'Oh, that one scene when you are watching them fighting and you shoot him, that look on your face, that joy when you're gonna kill him!!' I said, 'Joy?!' [laughs]. They find all kinds of things in your performance that aren't there at all. As a matter of fact, I could hardly see them because the camera was behind them off light and all I saw was this bright light, I couldn't see anything!"

Out of the Past (1947) still is a wonderful example of a 1940s film noir with Robert Mitchum[3] as a former private investigator who comes to a violent end, despite trying to lead a quiet, small town life as a gasoline station operator. He tells the greater part of the story in retrospect. Jane Greer plays a killer he falls for after their paths cross in Acapulco, while Kirk Douglas plays a gangster and Mitchum's one-time employer. It's a fascinating melodrama with the dialogue as a standout.

The film was a huge success and Miss Greer became one of RKO's leading actresses. Did she feel like a movie star? "No, I didn't. I considered myself more a working actress. After I finished *Out of the Past*, Howard Hughes bought the studio. He had me come into his office which was at the Goldwyn Studios; he never came onto the RKO lot. He said to me, 'I know you're not happy.' I said, 'What do you mean? I am happy, I have a baby now, and I hope to have more. I am happy!' He said, 'You're not happy with your husband, Edward Lasker.' I said, 'Yes, I am!' He knew Edward and he didn't like him. Then he said, 'Well, I'll tell you one thing, as long as I own the studio, you won't work.' So I said, 'This will kill my career!' He said, 'Yes, it will.' I went home and explained it to Edward. Hughes had this obsession

Jane Greer, Kirk Douglas and Robert Mitchum in *Out of the Past* (1947). (Courtesy of DOCIP Film Archive, Brussels, Belgium.)

with women. I thought, maybe he'll get over it. A female screenwriter at RKO once told me she had written something for me; she told Hughes, 'I don't think the stockholders would like it if you say I can't have Jane in it.' Well, he still wouldn't let me do that picture.

"When *The Big Steal* came along, Robert Mitchum had been arrested for possessing marijuana and his leading lady Lizabeth Scott already had her wardrobe. But when she found out he had to go to jail, she said, 'I don't want to do it.' So they were trying to find *someone* to work with him, because they wanted him to go to work in Mexico the next Tuesday. Several people were asked to do it, including Joan Bennett, but they all turned it down. I really wanted to do it, because I didn't want Bob to be hurt by all this turning down. Finally, and I guess they got stuck, the head of the studio, Sid Rogell, came to my house and said, "Howard's going to call you and he's gonna try to trap you, so be careful.' 'Trap me?!' He said, 'Don't tell him I was here!' I said, 'I won't!' Well, when the phone rang, it was Howard. 'Bettejane'—he always called me Bettejane—'Bettejane, are you interested in doing this picture with Bob Mitchum?' I said, 'I'd love to, Howard. I love Bob, you know that, I worked with him and I'd love to work with him again.' He said, 'Well then, all right, but you'd have to wear Lizabeth Scott's wardrobe. You leave next Tuesday.' 'All right.' 'You have anything else to tell me?' I said, 'No, I don't think so.' 'You liar, you're pregnant! You're knocked up!' I said, 'Am I?' 'Yes!' I said, 'I didn't know, they haven't called me yet. I did take a test, but I haven't gotten the result of the test yet.' 'Well I got it, and you're knocked up.' 'But I still can do the picture. If we start next Tuesday, I've still got some time cause it won't show until the fourth or fifth month.'

"Well, we went to Mexico and I realized that these costumes they had made, were going to be tough, a tight short skirt, a bolero, things like that—no big hats, nothing to hide behind. Everybody thought that, if Bob Mitchum is working, in Mexico especially, the judge will think, 'Well, we'll bring that guy back from Mexico, give him a light tap on the hand, send him back to Mexico and let him finish the picture.' No way! The judge sentenced him to sixty days. So Bob went to jail and regarding my pregnancy, it was a tight squeeze towards the end, cause we went back to Mexico and we worked another couple of months there. When we came back to America, we did most of the close-ups and the car chases; I could at least sit down."

Howard Hughes[4] acquired a controlling interest in RKO in 1948; during the first months of his reign, most of the RKO staff resigned due to his unpredictable management, and six years later he sold the studio. Miss Greer: "In 1945, while I was still living with my parents, we got along and I saw him quite a bit for a while. We often went to the Chi Chi bar on Hollywood Boulevard where he would eat the same things all the time: hamburgers, peas, mash potatoes, salad and a chocolate sundae. He would call me at odd hours, like at eleven o'clock in the evening, and ask me out to dinner. I would say, 'Howard, I've gone to bed.' 'But it's not that far, and please don't let me eat alone.' So I would get dressed.

"He loved to talk on the phone; we were once at the Chi Chi and he got up. 'I'm not going to make any phone calls,' he said, 'I'm just going to the men's room.' After a long time he came back and sat down. I said, 'You made some phone calls, didn't you?' 'I didn't, I swear, I didn't.' But his shirt was all wet. I said, 'What happened to your shirt?' 'I just washed it, I took it off and washed it, their was some chocolate sauce on it.' That's when I first noticed the washing syndrome, the compulsive washing hands syndrome that I had heard about. Years later he had a lot of problems with this compulsive behavior, but then I wasn't around him anymore.

"When he still refused to put me in a picture, my husband, who was doing a film at RKO with Howard Hawks at the time, said, 'As a stockholder of RKO, I want to get word to Mr. Hughes that I'm going to sue him and that he must let Jane go out of her contract." Finally he let me go and I paid him $11,000. By then *Out of the Past* and *The Big Steal* were already so long ago, I had lost so much time, it was terrible. So I never felt as a star, I was a working actress—when I was at work."

In all, Miss Greer made two films with Robert Mitchum as her co-star, *Out of the Past* and *The Big Steal*. "Bob Mitchum was the last person of my generation I kept in touch with. A lot of people I worked with, I liked, but it didn't result in friendships. I loved Bob, he was so wonderful and helpful to me. I remember when he was under contract at RKO and one day he was on this square, a little square at RKO. He had a dressing room on the third floor but wanted one on a lower floor. He was yelling, 'Goldberg, hey Goldberg!'—he was the studio manager. All the buildings were overlooking this square and when he stuck his head out, he said, 'What do you want?' Bob said, 'Okay Goldberg, do I get the dressing room, or do I drop the towel?' He only had a towel around his waist. 'Some actors have a dressing room on the first floor and they're not even on the lot, and I'm doing a picture here and one at Metro at the same time, so let me have a dressing room on the first floor.' All the secretaries and writers and so forth were all looking outside and were saying, 'Drop the towel!' [laughs]. Everybody was laughing, poor Goldberg was so embarrassed and finally, the head of the studio, Charlie Koerner, who was in the next office to Goldberg, stuck his head out and said, 'What's going on here?' Goldberg said, 'I told him he couldn't have a downstairs dressing room.' 'Why can't he have it?' 'Because they're all taken.' 'By who?' 'Bill Williams.' 'Well, he's not on the lot. Who else?' 'Lawrence Tierney.' 'He's not working. Give him a dressing room.' So he got it, but he would have dropped the towel, and they knew it!

"When I left RKO, Dore Schary had replaced Louis B. Mayer as the head of MGM; he was a friend of mine, but he was really too busy to help friends. He gave me pictures, such as *You for Me* with Peter Lawford, *Desperate Search* with Howard Keel, *The Clown* with Red Skelton, but even with *The Prisoner of Zenda* I really wasn't happy the way things were going, so I decided that would I get out of it and forget about movies. And I did until *Run for the Sun* in 1956.

"It gave me enough time to raise my children and I had no longer the professional ambition I had before. I didn't pursue anything, I even didn't have an agent. People would just call if anything came up and I would go out and see them. I remember that I once went to see Mr. Otto Preminger at Fox. This was for a loan-out, when I still was under contract to Howard. I walked into his office, he was getting through his mail and he simply ignored me. I said, 'Mr. Preminger, would you do me a favor? When you send this script back to RKO, don't let them know that I turned it down because they'll put me on suspension. So I'd appreciate it if you won't say anything.' I had no intention of doing it—and of course he let them know immediately [laughs]. I didn't really need it anymore.

Red Skelton (1913–1997), reading the Belgian film magazine *Film en Toneel*, was Jane Greer's co-star in *The Clown* (1952), a remake of *The Champ* (1931).

"So I didn't work again until *Run for the Sun* which was made in Mexico as well. When Jane Russell and her husband Robert Waterfield called me for the picture—he was the producer—I had a suspicion that Howard was sitting there too. She was under contract to Howard too; they were very good friends. After all, why would Jane Russell and Bob Waterfield suddenly want Jane Greer? Anyway, I did the picture and I enjoyed it. I loved Richard Widmark, he was marvelous. I got to see wonderful places like Acapulco, but unfortunately they were working in the swamps of Acapulco at a time when you had to watch out for a virus that was killing people. While doing a scene there, I had cracked my tail bone on a rock. I went back to the swamp but the wound was open and I didn't realize it. All of a sudden the swelling was terrible, but I didn't know what was happening. I went to an American doctor in Mexico who said this was a very serious matter and I had to go back home for a few weeks. But by the time I got back, it was very bad. What I didn't know then, was that it takes years for this virus to really hit you. it affects the pericardium and you're in terrible pain. We didn't know much about pericarditis in those days, I know my doctor didn't. We didn't even know what it was for a very long time. It causes tremendous pain, it is constantly strangling the heart. I went to a hospital in Texas, where doctor Michael Debakey, then very well known in America, could help me out and he really saved my life. During surgery, they take your heart out, peel it like a grape and they put it back in. Career-wise that put me down a long time too.

"When I made *Where Love Has Gone* in 1964, a year after the surgery, I was a basket case. I had had the surgery and while I was in the hospital, my husband had fallen in love with another woman. I said to him, 'Look, if you want to marry her, it's fine with me.' He said, 'Okay, we'd have to tell the boys first.' There was nothing wrong with our marriage, we never fought, we were always so happy and now we had to tell them we were going to divorce. Of course, they never expected anything like this. Film-wise, I was lucky that *Where Love Has Gone* came along, because it got me back in pictures so to speak."

How about the directors Miss Greer had worked with so far? How were they? "Most of them were wonderful, although I had two directors that were really vicious. One of them

Studio portrait of Jane Greer when she made *Run for the Sun* (1956).

was Sidney Lanfield. He directed *Station West* (1948) and he had a terrible reputation, especially with women. I don't know how I could have tolerated being treated so badly. He didn't want me in the picture in the first place, but the studio wanted me—I was under contract. He wanted Marlene Dietrich. He would say things like, 'I could walk down Hollywood Boulevard and pick out ten girls on the street who could act better than you can.' That was before the camera was rollin'. He then would say, 'Roll 'em!' He was cruel to everyone. He was impossible, absolutely impossible. The minute I got back here, I said, 'I'm not going to work with that man again. I can't.' Aggie [Agnes Moorehead] also had the worst time with him. He never became a great director, anyway.

"The other one was Henry Hathaway.[5] I worked with him on *You're in the Navy Now* (1951). I had heard a lot of stories about him. He always had a patsy that he could pick on. We were on location on a ship in the north of Virginia. His first victim was Jack Webb; Jack had to do something in a scene aboard the ship and he yelled, 'Who do think you are, you can't act that way!' That went on for two or three weeks until one day, Jack came down at six o'clock in the morning and said, 'I'm leaving. I'm going home. I called the Screen Actors Guild and they said I didn't have to take what he's been doing to me. And that's good enough for me.' Next thing, there's Henry Hathaway, 'Jack!!' [very friendly]. Anyway, Jack stayed on and then it was Eddie Albert's turn.

"Finally we got back to Hollywood and he brought along a captain of this ship, with his wife, as a sort of technical advisor—with a good salary. The guy was sitting next to Hathaway on the set, so he could advise him whenever it was necessary. At one point, he said, 'Mr. Hathaway, you see, Mr. Webb is running down the ladder and coming in this way and so forth, he wouldn't be allowed to do that.' 'What are you talking about?!' 'Well, it would not be the protocol, he couldn't do that.' 'Who the f.. asked you?! You get your f.. a... out of here!' Five minutes later, Henry said, 'Where's the captain!' 'He left.' 'He left what!' 'He left the lot.' 'He left the lot?! What do you mean, he left the lot!!' This man simply checked out of his hotel and went back home.

"Then it was my turn. But I didn't know it was my turn yet [laughs]. In one scene Henry Hathaway wanted me to do a triple take, but I didn't particularly like the idea. 'You...!!!' 'It's Jane, Henry!' [laughs]. I went to my dressing room, locked the door and I cried. I asked Gary Cooper how he could take it, after all he's done several pictures with this man. He said, 'I go to the back of the set and I bang my fist against the wall.'"

You're in the Navy Now (1951), a naval comedy set in World War II, was Miss Greer's first film made at another studio (Fox). She played the wife of Gary Cooper (with Charles Bronson, Jack Warden and Lee Marvin in their screen debuts) and, as mentioned, she then moved over to MGM to appear in such films as *The Clown* (1952, an updated version of *The Champ*) and *The Prisoner of Zenda* (1952, previously filmed in 1913, 1922 and 1937) opposite Stewart Granger in the dual role.

Studio portrait of Gary Cooper, Jane Greer's leading man in *You're in the Navy Now* (1951).

Other highlights in Miss Greer's career include Roy Boulting's engrossing and well-made adventure film *Run for the Sun* (1956, a remake of Robert Wise's *The Game of Death*); *Man of a Thousand Faces* (1957), a biography of the life of silent screen legend Lon Chaney portrayed by James Cagney with Miss Greer as his second wife; Edward Dmytryk's *Where Love Has Gone* (1964), playing the role of a juvenile probation officer, and *Against All Odds* (1984), a remake of *Out of the Past* with Miss Greer, now just as manipulative as the mother of Rachel Ward (cast in Miss Greer's original role) as she had been back then in the original—all much to the delight of film buffs. She also participated in an *Out of the Past* parody on TV's *Saturday Night Live* with her original co-star Robert Mitchum.

Watching the films she made over the years, talking about her dedication and professionalism with a few of her colleagues and people she worked with, and finally doing research about what has been written about her performances in prestigious American publications, it is not surprising that only superlatives are used to describe the talent of Miss Greer. What follows is a handful of comments written about some of her performances: "Jane

Greer is very effective in her role," "she is both beautiful and excellent in her portrayal," "she is particularly appealing in a difficult role," "she definitely makes her role count," "she enacts her role exceptionally well" and finally as *Variety* mentioned when reviewing *Run for the Sun* (1956), "it should be noted that Miss Greer should do *more* films, she has the looks and the ability." All of those quotes put together are perhaps the most accurate way to describe the essence of Miss Greer, both as an actress and as a person.

"I'd love to get back to work, but it's very difficult nowadays for actresses of my generation to get good parts. The only ones who get to play them, are Lauren Bacall and Gena Rowlands, and they're both so good at it that they get them right away. I don't go out to parties, so people don't think of me. If they don't see you, they certainly don't think of you," Miss Greer said. She enriched the screen over the years with impressive and powerful performances, and it would have been extremely interesting to see her in a new role again. Unfortunately, she died of cancer in August 2001.

Two of her sons, Lawrence and Alex Lasker, have also been successfully involved in pictures: Lawrence as producer of films such as John Badham's *WarGames* (1983), *Awakenings* (1990) and *Sneakers* (1992); Alex as the screenwriter of Clint Eastwood's *Firefox* (1982) and John Boorman's *Beyond Rangoon* (1995) starring Patricia Arquette. Her third son Steven Lasker is producing cassettes and CD albums; his latest was a large package of Duke Ellington CDs, which earned him a Grammy Award.

Interview: Bel Air, April 9,1999

Notes

1. Joan Harrison (1911–1994) joined Alfred Hitchcock's staff in 1933 as his secretary—she also played a secretary in *The Man Who Knew Too Much* (1934). Soon she started reading books and scripts and collaborated on his screenplays. In 1939 she accompanied Hitchcock to Hollywood. As a screenwriter she worked on a few of his films: *Jamaica Inn* (1939), *Rebecca* (1940), *Foreign Correspondent* (1941), *Suspicion* (1941) and *Saboteur* (1942). Later on, she also became a producer of films such as *Nocturne* (1946), *Ride the Pink Horse* (1947) and *They Won't Believe Me* (1947). From 1955 to 1962 she produced the suspense anthology TV series *Alfred Hitchcock Presents*. More information on Alfred Hitchcock: interview with Janet Leigh, note 5.
2. Robert Sparks (1900–1963), screenwriter, story editor and producer—including at Columbia, producing the *Blondie* films starring his wife Penny Singleton (b. 1908)—was an executive producer at RKO.
3. Robert Mitchum (1917–1997), one of Hollywood's top actors for several decades, appeared in such films as *The Story of G.I. Joe* (1945, Academy Award nomination for best supporting actor), *River of No Return* (1954), *Not as a Stranger* (1955), *Heaven Knows, Mr. Allison* (1957), *The Sundowners* (1960), *Cape Fear* (1962, as well as the 1991 remake), *The List of Adrian Messenger* (1963), *Ryan's Daughter* (1970), *Farewell, My Lovely* (1975), *The Last Tycoon* (1976) and *Maria's Lovers* (1985).
4. Howard Hughes (1905–1976), oil tycoon and billionaire with an estimated fortune of over $1,000,000,000, also produced films occasionally, including the classics *Hell's Angels* (1930, also dir., starring Jean Harlow), Lewis Milestone's *The Front Page* (1931), *Scarface* (a.k.a. *Scarface, The Shame of the Nation*, 1932), and *The Outlaw* (filmed in 1941, also dir.). Later on he became a total recluse who spent a lot of his time in a penthouse at the Desert Inn in Las Vegas, controlling and expanding his vast empire. He died from a stroke on an airplane *en route* from Acapulco to a Texas hospital.
5. Henry Hathaway (1898–1985), was the grandson of a Belgian marquis who had moved to San Francisco after he failed to acquire Hawaii for the Belgian king Leopold II (1835–1909). Known to be a very tough director, he entered films in 1908 at age ten appearing in films directed by Allan Dwan. He then worked for Thomas Ince, became a prop man for Universal and after World War I an assistant director, working frequently with Victor Fleming and Josef von Sternberg. He started directing low budget Westerns in 1932. He is best remembered for the several Westerns he made over the years, although he also worked in other genres. Films include *Lives of a Bengal Lancer* with Gary Cooper (1935, Academy Award nomination for best director), *Go West, Young Man* (1936, with Mae West), the World War II drama *13 Rue Madeleine* (1946), *Kiss of Death* (1947), *The Desert Fox* (1951), *How the West Was Won* (1962, episode "The Rivers, the Plains, the Outlaws"), *Circus World* (1964) and *True Grit* (1969, which finally earned John Wayne his Academy Award for his role as one-eyed U.S. Marshal Rooster Cogburn).

Filmography

As Bettejane Greer

Pan-Americana (RKO, 1945). DIR-PROD John H. Auer. SCR Lawrence Kimble (story by Frederick Kohner, John H. Auer). CAM Frank Redman. ED Harry Marker. MUS (songs) Ary Barroso, Margarita Lecuona, Gabriel Ruiz, others. RUNNING TIME 84 min. CAST: Phillip Terry (Dan); Audrey Long (Jo Anne); Robert Benchley (Charlie); Eve Arden (Hoppy); Ernest Truex (Uncle Rudy); **Bettejane Greer** (Hoppy's secretary).

Two O'Clock Courage (RKO, 1945). DIR Anthony Mann. PROD Ben Stoloff. SCR Robert E. Kent (novel by Gelett Burgess). CAM Jack Mackenzie. ED Philip Martin, Jr. RUNNING TIME 66 min. CAST: Tom Conway (The Man); Ann Rutherford (Patty); Richard Lane (Haley); Roland Drew (Mark Evans); Emory Parnell (Brenner); **Bettejane Greer** (Helen).

George White's Scandals (RKO, 1945). DIR Felix E. Feist. PROD George White. SCR Hugh Wedlock, Howard Snyder, Parke Levy, Howard Green. CAM Robert de Grasse. ED Joseph Noriega. MUS Jack Yellen, Sammy Fain. RUNNING TIME 94 min. CAST: Joan Davis (Joan Mason); Jack Haley (Jack Williams); Phillip Terry (Tom McGrath); Martha Holliday (Jill Martin); Ethel Smith (Swing Organist); **Bettejane Greer** (Billie Randall).

As Jane Greer

Dick Tracy, a.k.a. *Dick Tracy, Detective* (RKO, 1945). DIR William Berke. PROD Herman Schlom. SCR Eric Taylor (cartoon strip by Chester Gould). CAM Frank Redman. ED Ernie Leadley. MUS Roy Webb. RUNNING TIME 61 min. CAST: Morgan Conway (Dick Tracy); Anne Jeffries (Tess); Mike Mazurki (Splitface); **Jane Greer** (Judith Owens); Lyle Latell (Pat Patton); Joseph Crehan (Chief Brandon).

The Falcon's Alibi (RKO, 1946). DIR Ray McCarey. PROD William Berke. SCR Paul Yawitz (story by Dane Lussier and Manny Seff, based on the characters created by Michael Arlen). CAM Frank Redman. ED Philip Martin, Jr. MUS C. Bakaleinikoff. RUNNING TIME 63 min. CAST: Tom Conway (Falcon); Rita Corday (Joan); Vince Barnett (Goldie); **Jane Greer** (Lola); Elisha Cook, Jr. (Nick); Emory Parnell (Metcalf).

The Bamboo Blonde (RKO, 1946). DIR Anthony Mann. PROD Herman Schlom. SCR Olive Cooper, Lawrence Kimble (story by Wayne Whittaker). CAM Frank Redman. ED Les Millbrook. MUS Charles O'Curran. RUNNING TIME 68 min. CAST: Frances Langford (Louise Anderson); Ralph Edwards (Eddie Clark); Russell Wade (Patrick Ransom, Jr.); Iris Adrian (Montana); Richard Martin (Jim Wilson); **Jane Greer** (Ellen Sawyer).

Sunset Pass (RKO, 1946). DIR William Berke. PROD Herman Schlom. SCR Norman Houston (novel by Zane Grey). CAM Frank Redman. ED Samuel K. Beetley. MUS Paul Sawtell. RUNNING TIME 60 min. CAST: James Warren (Rocky); Nan Leslie (Jane); John Laurens (Chito); **Jane Greer** (Helen); Robert Barrat (Curtis); Harry Woods (Cinibar).

Sinbad the Sailor (RKO, 1947). DIR Richard Wallace. PROD Stephen Ames. SCR John Twist, George Worthington Yates. CAM George Barnes. ED Sherman Todd, Frank Doyle. MUS Roy Webb. RUNNING TIME 116 min. CAST: Douglas Fairbanks, Jr. (Sinbad); Maureen O'Hara (Shireen); Walter Slezak (Melik); Anthony Quinn (Emir); George Tobias (Abbu); **Jane Greer** (Pirouze).

They Won't Believe Me (RKO, 1947). DIR Irving Pichel. PROD Joan Harrison. SCR Jonathan Latimer (story by Gordon McDonell). CAM Harry J. Wild. ED Elmo Williams. MUS Roy Webb. RUNNING TIME 95 min. CAST: Robert Young (Larry); Susan Hayward (Verna); **Jane Greer** (Janice); Rita Johnson (Gretta); Tom Powers (Trenton); George Tyne (Lt. Carr).

Out of the Past (RKO, 1947). DIR Jacques Tourneur. PROD Warren Duff. SCR Geoffrey Homes [Daniel Mainwaring] (also novel). CAM Nicholas Musuraca. ED Samuel E. Beetley. MUS Roy Webb. RUNNING TIME 95 min. CAST: Robert Mitchum (Jeff Bailey); **Jane Greer** (Kathie Moffat); Kirk Douglas (Whit Sterling); Rhonda Fleming (Meta Carson); Richard Webb (Jim); Steve Brodie (Fisher).

Station West (RKO, 1948). DIR Sidney Lanfield. PROD Robert Sparks. SCR Frank Fenton, Winston Miller (novel by Luke Short). CAM Harry J. Wild. ED Frederic Knudtson. MUS Heinz Roemheld. RUNNING TIME 91 min. CAST: Dick Powell (Haven); **Jane Greer** (Charlie); Agnes Moorehead (Mrs. Calson); Burl Ives (Hotel Clerk); Tom Powers (Captain); Gordon Oliver (Prince).

The Big Steal (RKO, 1949). DIR Don Siegel. PROD Jack J. Gross. SCR Geoffrey Homes, Gerald Drayson Adams (story by Richard Wormser). CAM Harry J. Wild. ED Samuel E. Beetley. MUS Leigh Harline. RUNNING TIME 71 min. CAST: Robert Mitchum (Duke); **Jane Greer** (Joan); William Bendix (Blake); Patric Knowles (Fiske); Ramon Novarro (Colonel Ortega); Don Alvadaro (Lt. Ruiz).

The Company She Keeps (RKO, 1950). DIR John Cromwell. PROD John Houseman. SCR Ketti Frings (also story). CAM Nicholas Musuraca. ED Robert Swink. MUS Leigh Harline. RUNNING TIME 82 min. CAST: Lizabeth Scott (Joan); **Jane Greer** (Diane); Dennis O'Keefe (Larry); Fay Baker (Tilly); John Hoyt (Judge Kendall); James Bell (Mr. Neeley).

You're in the Navy Now, a.k.a. *U.S.S. Teakettle* (20th Century Fox, 1951). DIR Henry Hathaway. PROD Fred Kohlmar. SCR Richard Murphy (from an article in the *New Yorker* by John W. Hazard). CAM Joe MacDonald.

ED James B. Clark. MUS Cyril Mockridge. RUNNING TIME 92 min. CAST: Gary Cooper (Lt. John Harkness); **Jane Greer** (Ellie); Millard Mitchell (Larrabee); Edward Albert (Lt. Bill Barron); John McIntire (Commander Reynolds); Ray Collins (Admiral Tennant).

You for Me (MGM, 1952). DIR Don Weis. PROD Henry Berman. SCR William Roberts (also story). CAM Paul C. Vogel. ED Newell P. Kimlin. MUS Alberto Columbo. RUNNING TIME 70 min. CAST: Peter Lawford (Tony Brown); **Jane Greer** (Katie McDermad); Gig Young (Dr. Jeff Chadwick); Paula Corday (Lucille Brown); Howard Wendell (Oliver Wherry).

The Prisoner of Zenda (MGM, 1952). DIR Richard Thorpe. PROD Pandro S. Berman. SCR John L. Balderston, Noel Langley (novel by Anthony Hope). CAM Joseph Ruttenberg. ED George Boemler. MUS Alfred Newman. RUNNING TIME 100 min. CAST: Stewart Granger (Rudolf Rassendyll/King Rudolf V); Deborah Kerr (Princess Flavia); Louis Calhern (Colonel Zapt); **Jane Greer** (Antoinette de Mauban); Lewis Stone (The Cardinal); Robert Douglas (Duke of Streslau).

Desperate Search (MGM, 1952). DIR Joseph Lewis. PROD Matthew Rapf. SCR Walter Doniger (novel by Arthur Mayse). CAM Harold Lipstein. ED Joseph Dervin. RUNNING TIME 71 min. CAST: Howard Keel (Vince Heldon); **Jane Greer** (Julie Heldon); Patricia Medina (Nora Stead); Keenan Wynn ("Brandy"); Robert Burton (Wayne Langmuir); Lee Aaker (Don).

The Clown (MGM, 1952). DIR Robert Z. Leonard. PROD William H. Wright. SCR Martin Rackin (adaptation by Leonard Praskins, story by Frances Marion). CAM Paul C. Vogel. ED Gene Ruggiero. MUS David Rose. RUNNING TIME 91 min. CAST: Red Skelton (Dodo Delwyn); Tim Considine (Dink Delwyn); **Jane Greer** (Paula Henderson); Loring Smith (Goldie); Philip Ober (Ralph Z. Henderson); Lou Lubin (Little Julie).

Down Among the Sheltering Palms (20th Century Fox, 1953). DIR Edmund Goulding. PROD Fred Kohlmar. SCR Claude Binyon, Albert Lewin, Burt Styler (story by Edward Hope). CAM Leon Shamroy. ED Louis Loeffler. MUS Alfred Newman. RUNNING TIME 86 min. CAST: William Lundigan (Capt. Bill Willoby); **Jane Greer** (Diana Forrester); Mitzi Gaynor (Rozouila); David Wayne (Lt. Carl O. Schmidt); Gloria De Haven (Angela Toland); Gene Lockhart (Rev. Edgett).

Run for the Sun (United Artists, 1956). DIR Roy Boulting. PROD Harry Tatelman. SCR Dudley Nichols, Roy Boulting (novel by Richard Connell). CAM Joe LaShelle. ED Fred Knudtsen. MUS Frederic Steiner. RUNNING TIME 98 min. CAST: Richard Widmark (Mike Latimer); **Jane Greer** (Katie Connors); Trevor Howard (Browne); Peter Van Eyck (Van Anders); Carlos Henning (Jan); Juan Garcia (Fernandez).

Man of a Thousand Faces (Universal, 1957). DIR Joseph Pevney. PROD Robert Arthur. SCR R. Wright Campbell, Ivan Goff, Ben Roberts (story by Ralph Wheelwright). CAM Russell Metty. ED Ted J. Kent. MUS Frank Skinner. RUNNING TIME 122 min. CAST: James Cagney (Lon Chaney); Dorothy Malone (Cleva Creighton Chaney); **Jane Greer** (Hazel Bennett); Marjorie Rambeau (Gert); Jim Backus (Clarence Logan); Robert J. Evans (Irving Thalberg).

Where Love Has Gone (Paramount, 1964). DIR Edward Dmytryk. PROD Joseph E. Levine. SCR John Michael Hayes (novel by Harold Robbins). CAM Joseph MacDonald. ED Frank Bracht. MUS Walter Scharf. RUNNING TIME 111 min. CAST: Susan Hayward (Valerie Hayden Miller); Bette Davis (Mrs. Gerald Hayden); Michael Connors (Luke Miller); Joey Heatherton (Danielle Valerie Miller); **Jane Greer** (Marian Spicer); DeForest Kelly (Sam Corwin).

Billie (United Artists, 1965). DIR-PROD Don Weis. SCR Ronald Alexander (also play). CAM John L. Russell. ED Adrienne Fazan. MUS Dominic Frontiere. RUNNING TIME 87 min. CAST: Patty Duke (Billie); Jim Backus (Howard Carol); **Jane Greer** (Agnes Carol); Warren Berlinger (Mike Benson); Billy DeWolfe (Mayor Davis); Charles Lane (Coach Jones).

The Outfit (MGM, 1973). DIR John Flynn. PROD Carter De Haven. SCR John Flynn (novel by Richard Stark). CAM Bruce Surtees. ED Ralph E. Winters. MUS Jerry Fielding. RUNNING TIME 102 min. CAST: Robert Duvall (Macklin); Karen Black (Bett); Joe Don Baker (Cody); Robert Ryan (Mailer); Timothy Carey (Menner); Sheree North (Buck's Wife); **Jane Greer** (Alma).

Against All Odds (Columbia, 1984). DIR Taylor Hackford. PROD Taylor Hackford, William S. Gilmore. SCR Eric Hughes (based on the film *Out of the Past* [1947], written by Daniel Mainwaring). CAM Donald Thorin. ED Frederic Steinkamp, William Steinkamp. MUS Michel Colombier, Larry Carlton. RUNNING TIME 128 min. CAST: Rachel Ward (Jessie Wyler); Jeff Bridges (Terry Brogan); James Woods (Jake Wise); Alex Karras (Hank Sully); **Jane Greer** (Mrs. Wyler); Richard Widmark (Ben Caxton).

Just Between Friends (Orion, 1986). DIR-SCR Allan Burns. PROD Allan Burns, Edward Teets. CAM Jordan Cronenweth. ED Anne Goursaud. COST Cynthia Bales. MUS Patrick Williams, Earl Klugh. RUNNING TIME 120 min. CAST: Mary Tyler Moore (Holly Davis); Ted Danson (Charles "Chip" Davis); Christine Lahti (Sandy Dunlap); Sam Waterston (Harry Crandall); Salome Jens (Helga); **Jane Greer** (Ruth Chadwick).

Immediate Family (Columbia, 1989). DIR Jonathan Kaplan. PROD Sarah Pillsbury, Midge Sanford. SCR Barbara Benedek. CAM John W. Lindley. ED Jane Kurson. MUS Brad Fiedel. RUNNING TIME 95 min. CAST: Glenn Close (Linda Spector); James Woods (Michael Spector); Mary Stuart Masterson (Lucy Moore); Kevin Dillon (Sam); Linda Darlow (Lawyer Susan Drew); **Jane Greer** (Michael's Mother).

Perfect Mate (1996). DIR-ED Karl Armstrong. PROD Tim Connors. SCR Kerry Armstrong. CAM Brad Rushing. MUS Murielle Hamilton. CAST: Carrie Armstrong (Jennifer); April Barnett (Terri); Kristin Banta (Val); Gwen Banta (Laurel); **Jane Greer** (Mom).

Television Movies

Columbo: Troubled Waters (1975). DIR Ben Gazzara. CAST: Peter Falk; Robert Vaughn; **Jane Greer** (Sylvia Danziger); Dean Stockwell; Robert Douglas.

The Shadow Riders (1982). DIR Andrew V. McLaglen. CAST: Tom Selleck; Sam Elliott; Ben Johnson; Katharine Ross; **Jane Greer** (Ma Traven); Harry Carey, Jr.

STANLEY KRAMER

The Defiant One

There is absolutely no doubt about it: Stanley Kramer was one of the best filmmakers ever, with a hugely impressive body of work and a list of films to his credit as producer and as producer/director which is nearly impossible for anyone else to achieve. After all, as a producer he was the driving force behind such films as *Champion* (1949, dir. Mark Robson, which made Kirk Douglas a star, portraying a boxer who showed how ruthless someone can be selling his soul to get to the top), *The Men* (1950, dir. Fred Zinnemann, Marlon Brando's first screen role, playing a bitter paraplegic as a result of a bullet in the lower back), *High Noon* (1952, dir. Fred Zinnemann, a compelling Western, launching Grace Kelly) and *The Caine Mutiny* (1954, dir. Edward Dmytryk, powerful drama based on Herman Wouk's Pulitzer Prize–winning novel)—just to name a few.

He then started producing *and* directing his own films as well, debuting with *Not as a Stranger* (1955, dealing with the medical profession), followed by such highly recommendable pictures as *The Defiant Ones* (1958, with Sidney Poitier and Tony Curtis as escaped, handcuffed convicts on the run), *On the Beach* (1959, depicting the end of the world caused by a nuclear war, told in a most gripping, honest and provoking way), *Inherit the Wind* (1960, focusing on the historical Scopes trial in the 1920s), *Judgment at Nuremberg* (1961, an absorbing drama about the trials of Nazi war criminals, with Spencer Tracy as the judge), *It's a Mad, Mad, Mad, Mad World* (1963, an amazing Mack Sennett–style slapstick comedy where everything perfectly overlapped), *Ship of Fools* (1965, superb filmization of Katherine Anne Porter's novel, Vivien Leigh's final film) and *Guess Who's Coming to Dinner* (1967, about a black man marrying a white girl, Spencer Tracy's final film)—once again, just to name a few.

It is clear that Mr. Kramer was more than just an august filmmaker: his wide range of powerful films are the ultimate example of what ingredients a solid drama should have. Themes usually show up in his films, and they often emerge as persuasive statements about human values or act as a focus on historical, social, political or environmental problems, always interesting topics to discuss. Or like Steven Spielberg once told him: "I could *never* have made *Schindler's List* if it weren't for *Judgment at Nuremberg*. You paved the way for me." Mr. Kramer is passing on his legacy to the next generation.

Did he always get the credit he rightfully deserved at the time when he was still making films? Mr. Kramer: "No, not at all. The press was very critical. My films often dealt with subjects that people were surprised one made a film about, and yet they still were successful. Some of my films were so much about what was going on in this country, and in the meantime they often were against what this country was standing for. When I made *Guess Who's Coming to*

Dinner, film critic Richard Schickel did a review in *Life* magazine—it was probably the worst review I had *ever* read in my life. Sometimes that kills a picture, but in this case it didn't: despite that terrible review, there were lines around the block to see the film. Only recently, when the American Film Institute was voting for the 100 best pictures of all time, I got a call from Mr. Schickel who said that *High Noon* and *Guess Who's Coming to Dinner* were voted as two of the 100 best pictures of all time. I said, 'Mr. Schickel, I have to tell you something. I am amused by this, as you gave *Guess Who's Coming to Dinner* one of the worst reviews ever back then and now you're telling me it is one of the 100 best pictures of all time!' He didn't know what to say! [laughs]. But he took it in good stride, though. Overall, the press could be very rough with my films. On the other hand, I also got great acclaim and sometimes those pictures didn't do anything at the box-office, except later on, when they were shown on television and became classics. You just never know."

Stanley Kramer. (Courtesy of Karen Sharpe Kramer.)

"I have very fond memories of all of my pictures, but *Guess Who's Coming to Dinner* has always been very special to me, since it was the last film of Spencer Tracy,[1] after we had worked together on *Inherit the Wind* [1960], *Judgment at Nuremberg* [1961] and *It's a Mad, Mad, Mad, Mad World* [1963]. It was a very special time: because of his weak health, he could only work in the mornings, so then we always did everyone's close-ups. A few weeks before we finished shooting, Spence came up to me and said, 'I think if I were to die on my way home tonight, you're protected and you'll be okay.' He was thrilled to do this film but the studio would not insure him because of his health problems, so Kate Hepburn and I put up our salaries as a guarantee that if he died during production, the studio would come out okay. The day we finished the film, Spence called his friends on the phone and said, 'I did it! I finished it! I'm so thrilled!' And then, ten days later, he passed away."

What made him such a special actor? Mr. Kramer: "He was my favorite actor. Period. People could easily identify with his interpretations. In any part he played, he had important lines to say and he made sure they meant something. The audience always believed what he said, because he was so powerful. When he said in *Judgment at Nuremberg*, 'This is what we stand for, truth, justice and value of a single human being,' and all that, he said it in a way that touched everybody. You could believe him, you could *trust* him. He reacted better than most

Spencer Tracy, Stanley Kramer's favorite actor.

actors acted. That gave him the personality of a *true* actor: he was a real plus in terms of where he was and where he belonged. He gave you the impression that he *invented* acting. I don't think you can find that in today's pictures. It's a shame that Spencer Tracy is hardly known to today's audiences."

Mr. Kramer discovered Marlon Brando,[2] another renowned actor, brought him to California and offered him his first screen role in *The Men* (1950). Mr. Kramer: "Marlon Brando changed acting, he *changed* the way of acting by bringing in the 'method.' It was the first time we had ever seen an actor like that. As far as the traditional way of acting we had ever seen before was concerned, he did everything wrong. But he found a way to bring a new kind of acting, a new kind of humanity to acting. I never ran into that range of tremendous pathos to violent power that could be so easily turned on or off as [director] Fred Zinnemann was able to show in *The Men*. I have always adored Brando and a few years later I produced another film he appeared in, *The Wild One*, way ahead of its time which is perhaps a strange thing to say, but we didn't know what we were doing, as it was so way ahead of its time.

"I think it was about a year ago, I got a phone call out of the blue. It was Marlon Brando who said to me, 'Stanley, I just have to tell you this: you are the *only* upstanding guy that I have ever known in my life, the *only* man with integrity, honesty, and you're a real leader. I just wanted to tell you this.' That was a very nice thing for him to say.

"James Dean[3] can easily be compared with Marlon. My wife knew James Dean quite well before he became *the* James Dean—he was dating her best friend at high school. He was just a little actor then, nothing special at that time. As actors are always out of work, her mother used to feed him, he was always hungry. One day, he told my wife he was going to New York and said he would come back as a star, he was very sure of himself. He was a strange little guy, he would go out and do all kind of improvisations. He was very believable and had a different way of working. Next time she met him, about five or six years later, both of them were working at Warner Bros.: she had just finished *The High and the Mighty* with John Wayne and he was working on *East of Eden*. Across the street from the Warner lot, there was a little drugstore and one day she was having a cup of coffee there with her mother and her agent. James Dean walked in, they talked, had coffee, and he told her, 'If anybody comes in here and I act strange to you, just go along with it. I just take on a different personality.' So somebody came in, he started humping over, he was hanging his head down, started mumbling—he was putting on an act, he fooled the world! That was not the James Dean she had known, but he became a great legend and a great actor.

"Well, there was something about him. She told me you just felt you *had* to be with him,

Marlon Brando (center with peaked cap) in *The Wild One* (1954), produced by Stanley Kramer. (Courtesy of DOCIP Film Archive, Brussels, Belgium.)

you wanted to be part of it. It seems that some people are destined for things, and then there's the rest of us [laughs]. It was wonderful to see what he accomplished: you can always wonder how he did it, and you want to be just like that yourself, but you know you probably never will be. I think that's what bonds us, what hooks us, why we—in this business—keep reaching for the impossible dream every day. It's magical when it happens and when it does happen, it's the most wonderful, rewarding thing that can ever happen to you as an artist. It's like when you have your first child, it's a magical experience, or when you get married to the person you're really in love with. Making films is mostly magical anyway."

Did Mr. Kramer ever have any problems with Marlon Brando? "No, never," he said, "although he caused problems when they were shooting *Mutiny on the Bounty* and they had an effect on me as well. You see, what happened was, they blamed him for all the problems and the delays on that film. But Marlon's explanation was that they promised to change the script in order to get him and they never did. I know that for sure, because *The Defiant Ones* was initially written for him and for Sidney Poitier, but due to the endless delays on *The Bounty*, Tony Curtis got his part."

How was *The Defiant Ones* received when it was released? Mr. Kramer: "The American Legion was opposed to the film, not because a black man was chained to a white man, but because Nathan E. Douglas, along with Harold Jacob Smith, two of the writers of the origi-

Stanley Kramer. (Courtesy of Karen Sharpe Kramer.)

nal story, were subpoenaed by the HUAC, the House Un-American Activities Committee, in 1953 and invoked the Fifth Amendment. Later on, Douglas and Harold Jacob Smith won the Academy Award by a great acclamation; it was a victory for freedom and the film turned out to be very successful."

Films like *The Defiant Ones* (1958), *On the Beach* (1959), *Inherit the Wind* (1960) and *Judgment at Nuremberg* (1961) are most certainly among the best films ever made. Watching those films and comparing them to most of the films made in the same period, one must agree that he made the kind of movies most of his contemporaries wouldn't even consider. Mr. Kramer explains: "I was born in New York in 1913 and attended the New York University. As I grew up in the Franklin Roosevelt era, I witnessed the social change of his administration. Like most college students, I admired him a lot—after all, he changed the static capitalism into a more vibrant preservation of the capitalistic system, which was very important at the time. I got very interested in the things he was dealing with like fear, freedom, peace—even though he got involved in the war—they became my choices for films. So I hoped I could make the films well enough to bridge the gap to massive entertainment.

"After working as a writer, editor and producer for several years, I started directing as well in the mid–1950s because I wanted to be a director from the very start. Combining the two, producing and directing, gave me more complete control over the films I made. It had nothing to do with power or ego or anything like that. It was very important though to have one vision to get up there on the screen, one vision all the way through. Film was a producer's medium at that time, it was not a director's choice: the producer hired the director to do his vision, he was always on the set, telling the director exactly how he expected everything to be directed. He hired the actors, supervised the editing, the scoring, etc. It would be the same analogy saying that it was Victor Fleming who made *Gone with the Wind*. You don't consider it his film, it will always be David O. Selznick's achievement; he made all the decisions."

That's why it will always be Stanley Kramer's *The Men*, *High Noon*, *The Member of the Wedding*, etc. Mr. Kramer explains: "I hired a wonderful director by the name of Fred Zinnemann in the early days of his career who directed those three films. Because of the fact that directors have taken a much more important position in the last decades, people will automatically assume if it's a well-known director, it is his film. I think this is a very interesting topic to discuss, because history will never record itself properly—it defused the role of the producer. I didn't become a director until the mid–1950s, because before that the director had no real power. The producer had first and last cut of every film and the director did more or less what the producer said anyway."

Mr. Kramer was known to be a very courageous independent producer. However, in order to start working with bigger budgets and stars, he moved his company to Columbia in 1951. Mr. Kramer: "The other independents were people like Sam Goldwyn or Selznick, they had been working several years before the war already. At that time taxes were not really what they were *after* the war and because of that, they had their own studios and back lots, which I did not have. I was a post-war *baby*! But when I started out, the producer was still the dreamer who had the original dream, he was still the one who wrote with the writer, he thought the thoughts, raised the money independently—I never financed an entire film myself, they were backed by retired oil men, lettuce growers from California, etc.—and as a producer, I went to the studio and said, 'I am not going to go under contract with you, I just want to rent your space to make my films.' Then you found your stars and you were on your way. The studios were intrigued by this."

Mr. Kramer must have been a man of tremendous charisma, power and vitality, ingredients which paved the way for him. He says: "Raising money for my films wasn't always easy. I once went to a lettuce grower in Salinas, California, to raise money for my first three films. The first one, *This Is New York*, lost money, but the second one, *Champion*, made enough money so I got him his money back. While telling him the story, I played all the parts. I played Kirk, the brother, I would go through the whole process, I literally played the picture to convince him, so he'd invest his money.

"When you have a successful film, everybody likes to take personal credit for why that film was so successful. 'If it hadn't been for my editing, it would never have been successful,' 'I pulled the rabbits out of my hat with my screenplay....' None of that is true. What really is true, you have a group of artists coming together and you have one captain of the ship, but everyone makes his contribution. Sometimes the majority of those contributions works and then you might have an extraordinary film that will *last*."

As Mr. Kramer was always very much involved with each phase of the process of filmmaking, he can easily be considered an all-round filmmaker. Could he then be compared with someone like Orson Welles?[4] "Orson was a wonderful filmmaker, but he was always very busy for taking credit of every phase of it. Unfortunately—and I think he was absolutely right—his peers resented the hell out of that because they knew they couldn't match it. What happened was that he had to face a lot of jealousy over that kind of thing, so they tried to get rid of him and they did a pretty good job at destroying him. You know, Christ was crucified, but He was so right about everything. They get afraid, I think it's human nature. People would say, 'Oh, look at him, I can't even match him, he's not down here with the rest of us, he's up *there* someplace, he's not even in the same category with us, let's get rid of him.' That's what happened to Orson Welles. It happened to others too. Although William Wyler was very successful when he was making films, I believe he is not remembered now the way he should be."

What about Charlie Chaplin—any comparisons between an all-round self-made man like Chaplin and Mr. Kramer? After all, Chaplin was able to keep on making the films he wanted to make and, just like Mr. Kramer, he was his own boss. Mr. Kramer: "Well, I haven't thought of that. Certainly, Chaplin was an extraordinary man, *really* extraordinary—but Orson Welles, you know, I think he could have gone on to do some remarkable things, certainly his first two films were amazing, *Citizen Kane* [1941], which he made when he was only 25, and *The Magnificent Ambersons* [1942]. I think they killed his soul and that he died a very tragic figure. It may be wrong of me to say that, but a lot of artists in this business never appreciated him or gave him his due. I think I was more independent than he was and I didn't care what anybody thought about my films, I only cared about what I thought about them, and as far as I was concerned, I thought there was something wrong with every single one of my films if they didn't reach the impossible dream."

Mr. Kramer's wife, former screen actress Karen Sharpe, is a current producer who produced *High Noon* (2000), a television remake of his film classic, and at this point there are plans to remake *The Caine Mutiny*, *The Men*, and *Champion* as well. Mr. Kramer: "Her remake of *High Noon* remained pretty faithful to the original screenplay. Now, it was about a man doing something important for the people he cared about, even when they wouldn't defend him and stand with him. It's about making the right choices for others, even with the risk of your own life, your own marriage or whatever is important to you. Since the 1950s, human nature hasn't changed that much. We haven't really progressed with our morality in this country, sometimes I feel that we have *regressed*, so the subject matter of that particular subject, or the Nuremberg situation or even *On the Beach* or *Inherit the Wind*, I think they are still very important to this day.

"My wife and I have been married for about 35 years now; before we got married, she was an actress and she had accomplished quite a number of things. She's the kind of person that wouldn't make any remake, unless it's about something very important that's uplifting us and inspires us. Unfortunately she has been criticized for it, but there's a whole generation that hasn't seen *High Noon*: I never expected a 22, 23 or 24 year old to have seen the film, I would have thought the 45 and 50 year olds did, considering they were the baby *boomers*. I was amazed that at the premiere of her film, my wife sat next to Pierce Brosnan who had never seen the original *High Noon*. Behind her sat David Hasselhoff and his wife—who our daughter Jennifer had just finished doing a play with—they had never seen it either. There must have been 700 or 800 people out there that evening, and the whole time she found herself defending the original, 'You ought to see Stanley Kramer's *High Noon*, that's really the great one!'

"When I made *High Noon*, Gary Cooper was really a *has-been*. We had never seen Grace

Kirk Douglas played a boxer in Stanley Kramer's *Champion* (1949).

Gary Cooper (left) and Lloyd Bridges in *High Noon* (1952), the second of three films Stanley Kramer made as producer with director Fred Zinnemann. (Courtesy of DOCIP Film Archive, Brussels, Belgium.)

Kelly or Katy Jurado before, they were brand new, Lloyd Bridges was a wonderful character actor but at that time quite unknown, it was made in black and white—most Westerns at that time were made in color. Sometimes things come together just right and something magical happens, you know. In the remake, Tom Skerritt underplays, just about like Cooper did, and my wife has opened it all a little bit more: the women are tougher, a little bit more involved, not just pretty decorations. She based the town on not wanting to support him out of cowardice which is what we wanted in the original, because it *was* cowardice—who could blame them, I wouldn't give up my life for my town, the odds were too great against the town for the people that were coming in to destroy it. In the new version it is more about money and about the heavy who's coming in with his group of people, while our sheriff was going out of town to marry. The town really wants to get rid of him, they want to hire a new Marshal from a bigger city, 'cause he is going to bring with him investors to make a bigger business for the town, that's why they want him to go. And they don't want bodies lying in the streets, it wouldn't look good when the investors would get into town [laughs]. So it was changed a little bit and they needed some answers which we didn't need in 1952. Opening up the script a little bit *does* work, but I think it lacks the magic of the original. Why? I don't know. You can have a wonderful screenplay, wonderful actors and it can come together and be just *less* than you had hoped. But in spite of that, my wife is happy about it, she says, 'The last thing I want to do is compete with you' [laughs].

"When I made *High Noon*, we had tremendous unrest in this country: they were looking for Communists under the bed. Some directors, actors or writers were involved with Communism, but I don't think we really understood Communism in the traditional sense of what it began to stand for and of course, today we say, 'Communism? So what?!' Isn't that funny, how history gets all excited and then kind of dies out because we're so unsophisticated about so many things. It obviously takes a lot of time to understand things and people sometimes get in those moods to find something to hate. In those days, Larry Parks was one of the people whose career was completely destroyed because he was fighting for the underdog; a lot of actors and performers are Democrats by nature, because we're all fighting for the 'little guy.' As Communism was fighting for the little guy, people got mixed up with it. Carl Foreman,[5] who wrote the adaptation of the story 'The Tin Star' [by John W. Cunningham] which became the screenplay of *High Noon*, was subpoenaed by the HUAC, and admitted he had been a Communist.

"At the end of my version of *High Noon*, there's this wonderful scene. Because the people of the town don't support him, they will not defend him while normally they'd help him defend their town, so Gary Cooper's character takes off his badge, throws it in the dirt as a gesture of disappointment and disgust. It was an emotional moment, but because of the times we were going through, they considered it a Communist gesture. The film was considered a Communist film and I was considered the Antichrist for having made it. It was picketed everywhere. John Wayne,[6] who was our leading star for so many years, was very much a reactionary at that time, he was a real protector of our country, of the American dream and he thought the film was totally un–American. He labeled it a Communist film and because he was our greatest star, many people picked up on that. Many years later, he apologized because he thought it was a very naïve statement on his part, which was true, but I thought he was a pretty fantastic guy to admit that he had made a terrible mistake. The picture still went on to win Academy Awards and it still is one of the most respected films of all time, in spite of the aura of being a Communist film."

"The funny thing about *High Noon* was, we had no title for the film. I just made up that title off the top of my head. You see, I was making *Home of the Brave* [1949], based on the play, which was about anti–Semitism during World War II. I thought it would be more interesting to make it about a black man in World War II. If the studio knew or found out that I was putting a black man [actor James Edwards] in that part, we would be thrown off the lot, so we made that film in secret and that picture was titled *High Noon*. I kept going into the office every day

John Wayne

and thought, 'High Noon, that's a good title, wish we had a film to go with it.' So when production designer Rudolph Sternad found the story of 'The Tin Star' and brought it to me, we bought the story rights from Mr. Cunningham and that little, short story evolved into the classic High Noon."

Throughout his entire career, he certainly took chances by making controversial, even provocative films—which all proved to be flawless and extremely rewarding in the end. And because they were so compelling, moving, tragic, sometimes chilling, and even offbeat, they often created a tense audience participation. Mr. Kramer: "To this day, there's still reaction to Inherit the Wind. I listen to the radio quite often and recently I heard this Christian station talking about 'Stanley Kramer and how he *dared* to make that movie Inherit the Wind about Darwinism!' I called up the station and said, 'Look, you missed the point of the film, which is about freedom of speech. I didn't want to press Darwinism at all, I don't believe in Darwinism over traditional religion, it is a fact that in every small town in the United States, there is fear of Darwinism versus traditional religion.'"

Mr. Kramer also cast some of the finest musical stars ever in less familiar but very convincing character roles: Fred Astaire as a scientist in On the Beach (1959), Gene Kelly as a journalist in Inherit the Wind (1960) and he revived Judy Garland's career by casting her as a German *hausfrau* who had sex with a Jew in Judgment at Nuremberg (1961, a role which earned her her second and final Academy Award nomination, after A Star Is Born) and as an employee in an institution for mentally disturbed children in John Cassavetes' A Child Is Waiting (1963, produced by Mr. Kramer)—at a time when nobody was interested in hiring her again. Mr. Kramer: "In a way that was a career risk. Judy Garland was heavy at the time, she had hardly made any films since A Star Is Born, was she still able to deliver a great performance? But I was never really afraid of taking risks." His films always indicated that same quality: from bringing paraplegics to the screen for the very first time, using real paraplegics and with an unknown in the leading role (Marlon Brando), or the very first motorcycle picture, The Wild One, based on a fascinating but true story, trying to find out why these motorcyclists were going up to this town in Northern California on the weekends and destroying property—for what reason? Mr. Kramer: "They didn't even know themselves why they were doing it, but the interesting part of it is the town complained like hell, but also 'loved' it because it was bringing a lot of attention to their little town. It was making a lot of money:

Judy Garland made a come-back in two Stanley Kramer films: *Judgment at Nuremberg* (1961) and *A Child Is Waiting* (1963).

(Left to right) Fred Astaire, Gregory Peck and Ava Gardner in *On the Beach* (1959), one of Stanley Kramer's many film classics. (Courtesy of DOCIP Film Archive, Brussels, Belgium.)

tourists were coming in to see it because of the fact those motorcyclists were there." So he took risks, from that subject matter to the killing of animals and animal rights in a little picture called *Bless the Beasts and the Children* (1972).

Can *On the Beach* be considered to be one of Mr. Kramer's greatest achievements? He says: "I think it certainly was a film with a vision, that's for sure. Scientists told me then, 'Mr. Kramer, the radioactivity would probably not carry all over the world, it would be just a certain percentage, like 90 or 95 percent would be contaminated by it, but it would not mean the *end* of the world.' I was criticized for that. After we moved from California to Washington State in the 1970s, the volcano Mount St. Helens erupted [1980] and its ash was carried all over the world. So the film proved right in the end: it *does* carry all over the world. Then somebody told me a serious filmmaker should never make a comedy. That's when I decided to make *It's a Mad, Mad, Mad, Mad World* [laughs]."

Screenwriter William Rose (1918–1987) wrote the screenplay for this film and later on he also wrote the screenplays of two other Kramer films, *Guess Who's Coming to Dinner* (earning him an Academy Award) and *The Secret of Santa Vittoria* (1969). Mr. Kramer: "Bill Rose was a wonderful writer who lived in London and then moved to the Isle of Jersey [one of the Channel Islands between France and Great Britain]. He was a very interesting person, we respected one another. *The Secret of Santa Vittoria* would have been a better film if we would have been

Sid Caesar, Edie Adams and Stanley Kramer on the set of *It's a Mad, Mad, Mad, Mad World* (1963). (Courtesy of Karen Sharpe Kramer.)

able to continue working on it, but he went through a hard time with his wife, they got divorced in the middle of it and he walked out of the film, so I got Ben Maddow to finish the screenplay. That film did not get its due because when it opened, United Artists which released and backed the film, thought it would save their company. We had a huge premiere but right across the street ran a little film called *Easy Rider*. The audience that came to see our film, thought, 'Mmm...' and they went over across the street to see *Easy Rider*, that was the new wave. It killed *The Secret of Santa Vittoria*, one of the more traditional films. I used to kid about this with Dennis Hopper, an extraordinary man in many ways and a wonderful artist in every way. People always talk about Jack Nicholson and his performance in that film and he certainly was very interesting. It made him a star and all that, but if you look at the film today, in retrospect, it was Dennis Hopper's film all the way. He's a remarkable filmmaker, highly criticized, but that film changed the business, just like Marlon Brando changed the business of acting. And then Dennis couldn't find a job, they wouldn't hire him, just because he was so extraordinary. So he's another one, like Welles. But he's acting now and he's a phenomenal photographer and artist, had a tremendous career, he's probably even more important to the art world than he is as an actor. He's a very good friend, he writes, acts, directs, he's a photographer, he's a *renaissance* man."

In the 1970s Mr. Kramer, his wife and their two daughters, Katharine and Jennifer, left Los Angeles and moved to Seattle (in the meantime, they have returned and now reside in the Los Angeles area). "We had two young children and I always considered myself a family man in the first place. My wife and I thought it was good to move to Seattle and live in a normal environment, away from Los Angeles. When the children were young, I always planned to work during school holidays so my family could come and stay with me. Whenever possible, I finished shooting by 5 or 5:30, so we could all have dinner together. Making films was my passion and it was terribly important to me, but I wanted my family to be at the center of it all.

"We shot the first full length film ever made in the Seattle area, *The Runner Stumbles* [1979]. It was supposed to be for Oskar Werner but he had a skiing accident so he was pulled out of the film. An actor like Albert Finney for example would have been an obvious choice to replace him for the part of the small-town priest who's accused of murdering a nun, but it turned out to be Dick Van Dyke. It was a wonderful experience, we cast a lot of the local talents, we shot it in the same little town which later became the town for the television series *Northern Exposure*. Those were very wonderful years. I also taught at the university and wrote a Sunday column in the *Seattle Times*."

"A lot of my film students became writers. One of them, Marc Norman, won an Academy Award for his screenplay of *Shakespeare in Love* [1998]—he was a protégé of mine who had studied and had worked on *Oklahoma Crude* [1973]. He had spent a lot of hours with me. However I feel that he won the Academy Award because he had the talent, not because I helped him out in those early stages."

What does it take to be a good director? Says Mr. Kramer: "Well, you can learn the technique. You can learn all the technical things you need to know as a director, but it must come from the heart. You must have a lot of energy and a cause, a *reason* to make those films. The long hours, the risks you have to take, it's even worse today. If you don't make those 20 million dollars on your first weekend, you're through! Two strikes and you're out! [laughs]. In films you have to make so much money to be able to at least continue, but money was never my first thought."

Despite all of his achievements, it seems strange however that he never got the recognition he deserved. His films garnered 85 Oscar nominations and 16 Oscars, he earned six nominations as producer in the best picture category and on top of that he was nominated three times as best director. Yet Mr. Kramer never received an Academy Award. He says: "I don't think people are aware of me anymore. A couple of years ago, my wife asked the American Film Institute to consider me as a recipient for the Life Achievement Award. But they prefer to honor actors now, so audiences would tune in to see the *stars*. Yet at that time, Ava Gardner, Gene Kelly, Fred Astaire, Marlene Dietrich, Anthony Quinn, Frank Sinatra ... they were all still alive, you could also have Kate Hepburn, Sidney Poitier, Gene Hackman, Tony Curtis, Ann-Margret, Faye Dunaway, Kirk Douglas, Marlon Brando, Gregory Peck, and many others who all appeared in my films." Mr. Kramer was never award-hungry though and was extremely pleased that the Academy awarded him the Irving G. Thalberg Award in 1961 (for consistently high quality in film making—"perhaps the biggest Oscar of them all," he says) and in 1991 he was the recipient of the Producers Guild's David O. Selznick Award for his entire *œuvre*.

Steven Spielberg, Barbra Streisand and a number of others got together a couple of years ago and tried to give him an honorary Oscar, but it was awarded to Mr. Kramer's discovery instead, Kirk Douglas. In spite of that, both Stanley Kramer and William Wyler hold the record for most nominations with their films.

It is striking that Mr. Kramer made several enriching *message* films over the years, featuring mostly strong characters, *male* characters. Mr. Kramer: "With the issues I was dealing with, it wasn't that easy to feature women. I did make a few romantic films over the years, like *The Four Poster* [1952, starring Lilli Palmer and Rex Harrison as a married couple, based on the play by Dutch writer Jan de Hartog which later on became the basis for the Broadway musical *I Do! I Do!*], but those films didn't really fit in my approach, that's why I didn't make too many of those. And speaking of message films, people often ask me if they can really change anyone's opinion. Let's put it this way, whether you like Bill Clinton or not, he is a great speaker and he has a gift for persuasion when making a speech to an audience. But can he really change their opinion? I don't know. So if you're talking about message films and their ability to change an audience's opinion, I don't think they can—if two people come out of the theater in New York or in Los Angeles and one person says to the other, 'Well, I never thought of it quite *that* way'—that's it!"

It was a unique and fascinating experience meeting and talking to Mr. Kramer at age 87, a man who made some of the most enduring and important films of all time. And even though the American Film Institute did make the terrible mistake of overlooking him as a recipient of their prestigious Life Achievement Award, Mr. Kramer is one of those legendary filmmakers whose films most definitely do stand the test of time.

Unfortunately, this interview turned out to be his last one. Six months later Mr. Kramer passed away (February 2001); anyone who grew up with his films one way or the other, or was influenced by his universal language of making a film straight from the heart, lost his ultimate mentor that day. I will never be able to describe—not even in Flemish, my own language—how honored and grateful I am that Mrs. Kramer allowed me to meet her husband who definitely made this world a better place to live in.

In 1997 Mr. Kramer published his autobiography *A Mad, Mad, Mad, Mad World—A Life in Hollywood* (published by Harcourt Brace & Company) which gives a detailed picture of his career as an honest, genuine, dedicated and extraordinary filmmaker. There is a possibility that in the future his daughter Katharine, who is Katharine Hepburn's godchild, might write a book on Mr. Kramer's life and career in films. Just as *High Noon* has a huge history of its own, so do all of Mr. Kramer's other films. A book focusing on his *body of work* should be absolutely more than just dealing with a series of interesting films and a lot of anecdotes about the actors on the set: he made films that nobody wanted to make at the time or even thought about making. Sometimes in history, there comes a leader, whether it is in politics, in science, in technology, in film, who paves the way for others as Mr. Kramer did for numerous other filmmakers. If you asked him *how* he did it, he couldn't really tell you. There's probably no real formula, perhaps he was on a mission and was touched by a number of things as he went along. He concluded the interview by saying, in all modesty, "I hope I did all right."

Interview: Los Angeles, August 20, 2000

Notes

1. Spencer Tracy (1900-1967), one of the best actors ever, debuted on the Broadway stage in the 1920s before making his film debut in John Ford's gangster drama *Up the River* (1930, with Humphrey Bogart in a supporting role). He won two Academy Awards (for best actor) for his leading roles in *Courageous* (1937) and *Boys Town* (1938, as Father Flanagan); other films for which he was nominated, were *San Francisco* (1936), *Father of the Bride* (1950), *Bad Day at Black Rock* (1955), *The Old Man and the Sea* (1958), *Inherit the Wind* (1960), *Judgment at Nuremberg* (1961) and *Guess Who's Coming to Dinner* (1967). He teamed up with Katharine Hepburn in a succession of heart-warming comedies or absorbing dramas: *Woman of the Year* (1942), *Keeper of the Flame* (1942), *Without Love* (1945), *The Sea of Grass* (1947), *State of the Union* (1948), *Adam's Rib* (1949), *Pat and Mike* (1952), *Desk Set* (1957) and *Guess Who's Coming to Dinner*. He was one of the most respected actors of his time, and the pallbearers at his funeral included actors Frank Sinatra and James Stewart, directors Stanley Kramer, John Ford and George Cukor, and screenwriter Garson Kanin who wrote the bestseller *Tracy and Hepburn: An Intimate Memoir* (1971).

2. Marlon Brando (b. 1924), one of the most talented and controversial actors of the past half century, was praised for the performances in most of his films, including in *The Men* (1950), *A Streetcar Named Desire*

(1951, Academy Award nomination for best actor), *Viva Zapata!* (1952, Academy Award nomination for best actor), *Julius Caesar* (1953, Academy Award nomination for best actor), *On the Waterfront* (1954, Academy Award for best actor), *The Godfather* (1972, Academy Award for best actor), *Last Tango in Paris* (1973, Academy Award nomination for best actor), *A Dry White Season* (1989, Academy Award nomination for best supporting actor) and *The Freshman* (1990).

3. James Dean (1931-1955), screen legend with an exceptionally short career in films. After four small screen roles in 1951-53 (*Sailor Beware, Fixed Bayonets, Has Anybody Seen My Gal?* and *Trouble Along the Way*), he only played three, but highly acclaimed leading roles in *East of Eden* (1954, Academy Award nomination for best actor), *Rebel Without a Cause* (1955) and *Giant* (1956, Academy Award nomination for best actor). A race car fanatic, he died in a car crash at age 24.

4. Orson Welles (1915–1985), genius filmmaker (actor, director, producer, screenwriter) who never got the opportunities and the credit he rightfully deserved, became frustrated and in the end had several unfinished projects waiting for the proper funds. A legend before he entered films, because of his sensational Mercury radio presentation *The War of the Worlds* (1938), which gave the impression Martians had landed in the U.S., he debuted on the screen with *Citizen Kane* (1941) and subsequently directed (and appeared in) other brilliant films such as *The Magnificent Ambersons* (1942), *The Lady from Shanghai* (1948), *Macbeth* (1948), *Othello* (1952), *Touch of Evil* (1958) and *The Trial* (1962). Over the years he acted in many films directed by others, and gave memorable performances in films such as *The Third Man* (1949, as Harry Lime), *The Long Hot Summer* (1958), *The Roots of Heaven* (1958), *Compulsion* (1959) and *A Man for All Seasons* (1966), and for several years he lived and worked in Europe. In 1970 he got an honorary Academy Award "for superlative artistry and versatility in the creation of motion pictures"; five years later the American Film Institute awarded him the Life Achievement Award, and in 1984 he received the Directors Guild of America's D. W. Griffith Award.

5. Carl Foreman (1914–1984), five time Academy Award nominated screenwriter who also became a producer and director, wrote six adaptations from short stories and plays for Stanley Kramer: *So This Is New York* (1948), *Champion* (1949), *Home of the Brave* (1949), *The Men* (1950), *Cyrano de Bergerac* (1951) and *High Noon* (1952), before he was blacklisted by the HUAC as he refused to give names, but admitted he had been a registered Communist. He then went into self-imposed exile in Great Britain and along with Michael Wilson wrote the Academy Award winning adaptation of *The Bridge on the River Kwai* (1957, both uncredited as they were blacklisted, but in 1985 they received a belated Academy Award), also *The Key* (1958), *Born Free* (1966) and *Mackenna's Gold* (1969). In 1975 he returned to the U.S.; at the time of his death, he was working on *The Yellow Jersey* about the Tour de France, the world's most important bicycle race, to be directed by Michael Cimino with Dustin Hoffman in the leading role. The project never materialized.

6. John Wayne (1907–1979), a.k.a. the "Duke," perhaps the most legendary actor of them all, who was the personification of everything America stood for, made over 250 films in his career which spanned nearly a half century. After his first major role in Raoul Walsh's *The Big Trail* (1930) and nearly a decade in B films, his role in John Ford's *Stagecoach* (1939) finally made him a star, and for many years to come he remained one of America's top box-office attractions. With John Ford he made ten more films; some of them became classics: *She Wore a Yellow Ribbon* (1949), *Rio Grande* (1950), *The Quiet Man* (1952) and *The Searchers* (1956). His other films include *Back to Bataan* (1945), *Sands of Iwo Jima* (1949), *Rio Bravo* (1959), *The Man Who Shot Liberty Valance* (1962), *Hatari!* (1962), *The Green Berets* (1968), *True Grit* (1969, which earned him an Academy Award for best actor) and *The Cowboys* (1972). In his final film, Don Siegel's melancholic and heart-warming *The Shootist* (1976), he played a former gunfighter who finds out he's got cancer and hopes to die peacefully. Ultimately cancer was Wayne's cause of death. In 1964 lung cancer was diagnosed for the first time. After two operations he was back on the right track, even though it cost him nearly an entire lung. Always a very outspoken patriot, he was known to be an anti–Communist and founded the Motion Picture Alliance for the Preservation of American Ideals.

Filmography

Note: Initially Stanley Kramer worked as a screenwriter and editor on movies for many years; those films are not included. In 1947 he formed his own production company, Stanley Kramer Productions, and from then on he produced all of his films.

So Ends Our Night (United Artists, 1941). DIR John Cromwell. PROD David L. Loew, Albert Lewin. PROD ASST **Stanley Kramer.** SCR Talbot Jennings (novel by Erich Maria Remarque). CAM William Daniels. ED William Reynolds. MUS Louis Gruenberg. RUNNING TIME 120 min. CAST: Fredric March (Josef Steiner); Margaret Sullavan (Ruth Holland); Frances Dee (Marie Steiner); Glenn Ford (Ludwig Kern); Anna Sten (Lilo); Erich von Stroheim (Brenner).

The Moon and Sixpence (United Artists, 1942). DIR Albert Lewin. PROD David L. Loew. ASST PROD **Stanley Kramer. SCR Albert Lewin (novel by W. Somerset Maugham). CAM John F. Seitz. ED Richard L. Van Enger. MUS Dimitri Tiomkin. RUNNING TIME 89 min. CAST: George Sanders (Charles Strickland); Herbert Marshall (Geoffrey Wolfe); Doris Dudley (Blanche Stroeve); Eric Blore (Captain Nichols); Albert Basserman (Doctor Coutras); Florence Bates (Tiare Johnson).

So This Is New York (United Artists, 1948). DIR Richard Fleischer. PROD **Stanley Kramer**. SCR Carl Foreman, Herbert Baker (novel by Ring Lardner). CAM Jack Russell. ED Walter Thompson. MUS Dimitri Tiomkin. RUNNING TIME 79 min. CAST: Henry Morgan (Ernie Finch); Rudy Vallee (Herbert Daley); Bill Goodwin (Jimmy Ralston); Hugh Herbert (Mr. Trumbult); Leo Gorcey (Sid Mercer); Virginia Grey (Ella Finch).

Champion (United Artists, 1949). DIR Mark Robson. PROD **Stanley Kramer**. SCR Carl Foreman (story "Champion" by Ring Lardner). CAM Frank F. Planer. ED Harry Gerstad. MUS Dimitri Tiomkin. RUNNING TIME 100 min. CAST: Kirk Douglas (Midge); Marilyn Maxwell (Grace); Arthur Kennedy (Connie); Paul Stewart (Haley); Ruth Roman (Emma); Lola Albright (Palmer).

Home of the Brave (United Artists, 1949). DIR Mark Robson. PROD **Stanley Kramer**. SCR Carl Foreman (play by Arthur Laurents). CAM Robert De Grasse. ED Harry Gerstad. MUS Dimitri Tiomkin. RUNNING TIME 86 min. CAST: Douglas Dick (Major Robinson); Steve Brodie (T. J.); Jeff Corey (Doctor); Lloyd Bridges (Finch); Frank Lovejoy (Mingo); James Edwards (Moss).

The Men (United Artists, 1950). DIR Fred Zinnemann. PROD **Stanley Kramer**. SCR Carl Foreman (also story). CAM Robert De Grasse. ED Harry Gerstad. MUS Dimitri Tiomkin. RUNNING TIME 85 min. CAST: Marlon Brando (Ken "Bud" Wilocek); Teresa Wright (Ellen); Everett Sloane (Dr. Brock); Jack Webb (Norm); Richard Erdman (Leo); Arthur Jurado (Angel).

Cyrano de Bergerac (United Artists, 1951). DIR Michael Gordon. PROD **Stanley Kramer**. SCR Carl Foreman (play by Edmond Rostand). CAM Frank F. Planer. ED Harry Gerstad. MUS Dimitri Tiomkin. RUNNING TIME 112 min. CAST: José Ferrer (Cyrano de Bergerac); Mala Powers (Roxane); William Prince (Christian); Morris Carnovsky (Le Bret); Ralph Clanton (De Guiche); Lloyd Corrigan (Ragueneau).

Death of a Salesman (Columbia, 1952). DIR Laszlo Benedek. PROD **Stanley Kramer**. SCR Stanley Roberts (play by Arthur Miller). CAM Frank F. Planer. ED William Lyon. MUS Alex North. RUNNING TIME 115 min. CAST: Fredric March (Willy Loman); Mildred Dunnock (Linda Loman); Kevin McCarthy (Biff); Cameron Mitchell (Happy); Howard Smith (Charley); Royal Beal (Ben).

My Six Convicts (Columbia, 1952). DIR Hugo Fregonese. PROD **Stanley Kramer**. SCR Michael Blankfort (book by Donald Powell Wilson). CAM Guy Roe. ED Gene Havlick. MUS Dimitri Tiomkin. RUNNING TIME 104 min. CAST: Millard Mitchell (James Connie); Gilbert Roland (Punch Pinero); John Beal (Doc); Marshall Thompson (Blivens Scott); Alf Kjellin (Clem Randall); Henry Morgan (Dawson).

The Sniper (Columbia, 1952). DIR Edward Dmytryk. PROD **Stanley Kramer**. SCR Harry Brown (story by Edna Anhalt, Edward Anhalt). CAM Burnett Guffey. ED Aaron Stell. MUS George Antheil. RUNNING TIME 87 min. CAST: Adolphe Menjou (Lt. Kafka); Arthur Franz (Eddie Miller); Gerald Mohr (Sgt. Ferris); Marie Windsor (Jean Darr); Frank Faylen (Inspector Anderson); Richard Kiley (Dr. James Kent).

High Noon (United Artists, 1952). DIR Fred Zinnemann. PROD **Stanley Kramer**. SCR Carl Foreman (story by John W. Cunningham). CAM Floyd Crosby. ED Elmo Williams. MUS Dimitri Tiomkin. RUNNING TIME 84 min. CAST: Gary Cooper (Will Kane); Thomas Mitchell (Jonas Henderson); Lloyd Bridges (Harvey Pell); Katy Jurado (Helen Ramirez); Grace Kelly (Amy Kane); Otto Kruger (Percy Mettrick).

The Happy Time (Columbia, 1952). DIR Richard Fleischer. PROD **Stanley Kramer**. SCR Earl Felton (play by Samuel Arthur Taylor, novel by Robert Fontaine). CAM Charles Lawton, Jr. ED William A. Lyon. MUS Dimitri Tiomkin. RUNNING TIME 94 min. CAST: Charles Boyer (Jacques Bonnard); Louis Jourdan (Uncle Desmond); Marsha Hunt (Susan Bonnard); Kurt Kasznar (Uncle Louis); Linda Christian (Mignonette Chappuis); Bobby Driscoll (Bibi).

The Four Poster (Columbia, 1952). DIR Irving Reis. PROD **Stanley Kramer**. SCR Allan Scott (play by Jan de Hartog). ED Henry Batista. MUS Dimitri Tiomkin. RUNNING TIME 103 min. CAST: Rex Harrison (John); Lilli Palmer (Abby).

Eight Iron Men (Columbia, 1952). DIR Edward Dmytryk. PROD **Stanley Kramer**. SCR Harry Brown (also play). CAM Roy Hunt. ED Aaron Stell. MUS Leith Stevens. RUNNING TIME 80 min. CAST: Bonar Colleano (Collucci); Arthur Franz (Carter); Lee Marvin (Mooney); Richard Kiley (Coke); Nick Dennis (Sapiros); James Griffith (Ferguson).

The Member of the Wedding (Columbia, 1953). DIR Fred Zinnemann. PROD **Stanley Kramer**. SCR Edna Anhalt, Edward Anhalt (book and play by Carson McCullers). CAM Hal Mohr. ED William A. Lyon. MUS Alex North. RUNNING TIME 88 min. CAST: Ethel Waters (Bernice Sadie Brown); Julie Harris (Frankie Addams); Brandon De Wilde (John Henry); Arthur Franz (Jarvis); Nancy Gates (Janice); William Hansen (Mr. Addams).

The Juggler (Columbia, 1953). DIR Edward Dmytryk. PROD **Stanley Kramer**. SCR Michael Blankfort (also novel). CAM Roy Hunt. ED Aaron Stell. MUS George Antheil. RUNNING TIME 84 min. CAST: Kirk Douglas (Hans Muller); Milly Vitale (Ya'El); Paul Stewart (Detective Karni); Joey Walsh (Yehoshua Bresler); Alf Kjellin (Daniel); Beverly Washburn (Susy).

The 5,000 Fingers of Dr. T. (Columbia, 1953). DIR Roy Rowland. PROD **Stanley Kramer**. SCR Dr. Seuss [Ted Geisel], Allan Scott (story by Dr. Seuss). CAM Frank F. Planer. ED Al Clark. MUS Frederick Hollander. RUNNING TIME 89 min. CAST: Peter Lind Hayes (Zabladowski); Mary Healy (Mrs. Collins); Hans Conried (Dr. Terwilliker); Tommy Rettig (Bart); John Heasley (Uncle Whitney); Robert Heasley (Uncle Judson).

The Wild One (Columbia, 1954). DIR Laszlo Benedek. PROD **Stanley Kramer**. SCR John Paxton (story by Frank Rooney). CAM Hal Mohr. ED Al Clark. MUS Leith Stevens. RUNNING TIME 79 min. CAST: Marlon Brando (Johnny); Mary Murphy (Kathie); Robert Keith (Harry Bleeker); Lee Marvin (Chino); Jay C. Flippen (Sheriff Singer); Peggy Maley (Mildred).

The Caine Mutiny (Columbia, 1954). DIR Edward Dmytryk. PROD **Stanley Kramer**. SCR Stanley Roberts (novel by Herman Wouk). CAM Frank F. Planer. ED William A. Lyon, Henry Batista. MUS Max Steiner. RUNNING TIME 125 min. CAST: Humphrey Bogart (Captain Queeg); José Ferrer (Lt. Barney Greenwald); Van Johnson (Lt. Steve Maryk); Fred MacMurray (Lt. Tom Keefer); Robert Francis (Ensign Willie Keith); May Wynn (May Wynn).

Not As a Stranger (United Artists, 1955). DIR-PROD **Stanley Kramer**. SCR Edna Anhalt, Edward Anhalt (novel by Morton Thompson). CAM Frank F. Planer. ED Frederic Knudtson. MUS George Antheil. RUNNING TIME 135 min. CAST: Olivia de Havilland (Kristina); Robert Mitchum (Lucas Marsh); Frank Sinatra (Alfred Boone); Gloria Grahame (Harriet Lang); Broderick Crawford (Dr. Aarons); Charles Bickford (Dr. Runkleman).

The Pride and the Passion (United Artists, 1957). DIR-PROD **Stanley Kramer**. SCR Edna Anhalt, Edward Anhalt (also story, novel by C. S. Forester). CAM Frank F. Planer. ED Frederic Knudtson, Ellsworth Hoagland. MUS George Antheil. RUNNING TIME 132 min. CAST: Cary Grant (Capt. Anthony Trumbull); Frank Sinatra (Miguel); Sophia Loren (Juana); Theodore Bikel (General Jouvet); John Wengraf (Sermaine); Jay Novello (Ballinger).

The Defiant Ones (United Artists, 1958). DIR-PROD **Stanley Kramer**. SCR Nathan E. Douglas [Nedrick Young], Harold Jacob Smith. CAM Sam Leavitt. ED Frederic Knudtson. MUS Ernest Gold. RUNNING TIME 97 min. CAST: Tony Curtis (John "Joker" Jackson); Sidney Poitier (Noah Cullen); Theodore Bikel (Sheriff Max Muller); Charles MacGraw (Capt. Gibbons); Lon Chaney (Big Sam); King Donovan (Solly).

On the Beach (United Artists, 1959). DIR-PROD **Stanley Kramer**. SCR John Paxton, James Lee Barrett (novel by Nevil Shute). CAM Giuseppe Rotunno. ED Frederic Knudtson. MUS Ernest Gold. RUNNING TIME 134 min. CAST: Gregory Peck (Dwight Towers); Ava Gardner (Moira Davidson); Fred Astaire (Julian Osborn); Anthony Perkins (Peter Holmes); Donna Anderson (Mary Holmes); John Tate (Admiral Bridie).

Inherit the Wind (United Artists, 1960). DIR-PROD **Stanley Kramer**. SCR Nathan E. Douglas [Nedrick Young], Harold Jacob Smith (play by Jerome Lawrence, Robert E. Lee). CAM Ernest Laszlo. ED Frederic Knudtson. MUS Ernest Gold. RUNNING TIME 126 min. CAST: Spencer Tracy (Henry Drummond); Fredric March (Matthew H. Brady); Gene Kelly (E. K. Hornbeck); Florence Eldridge (Mrs. Brady); Dick York (Bertram T. Cates); Donna Anderson (Rachel Brown).

Judgment at Nuremberg (United Artists, 1961). DIR-PROD **Stanley Kramer**. SCR Abby Mann (also teleplay [1959]). CAM Ernest Laszlo. ED Frederic Knudtson. MUS Ernest Gold. RUNNING TIME 190 min. CAST: Spencer Tracy (Judge Dan Haywood); Burt Lancaster (Ernst Janning); Richard Widmark (Col. Tad Lawson); Marlene Dietrich (Madame Bertholt); Maximilian Schell (Hans Rolfe); Judy Garland (Irene Hoffman); Montgomery Clift (Rudolph Petersen).

Pressure Point (United Artists, 1962). DIR Hubert Cornfield. PROD **Stanley Kramer**. SCR Hubert Cornfield, S. Lee Pogostin (story by Robert Mitchell Lindner). CAM Ernest Haller. ED Frederic Knudtson. MUS Ernest Gold. RUNNING TIME 91 min. CAST: Sidney Poitier (Doctor); Bobby Darin (Patient); Peter Falk (Young Psychiatrist); Carl Benton Reid (Medical Officer); Mary Munday (Bar Hostess); Barry Gordon (Patient as a Boy).

A Child Is Waiting (United Artists, 1963). DIR John Cassavetes. PROD **Stanley Kramer**. SCR Abby Mann. CAM Joseph LaShelle. ED Gene Fowler, Jr. MUS Ernest Gold. RUNNING TIME 102 min. CAST: Burt Lancaster (Dr. Matthew Clark); Judy Garland (Jean Hansen); Gena Rowlands (Sophie Widdicombe); Steven Hill (Ted Widdicombe); Bruce Ritchey (Reuben Widdicombe); Gloria McGehee (Mattie).

It's a Mad, Mad, Mad, Mad World (United Artists, 1963). DIR-PROD **Stanley Kramer**. SCR William Rose, Tania Rose (also story). CAM Ernest Laszlo. ED Frederic Knudtson, Robert C. Jones, Gene Fowler, Jr. MUS Ernest Gold. RUNNING TIME 192 min. CAST: Spencer Tracy (Capt. C. G. Culpeper); Milton Berle (J. Russell Finch); Sid Caesar (Melville Crump); Buddy Hackett (Benjy Benjamin); Ethel Merman (Mrs. Marcus); Mickey Rooney (Ding Bell).

Ship of Fools (Columbia, 1965). DIR-PROD **Stanley Kramer**. SCR Abby Mann (novel by Katherine Anne Porter). CAM Ernest Laszlo. ED Robert C. Jones. MUS Ernest Gold. RUNNING TIME 149 min. CAST: Vivien Leigh (Mary Treadwell); Simone Signoret (La Condesa); José Ferrer (Rieber); Lee Marvin (Tenny); Oskar Werner (Dr. Schumann); Elizabeth Ashley (Jenny).

Guess Who's Coming to Dinner (Columbia, 1967). DIR-PROD **Stanley Kramer**. SCR William Rose. CAM Sam Leavitt. ED Robert C. Jones. MUS Frank De Vol. RUNNING TIME 108 min. CAST: Spencer Tracy (Matt

Drayton); Sidney Poitier (John Prentice); Katharine Hepburn (Christina Drayton); Katharine Houghton (Joey Drayton); Cecil Kellaway (Monsignor Ryan); Beah Richards (Mrs. Prentice).

The Secret of Santa Vittoria (United Artists, 1969). DIR-PROD **Stanley Kramer**. SCR William Rose, Ben Maddow (novel by Robert Crichton). CAM Giuseppe Rotunno. ED William A. Lyon, Earle Herdan. MUS Ernest Gold. RUNNING TIME 138 min. CAST: Anthony Quinn (Italo Bombolini); Anna Magnani (Rosa Bombolini); Virna Lisi (Caterina Malatesta); Hardy Kruger (von Prum); Sergio Franchi (Tufa); Renato Rascel (Babbaluche).

R.P.M. (Columbia, 1970). DIR-PROD **Stanley Kramer**. SCR Erich Segal. CAM Michel Hugo. ED William A. Lyon. MUS Barry DeVorzon, Perry Botkin, Jr. RUNNING TIME 92 min. CAST: Anthony Quinn (Paco Perez); Ann-Margret (Rhoda); Gary Lockwood (Rossiter); Paul Winfield (Dempsey); Graham Jarvis (Thatcher); Alan Hewitt (Hewlett).

Bless the Beasts and Children (Columbia, 1971). DIR-PROD **Stanley Kramer**. SCR Mac Benoff (novel by Glendon Swarthout). CAM Michel Hugo. ED William A. Lyon. MUS Barry DeVorzon, Perry Botkin, Jr. RUNNING TIME 109 min. CAST: Bill Mumy (Teft); Barry Robins (Cotton); Miles Chapin (Shecker); Darel Glaser (Goodenow); Bob Kramer (Lally 1); Marc Vahanian (Lally 2).

Oklahoma Crude (Columbia, 1973). DIR-PROD **Stanley Kramer**. SCR Marc Norman. CAM Robert Surtees. ED Folmar Blangsted. MUS Henry Mancini. RUNNING TIME 111 min. CAST: George C. Scott (Noble Mason); Faye Dunaway (Lena Doyle); John Mills (Cleon Doyle); Jack Palance (Hellman); William Lucking (Marion); Harvey Jason (Wilcox).

The Domino Principle (Avco Embassy, 1977). DIR-PROD **Stanley Kramer**. SCR Adam Kennedy (also novel). CAM Fred Koenekamp, Ernest Laszlo. ED John Burnett. MUS Billy Goldenberg. RUNNING TIME 100 min. CAST: Gene Hackman (Roy Tucker); Candice Bergen (Ellie Tucker); Richard Widmark (Tagge); Mickey Rooney (Spiventa); Edward Albert (Ross Pine); Eli Wallach (General Tom Reser).

The Runner Stumbles (20th Century Fox, 1979). DIR-PROD **Stanley Kramer**. SCR Milan Stitt (also play). CAM Laszlo Kovacs. ED Pembroke J. Herring. MUS Ernest Gold. RUNNING TIME 99 min. CAST: Dick Van Dyke (Father Rivard); Kathleen Quinlan (Sister Rita); Maureen Stapleton (Mrs. Shanding); Ray Bolger (Monsignor Nicholson); Tammy Grimes (Erna); Beau Bridges (Toby).

JANET LEIGH

I always had the impression that over the years people repeatedly made a terrible mistake by thinking that Janet Leigh was *just* the lady in the shower scene of Alfred Hitchcock's *Psycho* (1960), a part she played so convincingly that it earned her an Academy Award nomination. She *was* that victim all right, perhaps one of the most famous "victims" in the history of picture making, but it would be most unfair to her and to the entire contribution to the film industry she has made in her lengthy career, if one ignored all her other films and performances which made her a star for several decades.

When I met her at her home, this impressive, down-to-earth lady also introduced me to a very energetic and enthusiastic film producer, Rick Schmidlin, who dropped by for a minute to say hello—he had done a tremendous job by restoring classics such as Orson Welles' *Touch of Evil* (1958), with Miss Leigh in the leading role (that's how they met), as well as Erich von Stroheim's *Greed* (1923), and he had just returned from Memphis, Tennessee, where he had shown a digitally remastered and completely re-edited version of *Elvis: That's The Way It Is* (originally released in 1970) to 2,500 Elvis fans on the 23rd anniversary of Elvis' death. Several months earlier, Mr. Schmidlin got hold of 65,000 feet of unused footage which enabled him to re-edit *Elvis* for Turner Entertainment and Turner Classic Movies; the film includes eight additional new musical numbers and he was able to portray the King even better as he really was when he was still at the height of his popularity. The movie was screened a few days later at the Motion Picture and Television Home in Woodland Hills in the presence of a number of people who had worked with Elvis, and it was great to see this wonderful piece of filmmaking which was unanimously well received by people who had worked their entire life in the film industry. Schmidlin told Miss Leigh all about the event in Memphis; it was indisputable that they shared the same passion—love and dedication for their craft.

Miss Leigh: "The restoration of *Touch of Evil* was based on a 58 page memo from Orson Welles to the studio when he saw what they had done to the picture after his cut. I got a call one day from Rick Schmidlin and he asked, 'Would you like to see what we've done with the film? Mr. Heston is coming too.' I remember I had an appointment, but I switched it and I went in the morning to Universal to see it. I was absolutely stunned. I was so thrilled to see what his team had brought back to the film. When they released it, we went all over the country and to Europe. The reception was just remarkable."

Miss Leigh, who dominated Hollywood in the 1950s as one of its leading ladies, has been in films now for over 50 years as she debuted in *The Romance of Rosy Ridge* (1947) opposite Van Johnson. Without any acting experience whatsoever, this then 20-year-old, fresh-faced actress

(Left to right) June Allyson, Janet Leigh, Peter Lawford and Richard Stapley in *Little Women* (1949). (Courtesy of DOCIP Film Archive, Brussels, Belgium.)

(born on July 6, 1927, in Merced, California, as Jeanette Helen Morrison), immediately got on the right track, or, as *Variety* wrote in its review: "The film introduces a newcomer, Janet Leigh, whose work indicates a bright future." *Voilà*.

Incidentally, it was former screen actress Norma Shearer[1] who discovered Miss Leigh by accident, just by looking at a photograph on the clerk's desk of a Northern California ski lodge where she was vacationing. She asked the clerk (Miss Leigh's father) for a copy of the picture, sent it to Lew Wasserman and in less than no time, Miss Leigh was on the MGM lot. "I am very grateful for that, as Norma Shearer was the one who started it all, although later on she didn't have anything to do with the pictures I made. It was just a matter of perfect timing," Miss Leigh says.

"At that time the studio system was a wonderful way for a young person like me to start in this business and to be initiated into the film industry. They built you as you went along, as you were ready for each next step. You never were given the responsibility of carrying a picture before you were ready for it. My first picture was with Van Johnson, who was the highest paid actor in Hollywood, with Thomas Mitchell, both great actors. I was surrounded by a lot of those wonderful people. Of course, I had to do what I had to do, but the responsibility of the picture didn't rest on my shoulders."

Her early roles were immediately leading roles, another remarkable achievement. Miss Leigh: "They allowed you to you grow as a person and as an actress as you developed, until your basic structure was solid. By the time you had your name above the title, you were ready for it. I was very fortunate in the way they guided my career in terms of the roles I got to play, and then there was the timing—I was in the right place at the right time. I didn't get cornered or get stuck in one genre, I was able to diversify, experiment and explore every genre, from drama, comedy, to musicals and Westerns."

Over the years, she was able to show her abilities as an actress who was equally at ease in musicals such as *Words and Music* (1948, biography of Rogers and Hart), *My Sister Eileen* (1955, with Miss Leigh singing songs as "I'm Great" and "Give Me a Hand and My Baby") and the highly amusing musical comedy *Bye, Bye Birdie* (1963), as well as the delightfully entertaining comedy *Confidentially Connie* (1953) and Anthony Mann's *The Naked Spur* (1953), one of the best Westerns of the decade. Her dramas include *Act of Violence* (1949, playing Van Heflin's wife), *That Forsyte Woman* (1949, adapted from Galsworthy's novel; in the late 1960s another adaptation was a hugely successful British TV series), *Houdini* (1953, based on the life of escape artist Harry Houdini, played by her then-husband Tony Curtis[2]), *Touch of Evil* (1958, one of Orson Welles' most inspiring films, with Miss Leigh as Charlton Heston's wife—the spectacular opening sequence by Russell Metty may be the best *ever*), Hitchcock's *Psycho* (more about that later), John Frankenheimer's breathtaking political thriller *The Manchurian Candidate* (1962, as Frank Sinatra's girlfriend) and the wonderful character study *Boardwalk* (1979) about an elderly couple (Lee Strasberg and Ruth Gordon) desperately trying to survive in their Brooklyn neighborhood (with Miss Leigh portraying their daughter). This is only a small summary of the many highlights of her career.

"I was very fortunate. Whatever God has graced me with, I was able to do. Instinct was given to me and as I started out, gradually I was able to open all the 'doors.' I worked very hard, I studied, I tried to learn my craft as best as I could and then use what was given to me. That combination made it work. But I could have gone through life and been a very happy person and not known this was ever inside of me, you just never know. When I was starting out, I used to see a lot of the older pictures and silents. I used to run them at the studio, especially because it had to do with the work I was doing at the time or a role I was playing, or just to see the actors and actresses of that period and how they approached a role.

"At that time the buck stopped at the studio heads, that is an expression that was used a lot. Louis B. Mayer made the final decision. When he looked at my first screen test and the test of another girl who was under contract and had already done a few pictures but was considered a little too sophisticated, because this character was a very naïve mountain girl, he said, 'We go with the new one.' That's how lucky I was. He made that decision. Then after that, the system took care of the training. Every studio had its string of people under contract. My second picture was *If Winter Comes* and they needed a young girl who gets pregnant, kills herself and then everyone blames Walter Pidgeon, so they looked at their list of people and thought I would be right for it. I had to learn an English accent which I studied very hard to do. Accents were never natural for me. Some people, like comics, they can tell a story and they can have any kind of accent there is. I've never been able to do that, if I do an accent in a picture, I study a long time with someone tutoring me. I just don't do it automatically."

As she was beginning her screen career, she appeared in Fred Zinnemann's *Act of Violence*. At that time his seven year contract at MGM was nearly up and he wouldn't renew it. Miss Leigh: "Fred Zinnemann was a wonderful man, absolutely wonderful. It was obvious to anyone who worked with him how talented he was, but at that time MGM didn't understand his type of work at all. He made dramatic films, which were not really the MGM style. They were used to the lavish, big extravaganzas, the musicals, and although he could do anything, he was used to drama and they just didn't understand his type of movies. But I'm glad I was at MGM because at least it gave me a chance to work with him. After Dore Schary[3] replaced Louis B. Mayer and took over MGM, you could see the changes in the studio policy. The whole

Jerry Lewis and Janet Leigh in *Living It Up* (1954). (Courtesy of DOCIP Film Archive, Brussels, Belgium.)

approach became different. It was focused on reality and hard-hitting kind of documentary style films, instead of what had been the MGM trademark. Dore Schary understood Zinnemann's approach of that kind of story, opposed to a *ladidadida* kind of thing, you know what I mean? It was the beginning of the age of realism.

"I didn't know Mr. Schary very well, but I did ask for my release at MGM. I had signed a seven year contract, they had a three month option, then another three month option and they could drop you. It was their right to exercise or not to exercise that option. Then it was six months and then it was yearly. They had rewritten my contract three times. I started at $50 a week which was a normal, standard contract. The first time they rewrote it, I was on location for my first picture. Then they rewrote it again around 1948 because I was doing some loan-outs and they were getting a lot of money from my loan-outs which was fine with me. You see, I never objected to that, because they took a big chance on me. Besides, I liked loan-outs, you got a chance to work with different people because you worked on a different lot, again opening more 'doors.' I was being handsomely paid by the studio, more than I ever dreamed of—by 1948 I think I was making $1,500 a week. I felt like a millionaire. When they loaned me to 20th Century Fox to do *Prince Valliant* [1954], 20th would pay MGM a lot more than what I was getting, but I thought that was right: they gave me the opportunity, they gave me *my* chance to earn $ 1.500 a week, where else would I have ever done that? And so, if they made the money, great! I'm glad that I could pay them back one way or the other. That's how I felt.

"Anyway, when Mr. Schary came in, I had been doing mostly loan-outs. When I came back to MGM, they weren't giving me the kind of pictures they gave at other studios on loan-outs. It just had changed: instead of a family, they started letting people go and not keeping them under contract; he was all for independency. You lost that continuity, that flow that seemed to come from MGM. I think the other studios had that as well. I was scared, because I didn't know if anyone else would want me if I weren't under contract to MGM. The agents were the ones who told me, 'You really have to ask for your release.' And I said to them, 'What if I don't get another job?' They said, 'We already have two offers from two studios for a non-exclusive deal.' I started to cry, because MGM was sort of my home, I had been there from my very first day, I was very emotional about it. At MGM they told me, 'Janet, we'll give you the release, but do this last picture with us.' So that's how I got my release. Then I signed a non-exclusive four picture deal over a period of five years with Universal and a five picture deal with Columbia over a period of seven years, something like that—meaning I could work anywhere else I wanted, but I owed them five pictures. I could turn down so many but it would get to the point where I had to take something, because I owed those pictures, both at Universal and at Columbia. It worked out beautifully.

"This wouldn't have been a good career decision earlier, I think it was just the right time. It wasn't really my decision, I was guided, I had the best agents in the world. It also gave me the opportunity to work with a lot of other actors and directors, even though I worked with many great people at MGM and I had been doing loan-outs in the meantime which gave me a lot of opportunities to work with people that weren't at MGM."

Miss Leigh worked also with some of the best and most prestigious directors in the business: Fred Zinnemann, George Sidney (*The Red Danube* [1949], *Scaramouche* [1952], *Who Was That Lady?* [1960], *Pepe* [1960], *Bye, Bye Birdie* [1963]), Mervyn LeRoy (*Little Women* [1949]), Josef von Sternberg (*Jet Pilot* [1957]), Orson Welles (*Touch of Evil*) and, last but not least, with Alfred Hitchcock (*Psycho*). How important is a good, talented, creative director? Miss Leigh: "They are *very* important. I worked with the best, some of them were really good, some were all right. Fortunately those came in a time when I was secure enough in my own ability to do a role, that I didn't depend alone on the director if they were average or all right. I realized that I

Janet Leigh and Tony Perkins in *Psycho* (1960). (Courtesy of DOCIP Film Archive, Brussels, Belgium.)

knew my craft well enough to know that maybe it wouldn't reach the height if I could rely on a director who made me do more, but I knew that I would do a good job. I don't mean that in an egotistical way, it is just that in those early years I would have panicked if the director wasn't the greatest. I love my work, the excitement and the exhilaration when I bring my contribution to the role. Take *Psycho* for example, Mister Tony Perkins[4] brought to his role what he wanted to contribute into the whole concept, and of course Mister Hitchcock[5] had it all planned from the beginning what he was going to do with the camera. So you get all those elements together and it's *wonderful*. It's not what I did that changed Marion, it just made it richer and fuller with what Hitchcock was doing with his camera, with the sets, what Tony was bringing to Norman. Then it sparked what I was doing with Marion and what I did with Marion sparked what he did to Norman ... you see what I'm saying? That the great excitement. If you happen to work with a director who does a good job but just isn't that creative, at least I can come in and I'm still sparked by someone else and ultimately we're all sparked—it may not reach the heights it could possibly have reached under someone else's guidance, but I know I'm okay. So a good director is always important, to anybody."

What was the impact of *Psycho* on Miss Leigh's career? "To most people, the first film they think of when they see my name, is *Psycho*. It wasn't a curse at all to me; it would have if it would have done to me what it did to Tony. He was so brilliant in his role that no one would allow him to play anybody else. They wouldn't allow him *not* to be Norman Bates. It was a curse for him. Because Marion Crane was done away with, I couldn't be brought back

Janet Leigh in *Psycho* (1960). (Courtesy of DOCIP Film Archive, Brussels, Belgium.)

so I was allowed to escape Marion Crane. After *Psycho* I did *Manchurian Candidate*, *Bye, Bye Birdie*, *Wives and Lovers* [1963], you know, drama, musical, comedy, ... I got scripts wanting me to do many other pictures à la *Psycho*, but I deliberately didn't do them. I didn't *want* to do them, there was no reason to, not when you have worked with Hitchcock and when you had that kind of response. You can't top that in that genre. So it was not a curse at all for me, it was a blessing. And, God bless his heart, Tony Perkins' career was damaged badly by *Psycho*, because he was so good. It even affected his children. His son Osgood told me once that Tony had carpool one week and Berry, his wife, didn't have the time to drive the car for some reason, so he was driving carpool. Osgood's friend wouldn't get in the car. He said, 'I'm not getting in the car with Norman Bates!' Osgood asked his father, 'Knowing the effect of *Psycho* on your career, if they gave you that script today, would you still do it?' Tony didn't answer him right away, about the next day he told Osgood, 'Yes, I would, because'—this is in essence, I don't remember the exact words, this is what he meant—'we're in a business of creating images. That's what we do. If I had been that successful in creating an image that people really believe, even to the point when they won't let me be anything else, I succeeded in my job, and yes I would'—which is pretty powerful."

What about Alfred Hitchcock, by many considered to be one of the greatest filmmakers in the history of the cinema? Miss Leigh: "Hitchcock's ability was to manipulate the audience and to create the kind of suspense, to take something absolutely normal like a shower and turn it into something evil. The reason why he was able to create what he did, was because he told the story with the camera so efficiently and he was so economical in his footage so that every frame in any of his films meant something. It was so tight and that is why you got that suspense. He was very well organized in his mind as to the directness of the story he was telling. He was brilliant and it was his kind of a crossword puzzle in a way to tell the story. He put all sorts of layers in it so that, if you really wanted to, you could see the story. If you wanted to look again, you could see another layer underneath, and another one, and another one. It was there if you saw it, and if you didn't, you could still enjoy the picture. But because of his brilliant mind, his fun was to do that. He was a very interesting man, unparalleled in his approach."

In the 1970s Miss Leigh's screen appearances became fewer and for the past few decades, she has been involved in several other activities as well which took a lot of her time and energy. In 1984 she published a bright and refreshing autobiography, *There Really Was a Hollywood*, which might be the basis for an upcoming documentary. Miss Leigh: "Right now, there's a possibility that a documentary-type show will be made based on the book. I would be taking the audience with me and introduce them to Hollywood as I saw it when I first came here and take them through those years. I might also update the book and re-release that, coinciding with the TV program."

When I met her, she had just finished her second novel: "I just turned it in. The first novel was called *House of Destiny*. To me writing a novel is an extension of performing—when doing a role, I create one character and when I'm writing, I create *all* the characters. So it is very similar how I approach a role: even though it's Janet playing the role—I can wear a black wig, like in *Bye, Bye Birdie*, it is still Janet playing a role. But I try to bring to that role a life, I create a life for that person, even if it has nothing to do with the script. It has something to do with her as a character. It gives me a reason for saying things and why I say them. In writing, I do the same thing. In each character, I give it a complete history so I know that character like my role when I play a role: where she went to school, what kind of a student she was, what is her favorite color…. It just makes a 'persona'; you're molding a person. It is great fun, I adore it. It was also fun writing my autobiography and it was fun writing the book on *Psycho*. I was asked to do that, but I thought, how can any more be said about *Psycho*, it has been examined upside down and inside out. They said, 'Well, that's right, but never by anyone who was actually there,' and that is true. I found things about *Psycho* that I hadn't thought about before. The novels are really more challenging because of the idea of creating characters, but the backgrounds are authentic. In *House of Destiny* the original family came from Sun Valley, Idaho, and as I love history, I read numerous books on the times. Then they arrived in Hollywood. It enabled me to use fictitious people, blending it with people that I've obviously known."

Miss Leigh has no time and no plans whatsoever to retire. "Retire? No, I don't think so, there is just so much to do. I am a consultant in my husband's business. Since he's not been as strong, I have incorporated my travels and travel for him as well. I have two children, two grandchildren and two four-legged children here [referring to her dogs] that I take care of, so it's a busy time. I am also putting my own archive together—I realize no one else can do it. They could put stills together, but they couldn't really put the other stuff together. USC will take the archives, they have the space. The Academy is good too and I would have gone there, but the USC has the room to put everything in one place, all the stills, the scripts, the playbills, etc. I have to at least get it all identified.

"I have also been working on the board of the Motion Picture and Television Fund in Woodland Hills[6] for almost 15 years now. There are thousands of people who go through all our various facilities which are located in the Los Angeles area. There's the home, the hospital, there are cottages, long-term care, short-term care. There's the board with all the studio heads and then there's the new generation with all of the younger producers, the children of the board members, like my daughter Jamie Lee—she doesn't work for them a lot because she doesn't have the time, but whenever she can, she does."

Her daughter and equally talented screen actress Jamie Lee Curtis,[7] with whom she appeared in films twice, *The Fog* (1980) and *Halloween H2O–Twenty Years Later* (1998)—to the joy of many film buffs—wrote the preface of Miss Leigh's autobiography. At one point she wrote: "She is one of the great *ladies* on and off the screen." I was familiar with her work as an actress, but now that I have met her in person, I can only confirm forcibly that statement.

Interview: Los Angeles, August 18, 2000

Notes

1. Norma Shearer (1900–1983) was one of MGM's most elegant leading stars—she was known as the "First Lady of the Screen." Referring to the wonderful parts she was offered at the studio, somebody once said, "No wonder, she sleeps with the boss." She married MGM's production executive Irving G. Thalberg in 1927, became one of the first actresses to win an Academy Award (for her role in *The Divorcee*, 1930) and gained four other nominations along the way, before retiring from the screen in 1942. Her numerous highlights include *Their Own Desire* (1929), *A Free Soul* (1931), *Strange Interlude* (1932), *The Barretts of Wimpole Street* (1934), *Romeo and Juliet* (1936, as Juliet), *Marie Antoinette* (1938), *Idiot's Delight* (1939) and *The Women* (1939).

2. Tony Curtis was Miss Leigh's husband from 1951 to 1962; they had two daughters, Kelly Lee (b. 1956) and Jamie Lee (b. 1958, note 7). After her divorce from Tony Curtis, Miss Leigh married businessman Robert Brandt. Tony Curtis (b. 1925) earned an Academy Award nomination for his role in Stanley Kramer's *The Defiant Ones* (1958); other films include *Some Like It Hot* (1959), *Operation Petticoat* (1959), *Spartacus* (1960), *The List of Adrian Messenger* (1963), *The Great Race* (1965), *The Boston Strangler* (1968), *The Last Tycoon* (1976), *Insignificance* (1985). In the early 1970s he appeared with Roger Moore in the British TV series *The Persuaders*. Tony Curtis is also a well-respected painter.

Studio portrait of Tony Curtis.

3. Dore Schary (1905-1980) was the head of MGM (replacing Louis B. Mayer—more information: interview with Kathryn Grayson, note 1) from 1951 to 1956. Originally a stage actor (appearing on Broadway in a play starring Spencer Tracy), a screenwriter and producer, he wrote the screenplays of such films as *Big City* (1937), *Boys Town* (1938, winning an Academy Award for the original story) and *Young Tom Edison* (1940), and contributed to *It's a Big Country* (1951). Films he produced include *The Spiral Staircase* (1946), *Crossfire* (1947), *Battleground* (1949), *The Swan* (1956), *Designing Woman* (1957) and *Sunrise at Campobello* (1960) which was based on the play he successfully had produced on Broadway after he was fired at MGM and which starred Ralph Bellamy as Franklin D. Roosevelt (a role he reprised in the film version). He also supervised the production of numerous other films as MGM's chief of production.

4. Anthony Perkins (1932–1992), the son of stage and screen actor Osgood Perkins (1892–1937), played the character of Norman Bates in Hitchcock's *Psycho* as well in its two sequels, *Psycho II* (1983) and *Psycho III* (1986, which he also directed), and in its prequel, *Psycho IV: The Beginning* (1990, TV movie). Other films he appeared in include *The Actress* (1953, his screen debut), *Friendly Persuasion* (1956, Academy Award nomination for best supporting actor), *Fear Strikes Out* (1957), *On the Beach* (1959), *Pretty Poison* (1968), *The Life and Times of Judge Roy Bean* (1972) and *Crimes of Pas-*

sion (1984). In 1973 he married actress-photographer Berry [Berinthia] Berenson (the sister of actress Marisa Berenson) who was one of the victims of American Airlines Flight 11 which crashed into the north tower of the World Trade Center on September 11, 2001; on the flight manifest, she was listed as Berinthia Perkins.

5. Alfred Hitchcock (1899–1980) hardly needs any introduction whatsoever. There was never another director whose films have been examined so thoroughly by journalists, film students or other filmmakers all over the world, just to have a better idea of his unique way of working. Films he made in his native Great Britain include *The Lodger* (1926), *Juno and the Paycock* (1930), *The Man Who Knew Too Much* (1934), *The 39 Steps* (1935), *The Lady Vanishes* (1938) and *Jamaica Inn* (1939). After that he was in the U.S. and made such films as *Rebecca* (1940, Academy Award nomination for best director), *Foreign Correspondent* (1940), *Suspicion* (1941), *Lifeboat* (1944, Academy Award nomination for best director), *Spellbound* (1945, Academy Award nomination for best director), *Notorious* (1946), *The Paradine Case* (1948), *I Confess* (1953), *Rear Window* (1954, Academy Award nomination for best director), *To Catch a Thief* (1954), *The Man Who Knew Too Much* (1956, remake of his 1934 version), *Vertigo* (1958), *North by Northwest* (1959), *Psycho* (1960, Academy Award nomination for best director), *The Birds* (1963), *Marnie* (1964) and his final film, *Family Plot* (1976). He was the recipient of the Life Achievement Award, given to him by the American Film Institute, in 1979.

6. The Motion Picture and Television Fund is the result of the combined efforts of film pioneers Mary Pickford, Charlie Chaplin, Douglas Fairbanks and D.W. Griffith when they founded the Motion Picture Relief Fund in 1921. In 1940, its president, Danish-born actor Jean Hersholt (1886–1956), purchased 48 acres in Woodland Hills, California, where the renowned full service nursing care facility the Motion Picture and Television Country Home has been based now for several decades and where people who have worked in the entertainment industry are taken care of. In addition to the spacious Woodland Hills campus, there are five Health Centers and a Children's Center located in the Los Angeles area, all meant to serve the entertainment community.

7. Jamie Lee Curtis starred in the TV series *Operation Petticoat* (1977-78) and after appearing in a series of horror films, including *Halloween* (1978), *Terror Train* (1980) and *Halloween II* (1981), she proved to be a highly versatile leading actress with interesting roles in *Trading Places* (1983), *A Fish Called Wanda* (1988), *My Girl* (1992), *Forever Young* (1992), *Virus* (1999) and *Halloween H2K: Evil Never Dies* (2001).

Filmography

The Romance of Rosy Ridge (MGM, 1947). DIR Roy Rowland. PROD Jack Cummings. SCR Lester Cole (novel by MacKinlay Kantor). CAM Sidney Wagner. ED Ralph E. Winters. MUS George Bassman. RUNNING TIME 105 min. CAST: Van Johnson (Henry Carson); Thomas Mitchell (Gill MacBean); **Janet Leigh** (Lissy Anne MacBean); Marshall Thompson (Ben MacBean); Selena Royle (Sairy MacBean); Charles Dingle (John Dessark).

If Winter Comes (MGM, 1948). DIR Victor Saville. PROD Pandro S. Berman. SCR Marguerite Roberts, Arthur Wimperis (novel by Arthur Stuart Menteth-Hutchinson). CAM George Folsey. ED Ferris Webster. MUS Herbert Stothart. RUNNING TIME 96 min. CAST: Walter Pidgeon (Mark Sabre); Deborah Kerr (Nona Tybar); Angela Lansbury (Mabel Sabre); Binnie Barnes (Natalie Bagshaw); **Janet Leigh** (Effie Bright); Dame May Whitty (Mrs. Perch).

Words and Music (MGM, 1948). DIR Norman Taurog. PROD Arthur Freed. SCR Fred Finklehoffe (story by Guy Bolton, Jean Holloway). CAM Charles Rosher, Harry Stradling. ED Albert Akst, Ferris Webster. MUS Lennie Hayton. RUNNING TIME 119 min. CAST: Perry Como (Eddie/Himself); Mickey Rooney (Lorenz "Larry" Hart); Ann Sothern (Joyce Harmon); Tom Drake (Richard "Dick" Rodgers); Betty Garrett (Peggy Lorgan McNeil); **Janet Leigh** (Dorothy Feiner).

Hills of Home (MGM, 1948). DIR Fred M. Wilcox. PROD Robert Sisk. SCR William Ludwig (sketches by Ian MacLaren). CAM Charles Schoenbaum. ED Ralph E. Winters. MUS Herbert Stothart. RUNNING TIME 94 min. CAST: Edmund Gwenn (William MacLure); Donald Crisp (Drumsheugh); Tom Drake (Tammas Milton); **Janet Leigh** (Margit Mitchell); Rhys Williams (Mr. Milton); Reginald Owen (Hopps).

Act of Violence (MGM, 1949). DIR Fred Zinnemann. PROD William H. Wright. SCR Robert L. Richards (story by Collier Young). CAM Robert Surtees. ED Conrad A. Nervig. MUS Bronislau Kaper. RUNNING TIME 82 min. CAST: Van Heflin (Frank R. Enley); Robert Ryan (Joe Parkson); **Janet Leigh** (Edith Enley); Mary Astor (Pat); Phyllis Thaxter (Ann); Berry Kroeger (Johnny).

Little Women (MGM, 1949). DIR-PROD Mervyn LeRoy. SCR Andrew Solt, Sarah Y. Mason, Victor Heerman (novel by Louisa May Alcott). CAM Robert H. Planck, Charles Schoenbaum. ED Ralph E. Winters. MUS Adolph Deutsch. RUNNING TIME 121 min. CAST: June Allyson (Jo March); Peter Lawford (Theodore Laurence); Margaret O'Brien (Beth March); Elizabeth Taylor (Amy March); **Janet Leigh** (Meg March); Rossano Brazzi (Professor Bhaer).

The Doctor and the Girl (MGM, 1949). DIR Curtis Bernhardt. PROD Pandro S. Berman. SCR Theodore Reeves (book by Maxence Van der Meersch). CAM Robert H. Planck. ED Ferris Webster. MUS Rudolph G. Kopp.

RUNNING TIME 97 min. CAST: Glenn Ford (Dr. Michael Corday); Charles Coburn (Dr. John Corday); Gloria De Haven (Fabienne); **Janet Leigh** (Evelyn Heldon); Bruce Bennett (Dr. Alfred Norton); Warner Anderson (Dr. Esmond).

The Red Danube (MGM, 1949). DIR George Sidney. PROD Carey Wilson. SCR Gina Klaus, Arthur Wimperis (novel by Bruce Marshall). CAM Charles Rosher. ED James E. Newcom. MUS Miklos Rozsa. RUNNING TIME 118 min. CAST: Walter Pidgeon (Col. Nicobar); Ethel Barrymore (Mother Superior); Peter Lawford (Major McPhimister); Angela Lansbury (Audrey Quail); **Janet Leigh** (Maria Buhlen); Louis Calhern (Col. Piniev).

That Forsyte Woman (MGM, 1949). DIR Compton Bennett. PROD Leon Gordon. SCR Jan Lustig, Ivan Tors, James B. Williams (novel by John Galsworthy). CAM Joseph Ruttenberg. ED Frederick Y. Smith. MUS Bronislau Kaper. RUNNING TIME 112 min. CAST: Errol Flynn (Soames Forsyte); Greer Garson (Irene Forsyte); Walter Pidgeon (Young Jolyon); Robert Young (Philip Bosinney); **Janet Leigh** (June Forsyte); Harry Davenport (Old Jolyon Forsyte).

Holiday Affair (MGM, 1949). DIR-PROD Don Hartman. SCR Isobel Lennart (novelette by John D. Weaver). CAM Milton Krasner. ED Harry Marker. MUS Roy Webb. RUNNING TIME 86 min. CAST: Robert Mitchum (Steve); **Janet Leigh** (Connie); Wendell Corey (Carl); Gordon Gebert (Timmy); Griff Barnett (Mr. Ennis); Esther Dale (Mrs. Ennis).

Jet Pilot (Universal, 1949, release delayed until 1957). DIR Josef von Sternberg. PROD-SCR Jules Furthman. CAM Philip G. Cochran, Winton C. Hoch. ED Michael R. McAdam, Harry Marker. MUS Bronislau Kaper. RUNNING TIME 112 min. CAST: John Wayne (Colonel Shannon); **Janet Leigh** (Anna); Jay C. Flippen (Major General Black); Paul Fix (Major Rexford); Richard Rober (George Rivers); Roland Winters (Colonel Sokolov).

Strictly Dishonorable (MGM, 1951). DIR-PROD Melvin Frank, Norman Panama. SCR Melvin Frank, Norman Panama (play by Preston Sturges). CAM Ray June. ED Cotton Warburton. MUS Lennie Hayton. RUNNING TIME 94 min. CAST: Ezio Pinza (Augustino Caraffa); **Janet Leigh** (Isabelle Perry); Millard Mitchell (Bill Dempsey); Gale Robbins (Marie Donnelly); Maria Palmer (Countess Szadvany); Esther Minciotti (Mme Maria Caraffa).

Angels in the Outfield (MGM, 1951). DIR-PROD Clarence Brown. SCR Dorothy Kingsley, George Wells (story by Richard Conlin). CAM Paul C. Vogel. ED Robert J. Kern. MUS Daniele Amfitheatrof. RUNNING TIME 99 min. CAST: Paul Douglas (Guffy McGovern); **Janet Leigh** (Jennifer Paige); Keenan Wynn (Fred Bayles); Donna Corcoran (Bridget White); Lewis Stone (Arnold P. Hapgood); Spring Byington (Sister Edwitha).

Two Tickets to Broadway (RKO, 1951). DIR James V. Kern. SCR Sid Silvers, Hal Kanter (story by Sammy Cahn). CAM Edward Cronjager. ED Harry Marker. MUS Walter Scharf. RUNNING TIME 106 min. CAST: Tony Martin (Dan); **Janet Leigh** (Nancy); Gloria DeHaven (Harriet); Eddie Bracken (Lew Conway); Ann Miller (Joyce Campbell); Bob Crosby (Bob).

It's a Big Country (MGM, 1951). DIR Richard Thorpe, John Sturges, Charles Vidor, Don Weis, Clarence Brown, William A. Wellman, Don Hartman. PROD Robert Sisk. SCR Dore Schary, William Ludwig, Helen Deutsch, George Wells, Allen Rivkin, Dorothy Kingsley, Isobel Lennart. CAM John Alton, Ray June, William Mellor, Joseph Ruttenberg. ED Ben Lewis, Frederick Y. Smith. MUS Johnny Green. RUNNING TIME 88 min. CAST: Ethel Barrymore (Mrs. Brian Riordan); Keefe Brasselle (Sgt. Maxie Klein); Gary Cooper (Texan); Nancy Davis (Miss Coleman); Van Johnson (Adam Burch); Gene Kelly (Icarus Xenophon); **Janet Leigh** (Rosa Szabo).

Just This Once (MGM, 1952). DIR Don Weis. PROD Henry Berman. SCR Sidney Sheldon (story by Max Trell). CAM Ray June. ED Frederick Y. Smith. MUS David Rose. RUNNING TIME 90 min. CAST: **Janet Leigh** (Lucy Duncan); Peter Lawford (Mark MacLane); Lewis Stone (Judge Samuel Colter); Marilyn Erskine (Gertrude Crome); Richard Anderson (Tom Winters); Douglas Fowley (Frank Pirosh).

Scaramouche (MGM, 1952). DIR George Sidney. PROD Carey Wilson. SCR Ronald Millar, George Froeschel (novel by Rafael Sabatini). CAM Charles Rosher. ED James E. Newcom. MUS Victor Young. RUNNING TIME 115 min. CAST: Stewart Granger (Andre Moreau); Eleanor Parker (Lenore); **Janet Leigh** (Aline De Gavrillac); Mel Ferrer (Marquis De Maynes); Henry Wilcoxon (Chevalier De Chabrillaine); Nina Foch (Marie Antoinette).

Fearless Fagan (MGM, 1952). DIR Stanley Donen. PROD Edwin H. Knopf. SCR Charles Lederer (story by Eldon W. Griffiths, Sidney Franklin, Jr.). CAM Harold Lipstein. ED George White. RUNNING TIME 79 min. CAST: **Janet Leigh** (Abby Ames); Carleton Carpenter (Floyd Hilston); Keenan Wynn (Sgt. Kellwin); Richard Anderson (Capt. Daniels); Ellen Corby (Mrs. Ardley); Barbara Ruick (Nurse).

The Naked Spur (MGM, 1953). DIR Anthony Mann. PROD William H. Wright. SCR Sam Rolfe, Harold Jack Bloom. CAM William Mellor. ED George White. MUS Bronislau Kaper. RUNNING TIME 91 min. CAST: James Stewart (Howard Kemp); **Janet Leigh** (Lina Patch); Robert Ryan (Ben Vandergroat); Ralph Meeker (Roy Anderson); Millard Mitchell (Jesse Tate).

Confidentially Connie (MGM, 1953). DIR Edward Buzzell. PROD Stephen Ames. SCR Max Shulman (story by Max Shulman, Herman Wouk). CAM Harold Lipstein. ED Frederick Y. Smith. MUS David Rose. RUNNING TIME 71 min. CAST: Van Johnson (Joe Bedloe); **Janet Leigh** (Connie Bedloe); Louis Calhern (Opie Bedloe); Walter Slezak (Emil Spangenberg); Gene Lockhart (Dean Magruder); Hayden Rorke (Simmons).

Houdini (Paramount, 1953). DIR George Marshall. PROD George Pal. SCR Philip Yordan (novel by Harold Kellock). CAM Ernest Laszlo. ED George Tomasini. MUS Roy Webb. RUNNING TIME 105 min. CAST: Tony Curtis (Houdini); **Janet Leigh** (Bess); Torin Thatcher (Otto); Angela Clarke (Mrs. Weiss); Stefan Schnabel (Pros. Attorney); Ian Wolfe (Fante).

Walking My Baby Back Home (Universal, 1953). DIR Lloyd Bacon. PROD Ted Richmond. SCR Don McGuire, Oscar Brodney (story by Don McGuire). CAM Irving Glassberg. ED Ted J. Kent. MUS Joseph Gershenson. RUNNING TIME 94 min. CAST: Donald O'Connor (Jigger Millard); **Janet Leigh** (Chris Hall); Buddy Hackett (Blimp Edwards); Lori Nelson (Claire); "Scat Man" Crothers (Smiley); Kathleen Lockhart (Mrs. Millard).

Prince Valiant (20th Century Fox, 1954). DIR Henry Hathaway. PROD Robert L. Jacks. SCR Dudley Nichols. CAM Lucien Ballard. ED Robert Simpson. MUS Franz Waxman. RUNNING TIME 100 min. CAST: James Mason (Sir Brack); **Janet Leigh** (Aleta); Robert Wagner (Prince Valiant); Debra Paget (Ilene); Sterling Hayden (Sir Gawain); Victor McLaglen (Boltar).

Living It Up (Paramount, 1954). DIR Norman Taurog. PROD Paul Jones. SCR Jack Rose, Melville Shavelson (musical comedy *Hazel Flagg* by Ben Hecht, Jule Styne, Bob Hilliard; story by James Street). CAM Daniel Fapp. ED Archie Marshek. MUS Walter Scharf. RUNNING TIME 94 min. CAST: Dean Martin (Steve); Jerry Lewis (Homer); **Janet Leigh** (Wally Cook); Edward Arnold (The Mayor); Fred Clark (Oliver Stone); Sheree North (Jitterbug Dancer).

The Black Shield of Falworth (Universal, 1954). DIR Rudolph Maté. PROD Robert Arthur, Melville Tucker. SCR Oscar Brodney (novel by Howard Pyle). CAM Irving Glassberg. ED Ted J. Kent. MUS Joseph Gershenson. RUNNING TIME 98 min. CAST: Tony Curtis (Myles Falworth); **Janet Leigh** (Lady Anne); David Farrar (Earl of Alban); Barbara Rush (Meg Falworth); Herbert Marshall (Earl of Mackworth); Rhys Williams (Diccon Bowman).

Rogue Cop (MGM, 1954). DIR Roy Rowland. PROD Nicholas Nayfack. SCR Sydney Boehm (novel by William P. McGivern). CAM John Seitz. ED James E. Newcom. MUS Jeff Alexander. RUNNING TIME 91 min. CAST: Robert Taylor (Christopher Kelvaney); **Janet Leigh** (Karen Stephanson); George Raft (Dan Beaumonte); Steve Forrest (Eddie Kelvaney); Anne Francis (Nancy Corlane); Robert Ellenstein (Sidney Y. Myers).

Pete Kelly's Blues (Warner Bros., 1955). DIR Jack Webb. SCR Richard L. Breen. CAM Hal Rosson. ED Robert M. Leeds. MUS Ray Heindorf, Sammy Cahn, Arthur Hamilton. RUNNING TIME 95 min. CAST: Jack Webb (Pete Kelly); **Janet Leigh** (Ivy Conrad); Edmond O'Brien (Fran McCarg); Peggy Lee (Rose Hopkins); Andy Devine (George Tenell); Lee Marvin (Al Gannaway).

My Sister Eileen (Columbia, 1955). DIR Richard Quine. PROD Fred Kohlmar. SCR Blake Edwards, Richard Quine (play by Joseph Fields, Jerome Chorodov). CAM Charles Lawton, Jr. ED Charles Nelson. MUS Morris Stoloff. RUNNING TIME 106 min. CAST: **Janet Leigh** (Eileen Sherwood); Betty Garrett (Ruth Sherwood); Jack Lemmon (Bob Baker); Robert Fosse (Frank Lippencott); Kurt Kasznar (Appopolous); Richard York (Wreck).

Safari (Columbia, 1956). DIR Terence Young. PROD Adrian D. Worker. SCR Robert Buckner, Anthony Veiller (story by Robert Buckner). CAM John Wilcox. ED Michael Gordon. MUS William Alwyn. RUNNING TIME 90 min. CAST: Victor Mature (Ken); **Janet Leigh** (Linda); John Justin (Brian Sinden); Roland Culver (Sir Vincent Brampton); Orlando Martins (Jerusalem).

Touch of Evil (Universal, 1958). DIR Orson Welles. PROD Albert Zugsmith. SCR Orson Welles (novel by Whit Masterson). CAM Russell Metty. ED Virgil M. Vogel. MUS Henry Mancini. RUNNING TIME 95 min. CAST: Charlton Heston (Ramon M. Vargas); **Janet Leigh** (Susan Vargas); Orson Welles (Hank Quinlan); Joseph Calleia (Pete Menzies); Akim Tamiroff ("Uncle" Joe Grandi); Joanna Moore (Marcia Linnekar).

The Vikings (United Artists, 1958). DIR Richard Fleischer. PROD Jerry Bresler. SCR Calder Willingham (novel by Edison Marshall). CAM Jack Cardiff. ED Hugo Williams. MUS Mario Nascimbene. RUNNING TIME 114 min. CAST: Kirk Douglas (Einar); Tony Curtis (Eric); Ernest Borgnine (Ragnar); **Janet Leigh** (Morgana); James Donald (Egbert); Alexander Knox (Father Godwin).

The Perfect Furlough (Universal, 1959). DIR Blake Edwards. PROD Robert Arthur. SCR Stanley Shapiro. CAM Philip Lathrop. ED Milton Carruth. MUS Frank Skinner. RUNNING TIME 93 min. CAST: Tony Curtis (Paul Hodges); **Janet Leigh** (Vicki Loren); Keenan Wynn (Harvey Franklin); Linda Cristal (Sandra Roca); Elaine Stritch (Liz Baker).

Who Was That Lady? (Columbia, 1960). DIR George Sidney. PROD-SCR Norman Krasna (also play). CAM Harry Stradling. ED Viola Lawrence. MUS André Previn. RUNNING TIME 116 min. CAST: Tony Curtis (David Wilson); Dean Martin (Michael Haney); **Janet Leigh** (Ann Wilson); James Whitmore (Harry Powell); John McIntire (Bob Doyle); Barbara Nichols (Gloria Coogle).

Psycho (Paramount, 1960). DIR-PROD Alfred Hitchcock. SCR Joseph Stefano (novel by Robert Bloch). CAM John L. Russell. ED George Tomasini. MUS Bernard Herrmann. RUNNING TIME 109 min. CAST: Anthony Perkins (Norman Bates); **Janet Leigh** (Marion Crane); Vera Miles (Lila Crane); John Gavin (Sam Loomis); Martin Balsam (Milton Arbogast); John McIntire (Sheriff Chambers).

Pepe (Columbia, 1960). DIR-PROD George Sidney. SCR Dorothy Kingsley, Claude Binyon (story by Leonard Spigelglass, Sonya Levien, play by L. Bush-Fekete). CAM Joe MacDonald. ED Viola Lawrence, Al Clark. MUS Johnny Green. RUNNING TIME 195 min. CAST: Cantinflas (Pepe); Dan Dailey (Ted Holt); Shirley Jones (Suzie Murphy); Carlos Montalban (Auctioneer); Vicki Trickett (Lupita); **Janet Leigh** (Herself).

The Manchurian Candidate (United Artists, 1962). DIR John Frankenheimer. PROD John Frankenheimer, George Axelrod. SCR George Axelrod (novel by Richard Condon). CAM Lionel Lindon. ED Ferris Webster. MUS David Amram. RUNNING TIME 126 min. CAST: Frank Sinatra (Bennett Marco); Laurence Harvey (Raymond Shaw); **Janet Leigh** (Rosie); Angela Lansbury (Raymond's Mother); Henry Silva (Chunjin); James Gregory (Sen. John Iselin).

Bye, Bye Birdie (Columbia, 1963). DIR George Sidney. PROD Fred Kohlmar. SCR Irving Brecher (play by Michael Stewart, Charles Strouse, Lee Adams). CAM Joseph Biroc. ED Charles Nelson. MUS Johnny Green. RUNNING TIME 112 min. CAST: **Janet Leigh** (Rosie DeLeon); Dick Van Dyke (Albert Peterson); Ann-Margret (Kim McAfee); Maureen Stapleton (Mama Petersen); Bobby Rydell (Hugo Peabody); Jesse Pearson (Conrad Birdie).

Wives and Lovers (Paramount, 1963). DIR John Rich. PROD Hal B. Wallis. SCR Edward Anhalt (play by Jay Presson Allen). CAM Lucien Ballard. ED Warren Low. MUS Lyn Murray. RUNNING TIME 103 min. CAST: **Janet Leigh** (Bertie Austin); Van Johnson (Bill Austin); Shelley Winters (Fran Cabrell); Martha Hyer (Lucinda Ford); Ray Walston (Wylie Driberg); Jeremy Slate (Gar Aldrich).

Kid Rodelo (Paramount, 1966). DIR Richard Carlson. PROD Jack O. Lamont, James J. Storrow, Jr. SCR Jack Natteford (story by Louis L'Amour). CAM Manuel Merino. ED Allan Morrison. MUS Johnny Douglas. RUNNING TIME 91 min. CAST: Don Murray (Kid Rodelo); **Janet Leigh** (Nora); Broderick Crawford (Joe Harbin); Richard Carlson (Link); José Nieto (Thomas Reese); Julio Peña (Balsas).

Harper (Warner Bros., 1966). DIR Jack Smight. PROD Jerry Gershwin, Elliott Kastner. SCR William Goldman (novel by Ross MacDonald). CAM Conrad Hall. ED Stefan Arnsten. MUS Johnny Mandel. RUNNING TIME 121 min. CAST: Paul Newman (Lew Harper); Lauren Bacall (Mrs. Sampson); Julie Harris (Betty Fraley); Arthur Hill (Albert Graves); **Janet Leigh** (Susan Harper); Pamela Tiffin (Miranda Sampson).

Three On a Couch (Columbia, 1966). DIR-PROD Jerry Lewis. SCR Bob Ross, Samuel Taylor (story by Arne Sultan, Marvin Worth). CAM W. Wallace Kelley. ED Russel Wiles. MUS Louis Y. Brown. RUNNING TIME 109 min. CAST: Jerry Lewis (Christopher Pride/Warren/Ringo/Rutherford/Heather); **Janet Leigh** (Dr. Elizabeth Acord); Mary Ann Mobley (Susan Manning); Gila Golan (Anna Jacque); Leslie Parrish (Mary Lou Mauve); James Best (Dr. Ben Mizer).

An American Dream (Warner Bros., 1966). DIR Robert Gist. SCR Mann Rubin (book by Norman Mailer). CAM Sam Leavitt. ED George Rohrs. MUS Johnny Mandel. RUNNING TIME 107 min. CAST: Stuart Whitman (Stephen Rojack); **Janet Leigh** (Cherry McMahon); Eleanor Parker (Deborah Rojack); Barry Sullivan (Lieutenant Roberts); Lloyd Nolan (Barney Kelly); Murray Hamilton (Arthur Kabot).

Grand Slam (Paramount, 1968). DIR Giuliano Montaldo. PROD Harry Colombo, George Papi. SCR Mino Roli, Marcello Fondato, Antonio de la Loma, Augusto Caminito, Marcello Coscia (story by Mino Roli, Augusto Caminito, Paolo Bianchini). CAM Antonio Macasoli. ED Nino Baragli. MUS Ennio Morricone. RUNNING TIME 121 min. CAST: **Janet Leigh** (Mary Ann); Robert Hoffman (Jean-Paul Audry); Edward G. Robinson (Prof. Anders); Adolfo Celi (Mark Milford); Klaus Kinski (Erich Weiss); Georges Rigaud (Gregg).

Hello Down There (Paramount, 1969). DIR Jack Arnold. PROD George Sherman. SCR John McGreevey, Frank Telford (story by Ivan Tors, Art Arthur). CAM Clifford Poland. ED Erwin Dumbrille. MUS (songs) Jeff Barry. RUNNING TIME 98 min. CAST: Tony Randall (Fred Miller); **Janet Leigh** (Vivian Miller); Jim Backus (T. R. Hollister); Roddy McDowall (Nate Ashbury); Ken Berry (Mel Cheever); Merv Griffin (Himself).

One Is a Lonely Number (MGM, 1972). DIR Mel Stuart. PROD Stan Margulies. SCR David Seltzer (story by Rebecca Morris). CAM Michael Hugo. ED David Saxon. MUS Michel Legrand. RUNNING TIME 97 min. CAST: Trish Van Devere (Amy); Monte Markham (Howard); **Janet Leigh** (Gert); Melvyn Douglas (Joseph); Jane Elliott (Madge); Jonathan Lippe (Employment Agent).

Night of the Lepus (MGM, 1972). DIR William F. Claxton. PROD A. C. Lyles. SCR Don Holliday, Gene R. Kearney (novel by Russell Braddon). CAM Ted Voigtlander. ED John McSweeney. MUS Jimmie Haskell. RUNNING TIME 88 min. CAST: Stuart Whitman (Roy); **Janet Leigh** (Gerry); Rory Calhoun (Cole); DeForest Kelley (Elgin); Paul Fix (Sheriff); Melanie Fullerton (Amanda).

Boardwalk (Atlantic, 1979). DIR Stephen Verona. PROD George Willoughby. SCR Stephen Verona, Leigh Chapman. CAM Billy Williams. RUNNING TIME 98 min. CAST: Ruth Gordon (Becky Rosen); Lee Strasberg (David Rosen); **Janet Leigh** (Florence); Joe Silver (Leo); Eli Mintz (Mr. Friedman); Eddie Barth (Eli).

The Fog (Avco Embassy, 1980). DIR-MUS John Carpenter. PROD Debra Hill. SCR John Carpenter, Debra Hill. CAM Dean Cundey. ED Tommy Wallace, Charles Bornstein. RUNNING TIME 91 min. CAST: Adrienne Barbeau (Stevie Wayne); Hal Holbrook (Father Malone); **Janet Leigh** (Kathy Williams); Jamie Lee Curtis (Elizabeth Solley); John Houseman (Machen); Tommy Atkins (Nick Castle).

Halloween H2O: Twenty Years Later (Miramax, 1998). DIR Steve Miner. PROD Paul Freeman. SCR Robert Zappia, Matt Greenberg (story by Robert Zappia). CAM Daryn Okada. ED Patrick Lussier. MUS John Ottman. RUNNING TIME 85 min. CAST: Jamie Lee Curtis (Laurie Strode/Keri Tate); Adam Arkin (Will Brennan); Michelle Williams (Molly); Adam Hann-Byrd (Charlie); Jodi Lyn O'Keefe (Sarah); **Janet Leigh** (Norma).

A Fate Totally Worse Than Death (2000). DIR John T. Kretchmer. PROD Bill Sheinberg, Jonathan Sheinberg, Sid Sheinberg. SCR Robert LoCash, Andrew Lane (novel by Paul Fleischman). MUS Suki Medencevic. ED Ross Albert. MUS Shawn K. Clement, Sean Murray. CAST: Julie Benz (Danielle); Nicole Bilderback (Tiffany); Monica Keena (Brooke); Suzanna Urszuly (Katarina); Jonathan Brandis (Drew); **Janet Leigh**.

Television Movies

The Monk (1969). DIR George McCowan. CAST: George Maharis; **Janet Leigh** (Janice Barns); Rick Jason; Carl Betz; Jack Albertson; Edward G. Robinson, Jr.

Honeymoon With a Stranger (1969). DIR John Peyser. CAST: **Janet Leigh** (Sandra Lathem); Rossano Brazzi; Joseph Lenzi; Cesare Danova.

Deadly Dream (1971). DIR Alf Kjellin. CAST: Lloyd Bridges; **Janet Leigh** (Laurel Hanley); Carl Betz; Leif Erickson; Don Stroud.

Murdock's Gang (1973). DIR Charles S. Dubin. CAST : Alex Dreier; **Janet Leigh** (Laura Talbot); Murray Hamilton; Frank Campanella.

Columbo: Forgotten Lady (1975). DIR Harvey Hart. CAST: Peter Falk; **Janet Leigh** (Grace Wheeler Willis); Sam Jaffe; John Payne.

Murder at the World Series (1977). DIR Andrew V. McLaglen. CAST: Linda Day George; Murray Hamilton; Karen Valentine; **Janet Leigh** (Karen Weese).

Telethon (1977). DIR David Lowell Rich. CAST: Lloyd Bridges; **Janet Leigh** (Elaine Cotton); Jill St. John; Polly Bergen; Sugar Ray Robinson.

Mirror, Mirror (1979). DIR Joanna Lee. CAST: **Janet Leigh** (Millie Gorman); Robert Vaughn; Loretta Swit; Chris Lemmon.

In My Sister's Shadow (1997). DIR Sandor Stern. CAST: **Janet Leigh** (Kay Connor); Nancy McKeon; Thomas McCarthy; Alexandra Wilson.

Literary Work

There Really Was a Hollywood (1984, autobiography)
Behind the Scenes of Psycho (1995)
House of Destiny (1995, novel)
The Dream Factory (2001, novel)

JOAN LESLIE

Remember the leading lady in those Warner Bros. classics *High Sierra*, *Sergeant York*, *The Hard Way*, *Yankee Doodle Dandy*, *Hollywood Canteen* and *Rhapsody in Blue*, all made in the early 1940s? It was Joan Leslie who played the female lead in all of them. The young audiences of today might perhaps not know who she is; after all, she hasn't made a film since 1956 (the last one was Raoul Walsh's *The Revolt of Mamie Stover* opposite Jane Russell and Richard Egan), when she virtually retired from the screen at age 31, but that doesn't mean she has vanished from the face of the earth.

To this day, Miss Leslie still resides in Hollywood and still keeps in touch with the film community, even though she does not participate in it anymore as a screen actress. Miss Leslie: "For many years now, I've been working for the Saint Anne's Maternity Home, located on the East Side of Los Angeles. I started there because my husband, who was an obstetrician, was a member of the voluntary medical staff. When we got married in 1950, he introduced me to Saint Anne's. I was very interested in it and they put me on the board of directors and the board of trustees. I also work with the fundraisers and get in touch with entertainers and stars.

"We have a lot of teenage girls there, 14, 15, 16 years old. They are pregnant, have nowhere to turn to and we spend a lot of money taking care of them. They don't know how to take care of a baby, they think it's going to be fun, they think it's going to be a doll they can play with, but they don't know how much they have to learn. You just can't wake up one morning and be a mother—that's what these girls need to learn. We have a lot of very good social workers, wonderful teachers and a very creative, loving atmosphere for these girls. We give them a lot of training as far as the baby is concerned; we also help them to learn a job so they can finish their schooling and work part-time. So it's a big assignment and that's why it is so interesting. It's a very handsome institution with a school next-door and it's very good to be a part of something like that."

Miss Leslie married Dr. William Caldwell in March 1950. "When I married, that would be the most important thing in my life. The only way to make a successful marriage, is to put it first, you have to *invest* yourself into marriage. And if it's with the right person, it's very much worth it. You have to close a door before you can open another one; sometimes it's hard to close that door. When you had a colorful life as an actress, it's not easy to say that, and to mean it as well: I *had* a very colorful life, there's nothing quite like it. But my husband was a doctor, that's a very engrossing field as well, a very meaningful part of life in the world today. I'm so proud of him and I respect him so much, and he respects me for what I have accomplished in my career. I stopped making films altogether when my two girls, my twins,

Joan Leslie

were born. When they went to school, I had a little bit more free time and I did some television and commercials and a picture now and then, but I'm saying *no* to everything now. Nobody is asking me to get back to work, and I don't think there's anything I'd really like to do. I've always liked to play a certain kind of part as I was a certain kind of person and I don't find that very much anymore. The business has changed so much."

And Miss Leslie (born Joan Agnes Theresa Sadie Brodel, on January 26, 1925, in Detroit, Michigan) knows what she's talking about; she made her professional stage debut at age nine with her two older sisters Mary[1] and Betty[2] as the Three Brodels. The trio specialized in singing, dancing, acrobatics, instrumental specialties (with Mary playing the saxophone, Betty at the piano and Joan playing the accordion) and impersonations (Joan did Garbo, Katharine Hepburn, Maurice Chevalier, ZaSu Pitts, Jimmy Durante and Luise Rainer).

They were so successful they toured Canada (Toronto, Montreal and Quebec) and the South, until an MGM talent scout spotted Joan when the girls played the Paradise Cafe in New York, and sent her and Mrs. Brodel to Hollywood. They signed her up for six months at $200 a week and she appeared in George Cukor's *Camille* (1937), opposite Greta Garbo and Robert Taylor. Miss Leslie: "Playing Robert Taylor's little sister in *Camille*—I was only 11—was a dream come true. I always wanted to be in pictures; I hoped to play Joan of Arc one day. It was remarkable the way MGM spent money to make it perfect. I was a minor, for the children they had a schoolhouse on the lot with a teacher under contract. I was in school with Mickey Rooney and Freddie Bartholomew.

"Costume designer Adrian had created two or three different costumes for me. I got to take home one of them and play around in, so that it looked as if it was played around in it. The idea was to show how Robert Taylor's family was strict and proper and yet, he was so in love with Camille. They wanted to show the contrast. In one scene, he was coming home to his country home and his little sister was supposed to make her first communion. I had a line to say, 'Oh Armand, Armand, so you did come all the way from Paris!' Well, I had a French coach to tell me how to say 'Armand,' and an English coach telling me how to say 'Paris'—I guess I said it with a Midwestern accent. That's the way MGM did things. I had been talking to Ann Rutherford, she was under contract for many years there, she always said, 'Oh, it was such fun!' But I never thought of it that way, it was work. She said, 'Well, we always had parties, all of us young people used to get together, the studio would provide us with buses and cars, we'd go to the beach and places like that!' MGM gave us the *deluxe* service. Cyd Charisse told me the other day she had a wonderful coach to help her with her Russian accent for her part of Ninotchka in *Silk Stockings*. Everybody got the best.

"After *Camille* I returned to New York and did modeling and a little radio work. My sister Mary was seen by a talent scout and was signed to a contract to come back here for Universal. She came out here, worked in a couple of pictures and kept telling Universal, 'You should have Joan here, because she would fit right into these Deanna Durbin pictures.' So finally she paved my way to come back out here, mother came with me and I started to get parts right away. I worked in all the different studios and when I did a part out at Warner Bros., they decided that I was contract material. They tested me for a contract, I sang and danced, did a couple of scenes and they signed me up. I was very happy about that. They said, 'We'll groom you and change your diction, so that you don't have a Midwestern accent anymore.' Within two weeks I was tested for *High Sierra*. It was a marvelous start for me."

To avoid confusion with Joan Blondell, her name was changed from Joan Brodel to Joan Leslie. At age 15 she played the part of the girl with a clubfoot in Raoul Walsh's *High Sierra*, opposite Humphrey Bogart[3] and Ida Lupino.[4] Miss Leslie: "My career really got started with *High Sierra*. He played this criminal in hiding, I was the crippled girl. He just meets me by accident and is very taken with me obviously and wants the operation done to fix my foot. That was such a good role—and I was only 15! I wish I had more such roles when I was older, I could have done more with them. Perhaps I was too young at that time to realize how precious such roles were, but I was lucky to just get through it."

From then on, it all went very fast. A week after finishing *High Sierra*, she enrolled in *The Wagons Roll at Night* (again opposite Bogart), then after a few days' rest she was cast in *The Great Mr. Nobody*. The day she finished that picture, she started a short, *Alice in Movieland*, and while she was doing that, she began working on *Sergeant York*, playing Gary Cooper's girlfriend.

In between there was no time to lose, as she had to rehearse, fit new costumes, do dialogue tests, get ready for new sets of still pictures and go to school every day. The board of education insisted she got a minimum of three hours' schooling a day, so when she was through with a scene, she rushed to her dressing room to get ready for her lessons with her teacher. Miss Leslie: "Jimmy Cagney did a lot of rewriting on the script of *Yankee Doodle Dandy* because he knew a lot about his character George M. Cohan. Whenever he made a suggestion, director Michael Curtiz said, 'Oh, that's good Jimmy, we'll use that.' After they had changed something here and there and I came back from school, it was always a little better. I would never be included in these discussions. They always made those changes when I was at school. So when I got back, they'd say, 'Joan, here is the script and this is what we're going to do.' So we always could keep on working."

She played the female leads opposite Gary Cooper in *Sergeant York* (1941) and James Cagney in *Yankee Doodle Dandy* (1942); both actors won Academy Awards as best actor for their roles. Miss Leslie: "I was never nominated but I don't feel I did anything up that caliber. And although Warner Bros. certainly had plans with me, times were changing. Television was coming in, that was a *big* threat." After *High Sierra* she was reunited with Ida Lupino in Vincent Sherman's fascinating *The Hard Way* (1942), telling the gripping story of Miss Lupino who pushes her younger sister (Leslie) in a show business career.

In the meantime, in the midst of World War II, Hollywood (and especially Warner Bros.) was almost working full-time to help and contribute to the home front and the war front, donating money to the Army Emergency Relief Fund, the Hollywood Canteen, etc. Michael Curtiz's musical *This Is the Army* (1943) was instrumental in promoting the cause to the audience to buy war bonds, as were two other Joan Leslie pictures, *Thank Your Lucky Stars* (1943, a star-studded musical with virtually all the stars and contract players on the Warner lot—

Joan Leslie and Humphrey Bogart in *High Sierra* (1941).

with Bette Davis singing "They're Either Too Young or Too Old") and *The Hollywood Canteen* (1944, based on the same idea as *Thank Your Lucky Stars*), another all-star picture, written and directed by Delmer Daves—he had also written the script for *Stage Door Canteen* (1943), a similar all-star extravaganza, this time set in New York's USO center.

The actual Hollywood Canteen[5] was a hugely popular place where movie stars would entertain the 'boys,' the men in uniform. The idea was conceived by Bette Davis[6] and John Garfield[7]

Joan Leslie

Bette Davis in *Thank Your Lucky Stars* (1943). She co-chaired the Hollywood Canteen with John Garfield.

and it was supported by the entire film industry. Miss Leslie: "I worked at the Hollywood Canteen every Tuesday. Every studio had one night of the week, Warner Bros. took Tuesdays. Bette Davis was very often down there, you saw Bob Hope, Bing Crosby, Marlene Dietrich, they all dropped in, they did their act and they'd sit around and talk with the boys. We'd pass out sandwiches, bring coffee, do the dishes or sometimes just talk. Quite often, we danced with the soldiers. When I was working on *Rhapsody in Blue*, I had some very dramatic hairdos with upswing, going against the way my hair was done usually, and I was dancing once with a boy who'd spin me across the floor. We were having a wonderful time until the pins started to come out, they dropped all over the floor and my hair was coming down [laughs]. We had a lot of fun, the boys laughed, they scattered all around to pick up the hair pins and help to put myself together again. My sisters would come with me, they helped to entertain, it was an all-out effort. We were proud and very happy to do that."

Was the atmosphere the same as in the film *Hollywood Canteen*? "I think better, although I don't remember exactly how it was in the picture. It was not a fancy room, it was just a café made over, a very plain structure. Sometimes the boys would be lined up for blocks. Then they made an announcement, 'You guys have all been in here an hour and a half now, so you go on out the back door cause we have to bring in some more fellows tonight'—or something like that. It also happened that I was asked to come over on other nights if they didn't have enough girls, or to have some pictures taken, or for autographs. Bette was very persuasive, she got Warner Bros. to donate a lot of money to the canteen, including from the premieres of films. She was *the* driving force behind it she co-chaired it together with John Garfield."

John Garfield

The film *The Hollywood Canteen* had an impressive cast with a lot of stars playing themselves or appearing in cameos and walk-ons. The storyline of the film begins when Robert Hutton, as a G.I., is on sick leave and can spend a few nights at the canteen before returning to active duty. When he enters, he happens to be the millionth guest to enjoy the hospitality of the canteen, earning him a prize. Miss Leslie: "He could have anything that he possibly wanted in Hollywood. In the plot he only wants a date with Joan Leslie and so, there's a scene when Bette calls me on the phone and says, 'Joan, will you come down to the canteen, I've got a special favor to ask you.' So I come over and she says, 'Joan, I'm so glad you could come, there's a boy here, he's the millionth guest of the canteen and he could have anything he wants, but all he wants is a date with you. Will you do it?' That was her line, and I was supposed to say, 'Oh sure, where is he? What are we going to do,' and things like that. But she was having trouble concentrating, she was also working on another picture with a very dramatic and demanding role. At one point, she said, 'Oh, cut! This is terrible. I just can't play myself, I don't know how, I can't be natural playing myself! But if you give me a cigarette or a drink or a gun, I'll play anything you want me to!' [laughs]. She had a great sense of humor—even about herself."

In all of her films at Warner Bros., Miss Leslie had prestigious leading men and co-stars, like Bogart, Cagney, Cooper, Henry Fonda, Olivia de Havilland and Fred Astaire (she was his youngest co-star ever, celebrating her 18th birthday with him on the set of *The Sky's the Limit*). Miss Leslie: "In most cases people were very supportive and the directors were very good. But I was so much younger than everybody that I didn't have the advantage of feeling like a *chum*. As I look back, it amazes me that neither was I in awe; I never said, 'I can't do this because this person is so famous and so wonderful, I'll be scared to death.' No, once I got up there and did the scene, I had every right to be there and I had to do the best I could because they were doing the best they could too. When you talk about working with the best, I'll always remember Jimmy Cagney. What a creative, dynamic person he was.

"Howard Hawks,[8] who directed *Sergeant York*, was very good. He had ways of telling you how to sit, how to look, what you should be emphasizing; we rehearsed and rehearsed, until we said, 'Don't you think we should start making some takes?' I think the production department must have gone mad, because if you didn't have a take already *in the can* as they say, by 9:15, they'd say, 'Well, what's wrong? What's holding you up?' But nobody could say that to Howard Hawks; if he didn't want to shoot anything till the afternoon, that would be fine. Cooper would do anything Hawks said, but he knew his craft and his capabilities too.

"Working with Michael Curtiz on *Yankee Doodle Dandy* was really wonderful, he was so happy with everything. With Jimmy Cagney and the whole creative atmosphere, that made it very easy. *This Is the Army* however, that was a terror; the script was non-existent, it was just a little plot thrown together to keep the musical numbers in a sort of a routine, and even though he had character actors like George Murphy and Ronald Reagan, it was very shallow. He was yelling and screaming at everyone, very critical and very tough on everybody."

Miss Leslie also appeared in *Rhapsody in Blue* (1945), the biography of George Gershwin, and in Busby Berkeley's *Cinderella Jones* (1946), both with Robert Alda. "By then television was coming in and they started to make a lot of lesser budget films and I was very unhappy with that. The last couple of pictures I had made, like *Cinderella Jones*, were terrible. I know Robert Alda didn't like it, but Busby Berkeley was directing it and there we were—all under contract. It's a big decision to say *no* to a big studio. But as TV was there already, they didn't know what to do, they didn't know what was coming next. Television in your home would be very attractive competition, so they had either to make the pictures cheaper, or make them better, something they never had to think of before. In the end, they adjusted, of course.

"Sometimes they'd tear up your contract and give you better terms, but they still had all the right to say, 'You're through, and we have no obligation to you and you are out there in the cold.' So I decided to sue Warner Bros. for freedom from my contract. The main reason why I did this, was that I wanted to have a say about the roles I had. It was a very risky thing to do and I don't think I would do it again, because there are other ways to fight their power and their strength over you. But it was a sad time: I did alienate myself, I *had* to alienate myself from everyone at Warner Bros. I was not supposed to contact anybody, cause I was suing them on a basis that a contract you sign when you are a minor, needs to be reaffirmed when you become a major at 21. Maybe you don't want to be under contract anymore, maybe someone talked you into it as a minor—that's the premise. Of course, I was happy to be under contract, but nevertheless, under some circumstances I should have had the right to reconsider at 21.

"However, they had a whole body of attorneys and they won a round, then I'd appeal and I won a round, and then finally it went to the District Court of Appeal and they won the decision 5 to 4. This decision was made on the basis that most contracts that are signed with a minor, can be re-examined when you become 21, except in three categories: if you are an actor/actress, a jockey or a prize-fighter [laughs]."

After appearing in such films as *Janie Gets Married* (1946, a sequel to *Janie* made two years before with Joyce Reynolds in the title role) and *Two Guys from Milwaukee* (1946, with Humphrey Bogart and Lauren Bacall in cameos), her last films for Warner Bros., Miss Leslie ranked number one in the "Future Star" poll of motion picture exhibitors (Yvonne De Carlo was number nine, Robert Mitchum ranked number ten). The future was bright indeed as she started working for various studios on a free-lance basis. In *Repeat Performance* (1947), her first picture since leaving Warner Bros., she was given the powerful role of a Broadway star who, on New Year's Eve, gets the chance to relive the past year, which leads up to the moment when she kills her husband, and in Nicholas Ray's *Born to Be Bad* (1950), Joan Fontaine played an unscrupulous woman who got what she wanted by manipulating everyone, including Miss Leslie.

She also appeared in such films as *Man in the Saddle* (1951) opposite Randolph Scott, as well as two films directed by pioneer and veteran Allan Dwan, *The Woman They Almost Lynched* (1953) and *Flight Nurse* (1954), followed by *Jubilee Trail* (1954) and *Hell's Outpost* (1954). As their titles indicate, these films, mostly made at Republic, were less rewarding than the films she was involved in in the 1940s; Miss Leslie found it difficult to get leading roles in first-rate pictures and years later, she speculated that the "gentleman's agreement" among the industry's executives that prevented her from working at other studios during and after the trial, definitely had its effect. They were made to think that she would be "difficult to work with ... a troublemaker." It took a while to overcome this.

It might not have made a difference in the end. After her marriage to Dr. Caldwell in 1950 and the birth of their twin daughters, she had other goals in her life: instead of being a screen actress, she intended to be a full-time mother for her children. She did make occasional appearances in TV series and commercials, but there were never any plans to make a comeback.

"I'm in the process now of refiling all my career scripts and contracts and as I look over all the stills I've got, I feel I could have done a little bit more, maybe I could have gotten around to playing Joan of Arc [laughs], but I'm really happy where I am now. It's a very tough business, *very* competitive. I certainly wasn't aware of that when I started at Warner Bros. at age 15. People were very nice to me. I honestly think if they didn't handle me carefully, I might have burst into tears, or run off the set or something because I was so young. They were getting the quality from me that they wanted: the young, innocent and sweet girl-next-door. It was during the war and that's what they wanted to project on the screen. Sometimes they refer to me as 'the ever sweet Joan Leslie,' which of course I don't particularly like, I was merely being myself in the 1940s, that's what it really was. It's a little too sweet for now, that's for sure [laughs]. But it's what the studio wanted then."

How would Miss Leslie like to be remembered in film encyclopedias? Certainly more than just "sweet"? "Well, I hope so. Vincent Sherman once told me, 'You had so much talent, you've been so surprising to me that at your age, you could do what you did.' Perhaps my career wasn't handled quite right or in a way that it could flower as it might have, but I couldn't wish any more than that, I'm a very modest person. I saw *Born to Be Bad* the other day and I liked it very much, it's the kind of thing I should have done more. I was beginning to look more like a secure, mature American girl, and not just the little girl-next-door, but one who could handle a profession, a romantic entanglement and make it interesting too. I was never given anything like that to do at Warner Bros."

Nevertheless, she left a legacy of more than 40 films, achieved stardom as a youngster, was equally at ease in dramatic and musical settings and, what's perhaps most important of all, has had a fascinating and full life *after* films. For a richly detailed look at her career, there is now the Joan Leslie Homepage, created by Kerry Kaneshiro, a graduate student at the University of California at Santa Barbara (www.picturegoer.com).

Interview: Hollywood, April 16, 1999

Notes

1. Mary Brodel (b. 1919) appeared in such films as *Reckless Living* (1938), *Men with Wings* (1938), *I Am the Law* (1938), *The Story of Vernon and Irene Castle* (1939), *Star Dust* (1940, with Joan Leslie), *The Bride Came C.O.D.* (1941), *One Foot in Heaven* (1941), *The Sunset Murder Case* (1941), *Million Dollar Baby* (1941), *Always in My Heart* (1942) and *Arsenic and Old Lace* (1944).

2. Betty Brodel (b. 1921) played small parts in *Hollywood Canteen* (1944), *Ladies Courageous* (1944), *Too Young to Know* (1945) and *Cinderella Jones* (1946).

3. Humphrey Bogart (1899–1957), a.k.a. "Bogey," who debuted on the screen in 1930, became one of the screen's most talented and beloved stars. He often portrayed hard-bitten, cynical, sarcastic and lonely characters and was known to be tough, both on and off screen—James Cagney once described him as a "Scotch and Soda athlete." His films include *The Petrified Forest* (1936), *Angels with Dirty Faces* (1938), *The Roaring Twenties* (1939), *High Sierra* (1941), *The Maltese Falcon* (1941), *Casablanca* (1943, Academy Award nomination for best actor), *To Have and Have Not* (1944), *The Big Sleep* (1946), *The Treasure of the Sierra Madre* (1948), *Key Largo* (1948), *The African Queen* (1951, Academy Award for best actor); *The Caine Mutiny* (1954, Academy Award nomination for best actor), *Sabrina* (1954), *The Barefoot Contessa* (1954) and *The Harder They Fall* (1956). His fourth wife (from 1945) was actress Lauren Bacall.

4. Ida Lupino (1918–1995), leading film actress, director, producer and screenwriter, was born in London as the daughter of actress Connie Emerald and comedian Stanley Lupino (1893–1942, brother of actor Barry Lupino [1884–1962], cousin of actors Lupino Lane [1892–1959] and Wallace Lupino [1897–1961]). She was discovered by veteran director Allan Dwan (1885–1981) when he was making a British film, *Her First Affair* (1933). The following year she went to Hollywood and appeared in such films as *Peter Ibbetson* (1935) and *The Adventures of Sherlock Holmes* (1939), but her biggest career break came when she was signed at Warner Bros., resulting in a succession of interesting roles in such films as *High Sierra* (1941), *Ladies in Retirement* (1941) and *The Hard Way* (1943). As a director she triumphed with *The Hitch-Hiker* (1953, also scr.) and *The Bigamist* (1955, also act.—the only time she directed herself), both with Edmond O'Brien in the lead.

5. The Hollywood Canteen, back then located in Hollywood at North Cahuenga Boulevard, just south of Sunset Boulevard, was demolished in 1966.

6. Bette Davis (1908–1989), prominent leading star who spent most of her career at Warner Bros. (1932–49; at the height of her popularity, she was called the "fourth Warner Brother"), though she had the reputation of being difficult because of her frequent disagreements with Jack L. Warner concerning her scripts, directors and co-stars. Films include *Dangerous* (1935, Academy Award for best actress), *The Petrified Forest* (1936), *Jezebel* (1938, Academy Award for best actress), *The Private Lives of Elizabeth and Essex* (1939), *The Letter* (1940), *Now, Voyager* (1942), *Mr. Skeffington* (1944), *All About Eve* (1950), *Whatever Happened to Baby Jane?* (1962), *Hush ... Hush, Sweet Charlotte* (1965). She was at her best playing outspoken, ambitious and selfish characters. Nominated ten times for an Academy Award, she died of cancer at a Paris hospital en route from a tribute in San Sebastian (Spain) to her West Hollywood home. She published her autobiography, *The Lonely Life*, in 1962, followed by a second volume, *This 'n' That*, in 1987.

7. John Garfield (1913–1952), leading actor of the 1940s who's mentor was playwright Clifford Odets (more information: interview with Luise Rainer, note 2) and who always thought himself to be a "theater actor who went to Hollywood," was twice nominated for an Academy Award for his performances in *Four Daughters* (1938) and *Body and Soul* (1947), and also appeared in *Saturday's Children* (1940), *The Sea Wolf* (1941), *Tortilla Flat* (1942), *Destination Tokyo* (1944), *The Postman Always Rings Twice* (1946, opposite Lana Turner), *Gentleman's Agreement* (1947) and John Huston's *We Were Strangers* (1949). He died in New York at age 39 of a heart attack. In his final years he was accused of being sympathetic to left-wing causes. When he refused to give names before the HUAC, he was constantly harassed by the government. His son John Garfield, Jr. (1943–1994), appeared in films during the 1960s and 1970s and became an editor in the 1980s. Daughter Julie Garfield (b. 1946) is a screen actress.

8. Howard Hawks (1896–1977), film director, producer and screenwriter, made films in nearly every genre and directed the biggest stars in some of their best films. His output includes *Bringing Up Baby* (1938), *Only Angels Have Wings* (1939), *His Girl Friday* (1940), *Sergeant York* (1941, Academy Award nomination for best direc-

tor), *To Have and Have Not* (1944), *The Big Sleep* (1946), *Red River* (1948), *Monkey Business* (1952), *Gentlemen Prefer Blondes* (1953), *Rio Bravo* (1959) and *Hatari!* (1962). In 1974 he received an honorary Academy Award with the inscription "Howard Hawks—A Master American filmmaker whose creative efforts hold a distinguished place in world cinema."

Filmography

As Joan Brodel

Camille (MGM, 1937). DIR George Cukor. SCR Zoë Akins, Frances Marion, James Hilton (novel by Alexandre Dumas). CAM William Daniels, Karl Freund. ED Margaret Booth. MUS Herbert Stothart. RUNNING TIME 108 min. CAST: Greta Garbo (Marguerite Gautier); Robert Taylor (Armand Duval); Lionel Barrymore (Monsieur Duval); Elizabeth Allan (Nichette); Jessie Ralph (Nanine); **Joan Brodel** (Marie Jeanette).

Men With Wings (Paramount, 1938). DIR-PROD William A. Wellman. SCR Robert Carson. CAM W. Howard Greene. ED Thomas Scott. MUS Boris Morros. RUNNING TIME 102 min. CAST: Fred MacMurray (Patrick Falconer); Ray Milland (Scott Barnes); Louise Campbell (Peggy Ranson); Andy Devine (Joe Gibbs); Lynne Overman (Hank Rinebow); Porter Hall (Hiram F. Jenkins); **Joan Brodel** (Patricia, age 11).

Nancy Drew, Reporter (Warner Bros., 1939). DIR William Clemens. SCR Kenneth Gamet. CAM Arthur Edeson. ED Frank Dewar. MUS Heinz Roemheld. RUNNING TIME 65 min. CAST: Bonita Granville (Nancy Drew); John Litel (Carson Drew); Frank Thomas, Jr. (Ted Nickerson); Mary Lee (Mary); Dickie Jones (Killer Parkins); **Joan Brodel** (Mayme).

Love Affair (RKO, 1939). DIR Leo McCarey. SCR Delmer Daves, Donald Ogden Stewart (story by Leo McCarey, Mildred Cram). CAM Rudolph Maté. ED Edward Dmytryk, George Hively. MUS Roy Webb. RUNNING TIME 87 min. CAST: Irene Dunne (Terry McKay); Charles Boyer (Michel Marnet); Maria Ouspenskaya (Grandmother); Lee Bowman (Kenneth Bradley); Astrid Allwyn (Lois Clarke); **Joan Brodel** (Autograph Seeker).

Winter Carnival (United Artists, 1939). DIR Charles F. Riesner. SCR Lester Cole, Budd Schulberg, Maurice Rapf (story by Corey Ford). CAM Merritt Gerstad. ED Otho Lovering, Dorothy Spencer. MUS Werner Janssen. RUNNING TIME 100 min. CAST: Ann Sheridan (Jill Baxter); Richard Carlson (Prof. Weldon); Helen Parrish (Ann Baxter); James Corner (Mickey Allen); Alan Baldwin (Don Reynolds); **Joan Brodel** (Betsy Philips).

Two Thoroughbreds (RKO, 1939). DIR Jack Hively. PROD Cliff Reid. SCR Joseph A. Fields, Jerry Cady (story by Joseph A. Fields). CAM Frank L. Redman. ED Theron Warth. MUS Roy Webb. RUNNING TIME 62 min. CAST: Jimmy Lydon (David Carey); **Joan Brodel** (Wendy Conway); Arthur Hohl (Thad); J. M. Kerrigan (Jack Lenihan); Marjorie Main (Hildegarde); Selmer Jackson (Bill Conway).

High School (20th Century Fox, 1940). DIR George Nichols, Jr. SCR Jack Jungmeyer, Edith Skouras, Harold Tarshis. CAM Lucien Androit. ED Harry Reynolds. MUS Samuel Kaylin. RUNNING TIME 74 min. CAST: Jane Withers (Jane Wallace); Joe E. Brown ("Slats" Roberts); Lloyd Corrigan (Henry Wallace); Claire Du Brey (Miss Huggins); Lynne Roberts (Carol Roberts); **Joan Brodel** (Patsy).

Young as You Feel (20th Century Fox, 1940). DIR Malcolm St. Clair. SCR Joseph Hoffman, Stanley Rauh (play by Lewis Beach). CAM Charles Clarke. ED Harry Reynolds. MUS Samuel Kaylin. RUNNING TIME 60 min. CAST: Jed Prouty (John Jones); Spring Byington (Mrs. John Jones); Joan Valerie (Bonnie); Russell Gleason (Herbert Thompson); Ken Howell (Jack Jones); **Joan Brodel**.

Star Dust (20th Century Fox, 1940). DIR Walter Lang. SCR Robert Ellis, Helen Logan (story by Jesse Malo, Keneth Earl, Ivan Kahn). CAM Peverell Marley. ED Robert Simpson. MUS David Buttolph. RUNNING TIME 84 min. CAST: Linda Darnell (Carolyn Sayres); John Payne (Bud Borden); Roland Young (Thomas Brooke); Charlotte Greenwood (Lola); William Gargan (Dane Wharton); Mary Brodel, **Joan Brodel** (College Girls).

Military Academy (Columbia, 1940). DIR D. Ross Lederman. PROD Wallace MacDonald. SCR Karl Brown, David Silverstein (story by Richard English). CAM Allen G. Siegler. ED Gene Milford. RUNNING TIME 65 min. CAST: Tommy Kelly (Tommy Lewis); Bobby Jordan (Dick Hill); David Holt (Sandy Blake); Jackie Searl (Prentiss Dover); Don Beddoe (Marty Lewis); **Joan Brodel** (Marjorie Blake).

Foreign Correspondent (United Artists, 1940). DIR Alfred Hitchcock. SCR Joan Harrison, Charles Bennett. CAM Rudolph Maté. ED Dorothy Spencer. MUS Alfred Newman. RUNNING TIME 119 min. CAST: Joel McCrea (Jones/Haverstock); Laraine Day (Carol Fisher); Herbert Marshall (Stephen Fisher); George Sanders (Herbert); Albert Basserman (Van Meer); **Joan Brodel** (Jones's sister).

Laddie (RKO, 1940). DIR Jack Hively. PROD Cliff Reid. SCR Bert Granet, Jerry Cady (novel by Gene Stratton-Porter). CAM Harry Wild. ED George Hively. MUS Roy Webb. RUNNING TIME 70 min. CAST: Tim Holt (Laddie Stanton); Virginia Gilmore (Pamela Pryor); Joan Carroll (Sister Stanton); Spring Byington (Mrs. Stanton); Robert Barrat (Mr. Stanton); **Joan Brodel** (Shelley Stanton).

As Joan Leslie

High Sierra (Warner Bros., 1941). DIR Raoul Walsh. SCR John Huston, W. R. Burnett (novel by W. R. Burnett). CAM Tony Gaudio. ED Jack Killifer. MUS Arthur Lange. RUNNING TIME 100 min. CAST: Ida Lupino (Marie Garson); Humphrey Bogart (Roy Earle); Alan Curtis (Babe Kozak); Arthur Kennedy (Red Hattery); **Joan Leslie** (Velma); Henry Hull (Doc Banton).

The Great Mr. Nobody (Warner Bros., 1941). DIR Ben Stoloff. SCR Ben Markson, Kenneth Gamet (story by Harold Titus). CAM Arthur Todd. ED Rudi Fehr. MUS Adolph Deutsch. RUNNING TIME 71 min. CAST: Eddie Albert (Dreamy); **Joan Leslie** (Mary); Alan Hale (Skipper); William Lundigan (Amesworth); John Titel (Wade); Charles Trowbridge (Dillon).

The Wagons Roll at Night (Warner Bros., 1941). DIR Ray Enright. SCR Barry Trivers, Fred Niblo, Jr. (novel by Francis Wallace). CAM Sid Hickox. ED Frederick Richards. MUS Heinz Roemheld. RUNNING TIME 84 min. CAST: Humphrey Bogart (Nick Coster); Sylvia Sidney (Flo Lorraine); Eddie Albert (Matt Varney); **Joan Leslie** (Mary Coster); Sig Rumann (Hoffman the Great); Cliff Clark (Doc).

Thieves Fall Out (Warner Bros., 1941). DIR Ray Enright. SCR Charles Grayson, Ben Markson (play by Irving Gaumont, Jack Sobel). CAM Sid Hickox. ED Clarence Kolster. MUS Heinz Roemheld. RUNNING TIME 72 min. CAST: Eddie Albert (Eddie Barnes); **Joan Leslie** (Mary Matthews); Jane Darwell (Grandma Allen); Alan Hale (Robert Barnes); William T. Orr (George Formsby); John Litel (Tim Gordon).

Sergeant York (Warner Bros., 1941). DIR Howard Hawks. PROD Jesse L. Lasky, Hal B. Wallis. SCR Abem Finkel, Harry Chandlee, Howard Koch, John Huston. CAM Sol Polito. ED William Holmes. MUS Max Steiner. RUNNING TIME 134 min. CAST: Gary Cooper (Alvin C. York); Walter Brennan (Pastor Rosier Pile); **Joan Leslie** (Gracie Williams); George Tobias (Michael T. Ross); Stanley Ridges (Major Buxton); Margaret Wycherly (Mother York).

The Male Animal (Warner Bros., 1942). DIR Elliott Nugent. PROD Hal B. Wallis. SCR Julius J. Epstein, Philip G. Epstein (play by Elliott Nugent, James Thurber). CAM Arthur Edeson. ED Thomas Richards. MUS Heinz Roemheld. RUNNING TIME 126 min. CAST: Henry Fonda (Tommy Turner); Olivia de Havilland (Ellen Turner); Jack Carson (Joe Ferguson); **Joan Leslie** (Patricia Stanley); Eugene Pallette (Ed Keller); Herbert Anderson (Michael Barnes).

Yankee Doodle Dandy (Warner Bros., 1942). DIR Michael Curtiz. PROD Jack L. Warner. SCR Robert Buckner, Edmund Joseph (story by Robert Buckner). CAM James Wong Howe. ED George Amy. MUS Leo F. Forbstein. RUNNING TIME 126 min. CAST: James Cagney (George M. Cohan); **Joan Leslie** (Mary); Walter Huston (Jerry Cohan); Richard Whorf (Sam Harris); George Tobias (Dietz); Irene Manning (Fay Templeton).

The Hard Way (Warner Bros., 1942). DIR Vincent Sherman. PROD Jerry Wald. SCR Daniel Fuchs, Peter Viertel. CAM James Wong Howe. ED Don Siegel. MUS Heinz Roemheld. RUNNING TIME 108 min. CAST: Ida Lupino (Helen Chernen); **Joan Leslie** (Katherine Chernen); Dennis Morgan (Paul Collins); Jack Carson (Albert Runkel); Gladys George (Lily Emery); Faye Emerson (Waitress).

This Is the Army (Warner Bros., 1943). DIR Michael Curtiz. PROD Jack L. Warner, Hal B. Wallis. SCR Casey Robinson, Capt. Claude Binyon. CAM Bert Glennon. ED George Amy. MUS Irving Berlin. RUNNING TIME 120 min. CAST: George Murphy (Jerry Jones); **Joan Leslie** (Eileen Dibble); George Tobias (Maxie); Alan Hale (Sgt. McGhee); Charles Butterworth (Eddie Dibble); Dolores Costello (Mrs. Davidson).

Thank Your Lucky Stars (Warner Bros., 1943). DIR David Butler. PROD Mark Hellinger. SCR Norman Panama, Melvin Frank, James V. Kern (story by Everett Freeman, Arthur Schwartz). CAM Arthur Edeson. ED Irene Morra. MUS Heinz Roemheld. RUNNING TIME 127 min. CAST: **Joan Leslie** (Pat Dixton); Humphrey Bogart (Himself); Eddie Cantor (Himself); Bette Davis (Herself); Olivia de Havilland (Herself); Errol Flynn (Himself); John Garfield (Himself); Ida Lupino (Herself).

The Sky's the Limit (RKO, 1943). DIR Edward H. Griffith. PROD David Hempstead. SCR Frank Fenton, Lynn Root. CAM Russell Metty. ED Roland Gross. MUS Leigh Harline. RUNNING TIME 90 min. CAST: Fred Astaire (Fred Atwell); **Joan Leslie** (Joan Manion); Robert Benchley (Phil Harriman); Robert Ryan (Reginald Fenton); Elizabeth Patterson (Mrs. Fisher); Marjorie Gateson (Canteen Hostess).

Hollywood Canteen (Warner Bros., 1944). DIR-SCR Delmer Daves. PROD Walter Gottlieb. CAM Bert Glennon. ED Christian Nyby. MUS Leo F. Forbstein. RUNNING TIME 124 min. CAST: Robert Hutton (Ed "Slim" Green); **Joan Leslie** (Herself); Dane Clark (Sgt. Nowland); Janis Paige (Angela).

Where Do We Go from Here? (20th Century Fox, 1945). DIR Gregory Ratoff. PROD William Perlberg. SCR Morrie Ryskind (story by Morrie Ryskind, Sig Hersig). CAM Leon Shamroy. ED J. Watson Webb. MUS David Raskin. RUNNING TIME 77 min. CAST: Fred MacMurray (Bill); **Joan Leslie** (Sally); June Haver (Lucille); Gene Sheldon (Genie); Anthony Quinn (Indian Chief); Carlos Ramirez (Benito).

Rhapsody in Blue (Warner Bros., 1945). DIR Irving Rapper. PROD Jesse L. Lasky. SCR Howard Koch, Elliot Paul (story by Sonya Levien). CAM Sol Polito, Merritt Gerstad, Ernest Haller, James Leicester, Roy Davidson, Willard Van Enger. ED Folmer Blangsted. MUS George Gershwin. RUNNING TIME 130 min. CAST: Robert

Alda (George Gershwin); **Joan Leslie** (Julie Adams); Alexis Smith (Christine Gilbert); Charles Coburn (Max Dreyfus); Julie Bishop (Lee Gershwin); Albert Basserman (Professor Frank).

Too Young to Know (Warner Bros., 1945). DIR Frederick De Cordova. PROD William Jacobs. SCR Joe Pagano (story by Harlan Ware). CAM Carl Guthrie. ED Folmer Blangsted. MUS H. Roemheld. RUNNING TIME 86 min. CAST: **Joan Leslie** (Sally Sawyer); Robert Hutton (Ira Enright); Dolores Moran (Patsy O'Brien); Harry Davenport (Judge Boller); Rosemary De Camp (Mrs. Enright); Barbara Brown (Mrs. Wellman).

Cinderella Jones (Warner Bros., 1946). DIR Busby Berkeley. PROD Alex Gottlieb. SCR Charles Hoffman (story by Philip Wylle). CAM Sol Polito. ED George Amy. MUS Frederick Hollander. RUNNING TIME 90 min. CAST: **Joan Leslie** (Judy Jones); Robert Alda (Tommy Coles); S. Z. Sakall (Gabriel Popik); Edward Everett Horton (Keating); Julie Bishop (Camille); William Prince (Bart Williams).

Janie Gets Married (Warner Bros., 1946). DIR Vincent Sherman. PROD Alex Gottlieb. SCR Agnes Christine Johnston (characters created by Josephine Bentham, Herschel V. Williams, Jr. in the stage play *Janie*). CAM Carl Guthrie. ED Christian Nyby. MUS Frederick Hollander. RUNNING TIME 89 min. CAST: **Joan Leslie** (Janie); Robert Hutton (Dick); Edward Arnold (Mr. Conway); Ann Harding (Mrs. Conway); Dorothy Malone (Spud); Hattie McDaniel (April).

Two Guys from Milwaukee (Warner Bros., 1946). DIR David Butler. PROD Alex Gottlieb. SCR Charles Hoffman, I. A. L. Diamond. CAM Arthur Edeson. ED Irene Morra. MUS Leonid Raab. RUNNING TIME 90 min. CAST: Dennis Morgan (Prince Henry); Jack Carson (Buzz Williams); **Joan Leslie** (Connie Reed); Janis Paige (Polly); S. Z. Sakall (Count Oswald); Lauren Bacall (Herself); Humphrey Bogart (Himself).

Repeat Performance (Eagle Lion, 1947). DIR Alfred Werker. PROD Aubrey Schenck. SCR Walter Bullock (novel by William O'Farrell). CAM Lew W. O'Connell. ED Louis H. Sackin. MUS George Antheil. RUNNING TIME 91 min. CAST: Louis Hayward (Barney Page); **Joan Leslie** (Sheila Page); Richard Basehart (William Williams); Virginia Field (Paula Costello); Tom Conway (John Friday); Natalie Schafer (Eloise Shaw).

Northwest Stampede (Eagle Lion, 1948). DIR-PROD Albert S. Rogell. SCR Art Arthur, Lillie Hayward (also story, suggested by *Wild Horse Roundup* by Jean Muir). CAM John W. Boyle. ED Philip Cahn. MUS Paul Sawtell. RUNNING TIME 79 min. CAST: **Joan Leslie** (Chris Johnson); James Craig (Dan Bennett); Jack Oakie (Mike Kirby); Chill Wills (Mileaway); Victor Kilian (Mel Saunders); Stanley Andrews (Bowles).

The Skipper Surprised His Wife (MGM, 1950). DIR Elliott Nugent. PROD William H. Wright. SCR Dorothy Kingsley (based on an article by Commander W. J. Lederer). CAM Harold Lipstein. ED Irvine Warburton. MUS Bronislau Kaper. RUNNING TIME 85 min. CAST: Robert Walker (Comm. W. Lattimer); **Joan Leslie** (Daphne Lattimer); Edward Arnold (Adm. H. Thorndyke); Spring Byington (Agnes Thorndyke); Leon Ames (Dr. Philip Abbott); Jan Sterling (Rita Rossini).

Born to Be Bad (RKO, 1950). DIR Nicholas Ray. PROD Robert Sparks. SCR Edith Sommer (novel by Anne Parrish). CAM Nicholas Musuraca. ED Frederic Knudtson. MUS Frederick Hollander. RUNNING TIME 93 min. CAST: Joan Fontaine (Christabel); Robert Ryan (Nick); Zachary Scott (Curtis); **Joan Leslie** (Donna); Mel Ferrer (Gobby); Harold Vermilyea (John Caine).

Man in the Saddle (Columbia, 1951). DIR-PROD William Berke. SCR Richard Landau, Dwight Babcock (story by Rupert Hughes). CAM Jack Greenhalgh. ED Phil Cahn. MUS Darrell Calker. RUNNING TIME 74 min. CAST: Randolph Scott (Owen Merritt); **Joan Leslie** (Laure Bidwell); Ellen Drew (Nan Melotte); Alexander Knox (Will Isham); Richard Rober (Fay Dutcher); John Russell (Hugh Clagg).

Hellgate (Lippert Pictures, 1952). DIR Charles Marquis Warren. PROD John C. Champion. SCR Charles Marquis Warren (story by Charles Marquis Warren, John C. Champion). CAM Ernest W. Miller. ED Elmo Williams. MUS Paul Dunlap. RUNNING TIME 87 min. CAST: Sterling Hayden (Gil Hanley); **Joan Leslie** (Ellen Hanley); Ward Bond (Lt. Tod Vorhees); Jim Arness (George Redfield); Marshall Bradford (Doctor Pelham); Peter Coe (Jumper Hall).

The Toughest Man in Arizona (Republic, 1952). DIR R. G. Springsteen. PROD Sidney Picker. SCR John K. Butler. CAM Reggie Lanning. ED Richard L. Van Enger. MUS R. Dale Butts. RUNNING TIME 91 min. CAST: Vaughn Monroe (Matt Landry); **Joan Leslie** (Mary Kimber); Edgar Buchanan (Jim Hadlock); Victor Jory (Frank Girard); Jean Parker (Della); Henry Morgan (Verne Kimber).

The Woman They Almost Lynched (Republic, 1953). DIR Allan Dwan. PROD Herbert J. Yates. SCR Steve Fisher (story by Michael Fessier). CAM Reggie Lanning. ED Fred Allen. MUS Stanley Wilson. RUNNING TIME 90 min. CAST: John Lund (Lance Horton); Brian Donlevy (Quantrill); Audrey Totter (Kate Quantrill); **Joan Leslie** (Sally Maris); Ben Cooper (Jesse James); James Brown (Frank James).

Flight Nurse (Republic, 1953). DIR Allan Dwan. PROD Herbert J. Yates. SCR Alan Le May. CAM Reggie Lanning. ED Fred Allen. MUS Victor Young. RUNNING TIME 90 min. CAST: **Joan Leslie** (Lt. Polly Davis); Forrest Tucker (Capt. Bill Eaton); Arthur Franz (Capt. Mike Barnes); Jeff Donnell (Lt. Ann Phillips); Ben Cooper (Private Marvin Judd); James Holden (Sgt. Frank Swan).

Jubilee Trail (Republic, 1954). DIR-PROD Joseph Kane. SCR Bruce Manning (novel by Gwen Bristow). CAM Jack Marta. ED Richard L. Van Enger. MUS Victor Young. RUNNING TIME 103 min. CAST: Vera Ralston (Florinda); **Joan Leslie** (Garnet); Forrest Tucker (John Ives); John Russell (Oliver Hale); Ray Middleton (Charles Hale); Pat O'Brien (Texas).

Hell's Outpost (Republic, 1955). DIR-PROD Joseph Kane. SCR Kenneth Gamet (novel by Luke Short). CAM Jack Marta. ED Richard L. Van Enger. MUS R. Dale Butts. RUNNING TIME 89 min. CAST: Rod Cameron (Tully Gibbs); **Joan Leslie** (Sarah Moffit); John Russell (Ben Hodes); Chill Wills (Kevin Russell); Jim Davis (Sam Horne); Kristine Miller (Beth Hodes).

The Revolt of Mamie Stover (20th Century Fox, 1956). DIR Raoul Walsh. PROD Buddy Adler. SCR Sydney Boehm (novel by William Bradford Huie). CAM Leo Tover. ED Louis Loeffler. MUS Hugo Friedhofer. RUNNING TIME 93 min. CAST: Jane Russell (Mamie Stover); Richard Egan (Jim); **Joan Leslie** (Annalee); Agnes Moorehead (Bertha); Jorja Curtright (Jackie); Michael Pate (Harry Adkins).

Television Movies

The Keegans (1976). DIR John Badham. CAST: Adam Roarke; Spencer Mulligan; Heather Menzies; Tom Clany; **Joan Leslie** (Mary Keegan); Priscilla Pointer.

Charley Hannah (1986). DIR Peter H. Hunt. CAST: Robert Conrad; Shane Conrad; **Joan Leslie** (Sandy Hannah); Red West.

Turn Back the Clock (1989). DIR Larry Elikann. CAST: Connie Sellecca; David Dukes; Gene Barry; **Joan Leslie** (Party Guest).

Fire in the Dark (1991). DIR David Hugh Jones. CAST: Olympia Dukakis; Lindsay Wagner; Jean Stapleton; **Joan Leslie** (Ruthie); Edward Herrmann.

SHEREE NORTH

Screen actress Sheree North, who was always considered a talented dancer (starting with *Living It Up* [1954]), a heart-warming comedienne (*Mardi Gras* [1958]) and, in later stages of her career, also a reliable character actress (*The Gypsy Moths* [1969], *The Shootist* [1976] among others), is one of the very few actresses who was born in Hollywood (in 1933), grew up there and became a star in her own right.

She got her first starring role in Nunnally Johnson's rock 'n' roll comedy *How to Be Very, Very Popular* (1955, with Betty Grable in her final film) and stole the show with her delightful "Shake, Rattle and Roll" dance sequence. Many people thought this new discovery was to become *the* new star of the 1950s and for a while it did seem that way, as she was groomed by her studio, 20th Century Fox, to go straight to the top. Yet, initially it was her goal to make it as a dancer, rather than becoming an actress, something she had already pursued during her teens. Dancing paved the way for her first success on Broadway, until she was lured back to her native Hollywood.

Starting her career at age three, after an agreement with her mother to cease impromptu in storefront windows in exchange for dancing lessons, she reappeared eight years later dancing on the stage of the Greek Theatre in Los Angeles. What happened then? Miss North: "When I was about 18, I worked in a small night club in Santa Monica and I was spotted there for a Broadway show which I wasn't at all interested in. But I had a little baby and I wanted to do something more stable. They kept calling me to come for an interview and finally I did. They wanted to know if I could sing and play the piano. The first song that came to my mind, was a song I heard Sophie Tucker sing, called "One of These Days." But as I was too embarrassed to sing it, I suggested they would play it on the piano and I would sing it in the other room, so that is what happened. The choreographer, Bob Alton, who had seen me originally and who had called me, asked if I could dance which I did and then they asked me to come to New York to appear in a Broadway show called *Hazel Flagg*. When they offered a girl friend of mine a job as well, I agreed.

"We were 18, we got free tickets to go to New York and didn't think about a career at all. I got discovered in the show, got good reviews, they used me to keep the show going and I made the cover of dozens of magazines [it earned her a Drama Desk Award and the Critics' Award]. Hollywood was interested in me, but my manager, who worked in New York, didn't want me to go back. He suggested I'd have a Broadway career instead and that I would come over to do a film only now and then, which was an excellent idea.

"When I came back here to do a screen test with George Cukor at Columbia, they were

Marilyn Monroe

looking for someone to replace Judy Holliday[1]—she was under contract there, but they felt they couldn't control her enough. So they were looking for a young blonde actress who also could do comedy. I did a screen test there and another one at Fox; Marilyn Monroe was put on suspension because there was a film she didn't want to do, so Fox wanted to cash in on all of my publicity and hired me. Unfortunately, my manager wasn't here and my agent had me sign this contract. My manager was very upset that I had this contract with Fox.

"He was a very good manager; my agent who was based in Los Angeles, mostly had male stars, including Rock Hudson, and his idea was to get you under contract so he got his steady check in the mail every week. He really didn't care about discussing your career or anything else. So there wasn't any guidance and I didn't understand the business, how to maneuver it or even to say, 'I don't want to do this script.'

"I had come out here to do a film version of the Broadway musical *Hazel Flagg*. Dean Martin and Jerry Lewis had bought the property; it became the basis for their comedy *Living It Up* [1954]. In the meantime, Bing Crosby was doing his first TV show. I was invited to be his guest and I played Jack Benny's girlfriend. That was really fun. I had grown up listening to Jack Benny on the radio; he was a very sweet man. Every day, we stopped at four o'clock, turned a couple of boxes on the set up, he took a hankie out, put it over the boxes and we'd have tea—tea and a cigar! That was very pleasant. I enjoyed that because it was more like doing theater, which interested me more than working in front of a camera.

"So meanwhile I had signed with Fox, I had to stay here in Hollywood and honor my seven year contract. I wasn't very happy, I really preferred the theater and the stage, and I was very unaccustomed to the camera. I also saw they were so cruel and made so much fun of Marilyn Monroe,[2] who was also under contract at Fox, that it frightened me to go against company policy as it were—you have your own individual taste and your own individual ideas, which make you an individual. The studios had a different idea at that time, they had their own idea how you should look or should dress and it sort of kills your individual character. I was afraid to say anything because I saw what fun they made of Marilyn. She was willing to fight them, to express and be her own self.

"She had a great sense of humor, a lot more power than she thought she had and she didn't know how to use it to call the shots. First you always want to get noticed, and then you want respect—at that time, she was searching for that respect, but she didn't feel strong enough within herself. I always thought she needed a really good friend, a mother image, somebody she really could trust.

"The way they made fun of her—she wouldn't know it particularly, but when she walked

(Left to right) Sheree North, Tommy Noonan and Charles Coburn in *How to Be Very, Very Popular* (1955). (Courtesy of DOCIP Film Archive, Brussels, Belgium.)

down the street at the studio, several people would walk behind her and imitate her walk, things like that. When she turned around, she would not know it, but still they'd all be laughing at her. When she went in to do her make-up and her hair, the other people would come out, talk about her and say terrible things, because she didn't want her make-up and her hair done according to the 'formula' of the studio. It was very difficult to fight that and she fought it. In fighting it, you cause a lot of bad feelings amongst people. I don't know if she was so much aware of it as I was, because I was the recipient of what everybody had to say about her. So I wasn't terribly happy with my seven year contract, but I did the films, although I really didn't know how to act. In fact, I thought they had hired me as a dancer. Twentieth Century Fox had signed me as a star, but when I found out they expected me to *act*, I went to Mr. Zanuck[3] and said, 'Mr. Zanuck, I know how to dance, but I don't act.' He said, 'If we need a dancer, we'll get Eleanor Powell! That's what we hired you for!'

"When I arrived at 20th Century Fox, I was a platinum blonde and I had my own idea how I wanted to look: I was very individual. Immediately they did several tests every day—I must have tested over 500 wigs for color, style, length, and make-up. Then they decided how you should look, how you should speak. I went along with all of it: the hair, the make-up, the diction teacher, but not the acting, that's when I found my own acting teacher. They did a lot of things—they would send you to publicize a film, not necessarily your own, but also somebody else's film. The publicity people made all the appointments for you, where, when and what you should eat and drink, they kept everything under control and made sure the image was the way they wanted it.

"The first film I did was the sequel to *How to Marry a Millionaire* [1953], called *How to Be Very, Very Popular* [1955]. I was very concerned about having to *speak*, and when I went on the set, I was totally unprepared. I hadn't studied acting, I didn't know anything about it. So here were all those people standing around and in the beginning I just talked very fast when they were shooting the scenes, because I didn't want to take anybody's time. The only time I felt comfortable, was during the dance sequence I got to do [the "Shake, Rattle and Roll" number]. That was put in as an afterthought—the studio didn't really know too much about rock 'n' roll then, they just decided to put a sort of rock 'n' roll dance number in it. I was allowed to do with that what I knew and Betty Grable also made me very comfortable. She was wonderful; with all of her fame and all of the films she did, she was a totally real human being, she had no ego. Robert Cummings was very nice too.

"When I grew up, the saying was *be seen and not heard*. Perhaps I took that too literally [laughs]: I was *very* quiet, I hardly spoke, the only way I knew how to express myself, was through dance. When I was young, I was an extremely quiet and shy person. If you'd put me on a stage, I could dance and be very outgoing, totally free—the only place where I felt freedom, was on the stage. I never felt freedom in life itself, which is not so unusual: many performers are like that. In fact, when I appeared on Broadway, after we opened and I got all the notices, Ben Hecht came to me and said, 'We're having a special rehearsal and we want you to come. I have written something.' I said, 'Not if I have to speak, I won't do it.' He said, 'Oh no, don't worry about that, just come to the rehearsal.' So I did and he rewrote the show and had written a speaking role for me. I just put the script down and said, 'You know, I told you, I don't speak.' He then changed it again—the only way I knew to express myself was through dance.

"So when *How to Be Very, Very Popular* was released, I was horrified. I apologized to everybody because I had put something on film which made me feel very uneasy. At that point, I said I would never do it again. But the studio talked me into doing a second film, which was the sequel to another Monroe film, *The Seven Year Itch* [1955], called *The Lieutenant Wore Skirts* [1956], also with Tom Ewell. I suffered the whole film, knowing I didn't know how to act and when this film was finished, I said, 'That's it. I will never do this again.' I *hated* doing it, but my manager suggested I study acting, it would make me feel more at ease. So I went to Jeff Corey, a

Betty Grable (1916–1973) was Sheree North's co-star in Grable's final film, *How to Be Very, Very Popular*

very talented acting teacher who had been blacklisted but who had a very good reputation—he was recommended to me by James Dean. When the studio found out about it, they said, 'Well, if you'll go to him, we'll put you on suspension.' So I said, 'Jimmy Dean had told me about him, and it wouldn't look nice if you would do that, because he has just been killed in a car crash.' So in the end, they didn't suspend me, they let me go to him and they finally hired him to help other people as well. I went there every day, he taught me about literature, gave me books to read, gave me a good education and he made me feel much more secure about acting. That helped tremendously. So as I continued to work, I became much more comfortable."

In the late 1950s, Miss North appeared in several other films at 20th Century Fox, including Michael Curtiz' *The Best Things in Life Are Free* (1956, telling the story of Tin Pan Alley's team of Buddy De Sylva, Lew Brown and Ray Henderson, with Miss North singing "It All Depends on You" and "Sunny Side Up," and she's at her best in the dance sequences, especially "The Birth of the Blues" with Jacques d'Amboise); *The Way to the Gold* (1957, solid action drama with Miss North as a waitress in search of a better life as she joins Jeffrey Hunter in a treasure hunt); Martin Ritt's second film, *No Down Payment* (1957, interesting story about young married couples with Miss North in a straight role as the wife of Tony Randall); *Mardi Gras* (1958, an upbeat musical with Pat Boone, with Miss North singing the song "That Man") and *In Love and War* (1958, set in World War II, based on Edward Anhalt's intriguing screenplay).

"By the time I did my last films for Fox, I felt reasonably comfortable, though never as comfortable as on stage. Never. There's something about people, about a live audience. I can relate to them and *feel*, and I can't feel anything from a camera. When my contract was finished, I was into a second marriage and I was more pursuing life as a mother. That was the reason why I hardly appeared in films. Later on I returned to Broadway, but my main concern was raising my two daughters. Mostly I took work in order to finance what I thought was my real career. The years at Fox might have given the impression that I lived the life of a star, but after that—when I was on my own—I didn't pursue any publicity at all as that just comes naturally when you're under contract at a studio."

In the 1960s, she appeared on the stage frequently, and she returned successfully to Broadway for *I Can Get It for You Wholesale*. Miss North: "Several television series were offered to me and I turned those down, because they would take me away from my house too much. Then I would just pay someone else to raise my children—why would I do that? So I preferred to live more humbly, not have so much money but be at home. That was my choice and I never regretted it anyway. Then if I did a TV show, I would only be gone for seven hours a day and I was home every night. After a week I would be off again, so it only took a week at a time. That proved to be very flexible and if I did a film, again, I wasn't gone that much, I was always around. I didn't take locations, I didn't go away and if I did a play, I did that in the Summer so the children went with me back East. The quality of the theater back East at that time was better than here in California, the professionalism was much higher than it was here—now it has become much improved. Back East, there were a lot of shows you could do and you could tour with your show around the country. The theater is more a family and it's a very nice feeling for children, it was a very nice atmosphere for the children. Actors can be very childlike too and they'd be on the floor with the coloring books with them.

"When I look back now and see the early films I appeared in, I think it wasn't *that* bad, but at the time I thought it was horrible. I knew how expressive I was as a dancer and I was not expressive as an actress—I knew the difference, I had some comparison what it felt like when you knew what you were doing. Still, if I could do it all over again, I would much rather have stayed in New York, I would have had a much better career, doing Broadway shows and

I would have chosen the properties I wanted to do. In films, I turned things down, unless I had to pay the rent or put my children through school. I turned a lot of things down that maybe I shouldn't have turned down, and I took a lot of things that I probably shouldn't have taken—I sort of adjusted according to what was necessary for an income at that time.

"When people ask, 'What's your favorite film?' I probably would say, 'I haven't done it yet.' I mean, if I compare it to the characters one gets to act in a play in a theater, those well-rounded, beautifully fleshed out characters, there's so much more to it. I guess if I compare the characters I played in the theater to the films I've done, then I feel the characters I played in films were not as fully realized. I just did a Tennessee Williams play at the Laguna Playhouse, *The Glass Menagerie* [December 1999–January 2000] that I'm very proud of. I feel I conquered a lot of difficult things in this play and brought a lot to the character that has never been brought to before. I have seen it many times and I never wanted to do it myself—I always thought they played my character as such a neurotic and that's not what Tennessee Williams meant to do with it. The director didn't feel that way either and together we realized a character of more depth.

"However, if someone would offer me a part in a play and at the same time I would get the opportunity to play the same part in a film, I would accept the screen role because you have to do a certain amount of things to keep your name going. There once was a film that came along, with Jack Nicholson and myself starring, it was an excellent script. Martin Ritt had sent it to me and I thought, 'This is too good to be true.' It turned out Martin got a heart attack and the doctor told him that, if he went on location, he probably wouldn't live to come back. So it was canceled and that was too bad. It was in the right period, we would have been a great combination. I don't know what happened to the script, perhaps I should have pursued it, but I am not good at that. Some actors are really gifted at that talent, I am not."

Miss North appeared in one film directed by Martin Ritt [*No Down Payment*] and she was the favorite character actress of Don Siegel[4] as she appeared in four of his films: *Madigan* (1968) with Richard Widmark in the title role as a New York detective, *Charley Varrick* (1973), a thriller with Walter Matthau playing a bank robber, John Wayne's final film *The Shootist* (1976) and *Telefon* (1977), an espionage thriller based on the novel by Walter Wager. Miss North: "Martin Ritt was a wonderful director, he was an actor's director. But some directors don't really know about acting and they don't discuss it or don't allow you time to prepare. They talk to you and are kidding with you, right up until they say, 'Roll 'em!' And then you're supposed to go right into the acting. They don't understand the process that you have to go through. Of course, that doesn't mean they're not good directors, they're wonderful film directors. Don Siegel was wonderful for what he did: he was a very sweet, funny and amusing man, but he didn't understand acting at all. You could

Sheree North in the mid–1970s when she appeared in the television series *Big Eddie*.

never discuss acting with him. *Roll 'em—you do it!* His talent was in telling a story, in casting and editing, he was an editor previously. I probably could have done more with my role in *The Shootist*; we had to shoot very quickly and Don was talking the whole time—I maybe didn't do as much as I maybe could have with it."

"Sometimes you'd say, 'Oh, I didn't do that scene very well.' And then, when you see it, 'Well, it's better than I thought it was.' Then, years later, 'Oh my God, that was just terrible! What was I thinking of?' You keep rejudging things, it's interesting how that goes on film. What I am always looking for though, is, 'Was it really happening at that moment, were you fully there?' You have to *dredge* up your whole soul. That is more an American acting requirement, the Stanislavski method that I grew up with when I started acting. Every moment should be real, and if you're not fully present, it isn't really happening or if you're just making believe it happens, it's not as good."

Not all actors had the same background or the same training ground. Did that ever have any impact on her work? Miss North: "I made two films with Burt Lancaster, *The Gypsy Moths* [1969] and *Lawman* [1971]; he was from another school of acting. With certain actors you decide at the time how you're going to play it, and then you just go on and play it—every little nuance is important. If I look at them and start with a smile, it will change the way they react, they act and react from moment to moment, that's very rare. Then there are actors you can't affect no matter what you do—Burt Lancaster was going to play it *that* way. It wouldn't matter if I gave him the wrong reaction. Most actors decide what they're going to do, so it doesn't matter what the other actor does. In that case they are not really reacting to you as much as just acting at you.

"I made two films with Robert Ryan, *Lawman* and *The Outfit* [1974]. He was a pleasure to be with on the set. He was such a real man, not an actor. In America there is a difference between real men and actors, much more so than in Europe. They forget that they are part of the human race and they become something apart. It is unfortunate if that happens to great actors. Karl Malden also remains a man and a human being, with all of the real feelings and emotions that a real human being is supposed to have.

"I appeared with Elvis Presley[5] in *The Trouble with Girls (and How to Get Into It)* [1969]. When he wasn't forced to be in his *star* position, he was extremely vulnerable, troubled, human and searching and was not really allowed to pursue that search. There was a lot of pressure on him about everything, all the time. He didn't know how to deal with it, He had gone through terrible depressions. He would go back to Graceland, just stay in his room and couldn't eat. His father would bring up a tray and put it at the door. His friends, the group he stayed loyal to, they didn't know how to help him

Recent portrait of Sheree North. (Courtesy of Sheree North and Phill Norman.)

out of it. He was pushed too much to work and ultimately take various medicines to continue to work, denying his own self. It doesn't show in his work, but being on the set with him for 12 hours a day, he revealed so much more of himself than most people do, I was quite stunned to see what a sad soul in search of a life he was. We got along very well. He knew I had been a rock 'n' roll dancer and I was now comfortable as an actress. He was not comfortable as an actor. We had a sort of identifying history by the time we worked on that film."

For her performances on TV, she was nominated for an Emmy trice; she appeared in three TV series (including the comedy series *Big Eddie* [1975]), and in countless TV movies, including *Vanished* (1971, the first TV movie shown in two parts), Richard Donner's *A Shadow in the Streets* (1975), *A Real American Hero* (1978), *Marilyn: The Untold Story* (1980) and *Dead on the Money* (1991, with Eleanor Parker and Kevin McCarthy). In recent years, however, she hasn't been seen too much in films.

After a career of more than 50 years in show business, what are her goals at this point? "I don't have any goals right now that I actively pursue. There are some plays that I'd like to do. I did a play a couple of years ago called *Breaking Up the Act* by Terry Kingsley, it was kind of nostalgic and it gave people a lot of laughs. I would like to do that with Shirley Jones and Angie Dickinson. We are all more or less from the same period. It is a very American play but I think people in England would enjoy it very much too. It is sort of like the Andrews Sisters, they're asked to come back years later to perform at the White House and they're all gone off in other directions, so they're trying to get the act back together. It's a simple play, but it is fun and it would be wonderful to entertain an audience with it."

Miss North on the other hand doesn't have to get *her* act back together—she still has all the qualities a solid performer needs.

Interview: Beverly Hills, August 17, 2000

Notes

1. Judy Holliday (1922–1965) was a successful stage and screen comedienne and Academy Award winning actress for her role of Billie Dawn in *Born Yesterday* (1950, a role she also had played on the Broadway stage). Her short career included other Broadway plays such as *Bells Are Ringing* and *Kiss Them for Me*, as well as films like *Adam's Rib* (1949), *It Should Happen to You* (1954), *Phffft* (1954), *The Solid Gold Cadillac* (1956) and her final film, Vincente Minnelli's *Bells Are Ringing* (1960). She died of cancer at age 43.

2. Marilyn Monroe (1926–1962), screen goddess and probably Hollywood's most famous post-war screen legend, appeared in such films as *The Asphalt Jungle* (1950), *All About Eve* (1950), *Monkey Business* (1952), *Gentlemen Prefer Blondes* (1953), *How to Marry a Millionaire* (1953), *River of No Return* (1954), *The Seven Year Itch* (1955), *Bus Stop* (1956), *The Prince and the Showgirl* (1957), *Some Like It Hot* (1959), *Let's Make Love* (1960) and *The Misfits* (1961). Even now, 40 years after her death, books are still being published about Marilyn Monroe, focusing on her impact and the life she lived as a star, rather than concentrating on her films and acting abilities.

3. Darryl F. Zanuck (1902–1979), from 1934 to 1956 studio executive at 20th Century Fox, after he co-founded 20th Century Pictures with Joseph M. Schenk which merged with Fox in 1933 to form 20th Century Fox. When the studio ran into financial difficulties with *Cleopatra* (1963), he bounced back and became president of the company until 1969. He then appointed his son Richard D. (b. 1934) as president, fired him later on after irreconcilable differences in studio policy and became studio executive himself until 1971. Films he made as producer include *Young Mr. Lincoln* (1939), *The Grapes of Wrath* (1940), *How Green Was My Valley* (1941, Academy Award for best picture), *The Razor's Edge* (1946), *Gentleman's Agreement* (1947), *All About Eve* (1950), *The Sun Also Rises* (1957), *The Roots of Heaven* (1958), and *The Longest Day* (1962). He was the recipient of the Irving G. Thalberg Award in 1937, 1944 and 1950.

4. Don Siegel (1912–1991), filmmaker who directed Clint Eastwood in *Coogan's Bluff* (1968), *Two Mules for Sister Sara* (1970), *The Beguiled* (1971), *Dirty Harry* (1971) and *Escape from Alcatraz* (1979). He also made other highly interesting films like *The Verdict* (1946), *The Big Steal* (1949), *Riot in Cell Block 13* (1954), *Invasion of the Body Snatchers* (1956), *Flaming Star* (1960), *The Killers* (1964) and *The Shootist* (1976). He frequently made cameo appearances in films, as in *Play Misty for Me* (1971, directed by Clint Eastwood) and in the remake of *Invasion of the Body Snatchers* (1978).

5. Elvis Presley (1935–1977), a.k.a. the "King of Rock 'n' Roll," who became the world's most successful recording artist ever, debuted on the screen in *Love Me Tender* (1956). Although he was definitely not the most talented actor around, his films managed to be profitable all the way. They include *Jailhouse Rock* (1957), *King Creole* (1958), *G.I. Blues* (1960), *Flaming Star* (1960), *Wild in the Country* (1961), *Viva Las Vegas* (1964), *Kissin' Cousins* (1964) and *Roustabout* (1964). His two concert films are *Elvis: That's the Way It Is* (1970) and *Elvis on Tour* (1972).

Filmography

Excuse My Dust (MGM, 1951). DIR Roy Rowland. PROD Jack Cummings. SCR George Wells. CAM Alfred Gilks. ED Irvine Warburton. MUS Arthur Schwartz, Dorothy Fields. RUNNING TIME 82 min. CAST: Red Skelton (Joe Belden); Sally Forrest (Liz Bullitt); Macdonald Carey (Cyrus Random, Jr.); William Demarest (Harvey Bullitt); **Sheree North** (Club Member).

Here Come the Girls (Paramount, 1953). DIR Claude Binyon. PROD Paul Jones. SCR Edmund Hartmann, Hal Kanter (story by Edmund Hartmann). CAM Lionel Lindon. ED Arthur Schmidt. MUS Lyn Murray. RUNNING TIME 77 min. CAST: Bob Hope (Stanley Snodgrass); Tony Martin (Allen Trent); Arlene Dahl (Irene Bailey); Rosemary Clooney (Daisy Crockett); Millard Mitchell (Albert Snodgrass); **Sheree North**.

Living It Up (Paramount, 1954). DIR Norman Taurog. PROD Paul Jones. SCR Jack Rose, Melville Shavelson (musical comedy by Ben Hecht, Jule Styne, Bob Hilliard; story by James Street). CAM Daniel Fapp. ED Archie Marshek. MUS Walter Scharf. RUNNING TIME 94 min. CAST: Dean Martin (Steve); Jerry Lewis (Homer); Janet Leigh (Wally Cook); Edward Arnold (The Mayor); Fred Clark (Oliver Stone); **Sheree North** (Jitterbug Dancer).

How to Be Very, Very Popular (20th Century Fox, 1955). DIR-PROD Nunnally Johnson. SCR Nunnally Johnson (play by Howard Lindsay based on the novel by Edward Hope and a play by Lyford Moore, Harlan Thompson). CAM Milton Krasner. ED Louis Loeffler. MUS Cyril J. Mockridge. RUNNING TIME 89 min. CAST: Betty Grable (Stormy); **Sheree North** (Curly); Robert Cummings (Wedgewood); Charles Coburn (Tweed); Tommy Noonan (Eddie); Orson Bean (Toby).

The Lieutenant Wore Skirts (20th Century Fox, 1956). DIR Frank Tashlin. PROD Buddy Adler. SCR Albert Beich, Frank Tashlin (story by Albert Beich). CAM Leo Tover. ED James B. Clark. MUS Cyril J. Mockridge. RUNNING TIME 98 min. CAST: Tom Ewell (Gregory Whitcomb); **Sheree North** (Kathy Whitcomb); Rita Moreno (Sandra); Rick Jason (Capt. Barney Sloan); Les Tremayne (Henry Gaxton); Alice Reinheart (Capt. Briggs).

The Best Things in Life Are Free (20th Century Fox, 1956). DIR Michael Curtiz. PROD Henry Ephron. SCR William Bowers, Phoebe Ephron (story by John O'Hara). CAM Leon Shamroy. ED Dorothy Spencer. MUS Lionel Newman. RUNNING TIME 104 min. CAST: Gordon MacRae (R. G. De Sylva); Dan Dailey (Henderson); Ernest Borgnine (Brown); **Sheree North** (Kitty); Tommy Noonan (Carl); Murvyn Vye (Manny).

The Way to the Gold (20th Century Fox, 1957). DIR Robert D. Webb. PROD David Weisbart. SCR Wendell Mayes (novel by Wilbur Daniel Steele). CAM Leo Tover. ED Hugh S. Fowler. MUS Lionel Newman. RUNNING TIME 95 min. CAST: Jeffrey Hunter (Joe Mundy); **Sheree North** (Waitress Clifford); Barry Sullivan (Marshall Hannibal); Walter Brennan (Uncle George); Neville Brand (Little Brother); Jacques Aubuchon (Clem).

No Down Payment (20th Century Fox, 1957). DIR Martin Ritt. PROD Jerry Wald. SCR Philip Yordan (novel by John McPartland). CAM Joseph LaShelle. ED Louis Loeffler. MUS Leigh Harline. RUNNING TIME 105 min. CAST: Joanne Woodward (Leola Boone); **Sheree North** (Isabelle Flagg); Tony Randall (Jerry Flagg); Jeffrey Hunter (David Martin); Cameron Mitchell (Troy Boone); Patricia Owens (Jean Martin).

Mardi Gras (20th Century Fox, 1958). DIR Edmund Goulding. PROD Jerry Wald. SCR Winston Miller, Hal Kanter (story by Curtis Harrington). CAM Wilfrid M. Cline. ED Robert Simpson. MUS Lionel Newman. RUNNING TIME 107 min. CAST: Pat Boone (Pat Newell); Christine Carere (Michelle Marton); Tommy Sands (Barry Denton); **Sheree North** (Eadie); Gary Crosby (Tony Runkle); Fred Clark (Curtis).

In Love and War (20th Century Fox, 1958). DIR Phillip Dunne. PROD Jerry Wald. SCR Edward Anhalt (novel by Anton Myrer). CAM Leo Tover. ED William Reynolds. MUS Hugo Friedhofer. RUNNING TIME 107 min. CAST: Robert Wagner (Frankie O'Neill); Dana Wynter (Sue Trumbell); Jeffrey Hunter (Nico Kantaylis); Hope Lange (Andrea Lenaine); Bradford Dillman (Alan Newcombe); **Sheree North** (Lorraine).

Destination Inner Space (Magna, 1966). DIR Francis D. Lyon. PROD Earle Lyon. SCR Arthur C. Pierce. CAM Brick Marquard. ED Robert S. Eisen. MUS Paul Dunlap. RUNNING TIME 83 min. CAST: Scott Brady (Comm. Wayne); **Sheree North** (Sandra); Gary Merrill (Dr. Le Satier); Mike Road (Hugh Maddox); Wende Wagner (Rene); John Howard (Dr. James).

Madigan (Universal, 1968). DIR Don Siegel. PROD Frank P. Rosenberg. SCR Henri Simoun, Abraham Polonsky (novel by Richard Dougherty). CAM Russell Metty. ED Milton Shifman. MUS Don Costa. RUNNING TIME

101 min. CAST: Richard Widmark (Det. Madigan); Henry Fonda (Comm. Russell); Inger Stevens (Julia Madigan); Harry Guardino (Det. Bonaro); James Whitmore (Chief Insp. Kane); **Sheree North** (Jonesy).

The Trouble with Girls (And How to Get Into It) (MGM, 1969). DIR Peter Tewksbury. PROD Lester Welch. SCR Arnold Peyser, Lois Peyser (story by Mauri Grashin). CAM Jacques Marquette. ED George W. Brooks. MUS Billy Strange. RUNNING TIME 97 min. CAST: Elvis Presley (Walter Hale); Marilyn Mason (Charlene); Nicole Jaffe (Betty); **Sheree North** (Nita Bix); Edward Andrews (Johnny); John Carradine (Drewcolt).

The Gypsy Moths (MGM, 1969). DIR John Frankenheimer. PROD Hal Landers, Bobby Roberts. SCR William Hanley (novel by James Drought). CAM Philip Lathrop. ED Henry Berman. MUS Elmer Bernstein. RUNNING TIME 106 min. CAST: Burt Lancaster (Mike Rettig); Deborah Kerr (Elizabeth Brandon); Gene Hackman (Joe Browdy); Scott Wilson (Malcolm Webson); William Windom (V. John Brandon); Bonnie Bedelia (Annie Burke); **Sheree North** (Waitress).

Lawman (United Artists, 1971). DIR-PROD Michael Winner. SCR Gerald Wilson. CAM Bob Paynter. MUS Jerry Fielding. RUNNING TIME 98 min. CAST: Burt Lancaster (Jered Maddox); Robert Ryan (Cotton); Lee J. Cobb (Vincent Bronson); **Sheree North** (Laura Selby); Joseph Wiseman (Lucas); Robert Duvall (Vernon Adams).

The Organization (United Artists, 1971). DIR Don Medford. PROD Walter Mirisch. SCR James R. Webb. CAM Joseph Biroc. ED Ferris Webster. MUS Gil Melle. RUNNING TIME 107 min. CAST: Sidney Poitier (Virgil Tibbs); Barbara McNair (Valerie Tibbs); Gerald S. O'Loughlin (Jack Pecora); **Sheree North** (Mrs. Morgan); Fred Beir (Bob Alford); Allen Garfield (Benjy).

Charley Varrick (Universal, 1973). DIR-PROD Don Siegel. SCR Howard Rodman, Dean Riesner (novel by John Reese). CAM Michael Butler. ED Frank Morriss. MUS Lalo Schifrin. RUNNING TIME 111 min. CAST: Walter Matthau (Charley Varrick); Joe Don Baker (Molly); Felicia Farr (Sybil Fort); Andy Robinson (Sullivan); John Vernon (Maynard Boyle); **Sheree North** (Jewell Everett).

The Outfit (MGM, 1974). DIR John Flynn. PROD Carter De Haven. SCR John Flynn (novel by Richard Stark). CAM Bruce Surtees. ED Ralph E. Winters. MUS Jerry Fielding. RUNNING TIME 103 min. CAST: Robert Duvall (Macklin); Karen Black (Bett); Joe Don Baker (Cody); Robert Ryan (Mailer); Timothy Carey (Menner); Richard Jaeckel (Chemey); **Sheree North** (Buck's Wife); Jane Greer (Alma).

Breakout (Columbia, 1975). DIR Tom Gries. PROD Robert Chartoff, Irwin Winkler. SCR Howard B. Kreitsek, Marc Norman, Elliott Baker (novel by Warren Hinckle, William Turner, Eliot Asinof). CAM Lucien Ballard. ED Bud Isaacs. MUS Jerry Goldsmith. RUNNING TIME 96 min. CAST: Charles Bronson (Nick); Robert Duvall (Jay); Jill Ireland (Ann); John Huston (Harris); Randy Quaid (Hawk); **Sheree North** (Myrna).

The Shootist (Paramount, 1976). DIR Don Siegel. PROD M. J. Frankovich, William Self. SCR Miles Hood Swarthout, Scott Hale (novel by Glendon Swarthout). CAM Bruce Surtees. ED Douglas Stewart. MUS Elmer Bernstein. RUNNING TIME 99 min. CAST: John Wayne (J. B. Books); Lauren Bacall (Bond Rogers); Ron Howard (Gillom Rogers); James Stewart (Dr. Hostetler); Richard Boone (Sweeney); **Sheree North** (Serepta).

Telefon (United Artists, 1977). DIR Don Siegel. PROD James B. Harris. SCR Peter Hyams, Stirling Silliphant (novel by Walter Wager). CAM Michael Butler. ED Douglas Stewart. MUS Lalo Schifrin. RUNNING TIME 103 min. CAST: Charles Bronson (Grigori Borzov); Lee Remick (Barbara); Donald Pleasence (Nicholai Dalchimsky); Tyne Daly (Dorothy Putterman); Alan Badel (Col. Malchenko); **Sheree North** (Marie Wills).

Rabbit Test (Avco Embassy, 1979). DIR Joan Rivers. PROD Edgar Rosenberg. SCR Joan Rivers, Jay Redack. CAM Lucien Ballard. ED Stanford C. Allen. MUS Mike Post. RUNNING TIME 84 min. CAST: Billy Crystal (Lionel); Joan Prather (Segoynia); Alex Rocco (Danny); Doris Roberts (Mrs. Carpenter); Edward Ansara (Newscaster); **Sheree North** (Mystery Woman); Joan Rivers (Second Nurse).

Only Once in a Lifetime (Movietime, 1979). DIR-SCR Alejandro Grattan. PROD Alejandro Grattan, Moctezuma Esparza. CAM Turner Browne. ED Esperanza Vasquez. MUS Robert O. Ragland. RUNNING TIME 97 min. CAST: Miguel Robelo (Dominguez); Estrellita Lopez (Consuelo); **Sheree North** (Sally); Claudio Brook (Jimenez).

Maniac Cop (Shapiro Glickenhaus Ent., 1990). DIR William Lustig. PROD-SCR Larry Cohen. CAM Vincent J. Rabe. ED David Kern. MUS Jay Chattaway. RUNNING TIME 92 min. CAST: Tom Atkins (Det. McCrae); Bruce Campbell (Jack Forrest); Laurene Landon (Teresa Mallory); Richard Roundtree (Pike); William Smith (Capt. Ripley); **Sheree North** (Sally Noland).

Cold Dog Soup (1990). DIR Alan Metter. SCR Stephen Dobyns, Thomas Pope (novel by Stephen Dobyns). CAM Frederick Elmes. ED Kaja Fehr. MUS Michael Kamen. CAST: Randy Quaid (Jack Cloud); Frank Whaley (Michael Latchmer); Christine Harnos (Sarah Hughes); **Sheree North** (Mrs. Hughes); Nancy Kwan (Madame Chang); Dante Basco (Chinese Boy).

Defenseless (Seven Arts/New Line Cinema, 1991). DIR Martin Campbell. PROD Renee Missell, David Bombyk. SCR James Hicks (story by James Hicks, Jeff Burkhart). CAM Phil Meheux. ED Lou Lombardo, Chris Wimble. MUS Curt Sobel. RUNNING TIME 104 min. CAST: Barbara Hershey (T. K. Katwuller); Sam Shepard (Det. Beutel); Mary Beth Hurt (Ellie Seldes); J. T. Walsh (Steven Seldes); Kellie Overbey (Janna Seldes); **Sheree North** (Mrs. Bodeck).

Susan's Plan (1998). DIR-SCR John Landis. CAM Ken Kelsch. ED Nancy Morrison. MUS Peter Bernstein. RUN-

NING TIME 89 min. CAST: Nastassja Kinski (Susan Holland); Billy Zane (Sam Myers); Michael Biehn (Bill); Rob Schneider (Steve); Dan Aykroyd (Bob); **Sheree North** (Mrs. Beyers).

Television Movies

Code Name: Heraclitus (1967). DIR James Goldstone. CAST: Stanley Baker; Leslie Nielsen; Jack Weston; **Sheree North**; Kurt Kasznar.
Then Came Bronson (1969). DIR William A. Graham. CAST: Michael Parks; Bonnie Bedelia; Akim Tamiroff; **Sheree North** (Gloria Oresko); Martin Sheen.
Vanished (1971). DIR Buzz Kulik. CAST: Richard Widmark; Skye Aubrey; James Farentino; Larry Hagman; Eleanor Parker; **Sheree North** (Beverly West).
Rolling Man (1972). DIR Peter Hyams. CAST: Dennis Weaver; Don Stroud; Donna Mills; **Sheree North** (Ruby); Slim Pickens; Agnes Moorehead.
Trouble Comes to Town (1972). DIR Daniel Petrie. CAST: Lloyd Bridges; Pat Hingle; Hari Rhodes; **Sheree North** (Mrs. Murdock); Joseph Bottoms.
Snatched (1973). DIR Sutton Roley. CAST: Howard Duff; Leslie Nielsen; **Sheree North** (Kim Sutter); Barbara Parkins; Robert Reed; John Saxon.
Maneater (1973). DIR Vince Edwards. CAST: Ben Gazzara; **Sheree North** (Gloria Baron); Richard Basehart; Kip Niven.
Key West (1973). DIR Philip Leacock. CAST: Stephen Boyd; Woody Strode; Tiffany Bolling; Simon Oakland; **Sheree North** (Brandi).
Winter Kill (1974). DIR Jud Taylor. CAST: Andy Griffith; John Larch; Tim O'Connor; Lawrence Pressman; **Sheree North** (Betty).
A Shadow in the Streets (1975). DIR Richard Donner. CAST: Tony Lo Bianco; Ed Lauter; Dana Andrews; **Sheree North** (Gina Pulaski).
Most Wanted (1976). DIR Walter Grauman. CAST: Stephen McNally; Robert Stack; **Sheree North** (Melissa Dawson); Tom Selleck; Percy Rodriguez.
The Night They Took Miss Beautiful (1977). DIR Robert Michael Lewis. CAST: Gary Collins; Chuck Connors; **Sheree North** (Layla Burden); Victoria Principal.
A Real American Hero, a.k.a. *Hard Stick* (1978). DIR Lou Antonio. CAST: Brian Dennehy; Forrest Tucker; **Sheree North** (Carrie Todd); Jason Hood.
Amateur Night at the Dixie Bar and Grill (1979). DIR Joel Schumacher. CAST: Frank Slaten; Candy Clark; Ed Begley, Jr.; **Sheree North** (Lettie Norman); Dennis Quaid.
Portrait of a Stripper (1979). DIR John A. Alonzo. CAST: Lesley Ann Warren; Edward Herrmann; **Sheree North** (Sally Evers).
Marilyn: The Untold Story (1980). DIR Jack Arnold, John Flynn. CAST: Catherine Hicks; Frank Converse; Jason Miller; **Sheree North** (Gladys Baker).
Legs (1983). DIR Jerrold Freedman. CAST: John Heard; Gwen Verdon; **Sheree North** (Ida); David Marshall Grant.
Scorned and Swindled (1984). DIR Paul Wendkos. CAST: Tuesday Weld; Keith Carradine; Peter Coyote; **Sheree North** (Maxine Wagner).
Jake Spanner, Private Eye, a.k.a. *The Old Dick* and *Hoodwinked* (1989). DIR Lee H. Katzin. CAST: Robert Mitchum; Ernest Borgnine; Stella Stevens; **Sheree North**; Edie Adams.
Dead on the Money (1990). DIR Mark Cullingham. CAST: Corbin Benson; Amanda Pays; Eleanor Parker; Kevin McCarthy; **Sheree North**.

JANIS PAIGE

Janis Paige, screen actress and full-fledged star of the 1940s who also worked extensively on the stage, in nightclubs and for television, still is as vivid as ever. I had the honor of meeting her on a sunny, early spring afternoon and although I only knew her from her films (her latest was *Welcome to Hard Times*, 1967—I never saw her perform live), she still has the very same spontaneity as back then when she was one of Warner Bros.' most reliable actresses.

She had quite a remarkable career, as she is one of those rare performers who's career has spanned every facet of show business. She is equally at home in drama, comedy or musicals.

Looking back to her early days in show business, Miss Paige recalls: "I was discovered by Ida Koverman, a talent scout who was Louis B. Mayer's right hand, when I was singing at the Hollywood Canteen. I was taken to Metro and put under contract for a year. I did one film there, *Bathing Beauty* [1944] with Red Skelton and Esther Williams—I had one line with about four words in it and a musical number, because I could sing and I could dance. But then they didn't know what to do with me, because they had Judy Garland, Gloria DeHaven, June Allyson, all these wonderful women. So they let me go and that very same day I was taken to the head of casting at Warner Brothers. He said, 'Wait a minute, I should introduce you to Delmer Daves.' I didn't know who Delmer Daves was, I knew so little about all those people. I was taken to the soundstage and this lovely man came over and talked to me for a few minutes. He then said, 'She is perfect!' and he put me in *The Hollywood Canteen* [1944] along with Joan Leslie and Dane Clark. That was my start at Warner Brothers. Five years in a row I made picture after picture."

At Warner Bros. from 1944 to 1949, Miss Paige's career really blossomed. She appeared in a wide variety of films, including the powerful 1946 remake of Somerset Maugham's brilliant novel *Of Human Bondage*, with Miss Paige in a strong supporting role as the third and final love of Paul Henreid; Raoul Walsh's exciting Western *Cheyenne* (1947), in which she played a delightful saloon singer (songs: "Going Back to Old Cheyenne" and "I'm So in Love"); the comedy *Wallflower* (1948), in which she appeared as Joyce Reynolds' sister with Robert Hutton as the object of their affections (and Miss Paige also singing "I May Be Wrong"), and the drama *Winter Meeting* (1948) in which she played a secretary—opposite Bette Davis.

However, film buffs will remember her mostly for the films she made with Jack Carson,[1] back then one of the leading actors at Warner Bros. Carson and Miss Paige appeared together in light films such as *Two Guys from Milwaukee* (1946), *The Place, the Time and the Girl* (1946),

Love and Learn (1947), *Romance on the High Seas* (1948), *Always Together* (1948) and *Mr. Universe* (1951).

"I worked a lot with Jack Carson and consider myself fortunate to have had the experience. Jack was from vaudeville and some burlesque I believe. When he and Robert Alda asked me to be a part of an extensive tour of theaters where motion pictures were played with a live show, I accepted readily and that began my on the job training for how to make a bow, how to 'milk' a bow and how to do skits. I learned all of it from Jack and also learned how to be a 'straight woman' to a comic. Along with singing and some dancing, I found a whole new niche for myself which helped me enormously when I worked with countless comics in night clubs. Bob Hope[2] did the same thing for me. I've forgotten how many of Bob's TV shows I did, but he put me to work and I got more and more experience from the greatest. The Milton Berles, the Bob Hopes, and the Jack Carsons of our profession were a gift to me in the development of my career. I shall always be in their debt. Through Bob, I saw Vietnam, Korea, twice, Japan, Cuba and Guantanamo, the Caribbean, Puerto Rico, and Panama. Along with Guam, Hawaii and the Philippines, I've been on aircraft carriers and flown in helicopters over the jungles of Thailand and the snow covered hills of Korea. How lucky can I be to have all this and a profession I love. Vaudeville is gone and so are all but a few who worked in that medium, but there is nothing to compare to it in today's world for that five and six hours a day where you could hone your craft. There are a few vaudevillians left who reside at the Actor's Fund in New Jersey which I support in every way I can. Today there is no vaudeville anymore, the vaudevillians are almost all gone, so people can't get a chance to see it anymore. So there are a few of them left, but you can count them on your two hands. I send all of my cassettes from the academy to the Actor's Fund Home, because they simply can't afford to buy them. They have three or four little screening rooms, so I pack up these boxes twice a year and ship all of my films to them. They just love it, cause now they get a chance to see new films as well, instead of only the old ones. It is wonderful to sit down with those former vaudevillians and talk to them. We even have an ex–Follies girl there, she's 99 now and still active and very vital.

Jack Carson, Janis Paige's frequent co-star.

"When I was under contract at Warner Bros., I was not in control of my own career, not at all. But I didn't care, I didn't even *think* about it. It was Jack [L.] Warner[3] who took care of us. He put me in all of those pictures, one after the other, with people who were big stars at the time, people like Jack, Zachary Scott, Dennis Morgan, Don DeFore, etc. We were kept so busy at Warner Bros., if we weren't working on a soundstage, they had us doing publicity tours in Texas, Colorado, Oregon, we all saw a lot of the country. Or we were taking dancing lessons,

Studio portrait of Janis Paige in the 1940s.

worked in the studio where they had portraits taken—I mean, I was on every major magazine cover in the world at one time. So it was all work, and I think the hardest thing for me was when Warner Brothers decided they didn't know what to do with me. Jack [L.] Warner said to me, 'Janis, I've got Ann Sheridan, I've got Jane Wyman, and I don't know what to do with you. You are one of those people I can't fit in.' I said, 'Well, maybe that's good, Mr. Warner.' 'But it's not good for the studio,' he said. And they let me go, but look what they had given me. I had this big name, at one time I was voted 4th in the nationwide Motion Picture Exhibitor's Poll—Elizabeth Taylor was 5th at the time. So when I left Warner Bros., I could go out and earn my living. The first thing I did, I went right into the theatre with my own act [1950].

"Before that, I had made a movie in [post-war] Italy [*Fugitive Lady*, released in 1951], one of the greatest experiences of my life, because we had no water there, except for the fountains and wells. I had this gorgeous apartment, but no water for the toilets, no water for the sink, no water to bathe in, no water to drink, so the maid would carry buckets of water from the fountain in the piazza. At the studio, they had generators so there I could take a shower, wash my hair, etc. I grew up *so* much in that time, adjusting myself to the circumstances, and I loved it. I was supposed to be there for a month and a half, I was there for five and a half months, living like an Italian.

"I did my first television show in the old ABC studios in New York, the first color broadcast with Bob Hope, that went from New York to California. That was in 1950, the first time I had ever been in front of a television camera. I began to work all the time for television for every major show, for Perry Como, Dinah Shore, Bob Hope, dramatic shows, then I did *The Pajama Game* in New York for a year and a half, and I also had my own series—so it was just a progression of television as it became the new medium."

Her leading role in *The Pajama Game* (1954) opposite John Raitt and Eddie Foy, Jr., was undoubtedly one of her greatest professional triumphs. She then appeared in her own comedy TV series *It's Always Jan* (1955-56, playing a nightclub entertainer and aspiring Broadway actress) and since then she has occasionally returned to the screen, usually in supporting roles, including in Rouben Mamoulian's *Silk Stockings* (1957, a musical remake of *Ninotchka*, 1939). Miss Paige: "*Silk Stockings* was one of the highlights of my film career, but it did come at the very end of it because then I went into television almost exclusively. The television business became so big at that time, and then I went to Broadway, so I had no time at all to do movies. I went into a whole new career.

"When they decided to do *That's Entertainment!* [1974], I was supposed to be in the first one, but Mrs. Astaire wouldn't give her okay to use the footage with Fred from *Silk Stockings* [dancing the famous "Stereophonic Sound"]. Then *Part 2* [1976] came along and again it wasn't included. When they were planning *That's Entertainment! 3* a few years ago, they finally released it.

"Working at the studios was something very special. No matter what soundstage I worked on back then, no matter what movie I was in, everybody who made that movie was part of this one big family. They treated my like one of their kids. We had invested in each other and we liked each other. We all were there for years. We had young men whose fathers were lightning experts, gaffers, cameramen, etc., who grew up to be cameramen too—it was a wonderful job and it was a tradition with pride. And when people say it was the golden age of pictures, believe me, it *was* the golden age. We'll never see it again. It has to be treasured and respected, just because our morals were different.

"I never thought it was hard work—I was born in Tacoma, Washington [on September 16, 1924, as Donna Mae Tjaden]. We could never afford to even buy any white clothes, because we couldn't afford to have them cleaned. I was a Depression kid and it was wonderful to be in this world of Warner Bros. where they wrap you in tissue paper and have a press department to protect you, to guide you, to dress you when they'd send you on junkets for motion pictures. My first time on a train was because of Warner Bros., my first time in a hotel, the first time ordering room service, my first time on a stage when they sent me to New York to promote a movie.... They treated me so wonderfully, I have nothing but praise for how I was treated. You know, I grew up with a work ethic: to work hard, to be on time, do what I was supposed to do and that's what I brought right into the studio. I think there were many big stars who had other agendas, who maybe couldn't stand the fame or didn't quite appreciate what they had and misbehaved—Errol Flynn was the perfect example of misbehavior and yet he was one of the biggest stars this business ever saw. So I suppose the bottom line is money, as long as the public accepts you, it must be all right I suppose, and they certainly accept a lot of stuff today, don't they.

"Actors are people, so we have to be good people too. Being in the spotlight makes it very difficult, the lack of privacy gets to you. When I was in pictures, we did not have that invasion of your privacy; they respected actors back then, the press left them alone. The press were given stories, they printed it and that was it; they didn't park outside your home with long lens cameras, looking into your bathroom. It's appalling, and they call it their civil right! So I don't blame actors who become sick and tired of it; aren't we all entitled to a private life, to a point? I think we are and I think the job has to stop sometime, and it doesn't for these people. Look at Julia Roberts, she's followed everywhere—I think she handles herself beautifully. She's got it together, that girl. But it still has got to be terrible, being *spied* on. You go on a vacation, and they're constantly spying on you....

"Much of what went on in the studio that could have been exploited, was not, because they protected their stars, they didn't believe in bad gossip, they didn't believe in babies out of wedlock, that was not a part of our life at the time. There are people who don't understand that anymore: the value system in the world is so mediocre today. Look around, you can see the misbehavior, the drugs, the ego, the flaunting of any kind of morality, ethics or integrity.

Where back then, that was essential, that's the way we conducted ourselves and I know I have to this day.

"When I was still in pictures, you couldn't show any cleavage, they couldn't use four letter words to get you excited, so the writers had to find another kind of language and be sensual in another way, they had to use their imagination. Take the lightning of two cigarettes between Paul Henreid and Bette Davis in Now, Voyager, that's one of the most sensual scenes ever seen, because they had to use their imagination. Sex was the same, we fell in love, we broke up, we married, we divorced, we had children, it was all just the same, except it was *private*. I think, when I grew up, the worst crime I could do, would be to embarrass my parents, to make them ashamed of me. That was the way things were then. When you left home and went to school, you went to your teachers who were an extension of your home. I remember I always had to raise my hand if I wanted to ask a question, we had to dress a certain way, we had to come in clean—it was such a different time. I have a sensibility about it, I understand it, but I do think we are carrying it too far. I don't know when this is going to stop. The next thing is going to be total nudity on the screen with nothing left to the imagination. The children who see this, don't have any childhood anymore—they're growing up sophisticated and street smart when they're five and six!

"Recently I went to the movies with a few friends. In front of us were a family, mother and father with their four children ranging from the age of five to about 12. However, it was not a movie for children. We were talking about it later on and said that it's no wonder we're having the problems we're having today with so many children: not all of them of course, but quite a number of them are defiant, they have no respect for teachers, no respect for the law, no respect for their parents, they have no respect for anyone. They're given the right somehow to demand their rights while they're still being educated, clothed, loved, fed and housed by their parents. And yet, there is no respect, because when they leave home, they go to a school with knives and guns, dirty language, no manners. When we were growing up, it was an aim to be elegant and to be graceful. When I went to the studio, I didn't know how to dress, I never had any good clothes, we simply couldn't afford them. They took me to wardrobe and put me in these beautiful things—it's like when you die and go to heaven, you know what I mean? It's a fantasy, I was in magic land all the time. But what I learned, was how to dress, what to leave off and what to put on, I grew up with the greatest couturiers the studio could offer, so I kept my eyes and ears open, learned from them and I grew up with a sense of how to dress, how to talk, etc. Look at the grammar today, they're not even taught to conjugate a verb. When I studied Por-

Janis Paige today. (Courtesy of Janis Paige.)

tuguese and Italian, I had to begin conjugating every single verb I could get my hands on, so that at least the grammar was good. Today, the grammar is really shocking to me. They don't know what the tenses are and I wonder what I've been paying for in the school system. It was mandatory to learn this, because if you didn't speak well, you didn't get a job. I've heard corporate people today speak without proper grammar; they do nothing to correct it because it *works* today, it *goes* today, it is *accepted* today. And I think a lot of it has to do with television; people can sit in their homes and say, 'Oh, I can put a funny thing on my head and be as funny as him, I can look like her,' etc.

"Many people have no concept of what it takes to put on a television show or a movie, from the script, to the casting, to the direction, to the photography, to the final editing, to the getting it out ... they haven't the slightest idea of the amount of work it takes to be an actor, to study, the countless hours of studying and being rejected, going back and learning again, taking singing and dancing lessons, etc. I do know that I certainly haven't been the biggest star in the world, but I've tried to be a credit to my industry and that's very important to me. I have no intention of retiring, because I feel better today than I've ever felt. I feel I'm smarter, wiser, more coordinated emotionally than I ever was before and I have some mental skills and tools with which I can live this life today.

"If you look at the films that are released now, for the most part, I think the Academy Award winning pictures of today really deserve that award—considering the kind of work, effort, thought and commitment that has gone into those movies. That's why they're given the Oscars, that's why we vote for them. I still vote. One of my private joys is to be a member of the Academy. There are so many good, decent, truly nice people in this business but you never hear about them because they go about their life quietly, with *manners* and *dignity*. I wish we could get some civility back in our country—civility was a primary requisite of life, how to grow up and be civil to people! Just look at the lyrics of the rap music, the violence, and then our kids are hearing this. What are we going to do a few generations from now, who are we going to be?"

Even though Miss Paige is in her late seventies now, she still won't even consider retiring. "I'm getting a one-woman show together, I'm talking about my career, about my singing, I do some funny stuff, tell a wonderful story about my first day with Fred Astaire—I have a history and I would like to give it to people. And I am still here, while many people of my time are not. So I hope I can say I must be doing something right. I only know that I love to wake up in the morning, love the day and I still work very hard. I have all of this incredible energy which I use up by the end of the day and I am pretty pulled together.

"If you listen to the world outside, they will count you out. As a woman, especially if you get older, you go through life and you say, 'Well, I guess they don't want me anymore.' I've had the good fortune to look young in my life because of my Norwegian bone structure or whatever it is, and I've been lucky to have wonderful health. But still I've counted myself out; I wanted to quit two or three hundred times. So whether there is a magic something going on like Disneyland with me or with my life, I don't know; all I know is that I am not ready to just go. When you think about it, there were seven studios back then and each had perhaps 15 contract players and then they'd borrow people. In the whole world, you know how small that was? And what an honor and what a privilege it was, how lucky we were to be *chosen*? Many fell along the way; for many of them it didn't work out, for one reason or the other—they got married, they decided to have a family, or the studio didn't want them anymore, but some of us were really lucky. Maybe the time was right for us, I don't know and there are certain things you really can't question. It's just the way it is.

"God gave me this *multitalent*, to be able to go from one medium to the next medium, so there was never any reason for me to quit. I always kept in shape, I always danced, I always worked and I also worked hard on my own emotional stability, how you survive as a human being, how you get better and get happier. I also attend a group therapy session once a week to keep my mind healthy and alive. When you get to be my age, you have to have made and found a way to make some peace with yourself, so I want to clear up my thinking, I want to understand more what this is all about, what we are going through, it's an adventure. Today I can describe myself as peacefully excited. The two don't really go together and I realize that, but there it is and that's the way I feel. We have a soul inside of us and we have to get in touch with that soul, with our true self, because we came in alone and we're going to go out alone. And every job I have done in my life, I did alone—*with* actors, but I was the one with the role, standing out there in front of all of those people, having learned the lines and done the work!

"One lifetime isn't enough for me, that's the worst of it! And yet, when I think about that, somebody said to me once, 'Janis, the secret of life is just to keep moving, you keep doing something. If you are waiting for a bus or a taxi, do something: keep moving, read, think, watch.' And so, I've done that and I think it stimulates your mind, it makes you interested. I take the best care of myself that I can and I am enjoying my life. I haven't been without my lows, *terrible* lows, I haven't been without pain in my life, but it hasn't killed me and it hasn't stopped me. You can't look outside for the answers, you always go into yourself. So those little, tiny water on rock lessons that we teach ourselves, are valuable in our approach to life.

"No matter how old you get, you always learn. Vietnam with Bob Hope was an incredible learning time. We were there to entertain the boys, and that's exactly what we did. I grew up loving a history book, *adoring* a history book. Today, our kids don't even know about American history, let alone world history. It seems to be *erased*, this American history, this young, amazing experiment called democracy, is being erased from school books! Is that the way to teach our children? No, I don't think so! I'd rather have them learn about the so-called politically incorrect times in our lives, in this country's birth and growth, than I would having them learn all the dirty four letter words. Because, at least if you teach them history, they learn how to make choices. That's what we were taught when we went to school: we were taught how bad slavery was, how it tore this country apart—when we were five or six years old, we *knew* that was bad! So I think we are doing our children a great injustice by not teaching them about the country they live in. We have so many immigrants here now who aren't learning about the country they're going to live and die in, while their children and their children's children will be born here."

As already mentioned, Miss Paige has the vitality of a 30 year old. And no doubt we will see and hear much more of this multitalented lady in the near future.

Interview: West Hollywood, March 1, 2001

Notes

1. Jack Carson (1910–1963), former vaudeville actor who entered films in 1937, was one the screen's notable character actors in the 1940s and 1950s. His score of screen credits include *You Only Live Once* (1937), *Bringing Up Baby* (1938), *Mr. Smith Goes to Washington* (1939), *The Strawberry Blonde* (1941), *Gentleman Jim* (1942), *The Hard Way* (1943), *Arsenic and Old Lace* (1944), *Mildred Pierce* (1945), *A Star Is Born* (1954) and *Cat on a Hot Tin Roof* (1958).

2. Bob Hope (b. 1903), British-born all-round entertainer and one of the screen's most successful and wealthiest actors and comedians ever, grew up in Cleveland and was among other things a newsboy and a boxer before becoming a vaudevillian, a popular star on 1930s radio and finally a screen star after debuting in *The Big Broadcast of 1938* (1938). His films include *The Cat and the Canary* (1939), *My Favorite Brunette* (1947), *Paleface* (1948), *The Seven Little Foys* (1955), *Beau James* (1957) and the seven *Road* pictures with Bing Crosby (1903–1977) and Dorothy Lamour (1914–1996): *Road to Singapore* (1940), *Road to Zanzibar* (1941), *Road to Morocco* (1942), *Road to Utopia* (1945), *Road to Rio* (1947), *Road to Bali* (1953) and *The Road to Hong Kong* (1962). To the

delight of the troops, he entertained the *boys* frequently during World War II, in Korea and in Vietnam. In all, he received five special Academy Awards—not for acting, but for the humanitarian causes he fought for over the years: in 1940 ("in recognition of his unselfish services to the Motion Picture Industry"), in 1944 ("for his many services to the Academy, a Life Membership in the Academy of Motion Picture, Arts and Science"), in 1952 ("for his contribution to the laughter of the world, his service to the Motion Picture Industry, and his devotion to the American premise"), in 1959 (Jean Hersholt Humanitarian Award) and in 1965 ("for his unique and distinguished service to our Industry and the Academy"). He has also authored several books, including *The Road to Hollywood: My 40-Year Love Affair with the Movies* (1977).

3. Jack L. Warner (1892–1978) was one of the four founders of Warner Bros. and became the company's production chief. The co-founders and other Warner brothers were Sam (1888–1927, chief executive), Harry (1881–1958, president) and Albert (1884–1967, treasurer). The studio's first star and initial money-maker was Rin Tin Tin, but after the success of their first talking picture *The Jazz Singer* (1927), they gathered a memorable list of stars such as Humphrey Bogart, James Cagney, Bette Davis, Olivia de Havilland and Errol Flynn. In 1956 Harry and Albert sold their interests in the company, while Jack remained the boss of the studio until 1967. He was not easy to work with and had "more enemies than friends" (he was sued frequently and Bette Davis once said: "I stabbed Jack [L.] Warner several times ... only in my mind."). His autobiography *My First Hundred Years in Hollywood* was published in 1965, a year after he made *My Fair Lady* which he considered his greatest cinematographic achievement. He was awarded the Irving G. Thalberg Award in 1958.

Filmography

Bathing Beauty (MGM, 1944). DIR George Sidney. PROD Jack Cummings. SCR Dorothy Kingsley, Allen Boretz, Frank Waldman (story by Kenneth Earl, M. M. Musselman, Curtis Kenyon). CAM Harry Stradling. ED Blanche Sewell. RUNNING TIME 101 min. CAST: Red Skelton (Steve Elliott); Esther Williams (Caroline Brooks); Basil Rathbone (George Adams); Bill Goodwin (Willis Evans); Jean Porter (Jean Allenwood); Nana Bryant (Dean Clinton), **Janis Paige** (Janis).

Hollywood Canteen (Warner Bros., 1944). DIR-SCR Delmer Daves. PROD Walter Gottlieb. CAM Bert Glennon. ED Christian Nyby. MUS Leo F. Forbstein. RUNNING TIME 124 min. CAST: Robert Hutton (Ed "Slim" Green); Joan Leslie (Herself); Dane Clark (Sgt. Nowland); **Janis Paige** (Angela).

Her Kind of Man (Warner Bros., 1946). DIR Frederick de Cordova. PROD Alex Gottlieb. SCR Gordon Kahn, Leopold Atlas (story by Charles Hoffman, Charles V. Kern). CAM Carl Guthrie. ED Frederick Richards. MUS Franz Waxman. RUNNING TIME 80 min. CAST: Dane Clark (Don Corwin); **Janis Paige** (Georgia King); Zachary Scott (Steve Maddux); Faye Emerson (Ruby Marino); George Tobias (Joe Marino); Howard Smith (Bill Fellows).

Of Human Bondage (Warner Bros., 1946). DIR Edmund Goulding. PROD Henry Blanke. SCR Catherine Turney (novel by W. Somerset Maugham). CAM Peverell Marley. ED Clarence Kolster. MUS Leo F. Forbstein. RUNNING TIME 106 min. CAST: Paul Henreid (Philip Carey); Eleanor Parker (Mildred Rogers); Alexis Smith (Nora Nesbitt); Edmund Gwenn (Athelny); Patric Knowles (Harry Griffiths); **Janis Paige** (Sally Athelny).

Two Guys from Milwaukee (Warner Bros., 1946). DIR David Butler. PROD Alex Gottlieb. SCR Charles Hoffman, I. A. L. Diamond. CAM Arthur Edeson. ED Irene Morra. MUS Leonid Raab. RUNNING TIME 90 min. CAST: Dennis Morgan (Prince Henry); Jack Carson (Buzz Williams); Joan Leslie (Connie Reed); **Janis Paige** (Polly); S. Z. Sakall (Count Oswald); Lauren Bacall (Herself); Humphrey Bogart (Himself).

The Time, the Place and the Girl (Warner Bros., 1946). DIR David Butler. PROD Alex Gottlieb. SCR Francis Swann, Agnes Christine Johnston, Lynn Starling (story by Leonard Lee). CAM William V. Skall, Arthur Edeson. ED Irene Morra. MUS Leo F. Forbstein. RUNNING TIME 105 min. CAST: Dennis Morgan (Steven Ross); Jack Carson (Jeff Howard); **Janis Paige** (Sue Jackson); Martha Vickers (Victoria Cassel); S. Z. "Cuddles" Sakall (Ladislaus Cassel); Alan Hale (John Braden).

Cheyenne (Warner Bros., 1947). DIR Raoul Walsh. PROD Robert Buckner. SCR Alan Le May, Thames Williamson (story by Paul I. Wellman). CAM Sid Hickox. ED Christian Nyby. MUS Max Steiner. RUNNING TIME 99 min. CAST: Dennis Morgan (James Wylie); Jane Wyman (Ann Kincaid); **Janis Paige** (Emily Carson); Bruce Bennett (Ed Landers); Alan Hale (Fred Durkin); Arthur Kennedy (The Sundance Kid).

Love and Learn (Warner Bros., 1947). DIR Frederick de Cordova. PROD William Jacobs. SCR Eugene Conrad, Francis Swann, I. A. L. Diamond (story by Harry Sauber). CAM Wesley Anderson. ED Frank McGee. MUS Max Steiner. RUNNING TIME 85 min. CAST: Jack Carson (Jingles); Martha Vickers (Barbara Wyngate); Robert Hutton (Bob Grant); **Janis Paige** (Jackie); Otto Kruger (Andrew Wyngate); Barbara Brown (Victoria Wyngate).

Romance on the High Seas (Warner Bros., 1948). DIR Michael Curtiz. PROD Alex Gottlieb. SCR Julius J. Epstein, Philip G. Epstein (story by S. Pondal Rios, Carlos A. Olivari). CAM Elwood Bredell. MUS Leo F. Forbstein. RUNNING TIME 97 min. CAST: Jack Carson (Peter Virgil); **Janis Paige** (Elvira Kent); Don DeFore

(Michael Kent); Doris Day (Georgia Garrett); Oscar Levant (Oscar Farrar); S. Z. Sakall (Lazlo Lazlo).

Wallflower (Warner Bros., 1948). DIR Frederick de Cordova. PROD Alex Gottlieb. SCR Phoebe Ephron, Henry Ephron (play by Reginald Denham, Mary Orr). CAM Karl Freund. ED Folmar Blangsted. MUS Leo F. Forbstein. RUNNING TIME 77 min. CAST: Robert Hutton (Warren James); Joyce Reynolds (Jackie); **Janis Paige** (Joy); Edward Arnold (Mr. Linnett); Barbara Brown (Mrs. Linnett); Jerome Cowan (Mr. James).

Always Together (Warner Bros., 1948). DIR Frederick de Cordova. PROD Alex Gottlieb. SCR Phoebe Ephron, Henry Ephron, I. A. L. Diamond. CAM Carl Guthrie. ED Folmer Blangsted. MUS Werner Heymann. RUNNING TIME 76 min. CAST: Joyce Reynolds (Jane Barker); Robert Hutton (Don Masters); Cecil Kellaway (Jonathan Turner); Ernest Truex (Mr. Bull); Don McGuire (McIntyre); **Janis Paige**, Humphrey Bogart, Dennis Morgan, Jack Carson, Alexis Smith (characters in movie).

Winter Meeting (Warner Bros., 1948). DIR Bretaigne Windust. PROD Henry Blanke. SCR Catherine Turney (novel by Ethel Vance). CAM Ernest Haller. ED Owen Marks. MUS Leo F. Forbstein. RUNNING TIME 104 min. CAST: Bette Davis (Susan Grieve); **Janis Paige** (Peggy Markham); James Davis (Lt. Slik Novak); John Hoyt (Stacy Grant); Florence Bates (Mrs. Castle); Walter Baldwin (Mr. Castle).

One Sunday Afternoon (Warner Bros., 1949). DIR Raoul Walsh. PROD Jerry Wald. SCR Robert L. Richards (play by James Hagan). CAM Sid Hickox, Wilfred M. Cline. ED Christian Nyby. MUS Ralph Blane. RUNNING TIME 90 min. CAST: Dennis Morgan (Biff Grimes); **Janis Paige** (Virginia Brush); Don DeFore (Hugo Barnstead); Dorothy Malone (Amy Lind); Ben Blue (Nick); Oscar O'Shea (Toby); Alan Hale, Jr. (Marty).

The Younger Brothers (Warner Bros., 1949). DIR Edwin L. Marin. PROD Saul Elkins. SCR Edna Anhalt (story by Mort Grant). CAM William Snyder. ED Frederick Richards. MUS Gregory Cava. RUNNING TIME 76 min. CAST: Wayne Morris (Cole Younger); **Janis Paige** (Kate Shephard); Bruce Bennett (Jim Younger); Geraldine Brooks (Mary Hathaway); Robert Hutton (Johnny Younger); Alan Hale (Sheriff Knudson).

The House Across the Street (Warner Bros, 1949). DIR Richard Bare. PROD Saul Elkins. SCR Russell Hughes (story by Roy Chanslor). CAM William Snyder. ED Frank Magee. MUS William Lava. RUNNING TIME 69 min. CAST: Wayne Morris (Dave Joslin); **Janis Paige** (Kit Williams); Bruce Bennett (Keever); Alan Hale (J. B. Grennell); James Mitchell (Marty Bremer); Barbara Bates (Beth Roberts).

This Side of the Law (Warner Bros., 1950). DIR Richard Bare. PROD Saul Elkins. SCR Russell Hughes (story by Richard Sale). CAM Carl Guthrie. ED Frank Magee. MUS William Lava. RUNNING TIME 74 min. CAST: Viveca Lindfors (Evelyn Taylor); Kent Smith (David Cummins); **Janis Paige** (Nadine Taylor); Robert Douglas (Philip Cagle); John Alvin (Calder Taylor).

Fugitive Lady, a.k.a. *The Dark Road* (Republic, 1951). DIR Sidney Salkow. PROD M. J. Frankovich. SCR John O'Dea (novel by Doris Miles Disney). CAM Tonino Delli Colli. ED Nino Baragli. MUS Willy Ferrero. RUNNING TIME 78 min. CAST: **Janis Paige** (Barbara Clementi); Binnie Barnes (Esther Clementi); Massimo Serato (Gene); Eduardo Clannelli (Ralph Clementi); Tony Centa (Jeff); Alba Arnova (Francine).

Mr. Universe (Eagle Lion, 1951). DIR-PROD Joseph Lerner. SCR Searle Kramer. CAM Gerald Hirschfeld. ED Geraldine Lerner. RUNNING TIME 89 min. CAST: Jack Carson (Jeff Clayton); **Janis Paige** (Lorraine); Vincent Edwards (Mr. Universe, Tommy Tomkins); Bert Lahr (Joe Pulaski); Robert Alda (Fingers Maroni).

Two Gals and a Guy (United Artists, 1951). DIR Alfred E. Green. PROD John W. Arents. SCR Searle Kramer. CAM Gerald Hirschfeld. MUS Gail Kubik. RUNNING TIME 75 min. CAST: Robert Alda (Deke Oliver); **Janis Paige** (Della Oliver/Sylvia Latour); James Gleason (Bill Howard); Lionel Stander (Mr. Seymour); Arnold Stang (Bernard).

Silk Stockings (MGM, 1957). DIR Rouben Mamoulian. PROD Arthur Freed. SCR Leonard Gershe, Leonard Spigelglass (musical play *Silk Stockings* based on book by George S. Kaufman, Leueen MacGrath, suggested by *Ninotchka* [1939], screenplay by Charles Brackett, Walter Reisch, Billy Wilder, story by Melchior Lengyel). CAM Robert Bronner. ED Harold F. Kress. MUS André Previn. RUNNING TIME 117 min. CAST: Fred Astaire (Steve Canfield); Cyd Charisse (Ninotchka); **Janis Paige** (Peggy Dayton); Peter Lorre (Brankov); George Tobias (Vassili Markovitch); Wim Sonneveld (Peter Ilyitch Boroff).

Please Don't Eat the Daisies (MGM, 1960). DIR Charles Walters. PROD Joe Pasternak. SCR Isobel Lennart (novel by Jean Kerr). CAM Robert Bronner. ED John MacSweeney. MUS David Rose. RUNNING TIME 111 min. CAST: Doris Day (Kate Mackay); David Niven (Lawrence Mackay); **Janis Paige** (Deborah Vaughn); Spring Byington (Mrs. Suzie Robinson); Richard Haydn (Alfred North); Patsy Kelly (Maggie).

Bachelor in Paradise (MGM, 1961). DIR Jack Arnold. PROD Ted Richmond. SCR Valentine Davies, Hal Kanter (story by Vera Caspary). CAM Joseph Ruttenberg. ED Richard Farrell. MUS Henry Mancini. RUNNING TIME 109 min. CAST: Bob Hope (Adam J. Niles); Lana Turner (Rosemary Howard); **Janis Paige** (Dolores Jynson); Jim Hutton (Larry Delavane); Paula Prentiss (Linda Delavane); Agnes Moorehead (Judge Peterson).

Follow the Boys (MGM, 1963). DIR Richard Thorpe. PROD Lawrence P. Bachmann. SCR David T. Chantler, David Osborn (story by Lawrence P. Bachmann). CAM Ted Scaife. ED John Victor Smith. MUS Ron Goodwin, Alexander Courage. RUNNING TIME 95 min. CAST: Connie Francis (Bonnie Pulaski); Paula Prentiss (Toni Denham); Dany Robin (Michele); Russ Tamblyn (Lt. Smith); Richard Long (Lt. Langley); **Janis Paige** (Liz Branville).

The Caretakers (United Artists, 1963). DIR-PROD Hal Bartlett. SCR Henry F. Greenberg (story by Hall Bartlett, Jerry Paris). CAM Lucien Ballard. ED William B. Murphy. MUS Elmer Bernstein. RUNNING TIME 97 min. CAST: Robert Stack (Donovan MacLeod); Polly Bergen (Lorna Melford); Joan Crawford (Lucretia Terry); **Janis Paige** (Marion); Diane McBain (Alison Horne).

Welcome to Hard Times (MGM, 1967). DIR Burt Kennedy. PROD Max E. Younstein. SCR Burt Kennedy (novel by E. L. Doctorow). CAM Harry Stradling, Jr. ED Aaron Stell. MUS Harry Sukman. RUNNING TIME 103 min. CAST: Henry Fonda (Blue Shane); Janice Rule (Molly Riordan); Keenan Wynn (Zar); **Janis Paige** (Adah); John Anderson (Ezra/Isaac Maple); Warren Oates (Jenks).

Natural Causes (1994). DIR James Beckett. PROD-SCR Jake Raymond Needham. CAM Denis Maloney. ED Richard Fields. MUS Nathan Wang. CAST: Linda Purl (Jessie); Cary-Hiroyuki Tagawa (Maj. Somchai); Ali MacGraw (Fran); **Janis Paige** (Mrs. MacCarthy).

Television Movies

Colombo: Blueprint for Murder (1972). DIR Peter Falk. CAST: Peter Falk; Patrick O'Neal; **Janis Paige** (Goldie Williamson); Forrest Tucker.

The Turning Point of Jim Malloy, a.k.a. *Gibbsville: The Turning Point of Jim Malloy* and *John O'Hara's Gibbsville* (1975). DIR Frank D. Gilroy. CAST: John Savage; Biff McGuire; Peggy McCay; Gig Young; Kathleen Quinlan; **Janis Paige** (Lonnie).

Cop on the Boat, a.k.a. *The Return of Joe Forrester* (1975). DIR Virgil W. Vogel. CAST: Lloyd Bridges; Don Stroud; **Janis Paige** (Irene); Jim Backus.

Lanigan's Rabbi (1976). DIR Lou Antonio. CAST: Art Carney; Stuart Margolin; **Janis Paige** (Kate Lanigan); Janet Margolin; Lorraine Gary.

Valentine Magic on Love Island, a.k.a. *Magic on Love Island* (1980). DIR Earl Bellamy. CAST: Adrienne Barbeau; Bill Daily; Howard Duff; Dominique Dunne; **Janis Paige** (Madge).

Angel on My Shoulder (1980). DIR John Berry. CAST: Peter Strauss; Richard Kiley; Barbara Hershey; **Janis Paige** (Dolly Blaine); Seymour Cassel.

Bret Maverick (1981). DIR Stuart Margolin. CAST: James Garner; Ed Bruce; Ramon Bieri; **Janis Paige** (Mandy Packer); Stuart Margolin.

The Other Woman (1983). DIR Melville Shavelson. CAST: Hal Linden; Anne Meara; Madolyn Smith-Osborne; **Janis Paige** (Mrs. Barnes).

LUISE RAINER

In Arthur Penn's *Little Big Man* (1970), William Hickey plays a young reporter who meets Dustin Hoffman for an interview. Hoffman, who plays a 121-year-old man, claims to be the only white survivor of the battle of Little Big Horn. He tells his overwhelming story and is able to capture a full life in a most fascinating way as a real storyteller, as a man with a unique and powerful personality—someone it is hard to catch up with. The reporter is totally in awe of him.

I felt exactly like that young reporter when I had the honor of meeting former screen actress (and to me always screen *legend*) Luise Rainer, in the 1930s one of MGM's most prominent leading actresses. She was the first person to win an Academy Award for best actress in two successive years (1937 and 1938) and that during the mere three and a half years she was in Hollywood!

Her premature and abrupt departure caused all kinds of things to be written about her: she didn't fit in the studio system, she was advised badly, she did not approve of and did not get on with Louis B. Mayer.... You can't always believe what is read or said, good or bad.

Miss Rainer, now 92, has lived in her adopted London since 1992, having returned from her Swiss home after her English husband's death. She is a wonderful, charming and most gracious lady, very vivid, bright, energetic, dynamic and literate, with a great sense of humor and she still looks at life through the eyes of someone who's eager to learn all that's new, fascinating and enriching.

She and Katharine Hepburn are the only 1930s stars who are still alive and who are able to talk about that time and era which, it seems, has become more and more important as time goes by, a decade that was dominated as well by stars such as Garbo, Dietrich, Norma Shearer and Joan Crawford.

The main difference between Miss Rainer and all other magnificent actresses is that her film career was so extraordinarily short. In a mere three and a half years and before she turned her back on Hollywood, she appeared in only eight films, most of which today's youngsters have not seen and are not familiar with. Yet, she deserves to be called a versatile and prolific actress.

She never felt herself a "star" or considered so-called stardom important; to her, being a truly first-class actress was the only important thing. The great Max Reinhardt,[1] the most influential stage director and producer on the German speaking stage, took her into his ensemble in Vienna, an ensemble that included amongst selected artists Emil Jannings, Conrad

Veidt and Elisabeth Bergner. Miss Rainer: "Reinhardt, though never titled, was a 'prince,' a true aristocrat from inside out, he was wonderful. There was an extraordinary aura about him, he sensed people and artists, he sensed their talent. When someone needed help and advice, he was there. Otherwise he would watch, let go, which made one feel his approval, giving encouragement and confidence to make one better."

Miss Rainer appeared in a few Austro-German films—"absolutely laughable," she claims; otherwise she appeared only on the stage. Lured to Hollywood in 1935 she was soon to be heralded as the new Garbo. Her U.S. screen debut was in *Escapade* (1935); *Variety* wrote in its film review: "Miss Rainer, entirely new to America, brings from Europe a wealth of skill in theatrical art. She acts with feeling." A talent had arrived and before the studio bosses were aware, she had, by her first film, proved herself to be a "star."

Her next film, *The Great Ziegfeld* (1936), a hugely entertaining biography of flamboyant impresario Florenz Ziegfeld, was an ode to showmanship with Miss Rainer impersonating Ziegfeld's first wife, Anna Held, a former famous actress-singer. A telephone scene Miss Rainer had to make became very famous. Ziegfeld had divorced Anna Held; by phone, the broken hearted Anna—holding back her tears—congratulated Ziegfeld on his next marriage. This scene earned Miss Rainer her first Academy Award.

The Great Ziegfeld was followed by *The Good Earth* (1937), based on Pearl S. Buck's 1931 Pulitzer Prize–winning novel about a hard-working Chinese farmer and his family. It proved again to be a great triumph for Miss Rainer who played the demanding role of O-Lan, the ever-patient wife of Paul Muni. She stole the show. Her part, she said, had dialogue of no more than three pages. Her feelings and deepest emotions had to be expressed

Luise Rainer during her famous telephone scene in *The Great Ziegfeld* (1936). (Courtesy of DOCIP Film Archive, Brussels, Belgium.)

through eyes and action. At the end of the film and after Olan's death, Muni, in deep sorrow, touched a peach tree she had planted, saying "O-Lan, you were the earth!"—providing one of the most powerful closing lines ever seen on film.

Miss Rainer: "Louis B. wanted me to be beautiful, nothing else, just one more horse in his stable. He was horrified at Irving Thalberg's insistence for me to play O-Lan, the poor uncomely little Chinese peasant. I myself, with the meager dialogue given to me, feared to be a hilarious bore. I had not then read Pearl Buck's famous novel; I felt I should not do so now, but instead do my best with the lines and situations given in the script."

Although up against Garbo's role of Marie Walewska in *Conquest*, the part of O-Lan earned Miss Rainer her second Academy Award.

Miss Rainer: "It may sound strange to say so, but I never felt to be what is called 'an actress.' Whatever I was able to do or give in my work came from inside out. It is in real life that people often act or need to act. On stage or screen, to be convincing, you have to be true, as true as you can be. For better or for worse you have to find within yourself that color and shade most similar to the character you have to play, build it up with the help of memory and intuition to be *it*. It should not be *acting*, it must be *being!*"

What is her greatest achievement? Is it perhaps this realism (for the part of O-Lan for example, she refused to wear the rubber mask Chinese look suggested by the make-up department) which made her performances so genuine, honest, down-to-earth? Miss Rainer: "I don't feel I have achieved anything, though I am told I have. I am grateful to have been permitted to give out a tiny bit of what was given to me in the cradle. I've been asked often why I don't teach acting. I couldn't! My sole schooling was to live alert and open-eyed, to feel and to sense. How could I teach that? I wouldn't know!"

Irving G. Thalberg, MGM's production executive and Mr. Mayer's right hand, died of pneumonia in September 1936 at age 37, a few weeks after the principal photography of *The Good Earth* was completed; the film was dedicated "To the memory of Irving Grant Thalberg—His last great achievement." What was Miss Rainer's impression of him? "His dying was a terrible shock to us. He was young and ever so able. Had it not been that he died, I think I may have stayed much longer in films."

After his death, she felt lost and Louis B. Mayer didn't know how to handle her. Being under a long contract, Miss Rainer went on to make five more films at Metro: a suspense film *The Emperor's Candlesticks* (1937, her third film with William Powell), *Big City* (1937) opposite Spencer Tracy, *The Toy Wife* (1938) with Melvyn Douglas, her favorite leading man who was, as she says, interested in more things than acting, Julien Duvivier's *The Great Waltz* (1938), playing Mrs. Johan Strauss, and finally *Dramatic School* (1938). She returned to the screen three years later in Paramount's *Hostages* (a film, she says, only her mother-in-law saw and she held it against her for ever after!).

"I was not happy in Hollywood. I felt I did not belong there. Getting the two Academy Awards put me on too high a pedestal, the whole surrounding world seemed to look at me, somehow preventing me from doing the looking which was a necessity to me, the way I needed to live. As a teenager, as a beginner in the theater, when I had enough money I could sit forever so long just looking around at the people, wondering what they may do, or how they may feel, or how they belong together, what was their activity, what made them look or act this or that way. I could no more do so. Of course I yearned to be successful, I was aware one has to make allowance to success, but it all changed my life the way I had not planned.

"It was only so very much later, long after I stopped filming and lived a different life that I realized how many human beings I had reached with my work; somehow it was a revelation and quite wonderful when doors opened for and to me I had never expected to open."

During World War II Miss Rainer spoke at bond drives all over the United States, sometimes together with journalists, at other times also together with America's First Lady Eleanor Roosevelt who had become an admirer of her's. When asked to go to Africa and Italy to entertain the troops, she did. It was combined with a kind of social welfare job, finding out the men's grudges or needs, matters they might not have wanted to or dared discuss with their commanding officers.

During her Hollywood years she was married to Clifford Odets.[2] "He was wonderful and extraordinary. Whatever time I could steal during my absorbing work, I gave to Clifford. I longed to be with him, I was much in love." What about her social life? "I think we did not partake in what's called 'Hollywood social life.' Clifford was as successful and well known as I was. Of course we had friends and of course we saw them, but mainly in small circles. Clifford's homestead was New York, mine was Hollywood. The spare time together was precious to us, the failure of our marriage was a distress.

Studio portrait of Luise Rainer when she made *Hostages* (1943). (Courtesy of Luise Rainer.)

"Life with another human being is never just easy, especially not when both partners are artists. No matter his belief in me as an actress and his pride in my success, Clifford Odets wanted me to himself and I think he suffered under my fame and his having to share me too much with the rest of the world. My second husband seemed to have been sent to me from heaven. He was a publisher, involved in books and ideas. We were married for 45 years and from the beginning till his death he was my rock of Gibraltar."

What about the so-called "Hollywood colony," often described as the place to be for numerous Europeans who worked in Hollywood back then? Miss Rainer: "I was frequently invited to Salka Viertel's house [more information: interview with Fred Zinnemann, note 6]; she kept the European colony together. She also was a close friend of Greta Garbo whose beauty I admired and adored."

To the joy of her friends and her still many fans Miss Rainer returned to films after more than 50 years to play a part in *The Gambler* (1997). The film, made in Hungary, was directed by Károly Makk. Miss Rainer: "At a party Roddy McDowall, one of my very best friends who unfortunately passed away, came to me with Anthony Hopkins whom I had not known before and they kind of chased me into doing that part. 'You simply have to do it,' both said. It was the film of Dostoyevsky's *Gambler*. I did it for the 'lark' of it!

"Károly Makk was dear but worried I may forget the lines and could I still act, he asked me. It made me laugh! As a matter of fact, I had been on the stage on and off; I also had made a small, lovely film for television in the 1980s called *A Dancer* in which I played a retired ballerina. Anyway I had enormous fun doing *The Gambler*, except it inflamed the spark in me again: suddenly, after all the years, I feel I must do more. But now, what's happening? The scripts that are thrown at me, are not quality but just any dame more than 75 years old."

She adds: "If I find a story and a part worthy of doing, I'll do it. But I've had a full life. I have lived it and seen much. I had two husbands, both special, both wonderful, both the envy of many women! I have my beloved child, my daughter. Sorrows were mixed with very great joys."

And with a little luck that right part may still come along, so we get to see a living legend at work once again.

I received a very warm welcome when visiting Miss Rainer at her London home and I am terribly grateful for her hospitality. Besides talking about her career in films, I also saw some of the impressive art work she had done over the years and which decorates the back rooms in her spacious, tasteful apartment. Both her Academy Awards have a special spot in her study.

I hope we can all see her again soon at the movies: "Luise Rainer—in a theater near you!"

Interview: London, March 26, 2000

Notes

1. Max Reinhardt (1873–1943), Austrian-born stage producer and director of the famous Deutsches Theater who worked mostly in Salzburg and Berlin, had an enormous influence on German, European and later also on Americans films as he had trained several leading actors (including Marlene Dietrich) and directors (such as Otto Preminger, William Dieterle and Ernst Lubitsch) who all went to and worked in the U.S. When the Nazis came to power in Germany, he too moved to the U.S. where he co-directed *A Midsummer Night's Dream* (1935) with William Dieterle. Before he died, he asked his friends and colleagues: "No flowers, instead make a contribution that will destroy Hitler." His two sons, Wolfgang Reinhardt (1909–1979, producer) and Gottfried Reinhardt (1911–1994, screenwriter, producer and director) also worked on both sides of the Atlantic.

2. Playwright, screenwriter and director Clifford Odets (1906–1963) was one of America's leading dramatists who wrote a number of screenplays and directed two solid dramas, *None but the Lonely Heart* (1944) and *The Story on Page Three* (1959). He and Miss Rainer were married from 1937 to 1940.

Filmography

Ja der Himmel über Wien (RKO, 1930).

Sehnsucht 202 (Cine-Allianz, 1932). DIR Max Neufeld. CAM Otto Kanturek. MUS Richard Fall. RUNNING TIME 88 min. CAST: Magda Schneider; Fritz Schulz; **Luise Rainer**; Rolf von Goth; Attila Horbiger; Mizzi Griebl; Hans Thimig.

Heute Kommt's Drauf An (RKO, 1933).

Escapade (MGM, 1935). DIR Robert Z. Leonard. PROD Bernard H. Hyman. SCR Herman J. Mankiewicz, Ethel Borden (based on the Austrian film *Maskerade* [1934]). CAM Ernest Haller. ED Tom Held. MUS Bronislau Kaper, Walter Jurmann. RUNNING TIME 93 min. CAST: William Powell (Fritz Heideneck); **Luise Rainer** (Leopoldine); Frank Morgan (Karl Harrandt); Virginia Bruce (Gerta Keller); Reginald Owen (Paul Harrandt); Mady Christians (Anita Keller).

The Great Ziegfeld (MGM, 1936). DIR Robert Z. Leonard. PROD Hunt Stromberg. SCR William Anthony McGuire (suggested by the life of Florenz Ziegfeld, Jr.). CAM Oliver T. Marsh. ED William S. Gray. MUS Arthur Lange. RUNNING TIME 180 min. CAST: William Powell (Florenz Ziegfeld, Jr.); Myrna Loy (Billie Burke); **Luise Rainer** (Anna Held Ziegfeld); Frank Morgan (Jack Billings); Fanny Brice (Herself); Virginia Bruce (Audrey Dane).

The Good Earth (MGM, 1937). DIR Sidney Franklin. SCR Talbot Jennings, Tess Slesinger, Claudine West (novel by Pearl S. Buck). CAM Karl Freund. ED Basil Wrangell. MUS Herbert Stothart. RUNNING TIME 138 min. CAST: Paul Muni (Wang Lung); **Luise Rainer** (O-Lan); Walter Connolly (Uncle); Tilly Losch (Lotus); Charles Grapewin (Old Father); Jessie Ralph (Cuckoo).

The Emperor's Candlesticks (MGM, 1937). DIR George Fitzmaurice. PROD John W. Considine, Jr. SCR Monckton Hoffe, Harold Goldman, Herman Manckiewicz (novel by Baroness Orczy). CAM Harold Rosson, Oliver T. Marsh. ED Conrad A. Nervig. MUS Franz Waxman. RUNNING TIME 90 min. CAST: William Powell (Baron Wolensky); **Luise Rainer** (Countess Mironova); Robert Young (Grand Duke Peter); Maureen O'Sullivan (Maria Orlech); Frank Morgan (Colonel Baron Suroff); Henry Stephenson (Prince Johan).

Big City (MGM, 1937). DIR Frank Borzage. PROD Norman Krasna. SCR Dore Schary, Hugo Butler (story by

Norman Krasna). CAM Joseph Ruttenberg. ED Frederick Y. Smith. MUS William Axt. RUNNING TIME 80 min. CAST: **Luise Rainer** (Anna Benton); Spencer Tracy (Joe Benton); Charles Grapewin (Mayor); Janet Beecher (Sophie Sloan); Eddie Quillan (Mike Edwards); Victor Varconi (Paul Roya).

The Toy Wife (MGM, 1938). DIR Richard Thorpe. PROD Merian C. Cooper. SCR Zoë Akins (based on a play by Henri Meilhac and Ludovic Halévy, and a play by Augustin Daly). CAM Oliver T. Marsh. ED Elmo Veron. MUS Edward Ward. RUNNING TIME 93 min. CAST: **Luise Rainer** (Gilberte, Frou Frou); Melvyn Douglas (Georges Sartoris); Robert Young (Andre Vallaire); Barbara O'Neil (Louise Brigard); H. B. Warner (Victor Brigard); Alma Kruger (Madame Vallaire).

The Great Waltz (MGM, 1938). DIR Julien Duvivier. PROD Bernard H. Hyman. SCR Samuel Hoffenstein, Walter Reisch (story by Gottfried Reinhardt). CAM Joseph Ruttenberg. ED Tom Held. MUS Dimitri Tiomkin. RUNNING TIME 105 min. CAST: **Luise Rainer** (Poldi Vogelhuber); Fernand Gravet (Johan Strauss); Miliza Korjus (Carla Donner); Hugh Herbert (Julius Hofbauer); Lionel Atwill (Count Hohenfried); Curt Bois (Kienzl).

Dramatic School (MGM, 1938). DIR Robert B. Sinclair. PROD Mervyn LeRoy. SCR Ernest Vajda, Mary C. McCall, Jr. (play by Hans Szekely, Zoltan Egyed). CAM William Daniels, Joseph Ruttenberg. ED Frederick Y. Smith. MUS Franz Waxman. RUNNING TIME 80 min. CAST: **Luise Rainer** (Louise Mauban); Paulette Goddard (Nana); Alan Marshall (Andre D'Abbencourt); Lana Turner (Mabo); Genevieve Tobin (Gina Bertier); Anthony Allan (Fluery); Henry Stephenson (Pasquel, Sr.).

Hostages (Paramount, 1943). DIR Frank Tuttle. PROD Sol C. Siegel. SCR Lester Cole, Frank Butler (novel by Stefan Heym). CAM Victor Milner. ED Archie Marshek. MUS Victor Young. RUNNING TIME 88 min. CAST: Arturo de Cordova (Paul Breda); **Luise Rainer** (Milada Preissinger); William Bendix (Janoshik); Roland Varno (Jan Pavel); Oscar Homolka (Lev Preissinger); Katina Paxinou (Maria).

The Gambler (Channel Four, 1997). DIR Károly Makk. PROD Charles Cohen, Marc Vlessing. SCR Katharine Ogden, Charles Cohen, Nick Dear. CAM Jules van den Steenhoven. ED Kevin Whelan. MUS Brian Lock. RUNNING TIME 97 min. CAST: Michael Gambon (Dostoyevsky); Jodhi May (Anna Snitkina); Polly Walker (Polina); Dominic West (Alexei); John Wood (The General); Johan Leysen (De Grieux); **Luise Rainer** (Grandmother).

PAULA RAYMOND

Paula Raymond will always be remembered for her leading role as Cary Grant's wife in *Crisis* (1950), which was Richard Brooks' first film as a director. It turned out to be a great start for an impressive career for its director, but unfortunately, for Miss Raymond, who was destined to become a star in her own right as well and definitely had the talent to be a top leading lady, the film only became one of the *few* highlights in her career. By the mid–1950s, when she was supposed to be among Hollywood's leading ladies, she had virtually retired from acting.

What had happened? Why did this versatile actress vanish from the face of the earth and start working as a secretary at age 32, only a few years after appearing opposite stars like Cary Grant, Dick Powell, Van Johnson, Adolphe Menjou, Esther Williams and Kathryn Grayson? That was something I hoped to find out.

I was able to meet with Miss Raymond in person after being introduced to her by Jerry Anker, president of the Hollywood High School Alumni Association and a close friend of numerous screen personalities, including Miss Raymond.

But first things first. How did she make it all the way to Hollywood, being born in San Francisco in 1924 as Paula Ramona Wright? Miss Raymond: "My father was a corporate lawyer in San Francisco, but after my mother had divorced him, we arrived here in Los Angeles and my sister was really the talented one, I was always the 'little' sister. We had friends here, especially a lady who had an agent for one of her sons; this agent found my sister—and me as well—interesting enough to appear in films. They made an appointment for an interview for a Jane Withers movie [*Keep Smiling*, 1938] for me to play the bad girl to Janie's heroine role. They chose me to test and finally I got the role. But I was still at school, I was in the 8th grade then. My mother didn't want to press it too much.

"When I was 19, I got married: that was going to be for the rest of my life. I thought I was going to be a housewife. But my husband was abusive, he thought 'if I can't have her, nobody's going to have her'—how stupid, after all, he had me! But occasionally he would overindulge and whatever alcoholic beverage he chose, he would become abusive. I had to support myself and my three month old daughter, so I went to MCA, one of the top agencies at the time, years before they bought Universal. But, as I had just had my daughter, they said, 'You will have to lose five pounds.' I asked, 'But what will I do in the meantime?' They said, 'Well, why don't you try modeling?' So I went over to one of the photographers, a quite famous and very good cover photographer at the time—that's how I got started modeling at $25 an hour and [I] forgot all about acting, because I was earning a living. I was also working for other photographers like Tom Kelley.

"After about three months, this lady asked me if I could act. I said, 'Well, I *am* an actress.' We sat down, read a couple of scenes from a book she took from her shelf and she said, 'Well, I have a friend at Paramount, Al Lewis, a casting director—you should see him.' She took me over, we did a test from *Night and Day*, the Cole Porter story with Cary Grant and Alexis Smith, and they signed me to a contract—this was late 1946—but they did absolutely nothing with me.

"Meanwhile I was getting calls from various agencies, the last one I had spoken to was the Cukor-Lipton Agency. One day I got a call from a young woman who worked at Max Arnow's office at Columbia Studios and she asked me to make an appointment to have me come in to see him. I made the appointment, but I couldn't go into a strange man's office by myself, not when you had heard all those stories about Hollywood, casting couches and all that stuff. So I called the last agents I had spoken with, that was Elsie Cukor [sister of film director George Cukor¹] and her husband, Leon Lipton. They accompanied me, and we went up to Max's office who offered me a seven year contract, starting at $100 a week. The agents said it was fine and at least I was working again. They did put me in some of their movies, but they were all B films, so I ate my way out of that contract, I got free in six months. I got so plump they couldn't use me as a leading lady [laughs] and then I didn't feel like working for a little while.

"Then something happened. I was playing an English girl in a television show called *Storybook Theater*—Barry Fitzgerald's brother, Arthur Shield, was the host of the show and they were doing 'A Million Dollar Poundnote.' This was a half-hour show so it was shot in three days; the second day my agent Leon was on the set as well. I said to him, 'Well Leon, how nice of you to visit me.' He said, 'I'm not visiting, they *called* me. What have you been doing? They wanted to talk to me!' I said, 'All I've been doing, is my job.' I couldn't figure out exactly what could be wrong, until a little bit later in the afternoon he came down from this interview and he said, 'Well Paula, nothing's wrong. They just said, 'You're not going to waste this girl on television, are you?' So Leon went home to Elsie and she said, 'You know, we've never done that with a client before, but maybe we'd better take her to see George.' So they took me to George Cukor and he said, 'Okay, I think we should test her.' He directed my screen test at MGM and I was signed immediately to an MGM contract. The first role I played at MGM was a small role in *Adam's Rib* [1949], I played the part of David Wayne's girlfriend. I think Cukor had that thrown into the script, to introduce me to the studio. I also had one scene in *East Side, West Side* [1950] playing James Mason's secretary.

Paula Raymond in the early 1950s. (Courtesy of Paula Raymond).

"By then they were testing me for the

lead in *Devil's Doorway* [1950] with Robert Taylor. Director Anthony Mann[2] who directed most of Jimmy Stewart's Westerns, didn't really want to have that *nobody*—here he had Robert Taylor, Gilbert Roland, Louis Calhern, Ramon Navarro, all of these wonderful people, and then this little nobody from nowhere is going to play the lead? So when he was directing the test, he would tell me all the time to do it this or that way—and then he'd say, 'No, no! Cut! Cut!'—as though I were doing it all wrong. 'No, do it *this* way!' Then, after a while, finally I turned around and said, 'Tony, when you make up your mind how you *really* want me to do it, I'll do it *that* way.' So after the next take, he said, 'Print.'

"We were on location in Aspen, Colorado—I was trying to hide. Knowing I was playing opposite to Robert Taylor, I was trying to be very quiet among those movie veterans, so they wouldn't notice this nobody was there too [laughs]. But Tony Mann decided that he wanted to get me into his bed. I understand that the crew was even taking bets as to who and when. Because nobody knew who I was, my publicity man, Jim Campbell, was always by my side. The first time Tony asked me out to dinner, I went with him—alone. But he would try to get me into his cabin and I said, 'No no, forget it.' So, after that, when Tony would say, 'Paula, shall we have dinner tonight?' I'd turn to Jim and say, 'Well, that sounds wonderful, doesn't it, Jim? We'd love to!' Which reminds me of my one date with Spencer Tracy while we were shooting *Adam's Rib*. Our dressing rooms were in the same dressing room building and one day he was coming down from his dressing room while I was going up to mine. He stopped me halfway up and he halfway down, and he said, 'Paula!' I said, 'Mr. Tracy!' I always called him Mr. Tracy. He said, 'They're giving a reception for Prince Philip of Sweden at Romanoff's on Saturday, would you do the honor of accompanying me?' Of course, I was dying to say yes, but the way I was raised, a young woman does not go out with an older man unchaperoned, so I thought, how can I say yes? So I finally blurted out, 'My mother and I would love to!' God bless him, he got my mother a date! [laughs]. Of course I was very much in awe of Spencer Tracy, but needless to say he never asked me out again [laughs].

"I think my favorite role was in *The Duchess of Idaho* [1950] although it was only the second lead—Esther Williams played the leading role. It was a comedy and I loved the role. In fact, when I was on location for *Devil's Doorway*, I was already cast for Robert Z. Leonard's *Duchess of Idaho*, so I had the script with me on location in Aspen. But I heard much later that they were sending back the rushes of *Devil's Doorway* in which I played a very dramatic role, and because of that, director Robert Z. Leonard—we always called him 'Pop' Leonard—had said, 'Well, she can't play comedy, she's a dramatic actress!' So after two weeks I had been taken out of that role. But producer Joe Pasternak came back and he had said, 'No no, I want Paula.'

"Well, before shooting of *Duchess of Idaho* began, they decided they'd better rehearse first and the only scene they did, was the opening scene with my character in the night club. So the writers, Jerry Davis and Dorothy Cooper, were on the set, they were all so afraid I couldn't play this role. Well, one of the greatest compliments I ever received, was when we were getting into the studio limousine after the test was over. The two writers were there and Dorothy Cooper said, 'You know, Paula, we both wrote the script, but I wrote the part of Ellen and you *are* Ellen!'"

As said before, 1950 turned out to be a highly successful year for Miss Raymond. It concluded with *Crisis*, set in Latin America where Grant (playing a surgeon) and his wife Raymond are kidnapped by dictator José Ferrer who needs brain surgery. This acclaimed movie put director Richard Brooks on the map, although Miss Raymond recalls that he wasn't the most popular one on the set. "He was always yelling at everybody, except at Cary," she says, "and when he would shout at me, I'd put my arm around him and I'd say quietly, 'Now, calm down, Richard. What is it you want?' And he'd calm down!

"After *Crisis* I played in *Grounds for Marriage*, in the second lead to Kathryn Grayson. I had to play that pretty coldly, because the sympathy—script-wise—was with my character who was being ditched for this frantic diva who was making so much trouble for my fiancé. That wasn't really too satisfactory. Later on, when they had cast me in *Inside Straight*, I had to play the French girl: they didn't even ask me if I could do a French accent and I don't know if anybody knew that I had studied French with a tutor in my early youth, before coming down to Los Angeles."

Miss Raymond had quite a cultural and musical background indeed and in her childhood she devoted a lot of her time and energy to developing her musical skills. "When I was ten, my professor wanted to take me on the road as a child prodigy because I played Beethoven's 'Moonlight' Sonata on the piano that well, which is about ten pages, but my mother wouldn't hear of it. I wonder what would have happened if I had started a concert pianist's career instead of acting. When I was doing *Grounds for Marriage*, there was a sign over

Studio portrait of Paula Raymond. (Courtesy of Paula Raymond.)

my nameplate on my portable dressing room, I couldn't make out what it said. They told me, 'Oh, that's Bronislau Kaper; he's scoring the movie.' After meeting him, I would go over to Bronie's bungalow, he would sit at the piano and play, I'd sing and I would bring a lot of my collection of music—I had a huge collection of music in those years. But I never went back to the field of music. A couple years ago I started writing special material and I have written a musical, but I haven't done anything with it.

"In all, I was at MGM for three years. One day, I saw a script on Niki Nayfack's desk—he had produced *Devil's Doorway*—and I asked Leon, my agent, to talk about it to Niki; I said it was a role I would be suitable for. He said he couldn't do that. I wish I had asked why not, but I was so astounded that my agent couldn't talk to a producer who had hired me for an important role before—he couldn't or wouldn't even talk to him! By then I wasn't getting any publicity and here I had done all of these movies with these great and popular artists. So I called Elsie and asked, 'Will you talk to Howard Strickling and ask him why I am not getting any publicity?'—Strickling was the head of publicity. She called me later on and said, 'I made an appointment for you to see Howard Strickling on Saturday at 10 o'clock in the morning.' Now, to me that was not representing me; if I have to go in and represent myself, what's the use of having an agent? So I did, I kept the appointment and I asked him why I wasn't getting any publicity. His answer was, 'Well, if Gene Tierney would walk in front of the Pantages Theatre on Hollywood Boulevard, probably no one would take particular notice, but if Ava Gardner or Lana Turner walked there, they'd be *mobbed*.' I said, 'You mean, in order to have publicity, you have to be a *naughty* woman?' And he shook up his shoulders as if he had said 'Yes, well that's it!' I said, 'Well, in that case I will never get any publicity.' And that's what happened—just stating what I was doing professionally, but nothing else to really write about.

"On Monday I went into Billy Grady's office, he was the head of casting. What I didn't realize at the time, was that I was beyond casting directors; at my level I was dealing with directors and producers—I didn't know I was getting the star treatment until I was locked out of my permanent dressing room. The last year they kept me there for a whole year to bury me. There was a producer from Fox who wanted to borrow me from MGM for *The Steel Trap* [1952] with Joseph Cotten and Teresa Wright—she played the role they wanted me for—he said, 'I wanted you so badly for that film I can *taste* it, but they were pricing you out of the industry on loan-out.'

"They were using me assisting in tests. I assisted in Chuck Connors' first screen test, I even assisted in a wardrobe test with Clark Gable and evidently he knew what was happening to me—I noticed the expression on his face, like 'What are *you* doing here?' Finally Billy Grady asked me as a favor to play Red Skelton's sister in *Texas Carnival* [1951] and I said, 'Well, for you I will.' It was a nothing role, I had only a couple scenes at the end of the movie; it was really Esther Williams and Red Skelton who dominated it all.

"So Billy Grady had all the casting directors come in and asked, 'Have you seen her agents?' 'No no, not for a year!' There were two agents, Phil Kellog from William Morris and Harry Freedman from MCA, who had been wooing me to go with their agencies. On this day Billy Grady jumped at the chance to call in Harry Freedman, but I said, 'I don't want to do anything to hurt Elsie and Leon'—they were responsible for my contract. If I would sign with another agent, they would still get their commission of ten percent as long as I would be at MGM. By then I was earning $500 a week which would be something like $2,000 a week today, I think. So anyway, in the end I took Billy Grady's advice and I went with MCA."

"I was told later that George Cukor had slated me to star in his next movie *The Actress* [1953]—finally, he hired Jean Simmons to do it—and I heard that they would make me a top *top* star. It wasn't so much that I had fired Elsie and Leon, but that I went with MCA and he hated MCA, so therefore he hated me.

"By then, CBS wanted me for the role of a saloonkeeper in a new series called *Gunsmoke*. Well, I wouldn't even talk to them, because at the inception of the series, this was something cheap—in those years, in the 19th century, a dancehall girl was looked upon as *cheap*—a [good] woman wouldn't have anything to do with those beer parlors or saloons. If it were one role in a movie, I would have loved to play that character, but in a continuing series to be a cheap woman—I was so prudish in those years. So I said, 'Oh no, I couldn't do that,' and I didn't even talk to CBS about it. Well of course, you know the history, they got Amanda Blake for the role of Kitty and she turned out not to be a floozy, but a warm, wonderful woman.

"At that time I had been dating Richard Gully who was Jack [L.] Warner's right hand man socially, and I was lucky to get a role in *King Richard and the Crusaders*. I played Queen Berengaria to George Sanders' King Richard. After that I started dating George—he was no longer with Zsa Zsa Gabor at the time—we had a lot of fun together. After we had been dating for some time, we usually had dinner at his home because he was so visible and so recognizable when he'd go out—he was 6 ft. 4 and had been in so many movies—we were sitting in his living room after dinner and we usually played chess. I never won a game from him, he was much too clever for me. He said, 'You know Paula, I would never marry a woman with whom I didn't go to bed first.' And I said, 'Then you'll never marry me,' and that's exactly the way it worked out.

"But as I was running out of screen roles, I had to take care of my child and I needed steady employment. So I looked in the advertising pages of the *Los Angeles Times* and this one ad said, 'Filing Clerk Wanted.' I knew nothing about business, I thought all you had to know was your ABC. So I applied for the position and I got the job at $50 a week. That was 1955. The year before I had earned at least $25,000, but it was a steady income. They fired me after three months—I didn't drink coffee so when it was time to take the coffee break, I'd take my work with me and when one of the computer cards was missing, they blamed it on me because I had been taking my work with me into the coffee room.

"So I bought a book in a second-hand bookstore, I think it was called 'Speedwriting' or something like that, where you use symbols instead of shorthand, and I got a job at an architectural firm as a secretary to the engineers. They promised me a raise in three months—my word is my bond, I don't accept less from anyone. After three months, when they broke their promise, I quit. Then there was an ad for a secretary bookkeeper. I thought, well I know that two and two are five. It turned out to be all bookkeeping but after a year I decided to return to acting."

"I got myself a wonderful agent by the name of Paul Wilkins. I was with him for three months and he couldn't sell me for dust—I was completely forgotten in those years from 1955 to 1958. But television brought me back by [my] replacing Irene Papas in a TV show as I found out later—I always say she started my second career. George Cukor had nothing to do with television, so I could keep on working for television. I also made a few movies as well, but it was nothing great or nothing special—perhaps that stigma was still alive."

Ultimately Miss Raymond became one of the busiest actresses in TV shows, frequently appearing as a guest star in prestigious series such as *The Untouchables*, *Maverick*, *Perry Mason* and *Have Gun–Will Travel*. However this second boost in her career ended abruptly in August 1962 when a car (with Miss Raymond as a front seat passenger) hit a tree on Sunset Boulevard and rolled over several times. Across the street, Dean and Jeanne Martin were hosting a party; when they heard what had happened, they immediately called an ambulance and a few of their guests pulled her out of the automobile before it exploded. Miss Raymond was pronounced dead on arrival at the hospital but a neurologist was able to keep her alive and plastic surgery was a necessity. Miss Raymond: "The accident changed my life completely. I lost my real nose, I lost my sense of smell and I had difficulties getting back to work. The only thing actually that I'm missing now is the bridge on my nose. Now that I have to wear glasses, I have nothing on which to hang them."

The following year she went back to work and since then she occasionally appeared in small parts. In February 1993, she had another huge setback when her daughter passed away as a victim of cancer. Miss Raymond still lives in Hollywood and divides her time, as she says, between poetry, her music, fan mail and her income properties. She also has an agent once again but is wise enough to realize that in present-day Hollywood the chances are extremely limited of her making a come-back of any sort.

No matter what, though, in the early 1950s her star was being polished, that's for sure, and it would be a pity if she were to be overlooked or ignored in post-war Hollywood film history—she deserves better than that.

Interview: Hollywood, April 11, 1999

Notes

1. George Cukor (1899–1983), one of Hollywood's most influential directors, generally known as a *woman's director* as he directed nearly all the top actresses from the 1930s to the early 1980s. His many films include *What Price Hollywood?* (1932), *Dinner at Eight* (1934), *Romeo and Juliet* (1936), *Camille* (1937), *The Women* (1939), *The Philadelphia Story* (1940), *Her Cardboard Lover* (1942), *Gaslight* (1944), *Born Yesterday* (1950), *A Star Is Born* (1954), *Let's Make Love* (1960), *My Fair Lady* (1964, Academy Award for best director), *Travels with My Aunt* (1973), *Rich and Famous* (1981).

2. Anthony Mann (1906–1967) made his first feature in 1942 and directed James Stewart in the Western

Winchester '73 (1950, originally assigned to Fritz Lang). Later on they also collaborated on *Bend of the River* (1952), *The Naked Spur* (1953), *The Glenn Miller Story* (1954), *The Far Country* (1955), *The Man from Laramie* (1955) and *Strategic Air Command* (1955). He also scored with two historical epics, *El Cid* (1961) and *The Fall of the Roman Empire* (1964). He died of a heart attack in April 1967 in Berlin while he was on location for *A Dandy in Aspic* (the direction of the film was completed by its leading actor, Laurence Harvey).

Filmography

Keep Smiling (20th Century Fox, 1938). DIR Herbert I. Leeds. SCR Frances Hyland, Albert Ray (original idea by Lynn Root, Frank Fenton). CAM Edward Cronjager. ED Harry Reynolds. MUS Samuel Kaylin. RUNNING TIME 77 min. CAST: Jane Withers (Jane Rand); Gloria Stuart (Carol Walters); Henry Wilcoxon (Jonathan Rand); Helen Westley (Mrs. Willoughby); Jed Prouty (Jerome Lawson); Douglas Fowley (Cederic Hunt); Robert Allen (Stanley Harper); **Paula Raymond** (Credited as Paula Rae Wright).

Experiment Perilous (RKO, 1944). DIR Jacques Tourneur. PROD Warren Duff. SCR Warren Duff (novel by Margaret Carpenter). CAM Tony Gaudio. ED Ralph Dawson. MUS C. Bakaleinikoff. RUNNING TIME 91 min. CAST: Hedy Lamarr (Allida Bedereaux); George Brent (Dr. Bailey); Paul Lukas (Nick Bedereaux); Albert Dekker (Clag); Carl Esmond (Maitland); **Paula Raymond** (Singing voice for Hedy Lamarr—uncredited).

Rusty Leads the Way (Columbia, 1948). DIR Will Jason. PROD Robert Cohn. SCR Arthur Ross (story by Nedrick Young). CAM Vincent Farrar. ED James Sweeney. MUS Mischa Bakaleinikoff. RUNNING TIME 59 min. CAST: Ted Donaldson (Danny); Sharyn Mofett (Penny); John Litel (Hugh); Ann Doran (Ethel); **Paula Raymond** (Louise Adams); Peggy Converse (Mrs. Waters).

Racing Luck (Kay Pictures, 1948). DIR William Berke. PROD Sam Katzman. SCR Joseph Carole, Al Martin, Harvey Gates. CAM Ira H. Morgan. ED Henry Batista. MUS Mischa Bakaleinikoff. RUNNING TIME 65 min. CAST: Gloria Henry (Phyllis); Stanley Clements (Boots); David Bruce (Jeff); **Paula Raymond** (Nathalie); Harry Cheshire (Radcliffe); Dooley Wilson (Abe).

Blondie's Secret (Columbia, 1948). DIR Edward Bernds. SCR Jack Henley (based on the comic strip "Blondie" created by Chic Young). CAM Vincent Farrar. ED Richard Fantl. MUS Mischa Bakaleinikoff. RUNNING TIME 68 min. CAST: Penny Singleton (Blondie Bumstead); Arthur Lake (Dagwood); Larry Simms (Alexander); Marjorie Kent (Cookie); **Paula Raymond** (Nurse).

Challenge of the Range (Columbia, 1948). DIR Ray Nazarro. PROD Colbert Clark. SCR Ed. Earl Repp. CAM Rex Wimpy. ED Paul Borofsky. RUNNING TIME 56 min. CAST: Charles Starrett (The Durango Kid); **Paula Raymond** (Judy Barton); William Halop (Reb Watson); Steve Darrell (Cal Matson); Henry Hall (Jim Barton); Robert Filmer (Grat Largo).

The Gun That Won the West (Columbia, 1948). DIR William Castle. PROD Sam Katzman. SCR James B. Gordon (also story). CAM Henry Freulich. ED Al Clark. MUS Mischa Bakaleinikoff. RUNNING TIME 69 min. CAST: Dennis Morgan (Jim Bridger); **Paula Raymond** (Maxine Gaines); Richard Denning (Jack Gaines); Chris O'Brien (Sgt. Carnahan); Robert Bice (Chief Red Cloud); Michael Morgan (Afraid of Horses).

Adam's Rib (MGM, 1949). DIR George Cukor. PROD Lawrence Weingarten. SCR Ruth Gordon, Garson Kanin. CAM George J. Folsey. ED George Boemler. MUS Miklos Rozsa. RUNNING TIME 101 min. CAST: Spencer Tracy (Adam Bonner); Katharine Hepburn (Amanda Bonner); Judy Holliday (Doris Attinger); Tom Ewell (Warren Attinger); David Wayne (Kip Lurie); Jean Hagen (Beryl Caighn); **Paula Raymond** (Emerald).

East Side, West Side (MGM, 1950). DIR Mervyn LeRoy. PROD Voldemar Vetluguin. SCR Isobel Lennart (novel by Marcia Devenport). CAM Charles Rosher. ED Harold F. Kress. MUS Miklos Rozsa. RUNNING TIME 108 min. CAST: Barbara Stanwyck (Jesse Bourne); James Mason (Brandon Bourne); Van Heflin (Mark Dwyer); Ava Gardner (Isabel Lorrison); Cyd Charisse (Rose Senta); Nancy Davis (Helen Lee); **Paula Raymond** (Joan Peterson).

Devil's Doorway (MGM, 1950). DIR Anthony Mann. PROD Nicholas Nayfack. SCR Guy Trosper. CAM John Alton. ED Conrad A. Nervig. MUS Daniele Amfitheatrof. RUNNING TIME 84 min. CAST: Robert Taylor (Lance Poole); Louis Calhern (Verne Coolan); **Paula Raymond** (Orrie Masters); Marshall Thompson (Rodl); James Mitchell (Red Rock); Edgar Buchanan (Zeke Carmody).

Duchess of Idaho (MGM, 1950). DIR Robert Z. Leonard. PROD Joe Pasternak. SCR Dorothy Cooper, Jerry Davis. CAM Charles Schoenbaum. ED Adrienne Fazan. MUS Georgie Stoll. RUNNING TIME 98 min. CAST: Esther Williams (Christine Duncan); Van Johnson (Dick Layn); John Lund (Douglas J. Morrison, Jr.); **Paula Raymond** (Ellen Hallet); Clinton Sundberg (Matson); Connie Haines (Peggy Elliot).

Crisis (MGM, 1950). DIR Richard Brooks. PROD Arthur Freed. SCR Richard Brooks (short story by George Tabori). CAM Ray June. ED Robert J. Kern. MUS Miklos Rozsa. RUNNING TIME 96 min. CAST: Cary Grant (Dr. Eugene Ferguson); José Ferrer (Raoul Farrango); **Paula Raymond** (Helen Ferguson); Signe Hasso (Isabel Farrago); Ramon Navarro (Col. Adragon); Gilbert Roland (Roland Gonzales).

Grounds for Marriage (MGM, 1951). DIR Robert Z. Leonard. PROD Samuel Marx. SCR Allen Rivkin, Laura

Kerr (story by Samuel Marx). CAM John Alton. ED Frederick Y. Smith. MUS Bronislaw Kaper. RUNNING TIME 89 min. CAST: Van Johnson (Dr. Bartlett); Kathryn Grayson (Ina Massine); **Paula Raymond** (Agnes Young); Barry Sullivan (Chris Bartlett); Lewis Stone (Dr. Young); Reginald Owen (Delacorte).

Inside Straight (MGM, 1951). DIR Gerald Mayer. PROD Richard Goldstone. SCR Guy Trosper (also story). CAM Ray June. ED Newell P. Kimlin. MUS Lennie Hayton. RUNNING TIME 87 min. CAST: David Brian (Rip McCool); Arlene Dahl (Lily Douvane); Barry Sullivan (Johnny Sanderson); Mercedes McCambridge (Ada); **Paula Raymond** (Zoe Carnot); Claude Jarman, Jr. (Rip, young man); Lon Chaney, Jr. (Shocker).

The Tall Target (MGM, 1951). DIR Anthony Mann. PROD Richard Goldstone. SCR Art Cohn, George Worthing Yates (story by George Worthing Yates, Geoffrey Homes). CAM Paul C. Vogel. ED Newell P. Kimlin. RUNNING TIME 78 min. CAST: Dick Powell (John Kennedy); **Paula Raymond** (Ginny Beaufort); Adolphe Menjou (Caleb Jeffers); Marshall Thompson (Lance Beaufort); Ruby Dee (Rachel); Will Geer (Homer Crowley).

Texas Carnival (MGM, 1951). DIR Charles Walters. PROD Jack Cummings. SCR Dorothy Kingsley (story by Dorothy Kingsley, George Wells). CAM Robert Plank. ED Adrienne Fazan. MUS David Rose. RUNNING TIME 76 min. CAST: Esther Williams (Debbie Telford); Red Skelton (Cornie Quinell); Howard Keel (Slim Shelby); Ann Miller (Sunshine Jackson); **Paula Raymond** (Marilla Sabinas); Keenan Wynn (Dan Sabinas).

The Sellout (MGM, 1952). DIR Gerald Mayer. PROD Nicholas Nayfack. SCR Charles Palmer (story by Matthew Rapf). CAM Paul C. Vogel. ED George White. MUS David Buttolph. RUNNING TIME 82 min. CAST: Walter Pidgeon (Haven Allridge); John Hodiak (Chick Johnson); Audrey Totter (Cleo Bethel); **Paula Raymond** (Peggy Stauton); Thomas Gomez (Kellwin Burke); Cameron Mitchell (Randy Stauton); Karl Malden (Buck Maxwell).

The Bandits of Corsica (United Artists, 1953). DIR Ray Nazzaro. SCR Richard Schayer (story by Frank Burt). CAM George E. Diskant. ED Grant Whytock. MUS Irving Gertz. RUNNING TIME 81 min. CAST: Richard Greene (Mario/Carlos/Lucien); **Paula Raymond** (Christina); Raymond Burr (Jonatto); Dona Drake (Zelda); Raymond Greenleaf (Paoli); Lee Van Cleef (Nerva).

The Beast from 20,000 Fathoms (Warner Bros., 1953). DIR Eugene Lourie. PROD Hal Chester, Bernard W. Burton, Jack Dietz. SCR Lou Morheim, Fred Freiberger (story by Ray Bradbury). CAM Jack Russell. ED Bernard W. Burton. MUS David Buttolph. RUNNING TIME 80 min. CAST: Paul Christian (Tom Nesbitt); **Paula Raymond** (Lee Hunter); Cecil Kellaway (Professor Elson); Kenneth Tobey (Col. Evans); Donald Woods (Capt. Jackson); Jack Pennick (Jacob).

The City That Never Sleeps (Republic, 1953). DIR-PROD John H. Auer. SCR Steve Fisher. CAM John L. Russell. ED Fred Allen. MUS R. Dale Butts. RUNNING TIME 90 min. CAST: Gig Young (Johnny Kelly); Mala Powers (Sally Connors); William Talman (Hayes Stewart); Edward Arnold (Penrod Biddel); Chill Wills (Joe Chicago); **Paula Raymond** (Kathy Kelly).

The Human Jungle (Allied Artists, 1954). DIR Joseph M. Newman. PROD Hayes Goetz. SCR William Sackheim, Daniel Fuchs (story by William Sackheim). CAM Ellis Carter. ED Lester Sansom, Samuel Fields. MUS Hans Salter. RUNNING TIME 82 min. CAST: Gary Merrill (Danforth); Jan Sterling (Mary); **Paula Raymond** (Pat Danforth); Emile Meyer (Rowan); Regis Toomey (Geddes); Chuck Connors (Swados).

King Richard and the Crusaders (Warner Bros., 1954). DIR David Butler. PROD Henry Blanke. SCR John Twist (novel *The Talisman* by Sir Walter Scott). CAM J. Peverell Marley. ED Irene Morra. MUS Max Steiner. RUNNING TIME 113 min. CAST: Rex Harrison (Emir Ilderim/Sultan Saladin); Virginia Mayo (Lady Edith); George Sanders (King Richard I); Laurence Harvey (Sir Kenneth); Robert Douglas (Sir Giles Amaury); Michael Pate (Conrad); **Paula Raymond** (Queen Berengaria).

The Flight That Disappeared (United Artists, 1961). DIR Reginald Le Borg. PROD Robert E. Kent. SCR Ralph Hart, Judith Hart, Owen Harris. CAM Gilbert Warrenton. ED Kenneth Crane. MUS Richard La Salle. RUNNING TIME 72 min. CAST: Craig Hill (Tom Endicott); **Paula Raymond** (Marcia Paxton); Dayton Lummis (Dr. Morris); Gregory Morton (The Examiner); John Bryant (Hank Norton); Addison Richards (The Sage).

Hand of Death (20th Century Fox, 1962). DIR Gene Nelson. PROD-SCR Eugene Ling. CAM Floyd Crosby. ED Carl Pierson. MUS Sonny Burke. RUNNING TIME 60 min. CAST: John Agar (Alex Marsh); **Paula Raymond** (Carol Wilson); Steve Dunne (Tom Holland); Roy Gordon (Dr. Ramsey); John Alonzo (Carlos).

The Spy with My Face (MGM, 1966). DIR John Newland. PROD Sam Rolfe. SCR Clyde Ware, Joseph Calvelli. CAM Fred Koenekamp. ED Joseph Dervin. MUS Morton Stevens. RUNNING TIME 86 min. CAST: Robert Vaughn (Napoleon Solo); Senta Berger (Serena); David McCallum (Illya Kuryakin); Leo G. Carroll (Alexander Waverly); Michael Evans (Darius Two); **Paula Raymond** (Director).

Blood of Dracula's Castle (Crown Int. Pictures, 1969). DIR Al Adamson. PROD Al Adamson, Rex Carlton. SCR Rex Carlton. CAM Leslie Kovacs. ED Peter Berry. MUS Lincoln Mayorage. RUNNING TIME 84 min. CAST: John Carradine (George); **Paula Raymond** (Countess); Alex D'Arcy (Count); Robert Dix (Johnny); Gene Shane (Glen Cannon); Barbara Bishop (Liz Arden).

JOHN SAXON

In the late 1950s John Saxon was one of America's prominent screen actors, both as a dramatic leading man in films like *The Unguarded Moment* (1956) and *Cry Tough* (1959) and as a juvenile star in *Rock, Pretty Baby* (1957) and its sequel *Summer Love* (1958). From the early 1960s he gradually became a very distinguished character actor, in major productions such as *The Unforgiven* (1960), *The Cardinal* (1963), *The Appaloosa* (1966) and *The Electric Horseman* (1979), as well as in independent and international productions including *Agostino* (1962) and *Tenebre* (1982). Today, nearly half a century after his screen debut, John Saxon takes the time to sit back and relax as he reminisces about his long and rewarding career in front of the camera.

He was born in 1936 in Brooklyn, where he also grew up. As a teenager, he became fascinated with films. Mr. Saxon: "When you're still a kid, you can distinguish something that has a certain *effect*. The same thing happened to me when I grew up and watched pictures. As I look back, from time to time I saw a movie that was very special, directed by somebody really *good*—back then I couldn't tell anything of what they were doing exactly, because I'm talking about when I was maybe 10 or 11 years old—but something could open my eyes because it seemed so real and had a kind of a feel to it that it made me think, 'Waw, this is great!' And it was probably directed by Robert Wise who had made it at a studio when he was a younger director.

"A few years later, when I was about 16, I started to go to an acting school in Manhattan and made some rounds in the city, worked at the theater and for television, holding a spear, things like that. When I came on my own to Los Angeles, I guess it was more out of desperation. I wanted to get out of New York and it seemed like an opportunity. I spent the summer of 1953 doing illustrations for magazines like *True Romance, Modern Romance* and *True Story*; I had an agent who gave me these jobs, he told me where to go and he had another job for me coming up. 'Did you ever think about being an actor?' he asked me. I said, 'Sure, I go to acting school.' As it turned out, he had been in Los Angeles and had given an agent there a few photographs of me. 'This agent is interested in handling you,' he said. So we talked on the phone to this man in Los Angeles whom I had never seen, about the contract which had to be signed by my parents because I was still a minor. A little while later, I had an agent in Hollywood while I was still in New York. Afterwards he wrote me a letter, telling me he could get me something, but I had to be in Los Angeles in order to do that. I saved everything I had, got on a plane and flew to Los Angeles. Within three weeks I auditioned at Universal; I guess I was good enough for them to consider and they signed me up—they didn't know I was

Judy Holliday and Jack Lemmon in George Cukor's *It Should Happen to You* (1954), John Saxon's debut film.

17, I had to lie about my age, because of child labor problems they might have. Growing up in Brooklyn, you acted like 21 when you were only 15, you know."

There was a very noticeable difference indeed between the Brooklyn he knew and Los Angeles where he had relocated in the meantime. Mr. Saxon: "The neighborhood I grew up in was predominantly Irish, Italian, Jewish and Greek; about a mile away from where I lived, was the Scandinavian section. So it was very European in many respects. That's why many parents didn't speak to other parents, they didn't understand each other. My mother came from Italy, she spoke English, but I don't think my grandfather knew more than 50 words of English. We had old world feelings, you know, like carefulness, a little bit of suspicion, and when I came to Los Angeles, I couldn't believe my eyes. Whenever I would drive by Hollywood High School, I would blink in astonishment, it was like something out of a movie then. The high school I went to had a sense of toughness, I think. Here were all these blonde girls with blue eyes, they all looked so picture-perfect. And when I'd meet these girls on the set of films like *Rock, Pretty Baby*, I still was astonished, it was like looking at different *creatures*. We were all a little suspicious, you know, if you came in and people opened the door for you, you'd look around and said, 'Who are you?' [laughs]. Here in California, people often didn't lock their cars or their houses; of course all of this has changed. There was a kind of exuberance and innocence at the same time."

What about his early days in films; how does he look back on his first pictures? Mr. Saxon: "The first film I did of any importance, *The Unguarded Moment* [1956], was a very interesting one. It was a kind of a dark psychological story, a good story. Then I made a couple of all–American beach party pictures like *Rock, Pretty Baby* [1957], *Summer Love* [1958]—to me, the roles I played in those films, were character roles [laughs]—and I did my first film with Sandra Dee called *The Restless Years* [1958], a sensitive drama about a small town in which a girl grew up with her mother and didn't know who her father was."

In all, Mr. Saxon made three pictures with Sandra Dee,[1] another screen idol at that time; their other films are *The Reluctant Debutante* (1958), shot in Paris, and *Portrait in Black* (1960). Mr. Saxon: "The last time I saw her was in 1991 when we did a reading for a play together. Unfortunately, from what I hear, she's not doing well. For a number of years, she had emotional setbacks. It hurts me in a sense—although we made a few films together, we weren't close—but she was sort of seduced into this fantasy of the studio, I think. I don't know if she was able to grow up emotionally—she was already a star at 16."

His other female co-star of *The Reluctant Debutante* was British screen comedienne Kay Kendall.[2] Mr. Saxon: "When we were making this film, I guess she was amused by me. I was 22 at that time. After I had arrived in Paris—I only spoke about a dozen words of French—I went to my hotel, took a shower, took a cab, and didn't return to the hotel for two days. She was always amused because I often was hanging out with girls and one day she insisted she'd take me to lunch. We were always very friendly and we were right in the middle of a scene one day when it was time for lunch, so that's exactly what we did. She bought a *big* bottle of red wine and she just kept pouring it. I said, 'We have to go back to work, you know.' 'Oh, stop worrying!' When we got back on the set, she was tipsy and she kept giggling all the time. The director, Vincente Minnelli, thought I had done this. Eventually we got through it, but it took a while because she kept giggling!"

Some of the first films he made were aimed at the youth market and that's exactly the audience they reached, ensuring him a strong appeal with the teenage audience back then. Mr. Saxon: "After we finished *Rock, Pretty Baby*, Sue George, Rod McKuen and I went on a tour to 26 cities in 26 days, driving or flying from one place to another, and I remember we went to a mall in New Orleans—a mall was a new concept at the time—there was a record store where we had to sign the records from the soundtrack. After we had been signing there for a while, this girl came up to me, and I told her, 'You've come here before, a few minutes ago, haven't you?' She said, 'Yes,' and a little while later she showed up again. 'You're here a third time, right?' She said, 'That's right, but you *need* us.' It took the wind out of me! [laughs]. These youngsters knew already that they were the market and we'd better not object [laughs]. Clark Gable once said about that, 'We signed a contract with the public and they've read the small print,' or something like that. I actually thought of that the moment this girl said that to me."

"I once went to Detroit in 1958 when I was on tour for *The Reluctant Debutante*. There was something [there] like a new festival or a conference. I was on a panel with Joan Fontaine and all of a sudden she said, 'All they want to do right now, is make pictures for young kids.' I felt guilty, you know [laughs], but maybe she was right, although now I am in the position of saying the same thing. The United States was and is very youth-oriented in many ways. On the other hand, I remember I went to countries like Argentina or Italy to attend a film festival, where there was such a reference to some old actor or actress; even though they may not have made a film for many years, there still was a certain respect. It seemed to me they respected old age or wisdom."

After being a very productive screen actor for nearly five decades, Mr. Saxon witnessed numerous changes along the way, both on and off screen. Did he have any particular thoughts on that subject that came to mind? Mr. Saxon: "When you're looking at what's going on in the world today, the dynamism and the culture, we're in the days of opportunism. In the 1950s there wasn't as much opportunism, it was just the beginning, like 'You don't like that job? Go

(Left to right) John Saxon, Sandra Dee and director Helmut Käutner on the set of *The Restless Years* (1958). (Courtesy of DOCIP Film Archive, Brussels, Belgium.)

get another job.' But nobody moved around in Brooklyn: you stayed around for years and years if you could afford it, you stayed at one job if it was decent. There once was a baseball player who played for the Chicago Cubs for many years. He never made more than $40,000 a year; yet, when his contract ended, he had the opportunity to go and play for somebody who would hire him for more money. He said, 'No, I'm a *Cub*, my fans are here and they care about me!' So his loyalty was to the team and the fans.

"I can give you a similar example from my business. In the 1950s I knew an elderly couple who lived in Beverly Hills and who took care of my fan mail. I was getting between a 1,000 and 1,500 letters a month; it used to cost me from $500 to $800 a month for postage, for the letters this couple wrote back—pretending to be me—the packaging, the photos, the envelopes, and so on. But I believed that the people who wrote to me were all fans. A couple of years ago however, I think about seven or eight years ago, I started to get a lot of mail at my home with requests for pictures. I thought, 'How nice.' So I would send photographs out, but sometimes you'd get a request to sign with a particular pen and with instructions how to sign it: *just sign here* or *just your name*. I was naive until a friend of mine brought me back one of these photos which he had bought at Larry Edmunds Bookstore on Hollywood Boulevard: he had seen it there and as a joke he had bought it for me. It was the very same photo I had sent to somebody a couple of months before; I had paid for it and this guy just sold it. I still get mail at my post office box and they include a photograph, *just sign here*, but when I smell that, I send it right back. Those people are not fans, this is a business. They're adopting me into an industry—on e-bay there are 15 objects being auctioned that have something to do with me, mostly pictures, I suppose. That's one big difference, it didn't happen in the 1950s: people were *fans*! Nobody sold this material, but we didn't think of everything as an opportunity. An old car was an old car, you know. We never thought that an old Cadillac would be worth $25,000, when it only cost $5,000 to start with.

"Right after the war, there was such a change. First of all, the war was over and the subsequent few years, right into the 1950s, were such an economic boom. The development here was incredible: everybody was getting enough money to buy a car, a house. In 1954 or 1955, if you drove out there on Ventura Boulevard and you got beyond Sepulveda Boulevard at night, you couldn't see anything: there *wasn't* anything. Look at it now! So there was a very upbeat change of lifestyle, energy and optimism. In 1963, I worked for Otto Preminger on a film called *The Cardinal*. What a lesson that was! He was a dynamic, talented and intelligent man, very difficult to work for, but he was one of the first to come up with something new, making documentaries like *The Making of...*: he had hired a crew to make a documentary of the making of *The Cardinal*. So on the set there were always people taking photographs, shooting footage of what was going on on the set; in addition, there were a lot of journalists that came by. I remember looking for a chair to sit on—I was one of the actors—I couldn't find one, but all the journalists had chairs [laughs]. The idea of *selling* was terribly important; the actor was there, he was already bought!"

This total and global economic change has affected, influenced and challenged the film industry in more than one way. Mr. Saxon: "Pictures are also made on the opportunity for alternative markets: T-shirts, all kinds of merchandising, you name it. I am not pessimistic, not at all, because the desire to do something artistic, close to the heart, is always there. There will *always* be people who have the courage to withstand the commercial pressure and they will *always* have the desire to produce something valuable. In the 1950s and certainly in the 1940s, when the studio system was still going strong, the obstacles were different: the studio system wasn't bad, but it certainly had its restrictions. If you were under contract, you were basically obliged to do what you were given. That wasn't terrible! People enjoyed themselves because there was a kind of camaraderie at the studios. Then it fell apart, television is probably what disrupted it. Also, the studio heads were passing away, those were the pioneers, they were autocratic and so on, but they liked what they did and they were close to what they did. By the end of the 1950s, many of the studios became part of conglomerates, like Paramount which was owned by Gulf and Western. All the decisions were made in New York: films were in the hands of people who weren't making any films.

"The studio I knew best, was Universal: I was under contract to Universal from 1954 till

Early studio portrait of John Saxon. (Courtesy of DOCIP Film Archive, Brussels, Belgium.)

1961; by the late 1960s it was converted largely and successfully into an MCA company and they were the first to succumb rather than resist television. There were several television series being made and at the same time came this opportunity for something new: tram tours that would go around the lot and the back lot. So all of a sudden, if you were working on the back lot, doing a Western or something, you had to stop while the tram was passing by and the tour guide would be describing what was going on. The moment you stopped, the dollars were coming in right there as the tram was passing by, so you could wait a few minutes.

"While being under contract to Universal, they were bringing over actors and directors from Germany—I guess they were thinking of the world market—like Curt Jurgens, I worked with a director called Helmut Käutner [*The Restless Years*], he had once made a famous picture with Horst Buchholz [*Monpti*, 1957]. Käutner came here and he made two pictures, one of them was *The Restless Years* [the other one was *A Stranger in My Arms* in 1959, with June Allyson, Jeff Chandler and Sandra Dee]. There were others too, and what I became very aware of, was that the film industry in Germany almost went *kaput* after the 1960s: they hardly made any films. I think it was a result of the Germans who wanted to see American films and didn't bother to see their own.

"Meanwhile, in Italy there was such a big expansion of production during a period I call 'Hollywood on the Tiber'—when I first went there in 1962, I wanted to work with the great Italian directors. I stayed there for a year and the closest I got to being in a good film, was *Agostino* [1962], directed by Mauro Bolognini with Ingrid Thulin, a Swedish actress. They were then trying to make all these copies of American films. Now they make mostly local films, they don't try to win the American market—they thought they could for a while to get hold of a portion of it by making copies or rip-offs of American films with less expensive American or international actors. Basically they made money with television and video rights, things like that, but I don't think those pictures ever made it to the cinemas here. The American production has dominated. The only thing that's questionable about it, is that there is a little bit of a tendency—and I realize it may be unfair to put it this way—to make everything *Disneyesque*, to reduce everything to action, special effects, or a view of the world that isn't very deep."

Academy Award winner Burt Lancaster (1913–1994) played the leading role in John Huston's The Unforgiven (1960), a Western co-starring Audrey Hepburn, Audie Murphy and John Saxon.

Films can go further than that: if they're good, they can be hopeful, uplifting and can have a huge impact on their audiences worldwide. Mr. Saxon: "Movies always relied on being able to take you someplace where you haven't been. They used to do this geographically, take you out of your realm and show you something you haven't seen before. But today, with travel being what it is, people have seen so many countries already, so now it has got to be something else, some content about what is going on to get you interested. Some kind of a breakthrough, or an insight. Television has that impact on people as well. In 1992 I was in Central Asia working on an Italian-financed miniseries about Ghengis Khan—what do you think everybody was watching on television? A Mexican serial called 'Even the Rich Cry,' a daytime soap opera. A year later I was in Moscow, people were still watching it there, it was the biggest hit you could imagine."

As he has worked extensively on both sides of the Atlantic Ocean, what are some of the most striking differences between working in the U.S. and working in Europe? Mr. Saxon: "The first time I went to work in Italy, I was on vacation. Compared to American productions at the same time, it was pretty unorganized. For example, when we finished after lunch and we'd have shot the day's work, they'd say, 'Everybody goes, leave, see you tomorrow.' So I would ask, 'Isn't there another scene to do?' In the U.S., if you finished the scenes for the day and you still had another two or three hours to go, they would rush and find you something else to do. In 1968 I worked on a Western that was shot partially in Italy and in Spain. When we got to Spain, lunch was usually at three o'clock. There were choices of maybe three entrees and several different kinds of wine. After lunch, very little was done. People *ate* a real meal, with three or four dishes, they had glasses of wine. Here in America, you go to the commissary, you have to be finished in one hour and get ready to be back on the set.

"Every country has got a little funny different thing. In Italy, you never found chairs on the set. I once asked, 'Can I have a chair?' They looked at each other and said in Italian, 'What does he want? A chair? Why?' You're on the set for ten or 12 hours and in between you want to sit down. Klaus Kinski once said the same thing, and when he got his chair, he said, 'I want my name on it.' The director got so angry he broke the chair [laughs], 'Who is this guy? He wants his name on a chair?!' [laughs].

"In Italy, when the director got annoyed, he'd say, 'I'm going home!' In America a director working in the studio system didn't dare to say a thing like that. That was a different system: there wasn't this hierarchy of organization. Cinecittà eventually became a major studio

Lana Turner (1920–1995), initially launched as the "Sweater Girl," made in her long and successful career one film with John Saxon: the mystery thriller *Portrait in Black* (1960).

in Italy, but who owned it? It always changed hands and so on. The producers were small, powerful guys like De Laurentiis, Carlo Ponti ... there were about half a dozen. They turned everything over to the director. If they worked with a director they admired or respected, *he* chose what was going to be shot, it wasn't the producer telling him you have to do this, you have to do that. The director was the *director*.

"I think my disposition for foreign films probably comes from two things: first of all, I am of Italian ancestors, but that's not the whole reason. To me, and I think to a lot of people here in America, films from the late 1950s coming from countries like France, Germany or Japan were very exciting. There were more people going to see foreign films in the 1960s than I believe there are today, perhaps because there is a greater indifference today: there used to be art houses all over the place, there still are but the American film took over, also production-wise. So in a number of countries, films have been produced for local consumption, certainly in Italy that was true. At one point we all looked up to foreign films: they were showing something we weren't getting here in America from a studio production. In a way they are produced closer to the *heart*, closer to an experience that is going on, more personal, they're not produced with an eye on the *huge world*."

In his entire career, he made one action film, *Enter the Dragon* (1973) with Bruce Lee; the picture became a classic in its genre. Mr. Saxon: "I was pleased with this film, but I never wanted to pursue it. I almost didn't do that film, I know I had agreed to do it but I hadn't signed anything yet, so after I reread the script—originally it was a very thin script, about 40 pages—and at the last minute, I called my agent and said, 'I want out of it.' Why? I am an actor, I want to *act*, this could be played by any good stuntman who knows a little bit about the martial arts—there weren't too many people who did at the time, which was my luck because I had practiced martial arts for about four years. Before the film came out, Chuck Norris told me this would be a tremendous hit. But still, it wasn't what I wanted to do. I didn't want to do something where every solution was *bing-pah-pooh*, you know. I am more interested in what we don't know about human nature and reveal solutions in an interesting way.

"The reason some of this has come about for me, is after having spent so much time in movies, you also *have* a lot of time, waiting in your dressing room for example, so I bring books and magazines with me. The biggest thing that I received from my career, was the opportunity to have time and investigate myself. I have been in psychoanalysis and I have been able to travel a lot and look around. The American solution in the action films is this one guy who becomes the hero; Errol Flynn did it, Stallone, Schwarzenegger, a lot of them have been the American action savior, taking care of the bad guys. I prefer to play other kinds of roles. Especially on television, I played a lot of heavies and it always surprised me and pleased me in a refreshing way that, while walking down the streets here in Beverly Hills, I could see that people recognized me with a *smile*. It wasn't like, oh, *that* guy, you know. So I suppose that people must feel something about me that is pleasant, or favorable. You know, I have worked very little this past year because of some injuries, but now, at 65, I feel more confident than I ever have. I was always very driven to take a job, I couldn't let an opportunity for a job [laughs]—it reminds me of my early years as an actor and also of my early years as a man, when at one point I couldn't let an opportunity of a woman go by [laughs], I couldn't say no!—but now I am more comfortable with a sense of optimism and anticipation that I am going to do something that I will enjoy more, I hope, in the next few years until I don't want to act at all, maybe. Who knows, maybe I will turn to just writing: I write in between and my own personal interest is not to write a blockbuster—I wouldn't know *how*—I prefer a small dramatic story, internally motivated drama with six characters, stuff like that. Writing is great, because I can do it anytime, and I like it, I get satisfaction from it. I have written about half a dozen screenplays, but I never made enough money on it as a writer. Just from the income as a writer, I think I made some $40,000 over a period of ten years. I would also like to direct a screenplay that I wrote."

Finally, what does he consider the most rewarding experience in his career so far? Mr. Saxon: "That was with a Western called *The Appaloosa* [1966]. I played the antagonist to Marlon Brando.³ Everything was against me in a way. I had an agent who recommended me to play the role, the studio thought it was a ludicrous idea. They didn't know I had played some roles of Latinos before, but they wouldn't even hear of it. Fortunately, my agent knew the secretary who was assigned to Sidney J. Furie, the director of the film. He called this secretary and said, 'Can you get John in to meet Sidney J. Furie?' She said, 'The only thing I can tell you, is that he comes here in the morning, he can sit in the waiting room and see what happens.' So that's what I did. I walked in, said hello to her, introduced myself and I sat in the chair. I waited and waited and all of a sudden the door opened from the inside office and there Sidney J. Furie came out, talking to one or two people, he pointed at me and said, 'You see, that's the kind of guy I am looking for.' And then he said, 'I know you, you're a good actor, let's arrange a screen test.' I tested and I got the role.

"I had met Marlon Brando several times before we started shooting. I loaned him a coat once when he had to go to New York, he never gave it back [laughs]. I started out not being in awe, you know, but he didn't want to play the first part of the film which was maybe 15 or 20 minutes, about his character's life before the drama starts—he played a buffalo hunter living amongst the Indians. He decided for some reason, I'm not sure why, that he didn't want to do that portion of the script—perhaps he may have felt that they weren't going to treat the subject matter of life amongst Indians in a serious enough fashion. So the first 15 minutes of the film disappeared and the story started with this encounter of two men that became like a vendetta or a rivalry. The second thing that happened, the screenwriter went on to another studio to write another script, so a second writer was assigned to do rewrites, but when those arrived on the set, they already didn't match with some other things that had been changed already—Brando also had made a number of changes.

"So one night we met in Marlon's trailer, there was the producer, the director, Marlon and myself, trying to figure out what to do the next day. I said, 'What about this,' and I suggested something, they were *desperate*. Marlon wanted to leave, he wanted to go to a Bob Dylan concert, so he left. The producer and the director then looked at me and said, 'Yeah, that's a great idea you got. But who's going to write it? Do you write?' I said, 'Yes.' So the next day I came on the set with the pages. I showed them to Marlon first—and I started rewriting scenes or making changes with some regularity and, in conversations with him, I was telling some experience I had and he'd come up with an idea. You remember the arm wrestling scene in the picture? I had worked in Durango, Mexico, about six years before with John Huston [while making *The Unforgiven*]. It was a wild, lawless place at the time, and there was a folklore about the scorpions of the region. So Marlon said, 'Why don't we have a contest where there's an arm wrestle with two scorpions tied down on the other side?' I said, 'That's pretty good.' I told him the story, he gave me the idea and I wrote the scene.

"So this was the most creative experience I've ever had. Unfortunately a couple of things happened. Marlon was not very keen about doing the picture; he wanted to play his role as a Mexican, but the studio said, 'No wait a minute, everybody's Mexican in this story, it's not a good idea if you'll be a Mexican too.' So he was disappointed and he was exhibiting his disappointment whenever he could. He had also prepared tests for the make-up and they weren't allowing him to use it. Furthermore he had a contract to work with Charles Chaplin and Sophia Loren on *A Countess from Hong Kong*; he had a date when that production was to start. So we were limping along, a little bit behind schedule; we were improvising how we were going to do the end of the film. Everybody was throwing in an idea before Marlon had to leave the set to start working with Chaplin, but finally the movie ended without a real resolution of some kind. Even though the picture didn't do that well, it still was the most creative experience I ever had."

If Mr. Saxon's ambition to concentrate on writing screenplays in the future can work out the way he hopes to, it might well be that other, even more rewarding film experiences will be added to his astonishing career. If he only won't forget to remain an actor as well!

Interview: Los Angeles, February 14, 2002

Notes

1. Sandra Dee (b. 1942), a former model, made her screen debut in Robert Wise's *Until They Sail* (1957) and rose to stardom as a teenager with films such as *The Restless Years, The Reluctant Debutante, Gidget* (1959), *Imitation of Life* (1959, as the daughter of Lana Turner) and the screen classic *A Summer Place* (1959). In 1960 she married Bobby Darin, her co-star in *Come September* (1961), *If a Man Answers* (1962) and *That Funny Feeling* (1965). By then the audience was losing interest in her pictures and after her marriage ended in divorce in 1967, she appeared in only a handful of films and a few television movies.
2. Kay Kendall (1926–1959), was married to Rex Harrison when she died of leukemia at age 33. She had joined the chorus line of the London Palladium in 1938 when she was 12 and appeared regularly in British films throughout the 1950s; her three final films were U.S. productions: *Les Girls* (1957, one of her biggest hits), *The Reluctant Debutante* and *Once More with Feeling* (1960).
3. Marlon Brando: interview with Stanley Kramer, note 2.

Filmography

It Should Happen to You (Columbia, 1954). DIR George Cukor. PROD Fred Kohlmar. SCR Garson Kanin. CAM Charles Lang. ED Charles Nelson. MUS Frederick Hollander. RUNNING TIME 86 min. CAST: Judy Holliday (Gladys Glover); Peter Lawford (Evan Adams III); Jack Lemmon (Pete Sheppard); Michael O'Shea (Brod Clinton); Constance Bennett (Herself); **John Saxon** (Uncredited).

A Star Is Born (Warner Bros., 1954). DIR George Cukor. PROD Sidney Luft. SCR Moss Hart (screenplay of *A Star Is Born* [1937] by Dorothy Parker, Alan Campbell, Robert Carson; original story by William A. Wellman, Robert Carson). CAM Sam Leavitt. ED Folmar Blangsted (restored version: Craig Holt). MUS Harold Arlen. RUNNING TIME 154 min. (restored version: 181 min.). CAST: Judy Garland (Esther Blodgett/Vicki Lester); James Mason (Norman Maine); Jack Carson (Matt Libby); Charles Bickford (Oliver Niles); Tommy Noonan (Danny McGuire); Amanda Blake (Susan Ettinger); **John Saxon** (Uncredited).

Running Wild, a.k.a. *The Girl in the Cage* (Universal, 1955). DIR Abner Biberman. PROD Howard Pine. SCR Leo Townsend (novel by Ben Benson). CAM Ellis W. Carter. ED Edward Curtiss, Ray Snyder. MUS Joseph Gershenson. RUNNING TIME 81 min. CAST: William Campbell (Ralph Barclay); Mamie Van Doren (Irma Bean); Keenan Wynn (Ken Osanger); Kathleen Case (Leta Novak); Jan Merlin (Scotty Cluett); **John Saxon** (Vince Pomeroy).

The Unguarded Moment (Universal, 1956). DIR Harry Keller. PROD Gordon Kay. SCR Herb Meadows, Larry Marcus (story by Rosalind Russell, Larry Marcus). CAM William Daniels. ED Edward Curtiss. MUS Herman Stein. RUNNING TIME 95 min. CAST: Esther Williams (Lois Conway); George Nader (Lt. Harry Graham); **John Saxon** (Leonard Bennett); Edward Andrews (Mr. Bennett); Les Tremayne (Mr. Pendleton); Jack Albertson (Prof.).

Rock, Pretty Baby (Universal, 1957). DIR Richard Bartlett. PROD Edmond Chevie. SCR Herbert H. Margolis, William Raynor. CAM Charlie Robinson. ED Fredrick Y. Smith. MUS Joseph Gershenson. RUNNING TIME 89 min. CAST: Sal Mineo (Angelo Barrato); **John Saxon** (Jimmy Daley); Luana Patten (Joan Wright); Edward Platt (Dr. Daley); Fay Wray (Beth Daley); Rod McKuen (Bentley); Shelley Fabares (Twinky Daley).

This Happy Feeling (Universal, 1958). DIR Blake Edwards. PROD Ross Hunter. SCR Blake Edwards (play *For Love or Money* by F. Hugh Herbert). CAM Arthur E. Arling. ED Milton Carruth. MUS Frank Skinner. RUNNING TIME 92 min. CAST: Debbie Reynolds (Janet Blake); Curt Jurgens (Preston Mitchell); **John Saxon** (Bill Tremaine); Alexis Smith (Nita Hollaway); Mary Astor (Mrs. Tremaine); Estelle Winwood (Mrs. Early).

Summer Love (Universal, 1958). DIR Charles F. Haas. PROD William Grady, Jr. SCR William Raynor, Herbert Margolis. CAM Carl E. Guthrie, Clifford Stine. ED Tony Martinelli. MUS Henry Mancini. RUNNING TIME 85 min. CAST: **John Saxon** (Jimmy Daley); Molly Bee (Alice); Rod McKuen (Bentley); Judi Meredith (Joan Wright); Jill St. John (Erica Landis); Troy Donahue (Sax Lewis); Shelley Fabares (Twinky Daley).

The Restless Years (Universal, 1958). DIR Helmut Käutner. PROD Ross Hunter. SCR Edward Anhalt (play *Teach Me How to Cry* by Patricia Joudry). CAM Ernest Laszlo. ED Albrecht Joseph. MUS Joseph Gershenson. RUNNING TIME 86 min. CAST: **John Saxon** (Will Henderson); Sandra Dee (Melinda Grant); Luana Patten (Polly Fisher); Margaret Lindsay (Dorothy Henderson); Virginia Grey (Miss Robeson); Teresa Wright (Elizabeth Grant).

The Reluctant Debutante (MGM, 1958). DIR Vincente Minnelli. PROD Pandro S. Berman. SCR William Douglas Home (also play). CAM Joseph Ruttenberg. ED Adrienne Fazan. MUS Eddie Warner. RUNNING TIME 94 min. CAST: Rex Harrison (Jimmy Broadbent); Kay Kendall (Sheila Broadbent); **John Saxon** (David Parkson); Sandra Dee (Jane Broadbent); Angela Lansbury (Mabel Claremont); Peter Myers (David Fenner).

Cry Tough (United Artists, 1959). DIR Paul Stanley. PROD Harry Kleiner. SCR Harry Kleiner (novel by Irving Shulman). CAM Irving Glassberg, Philip H. Lathrop. ED Frederic Knudtson. MUS Laurinda Almeida. RUNNING TIME 83 min. CAST: **John Saxon** (Miguel Estrada); Linda Cristal (Santa); Joseph Calleia (Sr. Estrada); Harry Townes (Carlos); Don Gordon (Incho); Perry Lopez (Toro).

The Big Fisherman (Buena Vista, 1959). DIR Frank Borzage. PROD Rowland V. Lee. SCR Howard Estabrook, Rowland V. Lee (novel by Lloyd C. Douglas) CAM Lee Garmes. ED Paul Weatherwax. MUS Albert Hay Malotte. RUNNING TIME 180 min. CAST: Howard Keel (Simon Peter); Susan Kohner (Fara); **John Saxon** (Voldi); Martha Hyer (Herodias); Herbert Lom (Herod Antipas); Ray Stricklyn (Deran); Beulah Bondi (Hannah).

The Unforgiven (United Artists, 1960). DIR John Huston. PROD James Hill. SCR Ben Maddow (novel by Alan Le May). CAM Frank Planer. ED Hugh Russell Lloyd. MUS Dimitri Tiomkin. RUNNING TIME 125 min. CAST: Burt Lancaster (Ben Zachary); Audrey Hepburn (Rachel Zachary); Audie Murphy (Cash Zachary); **John Saxon** (Johnny Portugal); Charles Bickford (Zeb Rawlins); Lillian Gish (Mattilda Zachary).

Portrait in Black (Universal, 1960). DIR Michael Gordon. PROD Ross Hunter. SCR Ivan Goff, Ben Roberts (play by Ivan Goff, Ben Roberts). CAM Russell Metty. ED Milton Carruth. MUS Frank Skinner. RUNNING TIME 112 min. CAST: Lana Turner (Sheila Cabot); Anthony Quinn (David Rivera); Richard Basehart (Howard Mason); **John Saxon** (Blake Richards); Sandra Dee (Cathy Cabot); Ray Walston (Cobb); Virginia Grey (Miss Lee).

The Plunderers (Allied Artists, 1960). DIR-PROD Joseph Pevney. SCR Bob Barbash. CAM Sol Polito. ED Tom McAdoo. MUS Leonard Rosenman. RUNNING TIME 94 min. CAST: Jeff Chandler (Sam Christy); **John Saxon** (Rondo); Dolores Hart (Ellie Walters); Marsha Hunt (Kate Miller); Jay C. Flippen (Sheriff); Ray Stricklyn (Jeb Lucas Tyler).

Posse from Hell (Universal, 1961). DIR Herbert Coleman. PROD Gordon Kay. SCR Clair Huffaker. CAM Clifford Stine. ED Frederic Knudtson. MUS Joseph Gershenson. RUNNING TIME 89 min. CAST: Audie Murphy (Banner Cole); **John Saxon** (Seymour Kern); Zohra Lampert (Helen Caldwell); Vic Morrow (Crip); Robert Keith (Capt. Brown).

War Hunt (United Artists, 1962). DIR Denis Sanders. PROD Terry Sanders. SCR Stanford Whitmore. CAM Ted McCord. ED John Hoffman, Edward Dutko. MUS Bud Shank. RUNNING TIME 81 min. CAST: **John Saxon** (Private Raymond Endore); Charles Aidman (Capt. Wallace Pratt); Sydney Pollack (Sgt. Owen Van Horn); Tommy Matsuda (Charlie); Gavin MacLeod (Private Crotty); Tom Skerritt (Sgt. Showalter); Robert Redford (Private Loomis).

Mr. Hobbs Takes a Vacation (20th Century Fox, 1962). DIR Henry Koster. PROD Jerry Wald. SCR Nunnally Johnson. CAM William C. Mellor. ED Marjorie Fowler. MUS Henry Mancini. RUNNING TIME 116 min. CAST: James Stewart (Roger Hobbs); Maureen O'Hara (Peggy Hobbs); Fabian (Joe); **John Saxon** (Byron); Marie Wilson (Mrs. Turner); Reginald Gardiner (Reggie McHugh).

Agostino (1962). DIR Mauro Bolognini. PROD Luigi Rovere. SCR Goffredo Parise (story by Alberto Moravia). CAM Aldo Tonti. ED Nino Baragli. MUS Carlo Rustichelli. RUNNING TIME 90 min. CAST: Paolo Colombo (Agostino); **John Saxon** (Renzo); Ingrid Thulin (Agostino's Mother).

The Cardinal (Columbia, 1963). DIR-PROD Otto Preminger. SCR Robert Dozier (novel by Henry Morton Robinson). CAM Leon Shamroy. ED Louis R. Roeffler. MUS Jerome Moross. RUNNING TIME 175 min. CAST: Tom Tryon (Stephen Fermoyle); Carol Lynley (Mona); Dorothy Gish (Celia); **John Saxon** (Benny Rampbell); John Huston (Cardinal Glennon); Burgess Meredith (Father Ned Halley); Romy Schneider (Annemarie).

La Ragazza Che Sapeva Troppo, a.k.a. *The Evil Eye* (1963). DIR-CAM Mario Bava. SCR Mario Bava, Enzo Corbucci, Ennio De Concini, Eliana De Sabata, Mino Guerrini. ED Mario Serandrei. MUS Les Baxter. CAST: Letícia Román (Nora Dralston); **John Saxon** (Marcello Bassi); Valentina Cortesa (Laura Terrani); Titti Tomaino.

Sette Contro la Morte, a.k.a. *The Cavern* (20th Century Fox, 1964). DIR Edgar G. Ulmer, Paolo Bianchini. PROD Edgar G. Ulmer. SCR Michael Pertwee, Jack Davies (story by Michael Pertwee, Jack Davies). CAM Gabor Pogany. ED Renato Cinquino. MUS Carlo Rustichelli. RUNNING TIME 83 min. CAST: **John Saxon** (Joe Cramer); Rosanna Schiaffino (Anna); Larry Hagman (Capt. Wilson); Peter Marshall (Pete Carter); Brian Aherne (General Braithwaite).

The Ravagers (Hemisphere, 1965). DIR Eddie Romero. SCR Cesar Adigo, E. F. Romero. CAM Tito Arevalo. ED Joven Calub. MUS Tito Arevaldo. RUNNING TIME 88 min. CAST: Robert Arevalo (Capt. Araulio); Jose Dagumboy (Joe); Vic Diaz (Cruz); Bronwyn Fitzsimmons (Sheila); **John Saxon** (Capt. Dermit Dowling).

Blood Beast from Outer Space, a.k.a. *Night Caller from Outer Space*, UK title *The Night Caller* (World Entertainment Corp., 1965). DIR John Gilling. PROD Ronald Liles. SCR Jim O'Connolly (novel *The Night Callers* by Frank Crisp). CAM Stephen Dade. ED Philip Barnikel. MUS Johnny Gregory. RUNNING TIME 84 min. CAST: **John Saxon** (Jack Costain); Alfred Burke (Hartley); Patricia Haines (Ann Barlow); Maurice Denham (Doctor Morley); Ballard Berkeley (Comm. Savage).

The Appaloosa (MGM, 1966). DIR Sidney J. Furie. PROD Alan Miller. SCR James Bridges, Roland Kibbee (novel by Robert MacLeod). CAM Russell Metty. ED Ted J. Kent. MUS Frank Skinner. RUNNING TIME 98 min. CAST: Marlon Brando (Matt Fletcher); Anjanette Comer (Trini); **John Saxon** (Chuy Medina); Emilio Fernández (Lazaro); Alex Montoya (Squint Eye).

Queen of Blood, a.k.a. *Planet of Blood* (American International Pictures, 1966). DIR-SCR Curtis Harrington. PROD George Edwards. CAM Vilis Lapenieks. ED Leo Shreve. MUS Leonard Morand. RUNNING TIME 81 min. CAST: **John Saxon** (Allan Brenner); Basil Rathbone (Dr. Farraday); Judi Meredith (Laura James); Dennis Hopper (Paul Grant); Florence Marly (Alien Queen).

I Tre Che Sconvolsero il West, Vado, Vedo e Sparo, a.k.a. *I Came, I Saw, I Shot* (1968). DIR Enzo G. Castellari. PROD Dario Sabatello. SCR Augusto Finocchi, Vittorio Metz, Enrique Llovet, José María Rodríuz (story by Augusto Finocchi, Vittorio Metz). CAM Alejandro Ulloa. ED Tatiana Casini. MUS Carlo Rusticelli. RUNNING TIME 95 min. CAST: Antonio Sabato (Moses Lang); **John Saxon** (Clay Watson); Frank Wolff (Edwin Kean); Agata Flori (Rosario); Leon Anchóriz (Garrito).

For Singles Only (Columbia, 1968). DIR Arthur Dreifuss. PROD Sam Katzman. SCR Arthur Dreifuss, Hal Collins (story by Arthur Hoerl, Albert Derr). CAM John F. Warren. ED Ben Lewis. MUS Fred Karger. RUNNING TIME 91 min. CAST: **John Saxon** (Bret Hendley); Mary Ann Mobley (Anne Carr); Lana Wood (Helen Todd); Peter Mark Richman (Gerald Pryor); Milton Berle (Mr. Parker).

Death of a Gunfighter (Universal, 1969). DIR Allen Smithee [i.e. Robert Totten replaced by Don Siegel]. PROD Richard E. Lyons. SCR Joseph Calvelli (novel by Lewis P. Patten). CAM Andrew Jackson. ED Robert F. Shugrue. MUS Oliver Nelson. RUNNING TIME 94 min. CAST: Richard Widmark (Marshal Frank Patch); Lena Horne (Claire Quintana); Carroll O'Connor (Lester Locke); David Opatoshu (Edward Rosenblum); Jacqueline Scott (Laurie Mills); **John Saxon** (Lou Trinidad).

Company of Killers (Universal, 1970). DIR Jerry Thorpe. PROD Jerry Thorpe, E. Jack Neuman. SCR E. Jack Neuman. CAM Jack Marta. ED John Elias. MUS Stanley Wilson. RUNNING TIME 86 min. CAST: Van Johnson (Sam Cahill); Ray Milland (George DeSalles); **John Saxon** (Dave Poohler); Brian Kelly (Nick Andros); Fritz Weaver (John Shankalien); Anna Capri (Maryjane).

Joe Kidd (Universal, 1972). DIR John Sturges. PROD Sidney Beckerman. SCR Elmore Leonard. CAM Bruce

Surtees. ED Ferris Webster. MUS Lalo Schifrin. RUNNING TIME 88 min. CAST: Clint Eastwood (Joe Kidd); Robert Duvall (Frank Harlan); **John Saxon** (Luis Chama); Don Stroud (Lamarr Simms); Stella Garcia (Helen Sanchez); James Wainwright (Olin Mingo).

Enter the Dragon (Warner Bros., 1973). DIR Robert Clouse. PROD Fred Weintraub, Paul Heller. SCR Michael Allin. CAM Gilbert Hubbs. ED Kurt Hirschler, George Watters. MUS Lalo Schifrin. RUNNING TIME 98 min (25th anniversary version: 110 min). CAST: Bruce Lee (Lee); **John Saxon** (Roper); Kien Shih (Han); Jim Kelly (Williams); Anna Capri (Tania); Robert Wall (Oharra).

Mr. Kingstreet's War (1973). DIR Percival Rubens. RUNNING TIME 92 min. CAST: **John Saxon** (Percival Kingstreet); Tippi Hedren (Maggie Kingstreet); Brian O'Shaughnessy (Morgan Kingstreet), Rossano Brazzi.

Baciano le Mani, a.k.a. *Family Killer* (Cannon, 1973). DIR-SCR Vittorio Schiraldi. CAM Marcello Gatti. ED Franco Fraticelli. MUS Enrico Simonetti. RUNNING TIME 95 min. CAST: Arthur Kennedy (Angelino Ferrante); **John Saxon** (Gaspare Ardizzone); Agostina Belli (Mariuccia Ferrante); Pino Colizzi (Massimo); Spiros Focás (Luca Ferrante).

Black Christmas (Ambassador, 1974). DIR Bob Clark. PROD Bob Clark, Gerry Arbeid. SCR Roy Moore. CAM Reg Morris. ED Stan Cole. MUS Carl Zittrer. RUNNING TIME 93 min. CAST: Olivia Hussey (Jess Bradford); Keir Dullea (Peter); Margot Kidder (Barb Coard); **John Saxon** (Lt. Fuller); Marian Waldman (Mrs. Mac); Andrea Martin (Phyl).

Metraletta Stein, a.k.a. *Fight to the Death* (1975). DIR-SCR José Antonio de la Loma. CAM Antonio Millan. ED Teresa Alcocer. MUS M. Molino, S. Cipriani, C. Rustichelli, D. Radici, D. Patacci. RUNNING TIME 106 min. CAST: **John Saxon** (Mariano Beltran); Francisco Rabal (Mendoza); Blanca Estrada (Ana); Frank Brana (Miner); David Carpenter (Carlitos).

Mitchell (Allied Artists, 1975). DIR Andrew V. McLaglen. PROD R. Ben Efraim. SCR Ian Kennedy Martin. CAM Harry Stradling, Jr. ED Fred A. Chulack. MUS Hoyt Axton, Jerry Styner. RUNNING TIME 97 min. CAST: Joe Don Baker (Mitchell); Martin Balsam (James Arthur Cummings); **John Saxon** (Walter Deaney); Linda Evans (Greta); Merlin Olsen (Benton).

The Swiss Conspiracy (S. J. International, 1975). DIR Jack Arnold. PROD Maurice Silverstein. SCR Norman Klenman, Howard Merrill, Philip Saltzman, Norman Sedawie, Michael Stanley (story by Norman Klenman, Howard Merrill, Norman Sedawie). CAM W. P. Hassenstein. ED Murray Jordan. MUS Klaus Doldinger. RUNNING TIME 89 min. CAST: David Janssen (David Christopher); Senta Berger (Denise Abbott); **John Saxon** (Robert Hayes); John Ireland (Dwight McGowan); Ray Milland (Johann Hurtil); Elke Sommer (Rita Jensen).

Una Magnum Special per Tony Saitta, a.k.a. *Strange Shadows in an Empty Room* (American International Pictures, 1976). DIR Alberto de Martino. PROD Edmondo Amati, Robert Ménard. SCR Frank Clark, Vincent Mann. CAM Anthony Ford. ED Vincenzo Tomassi. MUS Armando Trovajoli. RUNNING TIME 99 min. CAST: Stuart Whitman (Tony); **John Saxon** (Sgt. Matthews); Martin Landau (Doctor); Tisa Farrow (Julie); Carole Laure (Louise Saitta).

Napoli Violenta, a.k.a. *Violent Protection* (1976). DIR Umberto Lenzi. SCR Vincenzo Mannino. RUNNING TIME 95 min. CAST: Maurizio Merli (Betti); **John Saxon** (Francesco Capuana); Barry Sullivan (The General); Guido Alberti (Chief of Police); Pino Ferrara (Garage Owner).

La Legge Violenta della Squadra Anticrimine, a.k.a. *Cross Shot* (1976). DIR Stelvio Massi. PROD Teodoro Agrimi. SCR Lucio De Caro, Maurizio Mengoni, Dardano Sacchetti, Piero Poggio (story by Lucio De Caro). CAM Mario Vulpiani. ED Mauro Bonanni. MUS Pino Pintucci. CAST: Lee J. Cobb (Dante Ragusa); **John Saxon** (Javocella); Thomas Hunter (Turrini); Renzo Palmer (Maselli); Lino Capolicchio (Antonio Blasi).

Italia a Mano Armata (1976). DIR Marino Girolami. SCR Vincenzo Mannino. CAM Fausto Zuccoli. ED Vincenzo Tomassi. MUS Franco Micazilli. CAST: Maurizio Merli (Betti); Raymond Pellegrin (Arpino); **John Saxon** (Albertelli); Daniele Dublino (Luzi); Massimo Vanni (Fabi).

Moonshine County Express (New World, 1977). DIR Gus Trikonis. PROD Ed Carlin. SCR Hubert Smith, Daniel Ansley. CAM Gary Graver. ED Gene Ruggiero. MUS Fred Werner. RUNNING TIME 95 min. CAST: **John Saxon** (J. B. Johnson), Susan Howard (Dot), William Conrad (Starkey), Morgan Woodward (Sweetwater), Claudia Jennings (Betty), Jeff Corey (Preacher Hagen).

Mark Colpisce Ancora, a.k.a. *Mark Strikes Again* (1977). DIR Stelvio Massi. SCR Lucio De Caro, Dardano Sacchetti. RUNNING TIME 102 min. CAST: Franco Gasparri (Mark Patti); **John Saxon** (Altman); John Steiner (Paul Henkel); Marcella Michelangeli (Olga Kube).

Il Cinico, l'Infame, il Violento, a.k.a. *The Cynic, the Rat and the Fist* (1977). DIR Umberto Lenzi. PROD Luciano Martino. SCR Ernesto Gastaldi, Umberto Lenzi, Dardano Sacchetti (story by Sauro Scavolini). CAM Federico Zanni. ED Eugenio Alabiso. MUS Franco Micalizzi. RUNNING TIME 100 min. CAST: Tomas Milian (Luigi Maietto); Maurizio Merli (Leonardo Tanzi); **John Saxon** (Frank Di Maggio); Renzo Palmer (Astalli); Roberto Undari (Dario).

Shalimar, a.k.a. *Raiders of Shalimar* (1978). DIR Krishna Shah. PROD Suresh Shah. SCR Krishna Shah (story by Krishna Shah, Stanford Sherman). CAM Harvey Genkins. ED Teddy Darvas. MUS R. D. Burman. RUN-

NING TIME 85 min. CAST: Rex Harrison (Sir John Locksley); Sylvia Miles (Countess Rasmussen); **John Saxon** (Col. Columbus); Dharmendra (S. S. Kumar); Zeenat Aman (Sheila Enders).

The Glove (PRO International, 1978). DIR Ross Hagen. PROD Julian Roffman. SCR Julian Roffman, Hubert Smith. CAM Gary Graver. ED Bob Fitzgerald. MUS Robert O. Ragland. RUNNING TIME 90 min. CAST: **John Saxon** (Sam Kellough); Roosevelt Grier (Sheila Michaels); Joanna Cassidy (Sheila Michaels); Joan Blondell (Mrs. Fitzgerald); Jack Carter (Walter Stratton); Aldo Ray (Prison Guard); Keenan Wynn (Bill Schwartz).

The Bees (New World, 1978). DIR-PROD-SCR Alfredo Zacharias (also story). CAM Leon Sanchez. ED Mort Tubor, Sandy Nervig. MUS Richard Gillis. RUNNING TIME 86 min. CAST: **John Saxon** (John); Angel Tompkins (Sandra); John Carradine (Dr. Hummel); Claudio Brook (Dr. Miller); Alicia Encinas (Alicia); Julio Cesar (Julio).

Fast Company (1979). DIR David Cronenberg. PROD Michael Lebowitz, Peter O'Brian, Courtney Smith. SCR David Cronenberg, Phil Savath, Courtney Smith (story by Alan Treen). CAM Mark Irwin. ED Ronald Sanders. MUS Fred Mollin. RUNNING TIME 91 min. CAST: William Smith (Lonnie "Lucky Man" Johnson); **John Saxon** (Phil Adamson); Claudia Jennings (Sammy); Nicholas Campbell (Billy 'The Kid' Brooker); Don Franks (Elder).

The Electric Horseman (Columbia/Universal, 1979). DIR Sydney Pollack. PROD Ray Stark. SCR Robert Garland (story by Robert Garland, Paul Gaer, Shelley Burton). CAM Owen Roizman. ED Sheldon Kaen. MUS Dave Grusin. RUNNING TIME 121 min. CAST: Robert Redford (Sonny); Jane Fonda (Hallie); Valerie Perrine (Charlotta); Willie Nelson (Wendell); **John Saxon** (Hunt Sears).

Beyond Evil (IFI/Scope III, 1980). DIR Herb Freed. PROD Herb Freed, David Baughn. SCR Herb Freed, Paul Ross (story by David Baughn). CAM Ken Plotin. ED Richard E. Westover. MUS Pino Donaggio. RUNNING TIME 94 min. CAST: **John Saxon** (Larry Andrews); Linda Day George (Barbara); Michael Dante (Del); Mario Malino (Albanos); Janice Lynde (Alma).

Battle Beyond the Stars (New World, 1980). DIR Jimmy T. Murakami. PROD Ed Carlin. SCR John Sayles (story by John Sayles, Anne Dyer). CAM Daniel Lacambre. ED Allan Holtzman, Bob Kizer. MUS James Horner. RUNNING TIME 104 min. CAST: Richard Thomas (Shad); Robert Vaughn (Gelt); **John Saxon** (Sador); Darlanne Fluegel (Nanelia); George Peppard (Cowboy); Sam Jaffe (Dr. Hephaestus); Jeff Corey (Zed).

Running Scared (1980). DIR-PROD Paul Glickler. SCR David Odell (story by Paul Glickler). CAM Willy Kurant. ED Robert Q. Lovett. MUS Roger Kellaway. RUNNING TIME 96 min. CAST: Ken Wahl (Chas McClain); Judge Reinhold (Leroy Beecher); Annie McEnroe (Sally Mae Giddens); Bradford Dillman (Arthur Jaeger); **John Saxon** (Capt. Munoz); Pat Hingle (Sgt. McClain).

Apocalypse Domani, a.k.a. *Cannibals in the Street* (Almi Cinema 5, 1980). DIR Antonio Margheretti. PROD Maurizio Amati, Sandro Amati. SCR Antonio Margheretti, Jimmy Gould, Dardano Saghetti. CAM Fernando Arribas. ED Giorgio Serrallonga. MUS Alexander Blonksteiner. RUNNING TIME 91 min. CAST: **John Saxon** (Norman Hopper); Elizabeth Turner (Jane Hopper); Giovanni Lombardo Radice (Charlie Bukowski); Cinzia De Carolis (Mary); Tony King (Tom Thompson); Wallace Wilkinson (Lt. Hill).

Blood Beach (Gross, 1981). DIR Jeffrey Bloom. PROD Sidney Beckerman. SCR Jeffrey Bloom (story by Jeffrey Bloom, Steven Navelansky). CAM Steve Poster. ED Gary Griffen. MUS Gil Melle. RUNNING TIME 92 min. CAST: David Huffman (Harry); Marianna Hill (Catherine); **John Saxon** (Pearson); Otis Young (Piantadosi); Stefan Gierasch (Dimitrios).

Assassinio al Cimitero Etrusco (1982). DIR Sergio Martino. PROD Luciano Martino. SCR Ernesto Gastaldi, Dardano Sacchetti. CAM Giancarlo Ferrando. ED Daniele Alabiso, Eugenio Alabiso. MUS Fabio Frizzi. CAST: Elvire Audrey (Joan Barnard); Paolo Malco (Mike Grant); Claudio Cassinelli (Paolo Domelli); Marilù Tolo (Maria); Van Johnson (Mulligan); **John Saxon** (Arthur Barnard).

Tenebre, a.k.a. *Unsane* (Bedford/Film Gallery, 1982). DIR Dario Argento. PROD Claudio Argento. SCR Dario Argento, George Kemp (story by Dario Argento). CAM Luciano Tovoli. ED Franco Fraticelli. MUS Simonetti-Morante-Pignatelli. RUNNING TIME 91 min. CAST: Anthony Franciosa (Peter Neal); Daria Nicolodi (Anne); Christian Borromeo (Gianni); Mirella D'Angelo (Tilde); Veronica Lario (Jane McKerrow); **John Saxon** (Bullmer).

Wrong Is Wright, a.k.a. *The Man with the Deadly Lens* (Columbia, 1982). DIR-PROD Richard Brooks. SCR Richard Brooks (novel *The Better Angels* by Charles McCarry). CAM Fred J. Koenekamp. ED George Grenville. MUS Artie Kane. RUNNING TIME 117 min. CAST: Sean Connery (Patrick Hale); George Grizzard (President Lockwood); Robert Conrad (Gen. Wombat); Katharine Ross (Sally Blake); G. D. Spradlin (Philindros); **John Saxon** (Homer Hubbard); Henry Silva (Rafeeq); Leslie Nielsen (Mallory).

Una Donna Dietro la Porta (1982). DIR Pino Tosini. SCR Pino Tosini, Leros Pittoni (story by Leros Pittoni). CAST: **John Saxon** (The Notary); Dalila Di Lazzaro (Andrea); Clarita Gatto (Marina).

The Big Score (Almi, 1983). DIR Fred Williamson. PROD Michael S. Landes, Albert Schwartz. SCR Gail Morgan Hickman. CAM João Fernandez. ED Dan Lowenthal. MUS Jay Chattaway. RUNNING TIME 85 min. CAST: Fred Williamson (Hooks); Nancy Wilson (Angi); **John Saxon** (Davis); Richard Roundtree (Gordon); Ed Lauter (Parks).

Desire (1983). DIR Eddie Romero. CAST: Tetchie Agbayani (Bessie); Judith Chapman (Julie Seaver); Ken Metcalfe (Phil Seaver); Maria Richwine (Cris Arias); **John Saxon** (Joe Hale).

A Nightmare on Elm Street (New Line Cinema, 1984). DIR-SCR Wes Craven. PROD Robert Shaye. CAM Jacques Haitkin. ED Rick Shaine. MUS Charles Bernstein. RUNNING TIME 91 min. CAST: **John Saxon** (Lt. Thompson); Ronee Blakley (Marge); Heather Langenkamp (Nancy); Amanda Wyss (Tina Gray); Nick Corri (Rod); Johnny Depp (Glen); Robert Englund (Fred).

Fever Pitch (MGM/UA, 1985). DIR-SCR Richard Brooks. PROD Fedddie Fields. CAM William A. Fraker. ED Jeff Jones. MUS Thomas Dolby. RUNNING TIME 96 min. CAST: Ryan O'Neal (Taggert); Catherine Hicks (Flo); Giancarlo Giannini (Charley); Bridgette Anderson (Amy); Chad Everett (Dutchman); **John Saxon** (Sports Editor).

Mani di Pietra, a.k.a. *Hands of Steel* (Almi, 1986). DIR Martin Dolman [Sergio Martino]. PROD Luciano Martino. SCR Martin Dolman [Sergio Martino], Elizabeth Parker [Elisa Briganti], Ernesto Gastaldi, Dardano Sacchetti. CAM John McFerrand [Giancarlo Ferrando]. ED Eugenio Alabiso, Alan Devgen. MUS Claudio Simonetti. RUNNING TIME 94 min. CAST: Daniel Greene (Paco Querak); Janet Agren (Linda); George Eastman (Raoul Fernandez); **John Saxon** (Francis Turner); Claudio Cassinelli.

A Nightmare on Elm Street 3: Dream Warriors (New Line Cinema, 1987). DIR Chuck Russell. PROD Robert Shaye. SCR Wes Craven, Chuck Russell, Frank Darabont, Bruce Wagner (story by Wes Craven, Bruce Wagner). CAM Roy H. Wagner. ED Terry Stokes, Chuck Weiss. MUS Angelo Badalementi. RUNNING TIME 96 min. CAST: Heather Langenkamp (Nancy Thompson); Patricia Arquette (Kirsten Parker); Larry Fishburne (Max); Craig Wasson (Dr. Neil Gordan); Robert Englund (Freddy Krueger); **John Saxon** (Donald Thompson); Priscilla Pointer (Dr. Elizabeth Simms); Dick Cavett (Himself); Zsa Zsa Gabor (Herself).

House Made of Dawn (1987). DIR-PROD Richardson Morse. SCR Richardson Morse, N. Scott Momaday (novel by N. Scott Momaday). CAM Stevan Larner. ED William Brame. MUS Peter Morse. RUNNING TIME 90 min. CAST: Larry Littlebird (Abel); Judith Doty (Milly); Jay Varela (Benally); Mesa Bird (Grandfather); **John Saxon** (Tomasah).

Nightmare Beach (1988). DIR Umberto Lenzi. PROD William J. Immerman. SCR Harry Kirkpatrick [Umberto Lenzi] (story by Harry Kirkpatrick, Vittorio Rambaldi). MUS Claudio Simonetti. CAST: Nicolas De Toth (Skip); **John Saxon** (Strycher); Lance LeGault (Rev. Bates); Sarah Buxton (Gail).

My Mom's a Werewolf (Crown International, 1989). DIR Michael Fischa. PROD Stephen J. Wolfe. SCR Mark Pirro. CAM Bryan England. ED Claudia Finkle. MUS Barry Fasman. RUNNING TIME 84 min. CAST: Susan Blakely (Leslie Shaber); **John Saxon** (Harry Thropen); Katrina Caspary (Jennifer Shabert); John Schuck (Howard Shaber); Ruth Buzzi (Madame Gypsy); Marilyn McCoo (Celia Celica).

Crossing the Line (1989). DIR Gary Graver. PROD Gregory Vanger, Jonathan Vanger. SCR Rick Marcus (story by James Ryan). ED Dean Goodhill. RUNNING TIME 94 min. CAST: Rick Hearst (Rick Kagan); John Stafford (Zach Kapinsky); Paul L. Smith (Joe Kapinsky); Vernon Wells (Steve Sinclair); **John Saxon** (Jack Kagan).

Criminal Act, a.k.a. *Tunnels* (1989). DIR Mark Byers. SCR Daniel Yost. RUNNING TIME 93 min. CAST: Catherine Bach (Pam Weiss); Charlene Dallas (Sharon Fields); Nicholas Guest (Ron Bellard); **John Saxon** (Herb).

The Arrival (1990). DIR David Schmoeller. SCR Daniel Ljoka. RUNNING TIME 103 min. CAST: David Schmoeller (Dr. Carlyle); **John Saxon** (Agent Mills); Linda Ljoka (Laura); Robin Frates (Connie).

Blood Salvage (Paragon Arts, 1990). DIR Tucker Johnston. PROD Martin J. Fischer, Ken Sanders. SCR Tucker Johnston, Ken Sanders. CAM Michael Karp. ED Jacquie Freeman Ross. MUS Tim Temple. RUNNING TIME 98 min. CAST: Danny Nelson (Jake Pruitt); Lori Birdsong (April Evans); **John Saxon** (Clifford Evans); Ray Walston (Mr. Stone); Christian Hesler (Hiram Pruitt); Evander Holyfield (Boxer).

The Last Samurai (1990). DIR-SCR Paul Mayersberg. CAST: Lance Henricksen (Johnny Congo); **John Saxon** (Haroun Al-Kamin); Lisa Eilbacher (Susan); James Ryan (Miyagawa).

Aftershock (1990). DIR Frank Harris. SCR Michael Standing. CAST: **John Saxon** (Oliver Quinn); Russ Tamblyn (Hank Franklin); Christopher Mitchum (Col. Slater); James Lew (Mr. James).

The Final Alliance (1990). DIR Mario DiLeo. SCR Harel Goldstein, John Eubank. CAST: David Hasselhoff (Will Colton); Jeanie Moore (Carrie); Bo Hopkins (Sheriff Whistler); **John Saxon** (Ghost); Gary Ford (James).

Hellmaster (1992). DIR-SCR Douglas Schulze. RUNNING TIME 92 min. CAST: **John Saxon** (Professor Jones); David Emge (Robert); Amy Raasch (Shelly O'Deane); Edward Stevens (Drake Destroy).

Animal Instincts (1992). DIR Gregory Dark. SCR Jon Robert Samsel, Georges des Esseintes. RUNNING TIME 95 min. CAST: Maxwell Caulfield (David Cole); Jan-Michael Vincent (Fletcher Ross); Shannon Whirry (Joanne Cole); Delia Sheppard (Ingrid); Mitchell Gaylord (Rod Tennison); **John Saxon** (Otto Van Horne); David Carradine (Lamberti).

Maximum Force (1992). DIR Joseph Mehri. SCR John Weidner, Ken Lamplugh. CAST: Sam J. Jones (Michael Crews); Sherrie Rose (Cody Randal); Jason Lively (Rick Carver); **John Saxon** (Capt. Fuller); Mickey Rooney (Chief of Police).

No Escape, No Return (1992). DIR-SCR Charles T. Kanganis. CAST: Maxwell Caulfield (William Robert

Sloan); Dustin Nguyen (Tommy Cuff); Denise Loveday (Ali Weston); **John Saxon** (James Mitchell); Joey Travolta (Stark).

Jonathan Degli Orsi (1992). DIR Enzo G. Castellari. PROD Franco Nero, Vittorio Noia, Alexandre Skodo. SCR Enzo G. Castellari, Lorenzo De Luca (story by Lorenzo De Luca, Franco Nero). CAM Mikhail Agranovich. ED Alberto Moriani. CAST: Franco Nero (Jonathan); **John Saxon** (Fred Goodwin); Floyd "Red Crow" Westerman (Chief Tawanka); David Hess (Maddock); Bobby Rhodes (Williamson).

Frame-Up II: The Cover-Up (1993). DIR-SCR Paul Leder. RUNNING TIME 90 min. CAST: Margaux Hemingway (Jean Searage); Wings Hauser (Sheriff Baker); **John Saxon** (Charles Searage); Patti d'Arbanville (Barbara Griffin); Cole Hauser (Cal); Lauren Woodland (Sue).

The Baby Doll Murders (1993). DIR-SCR-ED Paul Leder. PROD Paul Leder, Ralph Tornberg. CAM Francis Grumman. MUS Dana Walden. CAST: Jeff Kober (Louis); **John Saxon** (John Maglia); Melanie Smith (Peggy Davis); Bobby Di Cicco (Larry); Tom Hodges (Les Parker);

Beverly Hills Cop III (Paramount, 1994). DIR John Landis. PROD Mace Neufeld, Robert Rehme. SCR Steven E. de Souza (characters created by Danilo Bach, Daniel Petrie, Jr.). CAM Mac Ahlberg. ED Dale Beddin. MUS Nile Rodgers. RUNNING TIME 109 min. CAST: Eddie Murphy (Alex Foley); Judge Reinhold (Billy Rosewood); Hector Elizondo (Joe Flint); Theresa Randle (Janice Perkins); **John Saxon** (Orrin Sanderson).

Killing Obsession (1994). DIR-PROD Paul Leder. CAST: John Savage (Albert); **John Saxon** (Dr. Sachs); Bobby Di Cicco (Pimp); Bernard White (Lt. Jackson); Victoria Dillard (Jean Wilson); Antonio Saxon.

Wes Craven's New Nightmare (New Line Cinema, 1994). DIR-SCR Wes Craven. PROD Marianne Maddalena. CAM Mark Irwin. ED Patrick Lussier. MUS J. Peter Robinson. RUNNING TIME 112 min. CAST: Robert Englund (Himself/Freddy Krueger); Heather Langenkamp (Herself); Miko Hughes (Dylan); David Newsom (Chase Porter); **John Saxon** (Himself).

Nonstop Pyramid Action (1995). DIR-SCR Ari Gold. CAST: Stephanie Ittelson (Amanda); **John Saxon** (Mr. Apple); Ari Gold (Rocker); Craig Stark (John-John).

The Killers Within (1995). DIR-SCR Paul Leder. CAST: Robert Carradine (Ben Wallace); Melanie Smith (Cynthia Alpert); Norbert Weisser (Bernhard Hiller); **John Saxon** (Det. Lewis); Ferdy Mayne (Gen. Von Weber).

From Dusk Till Dawn (Miramax, 1996). DIR-ED Robert Rodriguez. PROD Gianni Nunnari, Meir Teper. SCR Quentin Tarantino (story by Robert Kurtzman). CAM Guillermo Navaro. MUS Graeme Revell. RUNNING TIME 108 min. CAST: Harvey Keitel (Jacob Fuller); George Clooney (Seth Gecko); Quentin Tarantino (Richard Gecko); Juliette Lewis (Kate Fuller); Fred Williamson (Frost); **John Saxon** (FBI Agent).

Lancelot: Guardian of Time (1997). DIR Rubiano Cruz. PROD Jed Nolan, George Peirson. SCR Patricia Monville. ED John Rosenberg. CAST: Marc Singer (Lancelot du Lac); Claudia Christian (Katherine Shelley); **John Saxon** (Wolvencroft); Jerry Levine (Michael Shelley); Adam Carter (Arthur).

Joseph's Gift (1998). DIR Philippe Mora. SCR Patricia Monville. CAST: Freddy Rodríguez (Joseph); Joseph Bottoms (James); **John Saxon** (Jacob Kelly); Pamela Bellwood (Clara Childress); Sam Bottoms (Robert).

The Party Crashers (1999). DIR-SCR Phil Leirness. RUNNING TIME 77 min. CAST: **John Saxon** (Mr. Foster); Max Parrish (Gigolo); Peter Murnik (Former Athlete); Shawnee Smith (Carolyn); Phil Leirness (Writer); Burt Bulos (Actor).

Tripwire (1999). DIR Sidney J. Furie. SCR John Mark Sheppard (story by Paul Leo Friedman). RUNNING TIME 87 min. CAST: Darryl Hannah; Piper Laurie; Ricard Moll; Jean Reno; **John Saxon**; Michael York (Stan); Stephanie Zimbalist (Claire).

Living in Fear (2001). DIR Martin Kitrosser. CAST: William R. Moses (Chuck Hausman); Marcia Cross (Rebecca Hausman); Daniel Quinn (Art); Katherine Helmond (Mrs. Ford); **John Saxon** (Rev. Leo Hausman).

Night Class (2001). DIR Sheldon Wilson. SCR William R. Greenblatt, William Wennekers. CAST: Sean Young; Rick Peters; Ron Perlman; Edward Albert; **John Saxon**.

The Courier (2001). DIR Lorena David. SCR Scott Duncan, Ned Kerwin. CAST: Tim Sitarz (Brock); Mario López (David Morales); Ali Landry (Bella); Nancy O'Dell (Dr. Drake); **John Saxon** (James Darabont).

Television Movies

Winchester '73 (1967). DIR Herschel Daugherty. CAST: John Drew Barrymore; Dan Duryea; **John Saxon** (Dakin McAdam); Joan Blondell; Paul Fix.

Istanbul Express (1968). DIR Richard Irving. CAST: Gene Barry; Senta Berger; Philip Bournef; Jack Kruschen; John Marley; **John Saxon** (Cheval).

The Intruders (1970). DIR William Graham. CAST: Don Murray; Anne Francis; Edmond O'Brien; **John Saxon** (Billy Pye); Gene Evans; Harry Dean Stanton; Harrison Ford.

Snatched (1973). DIR Sutton Roley. CAST: Howard Duff; Leslie Nielsen; Sheree North; Barbara Parkins; Robert Reed; **John Saxon** (Paul Maxvill).

Linda (1973). DIR Jack Smight. CAST: **John Saxon** (Jeff Braden); Stella Stevens; Ed Nelson; John McIntire; Alan Fudge.

Can Ellen Be Saved? (1974). DIR Harvey Hart. CAST: Leslie Nielsen; Katherine Cannon; Michael Parks; **John Saxon** (James Hallbeck); Louise Fletcher; Kathleen Quinlan.

Planet Earth (1974). DIR Marc Daniels. CAST: **John Saxon** (Dylan Hunt); Janet Margolin; Ted Cassidy; Christopher Carey; Diane Muldaur; Sally Kemp.

Crossfire (1975). DIR William Hale. CAST: James Farentino; **John Saxon** (Dave Ambrose); Patrick O'Neal; Pamela Franklin; Ned Glass; Herb Edelman.

Strange New World (1975). DIR Robert Butler. CAST: Richard Farnsworth; Catherine Bach; **John Saxon** (Capt. Anthony Vico); James Olsen; Keene Curtis.

Once an Eagle (1976). DIR Richard Michaels, E. W. Swackhamer. CAST: Sam Elliott; Glenn Ford; Ralph Bellamy; Linda Gay George; Kim Hunter; **John Saxon** (Capt. Townshend).

Raid on Entebbe (1977). DIR Irvin Kershner. CAST: Peter Finch; Martin Balsam; Horst Buchholz; **John Saxon** (Benny Peled); Sylvia Sidney; Jack Warden; Charles Bronson; Jack Warden.

Harold Robbins' 79 Park Avenue (1977). DIR Paul Wendkos. CAST: Lesley Ann Warren; Marc Singer; David Dukes; Barbara Barrie; Polly Bergen; Raymond Burr; **John Saxon** (Harry Vito).

Greatest Heroes of the Bible (1978). DIR James L. Conway. CAST: Julie Adams; Lew Ayres; John Carradine; Jeff Corey; **John Saxon** (Adonijah); Dean Stockwell; Robert Vaughn.

Golden Gate (1981). DIR Paul Wendkos. CAST: Mary Crosby; Melanie Griffith; Perry King; **John Saxon** (Sagar); Jean Simmons.

Savage in the Orient (1983). DIR Vincent Sherman. CAST: Lew Ayres; Leif Erickson; Gayle Hunnicutt; Joe Penny; **John Saxon**.

Prisoners of the Lost Universe (1983). DIR Terry Marcel. CAST: Richard Hatch; Kay Lenz; **John Saxon** (Kleel); Peter O'Farrell (Malachi); Ray Charleson.

Solomon Northrup's Odyssey (1984). DIR Gordon Parks. CAST: Avery Brooks; Rhetta Greene; Mason Adams; Lee Bryant; **John Saxon** (Epps).

Brothers-in-Law (1985). DIR John Boulting, Roy Boulting. CAST: Mac Davis; Joseph Cortese; Robert Culp; **John Saxon** (Royal Cane); Daphne Ashbrook; Gerald S. O'Loughlin.

Payoff (1991). DIR Stuart Cooper. CAST: Keith Carradine; Jeff Corey; **John Saxon** (Rafael Concion); Harry Dean Stanton; William S. Taylor.

Blackmail (1991). DIR Ruben Preuss. CAST: Susan Blakely; Dale Midkiff; Beth Toussaint; **John Saxon** (Gene); Mac Davis; Kevin McNulty.

Liz: The Elizabeth Taylor Story (1995). DIR Kevin Connor. CAST: Sherilyn Fenn; Nigel Havers; Katherine Helmond; Kevin McCarthy; William McNamara; **John Saxon** (Richard Brooks).

VINCENT SHERMAN

Which director, who is considered to be one of the great craftsmen from the old studio system, do you think entered the film industry in the late 1930s, directed such actors as Humphrey Bogart, Claude Rains, Bette Davis, Joan Crawford, Clark Gable, Errol Flynn, Miriam Hopkins, Ava Gardner, Paul Newman, Ida Lupino, John Garfield, Richard Burton and so many others in some of their best films, published a fabulous autobiography in 1996 at age 90 and to this day is still doing extremely well? Right, veteran Vincent Sherman.

I had the honor of meeting Mr. Sherman in 1999 at his impressive Malibu home, overlooking the Pacific Ocean, and it was a wonderful experience to talk to this 93-year-old man. Or perhaps we should say 93-year-*young* man, as he looks at least 30 years younger than he actually is, and has the *drive* and the energy of someone half his age. Unlike you might expect, he remembers every detail of his entire *body of work* and during our talk, he gave us a very clear picture of how directors worked in the days of the studio system. As we were about to find out, he also has some great and new ideas for screenplays he's currently working on—on his computer in his spacious office. Its walls are decorated with posters from films he made (*The Hard Way, Old Acquaintance*, etc.), along with photographs from his films; he also has an extensive library of film books which includes a lot of biographies and autobiographies.

Mr. Sherman's autobiography, *Studio Affairs—My Life as a Film Director*,[1] rightfully deserves a special place in his own archive. In this book, he tells his story from his childhood on—he grew up in Vienna, Georgia, where he was born on July 16, 1906, into a Jewish family—and he reflects on how he first became an actor, then a screenwriter and finally one of Warner Bros.' most reliable and most dependable film directors in the 1940s, flourishing under the studio system.

"When in college, I was president of the Debating Society and I was pretty good at speaking, so ultimately my mother wanted me to be a lawyer. I *was* going to be a criminal lawyer, I was very much taken with the great lawyer Clarence Darrow who defended the Loeb-Leopold murder-case in Chicago. I thought, 'If I could only be that kind of a lawyer, with that kind of humanitarian quality!' When I got out of college, I started working as a reporter for the *Atlanta Journal* at the police station. There I got very disgusted with the law; young guys who were trying to make a living as a lawyer, would come to me and because I had access as a newspaper reporter to various actions, they'd ask me if I could tip them off about a damage suit. In return I would get a little piece of the action. I got disgusted with it. I said, 'Jesus, is that the way I have to make my living? I don't want any part of it.' So I gave up the law and that's when I started writing. I loved writing plays. I wrote a play with a friend of mine while attending

Oglethorpe University in Atlanta. We left the South, went to New York and when we couldn't sell the play, I became an actor because I had to eat. I went to work as an extra at the Theater Guild. It was the best thing that ever happened to me. It was a forward moving group with some great people. That's where I met Sanford Meisner, Clifford Odets, Claude Rains, etc."

So he became a stage actor in various Theater Guild productions until he was lured to Hollywood and debuted in a memorable portrayal as a young Communist opposite John Barrymore in William Wyler's *Counsellor at Law* (1933), followed by among others *Midnight Alibi* (1934), silent screen actor Richard Barthelmess' last film at Warner Bros. And he appeared in three films in the Inspector Trent police series at Columbia, with character actor Ralph Bellamy in the title role.

A few years later, under contract to Warner Bros., Mr. Sherman started writing screenplays for films starring actors such as Ronald Reagan and Humphrey Bogart, before turning to directing with *The Return of Dr. X* (1939) with Bogart as a creepy lab assistant. He then directed several other films, mostly at Warner Bros., including *Saturday's Children* (1940) starring John Garfield and Claude Rains; *All Through the Night* (1942), one of Bogart's best films prior to *Casablanca*; *The Hard Way* (1942), his first film with Ida Lupino and Joan Leslie; two of Bette Davis' best films, *Old Acquaintance* (1943) and *Mr. Skeffington* (1945); *The Adventures of Don Juan* (1949) with Errol Flynn in one of the last true swashbuckler films; and *Harriet Craig* (1950), *The Damned Don't Cry* (1950) and *Goodbye, My Fancy* (1951), all three with Joan Crawford. He reunited the team from *Gilda*, Rita Hayworth and Glenn Ford, in *Affair in Trinidad*, and directed a memorable Paul Newman in one of his early films, *The Young Philadelphians* (1959).

Humphrey Bogart appeared in two films directed by Vincent Sherman: *The Return of Dr. X* (1939) and *All Through the Night* (1941).

This incomplete list of his achievements contains several classics. Mr. Sherman: "I think *Mr. Skeffington* is the film people remember very well, but for me it's very difficult to say which film I prefer. It's like asking a mother which of her children she likes the most. I know I made several *bread and butter* pictures, films the studio wanted you to make and in those days you liked to keep on working. You just tried to do the best you could with what you were given to direct. But I still do have fond memories of films like *The Hard Way*. Ida Lupino played the leading role and at the time she hated it. Nobody at Warner Bros. liked it when it was made. Jack [L.] Warner didn't like it, the original writer of the script Irwin Shaw even took his name off the picture—yet when he died, it was the only film he ever got credit for. But when the film came out, Ida won the New York Film Critics Award for her performance. When it was shown at the Telluride Film Festival in 1995, I got a standing ovation.

"*Mr. Skeffington* reunited me with Claude

Claude Rains and Bette Davis get married in *Mr. Skeffington* (1945). (Courtesy of DOCIP Film Archive, Brussels, Belgium.)

Rains once more; he was an old friend from New York where we had appeared in a few plays together. It's a good film and still a very popular picture with a good story. *The Young Philadelphians* is also one of my favorites. I guess I have in all about 10 or 11 pictures that I like very much." It's very strange that, despite the classics Vincent Sherman made, people now are not familiar with him; audiences seem to remember his contemporaries like Billy Wilder, Hitchcock, Frank Capra and John Huston a little bit better. "Let's say there were about ten directors that were really well known. You ask the average man in the street who directed *Gone with the Wind*, he won't know. Before *Casablanca*, very few people knew who Michael Curtiz was. A lot of people still don't know and he was one of the best directors in this town. He made one success after another; he did seven pictures with Errol Flynn. Warner Bros. never gave publicity to directors. The stars got the publicity, not the writers or the directors, nor anybody else in the studio.

"In Europe, the director was the god on the set. I remember meeting Julien Duvivier in this town. I liked him very much, he was a very talented director. He was doing a picture at Metro, he hated it, he found it very difficult to adjust. He had to please a committee—there would be a producer, and assistant producer, the head of the studio, people were calling him all the time.... You had to win the respect, it was not automatically given to you. I got along very well at Warner Bros., I was well liked. I was there the first time almost 15 years steadily. My pictures made money and when I left, I left because of the political situation. When that was cleared up, they asked me to come back. The last time, I wanted to leave because they

Bette Davis and Vincent Sherman on the set of *Mr. Skeffington* (1945), one of the screen's most enduring film classics. (Courtesy of Vincent Sherman.)

weren't buying stories anymore and the studio was going downhill. Warner himself was becoming tired, television was beginning to come up and he was losing his touch and the enthusiasm he had as a young man. But they made some great pictures in all of the studios. The stories were better because they couldn't depend on just sex, violence and special effects.

"Now, I just talked about my political situation. I was never a member of the Communist Party, but I was a left-wing democrat and I certainly belonged to many organizations that were later accused of Communist affiliations." Mr. Sherman refers to the period in the late 1940s when several artists, accused of being members or once having been members of the Communist Party, were blacklisted by the American film industry and could only find work abroad or under pseudonyms. "The truth is," he continues, "I knew every one of the *guys*, also Elia Kazan.[2] I knew him when he first started with the Group Theater. I knew those of the Hollywood Ten like Alvah Bessie and Lester Cole; the only one I didn't know, was Dalton Trumbo. Some of them I didn't like personally, some of them were opportunistic and so forth. I knew Edward Dmytryk too, because Eddie and I had delivered lectures at a place called the Alliance on motion picture direction. Never anything about politics was discussed. Subsequently I found out that the school had been organized as a red front school, but never once was politics discussed.

"In fact, the two people that were most successful in terms of the lectures, were Dmytryk and myself. And we were very friendly, I saw Dmytryk very often at parties. I didn't like what he did or what Kazan did, but it was a different time, a different atmosphere, the world was different at that time. Both were very talented, but I thought the Academy was wrong in selecting Kazan for a Human Achievement Award at the latest Academy Award ceremonies. The category was not quite right, 'cause there's no question that what he did, hurt people and that was wrong. On the other hand, I don't know if he was thoroughly convinced in what he was doing. Maybe he did it to protect himself, so he could keep on working in the picture business. I talked to Dmytryk subsequently and he told me he had been a party member, at the time when we were lecturing together. I didn't know that because we never talked politics. Anyhow, Dmytryk told me he became disillusioned with the Communist Party before the HUAC got busy. But he felt that since he had been identified as having been a Communist, he had to go to jail even though he wanted to get out of the party already. But he felt, if he confessed to the HUAC at that time, they would have thought he'd do it to stay out of jail. So he went to jail, and then after jail he admitted it, so I felt sympathetic towards him; it took a lot of guts.

"I was very disappointed in Kazan at the 1999 Academy presentation when he received his honorary Oscar. I thought he had a chance, he could have said *something*, he could have said what Dalton Trumbo said: 'We were all victims.' Which I think was true. Kazan could have said something that at least left a better taste in the mouth of people, something like, 'I'm sorry I had to do what I did. I certainly never meant to hurt people. I'm grateful that the Academy is giving me this.' He could have said something about the times, he could have made some gesture of regret. The villain was not Kazan; it was the HUAC, because it was illegal in spirit, if not in fact. It caused great trouble because this is supposed to be a democracy.

"It was a terrible period in American history, terrible. The heads of the studio were businessmen who were protecting their business. Had they said 'No' to the HUAC, they would undoubtedly have lost their positions as president of the company and so forth, because what it comes down to, the dollar is the fundamental thing the business rests on. I think even Jack [L.] Warner was reluctant to do what he did [he said to the HUAC he wouldn't tolerate any Communist working for him], in fact he told me afterwards, 'But what else could I do?' The American Legion was ready to picket in front of the theaters if any company indicated that it was against the HUAC; it was a very rough time. As I look at the world and the changes that have been going on in my 93 years, I have a tendency not to pass judgment on people because it's very difficult to describe and to get the feeling of the times when Kazan made his confession. It's very difficult to understand that time.

"I knew Robert Rossen[3] very well. We worked right across from each other's office for at least seven, eight years. Every afternoon he'd come to my office, have a cup of coffee and we'd talk about world conditions, about a play he'd been working on for years—about pool sharks and so forth—later on he did the picture, *The Hustler*. And he was telling me how he criticized the people who confessed and how terrible it was. And what happened? I'll never forget. He came in one morning and said, 'Who do you think was sitting next to me on the plane from New York [he just came back from New York]? Earl Browder!' He had been the head of the Communist Party in the United States. That's when the party was leading to cooperation with the other parties and Rossen was telling me how wonderful he was. Six months later he confessed. I thought that was an opportunistic thing, you see. So it's very difficult to say how you were affected by it and believe me, you had to be strong to stand up and take a stand against them. Some people were headstrong, but not necessarily fully convinced that they were right.

"You have to remember that in this country the 1930s were very bad years. People were jobless, there were soup and bread lines, there were difficulties, milk strikes in the Midwest, farms were being confiscated, so there was a pent up anger inside the American people. So who do you let your anger out on? The minorities. These ancient hatreds come up when the conditions get bad. On three different occasions they came to me and asked me to join the Communist Party. I was very tempted. Also, here we saw the rise of Hitlerism and fascism in Europe and the feeling was that the only group that was doing anything about the rise of fascism and the rise of anti–Semitism in Europe, was the Communist Party. That's the reason why these guys drifted into the party. At least they were calling for social change. It's not that they wanted to destroy the American government, they wanted to destroy the political set-up that was inside the American government. They thought they would be helping America, not hurting it. You would have to sit down and re-create the entire atmosphere to understand the actions of some of the people. If you didn't live in those times, you can't know what they were like. So when people talk to me about Kazan and some of the others, I think, well, I don't know, I can't come down on them as hard as some people have. I don't know what I would have done if they would have told me, 'Either you work or you don't work.' I also had a family to support. I don't like to pass judgment.

"I could have been able to join the top rank of directors with John Huston and the others, if things had worked out slightly differently. I was *this* close to making *Casablanca*. The way that was given to me, I'll never forget. I was on my way to the office one morning when Bob Rossen asked me, 'Have you read that piece of crap that's been going around, "Everybody Comes to Rick's"?' I said, 'No, what is it about?' 'Well, it's a play they bought for $35,000. It was a try-out, it failed, it closed out of town before it opened in New York—but they bought the story. Now they wanna make a picture out of it. It's a piece of romantic nonsense.'

"The next day I came to my office and the play was on my desk. I read it and I said, 'My God, it's not a good play, but it's got wonderful material for a movie. There are the refugees trying to escape, people under pressure, an American who says, 'I'm disgusted with all politics.' He wants nothing to do with it and he's against everybody, he's there only for himself. There's a black man playing the piano for him, a sentimental number that reminds him of a girl he was in love with and who deserted him, and so forth. It had all the ingredients for what I call a good movie, not a great, important movie, but a good movie. When I read it, I went rushing up to the Epstein brothers, Julius [J.] and Philip [G.] Epstein,[4] who had written the script of *Saturday's Children* and they later wrote and produced *Mr. Skeffington*. I thought they were good writers and I told them the story. I said, 'Hey, it's a great story, guys. Why don't you do it?' They said, 'Well, we gotta go to New York a few days from now, why don't you talk to Wallis?' Hal B. Wallis was the head of the studio at that time. I went up to him and said, "Hal, I just read 'Everybody Comes to Rick's.'" 'Yeah, what do you think?' I said, 'It would make a great movie.' 'You're kidding?' 'No.' 'Well, nobody likes it around here.' 'I know, it's not really great, but if it's done properly, it's got all the romantic elements for a hell of a love story. I talked to the Epsteins about it, and they will do it.' He said, 'They won't do anything, they're on their way to New York.' I said, 'Okay, when they're back and the script is finished, will you let me do it?' 'Gee Vince, you're talking about six months from now, who knows what the situation is then? Maybe we'll never make it, I don't know.' I said, 'Well, okay, but please keep me in mind.' So I got the Epsteins on that script, but later, as I was set to do *The Hard Way*, Wallis offered *Casablanca* to Michael Curtiz. The same thing happened with *The Treasure of the Sierra Madre* a few years later. I brought it to the studio before John Huston did, I begged them to buy it, but they turned it down. I should have bought it myself, for God's sake. I could have bought it for $10,000."

A third film which he in the end didn't make, was "From Here to Eternity" (directed by Fred Zinnemann), made at Columbia. Mr. Sherman: "I called a friend of mine who had a bookstore in Hollywood. He talked to me about a new book he had read, called *From Here to Eternity* and he let me have a pre-publication copy. It had been bought by a man named Sylvan Simon who was Harry Cohn's executive producer at Columbia at the time. I read it and said it would make a hell of a movie. By that time I had just finished *Lone Star* with Clark Gable and I called Harry Cohn[5] for whom I had done *Harriet Craig* with Joan Crawford. I said, 'Harry, I just want you to know I read "From Here to Eternity" which Columbia bought. The book is great, I'd love to do it.' He said, 'Well Vince, that's a long way off. The Army doesn't want us to; they're reluctant to make it. But come over, I want to talk to you about something else.'

"So I went over to see him. He asked if I wanted to make the next picture of Rita Hayworth[6] instead, the first one after her divorce from Aly Khan. Who wouldn't, I thought. She was a wonderful star and a princess who got worldwide publicity. Harry gave me the first 15 pages of the screenplay. It was about a young man flying to Trinidad to rescue his brother where he got in some kind of trouble and needed help. Then I said to Harry, 'What about the rest of it? What happens then?' He said, 'Look, is it a deal, will you make it?' I said OK. Now, Harry Cohn was like a New York gangster in a way: you shake hands with him, that's the deal. I didn't sign the contract until the picture was finished. It was a matter of confidence.

"I went downstairs to see the producer, Burt Granet, and the writer, Virginia Van Upp—she also wrote the screenplay for *Gilda*. I said, 'I've read the first 15 pages of the screenplay and Harry told me you'd tell me the rest of the story.' But they couldn't. Then I knew I was in trouble; they only showed me the first 25 or 30 pages, that was it. When I walked out with Burt, he said to me, 'Vincent, you don't know what you're getting yourself into.' 'What do you mean?' 'I don't know about you, but I'm getting off the picture in the morning.' I said, 'But you're the producer!' 'No, I came here to produce a picture written by Garson Kanin starring Judy Holliday. Cohn had asked me to help him out on this one, to see if I could help Virginia with it. She's having trouble with her husband, she's drinking, she has no story, it's terrible and I don't wanna be blamed for it. I've only been here for a week trying to help her, but I'm getting off and my advice to you is you get off the picture too.' I said, 'Jesus Christ, I just shook hands with Harry, I said I'd do the picture!' He said, 'Well, that's up to you.'

"Whatever the original story was, it was nothing that I could work with. The next morning, I went up to Harry's office; he was sitting there, very angry-looking. He said, 'I don't like a quitter. Bert Granet just walked off the picture, he doesn't want to produce it.' I said, 'Well Harry, you told me you had a story, there is no story!' And he didn't wanna take the responsibility.' Harry said, 'Vince, don't you think I know that! Look, I'm in trouble, Rita came back, I had no notice she was coming back, I had to put her on salary, $3,500 a week, which is what she made when she married Aly Khan and her contract was in abeyance. If I want to make a picture with her, I *have* to put her on salary again. And of course we want to make a picture with her, but I didn't have a story for her, I didn't even know she was coming back. So I called Virginia and she said, "Yeah, I got a story for her," and I said, "All right, I'll pay $50,000 for a piece." Now New York is screaming! She has been sitting here for 16 weeks, getting paid $3,500 a week and I gotta make something with her. Help me out!'

"So I said, 'Oh well, that's a different story. Okay Harry, I'll do what I can. But get me a writer that I know I can work with.' So he got rid of Virginia Van Upp and got me Jimmy Gunn, who had worked with me already on a couple of scripts. He had a bright mind, not always very focused, he was drinking and was very unhappy, but he was talented. The next day, I sent for a copy of *Notorious*, the picture that Hitchcock made with Bergman and Claude Rains. I stole a little from that film, a little from this, a little from that, and I put together a melodrama that took place in Trinidad. As Harry said, get me 12 reels, three or four dance numbers, give me a love-hate relationship with Glenn Ford and Rita Hayworth, and get something meaningful. That's how *Affair in Trinidad* was made. When Harry had seen the first

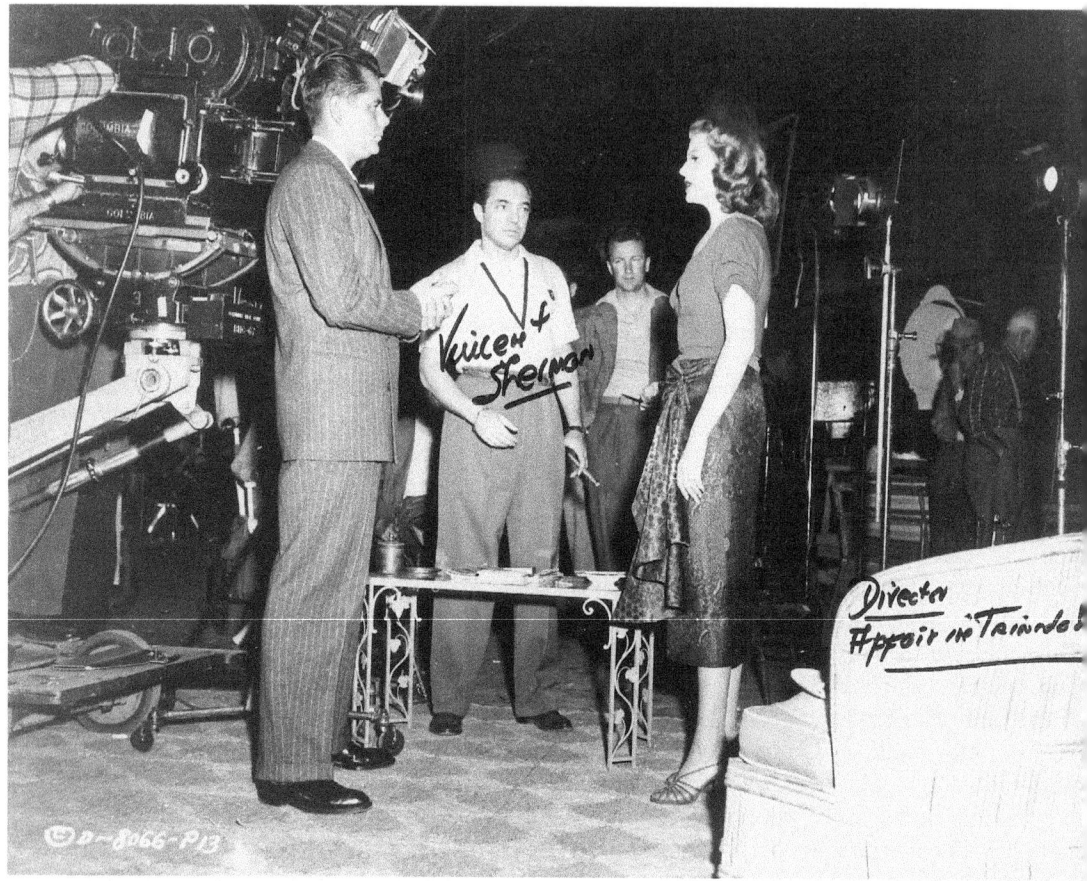

Glenn Ford, Vincent Sherman and Rita Hayworth on the set of *Affair in Trinidad* (1952). (Courtesy of Vincent Sherman.)

rough cut of the picture, he said, 'I want you to know how much I appreciate what you did for me,' and he gave me a check for $10,000 as a bonus. All the stories I heard about Harry Cohn, how bad he was—Jack [L.] Warner never gave me a bonus—but this man, I liked him. I'm not proud of *Affair in Trinidad*, but it did all right. It finally cost $1,300,000 and it grossed about $7,000,000.

"I thanked him, I said, 'Harry, that's the nicest thing that anyone has ever said to me since I've been in the picture business.' He said, 'Well okay, I know how hard you worked on it and, wait a minute, I'm not through with you yet, I'm also gonna give you two percent of our share of the profits. We have 75 percent, Rita has 25 percent, and you get two percent of our profits.' So the picture didn't do my reputation any good, but it paid me well. I got to know Rita and she was wonderful and very talented, but the saddest girl I've ever known. She had been used by every man who ever worked with her, they all went to bed with her and used her. She was very shy, uneducated, very insecure and had a terrible inferiority complex about herself. On the other hand, I'm sure that, being with Orson Welles [her husband from 1943 to 1948], anybody would have an inferiority complex."

Before *Affair in Trinidad*, Mr. Sherman had just finished *Lone Star* with Clark Gable. Mr. Sherman: "My agent Arthur Parks asked me if I'd like to make a Western with Clark Gable. I loved the idea, because I was tired of making women's pictures, I had made five or six of them, now I wanted to make a picture with men. So I went over to MGM and met Gable and the producer, Z. Wayne Griffin. Clark Gable, who's post-war films had been less successful, was a very nice man, but the script wasn't very good. I didn't say that exactly, I just said, 'It needs a lot of work.' We got along very well, but he said, 'I'm sorry that you don't feel too enthusiastic about this picture, maybe some other time we'll do another picture together.' The next day my agent called and said, 'Vincent, you don't have to worry about *Lone Star*, Howard Hawks will do it.' Another two weeks went by and I got another call from my agent who said, 'The Hawks deal didn't work out. Gable liked you and he would like you to do the picture. He felt that you were not a whore!' A whore is a man who will do any script as long as you pay him for it, and he respected me for being honest about it. When the producer called me in, he said, 'Well, you were right, it needs rewriting and we've engaged a woman who will rewrite the script.'

Rita Hayworth

"Then I met cameraman Hal Rosson[7] who had a very good reputation at MGM. He had made many great pictures and he seemed all right. When we went to look for locations, I said, 'What do you think of this?' 'It's up to you. If you like it, I'll shoot it,' he said. Well, I sensed something—at the end of the day I told him, 'Look Mr. Rosson, I want you to know I'm doing this picture because I get a chance to make a man's picture after a series of women's pictures, but I got a lousy script and I'm going to need all the help I can get.' He said, 'What? In that case, I owe you an apology, because the producer told me you thought it was a great script. And I said to myself, if he thinks it's a great script, he's not much of a director!'

"When I got through with the picture, there was one coming up with Spencer Tracy called *Plymouth Adventure*. Hal Rosson went up to the front office and recommended me to do the picture. He said, 'This guy is the best technically equipped director I ever worked with since Victor Fleming.' Well I was very appreciative, particularly since several people had warned me to watch out for Rosson. They told me he was a little Napoleon who would take over the picture. Never once did we have an argument, from the minute we started up till the very end. He was very solid as a craftsman and a very decent human being." Ultimately, Dore Schary, the head of MGM, gave *Plymouth Adventure* to veteran Clarence Brown.

A good script was obviously terribly important to a director from the "Golden Era" because it told a real story about real people. Mr. Sherman: "Today, the young audience is from 16 to 22, they buy the tickets and they go to see special effects, sex and violence. But there's also an audience out there from 35 to 65, they're all tired of the explosions, the special effects, they don't want to see any more car chases. Technically the film business has improved, there's no question about that. They're doing things now that we hardly could do. What Spielberg did in *Jurassic Park*, that was wonderful. But I do miss the stories of human

Errol Flynn played the title role in Vincent Sherman's *The Adventures of Don Juan* (1949).

beings. I prefer to see pictures in which men have the guts to face the odds and have to be up against failure—and win. Life is not always like that, for most of the time good men get buried and very few achieve greatness."

In between, Mr. Sherman is regularly invited to attend retrospectives of his films. "A few years ago I was invited to the Lumière Institute in Lyon, France, and the following year they invited me to Finland where I stayed for five or six days. They ran six of my pictures. The last day there was scheduled a 'Discussion with Vincent Sherman.' My grandson, who was with me, had a date to go fishing that day. I told him to go fishing, but he said, 'What about that discussion?' I said, 'I'll handle it, there will be maybe 25 or 30 people, you go ahead and have a good time.' I came to the meeting, there were 400 people and I was there for over three hours. It was a wonderful discussion. I could have stayed there for six hours, telling them stories about everybody, you know. They did a wonderful thing. They ran a picture of mine that Turner Classic Movies put together. A couple of years ago Turner Classic Films Television named me 'Director of the Month.' They showed 20 of my pictures and also invited me to come to Atlanta where they wanted me to join Robert Osborne who introduced my films. TNT got all my pictures by the way.

"I don't watch too much television now, but they tell me that some of the television shows are better than the movies. I look at the news and that is pretty discouraging these days, and yet we have to think that the world is getting better, medicine is progressing, people are living longer, but the only thing that isn't progressing is the humanity between people. I keep up with what's going on, I subscribe to about ten publications, I try to read them all but everything is so rapid today, it's very difficult. When I was growing up as a kid down South and something happened in Europe, we didn't find out about it for two weeks. Now it happens at one o'clock and at 2:30 the whole world knows it."

It was very fascinating to hear Mr. Sherman relate his experiences and thoughts. Next time we see one of his films again, we will enjoy them all the more, knowing now what an amazing man was standing behind the camera.

Interview: Malibu, April 8, 1999

Notes

1. His autobiography was published in 1996 by the University Press of Kentucky.
2. Elia Kazan (b. 1909) testified before the HUAC, admitted he had been a member of the Communist

Robert Vaughn and Paul Newman in *The Young Philadelphians* (1959).

Party and agreed to name names to avoid getting blacklisted. A hugely influential filmmaker, he was a co-founder of the Actors Studio (1947) and launched the Method, a new way of acting, first brought to the screen by actors such as Marlon Brando and James Dean. Kazan, one of America's leading post-war directors, made such films as *Gentleman's Agreement* (1947, Academy Award for best director), *A Streetcar Named Desire* (1951, Academy Award nomination for best director); *Viva Zapata!* (1952); *On the Waterfront* (1954, Academy Award for best director), *East of Eden* (1954, also prod., Academy Award nomination for best director); *Baby Doll* (1956, also prod.); *Wild River* (1960, also prod.); *Splendor in the Grass* (1961); *America, America* (1963, also prod. and screenplay, based on his own novel—Academy Award nominations for best picture, best director and best screenplay); and *The Last Tycoon* (1976). His autobiography *Elia Kazan: A Life* was published in 1988.

3. Robert Rossen (1908–1966), playwright, screenwriter and filmmaker who worked in films from the late 1930s to the 1960s. He wrote, produced and directed *All the King's Men* (1949, Academy Award winner as best picture) and *The Hustler* (1961)—both films earned him a total of six Academy Award nominations. Other films he directed were *Island in the Sun* (1957) and *Lilith* (1964). He too was a victim of the HUAC. First he denied membership in the Communist Party, for which he was blacklisted, and then a few years later he agreed to give names and as a result was able to work again. According to Ephraim Katz' *The MacMillan Film Encyclopedia* (published in 1994), he then "withdrew within himself and was described by friends as a tortured person."

4. Julius J. Epstein (1909–2000) and his twin brother Philip G. Epstein (1909–1952) won an Academy Award for their screenplay of *Casablanca* (1943) which they wrote in collaboration with Howard Koch. The Epsteins also wrote and produced *Mr. Skeffington* (1945). Philip G. died of cancer at age 43.

5. Harry Cohn (1891–1958), in 1924 co-founder and until his death the head of Columbia, personally guided the careers of several of his stars, including Jean Arthur (1905–1991), William Holden (1918–1981), Glenn Ford (b. 1916), and, most notably, his most powerful box-office attraction, Rita Hayworth (note 6). Cohn was known for being cruel, ruthless and vulgar (director Charles Vidor took him to court once for verbal abuse). As a result, he was nicknamed "Harry the Horror" and the "Czar," but on the other hand, he knew the business of filmmaking inside out. The other founders of Columbia were his brother Jack Cohn (1886–1956) and Joe Brandt (1883–1939) who sold his interests in the company to Harry Cohn in 1932.

6. Rita Hayworth (1918–1987), was originally a dancer but became Columbia's leading actress and most important box-office star in the 1940s. She was married for two years (1949–51) to Aly Khan, the son of the spiritual leader of millions of Muslims. Her films include *Only Angels Have Wings* (1939), *The Strawberry Blonde*

(1941), *You'll Never Get Rich* (1941, with Fred Astaire who later called her his favorite dancing partner), *Cover Girl* (1944, opposite Gene Kelly), *Gilda* (1946), *The Lady from Shanghai* (1948), *The Loves of Carmen* (1948), *Miss Sadie Thompson* (1953), *Fire Down Below* (1957), *Pal Joey* (1957), *Circus World* (1964) and her final film *The Wrath of God* (1972).

7. Hal Rosson (1895–1988), was once married to Jean Harlow (1933–35) and started his career as cinematographer in the 1910s. His numerous films include *Tarzan, the Ape Man* (1932), *Red Dust* (1932), *The Garden of Allah* (1936, honorary Academy Award for the color cinematography), *The Wizard of Oz* (1939), *Boom Town* (1940), *The Asphalt Jungle* (1950), *Lone Star* (1951), *Singin' in the Rain* (1952).

Filmography

Counsellor at Law (Universal, 1933). DIR William Wyler. PROD Carl Laemmle, Jr. SCR Elmer Rice (also play). CAM Norbert Brodine. ED Daniel Mandell. RUNNING TIME 78 min. CAST: John Barrymore (George Simon); Bebe Daniels (Regina "Rexy" Gordon); Doris Kenyon (Cora Simon); Melvyn Douglas (Roy Darwin); Thelma Todd (Lillian La Rue); **Vincent Sherman** (Harry Becker).

Speed Wings (Columbia, 1934). DIR Otto Brower. SCR Horace McCoy (also story). CAM Al Siegler. ED John Rawlins. RUNNING TIME 60 min. CAST: Tim McCoy (Tim); Evalyn Knapp (Mary); Billy Bakewell (Jerry); **Vincent Sherman** (Mickey); Hooper Atchley (Crandall); Ben Hewlett (Gregory).

The Crime of Helen Stanley (Columbia, 1934). DIR D. Ross Lederman. SCR Harold Shumate (story by Charles R. Condon). CAM Al Siegler. ED Otto Meyer. RUNNING TIME 58 min. CAST: Ralph Bellamy (Inspector Trent); Shirley Grey (Betty); Gail Patrick (Helen Stanley); Kane Richmond (Lee Davis); Bradley Page (George Noel); **Vincent Sherman** (Karl Williams).

Girl in Danger (Columbia, 1934). DIR D. Ross Lederman. SCR Harold Shumate (also story). CAM F. M. Browne. ED Otto Meyer. RUNNING TIME 57 min. CAST: Ralph Bellamy (Inspector Trent); Shirley Grey (Gloria Gale); J. Carrol Naish (Mike Russo); Charles Sabin (Dan Terrence); Ward Bond (Wynkoski); **Vincent Sherman** (Willie Tolini).

One Is Guilty (Columbia, 1934). DIR Lambert Hillyer. SCR Harold Shumate (also story). CAM John Stumar. RUNNING TIME 61 min. CAST: Ralph Bellamy (Inspector Trent); Shirley Grey (Sally Grey); Warren Hymer (Walters); Rita La Roy (Lola Deveroux); J. Carrol Naish (Jack Allan); **Vincent Sherman** (William Malcolm).

Hell Bent for Love (Columbia, 1934). DIR D. Ross Lederman. SCR Harold Shumate (also story). CAM Benjamin Kline. ED Otto Meyer. RUNNING TIME 58 min. CAST: Tim McCoy (Sgt. Tim Daley); Lilian Bond (Millie Garland); Bradley Page (Trigger Talano); **Vincent Sherman** (Johnny Frank); Lafe McKee (Dad Daley); Harry C. Bradley (Professor).

Midnight Alibi (Warner Bros., 1934). DIR Alan Crosland. SCR Warren Duff (story by Damon Runyon). CAM William Rees. ED Jack Killifer. RUNNING TIME 60 min. CAST: Richard Barthelmess (Lance McGowan/Robert Anders); Ann Dvorak (Joan); Helen Chandler (Abigail); Helen Lowell (The Old Doll); Henry O'Neill (Ardsley); Robert Barrat (Angie); **Vincent Sherman** (Black Mike).

Crime School (Warner Bros., 1938). DIR Lewis Seiler. SCR **Vincent Sherman**, Crane Wilbur (story by Crane Wilbur). CAM Arthur Todd. ED Terry Morse. MUS Max Steiner. RUNNING TIME 85 min. CAST: Humphrey Bogart (Mike Braden); Gale Page (Sue Warren); Billy Halop (Frankie Warren); Bobby Jordan (Squirt); Huntz Hall (Goofy); Leo Gorcey (Spike).

My Bill (Warner Bros., 1938). DIR John Farrow. SCR **Vincent Sherman**, Robertson White (play by Tom Barry). CAM Sid Hickox. ED Frank Magee. MUS Leo F. Forbstein. RUNNING TIME 60 min. CAST: Kay Francis (Mary Colbrook); Bonita Granville (Gwen Colbrook); John Litel (Mr. Rutlin); Anita Louise (Muriel Colbrook); Bobby Jordan (Reginald Colbrook); Dickie Moore (Bill Colbrook).

Heart of the North (Warner Bros., 1938). DIR Lewis Seiler. SCR **Vincent Sherman**, Lee Katz (novel by William Byron Mowery). CAM L. W. O'Connell. ED Louis Hesse. MUS Adolph Deutsch. RUNNING TIME 85 min. CAST: Dick Foran (Sgt. Alan Baker); Gloria Dickson (Joyce MacMillan); Gale Page (Elizabeth Spaulding); Allen Jenkins (Corp. Bill Hardsack); Patric Knowles (Corp. Montgomery); Janet Chapman (Judy Montgomery); James Stephenson (Inspector Gore).

King of the Underworld (Warner Bros., 1939). DIR Lewis Seiler. SCR **Vincent Sherman**, George Bricker (story by W. R. Burnett). CAM Sid Hickox. ED Frank Dewar. MUS Heinz Roemheld. RUNNING TIME 69 min. CAST: Humphrey Bogart (Joe Gurney); Kay Francis (Carol Nelson); James Stephenson (Bill Stephens); John Eldredge (Niles Nelson); Jessie Busley (Aunt Josephine); Arthur Aylesworth (Dr. Sanders).

Pride of the Blue Grass (Warner Bros., 1939). DIR William McGann. SCR **Vincent Sherman** (also story). CAM Ted McCord. ED Frank Dewar. MUS Howard Jackson. RUNNING TIME 65 min. CAST: Edith Fellows (Midge Griner); James McCallion (Danny Lowman); Granville Bates (Bob Griner); Aldrich Bowker (Judge); Arthur Loft (Dave Miller); DeWolf Hopper (Joe).

The Return of Dr. X (Warner Bros., 1939). DIR **Vincent Sherman**. SCR Lee Katz (story by William J. Makin).

CAM Sid Hickox. ED Thomas Pratt. MUS Bernhard Kaun. RUNNING TIME 60 min. CAST: Humphrey Bogart (Marshall Quesne, a.k.a. Dr. Xavier); Rosemary Lane (Joan Vance); Wayne Morris (Walter Barnett); Dennis Morgan (Michael Rhodes); John Litel (Dr. Francis Flegg); Lya Lys (Angela Merrova).

Saturday's Children (Warner Bros., 1940). DIR **Vincent Sherman**. PROD Jack L. Warner, Hal B. Wallis. SCR Julius J. Epstein, Philip G. Epstein (play by Maxwell Anderson). CAM James Wong Howe. ED Owen Marks. RUNNING TIME 101 min. CAST: John Garfield (Rims Rosson); Anne Shirley (Bobby Halevy); Claude Rains (Mr. Halevy); Roscoe Karns (Willie Sands); Lee Patrick (Florrie Sands); Dennie Moore (Gertrude Mills).

The Man Who Talked Too Much (Warner Bros., 1940). DIR **Vincent Sherman**. SCR Walter DeLeon, Earl Baldwin (play by Frank L. Collins). CAM Sid Hickox. ED Thomas Pratt. MUS Heinz Roemheld. RUNNING TIME 74 min. CAST: George Brent (Stephen Forbes); Virginia Bruce (Joan Reed); Brenda Marshall (Celia Farraday); Richard Barthelmess (J. B. Roscoe); William Lundigan (Johnny Forbes); George Tobias (Slug McNutt).

Flight from Destiny (Warner Bros., 1941). DIR **Vincent Sherman**. PROD Jack L. Warner. SCR Barry Trivers (story by Anthony Berkeley). CAM James Van Trees. ED Thomas Richards. RUNNING TIME 73 min. CAST: Geraldine Fitzgerald (Betty Farroway); Thomas Mitchell (Prof. Todhunter); Jeffrey Lynn (Michael Farroway); James Stephenson (Dr. Stephens); Mona Maris (Ketti Moret); Jonathan Hale (District Attorney).

Underground (Warner Bros., 1941). DIR **Vincent Sherman**. SCR Edwin Justus Mayer, Oliver H. P. Garrett. CAM Sid Hickox. ED Thomas Pratt. MUS Adolph Deutsch. RUNNING TIME 95 min. CAST: Jeffrey Lynn (Kurt Franken); Philip Dorn (Eric Franken); Kaaren Verne (Sylvia Helmuth); Mona Maris (Fraulein Gessner); Peter Whitney (Alex); Martin Kosleck (Heller).

All Through the Night (Warner Bros., 1941). DIR **Vincent Sherman**. PROD Jerry Wald. SCR Leonard Spigelgass, Edwin Gilbert (story by Leonard Spigelgass, Leonard Q. Ross). CAM Sid Hickox. ED Rudi Fehr. MUS Adolph Deutsch. RUNNING TIME 107 min. CAST: Humphrey Bogart (Gloves Donahue); Conrad Veidt (Hall Ebbing); Kaaren Verne (Leda Hamilton); Jane Darwell (Ma Donahue); Frank McHugh (Barney); Peter Lorre (Pepi).

The Hard Way (Warner Bros., 1942). DIR **Vincent Sherman**. PROD Jerry Wald. SCR Daniel Fuchs, Peter Viertel. CAM James Wong Howe. ED Thomas Pratt. MUS Heinz Roemheld. RUNNING TIME 108 min. CAST: Ida Lupino (Helen Chernen); Joan Leslie (Katherine Chernen); Dennis Morgan (Paul Collins); Jack Carson (Albert Runkel); Gladys George (Lily Emery); Faye Emerson (Waitress).

Old Acquaintance (Warner Bros., 1943). DIR **Vincent Sherman**. PROD Henry Blanke. SCR John Van Druten, Leonore Coffee. CAM Sol Polito. ED Terry Morse. MUS Franz Waxman. RUNNING TIME 110 min. CAST: Bette Davis (Katherine Marlowe); Miriam Hopkins (Millie Drake); Gig Young (Rudd Kendall); John Loder (Preston Drake); Dolores Moran (Deirdre); Philip Reed (Lucian Grant).

In Our Time (Warner Bros., 1944). DIR **Vincent Sherman**. PROD Jerry Wald. SCR Ellis St. Joseph, Howard Koch. CAM Carl Guthrie. ED Rudi Fehr. MUS Franz Waxman. RUNNING TIME 110 min. CAST: Ida Lupino (Jennifer Whittredge); Paul Henreid (Count Stephen Orvid); Nancy Coleman (Janina Orvid); Mary Boland (Mrs. Bromley); Victor Francen (Count Pavel Orvid); Alla Nazimova (Zofya Orvid).

Mr. Skeffington (Warner Bros., 1944). DIR **Vincent Sherman**. PROD-SCR Julius J. Epstein, Philip G. Epstein. CAM Ernest Haller. ED Ralph Dawson. MUS Franz Waxman. RUNNING TIME 146 min. CAST: Bette Davis (Fanny Trellis); Claude Rains (Job Skeffington); Walter Abel (George Trellis); Richard Waring (Trippy Trellis); George Coulouris (Dr. Byles); Marjorie Riordian (Fanny Junior); Robert Shayne (MacMahon).

Pillow to Post (Warner Bros., 1945). DIR **Vincent Sherman**. PROD Alex Gottlieb. SCR Charles Hoffman. CAM Wesley Anderson. ED Alan Crosland, Jr. MUS Frederick Hollander. RUNNING TIME 92 min. CAST: Ida Lupino (Jean Howard); Sidney Greenstreet (Col. Otley); William Prince (Don Mallory); Stuart Erwin (Capt. Jack Ross); Johnny Mitchell (Slim Clark); Ruth Donnelly (Mrs. Wingate).

Janie Gets Married (Warner Bros., 1946). DIR **Vincent Sherman**. PROD Alex Gottlieb. SCR Agnes Christine Johnston. CAM Carl Guthrie. ED Christian Nyby. MUS Frederick Hollander. RUNNING TIME 89 min. CAST: Joan Leslie (Janie); Robert Hutton (Dick); Edward Arnold (Mr. Conway); Ann Harding (Mrs. Conway); Dorothy Malone (Spud); Hattie McDaniel (April).

Nora Prentiss (Warner Bros., 1947). DIR **Vincent Sherman**. PROD William Jacobs. SCR N. Richard Nash. CAM James Wong Howe. ED Owen Marks. MUS Franz Waxman. RUNNING TIME 111 min. CAST: Ann Sheridan (Nora Prentiss); Kent Smith (Dr. Richard Talbot); Bruce Bennett (Dr. Joel Merriam); Robert Alda (Phil Dinardo); Rosemary De Camp (Lucy Talbot); John Ridgely (Walter Hailey).

The Unfaithful (Warner Bros., 1947). DIR **Vincent Sherman**. PROD Jerry Wald. SCR David Goodis, James Gunn. CAM Ernest Haller. ED Alan Crosland, Jr. MUS Max Steiner. RUNNING TIME 109 min. CAST: Ann Sheridan (Chris Hunter); Lew Ayres (Larry Hannaford); Zachary Scott (Bob Hunter); Eve Arden (Paula); Jerome Cowan (Prosecuting Attorney); Steven Geray (Martin Barrow).

The Adventures of Don Juan (Warner Bros., 1948). DIR **Vincent Sherman**. PROD Jerry Wald. SCR George Oppenheimer, Harry Kurnitz. CAM Elwood Bredel. ED Alan Crosland, Jr. MUS Max Steiner. RUNNING TIME 110 min. CAST: Errol Flynn (Don Juan); Viveca Lindfors (Queen Margaret); Robert Douglas (Duke de Lorca); Alan Hale (Leporello); Romney Brent (King Phillip III); Ann Rutherford (Donna Elena).

The Hasty Heart (Warner Bros., 1949). DIR **Vincent Sherman**. SCR Ranald McDougall (play by Joan Patrick). CAM Wilkie Cooper. ED E. B. Jarvis. MUS Jack Beaver. RUNNING TIME 99 min. CAST: Ronald Reagan (The Yank); Patricia Neal (Sister Margaret); Richard Todd (The Scot); Anthony Nicholls (Col. Dunn); Howard Crawford (The Tommy).

Backfire (Warner Bros., 1950). DIR **Vincent Sherman**. PROD Jerry Wald. SCR Larry Marcus. CAM Carl Guthrie. ED Thomas Reilly. MUS Ray Heindorf. RUNNING TIME 91 min. CAST: Virginia Mayo (Julie Benson); Gordon MacRae (Bob Corey); Edmond O'Brien (Steve Connolly); Dane Clark (Ben Arno); Viveca Lindfors (Lysa Randolph); Ed Begley (Capt. Garcia).

The Damned Don't Cry (Warner Bros., 1950). DIR **Vincent Sherman**. PROD Jerry Wald. SCR Jerome Weidman, Harold Medford. CAM Ted McCord. ED Rudi Fehr. MUS Daniele Amfitheatrof. RUNNING TIME 103 min. CAST: Joan Crawford (Ethel Whitehead); David Brian (George Castleman); Steve Cochran (Nick Prenta); Kent Smith (Martin Blackford); Hugh Sanders (Grady); Selena Royle (Patricia Longworth).

Harriet Craig (Columbia, 1950). DIR **Vincent Sherman**. PROD William Dozier. SCR Ann Froelich, James Gunn. CAM Joseph Walker. ED Viola Lawrence. MUS George Duning. RUNNING TIME 94 min. CAST: Joan Crawford (Harriet Craig); Wendell Corey (Walter Craig); Lucile Watson (Celia Fenwick); Allyn Joslyn (Billy Birkmire); William Bishop (Wes Miller); K. T. Stevens (Clare Raymond).

Goodbye, My Fancy (Warner Bros., 1951). DIR **Vincent Sherman**. PROD Henry Blanke. SCR Ivan Goff, Ben Roberts (play by Fay Kanin). CAM Ted McCord. ED Rudi Fehr. MUS Daniele Amphitheatrof. RUNNING TIME 107 min. CAST: Joan Crawford (Agatha Reed); Robert Young (Dr. J. Merrill); Frank Lovejoy (Matt Cole); Eve Arden (Woody); Janice Rule (Virginia Merrill); Lurene Tuttle (E. Griswold).

Lone Star (MGM, 1952). DIR **Vincent Sherman**. PROD Z. Wayne Griffin. SCR Borden Chase. CAM Harold Rosson. ED Ferris Webster. MUS David Buttolph. RUNNING TIME 94 min. CAST: Clark Gable (Devereaux Burke); Ava Gardner (Martha Ronda); Broderick Crawford (Thomas Craden); Lionel Barrymore (Andrew Jackson); Beulah Bondi (Minniver Bryan); Ed Begley (Anthony Demmet).

Affair in Trinidad (Columbia, 1952). DIR-PROD **Vincent Sherman**. SCR Oscar Saul, James Gunn (story by Virginia Van Upp, Berne Giler). CAM Joseph Walker. ED Viola Lawrence. MUS Morris Stoloff, Charles Duning. RUNNING TIME 98 min. CAST: Rita Hayworth (Chris Emery); Glenn Ford (Steve Emery); Alexander Scourby (Max Fabian); Valerie Bettis (Veronica); Torin Thatcher (Inspector Smythe); Howard Wendell (Anderson).

Garment Jungle (Columbia, 1957). DIR **Vincent Sherman**. PROD Harry Kleiner. SCR Harry Kleiner (based on articles by Lester Velie). CAM Joe Biroc. ED William Lyon. MUS Leith Stevens. RUNNING TIME 88 min. CAST: Lee J. Cobb (Walter Mitchell); Kerwin Mathews (Alan Mitchell); Gia Scala (Theresa); Richard Boone (Artie Ravidge); Valerie French (Lee Hackett); Robert Loggia (Tulio Renata).

The Naked Earth (20th Century Fox, 1958). DIR **Vincent Sherman**. PROD Adrian Worker. SCR Milton Holmes (also story). CAM Erwin Hillier. ED E. Jarvis. MUS Arthur Benjamin. RUNNING TIME 96 min. CAST: Richard Todd (Danny); Juliette Greco (Maria); Finlay Currie (Father Verity); John Kitzmiller (David); Laurence Naismith (Skins Trader); Christopher Rhodes (Al); Orlando Martins (Tribesman).

The Young Philadelphians (Warner Bros., 1959). DIR **Vincent Sherman**. SCR James Gunn (novel by Richard Powell). CAM Harry Stradling. ED William Ziegler. MUS Ernest Gold. RUNNING TIME 136 min. CAST: Paul Newman (Tony Lawrence); Barbara Rush (Joan Dickinson); Alexis Smith (Carol Wharton); Brian Keith (Mike Flannagan); Diane Brewster (Kate Judson); Billie Burke (Mrs. J. A. Allen); Robert Vaughn (Chester Gwynn).

Defend My Love (Titanus, 1959). DIR **Vincent Sherman**, Giulio Macchi. PROD Silvio Clementelli. SCR Giorgio Prosperi, Jacques Robert. CAM Gianni Di Venanzo. ED Mario Serandrei. RUNNING TIME 88 min. CAST: Martine Carol (Elisa); Gabriele Ferzetti (Pietro); Vittorio Gassman (Giovanni); Charles Vanel (Verdision).

Ice Palace (Warner Bros., 1960). DIR **Vincent Sherman**. PROD Henry Blanke. SCR Harry Kleiner (novel by Edna Ferber). CAM Joseph Biroc. ED William Ziegler. MUS Max Steiner. RUNNING TIME 143 min. CAST: Richard Burton (Zeb); Robert Ryan (Thor); Carolyn Jones (Bridie); Martha Hyer (Dorothy); Jim Backus (Dave Jusack); Ray Danton (Bay); Diane McBain (Christine).

A Fever in the Blood (Warner Bros., 1961). DIR **Vincent Sherman**. PROD Roy Huggins. SCR Roy Huggins, Harry Kleiner (novel by William Pearson). CAM J. Peverell Marley. ED William Ziegler. MUS Ernest Gold. RUNNING TIME 117 min. CAST: Efrem Zimbalist, Jr. (Judge Hoffman); Angie Dickinson (Cathy Simon); Jack Kelly (Dan Callahan); Don Ameche (Sen. A. S. Simon); Ray Danton (Marker); Herbert Marshall (Gov. Thornwall)

The Second Time Around (20th Century Fox, 1961). DIR **Vincent Sherman**. PROD Jack Cummings. SCR Oscar Saul, Cecil Dan Hansen (novel by Richard Emery Roberts). CAM Ellis Carter. ED Betty Steinberg. MUS Gerald Fried. RUNNING TIME 99 min. CAST: Debbie Reynolds (Lucretia Rogers); Steve Forrest (Dan Jones); Andy Griffith (Pat Collins); Juliet Prowse (Rena, a dancehall girl); Thelma Ritter (Aggie); Ken Scott (Sheriff John Yoss).

Cervantes, a.k.a. *The Young Rebel* (AIP, 1969). DIR **Vincent Sherman**. PROD Alexander Salkind. SCR David Karp (book by Bruno Frank). CAM Edmond Richard. ED Margarita Ochoa. MUS Jean Ledrut, Angel Arteaga.

RUNNING TIME 111 min. CAST: Horst Buchholz (Miguel de Cervantes); Gina Lollobrigida (Giulia); José Ferrer (Hassam Bey); Louis Jourdan (Cardinal Acquaviva); Francisco Rabal (Rodrigo); Fernando Rey (Philip II).

Television Movies

The Last Hurrah (1977). DIR **Vincent Sherman**. CAST: Carroll O'Connor; Dana Andrews; Mariette Hartley; Burgess Meredith; Patrick O'Neal.
Lady of the House (1978). CO-DIR with Ralph Nelson. CAST: Dyan Cannon; Armand Assante; Colleen Camp; Susan Tyrrell.
Women at West Point (1979). DIR **Vincent Sherman**. CAST: Linda Purl; Jameson Parker; Andrew Stevens; Paul Gleason.
Bogie: The Last Hero (1980). DIR **Vincent Sherman**. CAST: Kevin O'Connor; Kathryn Harrold; Ann Wedgeworth; Patricia Barry; Richard A. Dysart.
The Dream Merchants (1980). DIR **Vincent Sherman**. CAST: Morgan Fairchild; Eve Arden; Red Buttons; Robert Culp; José Ferrer; Fernando Lamas; Ray Milland.
Trouble in High Timber Country, a.k.a. *The Yeagers* (1980). DIR **Vincent Sherman**. CAST: Eddie Albert; Michael J. Fox; Kevin Brophy; Robin Dearden.
Savage in the Orient (1983). DIR **Vincent Sherman**. CAST: Lew Ayres; Leif Erickson; Gayle Hunnicutt; Joe Penny; John Saxon.

ROBERT WISE

A master craftsman and one of Hollywood's most skillful film directors for several decades, veteran Robert Wise has made several landmark films over the years. Not only his two major blockbusters, *West Side Story* (1961) and *The Sound of Music* (1965), are absolute highlights in the history of picture making, but also such films as *The Body Snatcher* (1945), *The Set-Up* (1949), *The Day the Earth Stood Still* (1951), *Somebody Up There Likes Me* (1956), *I Want to Live!* (1958), *Odds Against Tomorrow* (1959), *The Haunting* (1963), *The Sand Pebbles* (1966) and *Audrey Rose* (1977) are all amazing achievements that have stood the test of time quite remarkably.

An avid filmgoer, even as a young boy, Mr. Wise was born September 10, 1914, in Winchester, Indiana, and grew up in nearby Connersville, "a small town with three movie houses," he claims. One year he had a contest and subsequently got a free pass to see all the movies during the entire summer: "I admired Douglas Fairbanks [Sr.] a lot. He did all of his stunts and I just couldn't wait for his next picture to be out. When I was about ten, a new picture had been released and I went out to see it. I decided to stay in the theater and saw it again until I was about halfway through. All of a sudden I felt a hand on my shoulder: it was my brother who had come over to take me home.

"When I was still a student, I intended to major in journalism—I had worked on the high school newspaper. I had two older brothers and one of them came out here in 1928 to work at RKO studios. He came home about five years later and he convinced me to go to Los Angeles and find a job in the movies, which I did at age 19: he got me an appointment with the head of the film editing department. For my first job I carried films up to the projection room, checked the prints, things like that. A few weeks later, a man named T.K. Wood [Truman K. Wood], a sound effects and music editor, asked for me to be put up with him which I did for about a year and a half, but I thought that was a dead end. Some of those people had been doing that for years and years. I didn't want to stop there, you know, I wanted to go on. So I asked my boss to put me in what we called the 'picture side,' in the film editing department, which he did and I got the chance to work with Billy Hamilton [William Hamilton], one of the all-time great film editors, who was just brilliant. He taught me this craft. He showed me how a sequence could be improved and all that. The first picture I shared credit with, was *The Hunchback of the Notre Dame* [1939]. Later on I went on my own as an editor and edited pictures like *Citizen Kane* [1941] and *The Magnificent Ambersons* [1942].

"For somebody who has the ambition of being a director, it is very helpful to be an editor first: you learn about how much to shoot, which angles to use, you get acquainted with actors, actresses, performances, things like that. You learn an awful lot on the way up. I had just finished editing Garson's Kanin comedy *My Favorite Wife* (1940) starring Irene Dunne and Cary Grant, when my boss Jimmy Wilkinson called me up. 'You've heard about Orson Welles,[1] haven't you?' he asked. I did know about his reputation in New York, what he had done on the stage and we *all* knew about his radio broadcast that scared half the nation to death. He said, 'Orson Welles was about to shoot three tests for a picture, but they were *scenes* for this picture and they just decided to give him a green light to make the picture, but he wants another editor, not the old-time editor he has right now: he wants somebody his own age. Interested?' So I went over to RKO in Culver City where they were shooting and there I met him for the first time, dressed and made up as the old Charles Foster Kane. We talked for about ten minutes, I returned to the studio in Hollywood and about 20 minutes later I got a call: I got the job."

His contribution to a film like *Citizen Kane* must have been instrumental for the film to become a classic. Mr. Wise: "Yes, I think so. It also earned me my first Academy Award nomination. It was a wonderful film. It was Orson's first film; he was 25 years old at the time—that's remarkable, isn't it? When I was editing it, it was pretty clear this was a very special film. You could even see it when the rushes were coming in: all of those marvelous performances with actors who were all new to the screen—they all came from Orson's Mercury Theatre. [The film's end credits begin with the statement: "Most of the principal actors in *Citizen Kane* are new to motion pictures. The Mercury Theatre is proud to announce them."] He had this outstanding photographer, Gregg Toland. It was a combination of all of those things, we couldn't wait each day to see the rushes."

Sneak previews were pretty common back then: without being announced, a film would be screened at a theater prior to its release to test the reaction of the audience. If necessary, a film could be re-edited. Mr. Wise: "In those days we often had sneak previews: we would take a film to a nearby town like Santa Barbara or San Diego and *test* the film, but we didn't have any sneak previews on *Citizen Kane*. I had to take back a print of it to New York to show to the heads of all the studios, to see if they'd allow RKO to release the film. You see, there was some concern around, that it might be a sort of a left-handed look at William Randolph Hearst, the big publisher. They were afraid the papers would come down on us and get us into trouble. So I flew to New York and in the Radio City Music Hall, there's a little projection room where the heads of the studios and their lawyers could see it. I met them the next day and they suggested to make a few small dialogue changes, and that was easy because all of those actors were in New York. So I stayed there for a few weeks until everything they requested had been done. When they had seen the new print, they said, 'Okay, go ahead and release the film.'"

The film became a legendary classic and influenced countless filmmakers ever after. As

Orson Welles as Charles Foster Kane in his screen debut, *Citizen Kane* (1941). This movie was edited by Robert Wise.

a screenwriter, director, producer and actor, Orson Welles instantly became Hollywood's all-round *wunderkind* (later on he became its *enfant terrible*) whose next Mercury (film) production, The Magnificent Ambersons, based on the novel by Booth Tarkington and set in the 19th century, became his second great masterpiece. (While making this film, he also co-directed [uncredited], co-wrote, produced and appeared in Journey into Fear.)

Mr. Wise: "Originally The Magnificent Ambersons was a very long film, about three hours. The studio decided to have a sneak preview to see how it played. When we took the film out, the response was just terrible: the audience didn't like it at all, they laughed at it, they even literally walked out. We then knew we had a problem with the picture. What could we do about it? We edited it again and had another preview. By this time, we had cut so much that we had continuity problems so we needed to shoot an additional scene with George [played by Tim Holt] and his mother [Dolores Costello]. Because Orson was in Brazil by this time, I was asked to direct that scene; it was my first directorial job. That went into the picture and we took it out for another preview in Long Beach. This time it played well: there were no bad laughs, no walk outs, so that's what it had to be, and that's the picture that went out.

"Sneak previews were always very valuable. I haven't made a film for theaters for quite a number of years now, but if I would make one today, I would still take it out. Whenever you would get what we call a *bad laugh*, when the audience laughs at something that shouldn't be, the minute that happens you'd say, 'I should have known.' And you are able to change a line or a scene or whatever is necessary."

After being an editor for a couple of years, Mr. Wise was allowed to direct his first feature, The Curse of the Cat People, at RKO, replacing Gunther von Fritsch. The film was a very well-made sequel of Jacques Tourneur's classic Cat People (1942). But his best RKO films in the years that followed are undoubtedly The Body Snatcher (1945), a compelling low-budget thriller, based on Robert Louis Stevenson's short story, starring Boris Karloff and Bela Lugosi in their last film together, and The Set-Up (1949), his final RKO picture, a suspenseful and realistic boxing drama focusing on one night in the life of an aging heavyweight boxer, played by Robert Ryan in a superb role. At the Cannes Film Festival, Mr. Wise won the Critic's Prize for his work on the film.

He then signed a contract at 20th Century Fox where he was allowed to make bigger and even better films, while at that same time things got worse for a lot of people because of the hearings of the House Un-American Activities Committee. Mr. Wise: "Yes, that's right, it was a terrible period when people had to go and testify whether or not they had been a Communist. It was not the government's business or anybody else's business to know what we believed in. But I was never called up and whatever happened back then, never put any restrictions on my work. I remember when I did Odds Against Tomorrow [1959], Harry Belafonte had brought the script to me and I liked it very much. The script was written by a man called John O. Killens. I asked Harry who he was and he said, 'Oh, he's a black screenwriter.' So I said, 'Fine, that's great, I like it very much.' I thought that was the end of the story, and later on, I went back to New York and got ready to make the film. I had an apartment on Fifth Avenue. Harry called me one morning and told me he'd bring the screenwriter over. I was anxious to meet him so we could talk about the script. When they arrived, I expected a black man, but it turned out to be Abraham Polonsky who at that time could not write under his own name [in 1996, the Writers' Guild of America restored Polonsky's credit]. The one who broke that whole thing, was Dalton Trumbo when he wrote the script for Spartacus [1960]. I think it was Kirk Douglas who said that they would only make that film with the screenwriter's name on it."

One of his early achievements at Fox was The Day the Earth Stood Still (1951), a science fiction film about an alien named Klaatu (played by Michael Rennie) who comes to Wash-

Michael Rennie and Patricia Neal in *The Day the Earth Stood Still* (1951). (Courtesy of DOCIP Film Archive, Brussels, Belgium.)

ington, D.C., with an anti-nuclear, pacifist message and befriends Patricia Neal while finding shelter in her boarding house. Mr. Wise: "When I first read the script, I thought it would make an absolutely marvelous science fiction picture. It had everything you wanted: it told the world to start getting along and to work towards peace. We were thinking of casting Claude Rains for the part of Klaatu, but fortunately for us, as it turned out, he was not available at the time because he was appearing in a play in New York. We were thinking of other possibilities and one day, I got a call from Darryl F. Zanuck who had seen a young actor in a London play and he had signed him to a contract. He thought he might be interesting for the picture. That was Michael Rennie who was so *much* better for us: he had not been on the screen before while Claude Rains, a very fine actor, had been in films so often. So that was a big break for us. Unfortunately Michael Rennie never made it as a major star, but he was right for the film."

With a film like *The Day the Earth Stood Still*, Mr. Wise captured the attention of audiences worldwide with his sensitive direction and intellectual approach, and showed what a *good* film is capable of. Mr. Wise: "Films can bring people together and make us understand each other a little bit better, they can *educate* us to a certain extent. They can take us someplace, just look at the foreign-language films, coming from countries with different nationalities, different lifestyles, different cultures. At the same time we have so much in common: the love for our family, for our children, the passion for life. Also, every good story has some kind of a theme—sometimes it's very obvious, sometimes you'll have to look underneath. *The Sound of Music* is regarded as a family picture, and it *is*, but between the lines there is the threat of the Nazis who are coming to power as the story unfolds. In a way *The Sand Pebbles* referred to our involvement in Vietnam, *I Want to Live!* focused on capital punishment, *The Set-Up* was about professional boxing and the control it sometimes had by gangsters."

These are only a few examples. Looking at Mr. Wise's films, there are several other powerful pictures which do make a point, like *Three Secrets* (1950) whose three leading characters (played by Eleanor Parker, Patricia Neal and Ruth Roman) wait anxiously to hear which one's child survived a plane crash on a California mountain top; the remake *So Big* (1953), a wonderful family picture based on Edna Ferber's sentimental 1924 Pulitzer Prize–winning novel, with Jane Wyman in a story basically about sacrifice and motherly love (previously filmed in 1925 with Colleen Moore, and in 1932 with Barbara Stanwyck); *Somebody Up There Likes Me* (1956), the true, gripping story of middle-weight boxing champion Rocky Graziano and his rise from the streets of New York, with Paul Newman as "Rocky" and Pier Angeli as his wife; *Until They Sail* (1957), set in World War II New Zealand—an adult love story revolving around various events in the lives of four sisters (Joan Fontaine, Jean Simmons, Piper Laurie, Sandra Dee); *Run Silent, Run Deep* (1958), an effective and convincing war drama about the conflicts between World War II submarine commander Clark Gable and his lieutenant Burt Lancaster (this film indicated that a picture can succeed without a love interest); *I Want to Live!* (1958) with Susan Hayward; and *Odds Against Tomorrow* (1959), a taut and exciting crime drama of an unlikely trio of bank robbers (Robert Ryan, Harry Belafonte, Ed Begley) who plan robbing a bank of $150,000.

Robert Wise. (Courtesy of DOCIP Film Archive, Brussels, Belgium.)

Still, the best was yet to come. In September 1957, the significant stage musical *West Side Story* (conceived by its writer Arthur Laurents, composer Leonard Bernstein and stage director and choreographer Jerome Robbins[2]) had opened at the Winter Garden Theatre on Broadway and would run for 732 performances before going on tour. Inspired by Shakespeare's timeless story of *Romeo and Juliet* (1594), it focused on two teenage gangs, the Jets and the Sparks, both based in Manhattan's Upper West Side, with its leading characters Maria and Tony (originally played by Carol Lawrence and Larry Kert[3]) caught in the middle of the gangs' endless rivalry.

A few years later, the film version had an even more acclaimed success as it became a much-beloved classic, one of the best musicals ever made, one of the best *films* ever made, with Natalie Wood and Richard Beymer in the leading roles, and a strong supporting cast of young, equally dynamic and talented upcoming actors. Mr. Wise: "When we were casting the actors for *West Side Story*, somebody had told us there was a very good screen test over at Warner

Bros. of Warren Beatty for *Splendor in the Grass*. We thought he might be a very good bet for us for the part of Tony. So we thought we'd go over and see his test with Natalie Wood.[4] When we saw it, we knew immediately that was our Maria right there and we forgot all about Warren. On the stage, Chita Rivera had played the part of Anita, which Rita Moreno played in the picture, and we wanted to have her in the film as well. But she was out of town appearing in *Bye, Bye Birdie*, otherwise I think she would have been asked to play the part in the film. Jerome Robbins, my co-director on the film, who had done the musical in New York, said she would have been wonderful too in the picture."

Both Mr. Wise and Jerome Robbins directed *West Side Story*. "When I was approached to do the film, I was thrilled: I had seen the show in New York and I loved it. But then they asked me, 'What would you think about having a co-director on the film? It will be Jerome Robbins who created and directed the show in New York.' I said, 'Why don't you let him direct the picture?' 'Oh no no, he never directed a film.' So basically, Jerome Robbins handled the musical and dancing scenes and I took care of the dramatic scenes. That worked well for about 60 percent of the shooting, because then we started to run behind schedule. The studio took Robbins off the picture but as he had already rehearsed all of the remaining dance numbers, I was able to continue shooting and finish the film."

Susan Hayward won an Academy Award for best actress for her role of Barbara Graham in Robert Wise's *I Want to Live!* (1958).

The film got 11 Academy Award nominations and won all but one, including for best picture (Mr. Wise, producer), best director (Mr. Wise and Jerome Robbins), best supporting actor (George Chakiris) and best supporting actress (Rita Moreno). As a ten Oscar winner, the film is surpassed by only two films with 11 Academy Awards each: *Ben-Hur* (1959) and *Titanic* (1997). Mr. Wise: "I was in New York recently for an anniversary showing at the Radio City Music Hall of the film. It just played like if I had made it yesterday: it pleased me *so* much that it still played so wonderfully well, 40 years after it was made. There were over 5,000 people. It was just *so* gratifying."

With the exception of Natalie Wood, no one in the cast of *West Side Story* was able to make it afterwards. Richard Beymer, George Chakiris, Rita Moreno, Russ Tamblyn, they were all so wonderful in the picture but were out of the spotlight much too soon. Mr. Wise: "I think they weren't offered the right parts after *West Side Story*, that's the only explanation I can think of."

Anyone who thinks of Mr. Wise, has *West Side Story* in mind, as well as the other box-office hit musical he made a few years later, *The Sound of Music* (1965), an equally enjoyable picture, which also deals with social issues and was loosely based on the true-life story of Maria von Trapp (1905–1987), an Austrian nun who left the convent and became the governess of a widowed and retired naval officer's seven children. Her life story formed the basis of the

Natalie Wood (in white, shaking hands) and George Chakiris (to her immediate left) in *West Side Story* (1961). (Courtesy of DOCIP Film Archive, Brussels, Belgium.)

1959 Broadway musical (with Mary Martin and Theodore Bikel) which ran for three years on the New York stage. This film version, starring Julie Andrews and Christopher Plummer, earned Mr. Wise two more Academy Awards (best director and producer of the best picture), and all four of those statues still have a special place in his office along with the Irving G. Thalberg Award he was awarded by the academy in 1967 for his unique contribution to the cinema.

Mr. Wise: "I think that *The Sound of Music* is perhaps one of the best family pictures ever made and that's probably a reason why it became such a big success all over the world. Also the timing was terribly important, I guess. Whenever I travel abroad and people find out I made *The Sound of Music*, they always say, 'Aaaaah, what a wonderful picture!' If I remember well, we also did some previews with this film in the Midwest. The reactions were just terrific and then we were pretty sure it would be a successful film."

The Sound of Music came his way merely by coincidence. At the time he was ready to make *The Sand Pebbles* (1966)—an adventure drama set in China in 1926 with Steve McQueen as a cynical sailor aboard a U.S. gunboat patrolling the Yangtze River—his most difficult film to make, both physically and logistically. "First of all, we had severe weather problems, and on top of that I had never filmed on water, or on a boat. Because we weren't allowed into China

Julie Andrews and the seven Von Trapp children in *The Sound of Music* (1965). (Courtesy of DOCIP Film Archive, Brussels, Belgium.)

back then, we had problems with showing the Yangtze River. So we shot it outside Hong Kong, and I was forced to place the camera in such a way that the little juts of land and nearby islands looked like the Yangtze River."

When preparing the film, Mr. Wise needed a lot more time and let the studio know that in the meantime he could make another film while working out the problems of *The Sand Pebbles*. That's when they suggested he do *The Sound of Music* first. Initially, Stanley Donen and Gene Kelly had turned it down, then William Wyler was assigned to the project, but he left after an argument with the studio and instead made *The Collector* with Terence Stamp. To this day, *The Sound of Music* still is one of the most successful films of all time.

With so many classics to his credit, what is the secret of directing a picture? Mr. Wise: "The power of directing is a combination. The script is always the foundation for any film. I have been fortunate to work with very good screenwriters, but I don't think they get the credit they deserve for their contribution. My films were always announced as *Robert Wise's so-and-so*, but if it weren't for that wonderful script, I would never have had a successful film. Whenever I read something, it has to grab my attention completely so I *want* to turn the pages and go on reading. Another thing that is utterly important, is what it has to say. Any *good* story must tell you something one way or the other about people, about man, about his world and his problems. As far as the actors are concerned, if there are any problems, you can talk about them when you go over the script. There's one restriction, though: in this business, you don't have the time for lengthy rehearsals before you start to shoot. The minute you call an actor in for a rehearsal, he's on the payroll and you have to pay him.

Robert Wise (left) on the set of *The Andromeda Strain* (1971). (Courtesy of DOCIP Film Archive, Brussels, Belgium.)

"During the era of the film studios, once you had your script, the budget and the cast, you were pretty much your own boss if you were also producing the picture. On the other hand, I never had any problems working at Fox with Darryl F. Zanuck. The studios were interested in two things: who were the actors, the main characters in the picture, and what was the budget. Once you agreed on that, you could go and make the picture. That's where their involvement ended really."

Occasionally, Mr. Wise also had his disappointments. "*Star!* [1968], the biographical film of Gertrude Lawrence, is still a very good picture, I think, but for some reason it just didn't work out." In between he turned down a few offers, including *The Godfather*. "Somebody sent me the book, but when I read it, I thought I didn't want to make a picture about the Mafia, so I didn't pursue it at all," he claims. And based on the script he read, he refused to make *Alien*, but wishes to emphasize that director Ridley Scott did an "excellent job." Other films he remembers very fondly include *The Haunting* (1963), a hair-raising haunted-house picture, one of the best of its kind, set in New England and shot in England; *Audrey Rose* (1977), a superb thriller with Anthony Hopkins who tells Marsha Mason that her 12-year-old daughter is a reincarnation of his own child; and *Star Trek: The Motion Picture* (1979)—a big surprise to see Mr. Wise's name appear on the opening credits of this film, but he considered it a challenge to do.

It was an even bigger surprise when he returned behind the camera and made the television movie *A Storm in Summer* (2000), starring Peter Falk—his first directorial effort since his musical *Rooftops* (1989). Mr. Wise: "When they offered me [the chance] to do it, I agreed right away. Peter Falk was very good in this picture which was nominated for three Emmy Awards. I made it in Vancouver. It was a very interesting experience. But this is definitely my last film—I'll be 88 pretty soon, so I'll just take it easy now. I prefer to see films now rather than make them—but I was thrilled to do it."

In 1998 the American Film Institute presented him with the AFI Lifetime Achievement Award in honor of his long, highly interesting career. His career, in fact, is a succession of inventive, innovative, intelligent, often irresistible pictures. In addition, through the years he was able to move swiftly from one genre to another. "I think I have done about every genre there is, approaching them in a style which I think is right for that particular genre. And because I have done so many different genres, I don't have a specific mark," he says. But what a career!

Interview: Los Angeles, February 15, 2002

Notes

1. Orson Welles: interview with Stanley Kramer, note 4.
2. Jerome Robbins (1918–1998), choreographer, dancer and director, was, according to the *New York Times* dance critic Anna Kisselgoff, "the first American-born classical choreographer." He won a total of five Tony Awards for his Broadway hits *The King and I* (1951), *Peter Pan* (1954), *West Side Story* (1957), *Gypsy* (1959), and *Fiddler on the Roof* (1964). His first choreographic success was Leonard Bernstein's *Fancy Free* (1944) which was expanded later on into *On the Town*.
3. Carol Lawrence (b. 1934) and Larry Kert (1930–1991) also appeared in films occasionally. She was seen frequently in television movies and TV series. Her other Broadway musicals include *I Do, I Do* and *Kiss of the Spider Woman*. Larry Kert's most interesting screen role was opposite Liza Minnelli in *New York, New York* (1977), singing a lengthy duet with her in the delightful "Happy Endings" sequence.
4. Natalie Wood (1938–1981), the daughter of Russian *émigré* parents, made her screen debut in *Happy Land* (1943) and became a child star when she appeared as Susan Walker in George Seaton's Christmas classic *Miracle on 34th Street* (1947). At age 17, she played the female leading role in *Rebel Without a Cause* opposite James Dean which earned her her first of three Academy Award nominations—the others were for *Splendor in the Grass* (1961) and *Love with a Proper Stranger* (1966). Other highlights include *Gypsy* (1963) and *Bob & Carol & Ted & Alice* (1969). One of the screen's most talented actresses with more than 50 films to her credit, she died in 1981 (while shooting *Brainstorm*) as a result of a tragic boating accident.

Filmography

Top Hat (RKO, 1935). DIR Mark Sandrich. PROD Pandro S. Berman. SCR Dwight Taylor, Allan Scott (story by Dwight Taylor, based on the play *The Girl Who Dared* by Alexander Faragó, Aladar Laszlo). CAM David Abel. ED William Hamilton. MUS Max Steiner. MUS ED **Robert Wise**. RUNNING TIME 100 min. CAST: Fred Astaire (Jerry Travers); Ginger Rogers (Dale Tremont); Edward Everett Horton (Horace Hardwick); Helen Broderick (Madge Hardwick); Erik Rhodes (Alberto Beddini); Eric Blore (Bates); Lucille Ball (Flower Clerk).

The Story of Vernon and Irene Castle (RKO, 1939). DIR H. C. Potter. PROD George Haight. SCR Richard Sherman (adaptation by Oscar Hammerstein, Dorothy Yost, books *My Husband* and *My Memories of Vernon Castle* by Irene Castle). CAM Robert De Grasse. ED William Hamilton. ASST ED **Robert Wise**. MUS Victor Baravalle. RUNNING TIME 93 min. CAST: Fred Astaire (Vernon Castle); Ginger Rogers (Irene Castle); Edna May Oliver (Maggie Sutton); Walter Brennan (Walter); Lew Fields (Himself); Etienne Girardot (Pa Aubel).

Bachelor Mother (RKO, 1939). DIR Garson Kanin. PROD B. G. DeSylva. SCR Norman Krasna (original story by Felix Jackson). CAM Robert De Grasse. ED **Robert Wise**, Henry Berman. MUS Roy Webb. RUNNING TIME 81 min. CAST: Ginger Rogers (Polly Parrish); David Niven (David Merlin); Charles Coburn (J. B. Merlin); Frank Albertson (Freddie Miller); E. E. Clive (Butler).

Fifth Avenue Girl (RKO, 1939). DIR-PROD Gregory La Cava. SCR Allan Scott. CAM Robert De Grasse. ED William Hamilton, **Robert Wise**. MUS Robert Russell Bennett. RUNNING TIME 83 min. CAST: Ginger Rogers (Mary Gray); Walter Connolly (Alfred Borden); Verree Teasdale (Martha Borden); James Ellison (Mike); Tim Holt (Tim Borden); Kathryn Adams (Katherine Borden).

The Hunchback of Notre Dame (RKO, 1939). DIR William Dieterle. PROD Pandro S. Berman. SCR Sonya Levien (novel *Notre Dame de Paris* by Victor Hugo). CAM Joseph H. August. ED **Robert Wise**. MUS Alfred Newman. RUNNING TIME 116 min. CAST: Charles Laughton (Quasimodo); Cedric Hardwicke (Frollo); Thomas Mitchell (Clopin); Maureen O'Hara (Esmeralda); Edmond O'Brien (Gringoire); Alan Marshal (Phoebus).

My Favorite Wife (RKO, 1940). DIR Garson Kanin. PROD Leo McCarey. SCR Bella Spewack, Samuel Spewack (original story by Bella Spewack, Samuel Spewack, Leo McCarey). CAM Rudolph Maté. ED **Robert Wise**. MUS Roy Webb. RUNNING TIME 88 min. CAST: Irene Dunne (Ellen Arden); Cary Grant (Nick Arden); Randolph Scott (Stephen J. Burkett); Gail Patrick (Bianca Bates); Ann Shoemaker (Ma Arden).

Dance, Girl, Dance (RKO, 1940). DIR Dorothy Arzner. PROD Erich Pommer. SCR Frank Davis, Tess Slesinger (story by Vicki Baum). CAM Russell Metty. ED **Robert Wise**. MUS Edward Ward, Ernst Matray. RUNNING TIME 90 min. CAST: Maureen O'Hara (Judy O'Brien); Louis Hayward (Jimmy Harris); Lucille Ball (Bubbles); Virginia Field (Elinor Harris); Ralph Bellamy (Steve Adams); Maria Ouspenskaya (Lydia Basilova).

Citizen Kane (RKO, 1941). DIR-PROD Orson Welles. SCR Orson Welles, Herman J. Mankiewicz. CAM Gregg Toland. ED **Robert Wise**. MUS Bernard Herrmann. RUNNING TIME 119 min. CAST: Orson Welles (Charles Foster Kane); Joseph Cotton (Jedediah Leland); Dorothy Comingore (Susan Alexander Kazne); Agnes Moorehead (Mary Kane); Ruth Warrick (Emily Norton Kane); Everett Sloane (Bernstein); Ray Collins (James W. Gettys).

The Devil and Daniel Webster, a.k.a. *All That Money Can Buy* (RKO, 1941). DIR-PROD William Dieterle. SCR Dan Tetheroh, Stephen Vincent Benét. CAM Joseph August. ED **Robert Wise**. MUS Bernard Herrmann.

RUNNING TIME 100 min. CAST: Edward Arnold (Daniel Webster); Walter Huston (Mr. Scratch); Jane Darwel (Ma Stone); Simone Simon (Belle); Gene Lockhart (Squire Slossum); Jeff Corey (Tom Sharp).

The Magnificent Ambersons (RKO, 1942). DIR-PROD Orson Welles. SCR Orson Welles (novel by Booth Tarkington). CAM Stanley Cortez. ED **Robert Wise**. MUS Bernard Herrmann. RUNNING TIME 88 min. CAST Joseph Cotton (Eugene); Dolores Costello (Isabel); Anne Baxter (Lucy); Tim Holt (George); Agnes Moorehead (Fanny); Orson Welles (Narrator).

Seven Days' Leave (RKO, 1942). DIR-PROD Tim Whelan. SCR William Bowers, Ralph Spence, Curtis Kenyon Kenneth Earl. CAM Robert De Grasse. ED **Robert Wise**. MUS C. Bakaleinikoff. RUNNING TIME 87 min CAST: Victor Mature (Johnny Grey); Lucille Ball (Terrence "Terry" Havalok-Allen); Harold Peary (Gildersleeve); Mapy Cortés (Mapy); Ginny Simms (Ginny); Freddy Martin and His Orchestra.

Bombardier (RKO, 1943). DIR Richard Wallace. PROD Robert Fellows. SCR John Twist (story by John Twist Martin Rackin). CAM Nicholas Musuraca. ED **Robert Wise**. MUS Roy Webb. RUNNING TIME 97 min. CAST Pat O'Brien (Major Davis); Randolph Scott (Capt. Oliver); Anne Shirley (Burton Hughes); Eddie Albert (Tom Hughes); Walter Reed (Jim Carter); Robert Ryan (Joe Connors).

The Fallen Sparrow (RKO, 1943). DIR Richard Wallace. PROD Robert Fellows. SCR Warren Duff (novel by Dorothy B. Hughes). CAM Nicholas Musuraca. ED **Robert Wise**. MUS Roy Webb. RUNNING TIME 94 min CAST: John Garfield (John "Kit" McKittrick); Maureen O'Hara (Toni Donne); Patricia Morrison (Barby Taviton); Martha O'Driscoll (Whitney Parker); John Miljan (Inspector Tobin); Walter Slezak (Dr. Skaas).

The Iron Major (RKO, 1943). DIR Ray Enright. PROD Robert Fellows. SCR Warren Duff, Aben Kandel (story by Florence E. Cavanaugh). CAM Robert De Grasse. ED **Robert Wise**, Philip Martin, Jr. MUS Roy Webb. RUNNING TIME 85 min. CAST: Pat O'Brien (Frank Cavanaugh); Robert Ryan (Father Timothy Donovan); Ruth Warrick (Florence Ayres Cavanaugh); Leon Ames (Robert Stewart); Russell Wade (Manning); Bruce Edwards (Lt. Jones).

Mademoiselle Fifi (RKO, 1943). DIR **Robert Wise**. PROD Val Lewton. SCR Josef Mischel, Peter Ruric (stories by Guy de Maupassant). CAM Harry Wild. ED J. R. Whittredge. MUS Werner R. Heymann. RUNNING TIME 69 min. CAST: Simone Simon (Elizabeth Rousset); John Emery (Jean Cordunet); Kurt Kreuger (Lt. von Eyrick, a.k.a. "Fifi"); Alan Napier (Count de Breville); Helen Freeman (Countess de Breville); Jason Robards, Sr. (Wholesaler in wine).

The Curse of the Cat People (RKO, 1944). DIR **Robert Wise**, Gunther von Fritsch. PROD Val Lewton. SCR DeWitt Bodeen. CAM Nicholas Musuraca. MUS Roy Webb. RUNNING TIME 70 min. CAST: Simone Simon (Irena Reed); Kent Smith (Oliver Reed); Jane Randolph (Alicia Reed); Ann Carter (Amy Reed); Eve March (Miss Calahan); Julia Dean (Julia Farren).

The Body Snatcher (RKO, 1945). DIR **Robert Wise**. PROD Val Lewton. SCR Philip MacDonald, Carlos Keith. CAM Robert De Grasse. ED J. R. Whittredge (short story by Robert Louis Stevenson). MUS Roy Webb. RUNNING TIME 78 min. CAST: Boris Karloff (John Gray); Bela Lugosi (Joseph); Henry Daniell (Toddy MacFarlane); Edith Atwater (Meg Cameron); Russell Wade (Donald Fettes); Rita Corday (Mrs. Marsh).

Game of Death (RKO, 1945). DIR **Robert Wise**. PROD Herman Schlom. SCR Norman Houston (story by Richard Connell). CAM J. Roy Hunt. ED J. R. Whittredge. MUS Paul Sawtell. RUNNING TIME 72 min. CAST: John Loder (Rainsford); Audrey Long (Ellen); Edgar Barrier (Kreiger); Russell Wade (Robert); Russell Hicks (Whitney); Jason Robards, Sr. (Captain).

Criminal Court (RKO, 1946). DIR **Robert Wise**. PROD Martin Mooney. SCR Lawrence Kimble. CAM Frank Redman. ED Robert Swink. MUS Paul Sawtell. RUNNING TIME 60 min. CAST: Tom Conway (Stephen Barnes); Martha O'Driscoll (Georgia Gale); June Clayworth (Joan Mason); Steve Brodie (Frankie Wright); Addison Richards (DA Gordon); Pat Gleason (Joe West).

Born to Kill, UK title: *Lady of Deceit* (RKO, 1947). DIR **Robert Wise**. PROD Herman Schlom. SCR Eve Greene, Richard Macauley (novel *Deadlier Than the Male* by James Gunn). CAM Robert De Grasse. ED Les Millbrook. MUS Paul Sawtell. RUNNING TIME 92 min. CAST: Claire Trevor (Helen); Lawrence Tierney (Sam); Walter Slezak (Arnett); Phillip Terry (Fred); Audrey Long (Georgia); Elisha Cook, Jr. (Marty).

Mystery in Mexico (RKO, 1948). DIR **Robert Wise**. PROD Sid Rogell. SCR Lawrence Kimble (story by Muriel Roy Bolton). CAM Jack Draper. ED Samuel E. Beetley. MUS Paul Sawtell. RUNNING TIME 66 min. CAST: William Lundigan (Steve Hastings); Jacqueline White (Victoria Ames); Ricardo Cortez (John Norcross); Tony Barret (Carlos); Jacqueline Dalya (Dolores Fernandez); Walter Reed (Glenn Ames).

Blood on the Moon (RKO, 1948). DIR **Robert Wise**. PROD Theron Warth. SCR Lillie Hayward (novel *Gunman's Chance* by Luke Short). CAM Nicholas Musuraca. ED Samuel E. Beetley. MUS Roy Webb. RUNNING TIME 86 min. CAST: Robert Mitchum (Jim Garry); Barbara Bel Geddes (Amy Lufton); Robert Preston (Tate Riling); Walter Brennan (Kris Barden); Phyllis Thaxter (Carol Lufton).

The Set-Up (RKO, 1949). DIR **Robert Wise**. PROD Richard Goldstone. SCR Art Cohn (poem by Joseph Moncure March). CAM Milton Krasner. ED Roland Gross. MUS C. Bakaleinikoff. RUNNING TIME 72 min. CAST: Robert Ryan (Stoker); Audrey Totter (Julie); George Tobias (Tiny); Alan Baxter (Little Boy); Wallace Ford (Gus); Percy Helton (Red).

Two Flags West (20th Century Fox, 1950). DIR **Robert Wise**. PROD Casey Robinson. SCR Casey Robinson (story by Curtis Kenyon, Frank S. Nugent). CAM Leon Shamroy. ED Louis Loeffler. MUS Hugo Friedhofer. RUNNING TIME 92 min. CAST: Joseph Cotton (Col. Clay Tucker); Linda Darnell (Elena Kenniston); Jeff Chandler (Maj. Henry Kinniston); Cornel Wilde (Capt. Mark Bradford); Dale Robertson (Lem); Jay C. Flippen (Sgt. Duffy).

Three Secrets (20th Century Fox, 1950). DIR **Robert Wise**. PROD Milton Sperling. SCR Martin Rackin, Gina Kaus. CAM Sid Hickox. ED Thomas Reilly. MUS David Buttolph. RUNNING TIME 98 min. CAST: Eleanor Parker (Susan Chase); Patricia Neal (Phyllis Horn); Ruth Roman (Ann Lawrence); Frank Lovejoy (Bob Duffy); Leif Erickson (Bill Chase); Ted de Corsia (Del Prince).

The House on Telegraph Hill (20th Century Fox, 1951). DIR **Robert Wise**. PROD Robert Bassler. SCR Elick Moll, Frank Partos (novel *The Frightened Child* by Dana Lyon). CAM Lucien Ballard. ED Nick DeMaggio. MUS Sol Kaplan. RUNNING TIME 93 min. CAST: Richard Basehart (Alan Spender); Valentina Cortese (Victoria Kowelska); William Lundigan (Maj. Marc Bennett); Fay Baker (Margaret); Gordon Gebert (Chris); Kei Thin Chung (Houseboy).

The Day the Earth Stood Still (20th Century Fox, 1951). DIR **Robert Wise**. PROD Julian Blaustein. SCR Edmund H. North (story by Harry Bates). CAM Leo Tover. ED William Reynolds. MUS Bernard Herrmann. RUNNING TIME 92 min. CAST: Michael Rennie (Klaatu); Patricia Neal (Helen Benson); Hugh Marlowe (Tom Stevens); Sam Jaffe (Jacob Barnhardt); Billy Grady (Bobby Benson); Frances Bavier (Mrs. Barley).

The Captive City (United Artists, 1952). DIR **Robert Wise**. PROD Theron Warth. SCR Karl Kamb, Alvin Josephy, Jr. (story by Alvin Josephy, Jr.). CAM Lee Garmes. ED Ralph Swink. MUS Jerome Moross. RUNNING TIME 91 min. CAST: John Forsythe (Jim Austin); Joan Camden (Marge Austin); Harold J. Kennedy (Don Carey); Marjorie Crossland (Mrs. Sirak); Victor Sutherland (Murray Sirak); Ray Teal (Chief Gillette).

Something for the Birds (20th Century Fox, 1952). DIR **Robert Wise**. PROD Samuel G. Engel. SCR I. A. L. Diamond, Boris Ingster (story by Boris Ingster, Alvin M. Josephy, Joseph Petracca). CAM Joseph LaShelle. ED Hugh S. Fowler. MUS Sol Kaplan. RUNNING TIME 81 min. CAST: Victor Mature (Steve Bennett); Patricia Neal (Anne Richards); Edmund Gwenn (Johnnie Adams); Larry Keating (Patterson); Gladys Hurlbut (Mrs. Rice).

Destination Gobi (20th Century Fox, 1953). DIR **Robert Wise**. PROD Stanley Rubin. SCR Everett Freeman (story by Edmund G. Love). CAM Charles G. Drake. ED Robert Fritch. MUS Sol Kaplan. RUNNING TIME 89 min. CAST: Richard Widmark (Sam McHale); Don Taylor (Jenkins); Casey Adams (Walter Landers); Murvyn Vye (Kengtu); Darryl Hickman (Cohen); Martin Milner (Elwood Halsey).

The Desert Rats (20th Century Fox, 1953). DIR **Robert Wise**. PROD Robert L. Jacks. SCR Richard Murphy. CAM Lucien Ballard. ED Barbara McLean. MUS Leigh Harline. RUNNING TIME 88 min. CAST: Richard Burton (Capt. MacRoberts); Robert Newton (Bartlett); Robert Douglas (General); Torin Thatcher (Barney); James Mason (Erwin Rommel).

So Big (Warner Bros., 1953). DIR **Robert Wise**. PROD Henry Blanke. SCR John Twist (novel by Edna Ferber). CAM Ellsworth Fredericks. ED Thomas Reilly. MUS Max Steiner. RUNNING TIME 101 min. CAST: Jane Wyman (Selina DeJong); Sterling Hayden (Pervus DeJong); Nancy Olsen (Dallas O'Mara); Steve Forrest (Dirk DeJong); Martha Hyer (Paula Hempel); Richard Beymer (Roelf Pool, age 12-16); Tommy Rettig (Dirk DeJong, age 8).

Executive Suite (MGM, 1954). DIR **Robert Wise**. PROD John Houseman. SCR Ernest Lehman (novel by Cameron Hawley). CAM George Folsey. ED Ralph E. Winters. RUNNING TIME 115 min. CAST: William Holden (McDonald Walling); Fredric March (Loren Phineas Shaw); Barbara Stanwyck (Julia O. Tredway); June Allyson (Mary Walling); Walter Pidgeon (Frederick Alderson); Shelley Winters (Eva Bardeman); Paul Douglas (Josiah Dudley); Louis Calhern (George Nyle Caswell); Dean Jagger (Jesse Q. Grimm).

Helen of Troy (Warner Bros., 1956). DIR **Robert Wise**. SCR John Twist, Hugh Gray (adaptation by Hugh Gray, N. Richard Nash). CAM Harry Stradling. ED Thomas Reilly. MUS Max Steiner. RUNNING TIME 118 min. CAST: Rossana Podestà (Helen); Jack Sernas (Paris); Sir Cedric Hardwicke (Priam); Stanley Baker (Achilles); Niall McGinnis (Menelaus); Nora Swinburne (Hecuba).

Tribute to a Bad Man (MGM, 1956). DIR **Robert Wise**. PROD Sam Zimbalist. SCR Michael Blankfort (story by Jack Schaefer). CAM Robert Surtees. ED Ralph E. Winters. MUS Miklos Rozsa. RUNNING TIME 95 min. CAST: James Cagney (Jeremy Rodock); Don Dubbins (Steve Millar); Stephen McNally (McNulty); Irene Papas (Jocasta Constantine); Vic Morrow (Lars Peterson); Lee Van Cleef (Fat Jones).

Somebody Up There Likes Me (MGM, 1956). DIR **Robert Wise**. PROD Charles Schnee. SCR Ernest Lehman (autobiography by Rowland Barber). CAM Joseph Ruttenberg. ED Albert Akst. MUS Bronislau Kaper. RUNNING TIME 112 min. CAST: Paul Newman (Rocky Graziano); Pier Angeli (Norma); Everett Sloane (Irving Cohen); Eileen Heckart (Ma Barbella); Sal Mineo (Romolo); Harold Stone (Nick Barbella).

Until They Sail (MGM, 1957). DIR **Robert Wise**. PROD Charles Schnee. SCR Robert Anderson (story by James A. Michener). CAM Joseph Ruttenberg. ED Harold F. Kress. MUS David Raksin. RUNNING TIME 94 min. CAST: Jean Simmons (Barbara Leslie Forbes); Joan Fontaine (Anne Leslie); Paul Newman (Capt. Harding); Piper Laurie (Delia Leslie); Charles Drake (Capt. Richard G. Bates); Sandra Dee (Evelyn Leslie).

This Could Be the Night (MGM, 1957). DIR **Robert Wise**. PROD Joe Pasternak. SCR Isobel Lennart (short stories by Cordelia Baird Gross). CAM Russell Harlan. ED George Boemler. RUNNING TIME 104 min. CAST: Jean Simmons (Anne Leeds); Paul Douglas (Rocco); Anthony Franciosa (Tony Armotti); Julie Wilson (Ivy Corlane); Neile Adams (Patsy St Clair); Joan Blondell (Crystal); ZaSu Pitts (Mrs. Shea).

Run Silent, Run Deep (United Artists, 1958). DIR **Robert Wise**. PROD Harold Hecht. SCR John Gay (novel by Edward L. Beach). CAM Russell Harlan. ED George Boemler. MUS Franz Waxman. RUNNING TIME 93 min. CAST: Clark Gable (Comdr. Richardson); Burt Lancaster (Lt. Bledsoe); Jack Warden (Mueller); Brad Dexter (Cartwright); Don Rickles (Ruby); Nick Cravat (Russo).

I Want to Live! (United Artists, 1958). DIR **Robert Wise**. PROD Walter Wanger. SCR Nelson Gilling, Don M. Mankiewicz (articles by Ed Montgomery, letters of Barbara Graham). CAM Lionel Lindon. ED William Hornbeck. MUS John Mandel. RUNNING TIME 120 min. CAST: Susan Hayward (Barbara Graham); Simon Oakland (Ed Montgomery); Virginia Vincent (Peg); Theodore Bikel (Carl Palmberg); Wesley Lau (Henry Graham).

Odds Against Tomorrow (United Artists, 1959). DIR-PROD **Robert Wise**. SCR John O. Killens [pseudonym for Abraham Polonsky] (novel by William P. McGivern). CAM Joseph C. Brun. ED Dede Allen. MUS John Lewis. RUNNING TIME 96 min. CAST: Harry Belafonte (Ingram); Robert Ryan (Slater); Shelley Winters (Lorry); Ed Begley (Burke); Gloria Grahame (Helen); Will Kuluva (Bacco).

West Side Story (United Artists, 1961). DIR **Robert Wise** and Jerome Robbins. PROD **Robert Wise**. SCR Ernest Lehman (stage play by Robert E. Griffith, Harold S. Prince, book by Arthur Laurents). CAM Daniel L. Fapp. ED Thomas Stanford. MUS Leonard Bernstein. RUNNING TIME 153 min. CAST: Natalie Wood (Maria); Richard Beymer (Tony); Russ Tamblyn (Riff); Rita Moreno (Anita); George Chakiris (Bernardo); Simon Oakland (Lt. Schrank).

Two for the Seesaw (United Artists, 1962). DIR **Robert Wise**. PROD Walter Mirisch. SCR Isobel Lennart (play by William Gibson). CAM Ted McCord. ED Stuart Gilmore. MUS André Previn. RUNNING TIME 120 min. CAST: Robert Mitchum (Jerry Ryan); Shirley MacLaine (Gittel Mosca); Edmon Ryan (Taubman); Elisabeth Fraser (Sophie); Eddie Firestone (Oscar); Billy Gray (Mr. Jacoby)

The Haunting (MGM, 1963). DIR-PROD **Robert Wise**. SCR Nelson Gidding (novel *The Haunting of Hill House* by Shirley Jackson). CAM Davis Boulton. ED Ernest Walter. MUS Humphrey Searle. RUNNING TIME 112 min. CAST: Julie Harris (Eleanor Vance); Claire Bloom (Theodora); Richard Johnson (Dr. Markway); Russ Tamblyn (Luke Sanderson); Lois Maxwell (Grace); Rosalie Crutchley (Mrs. Dudley).

The Sound of Music (20th Century Fox, 1965). DIR-PROD **Robert Wise**. SCR Ernest Lehman (stage musical by Richard Rogers, Oscar Hammerstein II, book by Howard Lindsay, Russel Crouse). CAM Ted McCord. ED William Reynolds. MUS Richard Rogers, Oscar Hammerstein II. RUNNING TIME 174 min. CAST: Julie Andrews (Maria); Christopher Plummer (Captain von Trapp); Eleanor Parker (The Baroness); Richard Haydn (Max Detweiler); Peggy Wood (Mother Abbess); Charmain Carr (Liesl); Heather Menzies (Louisa).

The Sand Pebbles (20th Century Fox, 1966). DIR-PROD **Robert Wise**. SCR Robert W. Anderson (novel by Richard McKenna). CAM Richard Johnson. ED William Reynolds. MUS Jerry Goldsmith. RUNNING TIME 193 min. CAST: Steve McQueen (Jake Holman); Richard Attenborough (Frenchy Burgoyne); Richard Crenna (Capt. Rollins); Candice Bergen (Shirley Eckert); Marayat Andriane (Maily).

Star! (20th Century Fox, 1968). DIR **Robert Wise**. PROD Saul Chaplin. SCR William Fairchild. CAM Ernest Laszlo. ED William Reynolds. MUS Lennie Hayton. RUNNING TIME 175 min. CAST: Julie Andrews (Gertrude Lawrence); Richard Crenna (Richard Aldrich); Michael Craig (Sir Anthony Spencer); Daniel Massey (Noel Coward); Robert Reed (Charles Fraser); Bruce Forsyth (Arthur Lawrence).

The Baby Maker (National General, 1970). DIR-SCR James Bridges. PROD Richard Goldstone. EXEC PROD **Robert Wise**. CAM Charles Rosher, Jr. ED Walter Thompson. MUS Fred Karlin. RUNNING TIME 109 min. CAST: Barbara Hershey (Tish Gray); Collin Wilcox-Horne (Suzanne Wilcox); Sam Groom (Jay Wilcox); Scott Glenn (Tad Jacks); Jeannie Berlin (Charlotte); Lili Valenty (Mrs. Culnick).

The Andromeda Strain (Universal, 1971). DIR-PROD **Robert Wise**. SCR Nelson Gidding (novel by J. Michael Crichton). CAM Richard H. Kline. ED Stuart Gilmore, John W. Holmes. MUS Gil Melle. RUNNING TIME 137 min. CAST: Arthur Hill (Dr. Jeremy Stone); David Wayne (Dr. Charles Dutton); James Olson (Dr. Mark Hall); Kate Reid (Dr. Ruth Leavitt); Paula Kelly (Karen Anson).

Two People (Universal, 1973). DIR-PROD **Robert Wise**. SCR Richard DeRoy. CAM Henri Decae. ED William Reynolds. MUS David Shire. RUNNING TIME 100 min. CAST: Peter Fonda (Evan); Lindsay Wagner (Deirde); Estelle Parsons (Barbara); Alan Fudge (Fitzgerald); Philippe March (Gilles); Frances Sternhagen (Mrs. McCluskey).

The Hindenburg (Universal, 1975). DIR-PROD **Robert Wise**. SCR Nelson Gidding (story by Richard A. Levinson, William Link, book by Michael M. Mooney). CAM Robert Surtees. ED Donn Cambern. MUS David Shire. RUNNING TIME 125 min. CAST: George C. Scott (Ritter); Anne Bancroft (The Countess); William Atherton (Boerth); Roy Thinnes (Martin Vogel); Gig Young (Edward Douglas); Burgess Meredith (Emilio Pajetta); Charles Durning (Capt. Pruss).

Audrey Rose (United Artists, 1977). DIR **Robert Wise**. PROD Joe Wizan, Frank De Felitta. SCR Frank De

Felitta (also novel). CAM Victor J. Kemper. ED Carl Kress. MUS Michael Small. RUNNING TIME 113 min. CAST: Marsha Mason (Janice Templeton); Anthony Hopkins (Elliot Hoover); John Beck (Bill Templeton); Susan Swift (Ivy Templeton); Norman Lloyd (Dr. Steven Lipscomb); John Hillerman (Scott Velie).

Star Trek: The Motion Picture (Paramount, 1979). DIR **Robert Wise**. PROD Gene Roddenberry. SCR Harold Livingston (story by Alan Dean Foster, based on *Star Trek*, created by Gene Roddenberry). CAM Richard H. Kline. ED Todd Ramsay. MUS Jerry Goldsmith. RUNNING TIME 132 min. CAST: William Shatner (Capt. Kirk); Leonard Nimoy (Spock); DeForest Kelley (Dr. McCoy); James Doohan (Scotty); George Takei (Sulu); Majel Barrett (Dr. Chapel).

Wisdom (20th Century Fox, 1986). DIR-SCR Emilio Estevez. PROD Bernard Williams. EXEC PROD **Robert Wise**. CAM Adam Greenberg. ED Michael Kahn. MUS Danny Elfman. RUNNING TIME 108 min. CAST: Demi Moore (Karen Simmons); Emilio Estevez (John Wisdom); Tom Skerritt (Lloyd Wisdom); Veronica Cartwright (Samantha Wisdom); William Allen Young (Williamson).

Rooftops (New Vision Pictures, 1989). DIR **Robert Wise**. PROD Howard W. Koch, Jr. SCR Terence Brennan (story by Tony Mark, Allan Goldstein). CAM Theo van de Sande. ED William Reynolds. MUS David A. Stewart, Michael Kamen. RUNNING TIME 95 min. CAST: Jason Gedrick (T); Troy Beyer (Elana); Eddie Vélez (Lobo); Tisha Campbell (Amber); Alexis Cruz (Squeak); Allen Payne (Kadim).

At Night the Sun Shines (1992). DIR Guillermo Real. PROD Guillermo Real, Sue Ann Hirshenberg. SUP PROD **Robert Wise**. MUS John Tatgenhorst. CAST: Beata Pozniak (Anabelle); Robert Desiderio; Lawrence Dobkin.

The Stupids (New Line Cinema, 1996). DIR John Landis. PROD Leslie Belzberg. SCR Brent Forrester (characters created by James Marshall, Harry Allard). CAM Manfred Guthe. ED Dale Beldin. MUS Christopher Stone. RUNNING TIME 94 min. CAST: Tom Arnold (Stanley Stupid); Jessica Lundy (Joan Stupid); Bug Hall (Buster Stupid); Alex McKenna (Petunia Stupid); Scott Kraft (Policeman); David Cronenberg (Postal Supervisor); Costa-Gavras (Gas Station Guy); **Robert Wise** (Stanley's Neighbor).

Television Movie

A Storm in Summer (2000). DIR **Robert Wise**. CAST: Peter Falk; Aaron Meeks; Nastassja Kinski; Andrew McCarthy; Ruby Dee.

JANE WITHERS

The first Jane Withers film I ever saw was *Bright Eyes* (1934), with the ever-popular Shirley Temple[1] (in her first top billing role and the first film written for her) being tormented by a mischievous, noisy and jealous Jane Withers. It was hardly a sympathetic entrance into the world of moviemaking, but she played this angry, messy and wild character so convincingly that her talents were recognized instantly. The *New York Times* praised her performance in its film review very accurately: "There were those among the critical gentry who came right out and said that her performance topped that of Shirley." Incidentally, Shirley Temple became the top child star of the 1930s; the young Miss Withers quickly became the second in ranking and, still in terms of box-office, both were among the top stars of the decade, with Miss Withers in the top ten biggest money-makers in 1937 and 1938.

This role of the mischievous, noisy and jealous brat she played so well in *Bright Eyes* is completely the opposite of who she is in real life. I met this wonderful lady, who's in her mid–70s right now, in Los Angeles when she was preparing the auction of her huge collection of Hollywood memorabilia. She had a lot of things on her mind at that time, a lot more urgent things to take care of than meeting me, yet she took a whole afternoon off to show me some of the precious film props she had collected over the years and which were stored in a very spacious warehouse. In her office she also talked about her lengthy career in films, being a child star in the 1930s, her plans for the future, her upcoming books and, certainly most precious to her, she shared her thoughts about her family and her religious beliefs.

Miss Withers: "I am working very hard on this auction right now and although I will part with this movie memorabilia, I know I will never *lose* it, it will always stay in my heart. I had the fun of finding and saving these things which are very important to me, because it is all Hollywood history—for example I got the barber chair of *My Darling Clementine* [1946], the hat Clark Gable wore in a joyful scene in *Saratoga* [1937] with Jean Harlow, etc. I loved it very much, and because of that, I wanted to save it. But it has become a tremendous responsibility and it is taking so much of my time, while there are so many other things now that I could be doing and that I would like to do and haven't had a chance to do yet—I have always been working and I love it, but there are other things as well in life. I would like to travel again, visit many places I have never had the privilege of going to before and I'm looking forward to that."

During our conversation, it became clear that religion has been her driving force all her life: "Absolutely, from babyhood! It has affected everything I ever did. Both Shirley Temple and I were Depression babies. So much insecurity and so much unhappiness went on at that time; our films were always entertaining and funny, they would take anybody's mind of their problems. Because we were both children, the audience would associate their families with us and with the films we did. So it was logical that we were very successful at that time and it was a great help, because we brought love, we brought entertainment, we brought a lot of the things maybe they felt they were lacking in some way."

Born in Atlanta, Georgia, on April 12, 1926, Miss Withers debuted in *Handle with Care* (1932), and two years later already, before appearing in *Bright Eyes*, she was W. C. Fields' hopscotch girl in the film classic *It's a Gift*: both films launched one of the most successful careers of the 1930s, as her mother signed a seven year contract with 20th Century Fox. Miss Withers: "When my contract was signed—I was seven and a half years old—my mother supervised it all. I was blessed with extraordinary parents, they were very understanding, helpful and encouraging in everything I ever did. I always get very upset when I read articles or see television shows with some of the young people that grew up in films as I did, and who have unkind things to say about it. I couldn't possibly do anything but love it, from the very first time I ever walked on the stage when I was two and a half years old. I loved the people, I loved their reaction, I loved meeting the fans all over the world.

"So when my contract was signed, I told the people that were in charge of the studio that money didn't interest me, I loved the talents of the people I was privileged to work with, I hoped they would enjoy it and would like to come to work as much as I did. That makes all the difference in the world in whatever you're doing, whether you're a carpenter, a mechanic, a truck driver or whatever. Then you can give everything properly to it. I always felt that way about anything I've ever done. Sometimes I would get a script that was not written for me, but they thought I would be good in the role. If it was against what I believed in very strongly, I would say, 'I'm sorry, this is not for me, I can't do this.'

"I was just an extra on the set of *It's a Gift*. I remember W. C. Fields[2] told the director, 'I gotta pick out one of these kids to do a pantomime scene with me.' He asked us all to line up, then pointed at me and said, 'Little girl, what's your name?' I said, 'Jane Withers.' 'Oh my goodness, you got a Southern accent, where are you from?' I said, 'Atlanta, Georgia.' And he said, 'Come over here with me, I want to see if you can do this. I've got to get to that door which is the door of my store. Now I want you to do hopscotch, so don't let me get to that door. You hopscotch here as I start to move and then I get all kinda upset, you hopscotch there, etc. You think you can do that?' So I started hopscotching and was concentrating until he said, 'That was fantastic! You think you could do it again?' After we had shot it, he told me, 'Your timing is impeccable, it is wonderful! Is your mother here? Everybody has a mother, where's yours?' I said, 'Well, she's here somewhere, but she doesn't come anywhere near the camera.' She always told me, 'It's your talent, not mine. I'll be there if you need me, but you know what you have to do: you just take the direction that they give you and do it the very best you can. If you don't like what they tell you to do, you tell them about it.'

"So this man called over the megaphone, 'Will the mother of...—what's your name, honey—will the mother of Jane Withers come down by the camera?' W. C. Fields told me, 'Honey, you've done something very right and I think your mother should know about it.' So he turned to my mother and said, 'Miss Withers, I'm W. C. You have a very talented little girl here, I think she's gonna go very far.' He took *time* to talk to us, you know. It was so lovely and he asked me what I would be doing later on. 'If you get a good role, let me know, let me see it—I *mean* it. Kid, you got something special. You're gonna be a big star.'"

"When I got the role in *Bright Eyes*, my mother helped me write a letter to W. C. Fields and I wrote, 'I'm the little kid that hopscotched my way in your movie *It's a Gift*. I don't want to bother you, but you asked me to let you know when I got a good role in something. In my

Jane Withers (left) and Shirley Temple in *Bright Eyes* (1934). (Courtesy of Jane Withers.)

new film, I have lines, people can really see me and I play the meanest kid in the world. They're going to hate me because everyone loves Shirley Temple so much. If you get a chance, I hope you get to see it. Thank you for caring and sharing. Jane Withers.' Well, he saw the picture. I got the greatest letter from him. He wrote, 'Told you! You're gonna be a big star!' He kept up with my career and when my contract at Fox was signed, I wrote him and said, 'I'm so grateful, God has taken such good care of me. My first film will be *Ginger* and I'm starting on my eighth birthday.'"

Ginger (1935) was Miss Withers' first film in a leading role (the *New York Times* wrote: "Miss Withers took the screen world more or less by storm last December when she appeared as the thorn in Shirley Temple's side in *Bright Eyes*. With *Ginger* she emerges as a star in her own right"). She says: "We started the picture on my eighth birthday. Two huge baskets of flowers arrived on the set and they were given to me. I said to the man delivering them, 'Oh, Sir, you made a mistake. Shirley Temple is way at the other end of the lot.' 'No, they are for you!' he said. I guess everybody on the set was in on it, because they all said, 'What's on the card? Who are they from?' So I opened up one card and it read, 'To my little friend, Jane, one swell girl. Knock 'em dead kid, you're gonna be great. Your pen pal and fan, W. C.' My heart was just pounding, I was so thrilled to see he would take the time to send me those beautiful flowers. I still have the baskets. The other one said, 'To my little friend, Jane, God bless you, I know you are going to be one of our greatest stars in America. Your friend, Franklin Delano Roosevelt.'

"I met Franklin Delano Roosevelt through impersonations. Somebody of the Democratic Party saw me doing an impersonation of him. I had a little tuxedo on and it was on a newsreel that was shown to him. 'That's the best impersonation anyone has ever done of me,' he said. 'Where is that kid? Find out her name and how old she is!' He was then still the governor of New York, I think it was 1933 or 1934, just before he became President. He then wrote me a letter which said, 'Dear little Jane, I saw the newsreel where you impersonated me, it's terrific. Good luck in your career, you can't miss. Keep in touch with me and let me know when I can see you again in films. I'm sending you a little button to wear and ask your mom and dad to vote for me.' I still have that little pin—framed, with his letter. Then I wrote him a letter again, like with W. C., and said, 'I am very excited, I have done a film with Shirley Temple, the only thing is I am so mean to her that everybody is going to hate me. But it's a wonderful role and I'm very grateful for the opportunity. If you see *Bright Eyes*, I hope you'll enjoy my part. Jane Withers.'

"Then I also sent him another letter when my contract was signed, telling I would start my first starring film called *Ginger* on my eighth birthday, and that resulted in the flowers. In two biographies of President Roosevelt, they mentioned that an extraordinary group of gentlemen were having dinner with him one evening, and he said, 'Now, I have the best desert in the world planned for you—you're going to see my favorite actress Jane Withers in her first starring role, called *Ginger*.'

"Our friendship lasted until his death, we became pen pals, it was all incredible to me because he died on my birthday in 1945, April 12. It was the saddest birthday I ever had. He was a very kind man, sometimes we'd talk on the phone. I had a special number to call. When the war broke out, I called him and said, 'I'll go right to the front lines to entertain our boys, I'll do anything to help.' During the war I did 150 bond and camp tours, but they would never let me go beyond America. He said, 'Jane, you are one of our national treasures. I would like you to go to the hospitals where so many of the young people, who grew up with you, are hurt and they need to see you there.' So whenever I finished a picture, I would get a good night's sleep and the next morning we would leave with special orders from the President on another bond or camp tour. It was a wonderful experience—someday perhaps I should write a book about all that, about all the people I met, all the boys that I danced with. Sometimes I'd dance for four or five hours at the Hollywood Canteen or the Stage Door Canteen in New York, wherever I was.

"When I did appearances, it was like a one-gal show. We'd take a small piano, which is portable, it's like a little suitcase; I would take my accompanist with me and he would play on the portable. I did shows, sang, danced and did impersonations for hundreds of boys, and at night we'd go to the hospitals. It was wonderful, interesting, very unique. I don't know if another girl or boy, even Judy Garland, Joan Leslie or Ann Blyth, was ever able to do what I did.

"In the meantime, I would always take the time to keep up with people. Every Sunday afternoon, after Sunday school in church, we'd have anywhere from 50 to 100 people at our home on Sunset Boulevard. And after I finished a movie, I would have the entire crew and all their families come over to our house for a barbecue. I was very lucky, because at Fox I usually had the same group of sweet people that worked on all of my films. They would be there for *hours*; they'd come in like 11 o'clock in the morning and wouldn't leave until nine o'clock at night. We'd sing, dance, different people would entertain, we'd swim, play croquet, badminton—we had a *good* time. My parents had bought this house after we had moved to California. Later on, for my 14th birthday, we built the second level on this house where we also had a projection room and enough space for my enormous doll and teddy bear collection. I also had my own soda fountain—all of our friends really loved making chocolate soda.

"During World War II our house was known as Withers USO. Everybody always came over. And when I appeared in *Giant*, a wonderful experience, they dubbed my house where we were on location in Texas as "Withers USO" because at night, after work, we'd have Monopoly marathons, bridge tournaments, play records, etc. I'd always have simple, wholesome food and at night nobody wanted to go home. So I had this huge Chinese gong sent from the studio. We always had to get up at four o'clock in the morning, and at ten minutes to nine, I'd ring this gong and would say, 'Okay everybody, put the covers over the Monopoly games, we'll continue tomorrow night just where we left off.' It was fun, great fun." *Giant*, starring Liz Taylor, Rock Hudson and James Dean (his last film), turned out to be one of Miss Withers' final films.

However, going back to the 1930s, when she was one of the biggest money-makers in Hollywood, she certainly must have had *power* as a child? Miss Withers: "I never thought of that as a child, I didn't know what it meant to be sixth in the box-office. I did ask for the same group of people to work with every time, we were like a team and everybody had his own special talent, so each of us could contribute to this team. My mother taught Sunday school and my father taught bible class. God was my partner from the day I was born, but I started dedicating my life to the Lord's work when I was nine years old. My parents said, 'Well, that's such a great responsibility, are you sure you can live up to that?' I said, 'I would never give my word if I couldn't live up to that in anything I ever do.'

"Many of the friends I grew up with, like Joan Leslie and Ann Blyth, we all loved working helping other people and giving back to the world. We have all been so lucky, you know. I was privileged to learn that at a very early age. I was very blessed to grow up in films as I did and be able to start out so very young. I was first on the stage in Aunt Sally's Kiddie Review, I sang, danced and did impersonations of the stars of the thirties, like W. C. Fields, ZaSu Pitts, Maurice Chevalier, Fanny Brice, Eddie Cantor, Greta Garbo, Fifi D'Orsay, Joe E. Brown, etc. It was so much fun, pretending you were them. That's what always made me very different from all the other children that were in films at the same time. I also was on the radio all the time; in fact, the first radio show that I got a job on, we were so thrilled because it was the first paying job we had when we got to California. On that show was Mickey Rooney who was then Mickey McGuire of Mickey McGuire comedies, Judy Garland was then one of the Gumm Sisters, Sidney Miller who later on became quite renowned for working with Donald O'Connor, was the master of ceremonies on that show. He also became director of the Mickey Mouse Club. We had children guest stars, like Baby Rosemarie who was later billed as Rosemarie on *The Dick Van Dyke Show*. She was one of the first child stars I ever met; she was touring on a personal appearance tour and came to Atlanta, Georgia, when I was three and a half years old.

"She said, 'If you think I'm going to be interviewed by a three-and-a-half-year-old kid, you got another thought coming.' She was very hesitant about doing this radio show with me, but finally she did and when it was over, she told me, 'Well, I gotta admit kid, you were very good.' When I came out here to California, we ran into each other and I said, 'You don't remember me, do you?' She said, 'Sure, you are that kid from the radio show in Atlanta. How old are you now?' I said, 'Six and a half!' [laughs].

"There are very few things that I wanted to do and that I haven't done. I always wanted to work with Jimmy Stewart and Cary Grant—they were my supreme favorites. I knew Jimmy in a Christian way through church because of his wife. I would see them every Sunday. I taught Sunday school for years with Eleanor Powell and Gloria Stewart, Jimmy Stewart's wife, at the Beverly Hills Presbyterian Church. But I also adored Fred Astaire, Gene Kelly, Ray Bolger, … I always loved their musicals.

"But again, as I said, I didn't know what it meant being sixth in box-office. We were doing a film, *Checkers* in 1937—I was 11 at the time—with Una Merkel. We were on location on a big racetrack at Santa Anita, here in California. I had to really ride a race horse and I had been practicing learning to ride. Over the loudspeakers, I heard the man announcing to all of those who were working that day, 'Wow, we have the greatest news! Look what happened to our kid'—they all called me their "kid"—'she's sixth in the box-office in the whole world!' I had heard of the box-office, but I never paid any attention to it and until they told me what it stood for, I didn't have any clue what it really meant.

"Instead, I would rather share thoughts with the people that would write to me. I answered my fan mail with two secretaries, two nights a week. It was great fun and I truly loved it—it was never difficult because I loved it, but it was *hectic*. My mother always said, 'If you don't want to do this anymore, you certainly do not have to. We'll walk right out the door and we'll never come back.' But I could hardly wait everyday to get up and go to the studio. Then, when we'd finish a movie, I would have to wait three weeks before everybody would be together again for the next movie. In between I would do personal appearances, go to children's orphan homes in any city I would visit, so I could have church services with them on Sundays."

More than ever, fans wrote to their favorite idols in the 1930s, during the era when the major studios promoted their precious superstars. Miss Withers also got her share of fan mail. "At one time I had seven secretaries that handled the mail and we would spend three nights a week answering them. I asked them to separate it into five different categories. Mostly the fans asked the same questions: what your favorite movie is, things like that. Some of them had much deeper thoughts than that and those I always answered first myself. I still get fan mail: now they often send lobby cards and stills to autograph. The last two times I moved, everything had to go into boxes and crates, including the fan mail. But after I moved, I opened the boxes of mail and I did answer them.

"On the other hand, I also had three kidnap threats in my life. When they caught one of these men, he had a life sentence to pay. I said, 'That's very severe for just writing me a letter.' They said, 'But it was what the letter stood for and the idea behind it, and that's why he had been punished the way he was.' So I decided I would like to talk to him, I wanted to know why anyone would write me such a letter—if we didn't pay him $250,000 in small bills and all that, he threatened to kill me. I was interested in knowing *why* he had such bad feelings about me. I never got to talk to him, but he did correspond with me and I wrote him back, asking him why he threatened to kill me. He wrote me that he had been married and that they had a little daughter, but his wife had died in an automobile accident which also killed his little daughter when she was two years old. He wrote me that he loved my films and he just wanted to talk to me. I wrote him that he was certainly paying a very high price for it now—we corresponded for quite some time and he made me a few little things while he was in prison like a box to keep his letters in and several things for my doll collection. I prayed for him daily."

Miss Withers' doll collection, which totals 14,000, has become the largest and most extensive in the world. She started collecting them as a youngster when people sent her gifts at the studio. The collection has been on tour a couple of times, including during World War II when it went on a cross-country railroad tour to raise money for the war effort—by that time, the collection consisted of a mere 3,500 dolls.

"In the 1940s I didn't appear in films that much anymore, because of the war—I was doing all those bond and camp tours. That had priority over any movie I made. I always said I would work until I was 21, then I hoped to find Mr. Right and be married for the rest of my life. Well, I got married at 21, unfortunately it wasn't Mr. Right—we're still good friends though. We would have had our 50th wedding anniversary in September 1999. I called him that day and I asked, 'You know what day it is? It would have been our 50th wedding anniversary today

Jane Withers with a few dolls from her huge doll collection. (Courtesy of Jane Withers.)

and I called to say thank you.' 'Thank me?' he said. 'Yes, if it hadn't been for you, we'd never have had Wendy, Bill and Randy. They are three of my greatest wishes that came true and I'll always love you for that."

Miss Withers' first husband was Texas oilman and rancher Bill Moss. After their divorce in 1954, she met and married Kenneth Errair, one of the Four Freshmen,[3] in 1955. They had two children; one of them is Kendall Errair, renowned costume designer who worked on several films, including *Far and Away* (1992), *Mission: Impossible* (1996), *The Horse Whisperer* (1998) and *Stepmom* (1998).

"In the 1940s I *had* to leave Fox. I didn't want to, but they weren't letting me grow up and I was getting all these letters from kids I had grown *up* with, saying, 'Hey, you're still doing those movies like you did when you were 10 and you're not 10 anymore!' And boy, did I know it! In fact, when I was 15, I wrote one of my own films. It was called *Small Town Deb*. I wrote exactly about what was happening to me in my real life, only I put it in a small town. I had an older sister in the story and I had to blame it on the mother—it certainly wasn't that way in real life. I cast the entire movie myself and it gave me a chance to show in the film what my feelings as a teenager were, that the mother isn't allowing her to grow up, to be herself and to find herself. It was way ahead of its time, it was more like the films they're doing now, only now they use terrible language and the situations are very different. It was just the fact that the mother didn't realize; she was so concerned about her older daughter and she really didn't take into her heart the situation of her younger daughter who really needed her help and guidance.

"So I wrote the outline of the story, but I didn't have the guts to tell that I was the writer. I used my initials J. W. and I used the name Jerrie Walters—named after Jerrie, one of my godchildren, and after my father whose first name was Walter.

"For the first time in 20 pictures, I had a new producer, John Stone. I didn't know him very well, but I thought, 'What a way to start a new friendship, *asking* for something instead of cooperating with the films that they send me.' But I couldn't do it anymore; the stuff they sent me was the same as what I did four movies ago, only this time I was a little peasant girl. This was crazy! So finally, when they wouldn't listen, I took it in and I asked, 'Would you please ask Mr. Stone to read this?' They said, 'Well, who is Jerrie Walters?' I just said, 'Jerrie Walters wrote the script and I would very much like to do this.' The next day, they called me and said, 'Hey, that's a great story! We'd like to do the film, but we gotta buy the story from Jerrie Walters. Can you introduce us to him?' I said, 'Well, Jerrie Walters is very busy right now'—and I was, I was ready to go on another bond and camp tour. I said, 'But Jerrie and I have planned on getting together tomorrow afternoon after 12 o'clock. I can tell Jerrie you want to talk about the script.' I never said *him*, I didn't want to lie."

Henry Fonda (1905–1982), here as the United States President in Sidney Lumet's *Fail Safe* (1964), made one of his first films with Jane Withers as his co-star (*The Farmer Takes a Wife*, 1935).

"So the next day, I went up the stairs, I went in. Mr. Stone said, 'Ah, Jane! Where is Jerrie Walters?' I said, 'I have something to tell you, could we please go in your office for just a minute?' 'Sure, but we're most anxious to see Jerrie Walters.' Then I said, 'Mr. Stone, you're looking at Jerrie Walters...' 'I beg your pardon?' 'I'm Jerrie Walters, I wrote that story, but I didn't have the guts to put my own name on it, because I didn't know what your reaction would be. But everything I wrote is true, I could bring you hundreds of letters that I have received from fans who wrote to me. They all say, 'Why won't they let you grow up at Fox?' I *am* growing up, you *must* let me play in an honest role. The last roles I played have been so tacky, I've been ashamed of them and they're not true. You got to do something about it.' He said, 'You're right, that's why we were so thrilled when we got the story. How much do you want for your story?' 'I want 15 scholarships at $1,500 apiece for kids who want to study music and acting, we desperately need an upright piano for the kindergarten department and if you could throw in another upright piano, that would be great, because we need that one for the teenager department at Sunday school.' So in the end, I received 15 scholarships and two pianos. And I worked on the screenplay and I got credit as Jerrie Walters. That really meant an awful lot to me, and it was a very successful movie. Very few people had a clue that I wrote the story.

"I guess it all stems from the fact that I can't do something I don't believe in. If you don't believe in the things you do, it will show right in your eyes, right in your face and it wouldn't be honest.

"Nowadays, they would not give a child the time on the screen that they did in the earlier years. Did you see the film *The Sixth Sense*? I thought the little boy [Haley Joel Osment] did a wonderful job. I never met him but I hope someday I can just tell him, 'You did a great job.' That's why I saw that film, because of the little boy. I have always been interested in children that are in films today. I also liked Jodie Foster when she was very young, she was excellent. Back then, all of Shirley's and my films were written for us. No one writes films for children anymore and I'm sure there are very talented children out there, just waiting for the opportunity, but when is it going to come?"

Over the years, Miss Withers turned down approximately 30 interesting film roles. She had set other priorities and other goals in her life. She didn't turn her back on Hollywood, but she simply didn't have the time and energy to devote to the process of filmmaking. "I was raising my five children then, that was reason enough to stop making films. When I was 15, I told my mother I wanted five children: first a girl, then three boys and then a girl at the end—I needed those girls for bookends to help me take care of all those boys. I really believed that and it did come true.

"Right now, I am also working hard on my books. What started out as one, has become about four or five, because there are so many things to share about so many wonderful people. I want to do *The Films of Jane Withers*—I have been working for four years on it already—I don't want to leave anyone out, I want to include everyone, looking back on their jobs, their friendship, working with them the way we did. Usually books like that just give the synopsis, the cast and a few crew members. But they don't take under consideration that extraordinary team of people that make it all happen. That's what I want to talk about."

"Other books I plan to write, include *The Men in My Life* and *The Ladies in My Life*. In *The Men in My Life*, I start by saying, 'Dear Reader, if you think this is another exposé of a child growing up in Hollywood, get your money back. This is my appreciation and "thank you" to all the *gentlemen* that have come into my life and that have shared with me so many wonderful thoughts, emotions and experiences and that have taught me so much.' The book is dedicated to my father, my grandfathers and my sons. There might be one sentence about one person and there might be seven pages about another person, depending on when they came into my life, how important they were to me as friends and what I learned from each and every one of them. The same with *The Women in My Life*: my mother, my daughters, the teachers at the studio, my Sunday school teacher, etc. Another book I plan to publish is called *Spiritual Vitamins*—that's one of my favorites too. Everyone says, 'You have so much energy, do you take vitamins?' I always say, 'I take *spiritual* vitamins!' That can be anything from a beautiful rainbow or to seeing someone smile, a puppy dog's tail wag, something you read—to me those are all spiritual vitamins."

"My mother wanted my autobiography to be called *I Grew Up in Hollywood* and I wanted it to be called *God Is My Partner*. She said, 'No, use that for your second book. Let people get to know you through your autobiography and then, they will understand *why* God is your partner.' I always tried to listen to my mom but I don't know yet what it will be till I finish it. Those are the main books I'm working on."

Even though she turned down various screen roles, she revived her career in the 1960s playing Josephine the plumber in a lengthy series of TV commercials. One often reads that this character made her a very wealthy woman. Miss Withers: "That is true, but I never look at wealth in dollars and cents. To me it's the wealth of experience, the people you share your time with and what you do with your time, that's the real wealth in life. But I did put all my five children through school and college from what I made as Josephine the lady plumber. It was fun to do, it entertained a lot of people, they all got a big kick out of the character I played and I took it very seriously. There has never been a lady plumber shown in any way before. Although it was only a TV commercial, I went to school to learn all about plumbing. You have to be familiar with it all, you have to know about the job you're performing. It was a long course and I didn't have much time. The commercials were made in New York at the time and I still lived in California.

"Anywhere I would go in that period of my life, truck drivers would say to me, 'Hey Josy! I got a bad sink!' And I'd say, 'I'm on my way to a job, if I had more time I would be glad to fix it!' or something like that [laughs]. It was great fun and I did that for almost 20 years. After 16 years of commercials, my mother collapsed with a brain tumor in 1975. I always had in my contract that if my children or my mother needed me, I would be with them because that's where I belong. So the only thing I ever asked for in the very beginning of my contract, I would like to be eight commercials ahead, so I'd never hold them up. When my mother collapsed, I knew it would be very difficult. I was with my mother for about eight years, so one of the writers got an idea: why couldn't we have a young girl that Josephine has taught everything she has learned about plumbing? So we did two commercials introducing her. She had the same attitude and manners, saying things like, 'Well, I'm just like my aunt Josephine.'"

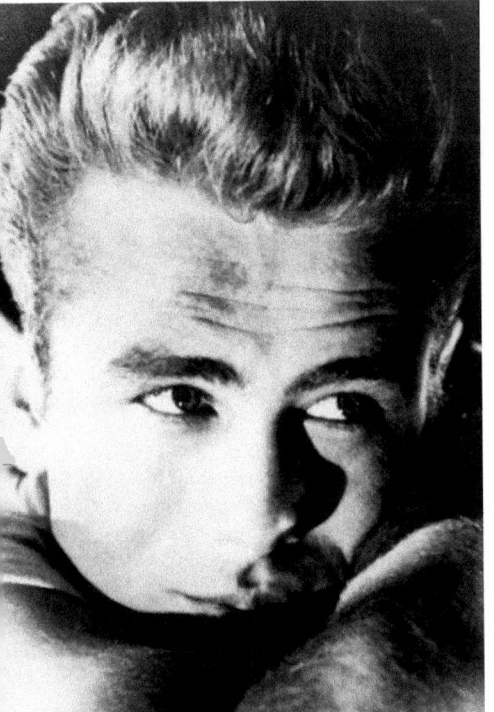

James Dean

Miss Withers' family and friends know her as a very strong and courageous woman. Despite the disappointments and tragedies she has faced in her life, she has always tried to make the world a better place. "The biggest blow in my life came when I lost one son with cancer. It's a great lesson, but it's also a terrible lesson. Somehow, I never felt he was gone: I always feel his presence, although he's not with me physically. I *know* he's there."

Miss Withers worked with many other great actors in her day. How does she look back on her friendship with James Dean, one of her leading men in *Giant*? "After we had spent some time in Texas, he came up to me and asked me, 'You don't like me, do you?' I said I did, but [advised him that] he had to change his attitude—instead of spitting on the ground or kicking up the dirt when he was talking to somebody, he could at least be more gentle and kind to all the others, be more appreciative of what they did for him. We talked about that and one evening when he came to my house, Withers USO, he wore a pink shirt he had been wearing for a few days already. As it was terribly hot in Texas, I told him, 'You should put on another shirt every day. Why don't you give it to me and I'll see to it that it has been washed by tomorrow, so you can drop by and pick it up.' That's what he did and whenever it was dirty or needed to be washed, he brought it over to me. At night he also came to Withers USO after all the other people left and we had long talks about acting, religion, etc. We got along just fine.

"He had set his mind on going to this race in California and he frequently asked George Stevens if he couldn't leave any sooner to drive up to California. George Stevens always said, 'No Jimmy, you have to stay here until your scenes are finished. You can't leave any sooner than that.' The day he left, he brought me his pink shirt before driving off. I still remember him leaving, I still remember him driving off, waving as he left, and when the news came late that same afternoon that he had been killed in this car accident, everybody on the set was heart-broken. I'll never forgot that day as long as I live!"

As I left her office, which is decorated with various posters from her films, she joined her staff again and resumed her preparations for the upcoming auction as there was still a lot of work to do. Miss Withers is an upbeat lady all the way and I'm looking forward to reading all of her books which undoubtedly will capture the essence of her colorful and enriching life, her work and all the wonderful things she stands for.

Interview: Los Angeles, March 8, 2000

Notes

1. Shirley Temple (b. 1928) was Hollywood's leading box-office attraction for four years in a row (1935–38) and most popular child star ever, adored by millions. She was the best cure for the Depression years, even though by the early 1940s she was considered a has-been. Retired from acting in 1949, she entered politics in 1968 and was among other things U.S. representative at the UN, and U.S. ambassador to Ghana and Czechoslovakia. Her films include *Little Miss Marker* (1934), *Bright Eyes* (1934), *The Little Colonel* (1935), *The Littlest Rebel* (1936), *Rebecca of Sunnybrook Farm* (1938), *The Little Princess* (1939), *The Bachelor and the Bobbysoxer* (1947), *Fort Apache* (1948) and *Mr. Belvedere Goes to College* (1949). Her autobiography, *Child Star*, was published in 1988.

2. W. C. Fields (1879–1946), began his career at age 14 as an amusement park juggler. Later on he became a vaudeville and stage star (touring Europe and performing at Buckingham Palace in 1901), worked with Flo Ziegfeld (from 1915 to 1921) and finally emerged as a screen actor from 1924. One of his first films was D. W. Griffith's *Sally of the Sawdust* (1925). Considered to be one of the great screen comedians of the 1930s, he gave one of his best and most unforgettable performances in a serious role as Micawber in George Cukor's *David Copperfield* (1935). His shorts include *The Dentist* (1932), *The Pharmacist* (1933), and *The Barber Shop* (1933), and he appeared in (and often wrote the story or screenplay for, under different pseudonyms) films such as *The Old-Fashioned Way* (1934), *It's a Gift* (1935), *The Man on a Flying Trapeze* (1935), *The Big Broadcast of 1938* (1938), *You Can't Cheat an Honest Man* (1939), *My Little Chickadee* (1940), *The Bank Dick* (1940) and *Never Give a Sucker an Even Break* (1941). His son W. C. Fields, Jr., who died in 1971, at age 67. Grandson Ronald J. Fields authored books about his illustrious grandfather and was the driving force behind the bestseller "W.C. Fields by Himself."

3. The Four Freshmen were a leading jazz-styled vocal and instrumental group formed in 1948. The group members were Kenneth Errair, Bob Flannagan, Ross Barbour, Ron Barbour. Their hits include "Day by Day" (1955), "Charmaine" (1955) and "Graduation Day" (1956).

Filmography

Handle with Care (Fox Film Corp., 1932). DIR David Butler. SCR Frank Craven, Sam Mintz (story by David Butler). CAM John Schmitz. ED Irene Morra. MUS George Lipschultz. RUNNING TIME 75 min. CAST: James

Dunn (Bill Gordon); Boots Mallory (Helen Barlow); El Brendel (Carl Lundstrom); Victor Jory (1st Public Enemy); Buster Phelps (Tommy); **Jane Withers** (Extra).

It's a Gift (Paramount, 1934). DIR Norman McLeod. PROD William Le Baron. SCR Jack Cunningham (story by Charles Bogle). CAM Henry Sharp. RUNNING TIME 70 min. CAST: W. C. Fields (Harold Bissonette); Kathleen Howard (Amelia Bissonette); Jean Rouverol (Mildred Bissonette); Julian Madison (John Durston); Tom Bupp (Norman Bissonette); **Jane Withers** (Hopscotch girl).

Bright Eyes (Fox Film Corp., 1934). DIR David Butler. PROD Sol M. Wurtzel. SCR William Conselman (story by David Butler, Edwin Burke). CAM Arthur Miller. MUS Samuel Kaylin. RUNNING TIME 83 min. CAST: Shirley Temple (Shirley Blake); James Dunn (Loop Merritt); Jane Darwell (Mrs. Higgins); Judith Allen (Adele Martin); Lois Wilson (Mary Blake); **Jane Withers** (Joy Smithe).

Ginger (Fox Film Corp., 1935). DIR Lewis Seiler. PROD Sol M. Wurtzel. SCR Arthur Kober (also story). CAM Bert Glennon. MUS Samuel Kaylin. RUNNING TIME 79 min. CAST: **Jane Withers** (Ginger); O. P. Heggie (Rexford Whittington); Jackie Searl (Hamilton Parker); Katharine Alexander (Mrs. Parker); Walter King (Daniel Parker); Donald Haines (Butch).

The Farmer Takes a Wife (Fox Film Corp., 1935). DIR Victor Fleming. PROD Winfield Sheehan. SCR Edwin Burke (play by Frank B. Elser, Marc Connelly). CAM Ernest Palmer. ED Harold Schuster. MUS Oscar Bradley. RUNNING TIME 91 min. CAST: Janet Gaynor (Molly Larkins); Henry Fonda (Dan Harrow); Charles Bickford (Jotham Klore); Slim Summerville (Fortune Friendly); Andy Devine (Elmer Otway); **Jane Withers** (Della).

This Is the Life (Fox Film Corp., 1935). DIR Marshall Neilan. SCR Lamar Trotti, Arthur Horman, Marshall Neilan (story by Gene Towne, Graham Baker, Lou Breslow, Sid Brod). CAM Daniel B. Clark. ED Fred Allen. MUS David Buttolph. RUNNING TIME 65 min. CAST: **Jane Withers** (Geraldine Revier); John McGuire (Michael Grant); Sally Blane (Helen Davis); Sidney Toler (Professor Breckinridge); Gloria Roy (Diane Revier); Gordon Westcott (Ed Revier).

Paddy O'Day (20th Century Fox, 1936). DIR Lewis Seiler. SCR Lou Breslow, Edward Eliscu. CAM Arthur Miller. ED Al De Gaetano. MUS Samuel Kaylin. RUNNING TIME 75 min. CAST: **Jane Withers** (Paddy O'Day); Pinky Tomlin (Ray Ford); Rita Cansino [changed her name the following year to Rita Hayworth] (Tamara Petrovitch); Jane Darwell (Dora); George Givot (Mischa); Francis Ford (Officer McGuire).

Gentle Julia (20th Century Fox, 1936). DIR John Blystone. SCR Lamar Trotti. CAM Ernest Palmer. ED Fred Allen. MUS Samuel Kaylin. RUNNING TIME 63 min. CAST: **Jane Withers** (Florence Atwater); Tom Brown (Noble Dill); Marsha Hunt (Julia Atwater); Jackie Searl (Herbert Atwater); Francis Ford (Mr. Tubbs); George Meeker (Mr. Crum).

Little Miss Nobody (20th Century Fox, 1936). DIR John Blystone. SCR Lou Breslow, Paul Burger, Edward Eliscu (short story by Frederick Hazlitt Brennan). CAM Bert Glennon. ED Al De Gaetano. MUS Samuel Kaylin. RUNNING TIME 72 min. CAST: **Jane Withers** (Judy Devlin); Jane Darwell (Martha Bradley); Ralph Morgan (Gerald Dexter); Sara Haden (Teresa Lewis); Harry Carey (John Russell); Betty Jean Hainey (Mary Dorsey).

Pepper (20th Century Fox, 1936). DIR James Tinling. SCR Lamar Trotti (story by Jefferson Parker, Murray Roth). CAM Daniel B. Clark. ED Fred Allen. MUS Samuel Kaylin. RUNNING TIME 61 min. CAST: **Jane Withers** (Pepper Jolly); Irvin S. Cobb (John Wilkes); Slim Summerville (Uncle Ben Jolly); Dean Jagger (Bob O'Ryan); Muriel Robert (Helen Wilkes); Ivan Lebedeff (Baron Von Stofel).

The Holy Terror (20th Century Fox, 1937). DIR James Tinling. SCR Lou Breslow, John Patrick. CAM Daniel B. Clark. ED Nick DeMaggio. MUS Samuel Kaylin. RUNNING TIME 66 min. CAST: **Jane Withers** ("Corky" Wallace); Anthony Martin (Danny Walkar); Leah Ray (Marjorie Dean); Joe Lewis (Pelican Beek); El Brendel (Alex Svenson); John Eldredge (Lt. Com. Wallace).

Angel's Holiday (20th Century Fox, 1937). DIR James Tinling. SCR Frank Fenton, Lynn Root (also story). CAM Daniel B. Clark. ED Nick DeMaggio. MUS Samuel Kaylin. RUNNING TIME 71 min. CAST: **Jane Withers** ("Angel" June Everett); Joan Davis (Stivers); Sally Blane (Pauline Kaye); Robert Kent (Nick Moore); Harold Huber (Bat Regan); Frank Jenks (Butch Broder).

Wild and Woolly (20th Century Fox, 1937). DIR Alfred Werker. SCR Lynn Root, Frank Fenton. CAM Harry Jackson. ED Al De Gaetano. MUS Samuel Kaylin. RUNNING TIME 65 min. CAST: **Jane Withers** (Arnette Flynn); Walter Brennan (Gramp Flynn); Pauline Moore (Ruth Morris); Carl "Alfalfa" Switzer (Zero); Jack Searl (Chaunce Ralston); Berton Churchill (Edward Ralston).

Can This Be Dixie? (20th Century Fox, 1937). DIR George Marshall. SCR Lamar Trotti (story by Lamar Trotti, George Marshall). CAM Bert Glennon, Ernest Palmer. ED Louis Loeffler. MUS Samuel Kaylin. RUNNING TIME 68 min. CAST: **Jane Withers** (Peg Gurgle); Slim Summerville (Robert Gurgle); Helen Wood (Virginia Peachtree); Thomas Beck (Ulysses S. Sherman); Sara Haden (Beauregard Peachtree); Claude Gillingwater (Col. Peachtree).

45 Fathers (20th Century Fox, 1937). DIR James Tinling. SCR Frances Hyland, Albert Ray (story by Mary Bickel, Edith Sparks). CAM Harry Jackson. ED Alex Troffey. MUS Samuel Kaylin. RUNNING TIME 71 min. CAST: **Jane Withers** (Judith Frazier); Thomas Beck (Roger Farragut); Louise Henry (Elizabeth Carter); The Hartmans (Joe & Flo McCoy); Richard Carle (Bunny Carothers); Nella Walker (Mrs. Carter).

Checkers (20th Century Fox, 1938). DIR H. Bruce Humberstone. SCR Lynn Root, Frank Fenton, Robert Chapin, Karen De Wolf (story by Lynn Root, Frank Fenton). CAM Daniel B. Clark. ED Jack Murray. MUS Samuel Kaylin. RUNNING TIME 78 min. CAST: **Jane Withers** (Checkers Judy); Edgar Connell (Stuart Erwin); Una Merkel (Mamie Appleby); Marvin Stephens (Jimmy Somers); Andrew Tombes (Tobias Williams); June Carlson (Sarah Williams).

Rascals (20th Century Fox, 1938). DIR H. Bruce Humberstone. SCR Robert Ellis, Helen Logan. CAM Edward Cronjager. ED Jack Murray. MUS Samuel Kaylin. RUNNING TIME 77 min. CAST: **Jane Withers** (Gypsy); Rochelle Hudson (Margaret Adams); Robert Wilcox (Tony); Borrah Minevitch (Gino); Minevitch Gang (Themselves); Steffi Duna (Stella).

Keep Smiling (20th Century Fox, 1938). DIR Herbert I. Leeds. SCR Frances Hyland, Albert Ray. CAM Edward Cronjager. ED Harry Reynolds. MUS Samuel Kaylin. RUNNING TIME 77 min. CAST: **Jane Withers** (Jane Rand); Gloria Stuart (Carol Walters); Henry Wilcoxon (Jonathan Rand); Helen Westley (Mrs. Willoughby); Jed Prouty (Jerome Lawson); Douglas Fowley (Cedric Hunt).

Always in Trouble (20th Century Fox, 1938). DIR Joseph Santley. SCR Karen De Wolf, Robert Chapin (story by Albert Treynor, Jeff Moffitt). CAM Lucien Andriot. ED Nick DeMaggio. MUS Samuel Kaylin. RUNNING TIME 70 min. CAST: **Jane Withers** (Jerry Darlington); Jean Rogers (Virginia Darlington); Arthur Treacher (Rogers); Robert Kellard (Pete Graham); Eddie Collins (Uncle Ed); Andrew Tombes (J. C. Darlington).

The Arizona Wildcat (20th Century Fox, 1939). DIR Herbert I. Leeds. SCR Barry Trivers, Jerry Cady. CAM Lucien Andriot. ED Fred Allen. MUS Samuel Kaylin. RUNNING TIME 69 min. CAST: **Jane Withers** (Mary Jane Patterson); Leo Carrillo (Manuel Hernandez); Pauline Moore (Caroline Reid); William Henry (Donald Clark); Henry Wilcoxon (Richard Baldwin).

Boy Friend (20th Century Fox, 1939). DIR James Tinling. SCR Joseph Hoffman, Barry Trivers (story by Lester Ziffren, Louis Moore). CAM Lucien Andriot. ED Norman Colbert. MUS Samuel Kaylin. RUNNING TIME 70 min. CAST: **Jane Withers** (Sally Murphy); Arleen Whelan (Sue Duffy); George Ernest (Billy Bradley); Douglas Fowley (Ed Boyd); Warren Hymer (Greenberg); Robert Kellard (Tommy Bradley).

Chicken Wagon Family (20th Century Fox, 1939). DIR Herbert I. Leeds. SCR Viola Brothers Shore (novel by John Barry Benefield). CAM Edward Cronjager. ED Fred Allen. MUS Samuel Kaylin. RUNNING TIME 64 min. CAST: **Jane Withers** (Addie Fippany); Leo Carrillo (Jean Paul Fippany); Marjorie Weaver (Cecile Fippany); Spring Byington (Josephine Fippany); Kane Richmond (Matt Hibbard); Hobart Cavanaugh (Henri Fippany).

Pack Up Your Troubles (20th Century Fox, 1939). DIR H. Bruce Humberstone. SCR Lou Breslow, Owen Francis. CAM Lucien Andriot. ED Nick DeMaggio. MUS Samuel Kaylin. RUNNING TIME 75 min. CAST: **Jane Withers** (Collette); The Ritz Brothers (Themselves); Lynn Bari (Yvonne); Joseph Schildkraut (Hugo Ludwig); Stanley Fields (Sgt. Walker); Fritz Leiber (Pierre Ferrand).

High School (20th Century Fox, 1940). DIR George Nichols, Jr. SCR Jack Jungmeyer, Edith Skouras, Harold Tarshis. CAM Lucien Andriot. ED Harry Reynolds. MUS Samuel Kaylin. RUNNING TIME 74 min. CAST: **Jane Withers** (Jane Wallace); Joe Brown, Jr. ("Slats" Roberts); Lloyd Corrigan (Dr. Henry Wallace); Claire Du Brey (Miss Huggins); Lynne Roberts (Carol Roberts); Paul Harvey (James Wallace).

Shooting High (20th Century Fox, 1940). DIR Alfred E. Green. SCR Lou Breslow, Owen Francis. CAM Ernest Palmer. ED Nick DeMaggio. MUS Samuel Kaylin. RUNNING TIME 65 min. CAST: **Jane Withers** (Jane Pritchard); Gene Autry (Will Carson); Marjorie Weaver (Marjorie Pritchard); Robert Lowery (Bob Merritt); Katharine Aldridge (Evelyn Trent); Hobart Cavanaugh (Clem Perkle).

The Girl from Avenue A (20th Century Fox, 1940). DIR Otto Brower. SCR Frances Hyland (play by Maude Fulton). CAM George Barnes, Lucien Andriot. ED Louis Loeffler. MUS Emil Newman. RUNNING TIME 73 min. CAST: **Jane Withers** (Jane); Kent Taylor (MacMillan Forrester); Katharine Aldridge (Lucy); Elyse Knox (Angela); Laura Hope Crews (Mrs. Forrester); Jessie Ralph (Mrs. Van Dyne).

Youth Will Be Served (20th Century Fox, 1940). DIR Otto Brower. SCR Wanda Tuchock (story by Ruth Fasken, Hilda Vincent). CAM Edward Cronjager. ED Nick DeMaggio. MUS Emil Newman. RUNNING TIME 66 min. CAST: **Jane Withers** (Edie May); Jane Darwell (Supervisor Stormer); Robert Conway (Bob Wilson); Elyse Knox (Pamela Wilson); Joe Brown, Jr. (Benjy); John Qualen (Clem Howie).

Golden Hoofs (20th Century Fox, 1941). DIR Lynn Shores. SCR Ben Grauman Kohn (story by Roy Chanslor, Thomas Langan). CAM Lucien Andriot. ED James B. Clark. MUS Cyril J. Mockridge. RUNNING TIME 67 min. CAST: **Jane Withers** (Jane Drake); Charles "Buddy" Rogers (Dean); Katharine Aldridge (Cornelia Hunt); George Irving (Timothy Drake); Buddy Pepper (Morty Witherspoon); Cliff Clark (Booth).

Her First Beau (Columbia, 1941). DIR Theodore Reed. PROD B. B. Kahane. SCR Gladys Lehman, Karen De Wolf (play by Florence Ryerson, Colin Clements). CAM George Meehan. ED Charles Nelson. MUS M. W. Stoloff. RUNNING TIME 77 min. CAST: **Jane Withers** (Penny Wood); Jackie Cooper (Chuck Harris); Edith Fellows (Milly Lou); Josephine Hutchinson (Mrs. Wood); William Tracy (Mervyn Roberts); Martha O'Driscoll (Julie Harris).

A Very Young Lady (20th Century Fox, 1941). DIR Harold Schuster. SCR Ladislas Fodor, Elaine Ryan (play by Ladislas Fodor). CAM Edward Cronjager. ED James B. Clark. MUS Cyril J. Mockridge. RUNNING TIME 80 min. CAST: **Jane Withers** (Kitty Russell); Nancy Kelly (Alice Carter); John Sutton (Dr. Meredith); Janet Beecher (Miss Steele); Richard Clayton (Tom Brighton); June Carlson (Madge).

Small Town Deb (20th Century Fox, 1941). DIR Harold Schuster. SCR Ethel Hill (story by **Jerrie Walters** [nom de plume of Jane Withers]). CAM Virgil Miller. ED Alexander Troffey. MUS Emil Newman. RUNNING TIME 72 min. CAST: **Jane Withers** (Patricia Randall); Jane Darwell (Katie); Bruce Edwards (Jack Richards); Cobina Wright (Helen Randall); Cecil Kellaway (Mr. Randall); Katharine Alexander (Mrs. Randall).

Young America (20th Century Fox, 1942). DIR Louis King. SCR Samuel G. Engel. CAM Glen MacWilliams, Lucien Andriot. ED Louis Loeffler. MUS Cyril J. Mockridge. RUNNING TIME 73 min. CAST: **Jane Withers** (Jane Campbell); Jane Darwell (Grandma Campbell); Lynne Roberts (Elizabeth Barnes); William Tracy (Earl Tucker); Robert Cornell (Jonathan Blake); Roman Bohnen (Mr. Barnes).

The Mad Martindales (20th Century Fox, 1942). DIR Alfred Werker. PROD Walter Morosco. SCR Francis Edwards Faragoh (play *Not for Children* by Wesley Towner). CAM Lucien Andriot. ED Nick DeMaggio. MUS Emil Newman. RUNNING TIME 65 min. CAST: **Jane Withers** (Kathy Martindale); Marjorie Weaver (Evelyn Martindale); Alan Mowbray (Hugo Martindale); Jimmy Lydon (Bobby); Byron Barr (Peter Varney); George Reeves (Julio Rigo).

Johnny Doughboy (Republic, 1942). DIR John H. Auer. SCR Lawrence Kimble (story by Frederick Kohner). CAM John Alton. ED Wallace Grissell, Edward Mann. MUS Walter Scharf. RUNNING TIME 63 min. CAST: **Jane Withers** (Ann/Penny); Henry Wilcoxon (Oliver Lawrence); Patrick Brook (Johnny Kelly); William Demarest (Harry Fabian); Ruth Donnelly (Biggsworth); Etta McDaniel (Mammy).

The North Star (RKO, 1943). DIR Lewis Milestone. PROD Samuel Goldwyn. SCR Lillian Hellman. CAM James Wong Howe. ED Daniel Mandell. RUNNING TIME 106 min. CAST: Anne Baxter (Marina); Dana Andrews (Kolya); Walter Huston (Dr. Kurin); Walter Brennan (Karp); Ann Harding (Sophia); **Jane Withers** (Claudia); Erich von Stroheim (Dr. von Harden).

My Best Gal (Republic, 1944). DIR Anthony Mann. SCR Olive Cooper, Earl Fenton (story by Richard Brooks). CAM Jack Marta. ED Ralph Dixon. MUS Morton Scott. RUNNING TIME 67 min. CAST: **Jane Withers** (Kitty O'Hara); Jimmy Lydon (Johnny McCloud); Frank Craven (Danny O'Hara); Fortunio Bonanova (Charlie); George Cleveland (Ralph Hodges); Franklin Pangborn (Mr. Porter).

Faces in the Fog (Republic, 1944). DIR John English. SCR Jack Townley. CAM Reggie Lanning. ED Tony Martinelli. MUS Richard Cherwin. RUNNING TIME 71 min. CAST: **Jane Withers** (Mary Elliott); Paul Kelly (Tom Elliott); Lee Patrick (Cora Elliott); John Litel (Dr. Fred Mason); Eric Sinclair (Joe Mason); Dorothy Peterson (Mrs. Mason).

Affairs of Geraldine (Republic, 1946). DIR George Blair. SCR John K. Butler (story by Lee Loeb, Arthur Strawn). CAM John Alton. ED Tony Martinelli. MUS Morton Scott. RUNNING TIME 68 min. CAST: **Jane Withers** (Geraldine Cooper); James Lydon (Willy Briggs); Raymond Walburn (Amos Hartwell); Donald Meek (Casper Millhouse); Charles Quigley (J. Edmund Roberts); Grant Withers (Henry Cooper).

Danger Street (Paramount, 1947). DIR Lew Landers. SCR Maxwell Shane, Winston Miller, Kae Salkow (story by Winston Miller, Kae Salkow). CAM Benjamin H. Kline. ED Howard Smith. MUS Darrell Calker. RUNNING TIME 66 min. CAST: **Jane Withers** (Pat Marvin); Robert Lowery (Larry Burke); Bill Edwards (Sandy Evans); Elaine Riley (Cynthia Van Loan); Audrey Young (Dolores Johnson); Lyle Talbot (Charles Johnson).

Giant (Warner Bros., 1956). DIR George Stevens. PROD George Stevens, Henry Ginsberg. SCR Fred Guiol, Ivan Moffat (novel by Edna Ferber). CAM William C. Mellor. ED William Hornbeck. MUS Dimitri Tiomkin. RUNNING TIME 168 min. CAST: Elizabeth Taylor (Leslie Benedict); Rock Hudson (Dick Benedict); James Dean (Jett Rink); Carroll Baker (Luz Benedict II); **Jane Withers** (Vashti Snythe); Chill Wills (Uncle Bawley).

The Right Approach (20th Century Fox, 1961). DIR David Butler. PROD Oscar Brodney. SCR Fay Kanin, Michael Kanin (play by Garson Kanin). CAM Sam Leavitt. ED Tom McAdoo. MUS Dominic Frontiere. RUNNING TIME 92 min. CAST: Frankie Vaughan (Leo Mack); Martha Hyer (Anne Perry); Juliet Prowse (Ursula Poe); Gary Crosby (Rip Hulett); David McLean (Bill Sikulovic); **Jane Withers** (Liz).

Captain Newman, M.D. (Universal, 1963). DIR David Miller. PROD Robert Arthur. SCR Richard Breen, Phoebe Ephron, Henry Ephron. CAM Russell Metty. ED Alma Macrorie. MUS Frank Skinner. RUNNING TIME 126 min. CAST: Gregory Peck (Capt. Newman); Tony Curtis (Corp. Laibowitz); Angie Dickinson (Lt. Corum); Bobby Darin (Corp. Tompkins); Eddie Albert (Col. Bliss); **Jane Withers** (Lt. Grace Blodgett).

The Hunchback of Notre Dame (Walt Disney Pictures, 1996). DIR Gary Trousdale, Kirk Wise. PROD Don Hahn. SCR Tab Murphy, Irene Mecchi, Bob Tzudiker, Noni White, Jonathan Roberts (story by Tab Murphy, novel *Notre Dame de Paris* by Victor Hugo). ED Ellen Keneshea. MUS Alan Menken. RUNNING TIME 85 min. Voices of: Tom Hulce (Quasimodo); Demi Moore (Esmeralda); Tony Jay (Judge Frollo); Kevin Kline (Capt. Phoebus); Paul Kandel (Clopin); Jason Alexander (Hugo); **Jane Withers** (additional dialogue Laverne).

Television Movies

All Together Now (1975). DIR Randal Kleiser. CAST: John Rubinstein; Glynnis O'Connor; Brad Savage; Helen Hunt; Dori Brenner; **Jane Withers** (Helen Drummond).

Video

The Hunchback of Notre Dame II (2001). Voices of: Tom Hulce; Demi Moore; Kevin Kline; Charles Kimbrough; **Jane Withers** (Laverne).

JANE WYATT

Jane Wyatt had a long, rewarding career as an actress. In the 1930s she played a leading part in *Lost Horizon*, followed by several "perfect wife" roles in the 1940s. In the 1950s she appeared as Margaret Anderson in one of America's most legendary television sitcoms, *Father Knows Best*, and in the six-year run she won three consecutive Emmy Awards. She kept working until the 1980s and triumphed once more as Mr. Spock's mother in *Star Trek: The Voyage Home* (1986), a role she had played previously in an episode of the original series.

Today, Miss Wyatt still lives in Los Angeles. Born in 1910 in New Jersey, she is a member of a renowned family. Miss Wyatt: "My family has lived in New York since the 17th century. My mother's family was Dutch, Van Rensselaer. It is still a big name in New York state. My father's family was English, they came over on the Mayflower." Two of her family members signed the Declaration of Independence and the Van Rensselaers were among the early Dutch settlers who at one point practically *owned* New York state.

She decided to become an actress when she was still a youngster, and was able to make it all the way to the New York stage in 1931 with *Give Me Yesterday*. Even though it was the Depression era, for Miss Wyatt one thing led to another: she appeared opposite actors like Louis Calhern and Charles Laughton, and was offered a contract by Carl Laemmle, Jr., Universal's president at the time, who had seen her in a Philip Barry play. Miss Wyatt: "I knew him very well. He was the one who came to New York, he recruited me personally and brought me out to Hollywood. I was in a play in New York and he'd take me out to dinner; I remember he always wanted champagne and half a pound of caviar. He was a sweet guy, he was the 'Prince of Universal,' but unfortunately he died a miserable death. When I first met him in New York, he was willing to give me a contract for the summer and then I'd come back to New York in the winter to do more plays. But it was not an interesting contract: they'd never have an important picture ready for you, so it didn't work out that way." However, Miss Wyatt did go out to Hollywood and stayed there.

"When I first went to Universal, back then there were those little cottages, the make-up room was in a former barn, there wasn't any floor in it, it was all pretty primitive. Coming from New York where you put your own make-up on before appearing on the stage, it was a big difference when I went to make-up at Universal. There was this guy who started to pull out my eyebrows. 'No no,' I said, 'stop! Stop!' 'Well, little girl,' he said, 'you don't know anything about make-up, do you? You have never been in the movies, I am the great Jack Pierce and I make up the greatest stars.' I looked up on the wall and there were pictures of Bela Lugosi, Boris Karloff, people like that [laughs]."

She made her screen debut in James Whale's powerful divorce drama *One More River* (1934). *Variety* wrote in its film review (April 14, 1934): "Jane Wyatt (out of legit) is an obvious find for the screen." As far as the film's stylish director was concerned, Miss Wyatt said, "I can't remember him giving me one piece of direction." In her next film *Great Expectations* (1934), she played the part of Estella, but it wasn't until *Lost Horizon* (1937) that she finally got recognized as a leading actress.

"I was under contract to Universal and at one time, they didn't have any picture for me; I was just sitting around and it drove me crazy. So they allowed me to do one outside picture. My agents saw they were casting for *Lost Horizon*; I did a test—there were a lot of actresses testing for the part, also some quite well-known people. I think one reason why I got the part was that I was a new actress, a fresh face, I had made only a couple of films by then. I didn't have any *name* or anything."

Lost Horizon is a splendid romantic fantasy, faithfully adapted from James Hilton's popular 1933 novel. It takes Ronald Colman[1] and his co-passengers of a crashed airplane to the beauty and the inner peace of the Valley of the Blue Moon in the Himalayan mountains which soon becomes their "Shangri-la," i.e. their own paradise on earth. Sam Jaffe played the High Lama, a former Belgian priest who had founded Shangri-la some three centuries before. Miss Wyatt: "*Lost Horizon* is still a wonderful picture. It has gotten better as it has gotten older. My character did not appear in the book, because in those days, the leading man wasn't supposed to fall in love with a half-caste character like the one Margo played, so they had to figure out how he could fall in love with a white girl. In the film you won't see any really dramatic scenes for this girl; she would be lying on the grass while they were talking to each other. It wasn't really an easy part to play, because there wasn't any scene with any plot in it, you know. It was a part without any character: I wasn't mean, I wasn't funny, they just had made it up. But I loved the picture. Ronald Colman was a wonderful actor to work with, he helped me a lot. He was a brilliant actor, a big star in the silent days, and he used his eyes marvelously: he used them to great advantage. Do you remember that scene when he decides to leave with his brother? It was an extraordinary acting scene and he played it all with his eyes. The film also brought the word Shangri-la into the English language."

Ronald Colman and Jane Wyatt in a publicity still for *Lost Horizon* (1938).

With a budget of $2,000,000 (half of Columbia's entire yearly budget), *Lost Horizon* became the studio's most expensive film up until then and the breathtaking Shangri-la set, built by Stephen

Goosson, was the largest set built in Hollywood. It took 150 workmen to finish the 1,000 feet long and almost 500 feet wide lamasery set. While James Hilton wrote the novel in only six weeks, it took director Frank Capra[2] nearly two years to finish the picture, for various reasons.

According to Miss Wyatt, Frank Capra used to handle studio boss Harry Cohn very well. "When Mr. Cohn came down on the set, Capra would say, 'Cut!' Then Harry Cohn would get so nervous that he'd finally leave the set: every minute the camera wasn't rolling, he was losing thousands of dollars, so he'd leave. But if he'd stayed on the set, he would have said things like, 'I don't like this, Frank, do it again.' Compared to other studios, at RKO, they were always getting through a new regime—I used to see Katharine Hepburn there all the time. But the Warners, Mr. Mayer and all those people *made* the big stars, there's no question about that. Dorothy McGuire[3] for example was a close friend of mine—her husband and my husband were in the same class at Harvard University—she had worked a lot with David O. Selznick and he chose just the right parts for her. When she was on her own, she often chose the *wrong* part for herself. I once asked Loretta Young, 'Loretta, why did Dorothy never become a big box-office star as you did?' She said, 'That's easy, Dorothy wanted to be an actress, I wanted to be a star.' Loretta Young was very smart, very astute. She knew exactly which way to go and she was right, she was quite frank about it."

Dorothy McGuire

Miss Wyatt also worked with other original and creative directors. She appeared in *Gentleman's Agreement* (1947) and *Boomerang* (1947), both directed by Elia Kazan. "Frank Capra was a darling man, a wonderful director, who allowed an actor to be himself and to expand, but from an actor's point of view, he wasn't like Elia Kazan: Elia was really into acting and could light up a scene for you. Frank Capra let you do the scene, and then he'd say, 'Well, this isn't good, this isn't right.'' Kazan always had the scene planned in his head and he'd tell you ahead of time exactly what he really wanted. It was more stimulating to work with a man like him."

Gentleman's Agreement starring Gregory Peck and Dorothy McGuire was a filmization of Laura Z. Hobson's novel dealing with anti-Semitism; back then it was a brave and daring approach to the subject. Miss Wyatt: "Kazan called me and said, 'Jane, it isn't a big part, but you would be perfect for it, because you and Dorothy McGuire look like sisters and I want you to play sisters.'" The film won several Academy Awards, including for best picture, best director, and best supporting actress (for Celeste Holm).

Throughout the 1940s Miss Wyatt played several leading and supporting roles in highly interesting and entertaining pictures. One of them was *None but the Lonely Heart* (1944), directed by playwright Clifford Odets, starring Cary Grant and a lot of actors of the Group Theatre. "Cary Grant was wonderful and great fun to work with, although the film was never much of a success. I remember one day things were pretty boring on the set and he said, 'Oh well, I'll

Loretta Young (1913–2000), leading screen actress during the 1930s and 1940s.

just walk on my hands.' So he walked on his hands [laughs]." Other films include Kazan's powerful semi-documentary *Boomerang* (1947), with Miss Wyatt as Dana Andrews' wife, and the André de Toth's *Pitfall* (1948), a suspenseful and melodramatic film noir, in which Miss Wyatt's husband Dick Powell has to deal with femme fatale Lizabeth Scott.

In October 1947, when Hollywood was suffering badly from the inquiries of the House Un-American Activities Committee, Miss Wyatt showed her braveness by accompanying actors like Danny Kaye, Paul Henreid, Humphrey Bogart, Lauren Bacall, John Huston, Gene Kelly, June Havoc, Geraldine Brooks, Sterling Hayden, Richard Conte and Marsha Hunt, when they flew to Washington to protest against the hearings and oppose the inquiries. The plane trip was organized by the Committee for the First Amendment ("a non-political organization campaigning only for honesty, fairness and the accepted rights of any American citizen") and got a lot of attention at the several stops made on its way to Washington. A number of those actors were blacklisted later on and couldn't find a job in Hollywood anymore. Miss Wyatt: "My agent called me one day and said, 'Look, I don't understand it. I had this deal all signed, and they just pulled out!'" After finishing *Criminal Lawyer* (1951) with Pat O'Brien, she decided to move to New York to avoid the blacklisting. She started a new career as a celebrated TV actress and did an awful lot of live television there. A couple of years later she was asked to return to Los Angeles and play the leading role in landmark comedy TV series, *Father Knows Best*, about an average American family living in Springfield. Robert Young played Jim, Miss Wyatt was his wife Margaret and they had three children.

Miss Wyatt: "*Father Knows Best* was a milestone in American television. I still see the two oldest children, Billy Gray and Elinor Donahue, all the time. At the time of the filming they were 16 or 17 and played my children; now we all seem to be the same age [laughs]. Robert Young was a very nice man to work with, very conscientious. He always knew his lines perfectly when he came on the set. There was a very strict discipline on our set, you weren't allowed to change one line in the dialogue. The producer had stacks of scripts all around his office and I once asked him, 'What are those?' He said, 'Those are the scripts for the first 15 weeks.' He was planning far ahead, that was incredible.

"With *Father Knows Best* we shot several days a week. You arrived at the studio, let's say at six o'clock in the morning, you said 'good morning' to the guard at the gate at Columbia studios where the series was shot—back then the studio was called Screen Gems—and you went to the make-up man. We had the same make-up man during all of those six years. We had the same crew, the same actors and we only had two directors. But when you're fortunate to work a lot in the movies or for television, you also do have to wait a lot in between on the set—that's a hard thing to get through. That's when I started studying Spanish so I could talk to the people at the gas station and places like that, because they speak Spanish here all the time and all over the place. I also read the Old Testament from the beginning till the end. Gary Cooper always went to sleep on the set: he would fall asleep just sitting in his chair, he'd be *sound* asleep. Then they'd call him, he'd shake himself, he'd get up and go to work.

"The first year of *Father Knows Best* was not so interesting for me, because they were using the old scripts from the radio shows and the best parts there were for Robert Young and Billy Gray, so I had very little to do. But in the second and in the third year my character had become very interesting."

Father Knows Best was a very good example of filmed television and there could be as many takes as needed or as the cast and crew wished. Live television, which Miss Wyatt had done in New York quite extensively, can be compared with working on the stage: if something went wrong, it was impossible to go back and fix it, there was *no* second take. The actors played their parts in front of the cameras *and* in front of this huge television audience which made it very exciting. Miss Wyatt enjoyed that thoroughly: the tension on the set, the countdown before getting live on the air when nothing could be changed anymore. She also remembers that at that time, live television was done in brand-new, fully air-conditioned studios in New York. For most of the big shows, they used five cameras on wheels (crab dolleys), they could wheel around and follow the actors everywhere. When she returned to Hollywood to do *Father Knows Best*, she was shocked to see how far behind the times the studios were: the sound stages were freezing in winter and boiling hot in summer, they were dirty and the cameras couldn't move. When they did a shot in which the actors were walking down the street, the camera was put on tracks that were laid down on the stage. As an actor, you could only walk in a straight line, and all the time you had to cope with the tracks. Making it look natural was not easy. Furthermore the crew were mostly older men that she had worked with 20 years before, whereas the people she worked with in New York were in their twenties or early thirties, and had started their careers with the newly invented TV cameras, the lights were easy to work with, everything went very smoothly. Miss Wyatt concludes: "Here in Hollywood, they said, 'Television isn't going to last,' but they didn't do anything about it: they had this *old* equipment, they were still using things that live television had abandoned."

When shooting a film, it often happened that the final scene of the film was the first one to be shot—for practical reasons—which made it very difficult as the actors didn't have the chance to do the script all the way through. Miss Wyatt: "That was one of the things I liked

Actress Geraldine Brooks (1925–1977) was one of the stars who flew to Washington to protest against the anti–Communist hearings and oppose the inquiries. In 1964 she married screenwriter and novelist Budd Schulberg (more information: interview Samuel Goldwyn, Jr., note 5).

Jane Wyatt (left) and Ann Blyth in *Our Very Own* (1950). (Courtesy of DOCIP Film Archive, Brussels, Belgium.)

best in live television: you begin at the beginning, and go right straight to the end. Everybody's nervous, everybody's in a rush, the wardrobe people have to get your clothes on and off in time, you have to *run run run* to get to the next set, that was always very exciting to me. And if the gun didn't go off, you were stuck there on the screen, nobody was going to help you.

"Looking back, *Father Knows Best* was quite celebrated and famous. *Lost Horizon* will go on forever. But on the stage I never got into a play that lasted more than a season, although they were plays by Clifford Odets or Somerset Maugham. But when I appeared on the stage, the Depression was not quite over and then we had a time when all the banks failed, it was a terrible time for the theater. I think the last play I did in New York was *Autumn Garden* by Lillian Hellman. I didn't like my part in it, but it was an important play and Fredric March was extremely good in it."

What about the actors now? Miss Wyatt: "I think the young actors today are awfully good, but there are no big stars like Gary Cooper or Ronald Colman. If you saw those men walking down the street, you knew them right away, even looking at their backs. The same thing with Henry Fonda, he had a strange way of walking, it was so distinctive, I don't think that is true now. I suppose it is because we don't have a studio like MGM to build them up to be big stars. If you take someone like Harrison Ford, he's a *wonderful* actor, but you won't easily recognize him in the street, his face isn't very distinctive. If I would see him in a restaurant,

I'm not sure that I'd recognize him, but you couldn't miss Gary Cooper, Ronald Colman, Jimmy Stewart or any of those people. They were stronger personalities, they were *always* very gracious and when it was your time to shine, they always let you have the whole thing. They never tried to grab it and keep it for themselves. I admired them.

"I still get a lot of fan mail for *Lost Horizon*, but it is very strange, most of my fan mail now is because of Star Trek, simply because I once played the mother of Mr. Spock. In the television series, I had a big part. Much later, I was in just one of the pictures [*Star Trek IV: The Voyage Home*, 1986] in a part I would call a cameo. I get a *lot* of mail, just because I played *the mother of*. It was a really big surprise, that such a small part could be that important, but those Trekkies are amazing. They have those big conventions and I once went to one of them. There were Trekkies coming from all over the world. The French people all got dressed up in Star Trek clothes and I had to stand up on the stage of this huge theater and answer their questions. Now, I didn't know too much about Star Trek, but I got through it all right. My little grandson had told me a lot about Star Trek that I didn't know. Trekkies know *everything*. When I got almost off the stage, I heard, 'One more question!' So I turned back and the question was, 'Miss Wyatt, what did it feel like to make love to a Vulcan'—I played a human who was married to a Vulcan. Well, I went dead white, what would I say to this question? [laughs]. So I suddenly said, 'I am not the kind of girl that kisses and tells' [laughs]. I was never so glad to get off the stage!

Henry Fonda in a scene from *A Big Hand for the Little Lady* (1966).

"Leonard Nimoy, who played Mr. Spock, used to live right across the street here for years. He also directed the film, but I don't think it is such a good idea to direct and act in the same picture. When we were doing a scene together, he'd be all over the place. When I was speaking to him, he was checking the lights or whatever to see if everything was right, but he wasn't looking at me, he wasn't concentrating on the scene.

"But I never regretted leaving New York in the 1930s and coming out to Hollywood. Once I settled down here, I began to garden and I loved it out here. I didn't think I'd ever go back to New York. I also did plays here in Los Angeles. In fact, the last play I did was *Driving Miss Daisy*. There are only two people in the play, the audience has to imagine the others. When driving the car, there were just four chairs on a platform—the driver sat in front and I sat on the chair behind him. It was real fun to do that. I think the play is much better than the picture. You really had to *act* the old age—there was no way you could change your wig for instance. I had to age 40 years without leaving the stage—that's difficult."

Still, Miss Wyatt, a most charming lady at age 91, is one of the very few actresses to conquer both films and television, and in between she was an experienced and skilled stage actress, which is more than a remarkable achievement.

Interview: Los Angeles, February 13, 2002

Notes

1. Ronald Colman (1891–1958) began his screen career in his native Great Britain, but arrived in the U.S. in 1920. There, Lillian Gish and director Henry King spotted him in a play (*La Tendresse*) and chose him as her leading man in *The White Sister* (1923). He soon became one of the most distinguished leading actors in American films and won an Academy Award for his dual role in *A Double Life* (1947). Other films include *Stella Dallas* (1925), *Beau Geste* (1926), *Bulldog Drummond* (1929), *The Prisoner of Zenda* (1937), *The Late George Apley* (1947) and his final film, *The Story of Mankind* (1957).
2. Frank Capra (1897–1991), three-time Academy Award winner as best director for *It Happened One Night* (1934), *Mr. Deeds Goes to Town* (1936) and *You Can't Take It with You* (1938), is considered to be one of the best directors ever, with other and equally impressive classics such as *Lady for a Day* (1933), *Lost Horizon* (1937), *Mr. Smith Goes to Washington* (1939), *Meet John Doe* (1941), *Arsenic and Old Lace* (1944), *It's a Wonderful Life* (1946), *State of the Union* (1948), *A Hole in the Head* (1959) and *A Pocketful of Miracles* (1961) to his credit. His autobiography *The Name Above the Title* was published in 1971. His son Frank Capra, Jr. (b. 1934), is a producer whose films include *The Black Marble* (1980), *An Eye for an Eye* (1981) and *Firestarter* (1984). Grandson Frank Capra III (b. 1959) has been an assistant director and producer since the early 1980s. In recent years he has worked on films such as *Ghosts of Mississippi* (1996), *Bulworth* (1998), *The Deep End of the Ocean* (1999) and *The Story of Us* (1999).
3. Dorothy McGuire (1916–2001) made her acting debut at age 13 opposite Henry Fonda at the Omaha Community Playhouse. She first appeared on Broadway in 1938 and five years later, David O. Selznick introduced her to movie audiences in *Claudia*, in which she reprised the role she had played on the Broadway stage. She was nominated for an Academy Award for best actress for her work in *Gentleman's Agreement*. Her many other screen highlights include Robert Siodmak's Hitchcock-like thriller *The Spiral Staircase* (1946, as the mute servant), *I Want You* (1951), *Three Coins in the Fountain* (1954), *Friendly Persuasion* (1956), *A Summer Place* (1959), *The Dark at the Top of the Stairs* (1960, as Robert Preston's wife), *Swiss Family Robinson* (1960) and *The Greatest Story Ever Told* (1965, as the Virgin Mary). She is the mother of actress Topo Swope.

Filmography

One More River (Universal, 1934). DIR James Whale. PROD Carl Laemmle, Jr. SCR R. C. Sherriff (novel by John Galsworthy). CAM John J. Mescall. ED Ted J. Kent. MUS W. Franke Harling. RUNNING TIME 85 min. CAST: Diana Wynyard (Claire); Frank Lawton (Tony); Mrs. Patrick Campbell (Aunt Em); **Jane Wyatt** (Dinny Cherrell); Colin Clive (Sir Gerald Corven); Reginald Denny (David Dornford).

Great Expectations (Universal, 1934). DIR Stuart Walker. PROD Stanley Bergerman. SCR Gladys Unger (novel by Charles Dickens). CAM George Robinson. ED Edward Curtiss. MUS Edward Ward. RUNNING TIME 100 min. CAST: Henry Hull (Abel Magwitch); Phillips Holmes (Pip); **Jane Wyatt** (Estella); Florence Reed (Miss Havisham); Alan Hale (Joe Gargery); Rafaela Ottiano (Mrs. Joe).

We're Only Human (RKO, 1935). DIR James Flood. PROD Edward Kaufman. SCR Rian James (story by Thomas Walsh). CAM J. Roy Hunt. ED Archie Marsheck. MUS Roy Webb. RUNNING TIME 67 min. CAST: Preston Foster (Pete McCaffrey); **Jane Wyatt** (Sally Rogers); James Gleason (Danny Walsh); Arthur Hohl (John Martin); John Arledge (Johnny O'Brien); Jane Darwell (Mrs. Walsh).

The Luckiest Girl in the World (Universal, 1936). DIR Edward Buzzell. SCR Herbert Fields, Henry Myers (story by Ann Jordan). CAM Merrit B. Gerstad. ED Dorothy Spencer. MUS Heinz Roemheld. RUNNING TIME 69 min. CAST: **Jane Wyatt** (Pat Duncan); Louis Hayward (Anthony McClellan); Nat Pendleton (Dugan); Eugene Pallette (Campbell); Catherine Doucet (Mrs. Duncan); Jason Robards, Sr. (Waiter).

Lost Horizon (Columbia, 1937). DIR-PROD Frank Capra. SCR Robert Riskin (novel by James Hilton). CAM Joseph Walker. ED Gene Havlick, Gene Milford. MUS Dimitri Tiomkin. RUNNING TIME 138 min. CAST: Ronald Colman (Robert Conway); **Jane Wyatt** (Sondra); John Howard (George Conway); Margo (Maria); Thomas Mitchell (Henry Barnard); Edward Everett Horton (Alexander P. Lovett); H. B. Warner (Chang); Sam Jaffe (High Lama).

Girl from God's Country (Republic, 1940). DIR Sidney Salkow. SCR Malcolm Stuart Boylan, Robert Lee Johnson, Elizabeth Meehan (story by Ray Milholland). CAM Jack A. Marta. ED William Morgan. MUS Cy Feuer. RUNNING TIME 75 min. CAST: Clem Bevens (Ben); Charles Bickford (Bill Bogler); John Bleifer (Ninimook); Ferike Boros (Mrs. Broken Thumb); Spencer Charters (Dealer); **Jane Wyatt** (Anne Webster).

Hurricane Smith (Republic, 1941). DIR Bernard Vorhaus. SCR Robert Presnell (story by Charles G. Booth). CAM Ernest Miller. ED Murray Seldeen. MUS Cy Feuer. RUNNING TIME 68 min. CAST: Ray Middleton (Bill "Hurricane" Smith); **Jane Wyatt** (Joan Blair Smith); Harry Davenport (Robert); J. Edward Bromberg (Bonelli); Henry Brandon (Sam Carson); Casey Johnson (Johnny Smith).

Weekend for Three (RKO, 1941). DIR Irving Reiss. PROD Tay Garnett. SCR Dorothy Parker, Alan Campbell (story by Budd Schulberg). CAM Russell Metty. ED Desmond Marquette. MUS Roy Webb. RUNNING TIME 66 min. CAST: Dennis O'Keefe (Jim Craig); **Jane Wyatt** (Ellen Graig); Phillip Reed (Randy); Edward Everett Horton (Stonebraker); ZaSu Pitts (Anna); Franklin Pangborn (Number Seven).

Kisses for Breakfast (Warner Bros., 1941). DIR Lewis Seiler. SCR Kenneth Gamet (play *The Matrimonial Bed* by Seymour Hicks, based on the French play *Au Premier de Ces Messieurs* by Yves Mirande, André Mouézy-Éon). CAM Arthur Edeson. ED James Gibbon. MUS Adolph Deutsch. RUNNING TIME 81 min. CAST: Dennis Morgan (Rodney Trask); **Jane Wyatt** (Laura Anders); Shirley Ross (Juliet Marsden); Lee Patrick (Betty Trent); Jerome Cowan (Lucius Lorimer).

The Navy Comes Through (RKO, 1942). DIR A. Edward Sutherland. PROD Islin Auster. SCR Roy Chanslor, Aeneas MacKenzie (story by Bordon Chase). CAM Nicholas Musuraca. ED Samuel E. Beetley. MUS Roy Webb. RUNNING TIME 82 min. CAST: Pat O'Brien (Michael Mallory); George Murphy (Lt. Sands); **Jane Wyatt** (Myra Mallory); Jackie Cooper (Joe "Babe" Dudson); Carl Esmond (Richard "Dutch" Kroner); Max Baer (Berringer); Desi Arnaz (Tarriba).

Army Surgeon (RKO, 1942). DIR A. Edward Sutherland. PROD Bert Gilroy. SCR Barry Trivers, Emmet Lavery. CAM Russell Metty. ED Samuel E. Beetley. MUS Roy Webb. RUNNING TIME 62 min. CAST: James Ellison (Capt. James Mason); **Jane Wyatt** (Beth Ainsley); Kent Taylor (Lt. Harvey); Walter Reed (Bill); James Burke (Brooklyn).

The Kansan (United Artists, 1943). DIR George Archainbaud. PROD Harry Sherman. SCR Harold Shumate (novel *Peace Marshal* by Frank Gruber). CAM Russell Harlan. ED Carrol Lewis. MUS Gerard Carbonara. RUNNING TIME 82 min. CAST: Richard Dix (John Bonniwell); **Jane Wyatt** (Eleanor Sager); Albert Dekker (Steve Barat); Eugene Pallette (Tom Waggoner); Victor Jory (Jeff Barat).

Buckskin Frontier (United Artists, 1943). DIR Lesley Selander. PROD Harry Sherman. SCR Norman Houston (novel *Buckskin Empire* by Harry Sinclair Drago). CAM Russell Harlan. ED Sherman A. Rose. MUS Victor Young. RUNNING TIME 76 min. CAST: Richard Dix (Stephen Brent); **Jane Wyatt** (Vinnie Marr); Albert Dekker (Gideon Skene); Lee J. Cobb (Jeptha Marr); Victor Jory (Champ Clanton).

None but the Lonely Heart (RKO, 1944). DIR Clifford Odets. PROD David Hempstead. SCR Clifford Odets (novel by Richard Llewellyn). CAM George Barnes. ED Roland Gross. MUS Hans Eisler. RUNNING TIME 112 min. CAST: Cary Grant (Ernest Verdun "Ernie" Mott); Ethel Barrymore (Ma Mott); Barry Fitzgerald (Henry Twite); June Duprez (Ada); **Jane Wyatt** (Aggie Hunter); Dan Duryea (Lew Tate).

The Bachelor's Daughters (United Artists, 1946). DIR-PROD-SCR Andrew L. Stone. CAM Theodore Sparkuhl. ED Duncan Mansfield. MUS Heinz Roemheld. RUNNING TIME 90 min. CAST: Gail Russell (Eileen McFarland); Claire Trevor (Cynthia); Ann Dvorak (Terry Wilson); Adolphe Menjou (Alexander Moody); Billie Burke (Molly Burns); **Jane Wyatt** (Marta).

Strange Conquest (Universal, 1946). DIR John Rawlins. PROD Marshall Grant. SCR Roy Chanslor (story by Lester Cole, Carl Dreher). CAM Charles Van Enger. ED Philip Cahn. MUS Paul Sawtell. RUNNING TIME 63 min. CAST: **Jane Wyatt** (Dr. Mary Palmer); Lowell Gilmore (Paul Harris); Julie Bishop (Virginia Sommers); Peter Cookson (William Sommers); Milburn Stone (Bert Morrow).

Gentleman's Agreement (20th Century Fox, 1947). DIR Elia Kazan. PROD Darryl F. Zanuck. SCR Moss Hart (novel by Laura Z. Hobson). CAM Arthur Miller. ED Harmon Jones. MUS Alfred Newman. RUNNING TIME 118 min. CAST: Gregory Peck (Philip Schuyler Green); Dorothy McGuire (Kathy Lacy); John Garfield (Dave Goldman); Celeste Holm (Anne Dettrey); Anne Revere (Mrs. Green); **Jane Wyatt** (Jane); Dean Stockwell (Tommy Green).

Boomerang! (20th Century Fox, 1947). DIR Elia Kazan. PROD Louis de Rochemont. SCR Richard Murphy (story *The Perfect Case* by Anthony Abbot). CAM Norbert Brodine. ED Harmon Jones. MUS Alfred Newman. RUNNING TIME 87 min. CAST: Dana Andrews (Henry L. Harvey); **Jane Wyatt** (Madge Harvey); Lee J. Cobb (Chief Robinson); Cara Williams (Irene Nelson); Arthur Kennedy (John Waldron); Sam Levene (Dave Woods).

Pitfall (United Artists, 1948). DIR André De Toth. PROD Samuel Bischoff. SCR Karl Kamb (novel by Jay Dratler). CAM Harry Wild. ED Walter Thompson. MUS Louis Forbes. RUNNING TIME 85 min. CAST: Dick Powell (John Forbes); Lizabeth Scott (Mona Stevens); **Jane Wyatt** (Sue Forbes); Raymond Burr (J. B. MacDonald); John Litel (DA); Byron Barr (Bill Smiley).

No Minor Vices (MGM, 1948). DIR-PROD Lewis Milestone. SCR Arnold Manoff (also story). CAM George Barnes. ED Robert Parrish. MUS Franz Waxman. RUNNING TIME 96 min. CAST: Dana Andrews (Perry Aswell); Lilli Palmer (April Aswell); Louis Jourdan (Octavio Quaglini); **Jane Wyatt** (Miss Darlington); Norman Lloyd (Dr. Sturdivant).

Bad Boy (Allied Artists, 1949). DIR Kurt Neumann. PROD Paul Short. SCR Robert D. Andrews (story by Robert D. Andrews, Paul Short). CAM Karl Struss. ED William Austin. MUS Paul Sawtell. RUNNING TIME 85 min. CAST: Lloyd Nolan (Marshall Brown); **Jane Wyatt** (Mrs. Brown); James Gleason (Chief); Stanley Clements (Bitsy Johnson); Martha Vickers (Lila Strawn); Audie Murphy (Danny Lester).

Task Force (Warner Bros., 1949). DIR-SCR Delmer Daves. PROD Jerry Wald. CAM Robert Burks, Wilfrid M. Cline. ED Alan Crosland, Jr. MUS Franz Waxman. RUNNING TIME 115 min. CAST: Gary Cooper (Jonathan

L. Scott); **Jane Wyatt** (Mary); Wayne Morris (McKinney); Walter Brennan (Pete Richard); Julie London (Barbara McKinney); Bruce Bennett (McCluskey).

Canadian Pacific (20th Century Fox, 1949). DIR Edwin L. Marin. PROD Nat Holt. SCR Jack DeWitt, Kenneth Gamet (story by Jack DeWitt). CAM Fred Jackman, Jr. ED Philip Martin. MUS Dimitri Tiomkin. RUNNING TIME 95 min. CAST: Randolph Scott (Tom Andrews); **Jane Wyatt** (Edith Cabot); J. Carroll Naish (Dynamite Dawson); Victor Jory (Dirk Rourke); Nancy Olson (Cecille Gauthier).

House by the River (Republic, 1950). DIR Fritz Lang. PROD Howard Welsch. SCR Mel Dinelli (novel by A. P. Herbert). CAM Edward Cronjager. ED Arthur D. Hilton. MUS George Antheil. RUNNING TIME 88 min. CAST: Louis Hayward (Stephen Byrne); **Jane Wyatt** (Marjorie Byrne); Lee Bowman (John Byrne); Dorothy Patrick (Emily Gaunt); Ann Shoemaker (Mrs. Ambrose); Jody Gilbert (Flora Bantam).

Our Very Own (RKO, 1950). DIR Dave Miller. PROD Samuel Goldwyn. SCR F. Hugh Herbert. CAM Lee Garmes. ED Sherman Todd. MUS Victor Young. RUNNING TIME 92 min. CAST: Ann Blyth (Gail Macauley); Farley Granger (Chuck); Joan Evans (Joan); **Jane Wyatt** (Lois Macaulay); Ann Dvorak (Mrs. Lynch); Natalie Wood (Penny Macauley).

My Blue Heaven (20th Century Fox, 1950). DIR Henry Koster. PROD Sol C. Siegel. SCR Lamar Trotti, Claude Binyon (story by S. K. Lauren). CAM Arthur E. Arling. ED James B. Clark. MUS Alfred Newman. RUNNING TIME 96 min. CAST: Betty Grable (Kitty Moran); Dan Dailey (Jack Moran); David Wayne (Walter Pringle); **Jane Wyatt** (Janet Pringle); Mitzi Gaynor (Gloria Adams); Una Merkel (Irma).

The Man Who Cheated Himself (20th Century Fox, 1950). DIR Felix E. Feist. PROD Jack M. Warner. SCR Seton I. Miller, Philip MacDonald (story by Seton I. Miller). CAM Russell Harlan. ED David M. Weishart. MUS Louis Forbes. RUNNING TIME 80 min. CAST: Lee J. Cobb (Ed Cullen); John Dall (Andy Cullen); **Jane Wyatt** (Lois Frazer); Lisa Howard (Janet); Alan Wells (Nito Capa).

Criminal Lawyer (Columbia, 1951). DIR Seymour Friedman. PROD Rudolph C. Folthow. SCR Harold Greene. CAM Philip Tannura. ED Charles Nelson. RUNNING TIME 74 min. CAST: Pat O'Brien (James Regan); **Jane Wyatt** (Maggie Powell); Carl Benton Reid (Tucker Bourne); Mary Castle (Gloria Lydendecker); Robert Shayne (Clark Simmons).

Interlude (Universal, 1957). DIR Douglas Sirk. PROD Ross Hunter. SCR Daniel Fuchs, Franklin Coen (adaptation by Inez Cocke, based on the screenplay of *When Tomorrow Comes* [1939] by Dwight Taylor, story "A Modern Cinderella" by James M. Cain). CAM William Daniels. ED Russell F. Schoengarth. MUS Frank Skinner. RUNNING TIME 90 min. CAST: June Allyson (Helen Banning); Rossano Brazzi (Toni Fischer); Marianne Cook (Reni Fischer); Françoise Rosay (Countess Reinhart); **Jane Wyatt** (Prue Stubbins).

Two Little Bears (20th Century Fox, 1961). DIR Randall Hood. PROD George W. George. SCR George W. George (story by George W. George, Judy George). CAM Floyd Crosby. ED Carl Pierson. MUS Henry Vars. RUNNING TIME 81 min. CAST: Eddie Albert (Harry Davis); **Jane Wyatt** (Anne Davis); Brenda Lee (Tina Davis); Soupy Sales (Officer McGovern); Butch Patrick (Billy Davis).

Never Too Late (Warner Bros., 1965). DIR Bud Yorkin. PROD Norman Lear. SCR Sumner Arthur Long (also play). CAM Philip Lathrop. ED William Ziegler. MUS David Rose. RUNNING TIME 105 min. CAST: Paul Ford (Harry Lambert); Connie Stevens (Kate Clinton); Maureen O'Sullivan (Edith Lambert); Jim Hutton (Charlie Clinton); **Jane Wyatt** (Grace Kimbrough).

Treasure of Matecumbe (Buena Vista, 1976). DIR Vincent McEveety. PROD Bill Anderson. SCR Don Tait (novel *A Journey to Matecumbe* by Robert Lewis Taylor). CAM Frank Phillips. ED Cotton Warburton. MUS Buddy Baker. RUNNING TIME 117 min. CAST: Robert Foxworth (Jim); Joan Hackett (Lauriette Paxton); Peter Ustinov (D. Ewing T. Snodgrass); Vic Morrow (Spangler); Johnny Doran (Davie); **Jane Wyatt** (Aunt Effie).

Star Trek IV: The Voyage Home (Paramount, 1986). DIR Leonard Nimoy. PROD Harve Bennett. SCR Harve Bennett, Steve Meerson, Peter Krikes, Nicholas Meyer (story by Leonard Nimoy, Harve Bennett; based on the TV series *Star Trek* created by Gene Roddenberry). CAM Don Peterman. ED Peter E. Berger. MUS Leonard Rosenman. RUNNING TIME 119 min. CAST: William Shatner (Admiral/Capt. James T. Kirk); Leonard Nimoy (Capt. Spock); DeForest Kelley (Leonard McCoy); James Doohan (Capt. Scott); **Jane Wyatt** (Amanda Grayson).

Television Movies

See How They Run (1964). DIR David Lowell Rich. CAST: John Forsythe; Senta Berger; **Jane Wyatt** (Augusta Flanders); Pamela Franklin; Franchot Tone; Leslie Nielsen; George Kennedy.

Weekend of Terror (1970). DIR Jud Taylor. CAST: Robert Conrad; Lee Majors; Carol Linley; Lois Nettleton; **Jane Wyatt** (Sister Frances); Ann Doran.

You'll Never See Me Again (1973). DIR Jeannot Szwarc. CAST: David Hartman; **Jane Wyatt** (Mary Alden); Ralph Meeker; Jess Walton; Ben Gazzara.

Tom Sawyer (1973). DIR James Neilson. CAST: Josh Albee; Jeff Tyler; Buddy Ebsen; **Jane Wyatt** (Aunt Polly); Vic Morrow; John McGiver.

Katherine (1975). DIR Jeremy Paul Kagan. CAST: Sissy Spacek; Art Carney; Henry Winkler; Julie Kavner; **Jane Wyatt** (Emily Alman).

Amelia Earhart (1976). DIR George Schaefer. CAST: Susan Clark; John Forsyth; Stephen Macht; Susan Oliver; Catherine Burns; **Jane Wyatt** (Amy Earhart).

A Love Affair: The Eleanor and Lou Gehrig Story (1978). DIR Fielder Cook. CAST: Blythe Danner; Edward Herrmann; Gerald S. O'Loughlin; Ramon Bieri; **Jane Wyatt** (Eleanor's Mother); Patricia Neal.

Superdome (1978). DIR Jerry Jameson. CAST: David Janssen; Edie Adams; Clifton Davies; Van Johnson; Donna Mills; **Jane Wyatt** (Fay Bonelli); Tom Selleck.

The Nativity (1978). DIR Bernard L. Kowalski. CAST: Madeleine Stowe; John Shea; **Jane Wyatt** (Anna); Leo McKern; John Rhys-Davies.

The Millionaire (1978). DIR Don Weis. CAST: Martin Balsam; Edward Albert; Ralph Bellamy; **Jane Wyatt** (Mrs. Mathews); William Demarest.

Missing Children: A Mother's Story (1982). DIR Dick Lowry. CAST: Richard A. Dysart; Kate Capshaw; **Jane Wyatt** (Judge Eloise Walker); Scatman Crothers.

Amityville: The Evil Escapes (1989). DIR Sandor Stern. CAST: Patty Duke; **Jane Wyatt** (Alice Leacock); Fredric Lehne; Lou Hancock; Norman Lloyd.

Simisola (1995). DIR Jim Goddard. CAST: George Baker; Christopher Ravenscroft; Jane Lapotaire; George Harris; **Jane Wyatt** (Newsreader).

FRED ZINNEMANN

I met film director Fred Zinnemann for the first time at his London office in April 1993; he had been living there for about 30 years after having spent several decades on the West Coast. Although he was born in Vienna, he spent the greater part of his career in America where he became one of the top men in his craft. He won a total of five Oscars and among his most impressive films, there are classics including *The Search* (1948), *High Noon* (1952), *From Here to Eternity* (1953), the musical *Oklahoma!* (1955), *The Nun's Story* (1959), *A Man for All Seasons* (1966) and, one of his final films, *Julia* (1977).

At the time, I was stunned to see that such an august film monument as Mr. Zinnemann was seemingly neglected, overlooked, nearly *ignored*, by audiences and film critics. He just lived quietly in London and enjoyed his retirement and the company of his many close friends (also from the film industry). As I entered his office, he was definitely not the tallest and physically the most impressive film personality I had ever met, but behind this "façade" there was a very intelligent man with a wonderful memory and he had, so to speak, a third eye for the tiniest details. It felt great to shake hands with the man who film-wise strongly influenced my youth: growing up with a large number of his movies, he broadened my horizon and showed me what the possibilities were of the art he still knew inside out.

In 1929 he arrived in Hollywood where he first started out as an extra (playing a German soldier in *All Quiet on the Western Front*, 1930) and he became the assistant of directors such as Berthold Viertel and Busby Berkeley. From 1937 he started making his own shorts at MGM. There he learned his craft and from 1942 he began directing features. Then his career really got started and it didn't take too long before he was praised for the sincerity of his films. Not all of them turned out to be major box-office successes, but he nevertheless made an incredible contribution to the American film industry with a number of admirable films about human beings and human relationships that had a terrific impact on both the press and the audience.

Since the Academy Awards provide the film industry each year with one of its highlights, it's interesting to know how he feels about all the fuzz that's created around those events. His films garnered more than 60 Academy Award nominations and won over 20 statues. Two of his films, *From Here to Eternity* and *A Man for All Seasons*, were voted by the Academy as best picture of the year. Mr. Zinnemann: "It's always nice if you can win an Oscar, and I am delighted to have the Oscars, but I'm not delighted by the system—it's a publicity kind of a thing. By and large, it's very important, but the mistakes that are made, are staggering. There

Deborah Kerr and Burt Lancaster in *From Here to Eternity* (1953). (Courtesy of DOCIP Film Archive, Brussels, Belgium.)

are so many pictures that are marvelous that never got an Oscar. There are a great number of directors who never got an Oscar, King Vidor and a number of others. He only got a charity Oscar when he was dying. It depends too much on politics, too much on publicity. Personally I don't believe that there's ever anything that's the *best*—it's a very façade kind of a thing to say this is the *best*. How can you say that Beethoven is better than Mozart? It's not right, so the whole concept of prizes is there really for the publicity and to get more people to pay their tickets to go to see movies. How can you say that *Citizen Kane* is the greatest picture ever made, when D. W. Griffith[1] made *Intolerance* a quarter of a century earlier?"

It's very striking that Mr. Zinnemann made not one single *bad* movie in his entire career. That's extremely rare, especially if you consider that respectable colleagues from the same generation such as John Huston[2] and Orson Welles, admitted that they did. Mr. Zinnemann: "All I looked for was that when people came out of the theater, they didn't have to be ashamed to be a member of the human race and that they could feel good about themselves, about being a person. And when you've seen a piece of good work, whatever it is, whether it is a good painting, or if you read a really good book, and not something that just kills time, it makes you feel good, it gives you a good feeling. I always wanted to make films that were more than just entertainment. I like people to be entertained, but I don't want it to be empty."

He did not fail. If you look at his filmography, you get all the examples you need. During and after World War II, he made three absorbing war dramas that were far and away ahead of their time. The first was *The Seventh Cross* (1944, starring Spencer Tracy) about seven men who are haunted by the Gestapo after their escape from a concentration camp. In 1948 he amazed everybody with the poignant drama *The Search* with Montgomery Clift (in his film debut) caring for a young boy who survived the concentration camp and whose mother keeps on searching for him. The third film is *From Here to Eternity* (1953), based on the novel by James Jones, which deals with Army life in Hawaii before the attack on Pearl Harbor in December 1941.

But Mr. Zinnemann had much more to offer. Everybody remembers Audrey Hepburn[3] as Sister Luke in *The Nun's Story* (1959, based on the book by Kathryn Hulme) about the Belgian nun who leaves the convent after 17 years. The film was completely prepared in Belgium (a number of scenes were shot in Bruges). There's also the powerful political thriller *The Day of the Jackal* (1973) about a plan to assassinate French President Charles De Gaulle, and a few years later Zinnemann came up with *Julia* (1977), at the time labeled a *women's picture*, with Jane Fonda and Vanessa Redgrave as two friends in the turbulent Europe of the 1930s. (*Julia* was also Meryl Streep's film debut.)

This is definitely a very incomplete summary of his career and the films he made, but isn't it strange that this man isn't as well known to the average audience as let's say John Huston or Billy Wilder? Isn't he a terribly underestimated director? "All those people are great filmmakers, they are very social, they get around, they look for publicity. If it comes their way, they'll take it. By instinct, I avoided it because it's like a merry-go-round, you know: once you get on it, you can't get off. If you're good with interviews, you get into it more and more, you get more on television. But that doesn't interest me very much. If people don't talk about me, *tant pis alors*, it doesn't bother me. In the context of what's happening in the world today, I don't think it's that important. Maybe it has to do with the fact that people don't know much about me—I feel what I have to contribute is on film."

Isn't he a little too modest? "No, I'm not. I know that I've made good pictures, I know the people whom I respect, like my pictures. I realize that the pictures I made are perhaps too up market, not for a broad audience. I also feel that from the seventies on, the whole trend of thinking has gone in a direction which isn't the way I look at life or the kind of pictures that I make. People like more films with entertainment values; maybe my pictures are more like lectures. I do what I do, and if people like it, I'm very happy and if they don't, I'm sorry that they don't like it but I don't feel desperate about it. I get depressed about it, yes.

"Now it would be very difficult for me to make another film and I have no great desire to do it," he says. "I don't speak the same language as the people who run the studios today—with all the respect for what they're doing. Now, the only thing that matters, is profit. Quality, it's nice if it's there, but it's not essential. That is very different from what it used to be. Sam Goldwyn once was producing a film he liked very much and he said, 'I don't give a damn if it makes a nickel, but I want everybody in America to see it.' He liked money but he was proud of quality, proud of having to say something positive, proud of giving people some substance, some nourishment, rather than just entertainment that they can't even remember.

"Right now I'm really more interested in seeing what's happening in the world rather than participating in the movie business," Mr. Zinnemann continues, "because the motion picture industry has to a large extent become so commercial that it has lost any sense of real importance, compared to what it may have had before. Commercially it is terribly important of course, but when you think of the contribution it has made, then I think it is very sad. We've contributed to the insanities of the world by showing an incredible amount of gruesome violence that should be reserved for psychiatric closed sessions. It's not that the pictures are not well made, they are wonderfully well made. Take *Silence of the Lambs*, that's a wonderfully made film, but what they are showing, is sick.

"If you imagine children of 8 or 10 years seeing this, they have no frame of reference, but

Fred Zinnemann and Audrey Hepburn on the set of *The Nun's Story* (1959). (Courtesy of DOCIP Film Archive, Brussels, Belgium.)

by looking at it, it becomes part of their education and they grow up with these impressions. Is it a wonder then that they go around killing people—for fun? Their sense of reality becomes distorted and they don't know where the dividing line is between reality and the video box.

"All you have to do is look at some old movies. Just before you came, I started to look at *The Grapes of Wrath*, directed by John Ford.[4] When you look at those performances and you look at what it's about, it breaks your heart, not only because it's so well made but because

Fred Zinnemann (left) and Maximilian Schell on the set of *Julia* (1977). Courtesy of DOCIP Film Archive, Brussels, Belgium.)

nobody can make pictures like that anymore. It's all happened in such a short time. I'm not pessimistic, because I'm sure there is a way that we will recover from all that, but I think there is an enormous crisis in the world in terms of values. Hopefully that is going to change. When and how—I don't know."

Those wonderful old movies and the equally wonderful artists who created them, were indeed right in various ways. Documentaries about the old Hollywood and their filmmakers often capture that same "magic" we're used to when watching the black and white classics. From 1937 to 1949 Mr. Zinnemann worked at MGM, the biggest and most influential studio of its era. His impression: "MGM was a factory, but fortunately the man at the top, Louis B. Mayer, had a very good idea of quality and he had terribly good people working there. You could really learn your profession, because you had to work on a contract that went on for several years. You could develop as a *craftsman* and learn how to direct. So by and large I think it was a very useful and helpful professional education.

"What was bad about it, was the constant demand from the studio to do things their way. In other words, for instance they'd say, 'Here's a script, and so and so is going to play those parts. You're going to start in three weeks on the sets of stage 24—is there anything else you want to know?' When you started out in the early stages, they were dictating what you could or could not do, and you were legally obligated to obey them without any objections, which made it difficult. Sometimes I would get scripts that were terrible and because I refused to do them, I got into trouble. That made me very cautious in many ways and I found out I

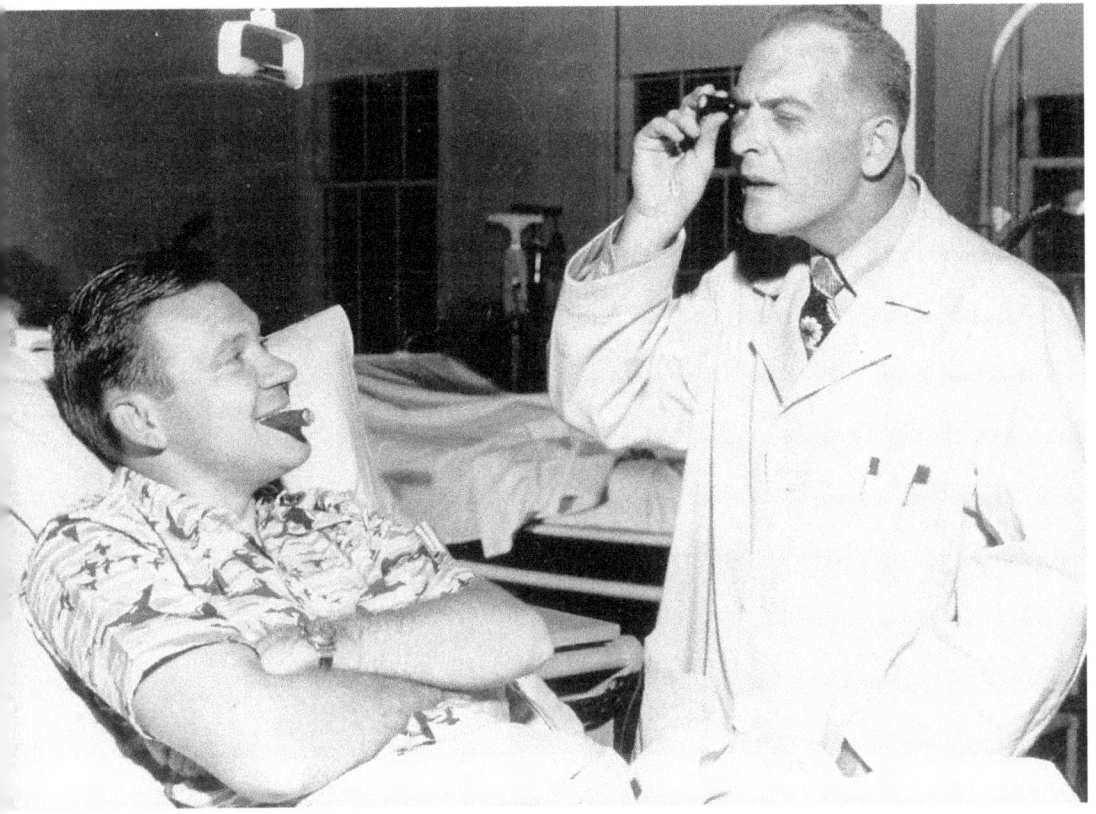

Richard Erdman (left), Everett Sloane in *The Men* (1950).

wasn't really a company man, I could not work that way. So when my contract was finished, I didn't renew it."

Result: Mr. Zinnemann couldn't find a job for a year. First he'd get three scripts a week, then two and after a while nothing. Then, a little later, Stanley Kramer and Carl Foreman asked him to direct *The Men*, which became Marlon Brando's first film. "If you had told the studio that you were going to make a film about paralyzed war veterans, they would have fainted, they wouldn't have dreamed of doing it. But Foreman and Kramer were very courageous young men and so it was a great pleasure to make that film. You didn't have to be told who was going to be in that picture. Eventually the film was a total flop: it was made for a postwar audience but it happened to come out just before the Korean war started. By then nobody wanted to see paralyzed war veterans." Yet, this highly acclaimed picture put Zinnemann back on the map.

Is Brando, as is often speculated, the greatest screen actor of all time? "No," Mr. Zinnemann says firmly, "Brando is a great actor, Montgomery Clift was a great actor, Audrey Hepburn and a number of others too—I can't say who is the best. If you would force me to give a name, I would say Spencer Tracy. Like Vanessa Redgrave, he's one of the very few film actors who doesn't have to do anything, he just has to *be* there; his reactions seem to me a lot better than the actions of a lot of actors. But the young audience hardly knows Tracy. The only one from that era that's still popular, is Humphrey Bogart, somehow he still represents the rebel spirit. Actors like Gary Cooper[5] are not nearly as popular as they should be.

"I never had any ambition of being an actor—I started out wanting to be a cameraman. I went to a school for cinematography in Paris; it still exists—now it is called National Lumière.

Spencer Tracy, here in *Dr. Jekyll and Mr. Hyde* (1941), played the leading role in Fred Zinnemann's absorbing drama *The Seventh Cross* (1944): "He is one of the few film actors who doesn't have to do anything; he just has to *be* there."

So I came out to America as a very well equipped second cameraman. In Hollywood I couldn't get in the union, so I got a job as an extra [*All Quiet on the Western Front*] and then, fortunately, also a job as assistant director. That's when I learned a lot about acting which I had no idea about. I knew nothing about acting, I still don't. All I know is that I believe in an actor or I don't believe in him. I don't want to tell an actor how to do a scene, I just want to see how he does it and tell him what I think could be perhaps better. You see, if you take a director like Kazan who was an actor himself, he can tell actors technically what he wants. I can tell the actors only what I want, but I can't tell them how to do it. So therefore I need to have actors who are terribly good, I can tell them what it is I'd like to get across and then it is up to them to do it. All I do, is suggest details, but the important thing for the actor is to be told what it is that the scene is about and what the character is about. Before I ever start working with an actor, I spend two, three, four hours talking about the character; about the development of the character, about the relationships of this person with the other characters—in detail. So when we come on the set and start rehearsing, I expect the actor to have formed an approach which I didn't see. I also believe that a film to a colossal extent depends on the proper casting, on the impact an actor can make on an audience. If you have a very good picture with actors that aren't quite talented enough, then the picture doesn't register the way it should."

What about the young stars of today? Take Tom Cruise for example. Can a true talent like Fred Zinnemann with his experience and his background take a youngster like Tom Cruise seriously? "I think Tom Cruise is a very talented actor and there are a tremendous amount of talented people working now. But I don't think it's really fair to compare his work under the conditions that his work is done with the actors of 30, 40 years ago. Now, they all work in a highly sophisticated technocratically oriented factory system. The whole basis of picture-making has changed from the ambition of doing something that has some positive value to things that make money. It doesn't matter all that much what it's about, whether it's positive or negative. So if you'd say that Tom Cruise may not be as good as let's say Montgomery Clift, it basically has to do with the fact that he doesn't work with material that's as good as what Clift had, you know. But I think that Tom Cruise is terribly good *today*. And you can see that everywhere. Where is the statesman today who is like Churchill or Roosevelt? I know I'm talking like a very old man, I *am* an old man, I've seen it all twice. Sometimes when I see what's happening in the world, it's a déjà vu. It all has happened before, 50 or 60 years ago."

What advice would Mr. Zinnemann give to a young director? "To a young director? Figure out for himself if he has got any talent to face his chances, because if he has no talent, he hasn't got anything else that would get him to fulfill himself. Talent is really the basic thing; the whole industry is based on talent, whether they are directors, actors or writers. There are a lot of people unfortunately who have a lot of self-confidence but who have no talent. They are not able to do it, but they think they can and their whole life becomes a complete frustration. But I could not give them any advice, unless it was something specific. General advice is usually not worth very much."

Studio portrait of Montgomery Clift who appeared in two films directed by Fred Zinnemann: *The Search* (1948) and *From Here to Eternity* (1953).

What is Mr. Zinnemann's opinion of the critics who reviewed his films over the years? "Some of them were very good, very articulate and very logical. But there were not very many who were really, really good critics like James Agee was, or like Pauline Kael. I always get surprised when I hear various critics doing very deep philosophical analyses of films like *High Noon*, one of the films I directed. I always have to laugh because it's so far away from what it's about. Somebody once said it's a parable on the war in Korea, somebody else with much more justification said it's an allegory on the days of McCarthy which is perhaps a little more to the point. But actually it's very simple: it's a story about compromise against commitment, you know, that you're really prepared to stand by something that you believe in and you don't compromise. That's what *High Noon* is about: a man who won't compromise. There are people who compromise for very good reasons, some have not very good reasons, so in a sense everybody recognizes himself. But it's got nothing to do with Korea or with McCarthy.

"It's curious, and I'm probably very detached about those things, but I was never too worried about what people thought. If I get an emotional response, that's nice. That's as far as it goes. Let me give you an example. You know about previews? You take a picture out, you

Gary Cooper and Grace Kelly in *High Noon* (1952). (Courtesy of DOCIP Film Archive, Brussels, Belgium.)

sit there and watch the audience. There are certain ground rules: if one person coughs, it's all right, but if ten people cough, it's not quite all right. Boy, if somebody starts lightning a cigarette, there's something wrong, or if they start whispering to each other, or if somebody gets up and walks out, even if he is just going to the toilet, he is a deadly enemy at that moment. Then, when you come out and if the picture is any good, the people are very enthusiastic. The lobby is full of people, they see you, they all come running toward you, clap you on the back and just talk in a very emotional way that makes very little sense—it's mostly sort of incoherent jabbering. If the picture is mediocre or not very good, the lobby is only half full and nobody moves. Instead of them running to you, you are going to them. As you walk, you can see that they think about what they are going to say. They'd say, 'Wasn't the music good!' Or, 'Wasn't the photography marvelous!' And if the picture is really bad, there's nobody out there. That is the most interesting kind of criticism, because I think film basically is not a rational thing. You bypass reason, the same way music really bypasses reason. Beyond a certain point, there's not much sense in trying to analyze it on a purely rational level, if you see what I mean. And it's the same with film. You can see a passage in a picture that's absolutely wonderful, and it is very hard trying to find the right words to explain *why* it's wonderful, all you know is that really shatters you. That's what I find for instance in John Ford's pictures: there are moments that are absolutely incredible."

Fred Zinnemann was born on April 29, 1907, in Vienna, a city that produced five other distinguished directors with an impressive career in the U.S.: Erich von Stroheim, Josef von Sternberg, Fritz Lang, Otto Preminger and Billy Wilder. That's a strange coincidence, isn't it? "Yes, it's very curious and it's a very interesting question. It's the same with all those marvelous musicians that came out of a small corner in Russia and Poland: Horowitz, Schnabel, the Gershwins, etc."

He didn't occupy himself too much with film when I met him, so what took up most of his time? "Well, I read an awful lot. It's marvelous to see how wonderful people used to write. I read mostly from the turn of the century, you know, the great writers of that era like Zola, Faulkner, Dostoyevski, etc. It's a very rich way of living because they are so good, so human.

They are so sensitive. Our communications have diminished by things like video and people become more and more isolated as against in the old days, when we were more concerned with each other. So my activities are more introspective than athletic.

"I used to do a lot of mountain climbing but that I can't do no more. *Five Days One Summer* was a sentimental sort of a thing. I wanted to show how people climbed mountains in those days which is quite different from the way they do it now and their whole attitude towards mountains: to some, it was almost sacred. I personally liked it. I don't know if the picture was any good, but I know that the climbing scenes were good.

"I can't go to the theater because I don't hear very well and I certainly don't watch my old movies on tv, not if I can help it. It's very upsetting because they very often get cut and commercials are put in between. I have prints of my old pictures if I want to watch those but it's no use looking back. That's all behind us, it's much better to look forward." And that is exactly what he did until his unfortunate death in March 1997, less than two months before his 90th birthday.

Sean Connery (background) and Fred Zinnemann on the set of Fred Zinnemann's final film *Five Days One Summer* (1982). (Courtesy of Fred Zinnemann.)

Three months later, the Zinnemann family organized a heartwarming tribute to his life and work at the Theatre Royal in London. His son Tim had compiled an impressive film tribute with clips and outtakes from his films and footage which showed daily life on the set, along with excerpts from interviews with Mr. Zinnemann. Producer David Puttnam and directors like John Schlesinger, Robert Wise and Alan Parker were all there, as well as actors like Paul Scofield, Edward Fox and Vanessa Redgrave who paid tribute to a director for whom they delivered perhaps their best performances so far.

Producer Tim Zinnemann, who lives in Los Angeles, has to carry on the family name now. He started out in the early 1960s as assistant editor, then became an assistant director on a number of prestigious films, including *Bullitt* (1968), *The Great White Hope* (1970), *Carnal Knowledge* (1971), *The Cowboys* (1972) and John Schlesinger's *The Day of the Locust* (1975) until he finally started producing as well. "Some of the pictures I made as a producer, like *The Running Man* [1987], *Pet Sematary* [1989] and *Street Fighter* [1994] did extremely well at the box-office, but I had decided I would not do these kind of things anymore. Films like these are like a trap: you start doing them and you get stuck doing them. Once you become identified with those kind of films, it's hard to break the cycle. I worked a lot with Ed Pressman, but after my father died, I decided to quit working with him and go out on my own.

"It is up to me to carry on the family name after all, so I want to be careful as to what I do. If they're going to be failures one way or the other, at least I want them to be my failures. I want to believe in what I'm doing. I now raise the money for my films independently, outside the system, and I feel very enthusiastic about it.

"When I was starting in the business, I tried to stay away from my father as far as I could. I never worked with him, I never asked for his help to get a job, I took an independent road. I tried to make my own way. It's not possible to live up to his accomplishments and I'm not trying to do that, but I'm very proud of who he was, what he did, what he meant to the film industry and I want him to be respected for who he was.

"After he passed away, there was a lot to do on his behalf, it took much more time than I had thought. My mother remained in England; she became ill and died over the course of nine months after he had died. So I spent pretty much the whole year with her in England, taking care of her, dealing with papers, what needed to be done. The Academy and the British Film Institute have basically all of my father's letters, all of his things. I thought it was good to share all that with students or scholars; it's out there now for them to see it and to use it. I wouldn't have the room for it here and I wouldn't know what to do with it other than stick it into a file cabinet. They have it beautifully organized, anyone who wants to go in and find out any aspect of his career, he can."

About his childhood, he says: "I grew up in this business, films were always in my life. As a kid growing up, I was always around actors, sets, etc. We lived in the Santa Monica Canyon. There were a lot of ex-patriot European Jews that had come over right before World War II. The Viertels[6] were a big theater family and they used to have these *salons* every week in Santa Monica, so they would have everybody from Aldous Huxley to Greta Garbo and all of these fascinating and colorful people. Those are the people I grew up with. This was the life I was used to. About Greta Garbo I don't remember that much, I was just a little kid. She was a very close friend of the Viertels, so she was always over there, but as far as I was concerned, she was just a regular person."

For those who want to know more about Tim Zinnemann's father, I can highly recommend *Fred Zinnemann, an Autobiography*, which is not like a traditional autobiography since it has a perfect balance between text and photographs (over 400). Should we anticipate *his* memoirs? was my final question to Fred Zinnemann back then. "No, I don't think I have the patience for that," he smiled.

As the people from the American Film Institute have been saying for the past 30 years or so, *good* films can "stand the test of time." Fred Zinnemann's contribution to the American film industry is the living proof that *his* films indeed can stand the test of time, *from here to eternity*.

Interviews: London, April 9, 1993 (Fred Zinnemann)
Santa Monica, April 12, 1999 (Tim Zinnemann)

Notes

1. D. W. Griffith (1875–1948), considered to be the "Father of the Cinema" who invented it all, was the man who gave *birth* to the movies by making milestones such as *The Birth of a Nation* (1915), *Intolerance* (1916), *Hearts of the World* (1918), *Broken Blossoms* (1919), *Way Down East* (1920) and *Orphans of the Storm* (1922). His contribution to the movies, when it was in its very early stages, has been so incredibly important, as he was the first one to use close-ups, flashbacks and fadeouts, and he experimented successfully with various other techniques with sets, lightning, camera angles, action sequences, etc. In 1935 he received an honorary Oscar "for his distinctive creative achievements and invaluable and lasting contributions to the progress of the film

industry," although he was nearly forgotten by then. In 1933 he sold all his holdings of United Artists, a company he had founded in 1919 with Charles Chaplin, Mary Pickford and Douglas Fairbanks, and he spent his final years as a bitter and lonely man at the Knickerbocker Hotel in Hollywood. His first wife, Linda Arvidson (1884–1949, a.k.a. Linda Griffith), met him at the turn of the century when both were acting in stock companies, and she played many leads in his early films (they married in 1906, were separated in 1911 and were not legally divorced until 1936). Her autobiography, *When the Movies Were Young* (1925), is a fabulous in-depth study of the silent era in general and Griffith's early work in particular. In later years, she also did film criticism for various magazines.

2. John Huston (1906–1987) was the son of actor Walter Huston (1884–1950) and father of actress Anjelica Huston (b. 1952). He became one of Hollywood's leading, most prominent and most creative filmmakers, directing nearly 40 films (and often writing the screenplay for them, alone or in collaboration), including *The Maltese Falcon* (1941, Academy Award nomination for best screenplay), *Across the Pacific* (1942), *The Treasure of the Sierra Madre* (1948, Academy Awards for best directing and best screenplay; also his father won for best supporting actor), *Key Largo* (1948), *The Asphalt Jungle* (1950, Academy Award nominations for best directing and best screenplay), *The Red Badge of Courage* (1951), *The African Queen* (1951, Academy Award nominations for best directing and best screenplay), *Moulin Rouge* (1952, Academy Award nominations for best directing and best screenplay), *Moby Dick* (1956), *Heaven Knows, Mr. Allison* (1957, Academy Award nomination for best screenplay), *The Misfits* (1961), *The List of Adrian Messenger* (1962), *The Night of the Iguana* (1964), *Fat City* (1972), *The Man Who Would Be King* (1975, with Sean Connery and Michael Caine, a film he originally wanted to make in the 1940s with Humphrey Bogart and Clark Gable—Academy Award nomination for best screenplay), *Annie* (1982), *Under the Volcano* (1984), and *Prizzi's Honor* (1985, Academy Award nomination for best directing; his daughter Anjelica received an Academy Award for best supporting actress). He also acted in numerous films, usually in supporting roles, including *The Cardinal* (1963, Academy Award nomination for best supporting actor) and *Chinatown* (1974). A colorful personality and a delightful storyteller, he was one of the founders of the Committee of the First Amendment in 1947 (along with William Wyler, Humphrey Bogart, Lauren Bacall, John Garfield, Gene Kelly, and others—more information: interview with Jane Wyatt) to stand up to the hearings by the HUAC. His autobiography, *An Open Book*, was published in 1980.

3. Audrey Hepburn (1929–1993), Belgian-born actress who grew up in the Netherlands and in England, as she had a Dutch mother and an English father, became one of the most elegant and most gracious actresses ever to grace the screen. After a few films in England, she went to the U.S., appeared on Broadway in the play *Gigi* and immediately took Hollywood by storm. Nominated five times for an Academy Award for best actress for *Roman Holiday* (1953, which earned her the Oscar), *Sabrina* (1954), *The Nun's Story* (1959), *Breakfast at Tiffany's* (1961) and *Wait Until Dark* (1967). Her other films include *Funny Face* (1957), *Love in the Afternoon* (1957), *The Unforgiven* (1960), *Charade* (1963), *My Fair Lady* (1964), *Two for the Road* (1967), *Robin and Marian* (1976) and *They All Laughed* (1981). She was married to Mel Ferrer from 1954 to 1968. In later years she devoted most of her time to being ambassador for UNICEF. Audrey Hepburn died of colon cancer.

4. John Ford (1895–1973), legendary film director and a favorite of the film critics, made several masterpieces in his career which began in 1917. Mostly associated with the Western genre, he won four Academy Awards as best director for *The Informer* (1935), *The Grapes of Wrath* (1940), *How Green Was My Valley* (1941) and *The Quiet Man* (1952)—none of them Westerns. Other highlights in his career were *Stagecoach* (1939), *They Were Expendable* (1945), *My Darling Clementine* (1946), *Fort Apache* (1948), *She Wore a Yellow Ribbon* (1949), *The Searchers* (1956) and *The Man Who Shot Liberty Valance* (1962). He frequently collaborated with John Wayne and Ward Bond.

5. Gary Cooper (1907–1961), leading actor from the 1930s through the 1950s. For many years he was the star on the Paramount lot and twice an Academy Award winner for *Sergeant York* (1941) and *High Noon* (1952). Cooper appeared in such films as *It* (1927), *Wings* (1928), *Morocco* (1930), *The Lives of a Bengal Lancer* (1935), *Mr. Deeds Goes to Town* (1936), *Beau Geste* (1939), *Meet John Doe* (1941), *The Pride of the Yankees* (1942), *For Whom the Bell Tolls* (1943), *Friendly Persuasion* (1956) and *The Naked Edge* (1961). He died of cancer in May 1961, a month after the Academy honored him with an honorary Oscar "for his many memorable screen performances and the international recognition he, as an individual, has gained for the motion picture industry." As Cooper was too ill, his friend James Stewart showed up to accept the award on his behalf.

6. Berthold Viertel (1885–1953) directed a number of German films before he arrived in Hollywood in 1928. In the U.S. he also directed plays and films (Fred Zinnemann worked with him for two years as his assistant in the early 1930s). After the war he returned to his native Vienna where he died in 1953. His wife Salka Viertel (1889–1978) was a close friend of Garbo's and screenwriter of five Garbo films (always in collaboration with others): *Queen Christina* (1933, co-story), *The Painted Veil* (1934), *Anna Karenina* (1935), *Conquest* (1937) and *Two-Faced Woman* (1941). She was also a stage and a screen actress who lived in Switzerland in her final years. Her autobiography, *The Kindness of Strangers*, was published in the 1970s. The Viertels organized those gatherings ("Sunday afternoon coffee-klatsches," as Fred Zinnemann calls them in his autobiography) for their close circle of friends. One of their children, Peter Viertel (b. 1920), became a screenwriter too; his credits include *Saboteur* (1942), *The*

Hard Way (1942), *We Were Strangers* (1949), *The Sun Also Rises* (1957), *The Old Man and the Sea* (1958) and *White Hunter, Black Heart* (1990, based on his 1953 novel). He married actress Deborah Kerr in 1962.

Filmography

Menschen am Sonntag (1930). DIR Curt Siodmak, Robert Siodmak, Edgar G. Ulmer, **Fred Zinnemann**. PROD Edgar G. Ulmer. SCR Billy Wilder, Curt Siodmak, Robert Siodmak. CAM Eugen Schüfftan. MUS Otto Stenzeel. RUNNING TIME 74 min. CAST: Erwin Splettstösser (Erwin); Brigitte Borchert (Brigitte); Wolfgang von Waltershausen (Wolfgang); Christl Ehlers (Cristl); Annie Schreyer (Annie).

All Quiet on the Western Front (Universal, 1930). DIR Lewis Milestone. PROD Carl Laemmle, Jr. SCR Del Andrews, Maxwell Anderson, George Abbott (novel *Im Westen Nichts Neues* by Erich Maria Remarque). CAM Arthur Edeson. ED Edgar Adams, Milton Carruth. MUS David Broekman. RUNNING TIME 140 min. CAST: Louis Wolheim (Katczinsky); Lew Ayres (Paul Baumer); John Wray (Himmelstoss); Raymond Griffith (Gerard Duval); George "Slim" Summerville (Tjaden); **Fred Zinnemann** (Uncredited).

The Wiser Sex (Paramount, 1932). DIR Berthold Viertel. ASST DIR **Fred Zinnemann**. SCR Harry Hervey, Caroline Franke (play *The Woman in the Case* by Clyde Fitch). RUNNING TIME 72 min. CAST: Claudette Colbert (Margaret Hughes); Melvyn Douglas (DA Rolfe); Lilyan Tashman (Claire Foster); William Boyd (Harry); Ross Alexander (Jimmy); Franchot Tone (Phil).

The Wave (1934). DIR **Fred Zinnemann**. PROD-CAM Paul Strand.

The Dark Angel (Paramount, 1935). DIR Sidney Franklin. ASST DIR **Fred Zinnemann**. PROD Samuel Goldwyn. SCR Lillian Hellman, Mordaunt Shairp (play by Guy Bolton). CAM Gregg Toland. ED Sherman Todd. MUS Alfred Newman. RUNNING TIME 105 min. CAST: Fredric March (Alan Trent); Merle Oberon (Kitty Vane); Herbert Marshall (Gerald Shannon); Janet Beecher (Mrs. Shannon); John Halliday (George Barton).

Peter Ibbetson (Paramount, 1935). DIR Henry Hathaway. SECOND UNIT DIR **Fred Zinnemann**. PROD Louis D. Lighton. SCR Vincent Lawrence, Waldemar Young (play by John Nathaniel Raphael based on novel by George du Maurier). CAM Charles Lang. ED Stuart Heisler. MUS Ernst Toch. RUNNING TIME 83 min. CAST: Gary Cooper (Peter Ibbetson); Ann Harding (Mary); John Halliday (Duke); Ida Lupino (Agnes); Douglass Dumbrille (Col. Forsythe).

Redes (1936). DIR Emilio Gómez Muriel, **Fred Zinnemann**. SCR Emilio Gómez Muriel, Henwar Rodakiewicz, **Fred Zinnemann** (story by Paul Strand, Agustin Velázquez Chávez). CAM Paul Strand. MUS Silvestre Revueltas. ED Emilio Gómez Muriel, Gunther von Fritsch. RUNNING TIME 65 min. CAST: Silvio Hernández; Antonio Lara; David Valle Gonzáles; Rafael Hinojosa.

Kid Glove Killer (MGM, 1942). DIR **Fred Zinnemann**. PROD Jack Chertok. SCR Allen Rivkin, John C. Higgins (story by John C. Higgins). CAM Paul C. Vogel. ED Ralph E. Winters. MUS David Snell. RUNNING TIME 74 min. CAST: Van Heflin (Gordon McKay); Marsha Hunt (Jane Mitchell); Lee Bowman (Gerald I. Ladimer); Samuel S. Hinds (Mayor Daniels); Cliff Clark (Capt. Lynch); Eddie Quillan (Eddie Wright); Ava Gardner (Car Hop).

Eyes in the Night (MGM, 1942). DIR **Fred Zinnemann**. PROD Jack Chertok. SCR Howard Emmett Rogers, Guy Trosper (novel by Baynard Kendrick). CAM Robert Planck, Charles Lawton. ED Ralph E. Winters. MUS Lennie Heyton. RUNNING TIME 79 min. CAST: Edward Arnold (Duncan Maclain); Ann Harding (Norma Lawry); Donna Reed (Barbara Lawry); Horace McNally (Gabriel Hoffman); Katherine Emery (Cheli Scott); Allen Jenkins (Marty).

The Seventh Cross (MGM, 1944). DIR **Fred Zinnemann**. PROD Pandro S. Berman. SCR Helen Deutsch (novel by Anna Seghers). CAM Karl Freund. ED Thomas Richards. MUS Roy Webb. RUNNING TIME 111 min. CAST: Spencer Tracy (George Heisler); Signe Hasso (Toni); Hume Cronyn (Paul Roeder); Jessica Tandy (Liessel Roeder); Herbert Rudley (Franz Marnet); Felix Bressart (Poldi Schlamm).

My Brother Talks to Horses (MGM, 1947). DIR **Fred Zinnemann**. PROD Samuel Marx. SCR Morton Thompson (also story). CAM Harold Rosson. ED George White. MUS Rudolph G. Kopp. RUNNING TIME 92 min. CAST: Jackie "Butch" Jenkins (Lewie); Peter Lawford (John S. Penrose); Edward Arnold (Mr. Bledsoe); Charlie Ruggles (Richard Roeder); Spring Byington (Mrs. Penrose); O. Z. Whitehead (Mr. Puddy).

Little Mister Jim (MGM, 1947). DIR **Fred Zinnemann**. PROD Orville O. Dull. SCR George Bruce (novel by Tommy Wadelton). CAM Lester White. ED Frank Hull. MUS George Bassman. RUNNING TIME 92 min. CAST: Jackie "Butch" Jenkins (Little Jim); James Craig (Capt. Big Jim Tukker); Frances Gifford (Jean Tucker); Luana Patten (Missey Choosey); Spring Byington (Mrs. Starwell); Chingwah Lee (Sui Jen).

The Search (MGM, 1948). DIR **Fred Zinnemann**. PROD Lazar Wechsler, Oscar Düby. SCR Richard Schweizer. CAM Emil Berna. ED Hermann Haller. MUS Robert Blum. RUNNING TIME 105 min. CAST: Montgomery Clift (Ralph Stevenson); Aline MacMahon (Mrs. Murray); Wendell Corey (Jerry Fisher); Jarmila Novotna (Mrs. Malik); Mary Patton (Mrs. Fisher); Ewart G. Morrison (Mr. Crookes), Ivan Jandl (Karen Malik).

Act of Violence (MGM, 1949). DIR **Fred Zinnemann**. PROD William H. Wright. SCR Robert L. Richards (story by Collier Young). CAM Robert Surtees. ED Conrad A. Nervig. MUS Bronislau Kaper. RUNNING TIME 82 min. CAST: Van Heflin (Frank R. Enley); Robert Ryan (Joe Parkson); Janet Leigh (Edith Enley); Mary Astor (Pat); Phyllis Thaxter (Ann); Berry Kroeger (Johnny).

The Men (United Artists, 1950). DIR **Fred Zinnemann**. PROD Stanley Kramer. SCR Carl Foreman (also story). CAM Robert De Grasse. ED Harry Gerstad. MUS Dimitri Tiomkin. RUNNING TIME 85 min. CAST: Marlon Brando (Ken "Bud" Wilocek); Teresa Wright (Ellen); Everett Sloane (Dr. Brock); Jack Webb (Norm); Richard Erdman (Leo); Arthur Jurado (Angel).

Teresa (MGM, 1951). DIR **Fred Zinnemann**. PROD Arthur M. Loew. SCR Stewart Stern (story by Alfred Hayes, Stewart Stern). CAM William J. Miller. ED Frank Sullivan. MUS Louis Applebaum. RUNNING TIME 101 min. CAST: Pier Angeli (Teresa); John Ericson (Philip); Patricia Collinge (Philip's Mother); Richard Bishop (Philip's Father); Peggy Ann Garner (Susan); Ralph Meeker (Sgt. Dobbs).

High Noon (United Artists, 1952). DIR **Fred Zinnemann**. PROD Stanley Kramer. SCR Carl Foreman (story by John W. Cunningham). CAM Floyd Crosby. ED Elmo Williams. MUS Dimitri Tiomkin. RUNNING TIME 84 min. CAST: Gary Cooper (Will Kane); Thomas Mitchell (Jonas Henderson); Lloyd Bridges (Harvey Pell); Katy Jurado (Helen Ramirez); Grace Kelly (Amy Kane); Otto Kruger (Percy Mettrick).

The Member of the Wedding (Columbia, 1953). DIR **Fred Zinnemann**. PROD Stanley Kramer. SCR Edna Anhalt, Edward Anhalt (book and play by Carson McCullers). CAM Hal Mohr. ED William A. Lyon. MUS Alex North. RUNNING TIME 88 min. CAST: Ethel Waters (Bernice Sadie Brown); Julie Harris (Frankie Addams); Brandon De Wilde (John Henry); Arthur Franz (Jarvis); Nancy Gates (Janice); William Hansen (Mr. Addams).

From Here to Eternity (Columbia, 1953). DIR **Fred Zinnemann**. PROD Buddy Adler. SCR Daniel Taradash (novel by James Jones). CAM Burnett Guffey. ED William Lyon. MUS George Duning. RUNNING TIME 118 min. CAST: Burt Lancaster (Sgt. Milton Warden); Montgomery Clift (Prewitt); Deborah Kerr (Karen Holmes); Donna Reed (Lorene); Frank Sinatra (Angelo Maggio); Philip Ober (Capt. Dana Holmes).

Oklahoma! (Columbia, 1955). DIR **Fred Zinnemann**. PROD Arthur Hornblow, Jr. SCR Sonya Levien, William Ludwig (adapted from the Rogers & Hammerstein musical play *Oklahoma!*, based on Lynn Riggs' dramatic play). CAM Robert Surtees. ED Gene Ruggiero. MUS Richard Rogers. RUNNING TIME 145 min. CAST: Gordon MacRae (Curly); Gloria Grahame (Ado Annie); Gene Nelson (Will Parker); Charlotte Greenwood (Aunt Eller); Shirley Jones (Laurey); Eddie Albert (Ali Hakim).

A Hatful of Rain (20th Century Fox, 1957). DIR **Fred Zinnemann**. PROD Buddy Adler. SCR Michael Vincente Gazzo, Alfred Hayes (play by Michael Vincente Gazzo). CAM Joseph MacDonald. ED Dorothy Spencer. MUS Bernard Herrmann. RUNNING TIME 109 min. CAST: Eva Marie Saint (Celia Pope); Don Murray (Johnny Pope); Anthony Franciosa (Polo); Lloyd Nolan (John Pope, Sr.); Henry Silva (Mother); Gerald O'Loughlin (Chuck).

The Old Man and the Sea (Warner Bros., 1958). DIR John Sturges, **Fred Zinnemann** [uncredited]. PROD Leland Hayward. SCR Peter Viertel (novel by Ernest Hemingway). CAM James Wong Howe. Ed Arthur P. Schmidt. MUS Dimitri Tiomkin. RUNNING TIME 86 min. CAST: Spencer Tracy (Old Man); Felipe Pazes (Boy); Harry Bellaver; Donald Diamond; Don Blackman.

The Nun's Story (Warner Bros., 1959). DIR **Fred Zinnemann**. PROD Henry Blanke. SCR Robert Anderson (book by Kathryn C. Hulme). CAM Frank F. Planer. ED Walter Thompson. MUS Franz Waxman. RUNNING TIME 149 min. CAST: Audrey Hepburn (Sister Luke); Peter Finch (Dr. Fortunati); Dame Edith Evans (Mother Emmanuel); Dame Peggy Ashcroft (Mother Mathilde); Dean Jagger (Dr. Van der Val); Mildred Dunnock (Sister Margharita).

The Sundowners (Warner Bros., 1960). DIR-PROD **Fred Zinnemann**. SCR Isobel Lennart (novel by Joe Cleary). CAM Jack Hildyard. ED Jack Harris. MUS Dimitri Tiomkin. RUNNING TIME 133 min. CAST: Deborah Kerr (Ida Carmody); Robert Mitchum (Paddy Carmody); Peter Ustinov (Venneker); Glynis Johns (Mrs. Firth); Dina Merrill (Jean Halstead); Chips Rafferty (Quinlan).

Behold a Pale Horse (Columbia, 1964). DIR-PROD **Fred Zinnemann**. SCR J. P. Miller (novel by Emeric Pressburger). CAM Jean Badal. ED Walter Thompson. MUS Maurice Jarre. RUNNING TIME 112 min. CAST: Gregory Peck (Manuel Artiguez); Anthony Quinn (Capt. Vinolas); Omar Sharif (Father Francisco); Mildred Dunnock (Pilar); Raymond Pellegrin (Carlos); Paolo Stoppa (Pedro).

A Man for All Seasons (Columbia, 1966). DIR-PROD **Fred Zinnemann**. SCR Robert Bolt (also play). CAM Ted Moore. ED Ralph Kemplen. MUS Georges Delerue. RUNNING TIME 120 min. CAST: Paul Scofield (Sir Thomas More); Wendy Hiller (Alice More); Leo McKern (Thomas Cromwell); Robert Shaw (King Henry VIII); Orson Welles (Cardinal Wolsey); Susannah York (Margaret More); Vanessa Redgrave (Anne Boleyn).

The Day of the Jackal (Universal, 1973). DIR **Fred Zinnemann**. PROD John Woolf. SCR Kenneth Ross (novel by Frederick Forsyth). CAM Jean Tournier. ED Ralph Kemplen. MUS Georges Delerue. RUNNING TIME 141 min. CAST: Edward Fox (The "Jackal"); Terence Alexander (Lloyd); Michel Auclair (Col. Rolland); Alan Badel (The Minister); Tony Britton (Inspector Thomas); Cyril Cusack (Gunsmith).

Julia (20th Century Fox, 1977). DIR **Fred Zinnemann**. PROD Richard Roth. SCR Alvin Sargent (story "Pentimento" by Lillian Hellman). CAM Douglas Slocombe. ED Walter Murch. MUS Georges Delerue. RUNNING TIME 116 min. CAST: Jane Fonda (Lillian Hellman); Vanessa Redgrave (Julia); Jason Robards (Dashiell Hammett); Maximilian Schell (Johan); Hal Holbrook (Alan Campbell); Rosemary Murphy (Dorothy Parker); Meryl Streep (Anne Marie).

Five Days One Summer (Warner Bros., 1982). DIR-PROD **Fred Zinnemann**. SCR Michael Austin (short story by Kay Boyle). CAM Giuseppe Rotunno. ED Stuart Baird. MUS Elmer Bernstein. RUNNING TIME 108 min. CAST: Sean Connery (Douglas); Betsy Brantley (Kate); Lambert Wilson (Johann); Jennifer Hillary (Sarah); Isabel Dean (Kate's Mother); Gerard Buhr (Brendal).

INDEX

Numbers in *italics* represent photographs.

Abbott, Bud 54
Abraham, F. Murray 20
The Absent Minded Professor (1961) 39
Across the Pacific (1942) 239
Act of Violence (1949) 95
The Actress (1953) 101, *152*
Adams, Edie 86
Adam's Rib (1949) 88, 128, 149, *150*
Adler, Buddy 5, 7, 12
Adrian 108
The Adventures of Don Juan (1949) 174, *182*
The Adventures of Sherlock Holmes (1939) 116
Affair in Trinidad (1952) 174, 179, 180, *180*
The African Queen (1951) 116, 239
Against All Odds (1984) 70
Agar, John 33
Agee, James 235
Agostino (1962) 156, 161
Airport 75 (1974) 38
Albert, Eddie 33, 69
Alda, Robert 114, 133
Alexander Hamilton (1931) 39
Alfred Hitchcock Presents (TV series) 71
Alice Adams (1935) 39
Alice in Movieland (1941, short) 109
Alien (1979) 196
All About Eve (1950) 116, 128
All Quiet on the Western Front (1930) 228, 234
All the King's Men (1949) 183
All Through the Night (1942) 174
Allen, Steve 14
The Alligator People (1959) 33, *35*, 38
Allyson, June 94, 132, 161
Alton, Bob 121
Always in My Heart (1942) 116
Always Together (1948) 133

America, America (1963) 183
An American in Paris (1951) 61
Anastasia (1956) 12
Anchors Aweigh (1945) 53, 54, *55*, 60
Andress, Ursula 14
Andrews, Dana 38, 220
Andrews, Julie 194, *195*
The Andrews Sisters 128
Andy Hardy's Private Secretary (1941) 53
Angeli, Pier 192
Angels with Dirty Faces (1938) 116
Anhalt, Edward 125
Anker, Jerry 148
Ann-Margret 14, 87
Anna Christie (1930) 60
Anna Karenina (1935) 47, 61, 239
Annie (1982) 239
Annie Get Your Gun (1950) 61
The Apartment (1960) 39
The Appaloosa (1966) 156, 164
April Love (1957) 6
Arden, Eve 64
Arliss, Anita 29
Arliss, Florence 38, 39
Arliss, George 29, 38
Arliss, Leslie 39
Arnow, Max 149
Around the World in Eighty Days (1956) 6
Arquette, Patricia 71
Arsenic and Old Lace (1944) 116, 132, 224
Arthur, Jean 183
Arvidson, Linda 239
As You Desire Me (1932) 61
The Asphalt Jungle (1950) 128, 184, 239
Astaire, Fred 57, 61, 84, *85*, 87, 114, 135, 137, 184, 206
Astaire, Mrs. 135
Attack of the 50 Foot Woman (1958) 39

Audrey Rose (1977) 188, 196
Autumn Garden (play) 222
Awakenings (1990) 71

Babes in Arms (1939) 61
Baby Doll (1956) 183
Baby Rosemarie 206
Bacall, Lauren 15, 71, 115, 116, 220, 239
The Bachelor and the Bobbysoxer (1947) 212
Back to Bataan (1945) 89
Bad Day at Black Rock (1955) 88
Bad Girl (1931) 61
Badham, John 71
Badlands of Montana (1957) 33
The Bank Dick (1940) 212
Banky, Vilma 50, 51
Bara, Theda 61
The Barber Shop (1933) 212
Barbour, Ron 212
Barbour, Ross 212
The Barefoot Contessa (1954) 116
Baretta (TV series) 20
The Barretts of Wimpole Street (1934) 101
Barry, Philip 217
Barrymore, John 174
Bartel, Paul 39
Barthelmess, Richard 174
Bartholomew, Freddie 108
Bathing Beauty (1944) 61, 132
Battleground (1949) 101
Beatty, Warren 183, 193
Beau Geste (1926) 224
Beau Geste (1939) 239
Beau James (1957) 138
Because You're Mine (1952) 61
Beethoven, Ludwig von 151, 229
Beethoven 2nd (1993) 20
Begley, Ed 192
The Beguiled (1971) 128

243

Index

Belafonte, Harry 190, 192
Bell, Book and Candle (play) 51
Bellamy, Ralph 101, 174
Bells Are Ringing (1960) 128
Bells Are Ringing (play) 128
Ben-Hur (1925) 43
Ben-Hur (1959) 193
Bend of the River (1952) 154
Beneath the Planet of the Apes (1970) 19
Bennett, Barbara 16
Bennett, Constance 16
Bennett, Joan *16*, 66
Benny, Jack 122
Berenson, Berry [Berinthia] 99, 102
Berenson, Marisa 102
Berg, Scott A. 47
Bergen, Candice 14
Bergman, Ingrid 15, 179
Bergner, Elisabeth 143
Berkeley, Busby 114, 228
Berle, Milton 133
Bernadine (1957) 5
Bernstein, Leonard 192
Bessie, Alvah 20, 176
The Best Things in Life Are Free (1956) 125
The Best Years of Our Lives (1946) 43
Beymer, Richard 7, 192, 193
Beyond Rangoon (1995) 71
Biberman, Herbert J. 20
The Big Broadcast of 1938 (1938) 138, 212
Big City (1937) 101, 144
Big Eddie (TV series) 128
The Big Fisherman (1959) 61
A Big Hand for the Little Lady (1966) 223
The Big Sleep (1946) 116, 117
The Big Steal (1949) 66, 67, 128
The Big Trail (1930) 89
The Bigamist (1955) 116
The Bing Crosby Show (TV series) 36
Bird on a Wire (1990) 20
The Birds (1963) 102
The Birth of a Nation (1915) 238
Bitter Sweet (1940) 14, 15, 60
The Black Marble (1980) 224
Blake, Amanda 152
Blake, Robert 20
Bless the Beasts and the Children (1972) 85
Blondell, Joan 109
Blondie (serial) 71
Blyth, Ann 205, 206, *222*
Boardwalk (1979) 95
Bob & Carol & Ted & Alice (1969) 197
Body and Soul (1947) 116
The Body Snatcher (1945) 188, 190
Bogart, Humphrey 88, 109, *110*, 114, 115, 116, 139, 173, 174, *174*, 220, 233, 239

Bogdanovich, Peter 39
Bohème, La (opera) 59
Bolger, Ray 206
Bolognini, Mauro 161
Bond, Ward 239
Boom Town (1940) 184
Boomerang (1947) 219, 220
Boone, Debbie 9
Boone, Pat 5, 6, *6*, 7, 8, 9, 10, 11, 12, 14, *17*, 125
Boorman, John 71
Born Free (1966) 89
Born to Be Bad (1950) 115
Born to Dance (1936) 61
Born Yesterday (1950) 128, 153
Borzage, Frank 54, 57, 61
The Boston Strangler (1968) 101
Boulting, Ray 70
Bow, Clara 50, 60
Boyer, Charles 35, 36, *36*
Boys Town (1938) 88, 101
Brahms, Johannes 59
Brainstorm (1983) 197
Brando, Marlon 75, 76, 77, 78, *78*, 84, 86, 87, 88, 164, 165, 183, 233
Brandt, Joe 183
Brandt, Robert 101
The Brave One (1956) 20
Breakfast at Tiffany's (1961) 239
Breaking Up the Act (play) 128
Brennan, Walter 6
Brice, Fanny 206
The Bride Came C.O.D. (1941) 116
Bride of the Gorilla (1951) 39
The Bridge on the River Kwai (1957) 89
Bridges, Lloyd 82, *82*
Brigadoon (1954) 54, 61
Bright Eyes (1934) 202, 203, 204, *204*, 205, 212
Bright Leaf (1950) 15
Bringing Up Baby (1938) 116, 138
The Broadway Melody of 1938 (1937) 61
Brodel, Betty 108, 116
Brodel, Joan Agnes Theresa Sadie 108
Brodel, Mary 108, 109, 116
Brodel, Mrs. 108
Brodie, Steve 65
Broken Blossoms (1919) 238
Bronson, Charles 39, 70
Brooks, Geraldine 220, *221*
Brooks, Louise 60
Brooks, Richard 148, 150
Brosnan, Pierce 81
Browder, Earl 177
Brown, Clarence 181
Brown, Joe E. 206
Brown, Les 125
Brute Force (1947) 15
Buchholz, Horst 161
Buck, Pearl [S.] 143, 144
Bulldog Drummond (1929) 224

Bullitt (1968) 237
Bullock, Sandra 39
Bulworth (1998) 224
Burnett, Carol 14
Burstyn, Ellen 14
Burton, Richard 7, 173
Bus Stop (1956) 7, 12, 128
Butch Cassidy and the Sundance Kid (1969) 19
Bye, Bye Birdie (1963) 95, 97, 99, 100
Bye, Bye Birdie (musical) 193

Caesar, Sid 86
Cagney, James 70, 109, 114, 116, 139
Cain, James M. 5
Caine, Michael 239
The Caine Mutiny (1954) 39, 75, 116
The Caine Mutiny (remake) 81
Caldwell, William 107, 115
Calhern, Louis 150, 217
Calhoun, Rory 33, *34*
California (1947) 15
Camelot (musical) 58
Camille (1937) 61, 108, 109, 153
Campbell, Jim 150
Can-Can (1960) 60, 61
The Canterville Ghost (1944) 62
Cantor, Eddie 206
Cape Fear (1962) 71
Cape Fear (1991) 71
Capra, Frank 175, 219, 224
Capra, Frank, Jr. 224
Capra, Frank, III 224
The Cardinal (1963) 156, 160, 239
Carnal Knowledge (1971) 237
Carson, Jack 132, 133, *134*, 138
Casablanca (1942) 116, 174, 175, 178, 183
Cassavetes, John 84
Cassel, Seymour 20
The Cat and the Canary (1939) 138
Cat on a Hot Tin Roof (1958) 138
Cat People (1942) 190
Chakiris, George 193, *194*
The Chalk Garden (play) 51
Chamberlain, Richard 14, 35
The Champ (1931) 68, 70
Champion (1949) 80, 81, 89
Champion (remake) 81
Chandler, Jeff 161
Chaney, Lon 70
Chaplin, Charlie 81, 102, 165, 239
Chaplin, Charles, Jr. 50
Chaplin, Sydney 50
Charade (1963), 239
Charisse, Cyd 54, 108
Charley Varrick (1973) 126
Checkers (1938) 207
Chevalier, Maurice 60, 108, 206
Cheyenne (1947) 132
A Child Is Waiting (1963) 84
Chinatown (1974) 16, 239

Index

Ching, William 29
Churchill, Winston (British Prime Minister) 1940-235
Cimino, Michael 89
Cinderella Jones (1946) 114, 116
Circus World (1964) 71, 184
Citizen Kane (1941) 65, 81, 89, 188, 189, 229
Clark, Dane 132
Claudia (1943) 224
Cleopatra (1963) 7, 128
Clift, Montgomery 230, 233, 235, *235*
Clinton, Bill 88
The Clock (1945) 61
The Clown (1952) 68, 70
Cobb, Lee J. 15
Coburn, Charles *123*
Cohan, George M. 109
Cohn, Harry 48, 179, 180, 183, 219
Cohn, Jack 183
Colbert, Claudette 39
Cole, Lester 20, 176
The Collector (1965) 195
Colman, Ronald 51, 218, *218*, 222, 223, 224
Color of Night (1994) 20
Come September (1961) 165
Como, Perry 134
Compulsion (1959) 89
Confidentially Connie (1953) 95
Connors, Chuck 152
Connory, Sean 237, 239
Conquest (1937) 61, 144, 239
Conte, Richard 220
Coogan's Bluff (1968) 128
Cooper, Dorothy 150
Cooper, Gary 14, 15, 16, 70, *70*, 71, 81, 82, *82*, 83, 109, 114, 221, 222, 223, 233, *236*, 239
Cooper, Jackie 43
Cooper, Ray 29
Coppola, Francis Ford 39
Corey, Jeff 14, 15, 16, 17, *17*, 18, 19, *19*, 124
Corman, Roger 14, 29, 30, 31 32, 33, 38, 39
Costello, Dolores 190
Costello, Lou 54
Cotten, Joseph 152
Counsellor at Law (1933) 174
A Countess from Hong Kong (1967) 165
The Country Girl (1954) 39
Courageous (1937) 88
Cover Girl (1944) 184
The Cowboys (1972) 89, 237
Crane, Richard 33
Crank, Fillmore 29, 38
Crawford, Joan 44, 47, 54, 142, 173, 174, 179
Crimes of Passion (1984) 101, 102
Criminal Lawyer (1951) 220

Crisis (1950) 148, 150, 151
Crosby, Bing 5, 7, 29, 36, 37, 39, 113, 122, 138
The Cross and the Switchblade (1970) 6, 7
Crossfire (1947) 101
Cruise, Tom 234, 235
Cry Tough (1959) 156
Cukor, Elsie 149, 151, 152
Cukor, George 88, 108, 121, 149, 152, 153, 212
Cummings, Jack 54, 61
Cummings, Robert 124
Cunningham, John W. 83, 84
The Curse of the Cat People (1944) 190
Curtis, Jamie Lee 101, 102
Curtis, Kelly Lee 101
Curtis, Tony 75, 78, 87, 95, 101, *101*
Curtiz, Michael 15, 45, 48, 57, 109, 114, 125, 175, 178
Curucu, Beast of the Amazon (1956) 32
Cyrano de Bergerac (1951) 89

d'Amboise, Jacques 125
The Damned Don't Cry (1951) 174
A Dancer (1988) 145
Dandridge, Dorothy 14
A Dandy in Aspic (1968) 154
Dangerous (1935) 116
Dante, Joe 39
Darby, Kim 14
Darin, Bobby 165
The Dark Angel (1925) 51
The Dark at the Top of the Stairs (1960) 224
Darrow, Clarence 173
Dassin, Jules 15
A Date with Judy (1948) 61
Daves, Delmer 110, 132
David Copperfield (1935) 212
Davis, Bette 44, 47, 57, 110, *112*, 113, 116, 132, 136, 139, 173, 174, *175*, 176
Davis, Jerry 150
Davis, Marion 54
Day of the Bad Man (1958) 39
The Day of the Jackal (1973) 230
The Day of the Locust (1975) 237
The Day the Earth Stood Still (1951) 188, 190, 191, *191*
Dead on the Money (1991) 128
Dean, James 14, 77, 89, 125, 183, 197, 206, 211, *211*, 212
Debakey, Michael 69
De Carlo, Yvonne 115
Deception (1992) 20
Decoy (TV series) 29, 33, 34
Dee, Sandra 158, *159*, 161, 165, 192
The Deep End of the Ocean (1999) 224
The Defiant Ones (1958) 75, 78, 79, 101
DeFore, Don 133

De Gaulle, Charles (French President) 230
de Hartog, Jan 88
DeHaven, Gloria 132
de Havilland, Olivia 114, 139
De Laurentiis, Dino 163
Del Rio, Dolores 60
Del Ruth, Roy 33, 35
De Mille, Cecil B. 15, 43
Demme, Jonathan 39
De Niro, Robert 18, 39
The Dentist (1932) 212
Dern, Bruce 39
The Desert Fox (1951) 71
The Desert Song (1953) 58
Designing Woman (1957) 101
Desire (1936) 61
Desk Set (1957) 88
The Desperate Hours (1955) 30
Desperate Search (1952) 68
Destination Tokyo (1944) 116
Destry Rides Again (1939) 61
De Sylva, Buddy 125
de Toth, André 220
The Devil (1921) 39
The Devil and Daniel Webster (1941) 15
Devil's Doorway (1950) 150, 151
Dick Tracy (1945) 65
The Dick Van Dyke Show (TV series) 206
Dickinson, Angie 128
Dieterle, William 15, 146
Dietrich, Marlene 61, 69, 87, 113, 142, 146
Diner (1982) 44
Dinner at Eight (1934) 153
Dirty Harry (1971) 128
Disraeli (1921) 38, 39
Disraeli (1929) 38, 39
The Divorcee (1927) 101
Dmytryk, Edward 20, 70, 75, 176, 177
D.O.A. (1950) 29, 30
Dr. Jekyll and Mr. Hyde (1941) *234*
Dr. Kildaire (TV series) 35
Dr. Syn (1937) 39
Dodsworth (1936) 43
Don Giovanni (musical) 54
Donahue, Elinor 220
Donen, Stanley 195
Donner, Richard 128
D'Orsay, Fifi 206
Dostoyevski, Fyodor 145, 236
Double Indemnity (1944) 39
A Double Life (1947) 224
Douglas, Kirk 14, 16, 65, 66, 75, *81*, 87, 190
Douglas, Melvyn 144
Douglas, Michael 38
Douglas, Nathan E. 78, 79
Dramatic School (1938) 144
Driving Miss Daisy (play) 223

Index

A Dry White Season (1989) 89
Duchess of Idaho (1950) 150
Dunaway, Faye 87
Dunn, James 61
Dunne, Irene 189
Durante, Jimmy 108
Durbin, Deanna 54, 61, 109
Duvivier, Julien 144, 175
Dwan, Allan 71, 115, 116
Dylan, Bob 165

The Eagle (1925) 51
East of Eden (1954) 77, 89, 183
East Side, West Side (1950) 149
Easter Parade (1948) 61
Eastman, Carol 16
Eastwood, Clint 71, 128
Easy Rider (1969) 86
Easy to Love (1953) 61
Eddy, Nelson 14, 60
Edwards, James 83
Egan, Richard 107
The Egg and I (1947) 39
Eilers, Sally 61
El Cid (1961) 154
The Electric Horseman (1979) 156
Ellington, Duke 71
Elvis: That's the Way It Is (1970) 93, 129
Elvis on Tour (1972) 129
The Emperor's Candlesticks (1937) 144
Enter the Dragon (1973) 163
Epstein, Julius J. 178, 183
Epstein, Philip G. 178, 183
Erdman, Richard 233
Errair, Kendall 208
Errair, Kenneth 208, 212
Escapade (1935) 143
Escape from Alcatraz (1979) 128
E.T. The Extra-Terrestrial (1982) 18
Even the Rich Cry (TV series) 162
An Evening with Kathryn Grayson (one-woman show) 58
Everybody Comes to Rick's (play) 178
Ewell, Tom 45
An Eye for an Eye (1981) 224

A Face in the Crowd (1957) 51
Fail Safe (1964) 209
Fairbanks, Douglas, Jr. 65
Fairbanks, Douglas, [Sr.] 102, 188, 239
The Falcon's Alibi (1946) 65
Falk, Peter 196
The Fall of the Roman Empire (1964) 154
Family Plot (1976) 102
Far and Away (1992) 208
The Far Country (1955) 154
A Farewell to Arms (1932) 61
Farewell, My Lovely (1975) 71
The Farmer Takes a Wife (1935) 209

Fat City (1972) 239
Father Knows Best (TV series) 217, 220, 221, 222
Father of the Bride (1951) 88
Faulkner, William 236
Faust (operetta) 60
Fear Strikes Out (1957) 101
Fenner, John 46
Ferber, Edna 192
Ferrer, José 150
Ferrer, Mel 239
Fessenden, Beverly Lucy 29
Fiddler on the Roof (Broadway musical) 197
Fields, Ronald J. 212
Fields, W.C. 203, 204, 206, 212
Fields, W.C., Jr. 212
Finney, Albert 87
Fire Down Below (1957) 184
Firefox (1982) 71
Firestarter (1984) 224
The Firm (1993) 16
A Fish Called Wanda (1988) 102
Fitzgerald, Barry 149
Five Days One Summer (1982) 237, *237*
Five Easy Pieces (1970) 16
Fixed Bajonets (1951) 89
Flaming Star (1960) 128, 129
Flanagan, Bob 212
Fleming, Victor 55, 71, 80, 181
Flesh and the Devil (1927) 60
Flight Nurse (1954) 115
Flynn, Errol 135, 139, 164, 173, 174, 175, *182*
The Fog (1980) 101
Foley, Shirley 9
Fonda, Henry 114, *209*, 222, *223*, 224
Fonda, Jane 14, 39, 230
Fonda, Peter 14
Fontaine, Joan 115, 158, 192
For Me and My Gal (1942) 61
For Whom the Bell Tolls (1943) 239
Ford, Glenn 174, 179, *180*, 183
Ford, Harrison 222
Ford, John 51, 88, 89, 231, 236, 239
Foreign Correspondent (1941) 71, 102
Foreman, Carl 83, 89, 233
Forever Young (1992) 102
Forrestal, James 18
Fort Apache (1948) 212, 239
Foster, Jodie 210
Four Daughters (1938) 116
The Four Freshmen 208, 212
The Four Poster (1952) 87
Fox, Edward 237
Fox, William 48
Foy, Eddie, Jr. 134
Francis Joins the Wacs (1954) 39
Frankenheimer, John 95
A Free Soul (1931) 101
Freed, Arthur 54, 61

Freedman, Harry 152
The Freshman (1990) 89
Friendly Persuasion (1956) 224, 239
Fritsch, Gunther von 190
From Here to Eternity (1953) 12, 60, 178, 179, 228, *229*, 230, 235
The Front Page (1931) 71
Fugitive Lady (1951) 134
The Full Monty (1997) 49
Funny Face (1957) 239
Funny Girl (stage musical) 50
Furie, Sidney J. 164

Gable, Clark 60, 64, 152, 173, 179, 180, 181, 192, 202, 239
Gabor, Zsa Zsa 152
Gaby-A True Story (1987) 51
Galsworthy, John 95
The Gambler (1997) 145
The Game of Death (1946) 70
Garbo, Greta 53, 54, 60, 108, 142, 143, 144, 145, 206, 238, 239
The Garden of Allah (1936) 184
Gardner, Ava 15, 60, *85*, 87, 151, 173
Garfield, John 110, 112, 113, *113*, 116, 173, 174, 239
Garfield, John, Jr. 116
Garfield, Julie 116
Garland, Beverly 29, 30, *31*, 32, *32*, 33, *33*, 34, *34*, 35, *35*, 36, 37, 38, *38*
Garland, Judy 84, *84*, 132, 205, 206
Garland, Richard 38
Garson, Greer 54, 58, *58*
Gaslight (1944) 153
Gates, Bill 48
Gaynor, Janet 5, 61
Gentleman Jim (1942) 138
Gentleman's Agreement (1947) 116, 128, 183, 219, 224
Gentlemen Prefer Blondes (1953) 117, 128
George, Sue 158
Gershwin, George 114, 236
Gershwin, Ira 236
Ghost (1990) 51
Ghosts of Mississippi (1996) 224
G.I. Blues (1960) 129
Giant (1956) 206, 211
Gidget (1959) 165
Gigi (1958) 61
Gigi (Broadway play) 239
Gilbert, Melissa 14
Gilda (1946) 174, 179
The Gilded Lady (1935) 39
Ginger (1935) 204, 205
Girl of the Golden West (1938) 60
Les Girls (1957) 165
Gish, Annabeth 45
Gish, Lillian 224
Give Me Yesterday (play) 217
The Glass Menagerie (play) 126

The Glass Web (1953) 30
The Glenn Miller Story (1954) 154
Go West, Young Man (1936) 71
The Godfather (1972) 89, 196
Going Hollywood (1933) 39
Going My Way (1944) 39
Goldwyn, Samuel, Jr. 43, 44, 45, 48, 49, *49*, 50, 51, 221
Goldwyn, Samuel, [Sr.] 43, 44, *44*, 47, 48, 51, 80, 230
Goldwyn, Tony 51
Gone with the Wind (1939) 47, 48, 64, 80, 175
The Good Earth (1937) 143
Goodbye, My Fancy (1951) 174
Goosson, Stephen 218, 219
Gordon, Ruth 95
Grable, Betty 121, 124, *124*
Grady, Billy 152
Grady, Don 37
Graham, Barbara 193
Grand Hotel (1932) 61
Granet, Burt 179
Granger, Stewart 70
Grant, Cary 64, 148, 149, 150, 189, 206, 219
The Grapes of Wrath (1940) 128, 231, 239
Gray, Billy 220, 221
Grayson, Kathryn 53, 54, *55*, 56, 57, *57*, 58, *59*, 60, 61, 101, 148, 151
Graziano, Rocky 192
The Great Caruso (1951) 61
The Great Mr. Nobody (1941) 109
The Great Race (1965) 101
The Great Waltz (1938) 144
The Great White Hope (1970) 237
The Great Ziegfeld (1936) 143
The Greatest Story Ever Told (1965) 224
Greed (1923) 93
The Green Berets (1968) 89
Greer, Bettejane 65, 66
Greer, Jane 64, 65, 66, *66*, 67, 68, 69, *69* 70, 71
Griffin, Z. Wayne 181
Griffith, D.W. 89, 102, 212, 229, 238, 239
Griffith, Linda 239
Grounds for Marriage (1951) 151
Guess Who's Coming to Dinner (1967) 75, 76, 85, 88
Gully, Richard 152
Gunn, Jimmy 179
Gunslinger (1956) 30, *32*
Gunsmoke (TV series) 152
Guys and Dolls (1955) 43
Gypsy (Broadway musical) 197
Gypsy (1963) 197
The Gypsy Moths (1969) 121

Hackford, Taylor 14

Hackman, Gene 87
Halloween (1978) 102
Halloween H2K: Evil Never Dies (2001) 102
Halloween H2O-Twenty Years Later (1998) 101
Halloween II (1981) 102
Hamilton, Billie 188
Hamilton, William 188
Handle with Care (1932) 203
Hands Across the Table (1935) 39
Hannibal (2001) 9
Happy Land (1943) 197
The Hard Way (1942) 107, 109, 116, 132, 173, 174, 178, 240
The Harder They Fall (1956) 116
Harlow, Jean 71, 184, 202
Harriet Craig (1950) 174, 179
Harrison, Joan 65, 71
Harrison, Rex 87, 165
Hart, Lorenz 95
Harvey, Laurence 154
The Harvey Girls (1946) 61
Has Anybody Seen My Gal? (1952) 89
Hasselhoff, David 81
Hatari! (1962) 89, 117
Hathaway, Henry 6, 19, 69, 70, 71
The Haunting (1963) 188, 196
Have Gun-Will Travel (TV series) 153
Haver, June 39
Havoc, June 220
Hawks, Howard 67, 114, 116, 181
Hawthorne, Nigel 46
Hayden, Sterling 220
Hayes, Allison 30, 39
Hayward, Susan 65, 192, *193*
Hayworth, Rita 174, 179, 180, *180*, *181*, 183
Hazel Flagg (Broadway show) 121, 122
Hearst, William Randolph 189
Hearts of the World (1918) 238
Heaven Knows, Mr. Allison (1957) 12, 71, 239
Hecht, Ben 124
Hedda Gabler (play) 20
Hedrick, Zelma Kathryn 53
Heflin, Van 95
Held, Anna 143
Hellman, Lillian 222
Hell's Angels (1930) 71
Hell's Outpost (1954) 115
Henderson, Ray 125
Henreid, Paul 132, 136, 220
Hepburn, Audrey 162, 230, *231*, 233, 239
Hepburn, Katharine 39, 53, *54*, 65, 87, 88, 108, 142, 219
Her Cardboard Lover (1942) 153
Her First Affair (1933) 116
Hersholt, Jean 60, 102, 139
Heston, Charlton 36, 95
Hickey, William 142

The High and the Mighty (1954) 77
High Noon (1952) 75, 76, 80, 81, *82*, 83, 84, 88, 89, 228, 235, *236*, 239
High Noon (remake, 2000) 81
High Sierra (1941) 107, 109, *110*, 116
High Society (1956) 39, 60
Higher and Higher (1943) 60
Hilton, James 218, 219
His Girl Friday (1940) 116
Hitchcock, Alfred 65, 71, 93, 95, 97, 98, 99, 101, 102, 175, 179
The Hitch-Hiker (1953) 116
Hitler, Adolf 146
Hobson, Laura Z. 219
Hoffman, Dustin 19, 89, 142
Holden, William 183
A Hole in the Head (1959) 224
Holiday Inn (1943) 39
Holliday, Judy 122, 128, *157*, 179
Hollywood Canteen (1944) 107, 110, 113, 116, 132
The Hollywood Revue of 1929 (1929) 61
Holm, Celeste 219
Holt, Tim 190
Home in Indiana (1944) 6
Home of the Brave (1949) 15, 83, 89
Hope, Bob 37, 39, 113, 133, 134, 138
Hopkins, Anthony 145, 196
Hopkins, Miriam 173
Hopper, Dennis 86
Horowitz, Vladimir 236
The Horse Whisperer (1998) 208
Hostages (1943) 144, 145
Houdini (1953) 95
Houdini, Harry 95
House of Rothschild (1934) 39
Houseman, John 18
How Green Was My Valley (1941) 128, 239
How the West Was Won (1962) 71
How to Be Very, Very Popular (1955) 121, *123*, 124
How to Marry a Millionaire (1953) 124, 128
Howard, Frances 43
Howard, Leslie 14, 15
Howard, Ron 39
Hudson, Rock 122, 206
Hughes, Howard 64, 65, 66, 67, 68, 71
Humoresque (1920) 61
The Hunchback of the Notre Dame (1939) 188
Hunt, Marsha 220
Hunter, Jeffrey 125
Hunter, Tab 14
Hush ... Hush, Sweet Charlotte (1965) 116
The Hustler (1961) 177, 183
Huston, Anjelica 239

Huston, John 116, 162, 165, 175, 178, 220, 229, 230, 239
Huston, Walter 239
Hutton, Robert 113, 132
Huxley, Aldous 238
Hytner, Nicholas 46

I Am a Fugitive from a Chain Gang (1932) 49
I Am the Law (1938) 116
I Can Get It for You Wholesale (Broadway musical) 125
I Confess (1953) 102
I Do! I Do! (Broadway musical) 88, 197
I Want to Live! (1958) 188, 192
I Want You (1951) 224
Idiot's Delight (1939) 101
If a Man Answers (1962) 165
If Winter Comes (1948) 95
Imitation of Life (1959) 165
In Love and War (1958) 125
Ince, Thomas 61, 71
The Informer (1935) 239
Inge, William 7
Inherit the Wind (1960) 75, 76, 79, 81, 84, 88
The Inn of the Sixth Happiness (1958) 12
Inside Straight (1951) 151
Insignificance (1985) 101
Intolerance (1916) 229, 238
Invasion of the Body Snatchers (1956) 128
Invasion of the Body Snatchers (1978) 128
Ireland, John 32
Island in the Sun (1957) 183
It (1927) 239
It Conquered the World (1956) 31, 33
It Happened in Brooklyn (1947) 54
It Happened One Night (1934) 224
It Should Happen to You (1954) 128, 154
It's a Big Country (1951) 101
It's a Gift (1934) 203, 212
It's a Mad, Mad, Mad, Mad World (1963) 75, 76, 85, 86
It's a Wonderful Life (1946) 224
It's Always Jan (TV series) 134
It's My Turn (1980) 38

Jackson, Kate 36
Jaffe, Sam 218
Jailhouse Rock (1957) 129
Jamaica Inn (1939) 71, 102
Janie (1944) 115
Janie Gets Married (1946) 115
Jannings, Emil 142
The Jazz Singer (1927) 50, 139
Jet Pilot (1957) 97
Jezebel (1938) 116

Joan of Arc (1948) 15
Joe Smith, American (1942) 62
John, Elton 5
Johnson, Edward 59
Johnson, Rita 65
Johnson, Van 54, 58, 93, 94, 148
The Joker Is Wild (1957) 33
Jolson, Al 50
Jones, James 230
Jones, Shirley 6, 128
Journey Into Fear (1942) 190
Journey to the Center of the Earth (1959) 6, 7
Joyce, Adrien 16
Jubilee Trail (1954) 115
Judgment at Nuremberg (1961) 75, 76, 79, 84, 88
Julia (1977) 228, 230, 232
Julius Caesar (1953) 89
Juno and the Paycock (1930) 102
Jurado, Katy 82
Jurassic Park (1993) 181
Jurgens, Curt 161

Kael, Pauline 235
Kaneshiro, Kerry 116
Kanin, Garson 15, 88, 179, 189
Kaper, Bronislau 151
Karloff, Boris 190, 217
Katz, Ephraim 183
Käutner, Helmut 159, 161
Kaye, Danny 220
Kazan, Elia 18, 51, 176, 177, 178, 182, 183, 219, 220, 234
Keel, Howard 54, 68
Keep Smiling (1938) 148
Keeper of the Flame (1942) 88
Kellerman, Sally 14
Kelley, Tom 149
Kellog, Phil 152
Kelly, Gene 53, 54, 55, 57, 84, 87, 184, 195, 206, 220, 239
Kelly, Grace 39, 75, 81, 82, 236
Kendall, Kay 158
Kern, Jerome 54
Kerr, Deborah 229, 240
Kershner, Irvin 14
Kert, Larry 192, 197
The Key (1958) 89
Key Largo (1948) 116, 239
Khan, Aly 179, 184
Killens, John O. 190
The Killers (1946) 15
The Killers (1964) 128
King, Henry 224
The King and I (Broadway musical) 197
King Creole (1958) 129
King Kong (1933) 47
King Richard and the Crusaders (1954) 152
Kingsley, Terry 128

Kinski, Klaus 162
Kirkland, Sally 39
The Kiss (1929) 60
Kiss Me, Kate (1953) 53, 54, 55, 58
Kiss Me, Kate (musical) 58
Kiss of Death (1947) 71
Kiss of the Spider Woman (Broadway musical) 197
Kiss the Girls (1997) 51
Kiss Them for Me (play) 128
Kisselgoff, Anna 197
Kissin' Cousins (1964) 129
The Kissing Bandit (1948) 54, 57
Koch, Howard 183
Koerner, Charlie 67
Koster, Henry 61
Kosterlitz, Hermann 61
Koverman, Ida 132
Kramer, Jennifer 81, 86
Kramer, Karen [Sharpe] 76, 79, 81, 86, 88
Kramer, Katharine 86, 88
Kramer, Stanley 15, 16, 75, 76, 76, 77, 78, 79, 79, 80, 81, 82, 84, 85, 86, 87, 88, 89, 101, 165, 197, 233
Kuffs (1992) 51
Kwan, Nancy 8

Ladd, Diane 39
Ladies Courageous (1944) 116
Ladies in Retirement (1941) 116
Lady for a Day (1933) 224
The Lady from Shanghai (1948) 89, 184
The Lady Vanishes (1938) 102
Laemmle, Carl 48, 51
Laemmle, Carl, Jr. 50, 51, 217
Lamour, Dorothy 39, 138
Lancaster, Burt 15, 127, 162, 192, 229
Lane, Lupino 116
Lanfield, Sidney 69
Lang, Fritz 39, 154, 236
Lanza, Mario 54, 59, 61
Lardner, Ring, Jr. 18, 20
La Rocque, Rod 51
Lasker, Alex 71
Lasker, Edward 65
Lasker, Lawrence 71
Lasker, Steven 71
Lasky, Jesse L. 43
Lasky, Jesse L., Jr. 50
La Tendresse (play) 224
Last Tango in Paris (1973) 89
The Last Time I Saw Paris (1954) 61
The Last Tycoon (1976) 18, 71, 101, 183
The Late George Apley (1947) 224
Laughton, Charles 15, 217
Laurents, Arthur 192
Laurie, Piper 192
Lawford, Peter 68, 94
Lawman (1974) 127
Lawrence, Carol 192, 197
Lawrence, Gertrude 196

Index 249

Lawson, John Howard 20
Lazybones (1925) 61
Lee, Bruce 163
The Left Hand of God (1955) 12
Leigh, Janet 61, 93, 94, *94*, 95, 96, 97, 98, *98*, 99, *99*, 100, 101
Leigh, Vivien 55, 75
Lemmon, Jack *157*
Leonard, Robert Z. 150
Leopold, Nathan 173
Leopold II [van Saksen-Coburg-Gotha] (king of Belgium) 71
LeRoy, Mervyn 97
Leslie, Joan 107, 108, *108*, 109, *110*, *111*, 113, 114, 115, 116, 132, 174, 205, 206
Let's Make Love (1960) 39, 128, 153
The Letter (1940) 116
Levinson, Barry 45
Lewis, Al 149
Lewis, Jerry 96, 122
Lewis, Sinclair 43
The Lieutenant Wore Skirts (1956) 124
The Life and Times of Judge Roy Bean (1972) 101
Lifeboat (1944) 102
Lilith (1964) 183
Lipton, Leon 149, 151, 152
The List of Adrian Messenger (1963) 71, 101, 239
Little Big Man (1970) 19, *19*, 142
The Little Colonel (1935) 212
Little Miss Marker (1934) 212
The Little Princess (1939) 212
Little Women (1949) 94, 97
The Littlest Rebel (1936) 212
Lives of a Bengal Lancer (1935) 71, 239
Living It Up (1954) 96,121, 122
Livingston, Barry 37
Livingston, Stanley 37
The Lodger (1926) 102
Loeb, Richard 173
Lombard, Carole 15, 39
Lone Star (1952) 179, 180, 184
The Long Hot Summer (1958) 89
The Longest Day (1962) 128
Loren, Sophia 165
Lost Horizon (1937) 217, 218, *218*, 222, 223, 224
Love (1927) 60, 61
Love and Learn (1947) 133
Love in the Afternoon (1957) 239
Love Is a Many Splendored Thing (1955) 12
Love Letters (play) 58
Love Me Tender (1956) 129
The Love Parade (1929) 60
Love Slaves of the Amazon (1957) 39
Love with a Proper Stranger (1966) 197
Lovely to Look At (1952) 54, 58
The Loves of Carmen (1948) 184
Lubitsch, Ernst 60, 146

Lucia (opera) 59
Lugosi, Bela 190, 217
Lumet, Sidney 209
Lupino, Ida 35, 36, 109, 116, 173, 174
Lupino, Stanley 116
Lupino, Wallace 116
Lyn, Dawn 37

Macbeth (1948) 89
MacDonald, Jeanette 14, 53, 60
Mackenna's Gold (1969) 89
MacMurray, Fred 29, 36, 37, *37*, 39
Madame Butterfly (opera) 59
Maddow, Ben 86
Madigan (1968) 126
The Madness of King George (1994) 46
The Magic Flame (1927) 51
The Magnetic Monster (1953) 39
The Magnificent Ambersons (1942) 81, 89, 188, 190
The Main Attraction (1962) 8
Makk, Károly 145
Malden, Karl 127
The Maltese Falcon (1941) 116, 239
Maltz, Albert 20
Mamoulian, Rouben 135
A Man for All Seasons (1966) 89, 228
The Man from Laramie (1955) 154
Man in the Saddle (1951) 115
Man of a Thousand Faces (1957) 70
The Man on a Flying Trapeze (1935) 212
The Man Who Knew Too Much (1934) 71, 102
The Man Who Knew Too Much (1956) 102
The Man Who Played God (1922) 39
The Man Who Played God (1932) 39
The Man Who Shot Liberty Valance (1962) 89, 239
The Man Who Would Be King (1975) 239
The Man with the Golden Arm (1955) 60
The Manchurian Candidate (1962) 60, 95, 99
Manckiewicz, Joseph L. 15
Mann, Anthony 95, 150, 153
Mannequin (1938) 61
March, Fredric 222
Mardi Gras (1958) 121, 125
Maria's Lovers (1985) 71
Marie Antoinette (1938) 101
Marilyn: The Untold Story (1980) 128
Marnie (1964) 102
Martin, Dean 39, 122, 153
Martin, Jeanne 153
Marvin, Lee 70
Mason, James 149
Mason, Marsha 196
Mata Hari (1931) 61
Maté, Rudolph 29
Matthau, Walter 126

Maugham, Somerset 43, 132, 222
Maverick (TV series) 153
Mayer, Louis B. 48, 51, 53, 55, 57, 58, 59, 60, 61, 68, 95, 101, 132, 142, 144, 219, 232
Maytime (1937) 60
McCarthy, Joseph (Senator)17, 235
McCarthy, Kevin 128
McDonald, Darren 18
McDowall, Roddy 15, 145
McGuire, Dorothy 219, *219*, 224
McGuire, Mickey 206
McKuen, Rod 158
McQueen, Steve 194
Meet John Doe (1941) 224, 239
Meet Me in St. Louis (1944) 61
Meisner, Sanford 174
The Member of the Wedding (1953) 80
The Men (1950) 75, 76, 80, 88, 89, 233, *233*
The Men (remake) 81
Men with Wings (1938) 116
Menjou, Adolphe 148
Menschen am Sonntag (1930) 39
Merkel, Una 207
The Merry Widow (1934) 60
The Merry Widow (musical) 58
Metropolis (1926) 39
Metty, Russell 95
Meyer, Emile 33
Mickey One (1965) 19
Midnight Alibi (1934) 174
A Midsummer Night's Dream (1935) 146
Mildred Pierce (1945) 138
Milestone, Lewis 71
Milland, Ray 15
Miller, Ann 59
Miller, Arthur 17
Miller, Sidney 206
Million Dollar Baby (1941) 116
Minnelli, Liza 197
Minnelli, Vincente 128, 158
Miracle on 34th Street (1947) 197
The Misfits (1961) 128, 239
Miss Sadie Thompson (1953) 184
Mission: Impossible (1996) 208
Mississippi (1935) 39
Mr. Belvedere Goes to College (1949) 212
Mr. Deeds Goes to Town (1936) 224, 239
Mr. Skeffington (1944) 116, 174, *175*, 178, 183
Mr. Smith Goes to Washington (1939) 138, 224
Mr. Universe (1951) 133
Mitchell, Thomas 94
Mitchum, Robert 65, 66, *66*, 67, 70, 71, 115
Moby Dick (1956) 239
Modine, Matthew 14, 20

Monkey Business (1952) 117, 128
Monpti (1957) 161
Monroe, Marilyn 7, 8, 36, 45, 122, *122*, 124, 128
Moore, Colleen 192
Moore, Roger 101
Moorehead, Agnes 69
Moreno, Rita 14, 193
Morgan, Dennis 133
Morgan, Michèle 60
Morocco (1930) 239
Morris, William 152
Morrison, Jeanette Helen 94
The Mortal Storm (1940) 61
Moss, Bill 208
Moss, Randy 208
Moss, Wendy 208
Moulin Rouge (1952) 239
Mozart, Wolfgang Amadeus 59, 229
Muni, Paul 49, 143, 144
Murphy, Audie 162
Murphy, George 114
Mutiny on the Bounty (1962) 78
My Darling Clementine (1946) 202, 239
My Fair Lady (1964) 139, 153, 239
My Favorite Brunette (1947) 138
My Favorite Wife (1940) 189
My Friend Flicka (1943) 15
My Girl (1992) 102
My Little Chickadee (1940) 212
My Sister Eileen (1955) 95
My Three Sons (TV series) 36, 37
Mystic Pizza (1988) 44, *45*

The Naked Edge (1961) 239
The Naked Spur (1953) 95, 154
Naughty Marietta (1935) 60
Naughty Marietta (musical) 58
Navarro, Roman 150
Nayfack, Niki 151
Nazimova [Alla] 61
Neal, Patricia 15, 190, *191*, 192
Never Give a Sucker an Even Break (1941) 212
New Moon (1940) 60
New York, New York (1977) 197
Newman, Paul 173, 174, *183*, 192
Nicholson, Jack 14, 16, 86, 126
Night and Day (1946) 149
The Night of Love (1927) 51
The Night of the Iguana (1964) 239
Night Watch (play) 58
Nimoy, Leonard 223
Ninotchka (1939) 61, 135
Niven, David 35
Nixon (1995) 51
No Down Payment (1957) 125, 126
Nocturne (1946) 71
None but the Brave (1965) 60
None but the Lonely Heart (1944) 146, 219

Noonan, Tommy *123*
Norman, Marc 87
Norris, Chuck 163
North, Sheree 14, 121, *123*, 125, 126, *126*, 127, *127*, 128
North by Northwest (1959) 102
Northern Exposure (miniseries) 87
Not as a Stranger (1955) 71, 75
Notorious (1946) 102, 179
Now, Voyager (1942) 116, 136
The Nun's Story (1959) 228, 230, 231, 239

O'Brien, Edmond 29, 116
O'Brien, Pat 220
Odds Against Tomorrow (1959) 188, 190, 192
Odets, Clifford 15, 116, 145, 146, 174, 219, 222
Of Human Bondage (1946) 132
Oklahoma! (1955) 228
Oklahoma Crude (1973) 87
Old Acquaintance (1943) 173, 174
The Old-Fashioned Way (1934) 212
The Old Man and the Sea (1958) 88, 240
On the Beach (1959) 75, 79, 81, 84, 85, *85*, 101
On the Town (1949) 60
On the Waterfront (1954) 51, 89, 183
Once More with Feeling (1960) 165
One Foot in Heaven (1941) 116
One Hour with You (1931) 60
One More River (1934) 218
Only Angels Have Wings (1939) 116, 183
Operation Petticoat (1959) 101
Operation Petticoat (TV series) 102
Ornitz, Samuel 20
Orphans of the Storm (1922) 238
Osborne, Robert 181
Osment, Haley Joel 210
Othello (1952) 89
Our Very Own (1950) *222*
Out of the Past (1947) 64, 65, 66, 67, 70
The Outfit (1974) 127
The Outlaw (1941) 71

Paige, Janis 132, 133, 134, *134*, 136, 137, 138
The Painted Veil (1934) 239
The Pajama Game (Broadway musical) 134
Pal Joey (1957) 60, 184
Paleface (1948) 138
Palmer, Lilli 87
Pan-Americana (1945) 64
Papas, Irene 153
The Paradine Case (1948) 102
Parker, Alan 237
Parker, Eleanor 128, 192

Parks, Arthur 180
Parks, Larry 83
Party Girl (1958) 61
Pasternak, Joe 54, 57, 61, 150
Pat and Mike (1952) 88
Patrick, John 8
Peck, Gregory *85*, 87, 219
Peg o' My Heart (1933) 54
The Pelican Brief (1993) 51
Penn, Arthur 19, 142
Penn, Leo 20
Pennies from Heaven (1936) 39
Pepe (1960) 97
Perkins, Anthony 38, 64, 98, *98*, 99, 101
Perkins, Berinthia 102
Perkins, Osgood (Anthony's father) 101
Perkins, Osgood (Anthony's son) 99
Perry Mason (TV series) 153
The Persuaders (TV series) 101
Pet Sematary (1989) 237
Peter Ibbetson (1935) 116
Peter Pan (Broadway musical) 197
Petrie, Donald 45
The Petrified Forest (1936) 116
The Pharmacist (1933) 212
Phffft (1954) 128
The Philadelphia Story (1940) 153
Philip (prince of Sweden) 150
Pickford, Mary 102, 239
Pidgeon, Walter 95
Pierce, Jack 217
The Pirate (1948) 61
Pitts, ZaSu 108, 206
The Place, the Time and the Girl (1946) 132
Play Misty for Me (1971) 128
Plummer, Christopher 194
Plymouth Adventure (1952) 181
A Pocketful of Miracles (1961) 224
Poitier, Sidney 75, 78, 87
Polonsky, Abraham 190
Ponti, Carlo 163
Porgy and Bess (1959) 43
Porter, Cole 149
Porter, Katherine Anne 75
Portrait in Black (1960) 158, 163
The Postman Always Rings Twice (1946) 116
Powell, Dick 35, 36, 148, 220
Powell, Eleanor 58, 122, 206
Powell, William 144
Preminger, Otto 68, 146, 236
Presley, Elvis 5, 9, 10, 11, 39, 93, 127, 129
Presley, Priscilla 11
Pressman, Ed 238
Preston, Robert 224
Pretty Poison (1968) 38, 101
The Pride and the Passion (1957) 60
The Pride of the Yankees (1942) 43, 239

The Prince and the Showgirl (1957) 128
Prince Valiant (1954) 97
The Princess Comes Across (1936) 39
The Prisoner of Zenda (1937) 224
The Prisoner of Zenda (1952) 68, 70
The Private Lives of Elizabeth and Essex (1939) 116
Prizzi's Honor (1985) 239
Psycho (1960) 64, 93, 95, 98, 98, 99, 99, 100, 101, 102
Psycho II (1983) 101
Psycho III (1986) 101
Psycho IV: The Beginning (1990) 101
Puttnam, David 237

Queen Christina (1933) 61, 239
The Quiet Man (1952) 89, 239
Quinn, Anthony 14, 87

Raeburn, Frances 62
Rainer, Luise 108, 116, 142, 143, *143*, 144, 145, *145*, 146
Rains, Claude 173, 174, 175, *175*, 179, 191
Raitt, John 134
Randall, Tony 125
Ray, Nicholas 115
Raymond, Paula 148, 149, *149*, 150, 151, *151*, 152, 153
The Razor's Edge (1946) 128
Reagan, Ronald 114, 174
A Real American Hero (1978) 128
Rear Window (1954) 102
Rebecca (1940) 47, 71, 102
Rebecca of Sunnybrook Farm (1938) 212
Rebel Without a Cause (1955) 89, 197
Reckless (1995) 51
Reckless Living (1938) 116
The Red Badge of Courage (1951) 239
The Red Danube (1949) 97
Red Dust (1932) 184
Red River (1948) 117
Redgrave, Vanessa 230, 233, 237
Reed, Donna 14
Reinhardt, Gottfried 146
Reinhardt, Max 142, 143, 146
Reinhardt, Wolfgang 146
The Reluctant Debutante (1958) 158, 165
Rennie, Michael 190, 191, *191*
Repeat Performance (1947) 115
The Restless Years (1958) 159, 161, 165
The Return of Dr. X (1939) 174
The Revolt of Mamie Stover (1956) 107
Reynolds, Joyce 115, 132
Rhapsody in Blue (1945) 107, 113, 114
Rich, Robert 20
Rich and Famous (1981) 153
Ride the Pink Horse (1947) 71
Rin Tin Tin 139
Rio Bravo (1959) 89, 117
Rio Grande (1950) 89

Riot in Cell Block 13 (1954) 128
Ritt, Martin 125, 126
The River (1929) 61
River of No Return (1954) 71, 128
Rivera, Chita 193
Road to Bali (1953) 39, 138
Road to Hong Kong (1962) 39, 138
Road to Morocco (1942) 39, 138
Road to Rio (1947) 39, 138
Road to Singapore (1940) 39, 138
Road to Utopia (1945) 39, 138
Road to Zanzibar (1941) 39, 138
The Roaring Twenties (1939) 116
Robbins, Jerome 192, 193, 197
Roberta (1935) 54
Roberts, Julia 44, *45*, 135
Roberts, Marguerite 19
Robin and Marian (1976) 239
Robinson, Edward G. 30
Robson, Mark 75
Rock, Pretty Baby (1957) 156, 157, 158
Rogell, Sid 66
Rogers, Ginger 64
Rogers, Richard 95
Roland, Gilbert 150
Roman, Ruth 192
Roman Holiday (1953) 239
The Romance of Rosy Ridge (1947) 93
Romance on the High Seas (1948) 133
Romeo and Juliet (1936) 101, 153
Romeo and Juliet (operetta) 60
Romeo and Juliet (play) 192
Rooftops (1989) 196
Rooney, Mickey 53, 54, 108, 206
Roosevelt, Eleanor 145
Roosevelt, Franklin Delano (President) 79, 101, 204, 205, 235
The Roots of Heaven (1958) 89, 128
Rose, William 85
Rose Marie (1936) 60
Rossen, Robert 177, 178, 183
Rosson, Hal 181, 184
Roustabout (1964) 129
Rowlands, Gena 71
Run for the Sun (1956) 68, 69, 70, 71
Run Silent, Run Deep (1958) 192
The Runner Stumbles (1979) 87
The Running Man (1987) 237
Russell, Jane 68, 107
Rutherford, Ann 108
Ryan, Robert 127, 190, 192
Ryan's Daughter (1970) 71

Saboteur (1942) 71, 240
Sabrina (1954) 116, 239
The Saga of Hemp Brown (1958) 33, 34
Sailor Beware (1951) 89
Sally of the Sawdust (1925) 212
San Francisco (1936) 60, 88
The Sand Pebbles (1966) 188, 192, 194, 195
Sanders, George 152

Sands of Iwo Jima (1949) 89
Saratoga (1937) 202
Saturday Night Live (TV show) 70
Saturday's Children (1940) 116, 174, 178
Saxon, John 156, 157, 158, *159*, 160, 161, 162, 163, 164, 165
Sayles, John 39
Scaramouche (1952) 97
The Scarecrow and Mrs. King (TV series) 36
Scarface (1932) 71
Scarface, the Shame of the Nation (1932) 71
Schaffner, Franklin J. 7
Schary, Dore 55, 60, 61, 68, 95, 97, 101, 181
Schell, Maximilian 232
Schenk, Joseph M. 128
Schickel, Richard 76
Schindler's List (1993) 75
Schlesinger, John 237
Schmidlin, Rick 93
Schnabel, Artur 236
Schulberg, B.P. 50
Schulberg, Budd 50, 51, 221
Schwarzenegger, Arnold 164
Scofield, Paul 237
Scopes, John T. 75
Scorsese, Martin 39
Scott, Adrian 20
Scott, Lizabeth 66, 220
Scott, Randolph 115
Scott, Ridley 196
Scott, Zachary 133
The Sea of Grass (1947) 88
The Sea Wolf (1941) 116
The Search (1948) 228, 230, 235
The Searchers (1956) 89, 239
Seaton, George 197
The Secret of Santa Vittoria (1969) 85, 86
Selznick, David O. 47, 48, 51, 80, 87, 219, 224
Selznick, Irene Mayer 48, 51
Selznick, Lewis J. 48
Selznick, Myron 48
Sennett, Mack 75
Sergeant York (1941) 107, 109, 114, 116, 239
Serling, Rod 10
The Set-Up (1949) 188, 190, 192
Seven Brides for Seven Brothers (1954) 61
The Seven Little Foys (1955) 138
Seven Sweethearts (1942) 54, 57
The Seven Year Itch (1955) 45, 124, 128
The Seventh Cross (1944) 229, 234
Seventh Heaven (1927) 61
A Shadow in the Streets (1975) 128
The Shaggy Dog (1959) 39
Shakespeare, William 53, 192
Shakespeare in Love (1998) 87

Shaw, George Bernard 43
Shaw, Irwin 174
She Wore a Yellow Ribbon (1949) 89, 239
Shearer, Norma 53, 61, 94, 101, 142
Sheridan, Ann 134
Sherman, Sally 61
Sherman, Vincent 3, 109, 115, 173, 174, 175, 176, *176*, 178, 179, 180, *180*, 181, 182
Shield, Arthur 149
Ship of Fools (1965) 16, 75
Shire, Talia 39
The Shootist (1976) 89, 121, 126, 127, 128
Shore, Dinah 134
Show Boat (1951) 53, 54, 61
Show Boat (musical) 58
Sidney, George 57, 97
Siegel, Don 89, 126, 128
Silence of the Lambs (1991) 230
Silk Stockings (1957) 61, 109, 135
Simmons, Jean 152, 192
Simon, Sylvan 178, 179
Sinatra, Frank 33, 53, 54, *55*, 57, 60, 87, 88, 95
Sinbad the Sailor (1947) 65
Since You Went Away (1944) 47
Singin' in the Rain (1952) 61, 184
Singleton, Penny 71
Siodmak, Curt 32, 39
Siodmak, Robert 39, 224
The Sixth Sense (1999) 210
Skelton, Red 68, *68*, 132, 152
Skerritt, Tom 82
Skippy (1931) 43
Skouras, Spyros P. 7, 12
The Sky's the Limit (1943) 114
Sloane, Everett *233*
Small Town Deb (1941) 209
Smith, Alexis 149
Smith, Harold Jacob 78, 79
Sneakers (1992) 71
So Big (1953) 192
So This Is Love (1953) 58
So This Is New York (1948) 80, 89
The Solid Gold Cadillac (1956) 128
Some Came Running (1959) 60
Some Like It Hot (1959) 45, 101, 128
Somebody Up There Likes Me (1956) 188, 192
Something Evil (1972) 17
Somewhere in the Night (1946) 15
The Son of the Sheik (1926) 50, 51
Sondergaard, Gale 20, 65
The Sound of Music (1965) 188, 192, 193, 194, 195, *195*
South Pacific (1958) 12
Sparks, Robert 65, 71
Spartacus (1960) 101, 190
Spellbound (1945) 47

Spielberg, Steven 14, 17, *18*, 75, 87, 181
The Spiral Staircase (1946) 101, 224
Splendor in the Grass (1961) 183, 193, 197
The Squaw Man (1913) 43
Stage Door Canteen (1943) 61, 110
Stagecoach (1939) 89, 239
Stagecoach (1966) 39
Stallone, Sylvester 39, 164
Stamp, Terence 195
Stanislavski, Konstantin 127
Stanwyck, Barbara 15, 192
Stapley, Richard *94*
Star! (1968) 196
Star Dust (1940) 116
A Star Is Born (1937) 47
A Star Is Born (1954) 84, 138, 153
Star Trek: The Motion Picture (1979) 196
Star Trek: The Voyage Home (1986) 217, 223
Stark, Ray 8
State of the Union (1948) 88, 224
Station West (1948) 69
The Steel Trap (1952) 152
Steichen, Edward 18
Stella Dallas (1925) 224
Stella Dallas (1937) 43
Stepmom (1998) 208
Sternad, Rudolph 84
Sternberg, Josef von 71, 97, 236
Stevens, George 212
Stevenson, Robert Louis 190
Stewart, Gloria (Mrs. James Stewart) 206
Stewart, James 88, 150, 153, 206, 223, 239
Stockwell, Dean 14
Stone, John 209
A Storm in Summer (2000) 196
The Story of G.I. Joe (1945) 71
The Story of Mankind (1957) 224
The Story of Us (1999) 224
The Story of Vernon and Irene Castle (1939) 116
The Story on Page Three (1959) 146
Storybook Theater (TV show) 149
Strange Interlude (1932) 101
A Stranger in My Arms (1959) 161
Strasberg, Lee 95
Strategic Air Command (1955) 154
The Stratton Story (1949) 61
Strauss, Mrs. Johan 144
The Strawberry Blonde (1941) 138, 183
Streep, Meryl 230
Street Fighter (1994) 237
A Streetcar Named Desire (1951) 89, 183
A Streetcar Named Desire (play) 51
Streisand, Barbra 14, 50, 87
Strickling, Howard 151
Strike Up the Band (1940) 61

Stroheim, Erich von 93, 236
The Student Prince (1954) 61
The Substance of Fire (1996) 51
Summer Love (1958) 156, 158
Summer of '42 (1971) 7
A Summer Place (1959) 165, 224
The Sun Also Rises (1957) 128, 240
The Sundowners (1960) 71
Sunrise at Campobello (1960) 101
The Sunset Murder Case (1941) 116
Superman and the Mole Men (1951) 19
Susan Lenox: Her Fall and Rise (1931) 61
Suspicion (1941) 65, 71, 102
Swamp Women (1955) 30
The Swan (1956) 101
The Sweet Ride (1968) 61
Sweethearts (1938) 60
Swing High, Swing Low (1937) 39
Swing Out, Sister (1945) 62
Swiss Family Robinson (1960) 224
Swope, Topo 224

Take Me Out to the Ball Game (1949) 60
Tales of Frankenstein (1958) 39
Tamblyn, Russ 193
The Taming of the Shrew (play) 53
Tarzan, the Ape Man (1932) 184
Taylor, Elizabeth 7, 134, 206
Taylor, Lili *45*
Taylor, Robert 108, 150
Telefon (1977) 126
Temple, Shirley 64, 202, 204, *204*, 205, 210, 212
Tenebre (1982) 156
Terror Train (1980) 102
Texas Carnival (1951) 61, 152
Thalberg, Irving G. 60, 61, 87, 101, 128, 139, 144, 194
Thalberg, Irving, Jr. 50
Thank Your Lucky Stars (1943) 109, 110, *112*
That Forsyte Woman (1949) 95
That Funny Feeling (1965) 165
That Midnight Kiss (1949) 54, 61
That's Entertainment! (1974) 135
That's Entertainment, Part 2 (1976) 135
That's Entertainment! 3 (1994) 135
Their Own Desire (1929) 101
They All Laughed (1981) 239
They Knew What They Wanted (1940) 15
They Were Expendable (1945) 239
They Won't Believe Me (1947) 65, 71
The Third Man (1949) 89
13 Rue Madeleine (1946) 71
The 39 Steps (1935) 102
This Is the Army (1943) 109, 114
Thousands Cheer (1944) 54
Three Coins in the Fountain (1954) 224
Three Secrets (1950) 192

Index

Thulin, Ingrid 161
Tickle Me (1965) 39
Tierney, Gene 151
Tierney, Lawrence 67
Till the Clouds Roll By (1946) 54
Titanic (1997) 193
Tjaden, Donna Mae 135
To Catch a Thief (1954) 102
To Have and Have Not (1944) 116, 117
The Toast of New Orleans (1950) 54, 61
Toland, Gregg 189
Too Young to Know (1945) 116
The Torrent (1926) 60
Tortilla Flat (1942) 116
Touch of Evil (1958) 89, 93, 97
Tourneur, Jacques 64, 190
Towne, Robert 16, 39
The Toy Wife (1938) 144
Tracy, Spencer 58, 60, 75, 76, 77, 77, 88, 144, 150, 229, 233, 234
Trading Places (1983) 102
Trapp, Maria von 193
Travels with My Aunt (1973) 153
Traviata, La (opera) 59
The Treasure of the Sierra Madre (1948) 116, 178, 239
The Trial (1962) 89
Trouble Along the Way (1953) 89
The Trouble with Girls [and How to Get Into It] (1969) 127
True Confession (1937) 39
True Grit (1969) 19, 89
Trumbo, Dalton 20, 176, 177, 190
Tucker, Sophie 121
Turner, Lana 116, 151, *163*, 165
Twelve Angry Men (play) 20
$20 a Week (1924) 39
20,000 Leagues Under the Sea (1954) 6
Two-Faced Woman (1941) 60, 239
Two for the Road (1967) 239
Two Guys from Milwaukee (1946) 115, 132
Two Lovers (1927) 51
Two Mules for Sister Sara (1970) 128
Two Sisters from Boston (1946) 54

Unconquered (1947) 15
Under the Volcano (1984) 239
The Unfinished Dance (1947) 61
The Unforgiven (1960) 156, 162, 165, 239
The Unguarded Moment (1956) 156, 157
Until They Sail (1957) 165, 192
The Untouchables (TV series) 153
Up the River (1930) 88

The Vagabond King (1956) 57, 58
Valenti, Jack 9
Valentino, Rudolph 50, 51

Van Cleef, Lee 33
Van Dyke, Dick 14, 16, 87
Vanished (1971) 128
Van Upp, Virginia 179
Varsi, Diane 14
Vaughn, Robert 183
Veidt, Conrad 142, 143
The Verdict (1946) 128
Verne, Jules 6
Vertigo (1958) 102
Vidor, King 43, 229
Viertel, Berthold 228, 238, 239
Viertel, Peter 240
Viertel, Salka 145, 238, 239
Virus (1999) 102
Viva Las Vegas (1964) 61, 129
Viva Zapata! (1952) 89, 183
Von Ryan's Express (1965) 60

Wager, Walter 126
The Wagons Roll at Night (1941) 109
Wait Until Dark (1967) 239
Wallflower (1948) 132
Wallis, Hal B. 19, 178
Walsh, Raoul 89, 107, 109, 132
Walters, Jerrie 209, 210
War of the Worlds (1938 radio presentation) 89
Ward, Rachel 70
Warden, Jack 70
WarGames (1983) 71
Warner, Albert 139
Warner, Harry 139
Warner, Jack L. 48, 116, 133, 134, 139, 152, 174, 177, 180
Warner, Jack L., Jr. 50
Warner, Sam 139
Wasserman, Lew 94
Waterfield, Robert 68
Way Down East (1920) 238
The Way to the Gold (1957) 125
Wayne, David 149
Wayne, John 71, 77, 83, 83, 89, 126, 239
We Were Strangers (1949) 116, 240
Webb, Jack 69
Welcome to Hard Times (1967) 132
Weld, Tuesday 14, 38
Welles, Orson 65, 80, 86, 89, 93, 97, 180, 189, *189*, 190, 197, 229
Wells, H.G. 43
Werner, Oskar 87
West, Mae 36, 71
West Side Story (1961) 188, 193, *194*
West Side Story (Broadway musical) 192, 197
The Westerner (1940) 43
Whale, James 218
What Price Hollywood? (1932) 153
Whatever Happened to Baby Jane? (1962) 116
Where Do We Go from Here? (1945) 39

Where Love Has Gone (1964) 69, 70
Whitburn, Joel 5
White Christmas (1954) 39
White Hunter, Black Heart (1990) 240
The White Sister (1923) 224
Who Was That Lady? (1960) 97
Who's Been Sleeping in My Bed? (1963) 39
Widmark, Richard 68, 126
Wild in the Country (1961) 129
The Wild One (1954) 76, 78, 84
Wild River (1960) 183
Wilder, Billy 39, 44, 48, 175, 230, 236
Wilkerson, David 6
Wilkins, Paul 153
Wilkinson, Jimmy 189
Williams, Bill 67
Williams, Esther 55, 132, 148, 150, 152
Williams, Robin 14
Williams, Tennessee 126
Willis, Bruce 20
Wilson, Michael 89
Winchester '73 (1950) 154
Wind Across the Everglades (1958) 51
Windsor, Marie 19
Wings (1928) 239
The Winning of Barbara Worth (1926) 51
The Winning Ticket (1935) 61
Winter Meeting (1948) 132
Wise, Robert 70, 165, 188, 189, 190, 191, 192, *192*, 193, 194, 195, 196, *196*, 237
Withers, Jane 148, 202, 203, 204, 204 205, 206, 207, 208, *208*, 209, 210, 211, 212
Without Love (1945) 88
Wives and Lovers (1963) 99
The Wizard of Oz (1939) 184
A Woman of Affairs (1928) 60
Woman of the Year (1942) 88
The Woman They Almost Lynched (1953) 115
The Women (1939) 101, 153
Wood, Natalie 192, 193, *194*, 197
Wood, T.K. 188
Wood, Truman K. 188
Woodward, Joanne 7
Words and Music (1948) 95
Wouk, Herman 75
The Wrath of God (1972) 184
Wright, Paula Ramona 148
Wright, Teresa 152
Wyatt, Jane 217, 218, *218*, 219, 220, 221, 222, *222*, 223
Wyler, William 30, 80, 87, 174, 195, 239
Wyman, Jane 134, 192

Yankee Doodle Dandy (1942) 107, 109, 114

The Yellow Canary (1963) 10, 17
The Yellow Jersey (never materialized) 89
You Can't Cheat an Honest Man (1939) 212
You Can't Take It with You (1938) 224
You for Me (1952) 68
You Only Live Once (1937) 138
You'll Never Get Rich (1941) 184
Young, Clara Kimball 61
Young, Loretta 219, *220*

Young, Robert 65, 220, 221
Young Mr. Lincoln (1939) 128
The Young Philadelphians (1959) 174, 175, *183*
Young Tom Edison (1940) 101
You're in the Navy Now (1951) 69, 70

Zanuck, Darryl F. 12, 49, 123, 128, 191, 196
Zanuck, Richard D. 128
Zetterling, Mai 8

Ziegfeld, Florenz, [Jr.] 143, 212
Ziegfeld Follies (1945) 54
Zinnemann, Fred 3, 39, 48, 60, 75, 77, 80, 82, 95, 97, 145, 178, 228, 229, 230, *231*, 232, *232*, 233, 234, 235, 236, 237, *237*, 238, 239
Zinnemann, Tim 237, 238
Zola, Emile 236
Zontar, the Thing from Venus (1968) 33
Zukor, Adolph 48

www.ingramcontent.com/pod-product-compliance
Ingram Content Group UK Ltd.
Pitfield, Milton Keynes, MK11 3LW, UK
UKHW050536150426
5217IPUK00026B/1966